A GIFT OF FIRE

A GIFT OF FIRE

Social, Legal, and Ethical Issues for Computing Technology

FOURTH EDITION

SARA BAASE

San Diego State University

International Edition contributions by
ATRIYA SEN
Indian Statistical Institute, Kolkata

Boston Columbus Indianapolis New York San Francisco Upper Saddle River
Amsterdam Cape Town Dubai London Madrid Milan Munich Paris Montreal Toronto
Delhi Mexico City Sao Paulo Sydney Hong Kong Seoul Singapore Taipei Tokyo

Editorial Director Marcia Horton	*Project Editor, International Edition* Karthik Subramanian
Executive Editor Tracy Johnson	*Publishing Administrator, International Editions* Hema Mehta
Associate Editor Carole Snyder	*Senior Manufacturing Controller, Production, International Editions* Trudy Kimber
Editorial Assistant Jenah Blitz-Stoehr	*Operations Supervisor* Alan Fischer
Director of Marketing Christy Lesko	*Manufacturing Buyer* Lisa McDowell
Marketing Manager Yez Alayan	*Art Director* Anthony Gemmellaro
Marketing Coordinator Kathryn Ferranti	*Cover Designer* Anthony Gemmellaro
Director of Production Erin Gregg	*Manager, Visual Research* Karen Sanatar
Managing Editor Jeff Holcomb	*Manager, Rights and Permissions* Michael Joyce
Production Project Manager Kayla Smith-Tarbox	*Text Permission Coordinator* Danielle Simon
Publisher, International Edition Angshuman Chakraborty	*Cover Art* Crocodile Images/Glow Images,
Acquisitions Editor, International Edition Jayashree Arunachalam	Yuri Arcurs/AGE Fotostock
Publishing Assistant, International Edition Shokhi Shah	*Lead Media Project Manager* Daniel Sandin
Print and Media Editor, International Edition Ashwitha Jayakumar	*Full-Service Project Management* Windfall Software

Credits and acknowledgements. Excerpt from Mike Godwin speech: at Carnegie Mellon University, November 1994. Copyright © 1994 by Mike Godwin. Reprinted with permission. Excerpt from Jerrold H. Zar's "Candidate for a Pullet Surprise": from JOURNAL OF IRREPRODUCIBLE RESULTS, 39, no. 1 (Jan/Feb 1994). Copyright © 1994 Norman Sperling Publishing. Reprinted with permission. Excerpt from "Social and Legal Issues": From INVITATION TO COMPUTER SCIENCE, 1E by Schneider/Gertsing. Copyright © 1995 South-Western, a part of Cengage Learning, Inc. Reproduced by permission. www.cengage.com/permissions. Appendix A.1: The Software Engineering Code of Ethics and Professional Practice. THE SOFTWARE ENGINEERING CODE OF ETHICS AND PROFESSIONAL PRACTICE © 1999 by the Institute of Electrical and Electronics Engineers, Inc. and the Association for Computing Machinery, Inc. Reprinted by permission. Appendix A.2: The ACM Code of Ethics and Professional Conduct. ACM CODE OF ETHICS AND PROFESSIONAL CONDUCT. Copyright © 1999 by the Association for Computing Machinery, Inc. and the Institute for Electrical and Electronics Engineers, Inc. Reprinted by permission. Adi Kamdar Excerpt: Adi Kamdar, "EFF Denounces Flawed E-Verify Proposal That Would Trample on Worker Privacy," July 1, 2011, www.eff.org/deeplinks/2011/07/eff-denounces-flawede-verify-proposal, viewed July 31, 2011. Reprinted under the terms of the Creative Commons Attributions License. Calvin and Hobbes "today at school . . . " cartoon © 1993 Watterson. Reprinted with permission of UNIVERSAL PRESS SYNDICATE. All rights reserved. Calvin and Hobbes "what's all the fuss about computers . . . " cartoon © 1995 Watterson. Dist. By UNIVERSAL PRESS SYNDICATE. Reprinted with permission. All rights reserved. "Opus" cartoon used with the permission of Berkeley Breathed and the Cartoonist Group. All rights reserved.

Pearson Education Limited
Edinburgh Gate
Harlow
Essex CM20 2JE
England

and Associated Companies throughout the world

Visit us on the World Wide Web at: www.pearsoninternationaleditions.com

© Pearson Education Limited 2013

ISBN 10: 0-273-76859-X
ISBN 13: 978-0-273-76859-3

British Library Cataloguing-in-Publication Data
A catalogue record for this book is available from the British Library

10 9 8 7 6 5 4 3 2 1—CRW—14 13 12 11 10

Typeset in Adobe Garamond by Windfall Software
Printed and bound by Courier Westford in The United States of America

The publisher's policy is to use paper manufactured from sustainable forests.

To *Keith*, always

And to *Michelle Nygord Matson* (1959–2012)

For her love of life, learning, and adventure
For her laughter, wisdom, and determination
For her friendship

CONTENTS

PREFACE

This book has two intended audiences: students preparing for careers in computer science (and related fields) and students in other fields who want to learn about issues that arise from computing technology, the Internet, and other aspects of cyberspace. The book has no technical prerequisites. Instructors can use it at various levels, in both introductory and advanced courses about computing or technology.

Scope of This Book

Many universities offer courses with titles such as "Ethical Issues in Computing" or "Computers and Society." Some focus primarily on professional ethics for computer professionals. Others address a wide range of social issues. The bulky subtitle and the table of contents of this book indicate its scope. I also include historical background to put some of today's issues in context and perspective. I believe it is important for students (in computer and information technology majors and in other majors) to see and understand the implications and impacts of the technology. Students will face a wide variety of issues in this book as members of a complex technological society, in both their professional and personal lives.

The last chapter focuses on ethical issues for computer professionals. The basic ethical principles are not different from ethical principles in other professions or other aspects of life: honesty, responsibility, and fairness. However, within any one profession, special kinds of problems arise. Thus, we discuss professional ethical guidelines and case scenarios specific to computing professions. I include two of the main codes of ethics and professional practices for computer professionals in an Appendix. I placed the professional ethics chapter last because I believe students will find it more interesting and useful after they have as background the incidents, issues, and controversies in the earlier chapters.

Each of the chapters in this book could easily be expanded to a whole book. I had to leave out many interesting topics and examples. In some cases, I mention an issue, example, or position with little or no discussion. I hope some of these will spark further reading and debate.

Changes for the Fourth Edition

For this fourth edition, I updated the whole book, removed outdated material, added many new topics and examples, and reorganized several topics. New material appears throughout. I mention here some major changes, completely new sections and topics, and some that I extensively revised.

- This edition has approximately 85 new exercises.
- In Chapter 1, I added a section on kill switches for smartphone apps, tablets, and so on, i.e., the ability of companies to remotely delete apps and other items from a user's device (in Section 1.2.1).
- All parts of Section 1.2 have new material, including, for example, uses of smartphone data and social network data for social research.
- I added a brief section on social contracts and John Rawls' views on justice and fairness (in Section 1.4.2).

New topics in Chapter 2 include

- smartphones and their apps collecting personal data without permission (in Section 2.1.2)
- Fourth Amendment issues about tracking a person's location via cellphone, tracking cars with GPS devices, and search of cellphones (in Sections 2.2.2 and 2.2.3)
- applications of face recognition (several places in the chapter)
- privacy implications of some social networking applications and social network company policies
- a right to be forgotten (Section 2.3.4)

Chapter 3 includes new sections on

- sexting (Section 3.2.3)
- ethics of leaking sensitive information (in Section 3.3)
- shutting down cellphone service or access to social media during riots or protests (Section 3.5.3)

The chapter also has

- use of social media by freedom movements and countermeasures by governments
- more on Western countries selling surveillance systems to dictators.

Chapter 4 includes

- discussion of plagiarism
- expanded sections on the Digital Millennium Copyright Act (Sections 4.2.2 and 4.2.3)
- an expanded section on patents for software (Section 4.5)

Chapter 5 has new sections on

- hacking by governments to attack others (Section 5.2.4)

- expansion of the Computer Fraud and Abuse Act to cover actions it was not intended to cover (in Section 5.2.6)

Chapter 6 has new sections on

- how content of social media can affect getting hired and fired
- use of social media and personal devices at work

Chapter 7 has expanded sections on

- the "wisdom of the crowd"
- ways the Internet can narrow or restrict the points of view people see (in Section 7.1.1)

Chapter 8 has

- an introduction to high reliability organizations (in Section 8.3.1).

Chapter 9 contains

- two new scenarios.

This is an extremely fast-changing field. Clearly, some issues and examples in this book are so current that details will change before or soon after publication. I don't consider this to be a serious problem. Specific events are illustrations of the underlying issues and arguments. I encourage students to bring in current news reports about relevant issues to discuss in class. Finding so many ties between the course and current events adds to their interest in the class.

Controversies

This book presents controversies and alternative points of view: privacy vs. access to information, privacy vs. law enforcement, freedom of speech vs. control of content on the Net, pros and cons of offshoring jobs, market-based vs. regulatory solutions, and so on. Often the discussion in the book necessarily includes political, economic, social, and philosophical issues. I encourage students to explore the arguments on all sides and to be able to explain why they reject the ones they reject before they take a position. I believe this approach prepares them to tackle new controversies. They can figure out the consequences of various proposals, generate arguments for each side, and evaluate them. I encourage students to think in principles, rather than case by case, or at least to recognize similar principles in different cases, even if they choose to take different positions on them.

My Point of View

Any writer on subjects such as those in this book has some personal opinions, positions, or biases. I believe strongly in the principles in the Bill of Rights. I also have a generally positive view of technology. Don Norman, a psychologist and technology enthusiast who writes on humanizing technology, observed that most people who have written books about technology "are opposed to it and write about how horrible it is."* I am not one of those people. I think that technology, in general, has been a major factor in bringing physical well-being, liberty, and opportunity to hundreds of millions of people. That does not mean technology is without problems. Most of this book focuses on problems. We must recognize and study them so that we can reduce the negative effects and increase the positive ones.

For many topics, this book takes a problem-solving approach. I usually begin with a description of what is happening in a particular area, often including a little history. Next comes a discussion of why there are concerns and what the new problems are. Finally, I give some commentary or perspective and some current and potential solutions to the problems. Some people view problems and negative side effects of new technologies as indications of inherent badness in the technology. I see them as part of a natural process of change and development. We will see many examples of human ingenuity, some that create problems and some that solve them. Often solutions come from improved or new applications of technology.

At a workshop on Ethical and Professional Issues in Computing sponsored by the National Science Foundation, Keith Miller, one of the speakers, gave the following outline for discussing ethical issues (which he credited to a nun who had been one of his teachers years ago): "What? So what? Now what?" It struck me that this describes how I organized many sections of this book.

An early reviewer of this book objected to one of the quotations I include at the beginnings of many sections. He thought it was untrue. So perhaps I should make it clear that I agree with many of the quotations—but not with all of them. I chose some to be provocative and to remind students of the variety of opinions on some of the issues.

I am a computer scientist, not an attorney. I summarize the main points of many laws and legal cases and discuss arguments about them, but I do not give a comprehensive legal analysis. Many ordinary terms have specific meanings in laws, and often a difference of one word can change the impact of a provision of a law or of a court decision. Laws have exceptions and special cases. Any reader who needs precise information about how a law applies in a particular case should consult an attorney or read the full text of laws, court decisions, and legal analysis.

Class Activities

The course I designed in the Computer Science Department at San Diego State University requires a book report, a term paper, and an oral presentation by each student. Students do several presentations, debates, and mock trials in class. The students are very

---

* Quoted in Jeannette DeWyze, "When You Don't Know How to Turn On Your Radio, Don Norman Is On Your Side," *The San Diego Reader*, Dec. 1, 1994, p. 1.

enthusiastic about these activities. I include several in the Exercises sections, marked as Class Discussion Exercises. Although I selected some exercises for this category, I find that many others in the General Exercises sections are also good for lively class discussions.

It has been an extraordinary pleasure to teach this course. At the beginning of each semester, some students expect boredom or sermons. By the end, most say they have found it eye-opening and important. They've seen and appreciated new arguments, and they understand more about the risks of computer technology and their own responsibilities. Many students send me news reports about issues in the course long after the semester is over, sometimes after they have graduated and are working in the field.

Additional Sources

The notes at the ends of the chapters include sources for specific information in the text and, occasionally, additional information and comment. I usually put one endnote at or near the end of a paragraph with sources for the whole paragraph. In a few places the endnote for a section is on the section heading. (We have checked all the Web addresses, but files move, and inevitably some will not work. Usually a search on the author and a phrase from the title of a document will locate it.) The lists of references at the ends of the chapters include some references that I used, some that I think are particularly useful or interesting for various reasons, and some that you might not find elsewhere. I have made no attempt to be complete.

An italic page number in the index indicates the page on which the index entry is defined or explained. The text often refers to agencies, organizations, and laws by acronyms. If you look up the acronym in the index, you will find its expansion.

My website for this book (www-rohan.sdsu.edu/faculty/giftfire) contains updates on topics in the book and other resources. Pearson Education maintains a website (www .pearsoninternationaleditions.com/baase) with supplements for instructors, including PowerPoint slides and a testbank. For access to instructor material, please contact your Pearson Education sales representative or visit the site, where you will find instructions.

Feedback

This book contains a large amount of information on a large variety of subjects. I have tried to be as accurate as possible, but, inevitably, there will be errors. I appreciate corrections. Please send them to me at GiftOfFire@sdsu.edu.

Acknowledgments

I am grateful to many people who provided assistance for this edition: Susan Brown (Florida Atlantic University) for advice about citations; Charles Christopher for regularly sending me legal articles perfectly targeted to topics I am writing about; Mike Gallivan (Georgia State University) for checking the Web addresses in endnotes; Julie Johnson (Vanderbilt University) for research assistance, an exercise, and the scenario and analysis in Section 9.3.4; Patricia A. Joseph (Slippery Rock University) for research assistance and an exercise; Ellen Kraft (Richard Stockton College) for assisting with research and the revision of Section 7.2; Jean Martinez for lively conversations about privacy, security, and social media; Michelle Matson for conversations about several topics in the book; Jack Revelle for bringing kill switches to my attention and sending me excellent articles; Carol Sanders for reading and improving Chapter 2, finding useful sources, and for many conversations about privacy, security, and social media; Marek A. Suchenek (California State University, Dominguez Hills) for research on software patent history and for email conversations about ethics, intellectual property, and human progress; Sue Smith, Char Glacy, and Michaeleen Trimarchi for their observations about how researchers use the Web; and my birding buddies, who got me out looking at birds once a week instead of at a screen.

I thank the following people for reviewing the third edition at the beginning of this project and providing suggestions for the new edition: Ric Heishman (George Mason University); Starr Suzanne Hiltz (New Jersey Institute of Technology); Jim K. Huggins (Kettering University); Patricia A. Joseph (Slippery Rock University); Tamara Maddox (George Mason University); Robert McIllhenny (California State University, Northridge); Evelyn Lulis (DePaul University); and Marek A. Suchenek (California State University, Dominguez Hills).

This edition includes some material from earlier editions. Thus again, I thank all the people I listed in the prefaces of those editions.

I appreciate the efforts of the staff at Pearson Education who worked on this book: my editor Tracy Johnson, associate editor Carole Snyder, production project manager Kayla Smith-Tarbox, the marketing department, and the people behind the scenes who handle the many tasks that must be done to produce a book. I thank the production team: Paul Anagnostopoulos, Richard Camp, Ted Laux, Jacqui Scarlott, and Priscilla Stevens.

Last but most, I thank Keith Mayers, for assisting with research, managing my software, reading all the chapters, being patient, running errands, finding other things to do while I worked (building a guitar!), and being my sweetheart.

The publishers would like to thank Victor Chakraborty for reviewing the content of the International Edition.

PROLOGUE

Prometheus, according to Greek myth, brought us the gift of fire. It is an awesome gift. It gives us the power to heat our homes, cook our food, and run the machines that make our lives more comfortable, healthy, and enjoyable. It is also awesomely destructive, both by accident and by arson. The Chicago fire in 1871 left 100,000 people homeless. In 1990, the oil fields of Kuwait were intentionally set ablaze. Since the beginning of the 21st century, wildfires in the United States have destroyed millions of acres and thousands of homes. In spite of the risks, in spite of these disasters, few of us would choose to return the gift of fire and live without it. We have learned, gradually, how to use it productively, how to use it safely, and how to respond more effectively to disasters, be they natural, accidental, or intentional.

Computer technology is the most significant new technology since the beginning of the Industrial Revolution. It is awesome technology, with the power to make routine tasks quick, easy, and accurate, to save lives, and to create large amounts of new wealth. It helps us explore space, communicate easily and cheaply, find information, create entertainment, and do thousands of other tasks. As with fire, this power creates powerful problems: potential loss of privacy, multimillion-dollar thefts, and breakdowns of large, complex systems (such as air traffic control systems, communications networks, and banking systems) on which we have come to depend. In this book, we describe some of the remarkable benefits of computer and communication technologies, some of the problems associated with them, and some of the means for reducing the problems and coping with their effects.

1

UNWRAPPING THE GIFT

1.1 The Pace of Change

> *In a way not seen since Gutenberg's printing press that ended the Dark Ages and ignited the Renaissance, the microchip is an epochal technology with unimaginably far-reaching economic, social, and political consequences.*
>
> —Michael Rothschild[1]

In 1804, Meriwether Lewis and William Clark set out on a two-and-a-half-year voyage to explore what is now the western United States. Many more years passed before their journals were published. Later explorers did not know that Lewis and Clark had been there before them. Stephen Ambrose points out in his book about the Lewis and Clark expedition, *Undaunted Courage*, that information, people, and goods moved no faster than a horse—and this limitation had not changed in thousands of years.[2] In 1997, millions of people went to the World Wide Web to watch a robot cart called Sojourner roll across the surface of Mars. We chat with people thousands of miles away, and instantly view Web pages from around the world. We can tweet from airplanes flying more than 500 miles per hour.

Telephones, automobiles, airplanes, radio, household electrical appliances, and many other marvels we take for granted were invented in the late 19th and early 20th centuries. They led to profound changes in how we work and play, how we get information, how we communicate, and how we organize our family lives. Our entry into space was one of the most dramatic feats of technology in the 20th century. Sputnik, the first man-made satellite, launched in 1957. Neil Armstrong walked on the moon in 1969. We still do not have personal spacecraft, vacation trips to the moon, or a large amount of commercial or research activity in space. Space tourism for the very rich is in an early stage. The moon landing has had little direct effect on our daily lives. But computer systems in cars can now apply the brakes if a pedestrian is in the car's path. Some cars park themselves, and experimental cars drive themselves on city streets. Computer programs beat human experts at chess and *Jeopardy!*, and our smartphones answer our questions. Surgeons perform surgery with robotic instruments miles from the patient. Roughly five billion people use cellphones; U.S. texters send more than a trillion texts in a year; Facebook has more than 800 million members; Twitter users tweet hundreds of thousands of times a day; and these numbers will be out of date when you read them. A day without using an appliance or device containing a microchip is as rare as a day without turning on an electric light.

The first electronic computers were built in the 1940s. Scientists at Bell Laboratories invented the transistor—a basic component of microprocessors—in 1947. The first hard-disk drive, made by IBM in 1956, weighed more than a ton and stored only five megabytes of data, less than the amount of space we use for one photo. Now, we can walk around with 150 hours of video in a pocket. A disk with a terabyte (one thousand gigabytes, or one trillion bytes) of storage—enough for 250 hours of high definition video—is inexpensive. There are hundreds of billions of gigabytes of information on the Internet. The 1991 space shuttle had a 1-megahertz* computer onboard. Ten years later, some luxury automobiles had 100-megahertz computers. Speeds of several gigahertz are now common. When I started my career as a computer science professor, personal computers had not yet been invented. Computers were large machines in air-conditioned rooms; we typed computer programs onto punched cards. If we wanted to do research, we went to a library, where the library catalog filled racks of trays containing 3 × 5 index cards. Social-networking sites were neighborhood pizza places and bars. The point is not that I am old; it is the speed and magnitude of the changes. The way you use computer systems and mobile devices, personally and professionally, will change substantially in two years, in five, and in ten, and almost unrecognizably over the course of your career. The ubiquity of computers, the rapid pace of change, and their myriad applications and impacts on daily life characterize the last few decades of the 20th century and the beginning of the 21st.

It is not just the technology that changes so fast. Social impacts and controversies morph constantly. With PCs and floppy disks came computer viruses and the beginnings of a huge challenge to the concept of copyright. With email came spam. With increased storage and speed came databases with details about our personal and financial lives. With the Web, browsers, and search engines came easy access by children to pornography, more threats to privacy, and more challenges to copyright. Online commerce brought bargains to consumers, opportunities to entrepreneurs, and identity theft and scams. Cellphones have had so many impacts that we discuss them in more detail later in this chapter and in Chapter 2. With hindsight, it might seem odd that people worried so much about antisocial, anticommunity effects of computers and the early Internet. Now, with the popularity of social networking, texting, and sharing video, photos, and information, the Net is a very social place. In 2008, "experts" worried the Internet would collapse within two years because of the demands of online video. It did not. Privacy threats of concern several years ago seem minor compared to new ones. People worried about how intimidating computers and the Internet were; now toddlers operate apps on tablets and phones. Concerns about technology "haves" and "have-nots" (the "digital divide") waned as Internet access and cellphones spread throughout the United States and around the world, shrinking the digital divide far faster than long-standing global divides in, say, education and access to fresh water.

Discussions of social issues related to computers often focus on problems, and indeed, throughout this book we examine problems created or intensified by computer technologies. Recognizing the benefits is important too. It is necessary for forming a reasonable, balanced view of the impact and value of the technology. Analyzing and evaluating the

---

* This is a measure of processing speed. One megahertz is 1 million cycles per second; 1 gigahertz is 1 billion cycles per second. "Hertz" is named for the 19th-century physicist Heinrich Rudolf Hertz.

impact of new technologies can be difficult. Some of the changes are obvious. Some are more subtle. Even when benefits are obvious, the costs and side effects might not be, and vice versa. Both the technological advances brought about by computer technology and the extraordinary pace of development have dramatic, sometimes unsettling, impacts on people's lives. To some, this is frightening and disruptive. They see the changes as dehumanizing, reducing the quality of life, or as threats to the status quo and their well-being. Others see challenging and exciting opportunities. To them, the development of the technology is a thrilling and inspiring example of human progress.

When we speak of computers in this book, we include mobile devices such as smartphones and tablets, desktop computers and mainframes, embedded chips that control machines (from sewing machines to oil refineries), entertainment systems (such as video recorders and game machines), and the "Net," or "cyberspace." Cyberspace is built of computers (e.g., Web servers), communication devices (wired and wireless), and storage media, but its real meaning is the vast web of communications and information that includes the Internet and more.

In the next section, we look at some phenomena, often unplanned and spontaneous, that computer and communication technology made possible. They have deeply changed how we interact with other people, what we can accomplish, and how others can intrude into our relationships and activities. In the rest of the chapter, we introduce themes that show up often, and we present an introduction to some ethical theories that can help guide our thinking about controversies throughout the rest of the book. The next seven chapters look at ethical, social, and legal issues primarily from the perspective of any person who lives and works in a modern computerized society and is interested in the impact of the technology. The final chapter takes the perspective of someone who works as a computer professional who designs or programs computer systems or as a professional in any area who must make decisions and/or set policy about the use of computer systems. It explores the ethical responsibilities of the professional. The Software Engineering Code of Ethics and Professional Practice and the ACM Code of Ethics and Professional Conduct, in Appendix A, provide guidelines for professionals.

1.2 Change and Unexpected Developments

No one would design a bridge or a large building today without using computers, but the Brooklyn Bridge, built more than 130 years ago—long before computers, is both a work of art and a marvelous feat of engineering. The builders of the Statue of Liberty, the Pyramids, the Roman aqueducts, magnificent cathedrals, and countless other complex structures did not wait for computers. People communicated by letters and telephone before text messages, email, and Twitter. People socialized in person before social-networking sites. Yet we can identify several phenomena resulting from computer and communication technology that are far different from what preceded them (in degree, if not entirely in kind), several areas where the impacts are dramatic, and many that were unanticipated. In this section, we consider a brief sampling of such phenomena. Some are quite recent. Some are routine parts of our lives now. The point is to remind us that a generation ago they did not exist. They illustrate the amazingly varied uses people find for new tools and technologies.

> *It is precisely this unique human capacity to transcend the present, to live one's life by purposes stretching into the future—to live not at the mercy of the world, but as a builder and designer of that world—that is the distinction between human and animal behavior, or between the human being and the machine.*
>
> —Betty Friedan[3]

1.2.1 CONNECTIONS: CELLPHONES, SOCIAL NETWORKING, AND MORE

The Web, social networking, cellphones, and other electronic devices keep us connected to other people and to information all day, virtually everywhere. We look at a few connectivity applications, focusing on fast changes and unanticipated uses and side effects (good and bad). The discussion suggests issues we study throughout the book.

Cellphones

In the 1990s, relatively few people had cellphones. Business people and sales people who often worked outside their office carried them. High-tech workers and gadget enthusiasts liked them. Others bought the phones so they could make emergency calls if their cars broke down. We were used to being out of touch when away from home or office. We planned ahead and arranged our activities so that we did not need a phone when one was not available. Within a short time, however, cell service improved and prices dropped. Cellphone makers and service providers developed new features and services, adding cameras, video, Web connections, and location detection. Apple introduced the iPhone in 2007, and phones got "smart." People quickly developed hundreds of thousands of applications and embraced the term *app*. Consumers downloaded 10 billion apps from Apple's App Store. Within very few years, people all over the world used phones, rather than PCs or laptops, as their connection to the Internet. Millions, then hundreds of millions, then billions of people started carrying mobile phones. In 2011, there were approximately five billion cellphone subscriptions worldwide—an astoundingly fast spread of a new technology. Writers describe the dramatic changes with observations such as, "A Masai warrior with a smartphone and Google has access to more information than the President did 15 years ago" and "More folks have access to a cellphone than to a toilet."[4]

Cellphones became a common tool for conversations, messaging, taking pictures, downloading music, checking email, playing games, banking, managing investments, finding a restaurant, tracking friends, watching videos. Smartphones serve as electronic wallets and identification cards at store terminals or security checkpoints. Phones monitor security cameras at home or control home appliances from a distance. Professional people use smartphone apps for a myriad of business tasks. Smartphones with motion detectors remind obese teenagers to get moving. An app analyzes blood glucose levels for diabetics and reminds them when to exercise, take medication, or eat something. Military personnel on the front lines can use specialized apps to download satellite surveillance video and maps. More unanticipated uses include location tracking, sexting, life-saving medical apps, and malicious data-stealing apps. People use cellphones to organize flash mobs for street dances and pillow fights—or for attacking pedestrians and looting stores. Terrorists use cellphones to set off bombs. Apps designed for poor countries inform people when water is available and help perform medical imaging.

These examples suggest the number and variety of unanticipated applications of this one, relatively new "connection" device. The examples also suggest problems. We discuss privacy invasion by data theft and location tracking in Chapter 2. In Chapter 3, we consider whether phone service should be shut down during riots. Is the security of smartphones sufficient for banking and electronic wallets? (What if you lose your phone?) Do people realize that when they synch their phone with other devices, their files become vulnerable at the level of the weakest security?

As a side effect of cellphone use and the sophistication of smartphones, researchers are learning an enormous amount about our behavior. Laws protect the privacy of the content of our conversations, but smartphones log calls and messages and contain devices that detect location, motion, direction, light levels, and other phones nearby. Most owners carry their phones all day. Researchers analyze this trove of sensor data. (Yes, much of it can be stored.) Analysis of the data generates valuable information about traffic congestion, commuting patterns, and the spread of disease. In an example of the latter, by studying movement and communication patterns of MIT students, researchers could detect who had the flu, sometimes before the students knew it themselves. Researchers also can determine which people influence the decisions of others. Advertisers and politicians crave such information. Perhaps the eeriest result is that researchers who analyzed time and location data from millions of calls said that, with enough data, a mathematical model could predict where someone would be at a particular future time with more than 90% accuracy. Who will have access to that information?[5]

Rudeness is an issue with cellphones. People use them in inappropriate places, disturbing others. The fact that so many people carry small cameras everywhere (mostly in phones, but also hidden in other small objects such as pens*) affects our privacy in public

---

* At least one company sells a working pen that records high-resolution video.

and nonpublic places.[6] How well do people armed with cellphone cameras distinguish news events and evidence of crimes from voyeurism, their own rudeness, and stalking?

Talking on a phone while driving a car increases the risk of an accident. Some states prohibit use of handheld phones while driving (and a lot of drivers ignore the ban). Researchers developed an app that uses motion detection by smartphones to deduce that a phone is in a moving car and block incoming calls. A more sophisticated version locates the phone well enough to block only the driver's phone, not that of a passenger.

Here is an example of a subtle behavioral change. When people began carrying cellphones and could call for help, more headed out in the wilderness or went rock climbing without appropriate preparation. In many areas of life, people take more risk when technology increases safety. This is not unreasonable if the added risk and increased safety are in balance. When rescue calls surged, some rescue services began billing for the true cost of a rescue—one way to remind people to properly weigh the risk.

Kill switches

Soon after Amazon began selling electronic books for its Kindle ebook readers, the company discovered that a publisher was selling books in Amazon's online store that it did not have the legal rights to sell in the United States. Amazon deleted the books from its store and from the Kindles of people who had bought them; it refunded their payments. A reasonable and appropriate response? Not to many customers and media observers. Customers were outraged that Amazon deleted books from their Kindles. People were startled to learn that Amazon *could* do so.* The response was so strong that Amazon announced that it would not remove books from customer Kindles again. Few realized at that time that Apple's iPhones already had a *kill switch*—a way for Apple to remotely delete apps from phones. In 2011, when a software developer discovered malicious code in an app for Android phones, Google quickly removed the app from its store and from more than 250,000 phones. Although this was a good example of the purpose of a kill switch and a beneficial use, the fact that Google could do it disturbed people. One of the troubling side effects of our connectivity is that outsiders can reach into our devices and delete our stuff.

Perhaps this extended reach should not have been a surprise. In many businesses, the IT department has access to all desktop computers and can install—or delete—software. Software on personal computers and other electronic devices communicates with businesses and organizations regularly, without our direct command, to check for updates of software, news, and our friends' activities. When we enable updates of software, a company remotely deletes old versions.

Now, the operating systems for smartphones, tablets, and some computers (e.g., Windows) have kill switches. The companies do not disclose much information about

---

* Ironically, one of the books Amazon removed was George Orwell's *1984*—a novel about a totalitarian government that regularly sent documents down a "memory hole" to destroy them.

them. The main purpose is security—to remove malicious software that the company discovers in an app after users have downloaded it. Indeed, companies such as Google and Apple that provide popular app stores see it as a serious responsibility to protect users from malicious apps. Some companies tell us about their removal capability in their terms of use agreements, but such agreements can run to thousands of words and have vague, general statements. Few people read them.

What are some potential uses and risks? Kill switches could remove content that infringes copyrights. They could remove content that a company or government deems offensive. What if malicious hackers found a way to operate the kill switches on our devices? Governments in many countries have extensive censorship laws and require that communications services provide government access to communications. Governments, in free and unfree countries, pressure businesses to act as the government prefers. For more than 2000 years, governments and religious and social organizations have burned books that displeased them. What pressures might governments put on companies to use the kill switches? Will the impact of electronic kill switches be more devastating than attempts to prohibit printed material? Or will companies use them carefully for improved security? Our new tools are remarkably powerful and remarkably vulnerable.

Social networking

While all this razzle-dazzle connects us electronically, it disconnects us from each other, having us "interfacing" more with computers and TV screens than looking in the face of our fellow human beings. Is this progress?

—Jim Hightower, radio commentator, 1995[7]

Facebook, one of the first of the social networking sites, started at Harvard as an online version of the hardcopy student directories available at many colleges. At first, the sites were wildly popular with young people, while older people did not understand the appeal or worried about safety and privacy. Adults quickly discovered benefits of personal and business social networking. Social networks are enormously popular with hundreds of millions of people because of the ease with which they can share so many aspects of their lives and activities with family, friends, co-workers, and the public.

As with so many other digital phenomena, people found unanticipated uses of social networking, some good, some bad. Friends and ex-boyfriends and ex-girlfriends post pranks and embarrassing material. Stalkers and bullies stalk and bully. Politicians, advertisers, businesses, and organizations seek donations, volunteers, customers, and connections. Protesters organize demonstrations and revolutions. Jurors tweet about court cases during trials (causing mistrials, overturned convictions, and jail time for offending jurors). Social networking brought us more threats to privacy and a steady stream of updates on the trivial details of people's lives. Gradually, social network companies developed sophisticated privacy controls and feedback systems to reduce problems, though they certainly have not eliminated them. Overall, to most people, the benefits outweigh the problems, and social networking has become the new way of communicating.

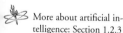
Privacy issues for social networks: Section 2.3.2

In a phenomenon called "crowd funding," social networks, Twitter, and other platforms make it easy to raise money in small amounts from a large number of people for charities, political causes, artistic projects, and investment in start-up companies.

How do social networking sites affect people and relationships? People can have hundreds of friends and contacts, but have they traded quality of in-person relationships for quantity of superficial digital relationships? Does the time spent online reduce the time spent on physical activity and staying healthy? It is still too early for definitive answers, but it appears that the many critics who anticipated a serious problem of social isolation were mistaken. Researchers find that people use social networks mostly to keep in touch with friends and family and that the easy, frequent contact enhances relationships, empathy, and a sense of community. On the other hand, young people who spend a lot of time on a social network do poorly in school and have behavioral problems. (Are these people who would have problems in any case? Does the access to the networks exacerbate preexisting emotional problems?)

Just as researchers study social phenomena using the masses of data that smartphone systems collect, they also mine the masses of data in social networks. For example, social scientists and computer scientists analyze billions of connections to find patterns that could help identify terrorist groups.[8]

A person you follow in social media might not be a person at all. A *socialbot* is an artificial intelligence program that simulates a human being in social media. Researchers tricked Twitter users into building relationships with artificial tweeting personalities, some of which gained large followings. Political activists launched socialbots to influence voters and legislators. The U.S. military raised concerns about automated disinformation campaigns by enemies. Advertising bots are likely to be common. When the Internet was new, someone commented (and many repeated) that "on the Internet, no one knows you're a dog." It meant that we could develop relationships with others based on common interests without knowing or caring about age, race, nationality, gender, or physical attractiveness. Some of those others might not even be people, and we might not know it. Should we be comfortable with that?

More about artificial intelligence: Section 1.2.3

Communication and the Web

Email and the Web are so much a part of our culture now that we might forget how new and extraordinary they are. Email was first used mostly by computer scientists. In the 1980s, messages were short and contained only text. As more people and businesses connected to computer networks, use of email expanded to science researchers, then to businesses, then to millions of other people. Limits on length disappeared, and we began attaching digitized photos and documents. People worldwide still send several billion emails daily (not counting spam), although texting, tweeting, and other social media have replaced email as the favored communication method in many contexts.[9]

High-energy physicists established the World Wide Web in Europe in 1990 to share their work with colleagues and researchers in other countries. In the mid- and late 1990s, with the development of Web browsers and search engines, the Web became an environment for ordinary users and for electronic commerce. Today there are billions of Web pages. The Web has grown from an idea to a huge library and news source, a huge shopping mall, an entertainment center, and a multimedia, global forum in less than one generation.

The Web gives us access to information and access to audiences unimaginable a generation ago. It empowers ordinary people to make better decisions about everything from selecting a bicycle to selecting medical treatments. It empowers us to do things that we used to rely on experts to do for us. Software tools, many available for free, help us analyze the healthiness of our diet or plan a budget. We can find references and forms for legal processes. We can read frank reviews of cameras, clothing, cars, books, and other products written by other buyers, not marketing departments. We can select our entertainment and watch it when we want to. We can fight back against powerful institutions by shaming them with videos that go viral* (see, for example, "United Breaks Guitars" on YouTube) or by posting legal documents intended to intimidate us (see, for example, chillingeffects.org). Businesses and organizations use "viral marketing"—that is, relying on large numbers of people to view and spread marketing messages in clever videos. We can start our own Web-based television network without the huge investment and government license requirements of broadcast television networks. A college student with a good idea and some well-implemented software can start a business that quickly grows to be worth millions or billions of dollars; several have. The openness of the Internet enables "innovation without permission," in the words of Vinton Cerf, one of the key people who has worked on Internet development since it began.[10]

Blogs (a word made up from "Web log") and videos are two examples of the many new forms of creativity that flourish because Web technology and special software make them so easy and inexpensive. They began as outlets for amateurs and now are significant sources of news and entertainment. They have created new paths for jobs—with news media, publishers, and advertising and entertainment companies. Of course, some amateur blogs and videos are dull, silly, and poorly written or made, but many are gems, and people find them. People blog on current events, celebrity gossip, hobbies, books, movies, dieting, law, economics, technology, political candidates, Internet issues, and virtually any other topic. They provide varied, sometimes quirky perspectives. The independence of

---

* "Going viral" describes the phenomenon where something posted in cyberspace catches the attention of people who view, copy, and spread it (or links to it) to millions more people.

"I've got pressure"

When asked by a young man to speak more quietly on his cellphone, a Hong Kong bus rider berated the man for nearly six minutes with angry insults and obscenities. In the past, a few other riders might have described the incident to friends, then soon forgotten it. But in this instance, another rider captured the scene on his cellphone. The video soon appeared on the Internet, and millions of people saw it. People provided subtitles in different languages, set the video to music, used clips as mobile-phone ringtones, and produced t-shirts with pictures and quotes. "I've got pressure" and other phrases from the rant slipped into conversations.

This incident reminds us that anything we do in a public place can be captured and preserved on video. But more, it illustrates how the Internet facilitates and encourages creativity and the quick creation and distribution of culture artifacts and entertainment, with the contribution of ideas, modifications, variations, improvements, and new works from thousands of people.

bloggers attracts readers; it suggests a genuine connection with what ordinary people are thinking and doing, not filtered through major news companies or governments. Businesses were quick to recognize the value of blogs, and many provide their own as part of their public relations and marketing programs. Inexpensive video cameras and video-manipulation tools have powered a burst of short amateur videos—often humorous, sometimes worthless, and sometimes quite serious. We can see a soldier's view of war, someone's encounter with aggressive whales, an arrest by police. Video sites also made it easy to post and trade professional videos, infringing copyrights owned by entertainment companies and individuals. We explore copyright issues in Chapter 4.

The Web connects students and teachers. At first, universities offered online courses within their area, benefitting people who work full-time, who have varying work schedules that conflict with normal class schedules, who have small children at home, or who cannot travel easily because of disabilities. Gradually a potential to revolutionize advanced education became clear.* More than 100 million people have viewed the thousands of free lessons on sciences, economics, and other subjects at the online Khan Academy. When two artificial intelligence experts offered a Stanford University graduate course for free online, they expected 500–1000 students to sign up. They got 160,000 people from around the world, and more than 20,000 completed the course, which included automatically graded homework assignments and exams.[11]

The impact of the connections provided by the Web and cellphones is more dramatic in remote or less developed areas of the world, many of which do not have landline telephones. Mountains and thick jungle, with no roads, separate villagers in one town in

---

* For elementary education, it appears that regular classes and in-person teachers still have the advantage.

Telemedicine

Telemedicine, or long-distance medicine, refers to remote performance of medical exams, analyses, and procedures using specialized equipment and computer networks. On long airplane flights, telemedicine can help treat a sick passenger and ascertain whether the plane needs to make an emergency landing. Prisons use telemedicine to reduce the risk of escape by dangerous criminals. Some small-town hospitals use video systems to consult with specialists at large medical centers—eliminating the expense, time, and possible health risk of transporting the patient to the medical center. A variety of health-monitoring devices send their readings from a patient's home to a nurse over the Internet. This technology eliminates the expense, time, and inconvenience of more frequent visits, while enabling more regular monitoring of patients and helping to catch dangerous conditions early.

Telemedicine goes well beyond transmission of information. Surgeons in New York used video, robotic devices, and high-speed communication links to remotely remove a gall bladder from a patient in France. Such systems can save lives in emergencies and bring a high level of surgical skills to small communities that have no surgeons.

Malaysia from the next, but the villagers order supplies, check the market price of rice to get a good deal when selling their crop, and email family photos to distant relatives. Farmers in Africa get weather forecasts and instruction in improved farming methods. An Inuit man operates an Internet service provider for a village in the Northwest Territories of Canada, where temperatures drop to −40°F. Villagers in Nepal sell handicrafts worldwide via a website based in Seattle. Sales have boomed, more villagers have regular work, dying local arts are reviving, and some villagers can now afford to send their children to school.

The Web abounds with examples of collaborative projects, some organized, such as Wikipedia* (the online encyclopedia written by volunteers), some spontaneous. Scientists collaborate on research with scientists in other countries much more easily and more often than they could without the Internet. Informal communities of programmers, scattered around the world, create and maintain free software. Informal, decentralized groups of people help investigate online auction fraud, a murder, stolen research, and other crimes. People who have never met collaborate on creating entertainment.

Some collaborative projects can have dangerous results. To reduce the flow of illegal immigrants, a governor of Texas proposed setting up night-vision webcams along the Mexican border that volunteers would monitor on the Internet. Will the people monitoring a border webcam go out and attack those they see coming across the border? What training or selection process is appropriate for volunteers who monitor these security cameras? In China, a man posted the online name of another man he believed was having

---

* A *wiki* is a website, supported by special software, that allows people to add content and edit content that others provide. Wikis are tools for collaborative projects within a business or organization or among the public.

an affair with his wife. Thousands of people participated in tracking down the man's real name and address and encouraging public action against him. Thousands of Twitterers in Saudi Arabia called for the execution of a young writer who they believed insulted the Prophet Muhammad. Mobs and individuals emotionally involved in a political, religious, or moral cause do not always pause for the details of due process. They do not carefully determine whether they identified the correct person, whether the person is guilty of a crime, and what the appropriate punishment is. On the other hand, police departments in cities in several countries effectively use instant messaging to alert residents who help find crime suspects or stolen cars in their neighborhoods. Enlisting volunteers is a useful new collaborative tool for crime fighting and possibly antiterrorism programs. How can we guide the efforts of thousands of individuals toward useful ends while protecting against mistakes, instant vigilantism, and other abuses?

1.2.2   E-commerce and Free Stuff

In the 1990s, the idea of commercial websites horrified Web users. The Web, they believed, was for research, information, and online communities. A few brick-and-mortar businesses and a few young entrepreneurs recognized the potential and benefits of online commerce. Among the earliest traditional businesses on the Web, United Parcel Service and Federal Express let customers check the status of packages they sent. This was both a novelty and a helpful service. Amazon.com, founded in 1994, started selling books on the Web and became one of the most popular, reliable, and user-friendly commercial sites. Many, many Web-based businesses followed Amazon, creating new business models—such as eBay with its online auctions. Traditional businesses established websites. Online sales in the United States now total hundreds of billions of dollars a year. The Web changed from a mostly academic community to a world market in little more than a decade.

Some of the benefits of e-commerce are fairly obvious: we can consider more products and sellers, some far away, in less time and without burning gasoline. Some benefits are less obvious or were not obvious before they appeared. Auction sites gave people access to customers they could not have found efficiently before. The lower overhead and the ease of comparison shopping on the Web brought down prices of a variety of products. Consumers save 10–40%, for example, by buying contact lenses online, according to a Progressive Policy Institute report. Consumers who do price-comparison research on the Web before buying a new car typically save about $400.[12] Small businesses and individual artists sell on the Web without paying big fees to middlemen and distributors. The Web enabled a peer-to-peer economy with websites where ordinary people sell or trade their skills, make small loans, and trade their homes for vacations.

Growth of commerce on the Web required solutions to several problems. One was trust. People were reluctant to give their credit card numbers on the Web to companies they had not dealt with or even heard of before. Enter PayPal, a company built on the idea of having a trusted intermediary handle payments. Encryption and secure servers also made payments safer.* The Better Business Bureau established a website where we can find out if consumers have complained about a company. Auction sites implemented rating and comment systems to help buyers and sellers determine whom to trust. Email confirmations of orders, consumer-friendly return policies, and easy packaging for returns all contributed to consumer comfort and more online sales. The University of Michigan's National Quality Research Center found that e-commerce businesses had a higher customer-satisfaction rating than any other sector of the economy. As online sales increased, competition led traditional stores to adopt some of the practices of e-commerce, such as consumer-friendly return policies.

Impacts of e-commerce on free speech: Section 3.2.5

Free stuff

Libraries have provided free access to books, newspapers, and journals for generations, and radio and television provided free news and entertainment before the Internet. But there is so much more free stuff now—a truly astounding amount—conveniently available on the Web.

For our computers, we can get free email programs and email accounts, browsers, filters, firewalls, encryption software, word processors, spreadsheets, software for viewing documents, software to manipulate photos and video, home inventory software, antispam software, antivirus software, antispyware software, and software for many other specialized purposes. This is a small sampling of software available for free.

We can find free game-playing programs for old board games and card games such as chess and bridge, as well as for new games. Phone service via Skype is free. There are free dating services on the Web. Major music festivals offer their concerts for free on the Internet, a nice alternative to paying $30 to $500 for a ticket. Craigslist, the classified ad site, one of the most popular websites in the world, is free to people who place ads and people who read them. Major (expensive) universities such as Stanford, Yale, and MIT provide video of lectures, lecture notes, and exams for thousands of their courses on the Web for free. We can download whole books from Google, Project Gutenberg, and other sources for free.† We can read news from all over the world for free. We can store our personal photographs, videos, and other files online for free. MySpace, Facebook, Twitter, LinkedIn, and YouTube are free; Google, Bing, and Yahoo are free. Specialized, scholarly encyclopedias (e.g., the Stanford Encyclopedia of Philosophy), Wikipedia, and hundreds of other references are free.

We pay for libraries with taxes. Advertisers pay for broadcasting radio and television programs. On the Web, advertising pays for many, many free sites and services, but far from all. Wikipedia carries no advertising—donations pay for its hardware and band-

---

* The ease and security of payment on the Web had a pleasant side effect: Many people contribute more to charitable organizations. That had the unpleasant side effect of spawning scam charity sites.

† Books available for free downloading are in the public domain (that is, out of copyright).

width. Craigslist charges fees of some businesses that post job announcements and brokers who post apartment listings in a few cities. That keeps the site free to everyone else and free of other paid ads. Businesses provide some free information and services for good public relations and as a marketing tool. (Some free programs and services do not have all the features of the paid versions.) Nonprofit organizations provide information as a public service; donations or grants fund them. One of the distinct and delightful features of the Internet is that individuals provide a huge amount of free stuff simply because it pleases them to do so. They are professionals or hobbyists or just ordinary people who enjoy sharing their expertise and enthusiasm. Generosity and public service flourish in the Web environment.

It is often obvious when we are viewing advertisements on websites or phones. Ads annoy some people, but they are not insidious, and their presence on a screen is not an unreasonable price to pay for free services. However, to earn ad revenue to fund multimillion-dollar services, many free sites collect information about our online activities and sell it to advertisers. This tracking is often not obvious; we consider it in Chapter 2.

1.2.3 ARTIFICIAL INTELLIGENCE, ROBOTICS, SENSORS, AND MOTION

Artificial intelligence

Artificial intelligence (AI) is a branch of computer science that makes computers perform tasks we normally (or used to) think of as requiring human intelligence. It includes playing complex strategy games such as chess, language translation, making decisions based on large amounts of data (such as approving loan applications), and understanding speech (where the appropriateness of the response might be the measure of "understanding"). AI also includes tasks performed automatically by the human brain and nervous system—for example, vision (the capture and interpretation of images by cameras and software). Learning is a characteristic of many AI programs. That is, the output of the program improves over time as it "learns" by evaluating results of its decisions on the inputs it encounters. Many AI applications involve *pattern recognition*, that is, recognizing similarities among different things. Applications include reading handwriting (for automatic sorting of mail and input on tablet computers, for example), matching fingerprints, and matching faces in photos.

Early in the development of AI, researchers thought the hard problems for computers were tasks that required high intelligence and advanced training for humans, such as winning at chess and doing mathematical proofs. In 1997, IBM's chess computer, Deep Blue, beat World Champion Garry Kasparov in a tournament. AI researchers realized that narrow, specialized skills were easier for computers than what a five-year-old does: recognize people, carry on a conversation, respond intelligently to the environment. In 2011, another specially designed computer system called Watson (also built by IBM) defeated human *Jeopardy!* champions by answering questions more quickly than the humans. Watson processes language (including puns, analogies, and so on) and general knowledge. It searches and analyzes 200 million pages of information in less than three seconds. Practical applications of the Watson technology include medical diagnosis and various business decision-making applications.

We briefly describe a few more examples of AI applications. They were astonishing advances not long ago.

When a man had a heart attack in a swimming pool in Germany, lifeguards did not see him sink to the bottom of the pool. An underwater surveillance system, using cameras and sophisticated software, detected him and alerted the lifeguards who rescued him. The software distinguishes a swimmer in distress from normal swimming, shadows, and reflections. It is now installed in many large pools in Europe and the United States. Just as AI software can distinguish a swimmer in trouble from other swimmers, AI software in video surveillance systems can distinguish suspicious behavior by a customer in a store that might indicate shoplifting or other crimes. Thus, without constant human monitoring, the AI-equipped video system can help prevent a crime, rather than simply identify the culprits afterwards.

Search engines use AI techniques to select search results. They figure out what the user meant if the search phrase contains typos, and they use context to determine the intended meaning of words that have multiple meanings. Automated websites that answer questions use AI to figure out what a question means and find answers.

Speech recognition, once a difficult research area, is now a common tool for hundreds of applications. Computer programs that teach foreign languages give instruction in correct pronunciation if they do not recognize what the user says. Millions of people who carry Apple smartphones can ask questions of Siri, Apple's "intelligent" personal assistant. Siri interprets our questions and searches the Web for answers. Air traffic controllers train in a mockup tower whose "windows" are computer screens. The trainee directs simulated air traffic. The computer system responds when the trainee speaks to the simulated pilots. Such simulation allows more intensive training in a safe environment. If the trainee mistakenly directs two airplanes to land on the same runway at the same time, no one gets hurt.

People continue to debate the philosophical nature and social implications of artificial intelligence. What does it mean for a computer system to be intelligent? Alan Turing, who developed fundamental concepts underlying computer science before there were computers, proposed a test, now called the Turing Test, for human-level intelligence. Let a person converse (over a network) with the system on any topics the person chooses. If the computer convinces the person that it is human, the computer passes the test. Is that enough? Many technologists think so (assuming the actual test is well designed). But is the computer intelligent? Philosopher John Searle argues that computers are not and cannot be intelligent. They do not think; they manipulate symbols. They do so at very high speed, and they can store (or access) and manipulate a huge quantity of data, but they are not conscious. They do not understand; they simulate understanding. Searle uses the following example to illustrate the difference: Suppose you do not know the

Chinese language. You are in a room with lots of boxes of Chinese symbols and a large instruction book written in English. People submit to you sequences of Chinese symbols. The instructions tell you how to manipulate the symbols you are given and the ones in the boxes to produce a new sequence of symbols to give back. You are very careful, and you do not get bored; you follow the instructions in the book exactly. Unknown to you, the sequences you receive are questions in Chinese. The sequences that you give back by following the instructions (just as a computer follows the instructions of a program) are the correct answers in Chinese. Everyone outside the room thinks you understand Chinese very well. Do you? Searle might say that although Watson won at *Jeopardy!*, Watson does not know it won.[13]

Whether we characterize machines as intelligent, or use the word metaphorically, or say that machines simulate intelligence, advances in AI are continuing at a very fast pace. It took IBM several years and millions of dollars to build Watson.[14] Technologist Ray Kurzweil thinks personal computers will have the power of Watson within 10 years.

The goal of 17th- and 18th-century calculators was modest: to automate basic arithmetic operations. It shocked people at the time. That a mindless machine could perform tasks associated with human intellectual abilities was disconcerting. Centuries later, Garry Kasparov's loss to a computer chess program generated worried articles about the value—or loss of value—of human intelligence. Watson generated more. So far, it seems that each new AI breakthrough is met with concern and fear at first. A few years later, we take it for granted. How will we react when *Jeopardy!* is oh, so trivial that anyone can do well

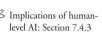 Implications of human-level AI: Section 7.4.3

at it? How will we react when we can go into a hospital for surgery performed entirely by a machine? Will it be scarier than riding in the first automatic elevators or airplanes? How will we react when we can have a conversation over the Net about any topic at all—and not know if we are conversing with a human or a machine? How will we react when chips implanted in our brains enhance our memory with gigabytes of data and a search engine? Will we still be human?

Robots

Robots are mechanical devices that perform physical tasks traditionally done by humans or tasks that we think of as human-like activities. Robotic machines have been assembling products in factories for decades. They work faster and more accurately than people can. Computer software with artificial intelligence controls most robotic devices now. Robotic milking machines milk hundreds of thousands of cows at dairy farms while the farmhands sleep or do other chores. Some robots dance, and some make facial expressions to convey emotions. However, just as general intelligence is a hard problem for AI, general movement and functioning is a hard problem for robots. Most robotic devices are special-purpose devices with a relatively limited set of operations.

McDonald's and other fast-food sellers use robotic food preparation systems to reduce costs and speed service. A robot pharmacist machine, connected to a patient database, plucks the appropriate medications from pharmacy shelves by reading bar codes, checks for drug interactions, and handles billing. One of its main goals is reduction of human error. Robots deliver medications and carry linens in hospitals. They navigate around obstacles and "push" elevator buttons with wireless signals. Physicians do complex and delicate surgery from a console with a 3-D monitor and joysticks that control robotic instruments. The software filters out a physician's shaky movements. Robots work in environments that are hazardous to people. They inspect undersea structures and communication cables. They search for survivors in buildings collapsed by bombs or earthquakes. They explore volcanoes and other planets. They move or process nuclear and other hazardous wastes.

For several years, Sony sold a robot pet dog, Aibo. It walked (with a camera system providing vision). It responded to commands, and it learned. Several companies make robots with a more-or-less human shape. Honda's Asimo, for example, walks up and down stairs. Various companies and researchers are developing robots with more general abilities. One goal is to develop robots that can act intelligently and perform a variety of operations to assist people. Robots (doglike or humanlike) can serve as companions to elderly people. Is an emotional connection with a machine dehumanizing, or is it an improvement over living alone or in a nursing home where the staff cannot provide regular companionship? Will knowing that Grandma has a robot companion ease the guilt of family members and lead them to visit less often? Will we come to view robot companions as positively as pets?

Smart sensors, motion, and control

How do robots walk, climb stairs, and dance? Tiny motion-sensing and gravity-sensing devices collect status data. Complex software interprets the data and determines the necessary motions, and then sends signals to motors. These devices—accelerometers, or *mems* (for microelectromechanical systems)—help robots, and Segway's motorized scooters, stay upright.

A sharp price drop for mems triggered a burst of applications.[15] They provide image stabilization in digital cameras. They detect when a car has crashed, when someone has dropped a laptop, or when an elderly person has fallen. (In those applications, the system deploys an airbag, triggers a lock on the disk drive to reduce damage, or calls for help.) The Wii game console, whose controller detects the user's motion, and motion detectors in smartphones brought motion-sensing applications to millions of consumers.

Tiny microprocessors with sensors and radio transmitters (sometimes called smart dust, though they are still larger than dust particles) are finding all sorts of applications. Some are in use; some are in development. We mention a few examples. These examples have many obvious benefits. What are some potential problems?

Oil refineries and fuel storage systems uses thousands of sensors to detect leaks and other malfunctions. Sandia National Laboratory developed a "chemical lab on a chip" that can detect emissions from automobiles, chemical leaks, dangerous gases in fires (reducing risk for firefighters), and many other hazards. Similar chips could detect chemical warfare agents.

Sensors detect temperature, acceleration, and stress in materials (such as airplane parts). Sensors distributed throughout buildings and bridges can detect structural problems, report on damage from earthquakes, and so on. These applications increase safety while reducing maintenance costs.

Sensors in agricultural fields report on moisture, acidity, and so on, helping farmers to avoid waste and to use no more fertilizer than needed. Sensors could detect molds or insects that might destroy crops. Sensors implanted in chickens monitor the birds' body temperature. A computer automatically reduces the temperature in the chicken coop if the birds get too hot, thus reducing disease and death from overheating. Sensors in food products monitor temperature, humidity, and other factors to detect potential health problems while the food is in transit to stores.

What will be the impact of tiny flying sensor/computers that communicate wirelessly and which the military can deploy to monitor movement of equipment and people, or with which police or criminals can spy on us in our homes and public places?

A Microsoft researcher developed a system with which a user manipulates 3-D images with hand movements, without touching a screen or any controls. Designers of buildings, machines, clothing, and so on, could use it to examine designs before implementing them. Someone with dirty (or sterile) hands (e.g., mechanics, cooks, surgeons) could examine reference materials while working. What other applications will people think of?

Sensors in baby clothes detect when a baby is sleeping face down, at risk for Sudden Infant Death Syndrome, and warn parents on their cellphone. A heart monitor in a firefighter's shirt alerts supervisors if the firefighter is too stressed and needs a break. Trainers plan to use sensors in special clothing to better train athletes. What other applications will we find for *wearware*?

Already we implant or attach microprocessor-controlled devices in or on human bodies: heart pacemakers and defibrillators and devices that restore motion to paralyzed people (which we describe in Section 1.2.4). These will likely see modifications that enhance performance for healthy people. At first it might be physical performance for athletes—for example, to help a competitive swimmer swim more smoothly. Then what? Biological sciences and computer sciences will combine in new ways.

1.2.4 Tools for Disabled People

One of the most heartwarming applications of computer technology is the restoration of abilities, productivity, and independence to people with physical disabilities.

Some computer-based devices assist disabled people in using ordinary computer applications that other people use, such as Web browsers and word processors. Some enable disabled people to control household and workplace appliances that most of us operate by hand. Some improve mobility. Some technologies that are primarily conveniences for most of us provide significantly more benefit for disabled people: consider that text messaging was very popular among deaf people before it was popular with the general population.

For people who are blind, computers equipped with speech synthesizers read aloud what a sighted person sees on the screen. They read information embedded in Web pages that sighted visitors do not need, for example, descriptions of images. Google offers search tools that rank websites based on how accessible they are for blind users. For materials not in electronic form, a scanner or camera, optical-character-recognition software, and a speech synthesizer combine to read aloud to a blind person. The first such readers were large machines. Now, handheld versions can read menus, bills, and receipts in restaurants, as well as magazines and mail at home. Where noise is a problem (or for a person both blind and deaf), a grid of buttons raised and lowered by the computer to form Braille characters can replace speech output. Braille printers provide hard copy. (Books have long been available in Braille or on tape, but the expense of production for a small market kept the selection limited.) Systems similar to navigation systems in cars help blind people walk around and find their way in unfamiliar neighborhoods.

Prosthetic devices, such as artificial arms and legs, have improved from heavy, "dumb" wood, to lighter materials with analog motors, and now to highly sensitive and flexible digitally controlled devices that enable amputees to participate in sports and fly airplanes. A person whose leg was amputated above the knee can walk, sit, and climb stairs with an artificial "smart" knee. Sensors attached to the natural leg measure pressure and motion more than a thousand times a second and transmit the data to a processor in the prosthetic leg. Artificial intelligence software recognizes and adapts to changes in speed and slope and the person's walking style. The processor controls motors to bend and straighten the knee and support the body's movement, replacing the normal complex interplay of nerves, muscles, tendons, and ligaments. Artificial arms use electrodes to pick up tiny electrical fields generated by contractions of muscles in the upper (natural) limb. Microprocessors control tiny motors that move the artificial limb, open and close fingers, and so on. For people with paralyzed legs or for others who cannot use an artificial leg, there are wheelchairs that climb stairs and support and transport a person in an upright position. In 2012, Exso Bionics sold its first exoskeleton, a device with sensors and tiny motors that straps to a person with paralyzed legs and enables the person to walk.[16]

Various conditions—loss of limbs, quadriplegia (paralysis in both arms and legs, often resulting from an accident), and certain diseases—eliminate all or almost all use of the hands. Speech recognition systems are an extremely valuable tool for these people and for others. (Deaf people can use speech-recognition systems to "hear" another speaker as the computer displays the spoken words on a screen.) People who cannot use their hands can dictate documents to a word processor and give commands to a computer to control household appliances.

To restore control and motion to people paralyzed by spinal injuries, researchers are experimenting with chips that convert brain signals to controls for leg and arm muscles.

Researchers in the United States and Europe are developing brain–computer interfaces so that severely handicapped people can operate a computer and control appliances with their thoughts.[17]

The impact of all these devices on the morale of the user is immense. Think about a person with an active mind, personality, and sense of humor—but who cannot write, type, or speak. Imagine the difference when the person gains the ability to communicate—with family and friends, and with all the people and resources available on the Internet.

1.3 Themes

Several themes and approaches to analysis of issues appear through this book. I introduce a few here.

Old problems in a new context

> Cyberspace has many of the problems, annoyances, and controversies of noncyber life, among them crime, pornography, violent fiction and games, advertising, copyright infringement, gambling, and products that do not work right.

Throughout this book, I often draw analogies from other technologies and other aspects of life. Sometimes we can find a helpful perspective for analysis and even ideas for solutions to new problems by looking at older technologies and established legal and social principles. The emphasis on the fact that similar problems occur in other areas is not meant to excuse the new problems. It suggests, however, that the root is not always the new technology but can be human nature, ethics, politics, or other factors. We will often try to analyze how the technology changes the context and the impact of old problems.

Adapting to new technology

> Changes in technology usually require adaptive changes in laws, social institutions, business policies, and personal skills, attitudes, and behavior.

When cellphones first came with built-in cameras, privacy laws in Pennsylvania (and elsewhere) were not sufficient to convict a man who used his cellphone to take a photo up a woman's skirt. (The man was found guilty of disorderly conduct.) A federal regulation requiring medical x-rays on film, rather than digital formats, was still in effect in 2011. During Japanese election campaigns in 2005, candidates were afraid to use email and blogs and to update their websites to communicate with voters, because a 1955 law that specifies the legal means of communicating with voters does not, of course, include these methods. It allows postcards and pamphlets.

We might naturally think some actions are criminal, and some should be legal, but legislators did not consider them when writing existing laws. The legal status of an action might be the opposite of what we expect, or it might be uncertain. Many new activities that new technology makes possible are so different from prior ways of doing things that we need a new set of "rules of the game."

We have to relearn standards for deciding when to trust what we read. The major impact of computer technology on privacy means we have to think in new ways about how to protect ourselves. We have to decide when privacy is important and when we are willing to put it at risk for some other benefit.

Varied sources of solutions to problems

Solutions for problems that result from new technology come from more or improved technology, the market, management policies, education and public awareness, volunteer efforts, and law.

The cycle of problems and solutions, more problems and more solutions, is a natural part of change and of life in general. Throughout this book, when we consider problems, we consider solutions from several categories. Technical solutions include hardware and software. "Hardware" might mean something other than part of a computer system; improved lighting near ATMs to reduce robberies is a hardware solution. Authentication technology helps reduce identity theft. Market mechanisms, such as competition and consumer demand, generate many improvements. We all must become educated about the risks of the high-tech tools we use and learn how to use them safely. Legal solutions include effective law enforcement, criminal penalties, lawsuits, legislation, and regulation. For example, there must be appropriate penalties for people who commit fraud online, and there must be appropriate liability laws for cases where system failures occur.

The global reach of the Net

The ease of communication with distant countries has profound social, economic, and political effects—some beneficial, some not.

The Net makes information and opportunities more easily available to people isolated by geography or by political system. It makes crime fighting and law enforcement more difficult, because criminals can steal and disrupt services from outside the victim's country. Laws in one country prohibiting certain content on the Web or certain kinds of Web services restrict people and businesses in other countries because the Web is accessible worldwide.

Trade-offs and controversy

Increasing privacy and security often means reducing convenience. Protecting privacy makes law enforcement more difficult. Unpleasant, offensive, or inaccurate information accompanies our access to the Web's vast amounts of useful information.

Some of the topics we discuss are not particularly controversial. We will sometimes address an issue more as a problem-solving exercise than as a controversy. We will look at the impact of electronic technology in a particular area, observe some problems that result, and describe solutions. On the other hand, many of the issues are controversial: leaking confidential information on the Internet, proper policies for privacy protection, how strict copyright law should be, offshoring of jobs, the impact of computers on quality of life.

We consider various viewpoints and arguments. Even if you have a strong position on one side of a controversy, it is important to know the arguments on the other side, for several reasons. Knowing that there are reasonable arguments for a different point of view, even if you do not think they are strong enough to win overall, helps make a debate more civilized. We see that the people on the other side are not necessarily evil, stupid, or ignorant; they may just put more weight on different factors. To convince others of your own viewpoint, you must counter the strongest arguments of the other side, so, of course, you first must know and understand them. Finally, you might change your own mind after considering arguments you had not thought of before.

Perfection is a direction, not an option.

In general, when evaluating new technologies and applications, we should not compare them to some ideal of perfect service or zero side effects and zero risk. That is impossible to achieve in most aspects of life. Instead, we should compare them to the alternatives and weigh the problems against the benefits. The ideal shows us the direction to go as we endeavor to seek improvements and solutions to problems.

Another reason that we cannot expect perfection is that we all have different ideas of what perfection is.

This does not excuse sloppiness. It is possible to meet extremely high standards.

Differences between personal choices, business policies, and law

The criteria for making personal choices, for making policies for businesses and organizations, and for writing laws are fundamentally different.

We can make a personal choice—for example, about what social networks to join, what apps to put on our phones, or what ebooks to buy—according to our individual values and situation. A business bases its policies on many factors, including the manager's perception of consumer preferences, what competitors are doing, responsibilities to stockholders, the ethics of the business owners or managers, and relevant laws.

Laws are fundamentally different from personal choices and organizational policies because they impose decisions by force on people who did not make them. Arguments for passing a law should be qualitatively different from reasons for adopting a personal or organizational policy. It might seem odd at first, but arguments on the merits of the proposal—for example, that it is a good idea, or is efficient, or is good for business, or is helpful to consumers—are not good arguments for a law. We can use these arguments to try to convince a person or organization to adopt a particular policy voluntarily. Arguments for a law must show why the decision should be enforced against someone who *does not agree* that it is a good idea. It is better to base laws on the notion of rights rather than on personal views about their benefits or how we want people to behave.

1.4 Ethics

Honesty is the best policy.

—English proverb, pre-1600

1.4.1 WHAT IS ETHICS, ANYWAY?

Sometimes, we discuss issues and problems related to computer technology from a somewhat detached perspective. We see how a new technology can create new risks and how social and legal institutions continually adapt. But technology is not an immutable force, outside of human control. People make decisions about what technologies and products to develop and how to use them. People make decisions about when a product is safe to release. People make decisions about access to and use of personal information. People make laws and set rules and standards.

Should you download movies from unauthorized websites? Should you talk on your cellphone while driving on a freeway? Should you hire foreign programmers who work at low salaries? Should you warn potential customers that the smartphone app you sell needs to copy their contact list? Should you fire an employee who is criticizing your business in social media? What information should you allow advertisers and other trackers to collect from visitors to the website you run? Someone sent you the contents of a friend's (a teacher's, a city council candidate's) email account; should you post it on the Web? In these examples, you are confronting practical and legal issues—and ethical ones. In each case you can restate the problem as a question in the form "Is it right to . . . ?" Is it right to make a significant change in your company's privacy policy without giving customers or members advance notice?

In this section, we introduce several ethical theories. We discuss some distinctions (e.g., between ethics and law) that are important to understand when tackling ethical issues.

Ethics is the study of what it means to "do the right thing." It is a complex subject that has occupied philosophers for thousands of years. This presentation is necessarily simplified.

Ethical theory assumes that people are rational and make free choices. Neither of these conditions is always and absolutely true. People act emotionally, and they make mistakes. A person is not making a free choice when someone else is pointing a gun at him. Some argue that a person is not making a free choice in a situation where she might lose a job. However, free choice and use of rational judgment are capacities and characteristics of

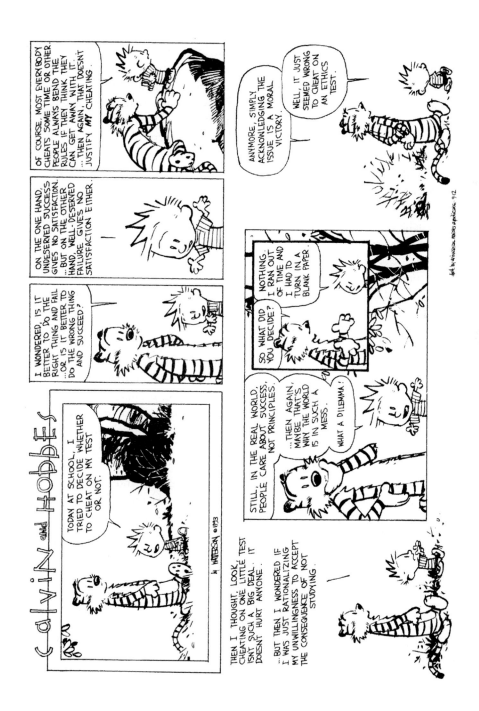

human beings, and they are reasonably assumed as the basis of ethical theory. We take the view that the individual is, in most circumstances, responsible for his or her actions.

Ethical rules are rules to follow in our interactions with other people and in our actions that affect other people. Most ethical theories attempt to achieve the same goal: to enhance human dignity, peace, happiness, and well-being. Ethical rules apply to all of us and are intended to achieve good results for people in general, and for situations in general—not just for ourselves, not just for one situation. A set of rules that does this well respects the fact that we are each unique and have our own values and goals, that we have judgment and will, and that we act according to our judgment to achieve our goals. The rules should clarify our obligations and responsibilities—and our areas of choice and personal preference.*

We could view ethical rules as fundamental and universal, like laws of science. Or we could view them as rules we make up, like the rules of baseball, to provide a framework in which to interact with other people in a peaceful, productive way. The titles of two books illustrate these different viewpoints. One is *Ethics:* Discovering *Right and Wrong*; the other is *Ethics:* Inventing *Right and Wrong*.[18] We do not have to decide which view is correct to find good ethical rules. In either case, our tools include reason, introspection, and knowledge of human nature, values, and behavior.

Behaving ethically, in a personal or professional sphere, is usually not a burden. Most of the time we are honest, we keep our promises, we do not steal, we do our jobs. This should not be surprising. If ethical rules are good ones, they work for people. That is, they make our lives better. Behaving ethically is usually practical. Honesty makes interactions among people work more smoothly and reliably, for example. We might lose friends if we often lie or break promises. Social institutions encourage us to do right: We might land in jail if caught stealing. We might lose our jobs if we do them carelessly. In a professional context, doing good ethically often corresponds closely with doing a good job in the sense of professional quality and competence. Doing good ethically often corresponds closely with good business in the sense that ethically developed products and ethical policies are more likely to please consumers. Sometimes, however, it is difficult to do the right thing. It takes courage in situations where we could suffer negative consequences. Courage is often associated with heroic acts, where one risks one's life to save someone in a dangerous situation—the kind of act that makes news. Most of us do not have those opportunities to display courage, but we do have many opportunities in day-to-day life.

1.4.2 A VARIETY OF ETHICAL VIEWS[19]

Although there is much agreement about general ethical rules, there are many different theories about how to establish a firm justification for the rules and how to decide what is

---

* Not all ethical theories fit this description. Ethical relativism and some types of ethical egoism do not. In this book, however, we assume these goals and requirements for ethical theories.

ethical in specific cases. We give very brief descriptions of a few approaches to ethics. Some ethicists* make a distinction between ethical theories that view certain acts as good or bad because of some intrinsic aspect of the action and ethical theories that view acts as good or bad because of their consequences. They call these deontological (or nonconsequentialist) and consequentialist theories, respectively. The distinction is perhaps emphasized more than necessary. If the criteria that deontologists use to determine the intrinsic goodness or badness of an act do not consider its consequences for people—at least for most people, most of the time—their criteria would seem to have little ethical merit.

Deontological theories

Deontologists tend to emphasize duty and absolute rules, to be followed whether they lead to good or ill consequences in particular cases. One example is: Do not lie. An act is ethical if it complies with ethical rules and you chose it for that reason.

Immanuel Kant, the philosopher often presented as the prime example of a deontologist, contributed many important ideas to ethical theory. We mention three of them here. One is the principle of universality: We should follow rules of behavior that we can universally apply to everyone. This principle is so fundamental to ethical theory that we already accepted it in our explanation of ethics.

Second, deontologists argue that logic or reason determines rules of ethical behavior, that actions are intrinsically good because they follow from logic. Kant believed that rationality is the standard for what is good. We can reason about what makes sense and act accordingly, or we can act irrationally, which is evil. The view that something is evil because it is illogical might seem unconvincing, but Kant's instruction to "Respect the reason in you"—that is, to use your reason, rationality, and judgment, rather than emotions, when making a decision in an ethical context—is a wise one.

Third, Kant stated a principle about interacting with other people: One must never treat people as merely means to ends, but rather as ends in themselves.

Kant took an extreme position on the absolutism of ethical rules. He argued, for instance, that it is always wrong to lie. For example, if a person is looking for someone he intends to murder, and he asks you where the intended victim is, it is wrong for you to lie to protect the victim. Most people would agree that there are cases in which even very good, universal rules should be broken—because of the consequences.

Utilitarianism

Utilitarianism is the main example of a consequentialist theory. Its guiding principle, as expressed by John Stuart Mill,[20] is to increase happiness, or "utility." A person's utility is what satisfies the person's needs and values. An action might decrease utility for some people and increase it for others. We should consider the consequences—the benefits and

---

* Ethicists are philosophers (and others) who study ethics.

damages to all affected people—and "calculate" the change in aggregate utility. An act is right if it tends to increase aggregate utility and wrong if it tends to decrease it.

Utilitarianism is a very influential theory, and it has many variations. As stated above, the utilitarian principle applies to individual actions. For each action, we consider the impact on utility and judge the action by its net impact. This is sometimes called "act utilitarianism." One variant of utilitarianism, called "rule utilitarianism," applies the utility principle not to individual actions but to general ethical rules. Thus, a rule utilitarian might argue that the rule "Do not lie" will increase total utility, and for that reason it is a good rule. Rule utilitarians do not do a utility calculation for each instance where they consider lying. Generally, a utilitarian would be more comfortable than a deontologist breaking a rule in circumstances where doing so would have good consequences.

There are numerous problems with act utilitarianism. It might be difficult or impossible to determine all the consequences of an act. If we can do so, do we increase what *we* believe will, or should, contribute to the happiness of the people affected, or what *they* choose themselves? How do we know what they would choose? How do we quantify happiness in order to make comparisons among many people? Should some people's utility carry more weight than others'? Should we weigh a thief's gain of utility equal to the victim's loss? Is a dollar worth the same to a person who worked for it and a person who received it as a gift? Or to a rich person and a poor person? How can we measure the utility of freedom?

A more fundamental (and ethical) objection to act utilitarianism is that it does not recognize or respect individual rights. It has no absolute prohibitions and so could allow actions that many people consider always wrong. For example, if there is a convincing case that killing one innocent person (perhaps to distribute his or her organs to several people who will die without transplants) or taking all of a person's property and redistributing it to other community members would maximize utility in a community, utilitarianism could justify these acts. A person has no protected domain of freedom.

Rule utilitarianism suffers far less than does act utilitarianism from these problems. Recognizing that widespread killing and stealing decrease the security and happiness of all, a rule utilitarian can derive rules against these acts. We can state these particular rules in terms of rights to life and property.

Natural rights

Suppose we wish to treat people as ends rather than merely means and we wish to increase people's happiness. These goals are somewhat vague and open to many interpretations in specific circumstances. One approach we might follow is to let people make their own decisions. That is, we try to define a sphere of freedom in which people can act freely according to their own judgment, without coercive interference by others, even others (including us) who think they are doing what is best for the people involved or for humanity in general. This approach views ethical behavior as acting in such a way that respects a set of fundamental rights of others, including the rights to life, liberty, and property.

These rights are sometimes called natural rights because, in the opinion of some philosophers, they come from nature or we can derive them from the nature of humanity. John Locke[21] argued that we each have an exclusive right to ourselves, our labor, and to what we produce with our labor. Thus, he argued for a natural right to property that we create or obtain by mixing our labor with natural resources. He saw protection of private property as a moral rule. If there is no protection for property, then the person who invents a new tool would be loathe to show it to others or use it in their view, as they might take it. Clearing land and planting food would be pointless, as one could not be present at all times to prevent others from picking all the crop. Thus, a right of private property increases overall wealth (utility) as well; the toolmaker or farmer has more to give or trade to others.

Respect for the rights to life, liberty, and property implies ethical rules against killing, stealing, deception, and coercion.

Those who emphasize natural rights tend to emphasize the ethical character of the *process* by which people interact, seeing acts generally as likely to be ethical if they involve voluntary interactions and freely made exchanges where the parties are not coerced or deceived. This contrasts with other ethical standards or approaches that tend to focus on the *result* or state achieved by the interaction, for example, seeing an action as likely to be unethical if it leaves some people poor.

Negative and positive rights, or liberties and claim rights

When people speak of rights, they are often speaking about two quite different kinds of rights. In philosophy books, these rights are usually called negative and positive rights, but the terms liberties and claim rights are more descriptive of the distinction.[22]

Negative rights, or liberties, are rights to act without interference. The only obligation they impose on others is not to prevent you from acting. They include the right to life (in the sense that no one may kill you), the right to be free from assault, the right to use your property, the right to use your labor, skills, and mind to create goods and services and to trade with other people in voluntary exchanges. The rights to "life, liberty, and the pursuit of happiness" described in the U.S. Declaration of Independence are liberties, or negative rights. Freedom of speech and religion, as guaranteed in the First Amendment of the U.S. Constitution, are negative rights: the government may not interfere with you, jail you, or kill you because of what you say or what your religious beliefs are. The right to work, as a liberty, or negative right, means that no one may prohibit you from working or, for example, punish you for working without getting a government permit. The (negative) right to access the Internet is so obvious in free countries that we do not even think of it. Authoritarian governments restrict or deny it.

Claim rights, or positive rights, impose an obligation on some people to provide certain things for others. A positive right to a job means that someone must hire you regardless of whether they voluntarily choose to, or that it is right, or obligatory, for the government to set up job programs for people who are out of work. A positive right to life means that some people are obligated to pay for food or medical care for others who cannot pay for them. When we interpret freedom of speech as a claim right, or positive right, it means that we may require owners of shopping malls, radio stations, and online services to provide space or time for content they do not wish to include. Access to the Internet, as a claim right, could require such things as taxes to provide subsidized access for poor people or foreign aid to provide access in poor countries. The last example suggests the following question: How far does the obligation to provide a positive right extend? Also, when thinking about what might be a positive, or claim, right, it is helpful to consider whether something should be a claim right if it depends on achieving a certain level of technology. For example, if access to the Internet is a positive right now, was it a positive right in the 1800s?

Here is a more fundamental problem: negative rights and positive rights often conflict. Some people think that liberties are almost worthless by themselves and that society must devise social and legal mechanisms to ensure that everyone has their claim rights, or positive rights, satisfied, even if that means diminishing the liberties of some. Other people think that there can be no (or very few) positive rights, because it is impossible to enforce claim rights for some people without violating the liberties of others. They see the protection of liberties, or negative rights, as ethically essential.

This is one of the reasons for disagreement on issues such as some privacy protection regulations, for example. Although we will not solve the disagreement about which kind of right is more important, we can sometimes clarify the issues in a debate by clarifying which kind of right we are discussing.

Golden rules

The Bible and Confucius tell us to treat others as we would want them to treat us. This is a valuable ethical guideline. It suggests a reciprocity, or a role reversal. We should not take the rule too literally however; we need to apply it at the appropriate level. It tells us to consider an ethical choice we are making from the perspective of the people it affects. No matter how much you enjoy fast driving on winding roads, it might not be kind to roar around those corners with a passenger who gets carsick easily. No matter how much you like your friends to share photos of you partying, it might not be good to share a photo of friend who prefers privacy. We want people to recognize us as individuals and to respect our choices. Thus, we should respect theirs.

Contributing to society

We are focusing on how to make ethical decisions. Some ethical theories take a wider goal: how to live a virtuous life. That is beyond the scope of this book, but some of the ideas relate to ethical choices. Aristotle says that one lives a virtuous life by doing virtuous acts. This leaves us with a question: What is a virtuous act? Most people would agree that helping to serve meals at a homeless shelter is a virtuous act. The view that this type of activity (doing unpaid charitable work) is the only or the main kind of virtuous act is common but is too limited. Suppose a nurse is choosing between spending one evening a week taking a course to learn new nursing skills or spending one evening a week helping at the homeless shelter. Or a programmer at a bank is choosing between a course on new computer security techniques and helping at the homeless shelter. There is nothing wrong with either choice. Is either one more virtuous than the other? The first choice increases the person's professional status and possibly the person's salary; you could see it as a selfish choice. The second choice is charitable work, helping unfortunate people. But the analysis should not stop there. A professional person, well trained and up-to-date in his or her profession, often can do far more to help a large number of people than the same person can accomplish performing low-skill tasks outside the person's professional area. The fact that the person is paid for his or her work is not significant in evaluating its contribution. Doing one's work (whether it is collecting garbage or performing brain surgery) honestly, responsibly, ethically, creatively, and well is a virtuous activity.

> *His philanthropy was in his work.*
>
> —Mike Godwin, writing about Apple co-founder Steve Jobs[23]

Social contracts and a theory of political justice[24]

Many topics we consider in this book go beyond individual ethical choices. They are social and legal policies. Thus we introduce (again, quite briefly) philosophical ideas about forming social and political systems.

The early foundations of social contract theory, the idea that people willingly submit to a common law in order to live in a civil society, are in the writings of Socrates and Plato but were not fully formed until the 1600s. Thomas Hobbes developed ideas of social contract theory in his book *Leviathan* (1651). Hobbes describes a starting point called the State of Nature, a dismal place where each man acts according to his own interests, no one is safe from physical harm, and there is no ability to ensure the satisfaction of one's needs. Hobbes believed that man is rational and will seek a better situation, even at the cost of giving up some independence in favor of common law and accepting some authority to enforce this "social contract." John Locke thought people could enforce moral rules, such as the rights to life, liberty and property, in a state of nature but that it was better to delegate this function to a government instituted by an implicit social contract.

The modern philosopher John Rawls[25] took social contract theory further, developing provisions of the "contract" based on his view of justice as fairness. I will criticize parts of his work, but some of his points provide useful ethical guidelines. Rawls sought to establish principles for proper political power in a society with people of varying religions, viewpoints, lifestyles, and so on. Rawls, like other social contract theorists, said that reasonable people, recognizing that a legal (or political) structure is necessary for social order, will want to cooperate on terms that all accept, and they will abide by the rules of society, even those they do not like. He argued that political power is proper only if we would expect all citizens to reasonably endorse its basic, or constitutional, principles. Tolerance is essential because deep questions are difficult, we answer them differently based on our life experiences, and people of good will can disagree. Thus, a proper political system protects basic civil liberties such as freedom of speech and free choice of occupation. It will not impose the views of some on the others.

To this point, Rawls' foundation is consistent with an emphasis on liberties (negative rights). Rawls distinguishes his system of justice by adding a strong requirement for claim rights (positive rights): a just and fair political system will ensure that all citizens have sufficient means to make effective use of their freedoms.* To Rawls, government financing of election campaigns is an essential feature of the system. This is a very specific political policy; people hotly debate its fairness and practical consequences. Rawls has made a leap that appears inconsistent with his emphasis that people of good will disagree on important issues and that a proper political system does not impose the views of one group on another.

In Rawls' view, an action or a social or political structure is not ethical if it has the effect of leaving the least-advantaged people worse than they were before (or would be in some alternative system). Thus, in a sense, Rawls gives far more weight (indeed, infinite weight) to the utility of the least-advantaged people than to anyone else. This is odd as an absolute rule, and its fairness is not obvious. His emphasis on concern for the least well off, however, is a reminder to consider impacts on such people; a loss or harm to them can be more devastating than to someone in a better position.

Rawls proposed a conceptual formulation termed the "veil of ignorance" for deriving the proper principles or policies of a just social or political system. By extension, we can use it as a tool for considering ethical and social issues in this book. We imagine that each person behind the veil of ignorance does not know his or her gender, age, race, talents, wealth, and so on, in the real world. Behind the veil of ignorance, we choose policies that would be fair for all, protecting the most vulnerable and least-advantaged members of society. Many writers use this tool to derive what they conclude to be the correct ethical positions on social policy issues. I find that sometimes when I go behind the veil of ignorance, I come to a different conclusion than the author. The tool is useful, like the principles of the ethical theories we described earlier, but, like them, it is not absolute. Even ignoring our status in society, people of good will come to different conclusions

---

* The meaning of fairness is not obvious. In various contexts and to different people, it can mean being judged on one's merits rather than irrelevant factors, getting an equal share, or getting what one deserves.

because of their knowledge of human behavior and economics and their understanding of how the world works.*

We illustrate with a policy example. The Children's Online Privacy Protection Act (COPPA) is a privacy law intended to protect a vulnerable population by requiring that websites get parental permission before collecting personal information from children under 13. After COPPA passed, because of the expense of complying with its requirements and the potential liability, some companies deleted online profiles of all children under 13, some canceled their free email and home pages for kids, and some banned children under 13 entirely. The *New York Times* does not allow children under 13 to register to use its website. Facebook's terms of use prohibit children under 13 from joining, but *Consumer Reports* estimates that more than seven million children under 13 have ignored the rule and joined.[26] The fiction that there are no members under 13 implies there is no need to provide mechanisms to protect them. Economists would have predicted these effects. We might have come up with COPPA behind a veil of ignorance, but it is not clear how well it actually helps and protects children. More knowledge helps us make better decisions and design better policies and laws.

No simple answers

We cannot solve ethical problems by applying a formula or an algorithm. Human behavior and real human situations are complex. There are often trade-offs to consider. Ethical theories do not provide clear, incontrovertibly correct positions on most issues. We can use the approaches we described to support opposite sides of many an issue. For example, consider Kant's imperative that one must never treat people as merely means to ends, but rather as ends in themselves. We could argue that an employer who pays an employee a very low wage, say, a wage too low to support a family, is wrongly treating the employee as merely a means for the employer to make money. But we could also argue that expecting the employer to pay more than he or she considers reasonable is treating the employer merely as a means of providing income for the employee. Similarly, it is easy for two utilitarians to come to different conclusions on a particular issue by measuring happiness or utility differently. A small set of basic natural rights might provide no guidance for many situations in which you must make ethical decisions—however, if we try to define rights to cover more situations, there will be fierce disagreement about just what those rights should be.

Although ethical theories do not completely settle difficult, controversial issues, they help to identify important principles or guidelines. They remind us of things to consider, and they can help clarify reasoning and values. There is much merit in Kant's principle of

---

* Rawls specifies that we assume people behind the veil of ignorance have knowledge of accepted economic principles, but in fact many philosophers and ordinary people do not—and of course, people will disagree about what is accepted.

Do organizations have ethics?

Some philosophers argue that it is meaningless to speak of a business or organization as having ethics. Individual people make all decisions and take all actions. Those people must have ethical responsibility for everything they do. Others argue that an organization that acts with intention and a formal decision structure, such as a business, is a moral entity.[27] However, viewing a business as a moral entity does not diminish the responsibility of the individual people. Ultimately, it is individuals who are making decisions and taking actions. We can hold both the individuals and the company or organization responsible for their acts.*

Whether one accepts or rejects the idea that a business can have ethical rights and responsibilities, it is clear that organizational structure and policies lead to a pattern of actions and decisions that have ethical content. Businesses have a "corporate culture," or a "personality," or simply a reputation for treating employees and customers in respectful and honest—or careless and deceptive—ways. People in management positions shape the culture or ethics of a business or organization. Thus, decisions by managers have an impact beyond the particular product, contract, or action a decision involves. A manager who is dishonest with customers or who cuts corners on testing, for example, is setting an example that encourages other employees to be dishonest and careless. A manager's ethical responsibility includes his or her contribution to the company's ethical personality.

* Regardless of whether or not we view businesses and organizations as moral agents, they are legal entities and can be held legally responsible for their acts.

universalism and his emphasis on treating people as intrinsically valuable "ends." "Do not lie, manipulate, or deceive" is a good ethical principle. There is much merit in utilitarianism's consideration of consequences and its standard of increasing achievement of people's happiness. There is much merit in the natural rights approach of setting minimal rules in a rights framework to guarantee people a sphere in which they can act according to their own values and judgment. The Golden Rule reminds us to consider the perspective of the people our actions affect. Rawls reminds us that it is especially important to consider the impact of our choices on the least-advantaged people.

1.4.3 Some Important Distinctions

A number of important distinctions affect our ethical judgments, but they are often not clearly expressed or understood. In this section, we identify a few of these. Just being aware of these distinctions can help clarify issues in some ethical debates.

Right, wrong, and okay

In situations with ethical dilemmas, there are often many options that are ethically acceptable, with no specific one ethically required. Thus, it is misleading to divide all acts into two categories, ethically right and ethically wrong. Rather, it is better to think of acts as either ethically obligatory, ethically prohibited, or ethically acceptable. Many actions might be virtuous and desirable but not obligatory.

Distinguishing wrong and harm

Carelessly and needlessly causing harm is wrong, but it is important to remember that harm alone is not a sufficient criterion to determine that an act is unethical. Many ethical, even admirable acts can make other people worse off. For example, you may accept a job offer knowing someone else wanted the job and needed it more than you do. You may reduce the income of other people by producing a better product that consumers prefer. If your product is really good, you might put a competitor out of business completely and cause many people to lose their jobs. Yet there is nothing wrong with doing honest, productive work.

Declining to give something (say, $100) to someone is not the same ethically as taking the thing away from the person. Both actions leave the person less well off by $100 than they would be otherwise. But if we took that simplistic view of harm, the harm would be essentially the same. To identify harm as wrong, we must identify what the person is due, what his or her rights are, and what our rights and obligations are.

On the other hand, there can be wrong when there is no (obvious or immediate) harm. Some hackers argue that breaking into computer systems is not wrong, because they do no harm. Aside from the fact that the hacker might do unintended harm, one can argue that hacking is a violation of property rights: a person has no right to enter your property without your permission, independent of how much harm is done in any particular instance.

Separating goals from constraints

Economist Milton Friedman wrote that the goal or responsibility of a business is to make a profit for its shareholders. This statement appalled some ethicists, as they believe it justifies, or is used to justify, irresponsible and unethical actions. It seems to me that arguments on this point miss the distinction between goals, on the one hand, and constraints on actions that may be taken to achieve the goals, on the other hand—or the distinction between ends and means. Our personal goals might include financial success and finding an attractive mate. Working hard, investing wisely, and being an interesting and decent person can achieve these goals. Stealing and lying might achieve them too. Stealing and lying are ethically unacceptable. Ethics tells us what actions are acceptable or unacceptable in our attempts to achieve the goals. There is nothing unethical about a business having the goal of maximizing profits. The ethical character of the company depends on whether the actions taken to achieve the goal are consistent with ethical constraints.[28]

Personal preference and ethics

Most of us have strong feelings about a lot of issues. It might be difficult to draw a line between what we consider ethically right or wrong and what we personally approve or disapprove of.

Suppose you get a job offer from a company whose products you do not like. You might decline the job and say you are doing so on ethical grounds. Are you? Can you convincingly argue that anyone who takes the job is acting unethically? Most likely you cannot, and that is not what you actually think. *You* do not want to work for a company you do not like. This is a personal preference. There is nothing ethically wrong with declining the job, of course. The company's freedom to produce its products does not impose an ethical obligation on you to assist it.

When discussing political or social issues, people frequently argue that their position is right in a moral or ethical sense or that an opponent's position is morally wrong or unethical. People tend to want to be on the "moral high ground." People feel the stigma of an accusation that their view is ethically wrong. Thus, arguments based on ethics can be, and often are, used to intimidate people with different views. It is a good idea to try to distinguish between actions we find distasteful, rude, or ill-advised and actions that we can argue convincingly are ethically wrong.

Law and ethics

What is the connection between law and ethics? Sometimes very little. Is it ethical to prohibit marijuana use by terminally ill people? Is it ethical for the government or a state university to give preference in contracts, hiring, or admissions to people in specific ethnic groups? Is it ethical for a bank loan officer to carry customer records on a laptop to work at the beach? The current law, whatever it happens to be at a particular time, does not answer these questions. In addition, history provides numerous examples of laws most of us consider profoundly wrong by ethical standards; slavery is perhaps the most obvious example. Ethics precedes law in the sense that ethical principles help determine whether or not we should pass specific laws.

Some laws enforce ethical rules (e.g., against murder and theft). By definition, we are ethically obligated to obey such laws—not because they are laws, but because the laws implement the obligations and prohibitions of ethical rules.

Another category of laws establishes conventions for business or other activities. Commercial law, such as the Uniform Commercial Code, defines rules for economic transactions and contracts. Such rules provide a framework in which we can interact smoothly and confidently with strangers. They include provisions for how to interpret a contract if a court must resolve a dispute. These laws are extremely important to any society and they should be consistent with ethics. Beyond basic ethical considerations, however, details could depend on historic conventions, practicality, and other nonethical criteria. In the United States, drivers must drive on the right side of the road; in England, drivers must drive on the left side. There is obviously nothing intrinsically right or wrong about either choice. However, once the convention is established, it is wrong to drive on the wrong side of the road because it needlessly endangers other people.

Unfortunately, many laws fall into a category that is not intended to implement ethical rules—or even be consistent with them. The political process is subject to pressure from special interest groups of all sorts who seek to pass laws that favor their groups or businesses. Examples include the laws (promoted by the television networks) that delayed the introduction of cable television and, later, laws (promoted by some cable television companies) to restrict satellite dishes. When margarine was first introduced, the dairy industry successfully lobbied for laws against coloring margarine yellow to look more like butter. After opposing re-sale auctions of event tickets for years, Ticketmaster accepted this popular online sales paradigm—and lobbied for laws restricting competitors.[29] Many prominent people in the financial industry reported receiving a large number of fundraising letters from members of Congress—in the week that Congress took up new regulations for their industry. Many political, religious, or ideological organizations promote laws to require (or prohibit) certain kinds of behavior that the group considers desirable (or objectionable). Examples include prohibitions on teaching foreign languages in schools (in the early 20th century),[30] prohibitions on gambling or alcohol, requirements for recycling, and requirements that stores close on Sundays. At an extreme, in some countries, this category includes restrictions on the practice of certain religions. Some politicians or political parties pass laws, no matter how public-spirited they sound, purely to give themselves and their friends or donors advantages.

Copyright law has elements of all three categories we have described. It defines a property right, violation of which is a form of theft. Because of the intangible nature of intellectual property, some of the rules about what constitutes copyright infringement are more like the second category, pragmatic rules devised to be workable. Powerful groups (e.g., the publishing, music, and movie industries) lobby for specific rules to benefit themselves. This is why some violations of copyright law are clearly unethical (if one accepts the concept of intellectual property), yet others seem to be entirely acceptable, sometimes even noble.

Legislators and their staffs draft some laws in haste, and they make little sense. Some laws and regulations have hundreds or thousands of pages and are full of specific detail that make many ethical choices illegal. When members of Congress debate whether pizza is a vegetable,[31] they are not debating an ethical issue.

Do we have an ethical obligation to obey a law just because it is a law? Some argue that we do: as members of society, we must accept the rules that the legislative process has created so long as they are not clearly and utterly ethically wrong. Others argue that, whereas this might often be a good policy, it is not an ethical obligation. Legislators are just a group of people, subject to errors and political influences; there is no reason to feel an ethical obligation to do something just because they say so. Indeed, some believe all laws that regulate personal behavior or voluntary economic transactions to be violations of the liberty and autonomy of the people forced to obey and, hence, to be ethically wrong.

Is it always ethically right to do something that is legal? No. Laws must be uniform and stated in a way that clearly indicates what actions are punishable. Ethical situations are complex and variable; the people involved might know the relevant factors, but it might not be possible to prove them in court. There are widely accepted ethical rules that would be difficult and probably unwise to enforce absolutely with laws—for example: Do not lie. New law lags behind new technology for good reasons. It takes time to recognize new problems associated with the technology, consider possible solutions, think and debate about the consequences and fairness of various proposals, and so on. A good law will set minimal standards that can apply to all situations, leaving a large range of voluntary choices. Ethics fills the gap between the time when technology creates new problems and the time when legislatures pass reasonable laws. Ethics fills the gap between general legal standards that apply to all cases and the particular choices made in a specific case.

While it is not ethically obligatory to obey all laws, that is not an excuse to ignore laws, nor is a law (or lack of a law) an excuse to ignore ethics.

EXERCISES

Review Exercises

1.1   What were two unexpected uses of social networking?

1.2   What are two ways free services on the Web are paid for?

1.3   Describe two applications of speech recognition.

1.4   List two applications mentioned in this chapter that help ordinary people to do things for which we used to rely on experts.

1.5   What are two of Kant's important ideas about ethics?

1.6   What is the difference between act utilitarianism and rule utilitarianism?

1.7   Give an example of a law that implements an ethical principle. Give an example of a law that enforces a particular group's idea of how people should behave.

1.8   Explain the distinction between the negative and positive right to freedom of speech.

1.9   When one goes behind Rawls' veil of ignorance, what is one ignorant of?

General Exercises

1.10 Write a short essay (roughly 300 words) about some topic related to computing technology or the Internet that interests you and has social or ethical implications. Describe the background; then identify the issues, problems, or questions that you think are important.

1.11 In your opinion, what are the pros and cons of Internet commerce, as compared to more conventional shopping?

1.12 Most libraries ban the use of cellphones. Some require that members switch off their phones before entering. What are some reasons for these policies? Do you think they are good policies? Explain.

1.13 What are some advantages and disadvantages of online tutoring (such as for school-goers), as compared to conventional tutoring? Give at least five distinct replies in total.

1.14 Videos containing violence, gore, recordings of surgery and childbirth, and so on, can be easily found on the Internet. In your opinion, should such material be publicly available? Discuss some social and ethical considerations.

1.15 Think of a useful application for a system in which the user wears virtual reality goggles.

1.16 Think of an application of artificial intelligence that does not yet exist, but that you would be very proud to help develop. Describe it.

1.17 List three applications of computing and communication technology mentioned in this chapter that reduce the need for planning events well in advance.

1.18 For each of the following tasks, describe how it was probably done 25 years ago (before the World Wide Web). Briefly describe the main difficulties or disadvantages of the older ways. Do you think there were advantages?

 (a) Planning a long holiday spanning multiple foreign countries.

 (b) Campaigning for a candidate in the presidential elections.

 (c) Conducting a survey of customer opinion of a product.

1.19 Many elderly and blind people have trouble navigating busy streets. Imagine an automated product designed with this problem in mind. What features would it have? What technologies would you use if you were designing it?

1.20 Which kind of ethical theory, deontologist or consequentialist, works better for arguing that it is wrong to drive one's car on the left side of a road in a country where people normally drive on the right? Explain.

1.21 Develop a code of ethics and etiquette for use of portable music players. Include provisions for music players in cellphones.

1.22 In the following (true) cases, tell whether the people are interpreting the right they claim as a negative right (liberty) or as a positive right (claim right). Explain. In each case, which kind of right should it be, and why?

 (a) A man sued his health insurance company because it would not pay for Viagra, the drug for treating male impotence. He argued that the insurer's refusal to pay denied his right to a happy sex life.

 (b) Two legislators who ran for reelection lost. They sued an organization that sponsored ads criticizing their voting records. The former legislators argued that the organization interfered with their right to hold office.

1.23 Advocacy groups have sued companies because blind people cannot use their websites.[32] The suits argue that the Americans With Disabilities Act requires that the sites be accessible. Should a law require all business and government websites to provide full access for disabled people? Discuss arguments for both sides. Identify the negative and positive rights involved. Which side do you think is stronger? Why?

1.24 If John Rawls were writing now, do you think he would include providing Internet access and cellphones for all citizens as an essential requirement of a just political system? Explain.

1.25 A citizen published morphed photographs of a public figure, depicting her in awkward situations. Do you think this was an ethical action? Why? How does it differ from using a caricature?

1.26 Following a debate among political candidates during a campaign, you quietly record video of candidates talking with individuals from the audience. One candidate, responding sympathetically to a person complaining about how an insurance company handled his insurance claim, says, "All insurance company executives ought to be shot." Another candidate, talking with a person who is angry about illegal immigration, says, "Anyone sneaking across the border illegally ought to be shot." Another candidate, sprawled on a chair in the back of the room, is snoring. And a fourth, a man, invites an attractive woman back to his hotel to continue their conversation over drinks.

Discuss the ethics of posting videos of the candidates' comments (or snoring) on the Web. Give reasons in favor of posting and reasons not to post.

Which, if any, would you post? To what extent would, or should, your support of or opposition to the candidate affect the decision?

1.27 (a) Thinking ahead to Chapter 4, identify any example, application, or service mentioned in this chapter that could have a major impact on intellectual property rights. Briefly explain how.

(b) Thinking ahead to Chapter 5, identify any example, application, or service mentioned in this chapter that could have a major impact on crime. Briefly explain how.

(c) Thinking ahead to Chapter 8, identify any example, application, or service mentioned in this chapter that could have a major impact on professional ethics. Briefly explain how.

Assignments

These exercises require some research or activity.

1.28 Go around your home and make a list of all the appliances and devices that contain a computer chip.

1.29 Arrange an interview with a disabled student on your campus. Ask the student to describe or demonstrate some of the computer tools he or she uses. (If your campus has a Disabled Student Center, its staff may be able to help you find an interview subject.) Write a report of the interview and/or demonstration.

1.30 Go to your campus library and look up a research paper in an old edition of a printed journal. Read it. Compare the convenience of reading printed journals to reading articles on the Web.

1.31 Computing technology has had a huge impact on the movie industry. Research such an application and write a short report on it.

1.32 Research any one application of computing technology in the legal industry and write a short report on it.

1.33 Over the next month or two (whatever is appropriate for the length of your course), collect news articles on (1) benefits and valuable applications of computer technology and (2) failures and/or problems that computer technology has caused. The articles should be current, that is, published during the time period of your course. Write a brief summary and commentary on two articles in each category indicating how they relate to topics covered in this book.

Class Discussion Exercises

These exercises are for class discussion, perhaps with short presentations prepared in advance by small groups of students.

1.34 The Eastman Kodak Company, which revolutionized consumer photography, filed for bankruptcy protection in January 2012. It is widely believed that the company was unable to keep up with fast-changing trends in technology. Ruminate on the risks and benefits that technological change poses to companies.

1.35 Is it ethically acceptable or ethically prohibited for an advocacy group to launch a socialbot on a social media system such as Twitter that pretends to be a person and subtly promotes the group's viewpoint? Consider the same question for a socialbot that promotes a particular company's products.

1.36 A car company offers as an option a system that will detect an upcoming collision using photographic sensors, immediately eject the driver and passengers from the car in protective airbags, and automatically steer the car away from danger if possible. The option is extremely expensive. If someone buys the car, does the person have an ethical obligation to buy the optional system to protect passengers?

BOOKS AND ARTICLES

Many of these references include topics that are covered throughout this book. Some of the references in Chapter 9 also include topics covered throughout this book.

- The Alliance for Technology Access, *Computer Resources for People With Disabilities*, 4th ed., Hunter House Publishers, 2004, www.ataccess.org.

- Stan Augarten, *Bit by Bit: An Illustrated History of Computers*, Ticknor & Fields, 1984. The early history, of course.

- Tim Berners-Lee, Usenet post describing the WorldWideWeb project, August 1991: groups.google.com/group/alt.hypertext/msg/395f282a67a1916c.

- Frances Cairncross, *The Death of Distance 2.0: How the Communications Revolution Is Changing Our Lives*, Harvard Business School Press, 2001.

- Peter J. Denning, ed., *The Invisible Future: The Seamless Integration of Technology Into Everyday Life*, McGraw Hill, 2001.

- Peter Denning and Robert Metcalfe, *Beyond Calculation: The Next Fifty Years of Computing*, Copernicus, 1997.

- Michael Dertouzos, *What Will Be: How the New World of Information Will Change Our Lives*, HarperEdge, 1997.

- Joseph Ellin, *Morality and the Meaning of Life: An Introduction to Ethical Theory*, Harcourt Brace Jovanovich, 1995.

- Neil A. Gershenfeld, *When Things Start to Think*, Henry Holt & Co., 1999.

- James Gleick, *The Information: A History, a Theory, a Flood*, Pantheon, 2011.

- Duncan Langford, ed., *Internet Ethics*, St. Martin's Press, 2000.

- Steven Levy, *In The Plex: How Google Thinks, Works, and Shapes Our Lives*, Simon & Schuster, 2011.

- Ben McConnell and Jackie Huba, *Citizen Marketers*, Kaplan Publishing, 2006. How ordinary people influence other consumers, democratizing marketing.

- Joel Mokyr, *The Gifts of Athena: Historical Origins of the Knowledge Economy*, Princeton University Press, 2002.

- Jan Narveson, *Moral Matters*, Broadview Press, 1993. The first chapter gives a good, very readable introduction to moral issues.

- Louis P. Pojman and James Fieser, *Ethical Theory: Classical and Contemporary Readings*, 6th ed., Wadsworth, 2010. Includes John Stuart Mill's "Utilitarianism," Kant's "The Foundations of the Metaphysic of Morals," John Locke's "Natural Rights," and other classical essays on various ethical theories.

- Michael J. Quinn, *Ethics for the Information Age*, 4th ed., Addison Wesley, 2011.

- Glenn Reynolds, *An Army of Davids: How Markets and Technology Empower Ordinary People to Beat Big Media, Big Government, and Other Goliaths*, Nelson Current, 2006.

- Richard A. Spinello and Herman T. Tavani, eds., *Readings in CyberEthics*, Jones and Bartlett, 2001.

- Don Tapscott and Anthony D. Williams, *Wikinomics: How Mass Collaboration Changes Everything*, Portfolio, 2006.

- Sherry Turkle, *Alone Together: Why We Expect More from Technology and Less from Each Other*, Basic Books, 2011. Includes results from many interviews with teenagers and college students about the impact on them of personal communications media.

- Vernor Vinge, *Rainbows End*, Tor, 2006. A science fiction novel, set in the near future, that imagines how computer technology may affect communication, education, medical care, and many facets of ordinary life.

NOTES

1. Michael Rothschild, "Beyond Repair: The Politics of the Machine Age Are Hopelessly Obsolete," *The New Democrat*, July/August 1995, pp. 8–11.

2. Stephen E. Ambrose, *Undaunted Courage: Meriwether Lewis, Thomas Jefferson and the Opening of the American West*, Simon & Schuster, 1996, p. 53.

3. Betty Friedan, *The Feminine Mystique*, W. W. Norton, 1963, p. 312.

4. In Chapters 1 and 2, respectively, of Peter H. Diamandis and Steven Kotler, *Abundance: The Future Is Better Than You Think*, Free Press, 2012. I paraphrased slightly.

5. Research centers doing this kind of research include the MIT Human Dynamics Laboratory, Harvard University, AT&T Labs, the London School of Economics, and others. For an overview of some of the research, see Robert Lee Hotz, "The Really Smart Phone," *Wall Street Journal*, Apr. 22, 2011, online.wsj.com/article/SB1000142405274870454 760457626326167984814.html, viewed Mar. 4, 2012.

6. Photos appear on the Web showing religious Muslim women with uncovered faces and other people in bathrooms or locker rooms or other embarrassing or awkward situations. This problem was more acute when cameras first appeared in cellphones and most people were unaware of them.

7. Quoted in Robert Fox, "Newstrack," *Communications of the ACM*, Aug. 1995, 38:8, pp. 11–12.

8. For a good overview, see Eric Beidel, "Social Scientists and Mathematicians Join The Hunt for Terrorists," *National Defense*, Sept. 2010, www.nationaldefense magazine.org, viewed Mar. 8, 2012.

9. "Email Statistics Report, 2011–2015," The Radicati Group, Inc., www.radicati.com; Heinz Tschabitscher, "How Many Emails Are Sent Every Day?" email.about.com/od/emailtrivia/f/emails_per_day.htm; both viewed Aug. 22, 2011.

10. Statement of Vinton G. Cerf, U.S. Senate Committee on the Judiciary Hearing on Reconsidering our Communications Laws, June 14, 2006, judiciary.senate.gov/testimony.cfm?id=1937&wit_id=5416.

11. Steven Leckart, "The Stanford Education Experiment," *Wired*, April 2012, pp. 68–77.
12. Robert D. Atkinson, "Leveling the E-Commerce Playing Field: Ensuring Tax and Regulatory Fairness for Online and Offline Businesses," Progressive Policy Institute Policy Report, June 30, 2003, www.ppionline.org, viewed Sept. 3, 2007. Jennifer Saranow, "Savvy Car Buyers Drive Bargains with Pricing Data from the Web," *Wall Street Journal*, Oct. 24, 2006, p. D5.
13. The last line of the paragraph is a paraphrase of the headline on an article Searle wrote, "Watson Doesn't Know It Won on 'Jeopardy!,'" *Wall Street Journal*, Feb. 17, 2011, online.wsj.com/article/SB10001424052748703407304576154313126987674.html, viewed Mar. 6, 2012. The original Chinese room argument is in John Searle, "Minds, Brains and Programs," *Behavioral and Brain Sciences*, Cambridge University Press, 1980, pp. 417–424.
14. IBM did not disclose the cost. I have seen estimates of $30–$100 million.
15. William M. Bulkeley, "Profit in Motion: Tiny Sensors Take Off," *Wall Street Journal*, May 10, 2007, p. B3.
16. Evan Ratliff, "Born to Run," *Wired*, July 2001, pp. 86–97. Rheo and Power Knees by Ossur, www.ossur.com, viewed Aug. 25, 2006. John Hockenberry, "The Human Brain," *Wired*, Aug. 2001, pp. 94–105. Aaron Saenz, "Ekso Bionics Sells its First Set of Robot Legs Allowing Paraplegics to Walk," Singularity Hub, Feb. 27, 2012, singularityhub.com/2012/02/27/ekso-bionics-sells-its-first-set-of-robot-legs-allowing-paraplegics-to-walk, viewed Mar. 7, 2012.
17. Hockenberry, "The Human Brain," describes various brain interface devices.
18. By Louis P. Pojman (Wadsworth, 1990) and J. L. Mackie (Penguin Books, 1977), respectively.
19. Sources for this section include: Joseph Ellin, *Morality and the Meaning of Life: An Introduction to Ethical Theory*, Harcourt Brace Jovanovich, 1995; Deborah G. Johnson, Computer Ethics, Prentice Hall, 2nd ed., 1994; Louis Pojman, *Ethical Theory: Classical and Contemporary Readings*, 2nd ed., Wadsworth, 1995 (which includes John Stuart Mill's "Utilitarianism," Kant's "The Foundations of the Metaphysic of Morals," and John Locke's "Natural Rights"); and James Rachels, *The Elements of Moral Philosophy*, McGraw Hill, 1993; "John Locke (1632–1704)," *Internet Encyclopedia of Philosophy*, Apr. 17, 2001, www.iep.utm.edu/locke, viewed Mar. 16, 2012; Celeste Friend, "Social Contract Theory," *Internet Encyclopedia of Philosophy*, Oct. 15, 2004, www.iep.utm.edu/soc-cont, viewed Mar. 16, 2012; Sharon A. Lloyd and Susanne Sreedhar, "Hobbes's Moral and Political Philosophy," *The Stanford Encyclopedia of Philosophy* (Spring 2011 Edition), Edward N. Zalta (ed.), plato.stanford.edu/archives/spr2011/entries/hobbes-moral; Leif Wenar, "John Rawls," *The Stanford Encyclopedia of Philosophy* (Fall 2008 Edition), Edward N. Zalta, ed., plato.stanford.edu/archives/fall2008/entries/rawls, viewed Mar. 16, 2012.
20. John Stuart Mill, *Utilitarianism*, 1863.
21. *John Locke, Two Treatises of Government*, 1690.
22. J. L. Mackie uses the term *claim rights* in Ethics: Inventing Right and Wrong. Another term for positive rights is entitlements.
23. Slightly paraphrased from Mike Godwin, "Steve Jobs, the Inhumane Humanist," *Reason*, Jan. 10, 2012, reason.com/archives/2012/01/10/steve-jobs-the-inhumane-humanist, viewed Mar. 14, 2012.
24. Julie Johnson assisted with the background for this section.
25. *A Theory of Justice*, 1971, and *Justice as Fairness*, 2001.
26. "That Facebook Friend Might Be 10 Years Old, and Other Troubling News," *Consumer Reports*, June 2011, www.consumerreports.org/cro/magazine-archive/2011/june/electronics-computers/state-of-the-net/facebook-concerns/index.htm, viewed Jan. 22, 2012.
27. Kenneth C. Laudon, "Ethical Concepts and Information Technology," *Communications of the ACM*, Dec. 1995, 38:12, p. 38.
28. Some goals appear to be ethically wrong in themselves—for example, genocide—although often it is because the only way to achieve the goal is by methods that are ethically unacceptable (killing innocent people).
29. Kent Smetters, "Ticketmaster vs. Ticket Buyers," American Enterprise Institute, Oct. 24, 2006, www.aei.org/publications/pubID.25049,filter.all/pub_detail.asp, viewed Nov. 1, 2006.
30. Nebraska, for example, banned teaching foreign languages in public or private schools below ninth grade.
31. Specifically, whether the tomato sauce should be counted as a vegetable to satisfy health requirements for school lunches.
32. For example, *National Federation for the Blind v. Target Corporation*.

2

PRIVACY

2.1 Privacy Risks and Principles

2.1.1 WHAT IS PRIVACY?

After the fall of the communist government in East Germany, people examined the files of Stasi, the secret police. They found that the government had used spies and informants to build detailed dossiers on the opinions and activities of roughly six million people— a third of the population. The informers were neighbors, co-workers, friends, and even family members of the people they reported on. The paper files filled an estimated 125 miles of shelf space.[1]

Before the digital age, surveillance cameras watched shoppers in banks and stores. And well into the era of computers and the Internet, pharmacies in Indiana disposed of hundreds of prescriptions, receipts, and order forms for medicines by tossing them into an open dumpster. Private investigators still search household garbage for medical and financial information, details of purchases, evidence of romantic affairs, and journalists' notes.

Computer technology is not necessary for the invasion of privacy. However, we discuss privacy at length in this book because the use of digital technology has made new threats possible and old threats more potent. Computer technologies—databases, digital cameras, the Web, smartphones, and global positioning system (GPS) devices, among others—have profoundly changed what people can know about us and how they can use that information. Understanding the risks and problems is a first step toward protecting privacy. For computer professionals, understanding the risks and problems is a step toward designing systems with built-in privacy protections and less risk.

There are three key aspects of privacy:

- Freedom from intrusion—being left alone
- Control of information about oneself
- Freedom from surveillance (from being followed, tracked, watched, and eavesdropped upon)

For the most part, in this book, we view privacy as a good thing. Critics of privacy argue that it gives cover to deception, hypocrisy, and wrongdoing. It allows fraud. It protects the guilty. Concern for privacy may be regarded with a suspicious "What do you have to hide?" The desire to keep things private does not mean we are doing anything wrong. We might wish to keep health, relationship, and family issues private. We might wish to keep religious beliefs and political views private from some of the people we interact with. Privacy of some kinds of information can be important to safety and security as well. Examples include travel plans, financial data, and for some people, simply a home address.

Privacy threats come in several categories:

- Intentional, institutional uses of personal information (in the government sector primarily for law enforcement and tax collection, and in the private sector primarily for marketing and decision making)
- Unauthorized use or release by "insiders," the people who maintain the information
- Theft of information
- Inadvertent leakage of information through negligence or carelessness
- Our own actions (sometimes intentional trade-offs and sometimes when we are unaware of the risks)

Privacy issues arise in many contexts. More topics with privacy implications appear in later chapters. We discuss spam, the intrusion of junk email and text messages, in Chapter 3. We address hacking and identity theft in Chapter 5. We discuss monitoring of workplace communications and other issues of privacy for employees in Chapter 6. Some privacy risks result from the fact that so much of the data stored about us is incorrect. Databases contain errors. Files are not updated. Records of different people with similar names or other similarities get comingled or confused. Chapter 8 discusses some of these problems. Privacy comes up again in Chapter 9, where we focus on the responsibilities of computer professionals.

It is clear that we cannot expect complete privacy. We usually do not accuse someone who initiates a conversation of invading our privacy. Many friends and slight acquaintances know what you look like, where you work, what kind of car you drive, and whether you are a nice person. They need not get your permission to observe and talk about you. Control of information about oneself means control of what is in other people's minds, phones, and data storage systems. It is necessarily limited by basic human rights, particularly freedom of speech. Nor can we expect to be totally free from surveillance. People see us and hear us when we move about in public (physically or on the Web).

If you live in a small town, you have little privacy; everyone knows everything about you. In a big city, you are more nearly anonymous. But if people know nothing about you, they might be taking a big risk if they rent you a place to live, hire you, lend you money, sell you automobile insurance, accept your credit card, and so on. We give up some privacy for the benefits of dealing with strangers. We can choose to give up more in exchange for other benefits such as convenience, personalized service, and easy communication with many friends. But sometimes, others make the choices for us.

I use many real incidents, businesses, products, and services as examples throughout this book. In most cases, I am not singling them out for special endorsement or criticism. They are just some of the many examples we can use to illustrate problems, issues, and possible solutions.

The man who is compelled to live every minute of his life among others and whose every need, thought, desire, fancy or gratification is subject to public scrutiny, has been deprived of his individuality and human dignity. [He] merges with the mass. . . . Such a being, although sentient, is fungible; he is not an individual.

—Edward J. Bloustein[2]

It's important to realize that privacy preserves not personal secrets, but a sense of safety within a circle of friends so that the individual can be more candid, more expressive, more open *with "secrets."*

—Robert Ellis Smith[3]

2.1.2 New Technology, New Risks

Computers, the Internet, and a whole array of digital devices—with their astounding increases in speed, storage space, and connectivity—make the collection, searching, analysis, storage, access, and distribution of huge amounts of information and images much easier, cheaper, and faster than ever before. These are great benefits. But when the information is about us, the same capabilities threaten our privacy.

Today there are thousands (probably millions) of databases, both government and private, containing personal information about us. In the past, there was simply no record of some of this information, such as our specific purchases of groceries and books. Government documents like divorce and bankruptcy records have long been in public records, but accessing such information took a lot of time and effort. When we browsed in a library or store, no one knew what we read or looked at. It was not easy to link together our financial, work, and family records. Now, large companies that operate video, email, social network, and search services can combine information from a member's use of all of them to obtain a detailed picture of the person's interests, opinions, realtionships, habits, and activities. Even if we do not log in as members, software tracks our activity on the Web. In the past, conversations disappeared when people finished speaking, and only the sender and the recipient normally read personal communications. Now, when we communicate by texting, email, social networks, and so on, there is a record of our words that others can copy, forward, distribute widely, and read years later. Miniaturization of processors and sensors put tiny cameras in cellphones that millions of people carry everywhere. Cameras in some 3-D television sets warn children if they are sitting too close. What else might such cameras record, and who might see it? The wireless appliances we carry contain GPS and other location devices. They enable others to determine our location and track our movements. Patients refill prescriptions and check the results of medical tests on the Web. They correspond with doctors by email. We store our photos and videos, do our taxes, and create and store documents and financial spreadsheets in a cloud of remote servers instead of on our own computer. Power and water providers might soon have metering and analysis systems sophisticated enough to deduce what appliances we are using, when we shower (and for how long), and when we sleep. Law enforcement agencies have very sophisticated tools for eavesdropping, surveillance, and collecting and analyzing data about people's activities, tools that can help reduce crime and increase security—or threaten privacy and liberty.

Combining powerful new tools and applications can have astonishing results. It is possible to snap a photo of someone on the street, match the photo to one on a social network, and use a trove of publicly accessible information to guess, with high probability of accuracy, the person's name, birth date, and most of his or her Social Security number. This does not require a supercomputer; it is done with a smartphone app. We see such systems in television shows and movies, but to most people they seem exaggerated or way off in the future.

All these gadgets, services, and activities have benefits, of course, but they expose us to new risks. The implications for privacy are profound.

> *Patient medical information is confidential. It should not be discussed in a public place.*
>
> —A sign, aimed at doctors and staff, in an elevator in a medical office building, a reminder to prevent low-tech privacy leaks.

Example: Search query data

After a person enters a phrase into a search engine, views some results, then goes on to another task, he or she expects that the phrase is gone—gone like a conversation with a friend or a few words spoken to a clerk in a store. After all, with millions of people doing searches each day for work, school, or personal uses, how could the search company store it all? And who would want all that trivial information anyway? That is what most people thought about search queries until two incidents demonstrated that it is indeed stored, it can be released, and it matters.

Search engines collect many terabytes of data daily. A terabyte is a trillion bytes. It would have been absurdly expensive to store that much data in the recent past, but no longer. Why do search engine companies store search queries? It is tempting to say "because they can." But there are many uses for the data. Suppose, for example, you search for "Milky Way." Whether you get lots of astronomy pages or information about the candy bar or a local restaurant can depend on your search history and other information about you. Search engine companies want to know how many pages of search results users actually look at, how many they click on, how they refine their search queries, and what spelling errors they commonly make. The companies analyze the data to improve search services, to target advertising better, and to develop new services. The database of past queries also provides realistic input for testing and evaluating modifications in the algorithms search engines use to select and rank results. Search query data are valuable to many companies besides search engine companies. By analyzing search queries, companies draw conclusions about what kinds of products and features people are looking for. They modify their products to meet consumer preferences.

But who else gets to see this mass of data? And why should we care?

If your own Web searches have been on innocuous topics, and you do not care who sees your queries, consider a few topics people might search for and think about why they might want to keep them private: health and psychological problems, bankruptcy, uncontrolled gambling, right-wing conspiracies, left-wing conspiracies, alcoholism, anti-abortion information, pro-abortion information, erotica, illegal drugs. What are some possible consequences for a person doing extensive research on the Web for a suspense novel about terrorists who plan to blow up chemical factories?

In 2006, the federal government presented Google with a subpoena* for two months of user search queries and all the Web addresses† that Google indexes.‡ Google protested, bringing the issue to public attention. Although the subpoena did not ask for names of users, the idea of the government gaining access to the details of people's searches horrified privacy advocates and many people who use search engines. Google and privacy advocates opposed the precedent of government access to large masses of such data. A court reduced the scope of the subpoena, removing user queries.[4]

A few months later, release of a huge database of search queries at AOL showed that privacy violations occur even when the company does not associate the queries with people's names. Against company policy, an employee put the data on a website for search technology researchers. This data included more than 20 million search queries by more than 650,000 people from a three-month period. The data identified people by coded ID numbers, not by name. However, it was not difficult to deduce the identity of some people, especially those who searched on their own name or address. A process called *re-identification* identified others. Re-identification means identifying the individual from a set of anonymous data. Journalists and acquaintances identified people in small communities who searched on numerous specific topics, such as the cars they own, the sports teams they follow, their health problems, and their hobbies. Once identified, a person is linked to all his or her other searches. AOL quickly removed the data, but journalists,

---

* A subpoena is a court order for someone to give testimony or provide documents or other information for an investigation or a trial.

† We use the term Web address informally for identifiers, or addresses, or URLs of pages or documents on the Web (the string of characters one types in a Web browser).

‡ It wanted the data to respond to court challenges to the Child Online Protection Act (COPA), a law intended to protect children from online material "harmful to minors." (We discuss COPA in Section 3.2.2.)

researchers, and others had already copied it. Some made the whole data set available on the Web again.[5]*

Example: Smartphones

With so many clever, useful, and free smartphone apps available, who thinks twice about downloading them? Researchers and journalists took a close look at smartphone software and apps and found some surprises.

Some Android phones and iPhones send location data (essentially the location of nearby cell towers) to Google and Apple, respectively. Companies use the data to build location-based services that can be quite valuable for the public and for the companies. (Industry researchers estimate the market for location services to be in the billions of dollars.) The location data is supposed to be anonymous, but researchers found, in some cases, that it included the phone ID.

Roughly half the apps in one test sent the phone's ID number or location to other companies (in addition to the one that provided the app). Some sent age and gender information to advertising companies. The apps sent the data without the user's knowledge or consent. Various apps copy the user's contact list to remote servers. Android phones and iPhones allow apps to copy photos (and, for example, post them on the Internet) if the user permits the app to do certain other things that have nothing to do with photos. (Google said this capability dated from when photos were on removable memory cards and thus less vulnerable.[6] This is a reminder that designers must regularly review and update security design decisions.)

A major bank announced that its free mobile banking app inadvertently stored account numbers and security access codes in a hidden file on the user's phone. A phone maker found a flaw in its phones that allowed apps to access email addresses and texting data without the owner's permission. Some iPhones stored months of data, in a hidden file, about where the phone had been and when, even if the user had turned off location services. Data in such files are vulnerable to loss, hacking, and misuse. If you do not know the phone stores the information, you do not know to erase it. Given the complexity of smartphone software, it is possible that the companies honestly did not intend the phones to do these things.[†]

Why does it matter? Our contact lists and photos are ours; we should have control of them. Thieves can use our account information to rob us. Apps use features on phones that indicate the phone's location, the light level, movement of the phone, the presence of other phones nearby, and so on. Knowing where we have been over a period of time (combined with other information from a phone) can tell a lot about our activities and

---

* Members of AOL sued the company for releasing their search queries, claiming the release violated roughly 10 federal and state laws.

† The various companies provided software updates for these problems.

1. Files on hundreds of thousands of students, applicants, faculty, and/or alumni from the University of California, Harvard, Georgia Tech, Kent State, and several other universities, some with Social Security numbers and birth dates (stolen by hackers).

2. Names, birth dates, and possibly credit card numbers of 77 million people who play video games online using Sony's PlayStation (stolen by hackers). Another 24 million accounts were exposed when hackers broke into Sony Online Entertainment's PC-game service.

3. Records of roughly 40 million customers of TJX discount clothing stores (T.J. Maxx, Marshalls, and others), including credit and debit card numbers and some driver's license numbers (stolen by hackers).

More about the TJX incident: Section 5.2.5

4. Bank of America disks with account information (lost or stolen in transit).

5. Credit histories and other personal data for 163,000 people (purchased from a huge database company by a fraud ring posing as legitimate businesses).

6. Patient names, Social Security numbers, addresses, dates of birth, and medical billing information for perhaps 400,000 patients at a hospital (on a laptop stolen from a hospital employee's car).

7. More than 1000 Commerce Department laptops, some with personal data from Census questionnaires. (Thieves stole some from the cars of temporary Census employees; others, employees simply kept.)

8. Confidential contact information for more than one million job seekers (stolen from Monster.com by hackers using servers in Ukraine).

Figure 2.1   Lost or stolen personal information.[7]

interests, as well as with whom we associate (and whether the lights were on). As we mentioned in Section 1.2.1, it can also indicate where we are likely to be at a particular time in the future.

Some of the problems we described here will have been addressed by the time you read this; the point is that we are likely to see similar (but similarly unexpected) privacy risks and breaches in each new kind of gadget or capability.

Stolen and lost data

Criminals steal personal data by hacking into computer systems, by stealing computers and disks, by buying or requesting records under false pretenses, and by bribing employees of companies that store the data. Shady information brokers sell data (including cellphone records, credit reports, credit card statements, medical and work records, and location of relatives, as well as information about financial and investment accounts) that they obtain illegally or by questionable means. Criminals, lawyers, private investigators, spouses, ex-spouses, and law enforcement agents are among the buyers. A private investigator could have obtained some of this information in the past, but not nearly so easily, cheaply, and quickly.

Hacking: Section 5.2

Another risk is accidental (sometimes quite careless) loss. Businesses, government agencies, and other institutions lose computers, disks, memory cards, and laptops containing sensitive personal data (such as Social Security numbers and credit card numbers) on thousands or millions of people, exposing people to potential misuse of their information and lingering uncertainty. They inadvertently allow sensitive files to be public on the Web. Researchers found medical information, Social Security numbers, and other sensitive personal or confidential information about thousands of people in files on the Web that simply had the wrong access status.

The websites of some businesses, organizations, and government agencies that make account information available on the Web do not sufficiently authenticate the person accessing the information, allowing imposters access. Data thieves often get sensitive information by telephone by pretending to be the person whose records they seek. They provide some personal information about their target to make their request seem legitimate. That is one reason why it is important to be cautious even with data that is not particularly sensitive by itself.

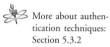
More about authentication techniques: Section 5.3.2

Figure 2.1 shows a small sample of incidents of stolen or lost personal information (the Privacy Rights Clearinghouse lists thousands of such incidents on its website). In many incidents, the goal of thieves is to collect data for use in identity theft and fraud, crimes we discuss in detail in Chapter 5.

A summary of risks

The examples we described illustrate numerous points about personal data. We summarize here:

- Anything we do in cyberspace is recorded, at least briefly, and linked to our computer or phone, and possibly our name.
- With the huge amount of storage space available, companies, organizations, and governments save huge amounts of data that no one would have imagined saving in the recent past.
- People often are not aware of the collection of information about them and their activities.
- Software is extremely complex. Sometimes businesses, organizations, and website managers do not even know what the software they use collects and stores.[8]
- Leaks happen. The existence of the data presents a risk.
- A collection of many small items of information can give a fairly detailed picture of a person's life.
- Direct association with a person's name is not essential for compromising privacy. Re-identification has become much easier due to the quantity of personal information stored and the power of data search and analysis tools.

- If information is on a public website, people other than those for whom it was intended will find it. It is available to everyone.

- Once information goes on the Internet or into a database, it seems to last forever. People (and automated software) quickly make and distribute copies. It is almost impossible to remove released information from circulation.

- It is extremely likely that data collected for one purpose (such as making a phone call or responding to a search query) will find other uses (such as business planning, tracking, marketing, or criminal investigations).

- The government sometimes requests or demands sensitive personal data held by businesses and organizations.

- We often cannot directly protect information about ourselves. We depend on the businesses and organizations that manage it to protect it from thieves, accidental collection, leaks, and government prying.

2.1.3 TERMINOLOGY AND PRINCIPLES FOR MANAGING PERSONAL DATA

We use the term *personal information* often in this chapter. In the context of privacy issues, it includes any information relating to, or traceable to, an individual person. The term does not apply solely to what we might think of as sensitive information, although it includes that. It also includes information associated with a particular person's "handle," user name, online nickname, identification number, email address, or phone number. Nor does it refer only to text. It extends to any information, including images, from which someone can identify a living individual.

Informed consent and invisible information gathering

The first principle for ethical treatment of personal information is *informed consent*. There is an extraordinary range to the amount of privacy different people want. Some blog about their divorce or illnesses. Some pour out details of their romantic relationships on television shows or to hundreds of social network friends. Others use cash to avoid leaving a record of their purchases, encrypt all their email,* and are angry when someone collects information about them. When a business or organization informs people about its data collection and use policies or about the data that a particular device or application collects, each person can decide, according to his or her own values, whether or not to interact with that business or organization or whether to use the device or application.

Invisible information gathering describes collection of personal information without the person's knowledge. The important ethical issue is that if someone is not aware of the collection and use, he or she has no opportunity to consent or withhold consent. We gave

---

* Encrypting data means putting it in a coded form so that others cannot read it.

several examples involving smartphones and their apps in the previous section. Here are examples from other contexts.

- A company offered a free program that changed a Web browser's cursor into a cartoon character. Millions of people installed the program but then later discovered that the program sent to the company a report of the websites its users visited, along with a customer identification number in the software.[9]

- "Event data recorders" in cars record driving speed, whether or not the driver is wearing a seatbelt, and other information.

- "History sniffers" are programs that collect information about a person's online activity based on the different colors a browser uses to display sites recently visited.

- Software called *spyware*, often downloaded from a website without the user's knowledge, surreptitiously collects information about a person's activity and data on his or her computer and then sends the information over the Internet to the person or company that planted the spyware. Spyware can track someone's Web surfing for an advertising company or collect passwords and credit card numbers typed by the user. (Some of these activities are illegal, of course.)

Sophisticated snooping technologies: Section 2.2.2

When our computers and phones communicate with websites, they must provide information about their configuration (e.g., the Web browser used). For a high percentage of computers, there is enough variation and detail in configurations to create a "fingerprint" for each computer. Some companies provide device fingerprinting software for combating fraud and intellectual property theft and for tracking people's online activity in order to target advertising. Both collection of configuration information and building of activity profiles are invisible. Financial firms that use device fingerprinting for security of customer accounts are likely to say so in a privacy policy. We are less likely to know when someone is using it to build marketing profiles.

Whether or not a particular example of data collection is invisible information gathering can depend on the level of public awareness. Some people know about event data recorders in cars; most do not.[10] Before the release of AOL user search data described in Section 2.1.2, collecting search query data was an example of invisible information gathering; for many people it still is. Many businesses and organizations have policy statements or customer agreements that inform customers, members, and subscribers of their policy on collecting and using personal data, but many people simply do not read them. And if they read them, they forget.

A legal remedy for secret data collection: Section 5.2.6

Thus, there can be a significant privacy impact from the many automated systems that collect information in unobvious ways, even when people have been informed. However, there is an important distinction between situations where people are informed but not aware and situations where the information gathering is truly covert, such as in spyware and in some of the smartphone apps we described in Section 2.1.2.

Cookies

Cookies are files a website stores on a visitor's computer.[11] Within the cookie, the site stores and then uses information about the visitor's activity. For example, a retail site might store information about products we looked at and the contents of our virtual "shopping cart." On subsequent visits, the site retrieves information from the cookie. Cookies help companies provide personalized customer service and target advertising to the interests of each visitor. They can also track our activities on many sites and combine the information. At first, cookies were controversial because the very idea that websites were storing files on the user's computer without the user's knowledge startled and disturbed people. Today, more people are aware of cookies and use tools to prevent or delete them. In response, some companies that track online activity developed more sophisticated "supercookies" that recreate deleted cookies and are difficult to find and remove.

Secondary use, data mining, matching, and profiling

> *My most private thoughts, my personal tragedies, secrets about other*
> *people, are mere data of a transaction, like a grocery receipt.*
>
> —A woman whose psychologist's notes were read by an insurer.[12]

Secondary use is the use of personal information for a purpose other than the one for which the person supplied it. Examples include sale of consumer information to marketers or other businesses, use of information in various databases to deny someone a job or to tailor a political pitch, the Internal Revenue Service searching vehicle registration records for people who own expensive cars and boats (to find people with high incomes), use of text messages by police to prosecute someone for a crime, and the use of a supermarket's customer database to show alcohol purchases by a man who sued the store because he fell down.

Data mining means searching and analyzing masses of data to find patterns and develop new information or knowledge. The research using social network data and smartphone data that we described in Section 1.2.1 are examples. *Matching* means combining and comparing information from different databases, often using an identifier such as a person's Social Security number or their computer's Internet address to match records. *Profiling* means analyzing data to determine characteristics of people most likely to engage in certain behavior. Businesses use these techniques to find likely new customers. Government agencies use them to detect fraud, to enforce other laws, and to find terrorists. Data mining, computer matching, and profiling are, in most cases, examples of secondary use of personal information.

We will see examples of secondary use throughout this chapter. One of the controversial issues about personal information is the degree of control people should have over secondary uses of information about them. The variety of uses illustrated by the few examples we gave above suggests that quite different answers are appropriate for different users and different uses.

After informing people about what personal information an organization collects and what it does with that information, the next simplest and most desirable privacy policy is to give people some control over secondary uses. The two most common forms for providing such choice are *opt out* and *opt in*. Under an opt-out policy, one must check or click a box on a contract, membership form, or agreement or contact the organization to request that they not use one's information in a particular way. If the person does not take action, the presumption is that the organization may use the information. Under an opt-in policy, the collector of the information may not use it for secondary uses unless the person explicitly checks or clicks a box or signs a form permitting the use. (Be careful not to confuse the two. Under an opt-out policy, more people are likely to be "in," and under an opt-in policy, more people are likely to be "out," because the default presumption is the opposite of the policy name.) Opt-out options are now common. Responsible, consumer-friendly companies and organizations often set the default so that they do not share personal information and do not send marketing emails unless the person explicitly allows it— that is, they use the opt-in policy. Particularly in situations where disclosing personal information can have negative consequences and it is not obvious to a customer that the organization might disclose it, a default of nondisclosure without explicit permission (that is, an opt-in policy) is the responsible policy.

Fair information principles

Privacy advocates have developed various sets of principles for protection of personal data. They are often called Fair Information Principles or Fair Information Practices.[13] Figure 2.2 presents such a list of principles. Informed consent and restrictions on secondary uses show up in the first and third principles. You will rarely see the last point in Figure 2.2 included among Fair Information Principles, but I consider it an important one. Some companies and organizations turn over personal data to law enforcement agents and government agencies when requested. Some do so only if presented with a subpoena or other court order. Some challenge subpoenas; some do not. Some inform their customers or members when they give personal data to the government; some do not. The entity that holds the data decides how far to go in protecting the privacy of its members or customers. The individual whose data the entity might release is rarely aware of the government request. Thus, the entities that hold the data have a responsibility to those people. Planning ahead for various possible scenarios, developing a policy, and announcing it (and following it) are all part of responsible management of other people's personal data.

1. Inform people when you collect information about them, what you collect, and how you use it.

2. Collect only the data needed.

3. Offer a way for people to opt out from mailing lists, advertising, and other secondary uses. Offer a way for people to opt out from features and services that expose personal information.

4. Keep data only as long as needed.

5. Maintain accuracy of data. Where appropriate and reasonable, provide a way for people to access and correct data stored about them.

6. Protect security of data (from theft and from accidental leaks). Provide stronger protection for sensitive data.

7. Develop policies for responding to law enforcement requests for data.

Figure 2.2   Privacy principles for personal information.

Many businesses and organizations have adopted some version of Fair Information Practices. Laws in the United States, Canada, and European countries (among others) require them in many situations. These principles are reasonable ethical guidelines. However, there is wide variation in interpretation of the principles. For example, businesses and privacy advocates disagree about what information businesses "need" and for how long.

It can be difficult to apply the fair information principles to some new technologies and applications. They do not fully address privacy issues that have arisen with the increase of cameras in public places (such as police camera systems and Google's Street View), the enormous amount of personal information people share in social networks, and the ubiquity and power of smartphones. For example, when someone puts personal information in a tweet to thousands of people, how do we determine the purpose for which he or she supplied the information? Can any recipient use the information in any way? How widely distributed must information be before it is public in the sense that anyone can see or use it? Even when people have agreed to share information, consequences of new

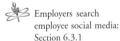 Employers search employee social media: Section 6.3.1 ways of sharing or new categories of information can be unexpected and problematic. For example, in Section 2.3.2 we discuss default settings for features in social networks that have significant consequences.

2.2 The Fourth Amendment, Expectation of Privacy, and Surveillance Technologies

In George Orwell's dystopian novel *1984*, Big Brother (the government) could watch everyone via "telescreens" in all homes and public places. There was little crime and little political dissent—and no love and no freedom. Today, the government does not have to watch every move we make, because so many of our activities leave data trails in databases available to government agencies.* When Big Brother wants to take a direct look at us and our activities, he uses sophisticated new surveillance tools. In this section, we consider the impact of these tools on privacy and look into their compatibility with constitutional and legal protections from government intrusions.

2.2.1   The Fourth Amendment

> *The right of the people to be secure in their persons, houses, papers, and effects, against unreasonable searches and seizures, shall not be violated, and no Warrants shall issue, but upon probable cause, supported by Oath or affirmation, and particularly describing the place to be searched, and the persons or things to be seized.*

—Fourth Amendment, U.S. Constitution

The U.S. Constitution protects a right to privacy from government intrusion, most explicitly in the Fourth Amendment. The U.S. Supreme Court has interpreted other parts of the Bill of Rights to provide a constitutional right to privacy from government in other areas as well. England has a similar tradition, as expressed in William Pitt's colorful statement in 1763:

> The poorest man may in his cottage bid defiance to all the force of the Crown. It may be frail; its roof may shake; the wind may blow through it; the storms may enter; the rain may enter—but the King of England cannot enter . . . .[14]

Here, we look at how databases, surveillance technology, and popular consumer gadgets threaten this right. Although the discussion in this section is in the context of the U.S. Fourth Amendment and U.S. Supreme Court rulings, the new technological risks of intrusion by governments are similar in other countries.

The Fourth Amendment sets limits on the government's rights to search our homes and businesses and to seize documents and other personal effects. It requires that the government have probable cause for the search and seizure. That is, there must be good evidence to support the specific search. Two key problems arise from new technologies. First, much of our personal information is no longer safe in our homes or the individual offices of our doctors and financial advisors. We carry a huge amount of personal information on smartphones and laptops. Much personal information is in huge databases outside of our control. Many laws allow law enforcement agencies to get information from nongovernment databases without a court order. Federal privacy rules allow law enforcement agencies to access medical records without court orders. The USA PATRIOT

---

* The use of myriad personal-data systems to investigate or monitor people is sometimes called *dataveillance*, short for "data surveillance."

Act (passed after the terrorist attacks in 2001) eased government access to many kinds of personal information, including library and financial records, without a court order. The second factor weakening Fourth Amendment protections is that new technologies allow the government to search our homes without entering them, to search our persons from a distance without our knowledge, and to extract all the data on a cellphone (including deleted data and password protected data) in less than two minutes at a traffic stop.

As we consider all the personal information available to government agencies now, we can reflect on the worries of Supreme Court Justice William O. Douglas about the potential abuse from government access to only the records of someone's checking account. In 1974, he said:

> In a sense a person is defined by the checks he writes. By examining them agents get to know his doctors, lawyers, creditors, political allies, social connections, religious affiliation, educational interests, the papers and magazines he reads, and so on ad infinitum. These are all tied in to one's social security number, and now that we have the data banks, these other items will enrich that storehouse and make it possible for a bureaucrat—by pushing one button—to get in an instant the names of the 190 million Americans who are subversives or potential and likely candidates.[15]

Today's readers should not miss the irony of the last sentence: 190 million was almost the entire population of the United States at the time.

With each new data storage or search technology, law enforcement agencies and civil libertarians argue the question of whether the Fourth Amendment applies. In the next few sections, we discuss such technologies and some principles the Supreme Court has established.

> *When the American Republic was founded, the framers established a libertarian equilibrium among the competing values of privacy, disclosure, and surveillance. This balance was based on technological realities of eighteenth-century life. Since torture and inquisition were the only known means of penetrating the mind, all such measures by government were forbidden by law. Physical entry and eavesdropping were the only means of penetrating private homes and meeting rooms; the framers therefore made eavesdropping by private persons a crime and allowed government to enter private premises only for reasonable searches, under strict warrant controls. Since registration procedures and police dossiers were the means used to control the free movement of "controversial" persons, this European police practice was precluded by American governmental practice and the realities of mobile frontier life.*
>
> —Alan F. Westin, *Privacy and Freedom*[16]

2.2.2   New Technologies, Supreme Court Decisions, and Expectation of Privacy

> *The principles laid down in this opinion . . . apply to all invasions on the part of government and its employees of the sanctity of a man's home and the privacies of life. It is not the breaking of his doors, and the rummaging in his drawers, that constitutes the essence of the offense; but it is the invasion of his indefeasible right of personal security, personal liberty and private property.*
>
> —Justice Joseph Bradley, *Boyd v. United States*, 1886.

"Noninvasive but deeply revealing" searches

The title above is from Julian Sanchez's description of a variety of search and detection technologies.[17] Many sound like science fiction; they are not. These technologies can search our homes and vehicles but do not require police to physically enter or open them. They can search our bodies beneath our clothes from a distance without our knowledge. What restrictions should we place on their use? When should we permit government agencies to use them without a search warrant?

Noninvasive but deeply revealing search tools (some in use and some in development) include particle sniffers that detect many specific drugs and explosives, imaging systems that detect guns under clothing from a distance, devices that analyze the molecular composition of truck cargo without opening the truck, thermal-imaging devices (to find heat lamps for growing marijuana, for example), and devices that locate a person by locating his or her cellphone. These devices have obvious valuable security and law enforcement applications, but the technologies can be used for random searches, without search warrants or probable cause, on unsuspecting people. As Sanchez points out, we live "in a nation whose reams of regulations make almost everyone guilty of some violation at some point."[18] Before the government begins using these tools on, say, ordinary people bringing medications home from Canada, making their own beer, or keeping a banned sweetener or saturated fat in their home (or whatever might be illegal in the future), it is critical for privacy protection that we have clear guidelines for their use—and, in particular, clarification of when such use constitutes a search requiring a search warrant.

Supreme Court decisions and expectation of privacy

Several Supreme Court cases have addressed the impact of earlier technology on Fourth Amendment protection. In *Olmstead v. United States*,[19] in 1928, the government had used wiretaps on telephone lines without a court order. The Supreme Court allowed the wiretaps. It interpreted the Fourth Amendment to apply only to physical intrusion and only to the search or seizure of material things, not conversations. Justice Louis Brandeis dissented, arguing that the authors of the Fourth Amendment did all they could to protect liberty and privacy—including privacy of conversations—from intrusions by government based on the technology available at the time. He believed that the court should interpret the Fourth Amendment as requiring a court order even when new technologies give the government access to our personal papers and conversations without entering our homes. In *Katz v. United States*, in 1967, the Supreme Court reversed its position and ruled that the Fourth Amendment does apply to conversations and that it applies in public places in some situations. In this case, law enforcement agents had attached an electronic listening and recording device on the outside of a telephone booth to record a suspect's conversation. The court said that the Fourth Amendment "protects people, not places," and that what a person "seeks to preserve as private, even in an area accessible to the public, may be constitutionally protected." To intrude in places where a reasonable person has a reasonable expectation of privacy, government agents need a court order.

Although the Supreme Court's decision in *Katz v. United States* strengthened Fourth Amendment protection in some ways, there is significant risk in relying on reasonable "expectation of privacy" to define the areas where law enforcement agents need a court order. Consider the two technologies in the box nearby. One tracks private actions in public view; the other tracks people in private places.

As well-informed people come to understand the capabilities of modern surveillance tools, we might no longer expect privacy from government, in a practical sense. Does that mean we should not have it? The Supreme Court recognized this problem in *Smith v. Maryland*, in which it noted that, if law enforcement reduces actual expectation of privacy by actions "alien to well-recognized Fourth Amendment freedoms," this should *not* reduce our Fourth Amendment protection. However, the Court has interpreted "expectation of privacy" in a very restrictive way. For example, it ruled that if we share information with businesses such as our bank, then we have no reasonable expectation of privacy for that information (*United States v. Miller*, 1976). Law enforcement agents do not need a court order to get the information. This interpretation seems odd. We do expect privacy of the financial information we supply a bank or other financial institution. We expect confidentiality in many kinds of information we share with a few, sometimes carefully selected, others. We share our Web activity with ISPs, websites, and search engine companies merely by typing and clicking. We share many kinds of personal information at specific websites where we expect it to be private. Is it safe from warrantless search?

In *Kyllo v. United States* (2001), the Supreme Court ruled that police could not use thermal-imaging devices to search a home from the outside without a search warrant. The Court stated that where "government uses a device that is not in general public use, to explore details of the home that would previously have been unknowable without physical intrusion, the surveillance is a 'search.'" This reasoning suggests that when a technology becomes more widely used, the government may use it for surveillance without a warrant.

Tracking cars and cellphones

Law enforcement agents track thousands of people's locations each year. Sometime they have a court order to do so, and some times they do not. Do they need one? We describe two key cases as examples.

In 2012, the Supreme Court decided *U.S. v. Jones*, its first major case of digital technology surveillance. Does the Fourth Amendment prohibit police from secretly attaching a GPS tracking device to a person's vehicle without a search warrant? The police said no; they could have observed the suspect's car as it moved about on public streets. They argued the GPS device is a labor-saving device. The Court disagreed. There are two arguments in favor of Fourth Amendment protection in this case. First, a vehicle is one of a person's "effects" that the Fourth Amendment explicitly protects. Second, tracking a person's location for a month, 24 hours a day, as in this case, goes beyond someone observing the car pass by in public; it violates a person's expectation of privacy. The Court agreed (unanimously) with the first argument. Police need a search warrant to attach a surveillance device to a private vehicle. The justices recognized that expectation of privacy would be a key issue in tracking cases where directly attaching a device is not necessary, but the majority chose to leave a decision about that to future cases.*[20]

The police had one argument against expectation of privacy in *U.S. v. Jones*: the vehicle drove around in public view. Suppose a person is at home, at a friend's or lover's home, inside a church or a health facility, or in any private space. Law enforcement agencies use a device to locate a person by locating his or her cellphone, even when the person is not actively using the phone.† Police do not need to enter private premises or physically attach anything to a person's property. Thus, expectation of privacy is a key issue here. Law enforcement agenies argue that cellphone tracking (which they have used more than 1000 times, according to a *Wall Street Journal* investigation) does not require a search warrant because a person who uses a cellphone service has no expectation of privacy about the location data the phone transmits to cell towers. This view might surprise most cellphone owners. The Supreme Court has not yet heard a case about this technology.

---

*Four justices wrote an opinion that the tracking also violated expectation of privacy.

†The device pretends to be a cell tower. Agents drive around with it and get the target phone to connect to it in several locations. They then triangulate on the phone from the data the device collects.

This standard may allow time for markets, public awareness, and technologies to develop to provide privacy protection against the new technology. Is it a reasonable standard— a reasonable adaptation of law to new technology? Or should the court have permitted the search? Or should the government have to satisfy the requirements of the Fourth Amendment for every search of a home where a warrant would have been necessary before the technology existed?

Our use of these new technologies doesn't signal that we're less interested in privacy. The idea of the government monitoring our whereabouts, our habits, our acquaintances, and our interests still creeps us out. We often just don't know it's going on until it's too late.

—Judge Alex Kozinski[21]

2.2.3 SEARCH AND SEIZURE OF COMPUTERS AND PHONES

Privacy in group association may . . . be indispensable to preservation of freedom of association, particularly where a group espouses dissident beliefs.

—The Supreme Court, ruling against the state of Alabama's attempt to get the membership list of the National Association for the Advancement of Colored People (NAACP) in the 1950s[22]

The NAACP's membership list was not on a computer in the 1950s. It undoubtedly is now. We consider several issues about how the Fourth Amendment applies to searches of computers, phones, and other electronic devices. How far does a search warrant extend when searching a computer? When is a search warrant needed?

The Fourth Amendment requires that search warrants be specific about the object of the search or seizure. Courts traditionally take the view that if an officer with a warrant sees evidence of another crime in plain view, the officer may seize it and prosecutors may use it. But the amount of information or evidence that might be in plain view in a house or office is small compared to what is on a computer. A computer at a business will have information about a large number of people. Membership lists, business records, medical records, and myriad other things can be on the same computer that law enforcement agents may search with a search warrant for specific, limited items. Access by law enforcement agents to all the data on a computer or device can be a serious threat to privacy, liberty, and freedom of speech.

How should we interpret "plain view" for a search of computer or smartphone files? A broad interpretation—for example, "all unencrypted files"—invites abuse. Agents could get a warrant for a small crime for which they have supporting evidence, and then go on fishing expeditions for other information. This thwarts the Fourth Amendment's requirement that a warrant be specific. In one case, while searching a man's computer with a search warrant for evidence of drug crimes, an officer saw file names suggesting illegal content not related to the warrant. He opened files and found child pornography. An appeals court said the names of files might be considered to be in plain view, but the contents of the files were not.[23] Although the crime in this case is a very unpleasant one, the principle protects us from abuses by the police.

In an investigation of the use of performance-enhancing drugs by professional baseball players, law enforcement agents obtained a search warrant for computer files of laboratory records on drug tests for 10 specific players. The lab files they seized contained records on hundreds of baseball players, hockey players, and ordinary people who are not athletes. The agents found that more than 100 baseball players tested positive for steroid use. This case received much attention in the news when the names of prominent players who allegedly tested positive leaked to the news media. A federal appeals court ruled that the information on all but the original 10 players was beyond the scope of the search warrant and the government was wrong to seize it.[24]

Suppose law enforcement agents have a search warrant for a computer but find that the files are encrypted. Must the owner supply the encryption key? The Fifth Amendment to

More about encryption: Section 2.5.1

the U.S. Constitution specifies that a person cannot be forced to testify against himself. However, courts sometimes allow the government to require a person to provide keys or combinations to a safe. Rulings in federal courts have been inconsistent about whether such a requirement can apply to encryption keys. (In many cases, law enforcement agents decrypt the files by other means.)

> *What happened to the Fourth Amendment?*
> *Was it repealed somehow?*
>
> —A judge, commenting on the seizure of lab records for drug tests[25]

Phones and laptops

A mobile phone might contain contacts, numbers for calls made and received, email, text messages, documents, personal calendars, photos, a history of Web browsing, and a record of where the phone has been. For many people, the phone is a traveling office, containing proprietary and confidential information. A lawyer's phone might contain information about clients and cases—legally protected from access by police.

Police may search an arrested person (without a search warrant) and examine personal property on the person (in pockets, for example) or within his or her reach. Is a search warrant required before the police can search the contents of the person's cellphone? *Should* a search warrant be required?

This seems like a classic "no-brainer." The vast collection of information on a cellphone is the kind of information the Fourth Amendment is intended to protect. A judge who ruled against a cellphone search said the justifications for permitting police to search an arrested person were to find and take weapons and to prevent the person from hiding or destroying evidence. Once the police have custody of a phone, it is safe from destruction and police must wait until they have a search warrant before retrieving information from the phone. The Ohio Supreme Court ruled that searching an arrested person's phone without a search warrant is unconstitutional:* people have an expectation of privacy for the contents of their phones.[26]

But the California Supreme Court ruled otherwise. It said that search of the contents of a cellphone was permitted because the phone was personal property found on the arrested person. Police have searched cellphones taken from arrested people in dozens of cases without warrants. Eventually, a case raising this issue will be heard by the U.S. Supreme Court. The result will have profound implications for privacy. In the meantime, lawyers suggest leaving a cellphone out of reach while driving.

Customs and border officials search luggage when U.S. citizens return from another country and when foreigners enter the United States. Border officials search, and sometimes seize, laptops and phones of journalists, businesspeople, and other travelers. Is searching a laptop equivalent to searching luggage? Or, because of the amount and kind of personal information they contain, does searching them at the border require reasonable suspicion of a crime? A federal appeals court ruled that customs agents do not need reasonable suspicion of a crime to search laptops, phones, and other electronic devices. Lawsuits and debate on the issue are ongoing.[27]

2.2.4 Video Surveillance and Face Recognition

We are used to security cameras in banks and convenience stores. They help in investigations of crimes. Prisons use video surveillance systems for security. Gambling casinos use them to watch for known cheaters. Video surveillance systems monitor traffic and catch drivers who run red lights. In these cases, people are generally aware of the surveillance. After the 2001 terrorist attacks, the police in Washington, D.C., installed cameras that zoom in on individuals a half mile away.

Cameras alone raise some privacy issues. When combined with face recognition systems, they raise even more. Here are some applications of cameras and face recognition and some relevant privacy and civil liberties issues.

In the first large-scale, public application of face recognition, police in Tampa, Florida, scanned the faces of all 100,000 fans and employees who entered the 2001 Super Bowl (causing some reporters to dub it Snooper Bowl). The system searched computer files of criminals for matches, giving results within seconds. People were not told that their faces were scanned. Tampa installed a similar system in a neighborhood of popular restaurants and nightclubs. Police in a control room zoomed in on individual faces and checked for matches in their database of suspects.[28] In two years of use, the system did not recognize anyone that the police wanted, but it did occasionally identify innocent people as wanted felons.

---

* The court allowed for exceptions in certain kinds of emergencies.

The ACLU compared the use of the face recognition system at the Super Bowl to a computerized police lineup to which innocent people were subject without their knowledge or consent. Face recognition systems had a poor accuracy rate in the early 2000s,[29] but the technology improved, along with the availability of photos to match against (tagged photos in social networks, for example). A police officer can now snap a photo of a person on the street and run a cellphone app for face recognition. (Another app scans a person's iris and collects fingerprints.)

Some cities have increased their camera surveillance programs, while others gave up their systems because they did not significantly reduce crime. (Some favor better lighting and more police patrols—low tech and less invasive of privacy.) Toronto city officials refused to let police take over their traffic cameras to monitor a protest march and identify its organizers. In a controversial statement, the Privacy Commissioner of Canada argued that the country's Privacy Act required a "demonstrable need for each piece of personal information collected" to carry out government programs and therefore recording activities of large numbers of the general public was not a permissible means of crime prevention.[30]

England was the first country to set up a large number of cameras in public places to deter crime. There are millions of surveillance cameras in Britain. A study by a British university found a number of abuses by operators of surveillance cameras, including collecting salacious footage, such as people having sex in a car, and showing it to colleagues. Defense lawyers complain that prosecutors sometimes destroy footage that might clear a suspect.[31] Enforcing a curfew for young people is one of the uses of public cameras in England. This application suggests the kind of monitoring and control of special populations the cameras make easy. Will police use face recognition systems to track political dissidents, journalists, political opponents of powerful people—the kinds of people targeted for illegal or questionable surveillance in the past? In 2005, the British government released a report saying Britain's closed-circuit TV systems were of little use in fighting crime. The only successful use of the cameras was in parking lots where they helped reduce vehicle crime.[32] Later that year, photos taken by surveillance cameras helped identify terrorists who set off bombs in the London subway. After rioters burned and looted neighborhoods in England in 2011, police used recordings from street cameras and face recognition systems to identify rioters. It is rare for all the facts or strong arguments to support only one side of an issue. What trade-offs between privacy and identifying criminals and terrorists are we willing to make?

The California Department of Transportation photographed the license plates on cars driving in a particular area. Then it contacted the car owners for a survey about traffic in the area. Hundreds of drivers complained. These people objected vehemently to what they considered unacceptable surveillance by a government agency even when the agency photographed only their license plates, not their faces—for a survey, not a police action. Many ordinary people do not like being tracked and photographed without their knowledge.

Clearly, some applications of cameras and face recognition systems are reasonable, beneficial uses of the technology for security and crime prevention. But there is a clear need for limits, controls, and guidelines. How should we distinguish appropriate from inappropriate uses? Should international events such as the Olympics, which are sometimes terrorist targets, use such systems? Should we restrict technologies such as face recognition systems to catching terrorists and suspects in serious crimes, or should we allow them in public places to screen for people with unpaid parking tickets? Do people have the right to know when and where cameras are in use? In the United States, police must have a reason for requiring a person to be fingerprinted. Should similar standards apply to their use of face recognition and iris scanning? If we consider these issues early enough, we can design privacy-protecting features into the technology, establish well-thought-out policies for their use, and pass appropriate privacy-protecting legislation before, as the Supreme Court of Canada worries in the quote below, "privacy is annihilated."

> *To permit unrestricted video surveillance by agents of the state would seriously diminish the degree of privacy we can reasonably expect to enjoy in a free society. . . . We must always be alert to the fact that modern methods of electronic surveillance have the potential, if uncontrolled, to annihilate privacy.*
>
> —Supreme Court of Canada.[33]

> *This is a public meeting!*
>
> —Reporter Pete Tucker, upon his arrest for taking a photo with his cellphone at an open meeting of a U.S. government agency. Newsman Jim Epstein was then arrested for recording the arrest of Tucker on his own phone.[34]

2.3 The Business and Social Sectors

2.3.1 MARKETING AND PERSONALIZATION

> *Acxiom provides complete and accurate pictures of customers and prospects, powering all marketing and relationship efforts.*
>
> —Acxiom website[35]

Marketing is an essential task for most businesses and organizations. It is one of the biggest uses of personal information—by businesses, political parties, nonprofit organizations, and advocacy groups. Marketing includes finding new customers, members, or voters

Data mining and clever marketing[36]

Customers of the British retailing firm Tesco permit the company to collect information on their buying habits in exchange for discounts. The company identifies young adult males who buy diapers and sends them coupons for beer—assuming that, with a new baby, they have less time to go to a pub.

Target beats that. Target's data miners analyzed purchases of women who signed up for baby registries. They discovered that pregnant women tend to increase their purchases of a group of 25 products. So if a woman starts buying more of several of those products (e.g., unscented lotions and mineral supplements), Target starts sending coupons and ads for preg-nancy and baby products. It can even time them for stages of the pregnancy.

To compete with Wal-Mart, Tesco aimed to identify those customers who were most price conscious and hence most likely to be attracted to Wal-Mart's low prices. By analyzing purchase data, the company determined which customers regularly buy the cheapest version of products that are available at more than one price level. Then they determined what products those customers buy most often, and they set prices on those products below Wal-Mart's.

Are these examples of desirable competition or scary intrusiveness and manipulation of consumers?

and encouraging old ones to continue. It includes advertising one's products, services, or cause. It includes how to price products and when and to whom to offer discounts.

Through most of the 20th century, businesses sent out catalogs and advertisements based on a few criteria (age, gender, and neighborhood, for example). Computers and the increased storage capacity of the 1980s and 1990s began a revolution in targeted marketing. Now, businesses store and analyze terabytes of data, including consumer purchases, financial information, online activity, opinions, preferences, government records, and any other useful information to determine who might be a new customer and what new products and services an old customer might buy. They analyze thousands of criteria to target ads both online and offline. Online retailers make recommendations to you based on your prior purchases and on those of other people with similar buying patterns. Websites greet us by name and present us with options based on prior activity at that site.

To many, the idea that merchants collect, store, and sell data on their purchasing habits is disturbing. These activities impinge upon a key aspect of privacy: control of information about oneself. Privacy advocates and some consumers object to advertising based on consumer purchase histories and online activity. Marketers argue that finely targeted marketing is useful to the consumer and that it reduces overhead and, ultimately, the cost of products. L.L. Bean, a big mail-order business, says it sends out fewer catalogs as it does a better job of targeting customers. A Web ad company said users clicked on 16% of ads displayed based on the user's activity profile—many more than the 1% typical for untargeted Web ads. Another firm says that 20–50% of people used the personalized coupons it provided on screen or by email, compared with the 1–5% redemption rate for newspaper inserts. The companies say targeting ads via personal consumer information reduces the number of ads overall that people will see and provides ads that people are more likely to want.[37] Many people like the personalization of ads and recommendations. Targeting is so popular with some people that Google advertised that its Gmail displays no *untargeted* banner ads.

Some kinds of less obvious personalization trouble people more (when they learn of them). The displays, ads, prices, and discounts you see when shopping online might be different from those others see. Some such targeting is quite reasonable: A clothing site does not display winter parkas on its home page for a shopper from Florida. Some sites offer discounts to first-time visitors. Some display any of hundreds of variations of a page depending on time of day, gender, location, and dozens of other attributes of a person's session. (Some sites guess a visitor's gender based on clicking behavior.[38]) If a person hesitates over a product, a site might offer something extra, perhaps free shipping. Is this collection and use of behavioral information an example of inappropriate invisible information gathering? When we shop in stores, sales clerks can see our gender and our approximate age. They can form other conclusions about us from our clothing, conversation, and behavior. Good salespeople in expensive specialty stores, car dealerships, flea markets, and third-world street markets make judgments about how much a potential customer will pay. They modify their price or offer extras accordingly. Is the complex software that personalizes shopping online merely making up for the loss of information that would be available to sellers if we were shopping in person? Are some people uneasy mainly because they did not realize that their behavior affected what appears on their screen? Are people uneasy because they did not realize that websites can determine (and store) so much about them when they thought they were browsing anonymously? Is the uneasiness something we will get over as we understand the technology better? Or are there privacy threats lurking in these practices?

Companies can use face recognition systems in video game consoles and televisions to target ads to the individual person who is playing a game or watching TV. What risks to privacy does this entail? Is it unethical to include such features? Will most people come to like the customization? Do they understand that if they see ads targeted to their interests, someone somewhere is storing information about them?

Our examples so far have been commercial situations. The Democratic and Republican parties use extensive databases on tens of millions of people to profile those who might vote for their candidates. The parties determine what issues to emphasize (and which to omit) in personalized campaign pitches. The databases include hundreds of details such as job, hobbies, type of car, and union membership.[39] One party might send a campaign flyer to a conservative union member that emphasizes its labor policy but does not mention, say, abortion, while another party might do the opposite.

The issue is informed consent

Technological and social changes make people uncomfortable, but that does not mean the changes are unethical. Some privacy advocates want to ban all advertising targeted by online behavior. It should be clear that targeted or personalized marketing is not, in itself, unethical. Most of the legitimate concern has to do with how marketers get the data they use. In some cases there is consent, in some there is not, and in many the complexity of the situation makes consent unclear.

Collection of consumer data for marketing without informing people or obtaining their consent was widespread, essentially standard practice, until roughly the late 1990s. Sometimes, small print informed consumers, but often they did not see it, did not understand the implications, or ignored it. Gradually, public awareness and pressure for improvement increased, and data collection and distribution policies improved. Now websites, businesses, and organizations commonly provide explicit, multi-page statements about what information they collect and how they use the information. They provide opt-out and opt-in options. (Federal laws and regulations require specific privacy protections for financial and medical information.[40]) There are still many companies that get it wrong, whether out of lack of concern for people's privacy or by misjudging what people want. There is also a vast world of data collection over which we have little or no direct control. When someone consents to a company's use of his or her consumer information, the person probably has no idea how extensive the company is and how far the data could travel. Firms such as Acxiom (quoted at the beginning of this section), a large international database and direct-marketing company, collect personal data from a huge number of online and offline sources. Such companies that maintain huge consumer databases buy (or merge with) others, combining data to build more detailed databases and dossiers. They sell data and consumer profiles to businesses for marketing and "customer management." Most people do not know such firms exist.

Extensive and hidden tracking of online activity led to calls for a "Do Not Track" button in browsers. The exact meaning and effects of such buttons are yet to be determined. The idea is that users would have one clear place to indicate that they do not want their Web activity tracked and stored. Many advertisers, providers of popular Web browsers, and large Internet companies agreed to implement and comply with some version of Do Not Track.

Awareness varies among consumers, and many do not read privacy policies. Is it the user's responsibility to be aware of the data collection and tracking policies of a site he or she visits? Does a person's decision to interact with a business or website constitute implicit consent to its posted data collection, marketing, and tracking policies? How clear, obvious, and specific must an information-use policy be? How often should a site that runs (or allows third parties to run) tracking software remind users? Some people who allow extensive tracking and information collection might later regret specific decisions they made. Whose responsibility is it to protect them? Can we protect them without eliminating options for the people who use them sensibly? Potentially negative future consequences of choices we make now (such as not getting enough exercise) are common in life. We can educate consumers and encourage responsible choices. (At the end of the chapter, we list nonprofit organizations that help do this.) Respect for people's autonomy means letting them make their own choices. Designing systems ethically and responsibly means including ways to inform and remind users of unobvious data collection, of changes in policies or features, and of risks.

Paying for consumer information

When businesses first began building extensive consumer databases, some privacy advocates argued that they should pay consumers for use of their information. In many circumstances, they did (and do) pay us indirectly. For example, when we fill out a contest entry form, we trade data for the opportunity to win prizes. Many businesses give discounts to shoppers who use cards that enable tracking of their purchases. Many offer to trade free products and services for permission to send advertising messages or to collect information. Some privacy advocates criticize such programs. Lauren Weinstein, founder of Privacy Forum, argues that among less affluent people the attraction of free services may be especially strong, and it "coerces" them into giving up their privacy.[41] People do not understand all the potential uses of their information and the long-term consequences of the agreements. On the other hand, such programs offer an opportunity for people with little money to trade something else of value (information) for goods and services they desire. Free-PC started the trend, in 1999, with its offer of 10,000 free PCs in exchange for providing personal information and watching advertising messages. Hundreds of thousands of people swamped the company with applications in the first day.

In any case, these early programs are dwarfed by the development of social networking, free video sites, and a huge number of other websites that provide information and services for free. People understand that advertising funds them. Gmail targets ads to individual users by analyzing the user's email messages. Some privacy advocates were horrified: it reads people's email! In exchange for permission to do so, Gmail provides free email and other services. Millions of people signed up. The success of these businesses and services shows that many people do not object to retailers using their purchase history or email and do not consider the intrusion of online ads to be extremely bothersome, nor their Web surfing to be particularly sensitive. Do they understand the potential consequences?

2.3.2 Our Social and Personal Activity

Broadcast Yourself.
—Slogan on YouTube's home page[42]

Social networks—what we do

There are two aspects of social networks to consider: our own responsibility for what we share (how we risk our privacy and that of our friends) and the responsibilities of the companies that host our information.

Many young people post opinions, gossip, and pictures that their friends enjoy. Their posts might cause trouble if parents, potential employers, law enforcement agents, or various others see them. An 18-year-old who posts sexy photos of herself in bathing suits is thinking about her friends viewing them, not potential stalkers or rapists. People who try to clean up their online personas before starting a job search find that it is hard to eliminate embarrassing material. Some social network apps ask for personal information—such as religion, political views, and sexual orientation—about one's friends as well as oneself. Do people think about how the information might be used and whether their friends would like it disclosed?

Why was it for so long standard practice to stop mail and newspaper delivery when going away on a trip? This one detail about location ("away from home") was important to protect from potential burglars. Yet, now, a great many people post their location (and that of their friends) to social networks.

Social networkers, with hundreds or thousands of network friends they never met, probably do not give enough thought to the implications of the personal information they make available. When someone initially chooses privacy settings, will that person later remember who is getting real-time reports on his or her status and activities?

Government agencies and businesses do many things wrong, but individuals also do not always exercise appropriate thought and care for their own privacy, future, and safety.

> *Polls show that people care about privacy.*
> *Why don't they act that way?*
>
> —Ian Kerr

Social networks—what they do

We use Facebook for our examples here because it has so many features and so many members, and because it has made instructive mistakes. The principles apply to other social media and other websites.

Facebook regularly introduces new services, new ways to share with friends and stay up-to-date on their activities. Several times, Facebook seriously misjudged how members would react and made poor choices. Some of the examples we describe quickly generated storms of criticism from tens of thousands to hundreds of thousands of members as well as from privacy advocates.

News feeds send recent changes in a member's personal information, friends list, and activities to that member's friends.[44] Facebook said it did not change any privacy settings when it introduced the feeds. It sends the information only to people the members had already approved and who could already see it if they looked. Within a day or two, hundreds of thousands of Facebook members protested vehemently. Why? The ease of accessing information can sometimes be more important than the fact that it is available somewhere. Many people do not check on their hundreds of friends regularly. The feeds, however, spread information to everyone instantly. Here is just one kind of instance where it makes a difference: In the physical world, we might share information about the end of a relationship, a serious illness, or a family problem with a few, chosen, close friends. Gradually, as we adjust to the new situation, others might learn of the event. The feeds remove the emotionally protective delay.

When Facebook began telling members about purchases their friends made, problems ranged from spoiling surprise gifts to embarrassing and worrisome disclosures. Should Facebook introduce such features turned "on" for everyone? Or should the company announce them and let members opt in with a click? When Facebook introduced a face recognition tool to help members tag friends in photos, the default was that the tool was on for all members. There was a way to opt-out, but many users were not aware of the new feature, so they did not know to opt out. Facebook's Places feature lets users tag friends who are at their location (whether or not the friend is actually there). What should the default settings be?

Angry members are not good for business. These incidents demonstrate the importance, from both an ethical perspective and a business perspective, of giving careful thought to the implications and risks of new features and the selection of default settings. Changes that might seem small and subtle can have big impacts on people's perceptions of privacy, on risk, and on feelings of comfort. People might be happy if a few friends tag them in a few photos, but they might be very uneasy if an automated system tags every photo they appear in. Quantity can make a difference in perceived quality (in particular, in one's feeling of control of information about oneself). In complex environments, such as social networks with their many features and members, an opt-in policy is preferable— that is, a policy where members must explicitly turn the feature on, or else it remains off. In complex environments, it is also valuable to have a range of options. For example, for a tagging feature (for location or photos), options can include informing the person and allowing removal of the tag, requesting permission for each tag before it goes live, and allowing a member to completely opt out of being tagged. (Facebook modified Places to include a range of levels of protection.)

According to the Federal Trade Commission (FTC), Facebook violated its stated policies in several instances: by giving users' IDs to advertisers along with data on user activity, by allowing third-party apps full access to member personal data, and by failing to delete some of a member's data when the member deleted the account. Such actions, in violation of a company's own statements about its practices, are deceptive; they thwart informed decisions and agreements. We might dislike, denounce, debate, and disagree about the ethics of some data practices. Deceptive practices are more clearly unethical (or unethical at a stronger level) than mistakenly or carelessly making poor choices about defaults.

Responsibility of free services

We should appreciate the astounding amount of free service available to us from social network companies—as well as search engines, communication systems such as Twitter, websites full of expert information, and so on. We can choose to use them or not. At the same time, the businesses that run these free services have a responsibility to their users. If you invite your neighbors to use your car anytime they wish without asking, you have an ethical responsibility not to leave the keys in the car when the brakes are not working. It does not matter that you do not charge a fee. Companies may not, ethically, offer attractive services and then cause a significant risk of harm, especially when the risk is hidden or unexpected.

Life in the clouds

Soon after a woman started writing a personal blog, she discovered that someone she had not seen in years read it. This horrified her. Perhaps she thought only people to whom she gave the Web address read the blog. She did not realize that it showed up high in search results for her name.[45] Another woman liked the feature on a social network site that told her which members read her profile. She was surprised and upset to find that people whose profiles she read knew that she read them. After Facebook suggested that two women might want to be friends, one of them discovered that they were both married to the same man.

The first incident reminds us that some people do not know or understand enough about how the Web works to make good decisions about what to put there.* The second indicates that some people do not think carefully about it. It also illustrates a very common phenomenon: people often want a lot of information about others, but they do not want others to have access to the same kinds of information about themselves. The bigamist did not realize that Facebook would notice his two wives had something in common.

Some people include their birth date in online profiles or in résumés they post on job-hunting sites. Genealogy sites are very popular. People create family trees with complete profiles of family members, including birth dates and mother's maiden name. Medical and financial institutions used this same information (birth dates and mother's maiden name) to verify a customer's identity. We can change a disclosed password; we cannot change our birth date or mother's maiden name.

The Web is public. Most people are decent and harmless, but many are evil and dangerous. Pedophiles have websites that link to sites of Cub Scouts, Brownies (the young version of Girl Scouts), junior high school soccer teams, and so on—sites with pictures of children and sometimes names and other personal information. That is scary. It does not mean that such organizations should not put pictures on their websites. It suggests, however, that they consider whether to include children's names, whether to require registration for use of the site, and so on.

Years ago, when many homes had answering machines connected to telephones, some people, instead, used answering services. Messages left for them resided on recording machines at the service's business site. I recall my surprise that people were comfortable having their personal messages on machines outside their control. How quaint and old-

---

* In an unusual example of initiative, the woman studied the techniques used to rank search results and modified her blog so that it no longer showed up prominently in searches for her name.

fashioned that concern seems now. Our cellphone and email messages routinely reside on computers outside our home or office. Text messages are retrievable months later. After many incidents of exposure of embarrassing messages, we still see individuals, politicians, lawyers, celebrities, and businesspeople writing sensitive, rude, or compromising things in email, text, and tweets with the apparent belief that no one but the intended recipient will ever see them.

Millions of Americans prepare their tax returns online. Do they think about where their income and expenditure data are going? How long the data remain online? How well secured the data are? Small businesses store all their accounting information online (in the "cloud") on sites that provide accounting services and access from anywhere. Do the business owners check the security of the sites? Several medical websites provide an easy place for people to store their medical records. Various companies offer services where people store all their data (email, photos, calendars, files) on the company's servers, instead of on their own PC or laptop. You can store an inventory of your valuable property on the Web (for free) to help with insurance claims after a fire or tornado. The companies supplying this service might all be honest, but the data, if leaked or hacked, is a shopping list for thieves.

There are big advantages to all these services. They are convenient. We do not have to manage our own system. We do not have to do backups. We can get to our files from anywhere with Internet access. We can more easily share files and collaborate with others on projects. There are disadvantages too. We cannot access our files when the network is down or if there is a technical problem at the company that stores them. But the more serious risks are to privacy and security. We lose control. Outside our home, our files are at risk of loss, theft, misuse by employees, accidental exposure, seizure by government agencies, uses by the service provider described in an agreement or privacy policy we did not read, uses we ignored when signing up for the service, and later uses that no one anticipated. We might not care who else sees our vacation photos. We might decide the convenience of filling out tax forms online or storing our medical records online outweighs the risks. The point is to be aware and to make the decision consciously. For computer professionals, awareness of the risks should encourage care and responsibility in developing secure systems to protect the sensitive information people store online.

2.3.3 Location Tracking

Global positioning systems (GPS), cellphones, radio frequency identification (RFID) tags,* and other technologies and devices enable a variety of location-based applications— that is, computer and communications services that depend on knowing exactly where a person or object is at a particular time. Since the introduction of the iPhone, there has been an explosion in such applications. The applications are extraordinarily diverse

---

* RFID tags are small devices that contain an electronic chip and an antenna. The chip stores identification data (and possibly other data) and controls operation of the tag. The antenna transmits and receives radio signals for communicating with devices that read the tag.

and have significant benefits. However, they add detailed information about our current location and our past movements to the pool of information that computer systems store about us, with all the potential threats to privacy.

To analyze risks, we should always consider unintended, as well as intended, uses. Recall from Section 2.2.2 that law enforcement agencies locate people by locating their phone. Details of the technology are secret and the device is probably expensive. But that is temporary. Eventually there will be an app for that. So imagine that anyone can enter a person's ID number (perhaps a phone number) on their own mobile device and ask where that person is now. Or perhaps a device could sweep a particular location and detect identifying devices of the people there—or identify them by face recognition. Who might a person *not* want to get this information? Thieves. A violent spouse or ex-spouse. A divorce lawyer. An annoying or nosy neighbor. A stalker. Co-workers or business associates. Anyone else who might object to your religion, politics, or sexual behavior. The government. (Oh, we see that our new teacher is at a meeting of Alcoholics Anonymous. Who is in that medical marijuana store or gun store right now?) Extensive records of where we were provide more details to the ever-growing profiles and dossiers businesses and governments build about us. With fast search, matching, and analysis tools, they can add more detail about who we spend time with and what we are doing. In Chapter 1, we mentioned that researchers learn about social organization and the spread of disease (among other things) by studying huge amounts of cellphone data. Such statistical data can be extremely valuable to us all, but a cellphone identifies a person, and, thus, the tracking information (if associated with the phone's number or ID) is personal information and raises the usual issues of consent, potential secondary uses, risks of misuse, and so on. Care must be taken to ensure that such data are protected.

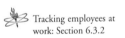 Tracking employees at work: Section 6.3.2

If accessed surreptitiously, stolen, disclosed accidentally, or acquired by government agencies, records of our location and movements pose threats to privacy, safety, and liberty. Privacy and industry organizations are developing guidelines for use of location-tracking applications to implement principles in Figure 2.2 and protect against some of the risks.[46]

Studying the behavior of customers in a store or other facility is a big potential application of location tracking. For example, a supermarket or an amusement park might want to analyze customer traffic patterns within the facility to plan a better layout, to determine how much time people spend inside, or to analyze waiting times. The privacy implications and risks of monitoring people's movements vary from little to great depending on how the tracking system does its work. Suppose, for example, an amusement park such as Disneyland wants to study visitor traffic patterns, detect crowds and long lines, and so on. It can do so with a location-emitting ticket that people get when they enter and discard when they leave. It need have no information connected to the person or family. For such a system, privacy is not an issue. There would be a temptation, however, to include demographic data and possibily identifying data on the tracker.

Who's at the Bar?

Hundreds of bars installed cameras with a face recognition system to provide data to a website and smartphone app. The app tells users the number of people at a particular bar, the male/female ratio, and the approximate age range. Each bar gets summary statistics on its patrons that could be useful for advertising or other business planning. The system does not identify individual people and does not store the video. So this is not a privacy issue. Or is it?

The point is that such an application can remain utterly unthreatening, or it can drift over the boundary into location tracking and privacy infringement. The bar owners do not control the system, so they cannot be certain that what they tell their customers about it is true. (There are many examples of systems collecting and storing data without the knowledge of the businesses that use the system.) The developer and operator of the system might exercise great care to protect patrons' privacy, or they might succumb to temptation to add new features that require storing video or identifying individuals. Awareness of potential risks and understanding of good privacy practices are essential for both the software developers who invent and upgrade such systems and the managers who make decisions about what features to implement.

Tools for parents

Many technologies help parents track their children's physical location. Cellphone services enable parents to check a child's location from the parent's mobile device. Devices installed in a car tell parents where their teens are and how fast they are driving. A company sells wireless watchband transmitters for children, so parents can monitor them. RFID tags in shoes and clothes can be monitored hundreds of feet away. These might be very helpful with young children who wander off in a crowded place.

Tracking children can increase safety, but there are parenting issues and risks involved in using tracking tools. At what age does tracking become an invasion of the child's privacy? Should parents tell children about the tracking devices and services they are using? Informed consent is a basic principle for adults. At what age does it apply to children? Will intense tracking and monitoring slow the development of a child's responsible independence?

A monitoring system that sends easily read or easily intercepted signals could decrease rather than increase the safety of a child. Child molesters and identity thieves could collect personal data. Parents need to be aware of potential for false alarms and for a false sense of security. For example, a child might lose a phone or leave a tagged article of clothing somewhere. Older kids might figure out how to thwart tracking systems. Clearly, how and when to use surveillance tools should involve thoughtful decisions for families.

Pets, prisoners, and people with Alzheimer's disease can wear devices that locate them if they wander off. Veterinarians implant ID chips under the skin of pets and farm animals.

Foiling poachers, following turtles, tracking guitars

Owners tag very valuable and extremely rare plants, both in the wild and in gardens, with tracking chips so they can locate them if stolen.

Satellite technology and microprocessors enormously improved animal tracking. Scientists now attach tiny transmitters to rare birds and other animals to study their behavior and learn how to protect their food sources. Researchers learned that some animals travel much farther than previously thought: Sea turtles swim from the Caribbean to Africa. A nesting albatross flew from Hawaii to the San Francisco Bay, a weeklong round-trip, to get food for its young. To encourage interest from the public, researchers set up websites where we can follow the animals' movements.[47]

These are valuable services. What happens when the same technologies track people?

I recently toured a guitar factory. The tour guide showed us a partially complete guitar neck. And there, on the front of the neck, was an RFID chip. The fret board, when attached to the neck, covers the chip. The guide explained how useful the chip was for tracking guitars through production and for finding a specific guitar in the stock room. The chip remains in the guitar when a customer buys it. Manufacturers put RFID tags in many other products, in addition to guitars, to track them through the manufacturing and sales processes. What is the potential for tracking people via the products they buy? Does it matter?

Some people have suggested doing this for prisoners and children. Does the suggestion of implanting tracking chips in people make you wonder if that is such a good idea? After heavy opposition from parents, a school dropped its proposal to require that all students wear an RFID-equipped device while on school grounds. The constant surveillance and the risks of misuse were enough, in the minds of many parents, to outweigh the benefits of a removable tracking device.

2.3.4   A Right to Be Forgotten

People sometimes want to remove information about themselves from the Internet or from a company's records. It could be an offensive comment made in anger, a photo on one's own social network page or a photo-sharing site, information in online directories, or personal data posted by others (e.g., on a genealogy site). It could be the profile an advertising company developed by tracking the person's Web activity, a collection of data gleaned from the person's smartphone use, or the collection of the person's search queries that a search engine stores. It could be unflatering images or information that other people posted. It could be a search engine's links to such material. Legislators and privacy

The right to be forgotten in the EU: Section 2.5.3

advocates in the United States and the European Union are promoting a legal right to demand that websites remove material about oneself. The right to have material removed, as a legal or ethical right, has come to be called the "right to be forgotten." The wide range of material a person might want to remove suggests many practical, ethical, social, and legal questions and criticisms about such a right.[48]

The policies of various websites about removing material vary. Some sites with members, such as social networks, respond to a member's request to delete material the user posted and to delete a member's material when the member closes the account. When the material is not in a user's account, the situation is more complicated. Some sites, such as directories, collect information automatically; thus, deleted information can reappear. A filter system to prevent reposting for a particular person has the problem of correctly distinguishing that person from others with the same or similar names.

Should a company or website always comply with a request to delete a particular item or a person's record any time a person makes such a request? We understand that people do foolish things and regret them later. It is reasonable to let many of them be forgotten. If a person wants to delete something he or she posted on a website, it is reasonable, courteous, good-spirited, and perhaps a good business policy to comply. If someone else posts compromising photos or information from a person's past, removing it raises issues of free speech and truth. If the person is not a public figure and the information has no broad social value, removing it might be the reasonable, courteous thing to do. Complying with the request could be ethically acceptable and admirable but not ethically obligatory. In some cases, it could be a bad idea. The information might matter to people in a particular community. The person who posted it might have a good reason. The appropriate decision in specific cases might be difficult.

What about the data that advertisers and search engines collect about us? Must they, from an ethical standpoint, comply with a request from a person who wants his or her record deleted? If the companies collected the data secretly, without permission, or in violation of their stated privacy policies and terms of use, then there are good reasons to require its deletion independent of any right to be forgotten. Suppose the information is the set of a person's search queries or something similar that a free website collects, and suppose the site makes its collection and use of the data clear in its terms of use. The company's use of the data is, in part, our payment for the free service it provides. If the company agrees to delete people's records upon request, it is providing its service to those people for free (or at a "discount" if they continue to view ads on the site). If a relatively small number of individuals request deletion of their data, a large company can probably afford to comply without significant inconvenience or reduction in the value it gets from analysis of user data. Many companies give some products and services for free. Again, complying with deletion requests could be ethically and socially admirable, good-spirited, and perhaps a good business policy. On the other hand, a person might make a deletion request to hide some illegal or offensive behavior or to remove evidence in a dispute of some kind.

If the right to be forgotten is a negative right (a liberty), it could mean that we may choose to stay off the Internet and become a recluse, but we cannot force someone else to remove a photo that we are in. As a positive right (a claim right), it is akin to requiring that others erase their minds, as well as their photos, blogs, and links. It can mean that others may not write about a person or exchange specified information about the person—information gained without violating any of the person's rights. This can infringe freedom of speech. In some applications, the right would mean that a person may break agreements (e.g., terms of use for a Web service) at will. There seems to be little if any basis for such an ethical right.

Are there contexts in which it makes sense to enforce a legal requirement to remove material when a person requests it? Perhaps for special populations, such as children (where parents might make the request or a young adult might want to remove seminude sexting photos sent to friends while in high school). Perhaps in other special situations. Legislators Sexting: Section 3.2.3 must carefully craft any such legal requirement to avoid conflict with free speech, free flow of information, and contractual agreements. A legal requirement to honor removal requests will be more of a burden to small sites than to large ones, which can develop software to help automate the process and have legal staffs to defend against complaints.

2.4 Government Systems

2.4.1 DATABASES

Federal and local government agencies maintain thousands of databases containing personal information. Examples include tax, property ownership, medical, travel, divorce, voter registration, bankruptcy, and arrest records. Others include applications for government grant and loan programs, professional and trade licenses, and school records (including psychological testing of children). And there are many, many more. Government databases help government agencies perform their functions, determine eligibility for government benefits programs, detect fraud in government programs, collect taxes, and catch people who are breaking laws. The scope of government activities is enormous, ranging from catching violent criminals to licensing flower arrangers. Governments can arrest people, jail them, and seize assets from them. Thus, the use and misuse of personal data by government agencies pose special threats to liberty and personal privacy. It seems reasonable to expect governments to meet an especially high standard for privacy protection and adherence to their rules.

The Privacy Act of 1974 is the main law about the federal government's use of personal data. A summary of the provisions of the Act appears in Figure 2.3. Although this law was an important step in attempting to protect our privacy from abuse by federal agencies, it has problems. The Privacy Act has, to quote one expert on privacy laws, "many loopholes, weak enforcement, and only sporadic oversight."[49] The E-Government Act of 2002 added some privacy regulations for electronic data and services—for example, requiring agencies

- Restricts the data in federal government records to what is "relevant and necessary" to the legal purpose for which the government collects it
- Requires federal agencies to publish a notice of their record systems in the Federal Register so that the public may learn about what databases exist
- Allows people to access their records and correct inaccurate information
- Requires procedures to protect the security of the information in databases
- Prohibits disclosure of information about a person without his or her consent (with several exceptions)

Figure 2.3 Provisions of the Privacy Act of 1974.

to conduct privacy impact assessments for electronic information systems and to post privacy policies on agency websites used by the public.

The Government Accountability Office (GAO) is Congress' "watchdog agency." Over the past 25 years, the GAO has released numerous studies showing lack of compliance with the Privacy Act and other privacy risks and breaches. The GAO reported in 1996 that White House staffers used a "secret" database with records on 200,000 people (including ethnic and political information) without adequate access controls. A GAO study of 65 government websites found that only 3% of the sites fully complied with the fair information standards for notice, choice, access, and security established by the Federal Trade Commission (FTC) for commercial websites. (The FTC's site was one that did not comply.) The GAO reported that the Internal Revenue Service (IRS), the Federal Bureau of Investigation (FBI), the State Department, and other agencies that use data mining to detect fraud or terrorism did not comply with all rules for collecting information on citizens. The GAO found dozens of weaknesses in the operation of the government's communication network for transmitting medical data in the Medicare and Medicaid programs—weaknesses that could allow unauthorized access to people's medical records.[50]

The IRS is one of several federal government agencies that collects and stores information on almost everyone in the country. It is also a major secondary user of personal information. Year after year, hundreds of IRS employees are investigated for unauthorized snooping in people's tax files. (An IRS employee who was a Ku Klux Klan member read tax records of members of his Klan group looking for income information that would indicate that someone was an undercover agent.) These abuses led to a law with tough penalties for government employees who snoop through people's tax information without authorization. However, a GAO report a few years later found that while the IRS had made significant improvements, the tax agency still failed to adequately protect people's financial and tax information. IRS employees were able to alter and delete data without authorization. Employees disposed of disks with sensitive taxpayer information without erasing files. Hundreds of tapes and diskettes were missing. A report by the Treasury's Inspector General said that the IRS did not adequately protect taxpayer information on more than 50,000 laptops and other storage media. Personal financial information that taxpayers provide to the IRS is "at risk" from hackers and disgruntled employees because many of the 250 state and federal agencies to which the IRS provides taxpayer information do not have adequate safeguards.[51]

Various reviews of compliance with the Privacy Act and the E-Government Act have highlighted weaknesses in these laws. The GAO advocated modifying the Privacy Act to cover all personally identifiable information collected and used by the federal government, thus closing gaping loopholes that exempt much government use of personal information from the law's provisions. The GAO advocated stricter limits on use of personal information. Recognizing that most people do not read the *Federal Register,* the GAO suggested better ways of informing the public about government databases and privacy policies. The Information Security and Privacy Advisory Board (a government advisory board) pointed out: "The Privacy Act does not adequately cover government use of commercially-compiled databases of personal information. The rules about the federal government's use of commercial databases, and even use of information gleaned from commercial search engines, have been vague and sometimes non-existent." Thus, agencies can bypass the protections of the Privacy Act by using private-sector databases and searches, rather than collecting the information itself.[52]

> *Quis custodiet ipsos custodes? (Who will guard the guards themselves?)*
>
> —Juvenal

Database example: tracking college students

The U.S. Department of Education proposed establishing a database to contain the records of every student enrolled in a college or university in the United States. The proposal would require colleges and universities to provide and regularly update the records including each student's name, gender, Social Security number, major, courses taken, courses passed, degrees, loans, and scholarships (public and private). The government would keep the data indefinitely. The department has not yet implemented the proposal because of intense opposition. The government already has similar databases, and proposals for massive government databases of personal information appear regularly. We discuss this one as an example for analysis; the issues and questions we raise here apply in many other situations.

The student database would have many beneficial uses: The federal government spends billions of dollars each year on federal grants and loans to students but has no good way to measure the success of these programs. Do students who get aid graduate? What majors do they pursue? The database would help evaluate federal student aid programs and perhaps lead to improvements in the programs. The database would provide more accurate data on graduation rates and on actual college costs. The ability to track the number of future nurses, engineers, teachers, and so on, in the educational pipeline can help shape better immigration policy and business and economic planning.

On the other hand, the collection of so much detail about each student in one place generates a variety of privacy risks. Several of the points in the list in Section 2.1.2 are relevant here. It is very likely that the government would find new uses for the data that are not part of the original proposal. Such a database could be an ideal target for identity thieves. Leaks of many sorts are possible and likely. There is potential for abuse by staff members who maintain the data; for example, someone might release college records of a political candidate. And there would undoubtedly be errors in the database. If the department limits the data's use to generalized statistical analysis, errors might not have a big impact, but for some potential uses, the errors could be quite harmful.

 More about identity theft: Section 5.3

Some educators worry that a likely eventual link between the database and public school databases (on children in kindergarten through high school) would contribute to "cradle-to-grave" tracking of childhood behavior problems, health and family issues, and so on.[53]

The planned uses of the database do not include finding or investigating students who are breaking laws, but it would be a tempting resource for law enforcement agencies. A Virginia state law requires colleges to provide the names and other identifying information for all students they accept. State police then check if any are in sex-offender registries. What else might they check for? What other government agencies might want access to a federal student database? Would the Defense Department use the database for military recruiting? What potential risks arise if employers get access? All such uses would be secondary uses, without the consent of the students.

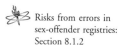 Risks from errors in sex-offender registries: Section 8.1.2

It makes sense for the government to monitor the effectiveness of the grants and loans it gives to college students. It is therefore reasonable to require data on academic progress and graduation from students who receive federal money or loan guarantees. But what justifies demanding the data on all other students? For statistics and planning, the government can do voluntary surveys, just as businesses and organizations, without the government's power of coercion, must do. Are the benefits of the database central enough to the fundamental responsibilities of government to outweigh the risks and to justify a mandatory reporting program of so much personal data on every student?*

---

* Critics of the proposal, including many universities, point out other risks and costs besides privacy. Colleges fear that collection of the data would lead to increased federal control and interference in management of colleges. The reporting requirements would impose a high cost on the schools. The whole project would have high costs to taxpayers.

The U.S. Census

The U.S. Constitution authorizes and requires the government to count the people in the United States every 10 years, primarily for the purpose of determining the number of Congressional representatives each state will have. Between 1870 and 1880, the U.S. population increased by 26%. It took the government nine years to process all the data from the 1880 census. During the 1880s, the population increased by another 25%. If the Census Bureau used the same methods, it would not complete processing data from the 1890 census until after the 1900 census was to begin. Herman Hollerith, a Census Bureau employee, designed and built punch-card processing machines—tabulators, sorters, and keypunch machines—to process census data.* Hollerith's machines did the complete 1890 population count in only six weeks—an amazing feat at the time. The Bureau completed the rest of the processing of the 1890 census data in seven years. It could have been done sooner, but the new machines allowed sophisticated and comprehensive analysis of the data that was not possible before. Here is an early example of computing technology enabling increased processing of data with the potential for good and bad effects: better use of information and invasion of privacy.

The Census Bureau requires everyone to provide name, gender, age, race, and relationship to people one lives with. It requires three million households a year to fill out a longer form that contains questions about marital history, ancestry, income, details about one's home, education, employment, disabilities, expenditures, and other topics.

Census information is supposed to be confidential. Federal law says that "in no case shall information furnished . . . be used to the detriment of any respondent or other person to whom such information relates."[54]

During World War I, the Census Bureau provided names and addresses of young men to the government to help find and prosecute draft resisters. During World War II, the Census Bureau assisted the Justice Department in using data from the 1940 census to find U.S. citizens of Japanese ancestry; the army rounded up Japanese-Americans and put them in internment camps. With the introduction of electronic computers and the advances in computing technology, using the data "to the detriment of any respondent" is easier. Some cities used census data to find poor families who violated zoning or other regulations by doubling up in single-family housing. They evicted the families. A few years after the 9/11 terrorist attacks, at the request of the Department of Homeland Security, the Census Bureau prepared lists showing the number of people of Arab ancestry in various zip codes throughout the United States. A government spokesperson said they needed the data to determine which airports should have signs in Arabic. Privacy and civil liberties organizations were skeptical.[55]

*The company Hollerith formed to sell his machines later became IBM.

When considering each new system or policy for personal data use or data mining by government, we should ask many questions: Is the information it uses or collects accurate and useful? Will less intrusive means accomplish a similar result? Will the system inconvenience ordinary people while being easy for criminals and terrorists to thwart?

How significant are the risks to innocent people? Are privacy protections built into the technology and into the rules controlling usage?

Fighting terrorism

Before the terrorist attacks on the United States on September 11, 2001, law enforcement agencies lobbied regularly for increased powers that conflicted with privacy. Sometimes they got what they wanted; sometimes they did not. Generally, people resisted privacy intrusion by government. After the attacks on the World Trade Center and the Pentagon, more people became willing to accept uses of personal data and forms of search and surveillance that would have generated intense protest before. Two examples are the intrusive searches at airports and the Transportation Security Administration's (TSA) requirement that airlines provide the name and birth date of every passenger to the TSA so that it can match people against its watch list. In 2012, the government extended to five years the amount of time the National Counterterrorism Center may store data on Americans with no known connection to terrorism or criminal activity.

 Errors in terrorism watch lists: Section 8.1.2

Proposals for new data mining programs to find terrorists and terrorist plots continue to appear. We summarize an interesting point Jeff Jonas and Jim Harper present about the suitability of data mining for this purpose.[56] Marketers make heavy use of data mining. They spend millions of dollars analyzing data to find people who are likely to be customers. How likely? In marketing, a response rate of a few percent is considered quite good. In other words, expensive, sophisticated data mining has a high rate of false positives. Most of the people whom data mining identifies as potential customers are not. Many targeted people will receive ads, catalogs, and sales pitches they do not want. Junk mail and pop-up ads annoy people, but they do not significantly threaten civil liberties. A high rate of false positives in data mining for finding terrorist suspects does. Data mining might be helpful for picking terrorists out of masses of consumer data, but appropriate procedures

Reducing privacy intrusions for air travel

Travelers are familiar with x-ray scanning machines at airports. The machines display on a computer screen the image of a person's body and any weapons and packets of drugs hidden under clothing and wigs. The American Civil Liberties Union (ACLU) describes the scan as "a virtual strip search." In response to strong objections from the public and privacy advocates, the TSA modified the software to display a generic line drawing of a body, instead of the x-ray image of the actual person scanned.[57]

Why didn't the TSA build in this obvious privacy-protecting feature at the beginning? There might be technical problems, but perhaps they did not because no law or regulation requires such privacy protection.

are essential to protect innocent but mistakenly selected people. Jonas and Harper argue that other methods for finding terrorists are more cost-effective and less threatening to the privacy and civil liberties of large numbers of people.

2.4.2 PUBLIC RECORDS: ACCESS VERSUS PRIVACY

Governments maintain "public records," that is, records that are available to the general public. Examples include bankruptcy records, arrest records, marriage license applications, divorce proceedings, property-ownership records (including mortgage information), salaries of government employees, and wills. These have long been public, but by and large they were available only on paper in government offices. Lawyers, private investigators, journalists, real estate brokers, neighbors, and others use the records. Now that it is so easy to search and browse through files on the Web, more people access public records for fun, for research, for valid personal purposes—and for purposes that can threaten the peace, safety, and personal secrets of others.

Public records include sensitive information such as Social Security numbers, birth dates, and home addresses. Maricopa County in Arizona, the first county to put numerous and complete public records on the Web, had the highest rate of identity theft in the United States.[58] Obviously, certain sensitive information should be withheld from public-record websites. That requires decisions about exactly what types of data to protect. It requires revisions to government software systems to prevent display of specified items. Because of the expense and lack of accountability, incentives within government agencies to do this are weak. A few have adopted policies to block display of sensitive data in files posted online, and some states have laws requiring it. Several software companies produced software for this purpose, using a variety of techniques to search documents for sensitive data and protect them. Until new systems—in which such security is part of the basic design—replace older systems, the patches and add-ons, while helpful, are likely to miss a lot of sensitive data.

 More about identity theft: Section 5.3

To illustrate more issues about public records and potential solutions, we describe a few kinds of specialized information (political contributions, flight information for private airplanes, and the financial statements of judges), then raise some questions.

Political campaign committees must report the name, address, employer, and donation amount for every donor who contributes more than $100 to a candidate for president. This information is available to the public. In the past, primarily journalists and rival campaigns examined it. Now it is on the Web and easy to search. Anyone can find out what candidate their neighbors, friends, employees, and employers support. We can also find the addresses of prominent people who might prefer to keep their address secret to protect their peace and privacy.

The pilots of the roughly 10,000 company airplanes in the United States file a flight plan when they fly. A few businesses have combined this flight information, obtained from government databases, with aircraft registration records (also public government records) to provide a service telling where a particular plane is, where it is going, when it will arrive, and so on. Who wants this information? Competitors can use it to determine with whom top executives of another company are meeting. Terrorists could use it to track movements of a high-profile target. The information was available before, but not so easily and anonymously.

Federal law requires federal judges to file financial disclosure reports.[59] The public can review these reports to determine whether a particular judge might have a conflict of interest in a particular case. The reports were available in print but not online. When an online news agency sued to make the reports available online, judges objected that information in the reports can disclose where family members work or go to school, putting them at risk from defendants who are angry at a judge. Ultimately, the reports were provided for posting online, with some sensitive information removed.[60]

The change in ease of access to information changes the balance between the advantages and disadvantages of making some kinds of data public. Whenever access changes significantly, we should reconsider old decisions, policies, and laws. Do the benefits of requiring reporting of small political contributions outweigh the privacy risks? Do the benefits of making all property ownership records public outweigh the privacy risks? Maybe. The point is that such questions should regularly be raised and addressed.

How should we control access to sensitive public records? Under the old rules for the financial statements of judges, people requesting access had to sign a form disclosing their identity. This is a sensible rule. The information is available to the public, but the record of who accessed it could deter most people intent on doing harm. Can we implement a similar system online? Technologies for identifying and authenticating people online are developing, but they are not yet widespread enough for use by everyone accessing sensitive public data on the Web. We might routinely use them in the future, but that raises another question: How will we distinguish data that requires identification and a signature for access from data the public should be free to view anonymously, to protect the viewer's privacy?[61]

2.4.3 NATIONAL ID SYSTEMS

In the United States, national identification systems began with the Social Security card in 1936. In recent decades, concerns about illegal immigration and terrorism provided the most support for a more sophisticated and secure national ID card. Opposition, based on concerns about privacy and potential abuse (and cost and practical problems), prevented significant progress on a variety of national ID proposals made by many government agencies. In this section, we review Social Security numbers, various issues about national ID systems, and the REAL ID Act, a major step toward turning driver's licenses into national ID cards.

Social Security numbers[62]

The history of the Social Security number (SSN) illustrates how the use of a national identification system grows. When SSNs first appeared in 1936, they were for the exclusive use of the Social Security program. The government assured the public at the time that it would not use the numbers for other purposes. Only a few years later, in 1943, President Roosevelt signed an executive order requiring federal agencies to use the SSN for new record systems. In 1961, the IRS began using it as the taxpayer identification number. So employers and others who must report to the IRS require it. In 1976, state and local tax, welfare, and motor vehicle departments received authority to use the SSN. A 1988 federal law requires that parents provide their SSN to get a birth certificate for a child. In the 1990s, the Federal Trade Commission encouraged credit bureaus to use SSNs. A 1996 law required that states collect SSNs for occupational licenses, marriage licenses, and other kinds of licenses. Also in 1996, Congress required that all driver's licenses display the driver's SSN, but it repealed that law a few years later due to strong protests. Although the government promised otherwise, the SSN has become a general identification number.

We use our Social Security number for identification for credit, financial services, and numerous other services, yet its insecurity compromises our privacy and exposes us to fraud and identity theft. For example, a part-time English teacher at a California junior college used the Social Security numbers of some of her students, provided on her class lists, to open fraudulent credit card accounts. Because the SSN is an identifier in so many databases, someone who knows your name and has your SSN can, with varying degrees of ease, get access to your work and earnings history, credit report, driving record, and other personal data. SSNs appear on public documents and other openly available forms. Property deeds, which are public records (and now online), often require SSNs. For decades, SSNs were the ID numbers for students and faculty at many universities; the numbers appeared on the face of ID cards and on class rosters. The state of Virginia included SSNs on published lists of voters until a federal court ruled that its policy of requiring the SSN for voter registration was unconstitutional. Some employers used the SSN as an identifier and put it on badges or gave it out on request. Many companies, hospitals, and other organizations to which we might owe a bill request our SSN to run a credit check. Some routinely ask for an SSN and record it in their files, although they do not need it.

More than 30 years ago, the U.S. Department of Agriculture (USDA) began including the SSN as part of the ID number for farmers who received loans or grants. In 2007, the USDA admitted that since 1996 it had inadvertently included the SSNs of more than 35,000 farmers on the website where it posted loan details.[63] This example illustrates how practices begun well before the Web have continuing repercussions. It also illustrates the importance of careful and thorough evaluation of decisions to put material on the Web. There are likely many similar examples that no one has yet noticed.

SSNs are too widely available to securely identify someone. Social security cards are easy to forge, but that hardly matters, because those who request the number rarely ask for the card and almost never verify the number. The Social Security Administration itself used to issue cards without verification of the information provided by the applicant. Criminals have little trouble creating false identities, while innocent, honest people suffer disclosure of personal information, arrest, fraud, destruction of their credit rating, and so on, because of problems with the SSN.

Gradually, governments and businesses began to recognize the risks of careless use of the SSN and reasons why we should not use it so widely. It could take a long time to undo the damage its widespread use has already done to privacy and financial security.

A new national ID system

> *Places like Nazi Germany, the Soviet Union, and apartheid South Africa all had very robust identification systems. True, identification systems do not cause tyranny, but identification systems are very good administrative systems that tyrannies often use.*

—Jim Harper, Director of Information Policy Studies, Cato Institute[64]

Various national ID card proposals in recent years would require citizenship, employment, health, tax, financial, or other data, as well as biometric information such as fingerprints or a retina scan, depending on the specific proposal and the government agency advocating it. In many proposals, the cards would also access a variety of databases for additional information.

More about biometrics: Section 5.3.3

Advocates of national ID systems describe several benefits: You would need the actual card, not just a number, to verify identity. The cards would be harder to forge than Social Security cards. A person would need to carry only one card, rather than separate cards for various services as we do now. The authentication of identity would help reduce fraud both in private credit card transactions and in government benefit programs. Use of ID cards for verifying work eligibility would prevent people from working in the United States illegally. Criminals and terrorists would be easier to track and identify.

Opponents of national ID systems argue that they are profound threats to freedom and privacy. "Your papers, please" is a demand associated with police states and dictatorships. In Germany and France, identification papers included the person's religion, making it easy for the Nazis to capture and remove Jews. Under the infamous pass laws of South Africa, people carried passes, or identification papers, that categorized them by race and controlled where they could live and work. Cards with embedded chips or magnetic strips and the large amount of personal information they can carry or access have even more potential for abuse. Most people would not have access to the machinery that reads the cards. Thus, they would not always know what information they are giving others about themselves. Theft and forgery of cards would reduce some of the potential benefits. Peter Neumann and Lauren Weinstein warned of risks that arise from the databases and communication complexes that would support a national ID card system: "The opportunities for overzealous surveillance and serious privacy abuses are almost limitless, as are opportunities for masquerading, identity theft, and draconian social engineering on a grand scale."[65]

A woman in Canada could not get her tax refund because the tax agency insisted she was dead. Her identification number had been mistakenly reported in place of her mother's when her mother died. She would still have been able to get a new job, withdraw money from her bank account, pay her rent, send email, and go to her doctor while she was resolving the problem with the tax agency. What if the worker verification database connected to the death records database? Or what if a mistake cancelled the one ID card required for all these transactions? A critic of a proposal for a national identification card in Australia described the card as a "license to exist."[66]

The REAL ID Act attempts to develop a secure national identification card by setting federal standards for driver's licenses (and state-issued ID cards, for people without driver's licenses). Licenses must meet the federal standards for use for identification by the federal government. Such purposes include airport security and entering federal facilities. By implication, they likely include working for the federal government and obtaining federal benefits. It is likely that the government will add many new uses, as it did with the Social Security number. Businesses and state and local governments are likely to require the federally approved ID card for many transactions and services. The federal government pays for approximatley half the medical care in the United States (for example, Medicare, benefits for veterans, and numerous federally funded programs). It is not hard to envision requiring the driver's license for federal medical services and eventually it becoming a de facto national medical ID card.

The REAL ID Act requires that, to get a federally approved driver's license or ID card, each person must provide documentation of address, birth date, Social Security number, and legal status in the United States. Motor vehicle departments must verify each person's information, in part by accessing federal databases such as the Social Security database. The departments must scan documents submitted by drivers and store them in transferable form, for at least 10 years (making motor vehicle records a desirable target for identity thieves). The licenses must satisfy various requirements to reduce tampering and counterfeiting, and they must include the person's photo and machine-readable information to be determined by the Department of Homeland Security.

The REAL ID Act puts the burden of verifying identity on individuals and the state motor vehicle departments. Errors in federal databases used for verification could prevent people from getting their driver's licenses. Many states object to the mandate and its high costs (estimated in billions of dollars). More than 20 states passed resolutions refusing to participate. Residents in states without a federally approved driver's license could experience serious inconvenience. Congress passed REAL ID in 2005, and it was originally to take effect in 2008. The Department of Homeland Security extended the deadline for

Accuracy of worker verification database: Section 6.3.1

compliance several times, while some members of Congress have been working to modify or repeal REAL ID. As I write this, the deadline remains in the future, and Congress has not repealed the law.

Many European and Asian countries require national ID cards. An unpopular plan for an expensive mandatory national ID card in the United Kingdom stalled when emails about weaknesses of the plan leaked from government offices. The government of Japan implemented a national computerized registry system that included assigning an ID number to every citizen of the country. The system is for government purposes, initially with approximately 100 applications, but eventually its uses will probably be in the thousands. The intention is to simplify administration procedures and make them more efficient. Privacy advocates and protesters have complained of insufficient privacy protection, potential abuse by government, and vulnerability to hackers. The Indian government is building a national ID database for its 1.2 billion people. The database will include each person's photo, fingerprints, iris scan, birth date, and other information. Its stated purposes include improving provision of government services and catching illegal immigrants.

> *As soon as you are willing to put your home, your office, your safe deposit box, your bike lock, your gym key, and your desk key all onto one and ask the government to issue that one key, you will be okay with the national ID. But until then, we need to think more in terms of diversification of identification systems.*
>
> —Jim Harper, Director of Information Policy Studies, Cato Institute[67]

2.5   Protecting Privacy: Technology, Markets, Rights, and Laws

2.5.1   TECHNOLOGY AND MARKETS

Many individuals, organizations, and businesses help meet the demand for privacy to some degree: Individual programmers post free privacy-protecting software on the Web. Entrepreneurs build new companies to provide technology-based privacy protections. Large businesses respond to consumer demand and improve policies and services. Organizations such as the Privacy Rights Clearinghouse provide excellent information resources. Activist organizations such as the Electronic Privacy Information Center inform the public, file lawsuits, and advocate for better privacy protection.

New applications of technology can often solve problems that arise as side effects of technology. Soon after "techies" became aware of the use of cookies by Web sites, they wrote cookie disablers and posted them on the Web. Software to block pop-up ads appeared soon after the advent of such ads. People figured out how to prevent ads from appearing in their Gmail and told the world. Companies sell software to scan for spyware;

some versions are free. We can install free add-ons to our browsers that block Web activity trackers. Several companies provide services, called anonymizers, with which people can surf the Web anonymously, leaving no record that identifies them or their computers. Some search engines do not store user search queries in a way that allows linking them together to one person.[68] Companies offer products and services to

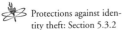 More about anonymizers: Section 3.4

prevent forwarding, copying, or printing email. (Lawyers are among the major customers.) There are services that fully erase email or text messages (on both the sender's and recipient's phones) after a user-specified time period. They can be helpful for doctors, who must follow very strict medical privacy regulations. Some tracking systems for laptops, tablets, and phones include a feature that allows the owner of a stolen or lost laptop to encrypt, retrieve, and/or erase files remotely.

These are a very few examples of the many products and technology applications that protect privacy. They illustrate that individuals, businesses, and organizations are quick to respond and make privacy-protecting tools available. They have advantages and disadvantages; they do not solve all problems.

Protections against identity theft: Section 5.3.2

Learning about, installing, and using privacy tools might be daunting to nontechnical, less educated users—a large part of the public—hence the importance of designing systems with privacy protection in mind, building in protective features, and having privacy-protecting policies.

Encryption

Cryptography is the art and science of hiding data in plain sight.
—Larry Loen[69]

It is possible to intercept email and data in transit on the Internet and to pick wireless transmissions out of the air. Someone who steals a computer or hacks into one can view files on it. Most eavesdropping by private citizens is illegal. Hacking and stealing laptops are crimes. The law provides for punishment of offenders when caught and convicted, but we can also use technology to protect ourselves.

Encryption is a technology, often implemented in software, that transforms data into a form that is meaningless to anyone who might intercept or view it. The data could be email, business plans, credit card numbers, images, medical records, cellphone location history, and so on. Software at the recipient's site (or on one's own computer) decodes encrypted data so that the recipient or owner can view the messages or files. Software routinely encrypts credit card numbers when we send them to online merchants. People are often not even aware that they are using encryption. The software handles it automatically.

Many privacy and security professionals view encryption as the most important technical method for ensuring the privacy of messages and data sent through computer networks. Encryption also protects stored information from intruders and abuses by employees. It is the best protection for data on laptops and other small data storage devices carried outside an office.

Encryption generally includes a coding scheme, or cryptographic algorithm, and specific sequences of characters (e.g., digits or letters), called *keys*, used by the algorithm. Using mathematical tools and powerful computers, it is sometimes possible to "break" an encryption scheme—that is, to decode an encrypted message or file without the secret key.

Modern encryption technology has a flexibility and variety of applications beyond protecting data. For example, it is used to create digital signatures, authentication methods, and digital cash. Digital signature technology allows us to "sign" documents online, saving time and paper for loan applications, business contracts, and so on. In one specialized authentication application, aimed at reducing the risk of unauthorized access to medical information online, the American Medical Association issues digital credentials to doctors that a laboratory website can verify when a doctor visits to get patient test results. There are likely to be thousands of applications of this technology.

Digital cash and other encryption-based privacy-protected transaction methods can let us do secure financial transactions electronically without the seller acquiring a credit card or checking account number from the buyer. They combine the convenience of credit card purchases with the anonymity of cash. With such schemes, it is not easy to link records of different transactions to form a consumer profile or dossier. These techniques can provide both privacy protection for the consumer with respect to the organizations he or she interacts with and protection for organizations against forgery, bad checks, and credit card fraud. However, cash transactions make it harder for governments to detect and prosecute people who are "laundering" money earned in illegal activities, earning money they are not reporting to tax authorities, or transferring or spending money for criminal purposes. Thus, most governments would oppose and probably prohibit a truly anonymous digital cash system. Some digital cash systems include provisions for law enforcement and tax collection. The potential illegal uses of digital cash have long been possible with real cash. It is only in recent decades, with increased use of checks and credit cards, that we lost the privacy we had from marketers and government when we used cash for most transactions.

The technologies of anonymity and cryptography may be the only way to protect privacy.

—Nadine Strossen, president of the American Civil Liberties Union[70]

Policies for protecting personal data

The businesses, organizations, and government agencies that collect and store personal data have an ethical responsibility (and in many cases a legal one) to protect it from misuse. Responsible data holders must anticipate risks and prepare for them. They must continually update security policies to cover new technologies and new potential threats.

Encryption Policy

For centuries before the Internet, governments, their military agencies, and their spies were the main users of codes. For decades, most of the cryptographers in the United States worked for the National Security Agency (NSA). The NSA almost certainly could break virtually any codes that were in use until the early 1970s.[71] The NSA worked hard to keep everything about encryption secret. In the 1970s, a private-sector breakthrough called public key cryptography produced encryption that was relatively easy to use and very difficult to crack. Keeping encryption as an exclusive tool of governments and spies was no longer an option.

More about the NSA: Section 2.6.3

Throughout the 1990s, when people began using encryption for email and other purposes, the U.S. government battled the Internet community and privacy advocates to restrict the availability of secure encryption (that is, encryption that is so difficult and expensive to crack that it is not practical to do so.) It maintained a costly and ultimately futile policy of prohibiting export of powerful encryption software. The government interpreted anything posted on the Internet as effectively exported. Thus, even researchers who posted encryption algorithms on the Net faced possible prosecution. The government argued that the export prohibition was necessary to keep strong encryption from terrorists and enemy governments. The U.S. policy was strangely out of date. The stronger encryption schemes were available on Internet sites all over the world.

The National Research Council (the research affiliate of the National Academy of Sciences) strongly supported the use of powerful encryption and the loosening of export controls. It argued that strong encryption provides increased protection against hackers, thieves, and terrorists who threaten our economic, energy, and transportation infrastructures.[72] The need for strong encryption in electronic commerce was becoming obvious as well.

Concurrently with the ban on export of strong encryption, the government attempted to ensure its access to encryption keys (or to the unencrypted content of encrypted messages) for encryption used within the United States. Pedophiles and child molesters encrypt child pornography on their computers. Other criminals encrypt email and files to hide their contents from law enforcement agents. The FBI supported a bill requiring a loophole, or "backdoor," in all encryption products made, sold, or used in the United States to permit immediate decryption of the encrypted data upon the receipt of a court order.[73] The FBI argued that authority to intercept telephone calls or email or seize computers meant nothing if agents could not read what they seized. Technical experts argued that such a law would be extraordinarily difficult to implement because encryption is now part of Web browsers and many other common computing tools. Implementation of an immediate decryption mechanism would threaten privacy and seriously weaken security of electronic commerce and communications.

During the same time, courts considered legal challenges to the export restrictions based on the First Amendment. The question is whether cryptography algorithms, and computer programs in general, are speech and hence protected by the First Amendment. The government argued that software is not speech and that control of cryptography was a national security issue, not a freedom-of-speech issue. The federal judge who heard the case thought otherwise. She said:

This court can find no meaningful difference between computer language . . . and German or French. . . . Like music and mathematical equations, computer language is just that, language, and it communicates information either to a computer or to those who can read it. . . . For the purposes of First Amendment analysis, this court finds that source code is speech.[74]

The U.S. government removed almost all export restrictions on encryption in 2000. Congress did not pass a law requiring all encryption to have a mechanism for law enforcement access. Among thousands of wiretaps approved for criminal investigations in 2010, law enforcement agents encountered encryption only six times and were able to obtain the plain text of the messages.[75]

Employers must train those who carry around personal data about the risks and proper security measures.

A well-designed database for sensitive information includes several features to protect against leaks, intruders, and unauthorized employee access. Each person with authorized access to the system should have a unique identifier and a password. A system can restrict users from performing certain operations, such as writing or deleting, on some files. User IDs can be coded so that they give access to only specific parts of a record. For example, a billing clerk in a hospital does not need access to the results of a patient's lab tests. The computer system keeps track of information about each access, including the ID of the person looking at a record and the particular information viewed or modified. This is an *audit trail* that can later help trace unauthorized activity. The knowledge that a system contains such provisions will discourage many privacy violations.

Databases with consumer information, Web-activity records, or cellphone location data are valuable assets that give businesses a competitive advantage. The owners of such data have an interest in preventing leaks and unlimited distribution. That includes providing security for the data and developing modes of operation that reduce loss. Thus, for example, mailing lists are usually not sold; they are "rented." The renter does not receive a copy (electronic or otherwise). A specialized firm does the mailing. The risk of unauthorized copying is thus restricted to a small number of firms whose reputation for honesty and security is important to their business. Other applications also use this idea of trusted third parties to process confidential data. Some car rental agencies access a third-party service to check the driving record of potential customers. The service examines the motor vehicle department records; the car rental company does not see the driver's record.

Website operators pay thousands, sometimes millions, of dollars to companies that do *privacy audits*. Privacy auditors check for leaks of information, review the company's privacy policy and its compliance with that policy, evaluate warnings and explanations on its website that alert visitors when the site requests sensitive data, and so forth. Hundreds of large businesses have a position called *chief privacy officer*. This person guides company privacy policy. Just as the Automobile Association of America rates hotels, the Better Business Bureau and similar organizations offer a seal of approval, an icon companies that comply with their privacy standards can post on websites.

Large companies use their economic influence to improve consumer privacy. IBM and Microsoft removed Internet advertising from websites that do not post clear privacy policies. Walt Disney Company and Infoseek Corporation did the same and, in addition, stopped accepting advertising on their websites from sites that do not post privacy policies. The Direct Marketing Association adopted a policy requiring its member companies to inform consumers when they will share personal information with other marketers and to give people an opt-out option. Many companies agreed to limit the availability of sensitive consumer information, including unlisted telephone numbers, driving histories, and all information about children.

There continue, of course, to be many businesses without strong privacy policies, as well as many that do not follow their own stated policies. The examples described here represent a trend, not a privacy utopia. They suggest actions responsible companies can take. As some problems are addressed, new ones continually arise.

2.5.2 RIGHTS AND LAW

In Section 2.2, we considered some aspects of law and Fourth Amendment principles related to protection of privacy. The Fourth Amendment protects the negative right (a liberty) against intrusion and interference by government. This section focuses mainly on discussion of principles related to rights and legal protections for personal data collected or used by other people, businesses, and organizations.

We separate legal remedies from technical, management, and market solutions because they are fundamentally different. The latter are voluntary and varied. Different people or businesses can choose from among them. Law, on the other hand, is enforced by fines, imprisonment, and other penalties. Thus, we should examine the basis for law more carefully. Privacy is a condition or state we can be in, like good health or financial security. To what extent should we have a legal right to it? Is it a negative right or a positive right (in the sense of Section 1.4.2)? How far should law go, and what should be left to the voluntary interplay of markets, educational efforts of public interest groups, consumer choices and responsibilities, and so forth?

Until the late 19th century, courts based legal decisions supporting privacy in social and business activities on property rights and contracts. There was no recognition of an independent right to privacy. In 1890, a crucial article called "The Right of Privacy," by Samuel Warren and Louis Brandeis[76] (later a Supreme Court Justice), argued that privacy was distinct from other rights and needed more protection. Judith Jarvis Thomson, an MIT philosopher, argued that the old view was more accurate, that in all cases where infringement of privacy is a violation of someone's rights, that violation is of a right distinct from privacy.[77] We present some of the claims and arguments of these papers. Then we consider a variety of other ideas and perspectives about laws to protect privacy.

One purpose of this section is to show the kinds of analyses that philosophers, legal scholars, and economists perform in trying to elucidate underlying principles. Another is to emphasize the importance of principles, of working out a theoretical framework in which to make decisions about particular issues and cases.

Warren and Brandeis: The inviolate personality

The main target of criticism in the 1890 Warren and Brandeis article is newspapers, especially the gossip columns. Warren and Brandeis vehemently criticize the press for "overstepping . . . obvious bounds of propriety and decency." The kinds of information of most concern to them are personal appearance, statements, acts, and interpersonal relationships (marital, family, and others).[78] Warren and Brandeis take the position that people have the right to prohibit publication of facts about themselves and photographs of themselves. Warren and Brandeis argue that, for example, if someone writes a letter in which he says he had a fierce argument with his wife, the recipient of the letter cannot publish that information. They base this claim on no property right or other right except privacy. It is part of the right to be let alone. Warren and Brandeis base their defense of privacy rights on, in their often-quoted phrase, the principle of "an inviolate personality."

Laws against other wrongs (such as slander, libel, defamation, copyright infringement, violation of property rights, and breach of contract) can address some privacy violations, but Warren and Brandeis argue that there remain many privacy violations that those other laws do not cover. For example, publication of personal or business information could constitute a violation of a contract (explicit or implied), but there are many cases in which the person who discloses the information has no contract with the victim. The person is not violating a contract but is violating the victim's privacy. Libel, slander, and defamation laws protect us when someone spreads false and damaging rumors about us, but they do not apply to true personal information whose exposure makes us uncomfortable. Warren and Brandeis say privacy is distinct and needs its own protection. They allow exceptions for publication of information of general interest (news), use in limited situations when the information concerns another person's interests, and oral publication. (They were writing before radio and television, so oral publication meant a quite limited audience.)

Judith Jarvis Thomson: Is there a right to privacy?

Judith Jarvis Thomson argues the opposite point of view. She gets to her point after examining a few scenarios.

Suppose you own a copy of a magazine. Your property rights include the right to refuse to allow others to read, destroy, or even see your magazine. If someone does anything to your magazine that you did not allow, that person is violating your property rights. For example, if someone uses binoculars to see your magazine from a neighboring building, that person is violating your right to exclude others from seeing it. It does not matter whether the magazine is an ordinary news magazine (not a sensitive privacy issue) or some other magazine you do not want people to know you read. The right violated is your property right.

You may waive your property rights, intentionally or inadvertently. If you absent-mindedly leave the magazine on a park bench, someone could take it. If you leave it on the coffee table when you have guests at your home, someone could see it. If you read a pornographic magazine on a bus, and someone sees you and tells other people that you read dirty magazines, that person is not violating your rights. The person might be doing something impolite, unfriendly, or cruel, but not something that violates a right.

Our rights to our person and our bodies include the right to decide to whom we show various parts of our bodies. By walking around in public, most of us waive our right to prevent others from seeing our faces. When a Muslim woman covers her face, she is exercising her right to keep others from viewing it. If someone uses binoculars to spy on us at home in the shower, they are violating our right to our person.

If someone beats on you to get some information, the beater is violating your right to be free from physical harm done by others. If the information is the time of day, privacy is not at issue. If the information is more personal, then they have compromised your privacy, but the right violated is your right to be free from attack. On the other hand, if a person peacefully asks whom you live with or what your political views are, they have violated no rights. If you choose to answer and do not make a confidentiality agreement, the person is not violating your rights by repeating the information to someone else, though it could be inconsiderate to do so. However, if the person agreed not to repeat the information, but then does, it does not matter whether or not the information was sensitive; the person is violating the confidentiality agreement.

In these examples, there is no violation of privacy without violation of some other right, such as the right to control our property or our person, the right to be free from violent attack, or the right to form contracts (and expect them to be enforced). Thomson concludes, "I suggest it is a useful heuristic device in the case of any purported violation of the right to privacy to ask whether or not the act is a violation of any other right, and if not whether the act really violates a right at all."[79]

Criticisms of Warren and Brandeis and of Thomson

Critics of the Warren and Brandeis position[80] argue that it does not provide a workable principle or definition from which to conclude that a privacy right violation occurs. Their notion of privacy is too broad. It conflicts with freedom of the press. It appears to make almost any unauthorized mention of a person a violation of the person's right.

Critics of Thomson present examples of violations of a right to privacy (not just a desire for privacy), but of no other right. Some view Thomson's notion of the right to our person as vague or too broad. Her examples might (or might not) be a convincing argument for the thesis that considering other rights can resolve privacy questions, but no finite number of examples can prove such a thesis.

Neither article directly refutes the other. Their emphases are different. Warren and Brandeis focus on the use of the information (publication). Thomson focuses on how it is obtained. This distinction sometimes underlies differences in arguments by those who advocate strong legal regulations on use of personal data and those who advocate more reliance on technical, contractual, and market solutions.

Applying the theories

How do the theoretical arguments apply to privacy and personal data today?

Throughout Warren and Brandeis, the objectionable action is publication of personal information—its widespread, public distribution. Many court decisions since the appearance of their article have taken this point of view.[81] If someone published information from a consumer databases (in print or by making it public on the Web), that would violate the Warren and Brandeis notion of privacy. A person might win a case if some-one published his or her consumer profile. But intentional publication is not the main concern in the current context of consumer databases, monitoring of Web activity, loca-tion tracking, and so on. The amount of personal information collected nowadays might appall Warren and Brandeis, but their article allows disclosure of personal information to people who have an interest in it. By implication, they do not preclude, for example, disclosure of a person's driving record to a car rental company from which he or she wants to rent a car. Similarly, it seems Warren and Brandeis would not oppose disclosure of information about whether someone smokes cigarettes to a life insurance company from whom the person is trying to buy insurance. Their view does not rule out use of (un-published) consumer information for targeted marketing, though they probably would disapprove of it.

The content of social networks would probably shock and appall Warren and Bran-deis. Their position would severely restrict the sharing of photos that include other people and of the location and activities of friends.

An important aspect of both the Warren and Brandeis paper and the Thomson paper is that of consent. They see no privacy violation if a person consented to the collection and use of the information.

Transactions

We have another puzzle to consider: how to apply philosophical and legal notions of privacy to transactions, which automatically involve more than one person. The following scenario will illustrate the problem.

One day in the small farm community of Friendlyville, Joe buys five pounds of potatoes from Maria, who sells him the five pounds of potatoes. (I describe the transaction in this repetitious manner to emphasize that there are two people involved and two sides to the transaction.)

Either Joe or Maria might prefer the transaction to remain secret. The failure of his own potato crop might embarrass Joe. Or Joe might be unpopular in Friendlyville, and Maria fears the townspeople will be angry at her for selling to him. Either way, we are not likely to consider it a violation of the other's rights if Maria or Joe talks about the purchase or sale of the potatoes to other people in town. But suppose Joe asks for confidentiality as part of the transaction. Maria has three options. (1) She can agree. (2) She can say no; she might want to tell people she sold potatoes to Joe. (3) She can agree to keep the sale confidential if Joe pays a higher price. In the latter two cases, Joe can decide whether to buy the potatoes. On the other hand, if Maria asks for confidentiality as part of the transaction, Joe has three options. (1) He can agree. (2) He can say no; he might want to tell people he bought potatoes from Maria. (3) He can agree to keep the purchase confidential if Maria charges a lower price. In the latter two cases, Maria can decide whether to sell the potatoes.

Privacy includes control of information about oneself. Is the transaction a fact about Maria or a fact about Joe? There does not appear to be a convincing reason for either party to have more right than the other to control information about the transaction. Yet this problem is critical to legal policy decisions about use of consumer information. If we are to assign control of the information about a transaction to one of the parties, we need a firm philosophical foundation for choosing which party gets it. (If the parties make a confidentiality agreement, then they have an ethical obligation to respect it. If the agreement is a legal contract, then they have a legal obligation to respect it.)

Philosophers and economists often use simple two-person transactions or relationships, like the Maria/Joe scenario, to try to clarify the principles involved in an issue. Do the observations and conclusions about Maria and Joe generalize to large, complex societies and a global economy, where, often, one party to a transaction is a business? All transactions are really between people, even if indirectly. So if a property right or a privacy right in the information about a transaction goes to one of the parties, we need an argument showing how the transaction in a modern economy is different from the one in Friendlyville. Later in this section, we describe two viewpoints on the regulation of information about consumer transactions: the free market view and the consumer protection view. The consumer protection view suggests treating the parties differently.

Ownership of personal data

Some economists, legal scholars, and privacy advocates propose giving people property rights in information about themselves. The concept of property rights can be useful even when applied to intangible property (intellectual property, for example), but there are problems in using this concept for personal information. First, as we have just seen, activities and transactions often involve at least two people, each of whom would have reasonable but conflicting claims to own the information about the transaction. Some personal information does not appear to be about a transaction, but there still can be problems in assigning ownership. Do you own your birthday? Or does your mother own it? After all, she was a more active participant in the event.

The second problem with assigning ownership of personal information arises from the notion of owning facts. (Copyright protects intellectual property such as computer programs and music, but we cannot copyright facts.) Ownership of facts would severely impair the flow of information in society. We store information on electronic devices, but we also store it in our minds. Can we own facts about ourselves without violating the freedom of thought and freedom of speech of others?

Although there are difficulties with assigning ownership in individual facts, another issue is whether we can own our "profiles," that is, a collection of data describing our activities, purchases, interests, and so on. We cannot own the fact that our eyes are blue, but we do have the legal right to control some uses of our photographic image. In almost all states, we need a person's consent to use his or her image for commercial purposes. Should the law treat our consumer profiles the same way? Should the law treat the collection of our search queries the same way? How can we distinguish between a few facts about a person and a "profile"?

Judge Richard Posner, a legal scholar who has extensively studied the interactions between law and economics, gives economic arguments about how to allocate property rights to information.[82] Information has both economic and personal value, he points out. It is valuable to us to determine if a business, customer, client, employer, employee, and so on, is reliable, honest, and so on. Personal and business interactions have many opportunities for misrepresentation and therefore exploitation of others. Posner's analysis leads to the conclusion that, in some cases, individuals or organizations should have a property right to information, while in other cases, they should not. That is, some information should be in the public domain. A property right in information is appropriate where the information has value to society and is expensive to discover, create, or collect. Without property rights to such information, the people or businesses that make investments in discovering or collecting the information will not profit from it. The result is that people will produce less of this kind of information, to the detriment of society. Thus, the law should protect, for example, trade secrets, the result of much expenditure and effort by a business. A second example is personal information, such as the appearance of one's naked body. It is not expensive for a person to obtain, but virtually all of us place value on protecting it, and concealment is not costly to society. So it makes sense to assign the property right in this information to the individual. Some privacy advocates want to protect information that can lead to denial of a job or some kind of service or contract (e.g., a loan). They advocate restrictions on sharing of information that might facilitate negative decisions about people—for example, landlords sharing a database with information about tenant payment histories. Posner argues that a person should not have a property right to negative personal information or other information whose concealment aids people in misrepresentation, fraud, or manipulation. Such information should be in the public domain. That means a person should not have the right to prohibit others from collecting it, using it, and passing it on, as long as they are not violating a contract or confidentiality agreement and do not obtain the information by eavesdropping on private communications or by other prohibited means.

In recent decades, the trend in legislation has not followed Posner's position. Some critics of Posner's point of view believe that moral theory, not economic principles, should be the source of property rights.

A basic legal framework

A good basic legal framework that defines and enforces legal rights and responsibilities is essential to a complex, robust society and economy. One of its tasks is enforcement of agreements and contracts. Contracts—including freedom to form them and enforcement of their terms by the legal system—are a mechanism for implementing flexible and diverse economic transactions that take place over time and between people who do not know each other well or at all.

We can apply the idea of contract enforcement to the published privacy policies of businesses and organizations. The Toysmart case is an example. Toysmart, a Web-based seller of educational toys, collected extensive information on about 250,000 visitors to its website, including family profiles, shopping preferences, and names and ages of children. Toysmart had promised not to release this personal information. When the company filed for bankruptcy, it had a large amount of debt and virtually no assets—except its customer database, which had a high value. Toysmart's creditors wanted the database sold to raise funds to repay them. Toysmart offered the database for sale, causing a storm of protest. Consistent with the interpretation that Toysmart's policy was a contract with the people in the database, the bankruptcy-court settlement included destruction of the database.[83]

A second task of a legal system is to set defaults for situations that contracts do not explicitly cover. Suppose a website posts no policy about what it does with the information it collects. What legal rights should the operator of the site have regarding the information? Many sites and offline businesses act as though the default is that they can do anything they choose. A privacy-protecting default would be that they can use the information only for the direct and obvious purpose for which they collected it. The legal system can (and does) set special confidentiality defaults for sensitive information, such as medical and financial information, that tradition and most people consider private. If a business or organization wants to use information for purposes beyond the default, it would have to specify those uses in its policies, agreements, or contracts or request consent. Many business interactions do not have written contracts, so the default provisions established by law can have a big impact.

A third task of a basic legal structure is to specify penalties for criminal offenses and breach of contracts. Thus, law can specify penalties for violation of privacy policies and negligent loss or disclosure of personal data that businesses and others hold. Writers of liability laws must strike a balance between being too strict and too lenient. If too strict, they make some valuable products and services too expensive to provide. If too weak, they provide insufficient incentive for businesses and government agencies to provide reasonable security for our personal data.

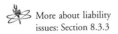 More about liability issues: Section 8.3.3

Regulation

Technical tools, market mechanisms, and business policies for privacy protection are not perfect. Is that a strong argument for regulatory laws? Regulation is not perfect either. We must evaluate regulatory solutions by considering effectiveness, costs and benefits, and side effects, just as we evaluate other kinds of potential solutions to problems caused by technology. The pros and cons of regulation fill entire books. We briefly make a few points here. (We will see similar problems in Section 8.3.3 when we consider responses to computer errors and failures.)

There are hundreds of privacy laws. When Congress passes laws for complex areas like privacy, the laws usually state general goals and leave the details to government agencies that write hundreds or thousands of pages of regulations, sometimes over many years. It is extremely difficult to write reasonable regulations for complex situations. Laws and regulations often have unintended effects or interpretations. They can apply where they do not make sense or where people simply do not want them.

Regulations often have high costs, both direct dollar costs to businesses (and, ultimately, consumers) and hidden or unexpected costs, such as loss of services or increased inconvenience. For example, regulations that prohibit broad consent agreements and instead require explicit consent for each secondary use of personal information have an attribute economists call "high transaction cost." The consent requirement could be so expensive and difficult to implement that it eliminates most secondary uses of information, including those that consumers find desirable.

Although regulations have disadvantages, we should remember that businesses sometimes overestimate the cost of privacy regulations. They also sometimes underestimate the costs, to themselves and to consumers, of not protecting privacy.[84]

Contrasting Viewpoints

> *When asked "If someone sues you and loses, should they have to pay your legal expenses?" more than 80% of people surveyed said "yes." When asked the same question from the opposite perspective: "If you sue someone and lose, should you have to pay their legal expenses?" about 40% said "yes."*

The political, philosophical, and economic views of many scholars and advocates who write about privacy differ. As a result, their interpretations of various privacy problems and their approaches to solutions often differ, particularly when they are considering laws and regulation to control collection and use of personal information by businesses.* We contrast two perspectives. I call them the free market view and the consumer protection view.

The free market view

People who prefer market-oriented solutions for privacy problems tend to emphasize the freedom of individuals, as consumers or in businesses, to make voluntary agreements; the diversity of individual tastes and values; the flexibility of technological and market solutions; the response of markets to consumer preferences; the usefulness and importance of contracts; and the flaws of detailed or restrictive legislation and regulatory solutions. They emphasize the many voluntary organizations that provide consumer education, develop guidelines, monitor the activities of business and government, and pressure

---

* There tends to be more agreement among privacy advocates when considering privacy threats and intrusions by government.

businesses to improve policies. They may take strong ethical positions but emphasize the distinction between the role of ethics and the role of law.

A free market view for collection and use of personal information emphasizes informed consent: Organizations collecting personal data (including government agencies and businesses) should clearly inform the person providing the information if they will not keep it confidential (from other businesses, individuals, and government agencies) and how they will use it. They should be legally liable for violations of their stated policies. This viewpoint could consider truly secret forms of invisible information gathering to be theft or intrusion.

A free market view emphasizes freedom of contract: People should be free to enter agreements (or not enter agreements) to disclose personal information in exchange for a fee, services, or other benefits according to their own judgment. Businesses should be free to offer such agreements. This viewpoint respects the right and ability of consumers to make choices for themselves based on their own values. Market supporters expect consumers to take the responsibility that goes with freedom—for example, to read contracts or to understand that desirable services have costs. A free market view includes free flow of information: the law should not prevent people (or businesses and organizations) from using and disclosing facts they independently or unintrusively discover without violating rights (e.g., without theft, trespass, or violation of contractual obligations).

We cannot always expect to get exactly the mix of attributes we want in any product, service, or job. Just as we might not get cheeseless pizza in every pizza restaurant or find a car with the exact set of features we want, we might not always be able to get both privacy and special discounts—or free services. We might not be able to get certain websites—or magazines—without advertising, or a specific job without agreeing to provide certain personal information to the employer. These compromises are not unusual or unreasonable when interacting with other people.

Market supporters prefer to avoid restrictive legislation and detailed regulation for several reasons. Overly broad, poorly designed, and vague regulations stifle innovation. The political system is a worse system than the market for determining what consumers want in the real world of trade-offs and costs. It is impossible for legislators to know in advance how much money, convenience, or other benefits people will want to trade for more or less privacy. Businesses respond over time to the preferences of millions of consumers expressed through their purchases. In response to the desire for privacy many people express, the market provides a variety of privacy protection tools. Market supporters argue that laws requiring specific policies or prohibiting certain kinds of contracts violate the freedom of choice of both consumers and business owners.

This viewpoint includes legal sanctions for those who steal data and those who violate confidentiality agreements. It holds businesses, organizations, and government agents responsible for loss of personal data due to poor or negligent security practices. To encourage innovation and improvement, advocates of this viewpoint are more likely to prefer penalties when a company loses, inappropriately discloses, or abuses the data, rather than regulations that specify detailed procedures that holders of personal information must follow.

The free market viewpoint sees privacy as a "good," both in the sense that it is desirable and that it is something we can obtain varying amounts of by buying or trading in the economy, like food, entertainment, and safety. Just as some people choose to trade some safety for excitement (bungee jumping, motorcycle riding), money (buying a cheaper but less safe product), or convenience, some choose different levels of privacy. As with safety, law can provide minimum standards, but it should allow the market to provide a wide range of options to meet the range of personal preferences.

The consumer protection view

Advocates of strong privacy regulation emphasize the unsettling uses of personal information we have mentioned throughout this chapter, the costly and disruptive results of errors in databases (which we discuss in Chapter 8) and the ease with which personal information leaks out, via loss, theft, and carelessness. They argue for more stringent consent requirements, legal restrictions on consumer profiling, prohibitions on certain types of contracts or agreements to disclose data, and prohibitions on businesses collecting or storing certain kinds of data. They urge, for example, that the law require companies to have opt-in policies for secondary uses of personal information, because the opt-out option might not be obvious or easy enough for consumers who would prefer it. They would prohibit waivers and broad consent agreements for secondary uses.

The focus of this viewpoint is to protect consumers against abuses and carelessness by businesses and against their own lack of knowledge, judgment, or interest. Advocates of the consumer protection view emphasize that people do not realize all the ways others may use information about them. They do not understand the risks of agreeing to disclose personal data. Those who emphasize consumer protection are critical of programs to trade free devices and services for personal information or consent for monitoring or tracking. Many support laws prohibiting collection or storage of personal data that could have negative consequences, if they believe the risks are more important than the value of the information to the businesses that want to collect it. Consumer advocate and privacy "absolutist" Mary Gardiner Jones objected to the idea of consumers consenting to dissemination of personal data. She said, "You can't expect an ordinary consumer who is very busy trying to earn a living to sit down and understand what [consent] means. They don't understand the implications of what use of their data can mean to them."[85] She said this roughly 20 years ago. Understanding the implications of the ways data are collected and used now is more difficult. A former director of the ACLU's Privacy and Technology Project expressed the view that informed consent is not sufficient protection. She urged a Senate committee studying confidentiality of health records to "re-examine the traditional reliance on individual consent as the linchpin of privacy laws."[86]

Those who emphasize the consumer protection point of view would argue that the Joe/Maria scenario in Friendlyville, described earlier in this section, is not relevant in a complex society. The imbalance of power between the individual and a large corporation is one reason. Another is that in Friendlyville the information about the transaction circulates to only a small group of people, whom Joe and Maria know. If someone draws inaccurate or unfair conclusions, Joe or Maria can talk to the person and present his or her explanations. In a larger society, information circulates among many strangers, and we often do not know who has it and what decisions about us they base on it.

A consumer cannot realistically negotiate contract terms with a business. At any specific time, the consumer can only accept or reject what the business offers. And the consumer is often not in a position to reject it. If we want a loan for a house or car, we have to accept whatever terms lenders currently offer. If we need a job, we are likely to agree to disclose personal information against our true preference because of the economic necessity of working. Individuals have no meaningful power against large companies like Google and Apple. They have to use search engines whether or not they know or accept a company's policy about use of their search queries.

In the consumer protection view, self-regulation by business does not work. Business privacy policies are weak, vague, or difficult to understand. Businesses sometimes do not follow their stated policies. Consumer pressure is sometimes effective, but some companies ignore it. Instead, we must require all businesses to adopt pro-privacy policies. Software and other technological privacy-protecting tools for consumers cost money, and many people cannot afford them. They are far from perfect anyway and hence not good enough to protect privacy.

The consumer protection viewpoint sees privacy as a right rather than something we bargain about. For example, a website jointly sponsored by the Electronic Privacy Information Center and Privacy International flashes the slogans "Privacy is a right, not a preference" and "Notice is not enough."[87] The latter indicates that they see privacy as a positive right, or claim right (in the terminology of Section 1.4.2). As a negative right, privacy allows us to use anonymizing technologies and to refrain from interacting with those who request information we do not wish to supply. As a positive right, it means we can stop others from communicating about us. A spokesperson for the Center for Democracy and Technology expressed that view in a statement to Congress, saying that we must incorporate into law the principle that people should be able to "determine for themselves when, how and to what extent information about them is shared."[88]

2.5.3 Privacy Regulations in the European Union

The European Union (EU) has a comprehensive Data Protection Directive (passed in 1995).[89] It covers processing of personal data, including collection, use, storage, retrieval, transmission, destruction, and other actions. The directive sets forth Fair Information Principles that EU member nations must implement in their own laws. Several are similar to the first five principles in Figure 2.2 (in Section 2.1.3). The EU has some additional or stronger rules. They include:

- Processing of data is permitted only if the person has consented unambiguously or if the processing is necessary to fulfill contractual or legal obligations or is needed for tasks in the public interest or by official authorities to accomplish their tasks (or a few other reasons).

- Special categories of data—including ethnic and racial origin, political and religious beliefs, health and sex life, and union membership—must not be processed without the person's explicit consent. Member nations may outlaw processing of such data even if the subject does consent.

- Processing of data about criminal convictions is severely restricted.

The EU's rules are stricter than those in the United States, as the next few examples illustrate.

Google modified its privacy policy in 2012 to allow the company to combine information it collects on members from its various services. The EU argued that average users could not understand how Google uses their data under the new policy and that that violates the EU's privacy regulations. A court in Germany said that some of Facebook's policies in its member agreement (for example, granting Facebook a license to use material a member posts or stores at Facebook) are illegal there. The German government told Facebook to stop running face recognition applications on German users; it violates German privacy laws.

The EU devised legal guidelines for social networking sites. The guidelines say the sites should set default privacy settings at a high level, tell users to upload a picture of a person only if the person consents, allow the use of psuedonyms, set limits on the time they retain data on inactive users, and delete accounts that are inactive for a long time.

The European Commission proposed granting a legal "right to be forgotten." It would, among other things, require that a website remove information, photos, and so on, of a particular person if that person requests it, whether that person posted the material or someone else did. It appears also to require that search engines remove links to material a person wants removed. Such a "right" clearly conflicts with freedom of speech in cases where another person posted the material and does not want it removed.

More about a right to be forgotten: Section 2.3.4

A Spanish government agency ordered Google to remove links from its search results to dozens of articles that have sensitive information about individual people. (Google fought the demand in European court, arguing that the order violated freedom of expression and that the government did not require news media to remove the articles.) Because of Germany's strict privacy laws, Google's Street View allowed anyone to request that their home or office be blurred out on its street images. Google won a lawsuit about Street View violating a homeowner's privacy, but the company discontinued taking photos for Street View in Germany.[90]

While the EU has much stricter regulations than the United States on collection and use of personal information by the private sector, some civil libertarians believe that the regulations do not provide enough protection from use of personal data by government agencies. Although the directive says that data should not be kept longer than necessary, European countries require that ISPs and telephone companies retain records of customer communications (date, destination, duration, and so on) for up to two years and make them available to law enforcement agencies. The EU said it needs this requirement to fight terrorism and organized crime.[91]

The EU's strict privacy directive does not prevent some of the same abuses of personal data that occur in the United States. In Britain, for example, the Information Commissioner reported that data brokers use fraud and corrupt insiders to get personal information. As in the United States, customers of illegal services include journalists, private investigators, debt collectors, government agencies, stalkers, and criminals seeking data to use for fraud.[92]

The EU Data Privacy Directive prohibits transfer of personal data to countries outside the European Union that do not have an adequate system of privacy protection. This part of the directive caused significant problems for companies that do business both in and outside Europe and might normally process customer and employee data outside the EU. The EU determined that Australia, for example, did not have adequate privacy protection. Australia allows businesses to create their own privacy codes consistent with the government's National Privacy Principles. The United States has privacy laws covering specific areas such as medical information, video rentals, driver's license records, and so on, but does not have comprehensive privacy laws covering all personal data. The EU agreed to the "Safe Harbor" plan, under which companies outside the EU that agree to abide by a set of privacy requirements similar to the principles in the Data Protection Directive may receive personal data from the EU.[93] After the terrorist attacks in 2001, screening of air travel passengers from Europe to the United States raised problems. The U.S. government wanted more information about the passengers than the EU wanted to provide.

Many privacy advocates describe U.S. privacy policy as "behind Europe" because the United States does not have comprehensive federal legislation regulating personal data collection and use. Others point out that the United States and Europe have different cultures and traditions. European countries tend to put more emphasis on regulation and centralization, especially concerning commerce, whereas U.S. tradition puts more emphasis on contracts, consumer pressure, flexibility and freedom of the market, and penalties for abuses of personal information by enforcement of existing laws (such as those against deceptive and unfair business practices).

2.6 Communications

Law enforcement agencies intercept communications to collect evidence of criminal activities. Intelligence agencies intercept communications to collect information about the activities and plans of hostile governments and terrorists. The Fourth Amendment to the U.S. Constitution and various laws put restraints on their activities to protect innocent people and reduce the opportunity for abuses. In this section, we consider how changing technologies and government policies affect the ability of law enforcement agencies to intercept the contents of communications and to obtain other information about communications. We begin with background on wiretapping of telephone conversations and laws about the privacy of telephone and email. We consider the Communications Assistance for Law Enforcement Act (CALEA), which requires that the technology used in communications systems be designed or modified to ensure the ability of law enforcement agencies to intercept communications. Then we consider interception of communications for national security.

2.6.1 WIRETAPPING AND EMAIL PROTECTION

Telephone

Within 10 years of the invention of the telephone, people (in and out of government) were wiretapping them.[94] Before that, people intercepted telegraph communications. Throughout the years when human operators made telephone connections and most people had party lines (one telephone line shared by several households), operators and nosy neighbors sometimes listened in on telephone conversations.

Increased wealth and new technology eliminated party lines and human operators, but telephones were still vulnerable to wiretapping. The legal status of wiretapping was debated throughout most of the 20th century. Federal and state law enforcement agencies, businesses, private detectives, political candidates, and others widely used wiretapping. In 1928, the Supreme Court ruled that wiretapping by law enforcement agencies was not unconstitutional, although Congress could ban it. In 1934, Congress passed the Communications Act. This law states that, unless authorized by the sender, no person could intercept and divulge a message; there is no exception for law enforcement agencies. A 1937 Supreme Court decision ruled that wiretapping violated this law.[95] Federal and state law enforcement agencies and local police ignored the ruling and continued to wiretap regularly for decades, sometimes with the approval of the U.S. Attorney General. In one well-publicized case, the FBI monitored the telephone calls between a defendant and her attorneys during her trial. Evidence obtained by illegal wiretapping is inadmissible in court, so the FBI kept a separate, secret file system. The FBI bugged and wiretapped members of Congress and the Supreme Court. Although there was publicity about extensive use of wiretapping by police, no prosecutions resulted. In many cases, of course, law enforcement agencies were wiretapping people suspected of crimes, but in many other cases, they tapped people with unconventional views, members of civil rights groups, and political opponents of powerful government officials.

A fierce debate on the wiretap issue continued. Congress repeatedly rejected proposals to allow wiretapping and electronic surveillance. In 1967 (in *Katz v. United States*, discussed in Section 2.2.2), the Supreme Court ruled that intercepting telephone conversations without a court order violated the Fourth Amendment to the U.S. Constitution. In 1968, as part of the Omnibus Crime Control and Safe Streets Act, Congress explicitly allowed wiretapping and electronic surveillance by law enforcement agencies, with a court order, for the first time in U.S. history. The main argument given for this change was the necessity to combat organized crime.

The government needs a court order to (legally) intercept or record the content of a telephone call for a criminal investigation.* Law enforcement agents must justify the request, and the wiretap permission is granted for a limited time period. Government agents may determine the telephone numbers called from a particular telephone and the number from which someone made a call with less court scrutiny and justification.

Senator Sam Ervin commented in 1968, "The mere fact of passing a law never resolves a controversy as fierce as this one."[96] He was right. Debate continued about whether the privacy protections in the Omnibus Crime Act were strong enough to be constitutional. Supreme Court justices disagreed. Wiretapping by government and politicians that was illegal or of questionable legality continued, most notably during the Vietnam War. Journalists and government employees were victims of unconstitutional wiretaps during the Nixon administration. In 1998, Los Angeles police officers admitted using wiretaps improperly in a large number of cases.

Most other countries have constitutional and legal protections for communications privacy, but police and intelligence agencies in many countries routinely perform illegal monitoring of political opponents, human rights workers, and journalists.[97]

Email and other new communications

Old laws did not explicitly cover email and cellphone conversations, and interception was common when email and cellphones were new. Driving around Silicon Valley eavesdropping on cellphone conversations was, reportedly, a popular form of industrial spying in the 1980s. Snoops intercepted cellphone conversations of politicians and celebrities. The Electronic Communications Privacy Act of 1986 (ECPA), with amendments in 1994, extended the 1968 wiretapping restrictions to electronic communications, including electronic mail, cordless and cellular telephones, and paging devices. This was a significant step toward protecting privacy in cyberspace from private and governmental snooping. It requires that the government get a court order to legally intercept email.† Controversy continued about the standard law enforcement agencies must meet to obtain copies of stored email. The government argued that people give up their expectation of privacy by allowing ISPs to store their email on the ISP's computers; thus, the strict requirements of the Fourth Amendment would

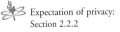
Expectation of privacy:
Section 2.2.2

---

* The government may intercept the content of communications without a court order in some emergencies.

† The ECPA allows businesses to read the email of employees on the business system. We discuss this issue of employee privacy in Chapter 6.

not apply. A federal appeals court ruled that people *do* have an expectation of privacy for email stored at their ISP and that police need a search warrant to get it.[98]

The USA PATRIOT Act (passed soon after the terrorist attacks in 2001) weakened the ECPA and loosened restrictions on government surveillance and wiretapping activities. It allows law enforcement agents to more easily get header information (such as destination and time) for email. Law enforcement agents use the looser standards to get cellphone location records without a search warrant. This practice is controversial. Some judges and many privacy advocates argue that the loosened provisions of the ECPA violate the Fourth Amendment.

2.6.2 Designing Communications Systems for Interception

New technologies, market competition, and varied customer needs have generated a great diversity of telecommunications services, equipment, protocols, algorithms, and companies. Law enforcement agencies argue that communication technologies developed in the past few decades have made their job of intercepting communications and obtaining communication records (for example, phone numbers called) more difficult. Internet telephone calls and email travel in small pieces (called packets) mingled with packets from other communications. Packets from one message might follow different routes to the destination. Thus, intercepting Internet communications is more difficult than attaching a clip to an old analog telephone wire. When people use call forwarding, the first number called—the number law enforcement agents can legally get fairly easily (without a search warrant)—does not give information about the actual recipient of the call.

The Communications Assistance for Law Enforcement Act (CALEA) requires that the design of telecommunications equipment ensure that the government can intercept telephone calls (with a court order or other authorization). CALEA passed in 1994, so it does not explicitly cover many newer ways of communicating. The law was controversial, and repeated attempts by the government to extend it continue to be controversial. In 2010, the government proposed legislation to require social networking sites and Internet phone services to modify their systems so that law enforcement agents can monitor the communications of users.[99]

In the past, engineers designed communications equipment for its communications purpose. The FBI developed its tools for interception, and communications providers had to assist. The significance of CALEA is that, previously, the government could not require the design and modification of communications equipment to meet the interception needs of law enforcement.

The essential argument in favor of CALEA (and other government programs to intercept communications) is to maintain the ability of law enforcement agencies to protect us from drug dealers, organized crime, other criminals, and terrorists in a changing technological environment. "The prospect of trying to enforce laws without a nationwide standard for surveillance would turn enforcement into a nightmare," according to the

The security of BlackBerrys

Research in Motion (RIM) provides encrypted, highly secure communications on its Black-Berrys. They are popular among business people, government agencies, and ordinary users around the world. Several governments (including China, India, Kuwait, and the United Arab Emeriates) pressured RIM to provide access to BlackBerry communications by government agents. Several threatened to ban BlackBerry (and other) services they could not monitor. RIM made agreements with some governments to allow access to users' communications when government requests comply with the country's laws.

FBI.[100] The problems with CALEA and other programs to intercept communications, according to critics, include threats to privacy and civil liberties, the potential for abuse by government, and the side effects of "backdoor" access that threaten the security of communications systems. Critics of CALEA also argue that requirements for determining the physical location of cellphone users and ensuring that the government could intercept Internet communications go beyond the scope of the law and extend the government's surveillance power beyond what Congress intended when it passed the law. The idea of designing communications technology for a "nationwide standard for surveillance" is a nightmare to those who place high value on privacy and civil liberties. Should the designers of communications systems be free to use the best technology available for achieving speed, convenience, low cost, and privacy?

More than 80% of the wiretaps courts authorize for criminal investigations are for drug cases.[101] Critics claim that wiretaps are a less useful law enforcement tool than informants, detective work, witnesses, and so on. Supporters of CALEA argue that wiretaps are essential for catching and/or convicting dangerous criminals. The focus of criminal wiretaps on drug crimes raises the question of whether the government really needs such extreme, system-wide controls on the communication systems used by 300 million Americans. If drug prohibition were to end, as alcohol prohibition did in the 1930s, would we find ourselves with a costly and privacy-threatening infrastructure of intrusion and relatively little legitimate need for it?

2.6.3 THE NSA AND SECRET INTELLIGENCE GATHERING[102]

The purpose of the National Security Agency (NSA) is to collect and analyze foreign intelligence information related to national security and to protect U.S. government communications and sensitive information related to national security. Because govern-

 The NSA and encryption policy: Section 2.5.1

ments encrypt their sensitive material, the NSA has long devoted a huge amount of resources to cryptology and has the most advanced code-breaking capabilities. A secret presidential order formed the NSA in 1952. Its budget is still secret, although its website says the NSA/CSS (NSA and Central Security Service) is about the size of one of the larger Fortune 500 companies.[103] The NSA builds and uses enormously powerful supercomputers.* It collects and stores huge masses of information.

Some of the NSA's activities go well beyond its purpose—or interpret the purpose to an extraordinarily broad degree—and potentially threaten the privacy and freedoms of U.S. citizens. Because the NSA uses methods that do not satisfy the Fourth Amendment, it was legally restricted to intercepting communications outside the United States (with some exceptions). Through its history, the agency generated much controversy by secretly violating restrictions on surveillance of people within the United States. In the 1960s and 1970s, the NSA monitored communications of specific American citizens (including civil rights leader Martin Luther King Jr. and entertainers who opposed the Vietnam War). A Congressional committee chaired by Senator Church found that the NSA had been secretly and illegally collecting international telegrams, including telegrams sent by American citizens, since the 1950s and searching them for foreign intelligence information. As a result, Congress passed the Foreign Intelligence Surveillance Act of 1978 (FISA) establishing oversight rules for the NSA. The law prohibited the agency from collecting masses of telegrams without a warrant and from compiling lists of Americans to watch without a court order. The law set up a secret federal court, the Foreign Intelligence Surveillance Court, to issue warrants to the NSA to intercept communications of people it could show were agents of foreign powers or involved in terrorism or espionage.

Secret access to communications and communications records

The NSA collects information by intercepting communications. While some newer technologies (such as fiber optic cable) made wiretapping more difficult, other technological changes in the past few decades make communications of ordinary people more vulnerable. Satellite communications were a boon to the NSA; it could pick messages out of the air. Increased wealth, travel, and trade generated more international communication—cluttering communications channels and potentially making it harder for the NSA to detect messages of interest. Then, vastly increased processing power of computer systems enabled the NSA to filter and analyze huge quantities of communications of innocent people instead of targeting only specific suspects. In cyberspace, our email, cellphone conversations, tweets, searches, purchases, financial information, legal documents, and so on, mix with military, diplomatic, and terrorist communications. The NSA sifts through it all. It does "deep packet inspection," analyzing the packets of information traveling through the Internet, and collects whatever is of interest. It collects all communications to and from approximately a million people on its watch lists. Its interception activity is

---

* As of 2012, the government had an IBM supercomputer that operated at 16.32 petaflops (16.32 million billion operations per second), officially the fastest in the world.[104]

extremely controversial because the NSA processes and collects data on Americans with no court order and no approval from the FISA court.

In 2006, an AT&T employee described (under oath) a secret, secure room the NSA set up at an AT&T switching facility. From this room, the NSA had access to email, telephone, and Web communications of AT&T users.[105] The NSA built a database of telephone and email records of millions of Americans. The government argued that the NSA was not intercepting or listening to telephone calls and was not collecting personal identifying information. It used sophisticated data mining technology to analyze calling patterns to learn how to detect communications of terrorist cells. The agency analyzes calling patterns because the sources of terrorism are diffuse and require broader means of detection and surveillance than old-time spy work. The NSA can no longer rely on monitoring only the telephone traffic of a few hostile governments and a small number of known suspects. It can no longer monitor just those specific physical telephone lines or communications links that connect specific military facilities or other sites of interest. Analysis of communications traffic helps the NSA determine what is suspicious. Opponents of the monitoring program argued that it was a huge intrusion on privacy. Even if the NSA did not collect customer names, it is quite easy to re-identify people from their phone records. Opponents said the warrantless collection of the records by the NSA was illegal, and it was illegal for a telephone company to provide them. Several groups filed suits against AT&T for violating its stated privacy policies and communications privacy law by assisting the NSA.

Congress passed the FISA Amendments Act in 2008. This law retroactively protects AT&T (and other entities that assist the NSA) from lawsuits. Although it includes provisions to restrict domestic surveillance, overall it reduces previous protections. The FISA Amendments Act is controversial, and a lawsuit challenging its constitutionality is ongoing.[106] In the meantime, it became clear that the NSA installed and continues to operate secret monitoring rooms at other major U.S. telecommunications company facilities, where it can filter and collect whatever domestic communications it chooses. The NSA built an enormous new data center to store, decrypt, and analyze billions of gigabytes of communications and files.[107] What it cannot decrypt now, it stores to decrypt later when it develops faster computers or better algorithms. Civil libertarians are concerned that the NSA is collecting huge quantities of ordinary business and personal encrypted data that have nothing to do with terrorism or foreign intelligence.

Before the USA PATRIOT Act, there was a sharp boundary between legal rules for terrorism investigations (involving foreigners) and criminal investigations (involving people within the United States). The PATRIOT Act allows information obtained in terrorism investigations under FISA warrants to be used in criminal cases. Government officials do not follow the normal protections and rules for search warrants in terrorism cases. In addition, prosecutors normally provide defense attorneys in a criminal case with recordings of intercepted messages. When obtained as part of a terrorism case, the government does not have to provide transcripts. Thus, the broader powers to violate privacy of communications in terrorism investigations can have serious impacts on people accused of ordinary crimes.

How can we evaluate the NSA's programs of massive collection of communications? How should we react when powerful government agencies break laws that protect privacy of communications? Accessing data on specific suspects is a reasonable, essential, and responsible part of criminal and terrorist investigations. Broad access and data mining are more questionable because they threaten the safety and freedom of innocent people if investigators mistakenly decide someone's transactions look suspicious. They provide the mechanisms for totalitarian control. Is the secrecy justifiable? Is the secrecy essential? Exposure of monitoring programs leads terrorists to take new measures to hide their activities, communications, and transactions. Temporary secrecy is essential for many criminal and terrorist investigations, but secret programs to monitor and collect communications present a huge potential for abuse, as we have seen often in the past. We have also seen the hideous effects of terrorism. Is the fact that there were no successful terrorist attacks in the United States after 2001 (up to the time I write this) due in part to the secret communications monitoring and analysis programs of the NSA and other intelligence agencies?

EXERCISES

Review Exercises

2.1   What does the term *personal information* mean?

2.2   What does the term *secondary use* mean? Give an example.

2.3   What does the term *re-identification* mean? Give an example.

2.4   Explain the difference between *opt-in* and *opt-out* policies for secondary uses of personal information.

2.5   Describe one application of face recognition that infringes privacy.

2.6   Describe two tools people can use to protect their privacy on the Web.

2.7   Describe two methods a business or agency can use to reduce the risk of unauthorized release of personal information by employees.

General Exercises

2.8   A social networking website stores the information provided by its users. It also provides anonymous statistical data to government agencies. Unknown to the website's developers and users, these agencies used the data for sociological studies. Was this a privacy violation? Why or why not?

2.9   "Caller ID" is the feature that displays the telephone number of the caller on the telephone of the person he or she calls. With Caller ID now routine and widely used, it might be surprising that when the service was first available, it was very controversial because of privacy implications.

(a) What aspect of privacy (in the sense of Section 2.1.1) does Caller ID protect for the recipient of the call? What aspect of privacy does Caller ID violate for the caller?

(b) What are some good reasons why a nonbusiness, noncriminal caller might not want his or her number displayed?

2.10 In jury trials, attorneys receive the list of people in the jury pool shortly before the jury selection process begins. Some attorneys bring staff members to court to search for information about prospective jurors on social networks. The attorneys use this information in deciding which potential jurors to accept. Which of the points at the end of Section 2.1.2 does this use of personal information illustrate?

2.11 A social networking website displays information about games played and apps run by users to other users who are connected to them. List several ways you can think of that this information could embarrass or cause problems for a person.

2.12 Which of the guidelines in Figure 2.2, if any, did AOL's release of user search queries (Section 2.1.2) violate?

2.13 The AOL search-query database released on the Web (Section 2.1.2) included the search query "How to kill your wife" and other related queries by the same person. Give arguments for and against allowing law enforcement agents to search the query databases of search engine companies periodically to detect plans for murders, terrorist attacks, or other serious crimes so that they can try to prevent them.

2.14 One of the risks associated with databases of personal information is that criminals steal and use the information. How is this statement similar to and how does it differ from saying, "One of the risks associated with buying an expensive car or stereo is that criminals steal them"? Can you draw any useful insights from the analogy?

2.15 (a) Some small businesses (a dry cleaner or a theater, for example) use telephone numbers to access customer or subscriber records in their database. The records are not available to the public online; they do not include credit card numbers. Is the use of the telephone number in such situations secure enough to protect privacy? Why?

(b) Some cellphone service providers let customers retrieve voice mail messages without entering a PIN when they call from their own phone. But someone else can fake the calling number with a Caller ID spoofing service and retrieve a person's messages. Is pinless retrieval a reasonable trade-off between convenience and privacy? Give your reasons.

2.16 Bills introduced in the U.S. Congress (and proposed in other countries) would require that anyone buying a prepaid cellphone must show identification and/or register the cellphone. Give arguments for and against passage of such a law.

2.17 Law enforcement agencies argue that cellphone users have no expectation of privacy about their location. Indeed, many people share their location with hundreds or thousands of friends on social networks. Make and evaluate arguments on each side of the question of whether we should require law enforcement agents to get a search warrant before tracking someone's cellphone.

2.18 A member of the Tampa, Florida, City Council described the camera and face recognition system installed in a Tampa neighborhood (Section 2.2.4) as "a public safety tool, no different from having a cop walking around with a mug shot."[108] Is he right? What are some similarities and differences, relevant to privacy, between the camera system and a cop walking around?

2.19 Discuss the privacy implications of full-length body scanners at airports. Discuss the pros and cons of such a system. What features or operational guidelines should they include to protect privacy?

2.20 A company planned to sell a laser device a person can wear around his or her neck that makes photographs taken of the person come out streaked and useless. The company marketed it to celebrities hounded by photographers. Suppose the device works well against surveillance cameras commonly used in public places and in many businesses. Suppose many people begin to use the device routinely when outside their homes. Suppose law enforcement agencies propose making its use illegal. Give arguments for and against such a proposal.

2.21 A college student set up a hidden webcam to record his roommate having sex with a date in their dorm room. He gave a password to several friends so they could watch on the Web. This is clearly an unethical, crude, cruel, and boorish invasion of privacy. How should the university respond? If you think legal action is appropriate, describe reasonable penalties, using analogies with other offenses.

2.22 Choose one or two of the marketing practices described in Section 2.3.1 that you consider unethical. If there are none, choose two for which you think there are some good arguments against them on ethical grounds. Give the arguments.

2.23 Life insurance companies are experimenting with analysis of consumer profiles (to determine whether a person eats healthy food, exercises, smokes or drinks too much, has high-risk hobbies, and so on) to estimate life expectancy. Companies might use the analysis to find populations to market policies to. From the perspective of privacy, what are some of the key ethical or social issues raised? Evaluate some of them.

2.24 A children's hospital began collecting and analyzing DNA from 100,000 children for a DNA-profile database. The database will be anonymous; the hospital will not store the DNA information with other information that identifies the individual it came from. Discuss potential valuable uses of such databases. Discuss potential risks and problems. If you were the head of a hospital, would you approve the project? As an individual, if you and your family were asked to provide DNA for the database, would you agree? Give reasons.

2.25 Under what circumstances, if any, do you think a person should ask another person's permission before posting a photo that the other person is in? When is it simply a courtesy, and when is it an ethical obligation? Explain your reasons.

2.26 A very large social network company analyzes all data it gathers through its service on its members' activities to develop statistical information for marketers and to plan new services. The information is very valuable. Should the company pay its members for its use of their information?

2.27 A university professor working with sensitive medical records shares a confidential file with a graduate student, who shares it on a public Internet forum. What are some ways to prevent such a leakage of sensitive data?

2.28 A court ordered a social media company and a search engine company to remove racy photos of a pop star and links to the photos. The companies removed all references to the person. What do you think of this incident?

2.29 People who flee severe hurricanes and other destructive events leave behind and lose important documents and records such as birth certificates, credit cards, property records, and employment records. A U.S. government agency proposed a new database where people could voluntarily store essential personal records in case of similar natural disasters. Discuss pros and cons of this proposal.

2.30 As part of the defense against terrorism, the U.S. government wanted to build a database of drivers of large trucks, people trained as scuba divers, and others with similar kinds of skills that could be used in future terrorist attacks. The FBI asked a large scuba diving business for its customer database.

(a) Discuss the request from the point of view of the board of directors of the scuba business.

(b) Discuss, from the point of view of a privacy organization, a possible law authorizing the FBI to build such a database.

(c) Describe how best the FBI might respond to the privacy objections.

2.31 Some cities and counties post maps on their websites showing property lines, property ownership information, property values, locations of roads, and aerial photos of all properties. Some residents oppose putting such information on the Web. What are some benefits of posting it? What are some risks or objections? Do you think the records should be on the Web? If so, why? If not, what alternative access would you suggest?

2.32 Give an explanation, with examples and/or analogies, to describe what it means for privacy to be a negative right (liberty). Do the same for privacy as a positive right (claim right). (See Section 1.4.2 for explanations of negative and positive rights.) Which kind of right, if either, seems more appropriate for privacy? Why?

2.33 Implementations of digital cash can allow secure and anonymous transactions. Do people have a negative right (in the sense of Section 1.4.2) to use anonymous digital cash? Considering the privacy benefits and the potential for use by tax evaders, criminals, and terrorists, do you think fully anonymous digital cash should be legal? Give your reasons.

2.34 Section 2.5.1 gave two examples of uses of trusted third parties to reduce access to personal information (see page 117). Give another example, either a real one you know of or an application you think would be useful.

2.35 A business maintains a database containing the names of shoplifters. It distributes the list to stores that subscribe.

(a) Should such a service be illegal to protect privacy? (Give reasons.)

(b) Describe the likely position of each of Warren and Brandeis, Judith Thomson, and Richard Posner (Section 2.5.2), with their reasons, on this question.

(c) Would your answer to part (a) differ if the question were about a database of tenant history available to landlords? Or a database available to the public with comments from tenants about landlords? How and why?

2.36 A company called, say, Digitizer provides a service for many other companies by converting their paper documents to digital files. The documents include employee information, medical records, business records, and many others. Digitizer hires relatively unskilled employees to organize the documents and prepare them for scanning.

(a) What are some potential risks here?

(b) Describe some actions Digitizer can take or policies it can adopt to reduce the risks.

2.37 A researcher advocates counter-terrorism security ensured by pervasive, all-seeing sensors; automated reasoners; and autonomous, lethal robots. Is this a violation of privacy? Why or why not?

2.38 A health-information website has many articles on health and medical issues, a chat room where people can discuss health issues with other users, and provisions for people to send questions by email for doctors to answer. You work as an intern for a company hired to do a privacy audit. The audit team will examine the site, find privacy risks (or good privacy protection practices), and make recommendations for changes as needed. Describe at least three things you would look for, explain their significance, and tell what your recommendations would be if you do or do not find them.

2.39 An Ivy League university set up a website that student applicants could access, using their Social Security number and other personal information, to find out if the school had accepted them for admission. Officials at the university determined that computers in the Admissions Office of another Ivy League university accessed some student accounts. Many students apply to both schools. People suspected that the university that accessed the accounts wanted to determine which students the other school had accepted before making its own decisions. The personal information needed to access the site was in the students' applications, available to the Admissions Office.

Analyze this incident. Identify the things done wrong (assuming the suspicions about the snooping are accurate). What actions should the administrations of both universities take?

2.40 Suppose each of the following is a proposed law. For each one, choose a side, either supporting or opposing it, and defend your position.

(a) To protect the public, companies that provide Web searching services to members or to the public must maintain user search query records for two years in case law enforcement agencies or terrorism investigators need them.

(b) To protect privacy, companies that provide Web searching services to members or to the public must not store user search queries in a way that links the queries of any one person together for more than one week.

2.41 Consider the guidelines developed in the European Union for social network sites (at the end of Section 2.5.3). Evaluate these simply as guidelines, not legal requirements. Evaluate them as legal requirements. (Consider, among other issues, how to define the sites to which the rules would apply.)

2.42 Assume you are a professional working in your chosen field. Describe specific things you can do to reduce the impact of any two problems we discussed in this chapter. (If you cannot think of anything related to your professional field, choose another field that might interest you.)

Assignments

These exercises require some research or activity.

2.43 (a) Read the privacy policy of a large, popular website. Write a brief summary. Identify the site (name, Web address, type of site). Give examples of parts of the policy that are, or are not, clear or reasonable.

(b) Choose any smartphone app that includes a privacy statement or policy. Summarize and evaluate it. Can you think of any important things that are missing?

2.44 Local law enforcement agencies are increasingly using drones (small, relatively inexpensive, remote-controlled aircraft). With their cameras and heat sensors, the drones can locate missing hikers, monitor crowds, and track fleeing criminals. News reporters and other private individuals might also use them in the near future. Find a report of an actual use of a drone. Describe it briefly. Does it threaten privacy?

2.45 Google Street View's cameras occasionally capture people in embarrassing behavior and in places they would prefer the whole world not see them. Many people objected that Street View violated people's privacy. How, and how well, does Google address the privacy concerns?

2.46 Read the guidelines for computer searches written by Judge Alex Kozinski in the decision in *United States of America v. Comprehensive Drug Testing* (Ninth Circuit, U.S. Court of Appeals, September 13, 2010). Summarize and evaluate them.

Class Discussion Exercises

These exercises are for class discussion, perhaps with short presentations prepared in advance by small groups of students.

2.47 Discuss Google's policies from a privacy perspective. What does it do well? What has it done poorly? How could it improve?

2.48 What threats to privacy were prevalent in the past, but have been addressed by new computer, Internet, or smartphone applications in the last few years?

2.49 Your town is considering setting up a camera and face recognition system in the downtown area and in a neighborhood with a high crime rate. They hired you as a consultant to help design policies for use of the system. Consider a variety of aspects, such as who will have access to the system, what databases of photos the system will use for matching, how long the town will store the video, and other factors you consider important. Describe some of your most important recommendations to the city with your reasons for them.

2.50 (a) A large retailer mines its customer database to determine if a customer is likely to be pregnant. (See the box in Section 2.3.1.) It sends ads or coupons for products the customer might buy. Is this ethically acceptable or ethically prohibited?

(b) The retailer knows that customers are uncomfortable with the idea that the retailer can determine that they are pregnant. The retailer makes ad booklets or email that include many pregnancy and baby products along with unrelated products. The customers who receive them do not realize that the ads are targeted for them. Is this ethically acceptable or ethically prohibited?

2.51 Veterinarians implant computer chips into pets and farm animals to identify them if they get lost. Some people suggest doing so for children. Discuss benefits and privacy implications. Do the benefits outweigh the risks?

2.52 Several men contracted syphilis, a serious sexually transmitted disease, after arranging to meet partners through an online chat room used mostly by gay men. The public health department asked the company that hosted the site for the names and addresses of all people who used the chat room so that it could inform them about possible exposure to the disease. The public health department did not have a court order. The site's policy says it will not release information that links screen names with real names. Should it make an exception in this case? Give arguments on both sides. How do you weigh the trade-off between the possibility of an infected person remaining uninformed and the loss of privacy to all visitors to the chat room? How important is it that the company abide by its posted privacy policy?

2.53 A Massachusetts high school adopted a policy that allows administrators to seize cellphones from students and search the phones when they suspect a phone might contain evidence of illegal activity. Discuss benefits and risks of this policy. Does it appear consistent with the Fourth Amendment? Court decisions allow schools to search students if there is reasonable suspicion that the student has contraband. With respect to privacy, how does physically searching a student differ from searching a cellphone?

2.54 Are businesses that provide free Internet services or other benefits in exchange for tracking Web activity offering a fair option for consumers, or are they unfairly taking advantage of low-income people who must give up some privacy for these services?

2.55 In one of Vernor Vinge's science fiction novels,[109] an organization scatters false information about people on the Web. Does that sound nasty? The name of the organization is Friends of Privacy. Are they?

2.56 Consider a "right to be forgotten," as in Sections 2.3.4 and 2.5.3. In what situations, if any, is such a legal right a good idea?

2.57 The city of Philadelphia requires GPS systems in all taxicabs. Is a government requirement for a tracking system for private taxi cabs a reasonable public safety measure or an unreasonable intrusion on the privacy of drivers and passengers? Identify several differences between such a government requirement and a taxicab company choosing to install GPS systems in its cabs. Is either more objectionable than the other? Why?

2.58 Do young people today view privacy differently from the previous generation?

2.59 Develop a policy for a large social network company on how to respond to requests from members seeking to prevent other members from communicating with them (that is, blocking other members).

2.60 Which do you think should have larger storage capacity: Google or the National Security Agency? Why? (Try to find recent estimates on the storage capacity of each.)

BOOKS AND ARTICLES

- James Bamford, *Body of Secrets: Anatomy of the Ultra-Secret National Security Agency, from the Cold War Through the Dawn of a New Century*, Doubleday, 2001.

- Colin J. Bennett, *The Governance of Privacy: Policy Instruments in Global Perspective*, MIT Press, 2006.

- Alexander Charns, *Cloak and Gavel: FBI Wiretaps, Bugs, Informers, and the Supreme Court*, University of Illinois Press, 1992.

- Robert Corn-Revere, "The Fourth Amendment and the Internet," Testimony before the Subcommittee on the Constitution of the House Committee on the Judiciary, Apr. 6, 2000, www.house.gov/judiciary/corn0406.htm.

- Whitfield Diffie and Susan Landau, *Privacy on the Line: The Politics of Wiretapping and Encryption*, MIT Press 1998.

- Jim Harper, *Identity Crisis: How Identification Is Overused and Misunderstood*, Cato Institute, 2006.

- Jeff Jarvis, *Public Parts: How Sharing in the Digital Age Improves the Way We Work and Live*, Simon and Schuster, 2011.

- Orin Kerr, *Searching and Seizing Computers and Obtaining Electronic Evidence in Criminal Investigations*, U.S. Dept. of Justice, 2002, www.usdoj.gov/criminal/cybercrime/s&smanual2002.htm.

- Jacqueline Klosek, *Data Privacy in the Information Age*, Quorum Books, 2000. Describes the European Union data privacy directive, privacy laws in many European countries, and major U.S. privacy laws.

- Alex Kozinski, "On Privacy: Did Technology Kill the Fourth Amendment?" *Cato Policy Report*, Nov./Dec. 2011, www.cato.org/pubs/policy_report/v33n6/cprv33n6-3.html.

- Edith Lapidus, *Eavesdropping on Trial*, Hayden Book Co., 1974. Contains history of wiretapping and the relevant sections of the Omnibus Crime Control and Safe Streets Act of 1968.

- Helen Nissenbaum, *Privacy in Context: Technology, Policy, and the Integrity of Social Life*, Stanford Law Books, 2009.

- George Orwell, *1984*, 1948. Orwell's dystopian novel in which the totalitarian government controlled the people via ubiquitous telescreens. What did he foresee accurately, and what did he miss? (Orwell introduced the term "Big Brother" for the government.)

- Steve Posner, *Privacy Law and the USA PATRIOT Act*, LexisNexis, 2006.

- James Rachels, "Why Privacy Is Important," in *Philosophy and Public Affairs* 4(4), Princeton University Press, 1975 (appears in several anthologies, including Schoeman, *Philosophical Dimensions of Privacy*, listed below).

- Jeffrey Rosen, "The Right to Be Forgotten," *Stanford Law Review* (64 Stanford L. Rev. Online 88), Feb. 13, 2012, www.stanfordlawreview.org/online/privacy-paradox/right-to-be-forgotten.

- Jeffrey Rosen, *The Unwanted Gaze: The Destruction of Privacy in America*, Random House, 2000.

- Jeffrey Rosen and Benjamin Wittes, eds., *Constitution 3.0 Freedom and Technological Change*, Brookings Institution Press, 2011. Covers surveillance and the Fourth Amendment, free speech, neuroscience, and genetic technologies.

- Bruce Schneier, *Secrets and Lies: Digital Security in a Networked World*, John Wiley & Sons, Inc., 2000.

- Ferdinand David Schoeman, *Philosophical Dimensions of Privacy: An Anthology*, Cambridge University Press, 1984.

- Robert Ellis Smith, *Ben Franklin's Web Site: Privacy and Curiosity from Plymouth Rock to the Internet*, Privacy Journal, 2004.

- Robert Ellis Smith, publisher, *Privacy Journal*. A monthly newsletter covering news on many aspects of privacy.

- Daniel J. Solove, *Understanding Privacy*, Harvard University Press, 2010.

- Charles Sykes, *The End of Privacy: Personal Rights in the Surveillance Society*, St. Martin's Press, 1999.

- Eugene Volokh, "Freedom of Speech and Information Privacy: The Troubling Implications of a Right to Stop People from Speaking about You," *Stanford Law Review* (52 Stanford L. Rev. 1049), 2000. Also at www.law.ucla.edu/faculty/volokh/privacy.htm.

- Alan F. Westin, *Privacy and Freedom*, Atheneum, 1968.

ORGANIZATIONS AND WEBSITES

- Cato Institute: www.cato.org/privacy-issues

- Department of Homeland Security: www.dhs.gov

- Electronic Frontier Foundation: www.eff.org

- Electronic Frontiers Australia: www.efa.org.au

- Electronic Privacy Information Center: www.epic.org and www.privacy.org (jointly sponsored by EPIC and Privacy International)

- Federal Bureau of Investigation: www.fbi.gov

- Federal Trade Commission: www.ftc.gov

- The National Security Agency: www.nsa.gov

- Privacy Commission of Australia: www .privacy.gov.au

- Privacy Commissioner of Canada: www .privcom.gc.ca

- Privacy International: www.privacy international.org

- Privacy Rights Clearinghouse: www.privacy rights.org

- TRUSTe: www.truste.org

NOTES

1. James O. Jackson, "Fear and Betrayal in the Stasi State," *Time*, Feb. 3, 1992, pp. 32–33.

2. "Privacy as an Aspect of Human Dignity," in Ferdinand David Schoeman, ed., *Philosophical Dimensions of Privacy: An Anthology*, Cambridge University Press, 1984, pp. 156–203, quote on p. 188.

3. "Reading *Privacy Journal*'s Mail," *Privacy Journal*, May 2001, p. 2.

4. Nicole Wong, "Judge Tells DoJ 'No' on Search Queries," Google Blog, Mar. 17, 2006, googleblog.blogspot.com/ 2006/03/judge-tells-doj-no-on-search-queries.html.

5. Michael Barbaro and Tom Zeller Jr., "A Face Is Exposed for AOL Searcher No. 4417749," *New York Times*, Aug. 9, 2006, www.nytimes.com, viewed Sept. 19, 2006. AOL acknowledged that the release was a bad mistake, fired the employees responsible, and considered improvements in internal policies to reduce the chance of similar errors in the future.

6. Brian X.Chen and Nick Bilton, "Et Tu, Google? Android Apps Can Also Secretly Copy Photos," *New York Times*, Mar. 1, 2012, bits.blogs.nytimes.com/2012/03/01/ android-photos, viewed Mar. 20, 2012.

7. I collected many of these examples from news reports.

8. The offending software is sometimes buried in ads or other content provided by third parties. Some retailers do not know that the software they use stores credit card numbers. (It is not supposed to.) For example, see Verizon Business Investigative Response team, "2008 Data Breach Investigations Report," www.verizonbusiness.com/resources/security/ databreachreport.pdf.

9. Associated Press, "Popular Software for Computer Cursors Logs Web Visits, Raising Privacy Issue," *Wall Street Journal*, Nov. 30, 1999, p. B6.

10. The National Highway Traffic Safety Administration requires that car makers inform owners if a car is equipped with a data recorder and specifies that the owner's consent is needed to collect data from the recorder.

11. For an early history of cookies, see John Schwartz, "Giving Web a Memory Cost Its Users Privacy," *New York Times*, Sept. 4, 2001, www.nytimes.com/2001/09/04/ business/giving-web-a-memory-cost-its-users-privacy .html, viewed Sept. 2, 2011.

12. Quoted in Theo Francis, "Spread of Records Stirs Patient Fears of Privacy Erosion," *Wall Street Journal*, Dec. 26, 2006, p. A1.

13. The Privacy Rights Clearinghouse shows several specific sets of Fair Information Principles in "A Review of the Fair Information Principles," www.privacyrights.org/ar/ fairinfo.htm.

14. Quoted in David Banisar, *Privacy and Human Rights 2000: An International Survey of Privacy Laws and Developments*, EPIC and Privacy International, 2000.

15. *California Bankers Assn. v. Shultz*, 416 U.S. 21 (1974). caselaw.lp.findlaw.com/cgi-bin/getcase.pl?court=us& vol=416&invol=21.

16. Alan F. Westin, *Privacy and Freedom*, Atheneum, 1968, p. 67.

17. Julian Sanchez, "The Pinpoint Search," *Reason*, January 2007, pp. 21–28.

18. Sanchez, "The Pinpoint Search," p. 21.

19. The citations for the cases mentioned in this section are *Olmstead v. United States*, 277 U.S. 438(1928); *Katz v. United States*, 389 U.S. 347(1967); *Smith v. Maryland*, 442 U.S. 735(1979); *United States v. Miller*, 425 U.S. 435(1976); and *Kyllo v. United States*, 99-8508 (2001).

20. *U.S. v. Jones*, Jan. 23, 2012, www.supremecourt.gov/ opinions/11pdf/10-1259.pdf, viewed Jan. 24, 2012. The case began in 2004.

21. Alex Kozinski, "On Privacy: Did Technology Kill the Fourth Amendment?" *Cato Policy Report*, Nov./Dec. 2011, www.cato.org/pubs/policy_report/v33n6/ cprv33n6-3.html, viewed Dec. 5, 2011.

22. *NAACP v. Alabama*, 357 U.S. 449 (1958).

23. *United States v. Carey*, 1999, caselaw.findlaw.com/us-10th-circuit/1317424.html, link updated Oct. 23, 2011.

24. *United States of America v. Comprehensive Drug Testing*, decision Sept. 13, 2010.

25. Quoted by Appellate Judge Sydney Thomas, who dissented from the appeals court ruling allowing use of the lab records. *USA v. Comprehensive Drug Testing* No. 05-10067.

26. Stephanie Francis Ward, "States Split Over Warrantless Searches of Cellphone Data," *ABA Journal*, Apr. 1, 2011, viewed Aug. 30, 2011.

27. *U.S. v. Arnold*, Ninth Circuit Court of Appeals, 2008. Amanda Bronstad, "Computer Search Turned Back at the Border," Law.com, Oct. 23, 2006, www.law.com/jsp/article.jsp?id=1161335118318, viewed Nov. 7, 2006. Ellen Nakashima, "Clarity Sought on Electronic Searches," *Washington Post*, www.washingtonpost.com/wp-dyn/content/article/2008/02/06/AR2008020604763.html.

28. Dana Canedy, "TV Cameras Seek Criminals in Tampa's Crowds," *New York Times*, July 4, 2001, pp. A1, A11.

29. The National Institute of Standards and Technology, a federal government agency, reported an accuracy rate of 57%. Jesse Drucker and Nancy Keates, "The Airport of the Future," *Wall Street Journal*, Nov. 23, 2001, pp. W1, W12. David Banisar raised issues about accuracy in "A Review of New Surveillance Technologies," *Privacy Journal*, Nov. 2001, p. 1.

30. Ross Kerber, "Privacy Concerns Are Roadblocks on 'Smart' Highways," *Wall Street Journal*, Dec. 4, 1996, pp. B1, B7. Banisar, "A Review of New Surveillance Technologies." Michael Spencer, "One Major City's Restrictions on TV Surveillance," *Privacy Journal*, March 2001, p. 3. Murray Long, "Canadian Commissioner Puts a Hold on Video Cameras," *Privacy Journal*, November 2001, pp. 3–4.

31. Marc Champion and others, "Tuesday's Attack Forces an Agonizing Decision on Americans," *Wall Street Journal*, Sept. 14, 2001, p. A8.

32. "Cameras in U.K. Found Useless." *Privacy Journal*, March 2005, pp. 6–7.

33. Quoted in Long, "Canadian Commissioner Puts a Hold on Video Cameras."

34. Jim Epstein, "Why I Was Arrested Yesterday at a D.C. Taxi Commission Meeting," June 23, 2011, reason.tv/video/show/taxi-commission-arrest, viewed Sept. 4, 2011.

35. Acxiom Latin America website, "Customer Information Management Solutions," www.acxiom.com, viewed Nov. 26, 2006.

36. Cecilie Rohwedder, "No. 1 Retailer in Britain Uses 'Clubcard' to Thwart Wal-Mart," *Wall Street Journal*, June 6, 2006, p. A1. Charles Duhigg, "How Companies Learn Your Secrets," *New York Times*, Feb. 16, 2012, www.nytimes.com/2012/02/19/magazine/shopping-habits.html, viewed Feb. 20, 2012.

37. Julia Angwin, "A Plan to Track Web Use Stirs Privacy Concern," *Wall Street Journal*, May 1, 2000, pp. B1, B18. Paulette Thomas, "'Clicking' Coupons On-Line Has a Cost: Privacy," *Wall Street Journal*, June 18, 1998, pp. B1, B8.

38. Jessica E. Vascellaro, "Online Retailers Are Watching You," *Wall Street Journal*, Nov. 28, 2006, pp. D1, D3.

39. Yochi J. Dreazen, "Democrats, Playing Catch-Up, Tap Database to Woo Potential Voters," *Wall Street Journal*, Oct. 31, 2006, pp. A1, A10.

40. For example, regulations established under the Gramm-Leach-Bliley Act of 1999, which are responsible for the millions of privacy notices and opt-out forms mailed out by credit card companies.

41. Julia Angwin, "A Plan to Track Web Use."

42. www.youtube.com, accessed Oct. 13, 2006.

43. Quoted in *Privacy Journal*, April 2006, p. 2.

44. Ruchi Sanghvi, "Facebook Gets a Facelift," Sept. 5, 2006, blog.facebook.com/blog.php?post=2207967130. "An Open Letter from Mark Zuckerberg," Sept. 8, 2006, blog.facebook.com/blog.php?post=2208562130; and many news stories.

45. Vauhini Vara, "Covering your Tracks in an Online World Takes a Few Tricks," *Wall Street Journal*, July 7, 2006, pp. A1, A10.

46. See, for example, Center for Democracy and Technology, "CDT Working Group on RFID: Privacy Best Practices for Deployment of RFID Technology," May 1, 2006, www.cdt.org/privacy/20060501rfid-best-practices.php.

47. John L. Eliot, "Bugging Plants to Sting Poachers," *National Geographic*, March 1996, p. 148. Jon R. Luoma, "It's 10:00 P.M. We Know Where Your Turtles Are." *Audubon*, Sept./Oct. 1998, pp. 52–57.

48. Jeffrey Rosen covers many in his article "The Right to Be Forgotten," *Stanford Law Review*, Feb. 13, 2012, www.stanfordlawreview.org/online/privacy-paradox/right-to-be-forgotten, viewed Feb. 13, 2012. See also Eugene Volokh, "Freedom of Speech and Information Privacy: The Troubling Implications of a Right to Stop People from Speaking about You," *Stanford Law Review* (52 Stanford L. Rev. 1049), 2000, www.law.ucla.edu/faculty/volokh/privacy.htm.

49. Steven A. Bercu, "Smart Card Privacy Issues: An Overview," *BOD-T-001*, July 1994, Smart Card Forum.

50. "Information Security: The Centers for Medicare & Medicaid Services Needs to Improve Controls over Key Communication Network," Government Accountability Office, Aug. 2006, www.gao.gov/new.items/d06750.pdf. *Computers and Privacy: How the Government Obtains, Verifies, Uses, and Protects Personal Data*, U.S. General Accounting Office, 1990 (GAO/IMTEC-90-70BR). "House Panel Probes White House Database," *EPIC Alert*, Sept. 12, 1996. OMB Watch study, reported in "U.S. Government Web Sites Fail to Protect Privacy," *EPIC Alert*, Sept. 4, 1997. www.wired.com/news/politics/0,1283,37314,00.html.

Internet Privacy: Comparison of Federal Agency Practices with FTC's Fair Information Principles, U.S. General Accounting Office, Sept. 11, 2000 (GAO/AIMD-00-296R). U.S. Government Accountability Office, *Data Mining* (GAO 05-866), Aug. 2005, www.gao.gov/new.items/d05866.pdf. The GAO was called the General Accounting Office until 2004.

51. "GAO Finds IRS Security Lacking," *EPIC Alert*, Jan. 20, 1999; the GAO report is *IRS Systems Security*, Dec. 1998 (AIMD-99-38). Treasury Inspector General for Tax Administration, "Increased IRS Oversight of State Agencies Is Needed to Ensure Federal Tax Information Is Protected," Sept. 2005, Reference Number: 2005-20-184, www.treas.gov/tigta/auditreports/2005reports/2005 20184fr.html, viewed May 16, 2007. Kathleen Day, "IRS Found Lax in Protecting Taxpayer Data," *Washington Post*, Apr. 5, 2007, p. D1, www.washingtonpost.com, viewed May 16, 2007.

52. The Information Security and Privacy Advisory Board, *Toward A 21st Century Framework for Federal Government Privacy Policy*, May 2009, www.securityprivacyandthe law.com/uploads/file/ispab-report-may2009.pdf, viewed Sept. 8, 2011. U.S. Government Accountability Office, *Privacy: Congress Should Consider Alternatives for Strengthening Protection of Personally Identifiable Information* (GAO-08-795T), June 18, 2008, www.gao.gov/products/GAO-08-795T, viewed Sept. 8, 2011.

53. Robert Ellis Smith, "Ominous Tracking of University Students," *Privacy Journal*, Aug. 2006, p. 1.

54. U.S. Code, Title 13.

55. U.S. Census Bureau, American Community Survey, www.census.gov/acs/www/about_the_survey/american_ community_survey, viewed Sept. 5, 2011. Letter from Vincent Barabba, director of Census Bureau under Presidents Nixon and Carter, and comments from Tom Clark, Justice Department coordinator of alien control, quoted in David Burnham, *The Rise of the Computer State*, Random House, 1983, pp. 23–26. Margo Anderson, *The American Census: A Social History*, Yale University Press, 1988. James Bovard, "Honesty May Not Be Your Best Census Policy," *Wall Street Journal*, Aug. 8, 1989. Lynette Clemetson, "Homeland Security Given Data on Arab-Americans," *New York Times*, July 30, 2004, p. A14.

56. Jeff Jonas and Jim Harper, "Effective Counterterrorism and Limited Role of Predictive Data Mining," Cato Institute Policy Analysis No. 584, Dec. 11, 2006.

57. Reuters, "Critics: New Airport X-ray Is a Virtual Strip Search," CNet News.com, Feb. 24, 2007, viewed Feb. 27, 2007. Scott McCartney, "Aiming to Balance Security and Convenience," *Wall Street Journal*, Sept. 1, 2011, p. D3.

58. www.consumer.gov/idtheft. "Second Thoughts on Posting Court Records Online," *Privacy Journal*, Feb. 2006, pp. 1, 4.

59. The Ethics in Government Act.

60. Tony Mauro, "Judicial Conference Votes to Release Federal Judges' Financial Records," Freedom Forum, Mar. 15, 2000, www.freedomforum.org/templates/document .asp?documentID=11896, viewed Jan. 5, 2007.

61. The article "Can Privacy and Open Access to Records be Reconciled?" *Privacy Journal*, May 2000, p. 6, outlines principles and guidelines devised by Robert Ellis Smith for access to public records.

62. Sources for this section include: Chris Hibbert, "What to Do When They Ask for Your Social Security Number," cpsr.org/prevsite/cpsr/privacy/ssn/ssn.faq.html, link updated Oct. 22, 2011; "ID Cards to Cost $10 Billion," *EPIC Alert*, Sept. 26, 1997; Glenn Garvin, "Bringing the Border War Home," *Reason*, Oct. 1995, pp. 18–28; Simson Garfinkel, *Database Nation: The Death of Privacy in the 21st Century*, O'Reilly, 2000, pp. 33–34; "A Turnaround on Social Security Numbers," *Privacy Journal*, Dec. 2006, p. 2; *Greidinger v. Davis*, U.S. Court of Appeals, Fourth Circuit.

63. Ellen Nakashima, "U.S. Exposed Personal Data," *Washington Post*, Apr. 21, 2007, p. A05. "USDA Offers Free Credit Monitoring to Farm Services Agency and Rural Development Funding Recipients," www.usa.gov/usdaexposure.shtml, viewed May 24, 2007.

64. "Understanding and Responding to the Threat of Terrorism," *Cato Policy Report*, Mar./Apr. 2007, pp. 13–15, 19.

65. Peter G. Neumann and Lauren Weinstein, "Inside Risks," *Communications of the ACM*, December 2001, p. 176.

66. Quoted in Jane Howard, "ID Card Signals 'End of Democracy,'" *The Australian*, Sept. 7, 1987, p. 3.

67. "Understanding and Responding to the Threat of Terrorism," *Cato Policy Report*, Mar./Apr. 2007, pp. 13–15, 19.

68. Ixquick, www.ixquick.com, is one example. It is a meta-search engine; that is, it uses several other search engines to find results and provides what it considers the best results to the user.

69. "Hiding Data in Plain Sight," *EFFector Online*, Jan. 7, 1993, www.eff.org/effector/effect04.05.

70. Quoted in Steve Lohr, "Privacy on Internet Poses Legal Puzzle," *New York Times*, Apr. 19, 1999, p. C4.

71. An exception is a method called one-time pads, but it is inconvenient to use and is not significant in the issues discussed here.

72. Kenneth W. Dam and Herbert S. Lin, eds., National Research Council, *Cryptography's Role in Securing the*

Information Society, National Academy Press, 1996, books.nap.edu/html/crisis.

73. The Security and Freedom through Encryption Act (SAFE), as amended by the House Intelligence Committee, Sept. 11, 1997.

74. Judge Marilyn Patel, quoted in Jared Sandberg, "Judge Rules Encryption Software Is Speech in Case on Export Curbs," *Wall Street Journal*, Apr. 18, 1996, p. B7. The case, *Bernstein v. United States,* and others continued for several more years, but in 1999 and 2000 two federal appeals courts ruled that the export restrictions violated freedom of speech. One court praised cryptography as a means of protecting privacy.

75. "Wiretap Report 2010," www.uscourts.gov/Statistics/WiretapReports/WiretapReport2010.aspx, viewed Mar. 23, 2012. The government reports encryption in wiretaps because a federal law requires it to do so. I could not find data on how often law enforcement agents encounter encryption in seized computer files and whether they can decrypt the files.

76. Samuel D. Warren and Louis D. Brandeis, "The Right to Privacy," *Harvard Law Review*, 1890, v. 4, p. 193.

77. Judith Jarvis Thomson, "The Right to Privacy," in David Schoeman, *Philosophical Dimensions of Privacy: An Anthology*, Cambridge University Press, 1984, pp. 272–289.

78. The inspiration for the Warren and Brandeis article, not mentioned in it, was that gossip columnists wrote about extravagant parties in Warren's home and newspapers covered his daughter's wedding. The background of the article is described in a biography of Brandeis and summarized in the critical response to the Warren and Brandeis article by William L. Prosser ("Privacy," in Schoeman, *Philosophical Dimensions of Privacy: An Anthology*, pp. 104–155).

79. Thomson, "The Right to Privacy," p. 287.

80. See, for example, Schoeman, *Philosophical Dimensions of Privacy: An Anthology*, p. 15, and Prosser, "Privacy," pp. 104–155.

81. Cases are cited in Prosser, "Privacy."

82. Richard Posner, "An Economic Theory of Privacy," *Regulation*, American Enterprise Institute for Public Policy Research, May/June 1978, pp. 19–26. (Appears in several anthologies including Schoeman, *Philosophical Dimensions of Privacy*, pp. 333–345, and Johnson and Nissenbaum, *Computers, Ethics & Social Values*, Prentice Hall, 1995.)

83. New York State Office of the Attorney General, "Toysmart Bankruptcy Settlement Ensures Consumer Privacy Protection," Jan. 11, 2001, www.ag.ny.gov/media_center/2001/jan/jan11a_01.html, link updated Oct. 22, 2011.

84. See Robert Gellman, "Privacy, Consumers, and Costs," March 2002, www.epic.org/reports/dmfprivacy.html, viewed May 24, 2007.

85. Dan Freedman, "Privacy Profile: Mary Gardiner Jones," *Privacy and American Business* 1(4), 1994, pp. 15, 17.

86. Janlori Goldman, statement to the Senate Judiciary Subcommittee on Technology and the Law, Jan. 27, 1994.

87. www.privacy.org.

88. Deirdre Mulligan, statement to U.S. House of Representatives Committee on the Judiciary hearing on "Privacy and Electronic Communications," May 18, 2000, www.cdt.org/testimony/000518mulligan.shtml, viewed May 24, 2007. The quotation in her statement is from Alan F. Westin, *Privacy and Freedom*, Atheneum, 1968.

89. "Directive 95/46/EC of the European Parliament and of the Council of 24 October 1995 on the Protection of Individuals with Regard to the Processing of Personal Data and on the Free Movement of Such Data," available at European Commission, Justice and Home Affairs, ec.europa.eu/justice_home/fsj/privacy/law/index_en.htm.

90. Josh Halliday, "Europe's Highest Court to Rule on Google Privacy Battle in Spain," *The Guardian*, Mar. 1, 2011, www.guardian.co.uk/technology/2011/mar/01/google-spain-privacy-court-case, viewed Oct. 14, 2011. Caroline McCarthy, "German Court Rules Google Street View is Legal," *CNet News*, Mar. 21, 2011, news.cnet.com/8301-13577_3-20045595-36.html, viewed Oct. 14, 2011.

91. Jo Best, "EU Data Retention Directive Gets Final Nod," CNET News.com, news.com.com Feb. 22, 2006, viewed Oct. 26, 2006.

92. "Just Published," *Privacy Journal*, Aug. 2006, p. 6. Information Commissioner's Office, *What Price Privacy? The Unlawful Trade in Confidential Personal Information*, May 10, 2006, www.ico.gov.uk/upload/documents/library/corporate/research_and_reports/what_price_privacy.pdf.

93. Jacqueline Klosek, *Data Privacy in the Information Age*, Quorum Books, 2000. "Australia: We're 'Adequate'!" *Privacy Journal*, May 2001, p. 4.

94. The historic information in this section is from Alan F. Westin, *Privacy and Freedom*; Alexander Charns, *Cloak and Gavel: FBI Wiretaps, Bugs, Informers, and the Supreme Court*, University of Illinois Press, 1992 (Chapter 8); Edith Lapidus, *Eavesdropping on Trial*, Hayden Book Co., 1974; and Walter Isaacson, *Kissinger: A Biography*, Simon and Schuster, 1992.

95. *Nardone v. U.S.* 302 U.S. 379(1937).

96. The quote is in the foreword of Lapidus, *Eavesdropping on Trial*.

97. For examples, see U.S. Department of State, "Country Reports on Human Rights Practices," Mar. 6, 2007, www.state.gov/g/drl/rls/hrrpt/2006, viewed Mar. 13, 2007.

98. *Warshak v. U.S.*, Case 06-492, Sixth Circuit Court of Appeals, 2008.

99. Ellen Nakashima, "U.S. Seeks Ways to Wiretap the Internet," *Washington Post*, Sept. 28, 2010, www.washingtonpost.com/wp-dyn/content/article/2010/09/27/AR2010092706637.html, viewed Oct. 13, 2011.

100. John Schwartz, "Industry Fights Wiretap Proposal," *Washington Post*, Mar. 12, 1994, p. C1, C7.

101. 84% in 2010, according to *Wiretap Report 2010*, Table 3, pg. 17, www.uscourts.gov/Statistics/WiretapReports/WiretapReport2010.aspx, viewed Oct. 13, 2011. The rate was 81% in 2005.

102. Sources for this section include: James Bamford, *The Puzzle Palace: A Report on NSA, America's Most Secret Agency*, Houghton Mifflin, 1982; NSA FAQ: www.nsa.gov/about/faqs/about_nsa.shtml, link updated Oct. 22, 2011; Statement for the Record of NSA Director Lt. General Michael V. Hayden, USAF, House Permanent Select Committee on Intelligence, Apr. 12, 2000, www.nsa.gov/public_info/speeches_testimonies/12apr00_dirnsa.shtml, link updated Oct. 22, 2011; James Bamford, *Body of Secrets: Anatomy of the Ultra-Secret National Security Agency, from the Cold War Through the Dawn of a New Century*, Doubleday, 2001; James Bamford, "The Black Box,"

Wired, April 2012, pp.78–85, 122–124 (online at www.wired.com/threatlevel/2012/03/ff_nsadatacenter). Bamford has written extensively about the NSA over several decades. His sources include former long-time NSA employees.

103. NSA FAQ: www.nsa.gov/about/faqs/about_nsa.shtml, link updated Oct. 22, 2011.

104. At Lawrence Livermore National Laboratory.

105. Declaration of Mark Klein, June 8, 2006, www.eff.org/files/filenode/att/SER_klein_decl.pdf, viewed June 19, 2007, link updated Nov. 21, 2011.

106. *Amnesty et al. v. Clapper*.

107. To be completed in 2013 at a cost of $2 billion, according to Bamford, "The Black Box."

108. Robert F. Buckhorn Jr., quoted in Dana Canedy, "TV Cameras Seek Criminals in Tampa's Crowds."

109. Vernor Vinge, *Rainbows End*, Tor, 2006.

3

FREEDOM OF SPEECH

3.1 Communications Paradigms

Congress shall make no law . . . abridging the freedom of speech,
or of the press. . . .

—First Amendment, U.S. Constitution

As we observed in Chapter 1, the Internet brought us extraordinary opportunities for increasing free expression of ideas, easy and inexpensive communication between people of different countries, and extraordinary opportunities for access to many voices and points of view all over the world. But freedom of speech has always been restricted to some degree in the United States and to a large degree in many other countries. In this chapter, we examine how principles of freedom of speech from earlier media affect the Internet and how the Internet affects them.* We consider pornography on the Internet, attempts to restrict it, and attempts to restrict access by children; advertising and commerce on the Web; spam (mass, unsolicited email); and anonymity as a protection for speakers. Some forms of speech have long been contentious (pornography, for example), and some are new forms that developed with the Internet and other digital technology (spam and video games, for example). When the First Amendment protects some forms of controversial speech (such as violent video games or leaking sensitive documents) from legal restrictions, ethical and social issues are particularly relevant. Throughout this chapter, we describe various incidents and cases and discuss issues they raise. In Section 3.5, we examine how communications and surveillance technologies affect freedom of speech in different countries, especially some that have a long tradition of censorship.

3.1.1 REGULATING COMMUNICATIONS MEDIA

It is by now almost a cliché to say that the Internet lets us all be publishers. We do not need expensive printing presses or complex distribution systems. We need only a computer or a cellphone. Any business, organization, or individual can set up a website. We can "publish" whatever we wish; it is available for anyone who chooses to read it. In 1994, shortly before the Web became widely used, Mike Godwin, then an attorney with the Electronic Frontier Foundation, described the dramatic change that computer communications brought about:

> It is a medium far different from the telephone, which is only a one-to-one medium, ill-suited for reaching large numbers of people. It is a medium far different from the newspaper or TV station, which are one-to-many media, ill-suited for feedback from the audience. For the first time in history, we have a many-to-many medium,

---

* Although some of our discussion is in the context of the U.S. Constitution's First Amendment, the arguments and principles about the human right of freedom of speech apply globally.

in which you don't have to be rich to have access, and in which you don't have to win the approval of an editor or publisher to speak your mind. Usenet* and the Internet, as part of this new medium, hold the promise of guaranteeing, for the first time in history, that the First Amendment's protection of freedom of the press means as much to each individual as it does to Time Warner, or to Gannett, or to the *New York Times*.[1]

Individuals took advantage of that promise. As just one indication, the number of blogs passed 150 million by 2010.[2] Some are as widely read and as influential as traditional newspapers. However, while computer communications technologies *might* guarantee freedom of speech and of the press for all of us, the guarantee is not certain.

Telephone, movies, radio, television, cable, satellites, and, of course, the Internet did not exist when the Constitution was written. Freedom of the press applied to publishers who printed newspapers and books and to "the lonely pamphleteer" who printed and distributed pamphlets expressing unconventional ideas. One might think the First Amendment should apply to each new communications technology according to its spirit and intention: to protect our freedom to say what we wish. Politically powerful people, however, continually try to restrict speech that threatens them. From the Alien and Sedition Acts of 1798 to regulation of Political Action Committees, such laws have been used against newspaper editors who disagreed with the political party in power and against ad hoc groups of people speaking out on issues. Attempts to restrict freedom of speech and of the press flourish with new technologies. Law professor Eric M. Freedman sums up: "Historical experience—with the printing press, secular dramatic troupes, photographs, movies, rock music, broadcasting, sexually explicit telephone services, video games, and other media—shows that each new medium is viewed at first by governments as uniquely threatening, because it is uniquely influential, and therefore a uniquely appropriate target of censorship."[3]

In this section, we introduce the traditional three-part framework for First Amendment protection and government regulation of communications media that developed in the United States in the 20th century. As we will see, modern communications technology and the Internet required that the framework be updated. The three categories are:

- Print media (newspapers, books, magazines, pamphlets)
- Broadcast (television, radio)
- Common carriers (telephone, telegraph, and the postal system)

The first category has the strongest First Amendment protection. Although books have been banned in the United States and people were arrested for publishing information on certain topics such as contraception, the trend has been toward fewer government restraints on the printed word.

---

* An early (pre-Web) collection of Internet discussion groups.

Television and radio are similar to newspapers in their role of providing news and entertainment, but the government regulates both the structure of the broadcasting industry and the content of programs. The government grants broadcasting licenses. Licensees must meet government standards of merit—a requirement that would not be tolerated for publishers because of the obvious threat to freedom of expression. The government has used threats of license revocation to get stations to cancel sexually oriented talk shows or to censor them. Since 1971, the government has banned cigarette ads from radio, television, and electronic media under the control of the Federal Communications Commission (FCC), but the ads continued to be legal in magazines and newspapers. In a 1978 case challenging the constitutionality of a ban on broadcast "indecency," the Supreme Court upheld the ban.* The federal government frequently proposes requirements to reduce violence on television or increase programming for children, but the government cannot impose such requirements on print publishers. Whether you favor or oppose particular regulations, the point is that the government has more control over television and radio content than it has over communication methods that existed at the time the Bill of Rights was written. The main argument used to deny full First Amendment protection to broadcasters was scarcity of broadcast frequencies. There were only a handful of television channels and few radio frequencies in the early days of broadcasting. In exchange for the "monopoly" privilege of using the scarce, publicly owned spectrum, broadcasters were tightly regulated. With cable, satellites, hundreds of channels, and competition from the Internet, the argument based on scarcity and monopoly is irrelevant now, but the precedent of government control remains. A second argument, still used to justify government-imposed restrictions on content, is that broadcast material comes into the home and is difficult to keep from children.

Common carriers provide a medium of communication (not content) and must make their service available to everyone. In some cases, as with telephone service, the government requires them to provide "universal access" (i.e., to subsidize service for people with low incomes). Based on the argument that common carriers are a monopoly, the law prohibited them from controlling the content of material that passes through their system. Telephone companies were prohibited from providing content or information services on the grounds that they might discriminate against competing content providers who must also use their telephone lines. Common carriers had no control over content, so they had no responsibility for illegal content passing through.

Beginning in the 1980s, computer bulletin board systems (BBS), commercial services like CompuServe, Prodigy, and America Online (AOL), and ultimately the World Wide Web became major arenas for distribution of news, information, and opinion. Because of the immense flexibility of computer communications systems, they do not fit neatly into the publishing, broadcasting, and common carriage paradigms. Cable television strained these categories previously. In commenting on a law requiring cable stations to carry

---

* The FCC had fined comedian George Carlin for a radio program about the seven dirty words one could not say on the radio.

certain broadcasts, the Supreme Court said cable operators have more freedom of speech than television and radio broadcasters, but less than print publishers.[4] But the Web does not fit between the existing categories any better than it fits within any one of them. It has similarities to all three, as well as additional similarities to bookstores, libraries, and rented meeting rooms—all of which the law treats differently.

As new technologies blurred the technical boundaries between cable, telephone, computer networks, and content providers, the law began to adapt. The Telecommunications Act of 1996 changed the regulatory structure. It removed many artificial legal divisions of service areas and many restrictions on services that telecommunications companies may provide. It also significantly clarified the question of the liability of Internet Service Providers (ISPs) and other online service providers for content posted by third parties such as members and subscribers. Print publishers and broadcasters are legally liable for content they publish or broadcast. They can be sued for libel (making false and damaging statements) and copyright infringement, for example. They are legally responsible for obscene material in their publications and programs. Before passage of the Telecommunications Act, several people brought suits against BBS operators, ISPs, AOL, and other service providers for content that others put on their systems. To protect themselves from lawsuits and possible criminal charges, service providers would likely have erred on the side of caution and removed much content that was legal—seriously restricting the amount of information and opinion in cyberspace. The Telecommunications Act stated that "no provider or user of an interactive computer service shall be treated as the publisher or speaker of any information provided by another information content provider."[5] This statement removed uncertainty and protected service providers, thus encouraging the growth of user-created content.*

In 1996, the main parts of the first major Internet censorship law, the Communications Decency Act, were ruled unconstitutional. However, efforts to censor the Internet continued. We investigate arguments about, as well as the impacts of, censorship and other restrictive laws in Section 3.2. In addition, we will see in Section 3.2.5 that many innovative individuals and entrepreneurs who tried to publish information, advertise products, and provide services on the Web encountered legal problems (and sometimes fines), not because of explicit censorship laws, but because of long-standing laws that restricted commerce to benefit powerful organizations, businesses, and governments. In several cases, these confrontations between new technology and old laws resulted in increased freedom.

3.1.2 Free Speech Principles

As we proceed with our discussion of free speech issues, it is helpful to remember several important points.

---

* Service providers remain at risk in many countries. For example, the head of eBay in India was arrested because someone sold pornographic videos on eBay's Indian site even though the video itself did not appear on the site and the seller violated company policy by selling them.

The First Amendment was written precisely for offensive and/or controversial speech and ideas. There is no need to protect speech and publication that no one objects to. The First Amendment covers spoken and written words, pictures, art, and other forms of expression of ideas and opinions.

The First Amendment is a restriction on the power of government, not individuals or private businesses. Publishers do not have to publish material they consider offensive, poorly written, or unlikely to appeal to their customers for any reason. Rejection or editing by a publisher is not a violation of a writer's First Amendment rights. Websites, search engine companies, and magazines may decline specific advertisements if they so choose. That does not violate the advertiser's freedom of speech.

Over the course of many years and many cases, the Supreme Court has developed principles and guidelines about protected expression.* When a government action or law causes people to avoid legal speech and publication out of fear of prosecution—perhaps because a law is vague—the action or law is said to have a "chilling effect" on First Amendment rights. Courts generally rule that laws with a significant chilling effect are unconstitutional. Advocating illegal acts is (usually) legal; a listener has the opportunity and responsibility to weigh the arguments and decide whether or not to commit the illegal act. The First Amendment does not protect libel and direct, specific threats. Inciting violence, in certain circumstances, is illegal. Although the First Amendment makes no distinctions among categories of speech, courts have treated advertising as "second class" speech and allowed restrictions that would not be acceptable for other kinds of speech. However, cases in recent years have gone against that trend. Courts have begun to rule that restrictions on truthful advertising do indeed violate the First Amendment.[6] Similarly, since the 1970s, the government has severely regulated political campaign speech, but recent Supreme Court decisions have restored some First Amendment protection for it. Many court decisions have protected anonymous speech, but there are serious attempts to limit or prohibit anonymity on the Internet.

There is a censorship issue whenever the government owns or substantially subsidizes communications systems or networks (or controversial services). For example, in the 1980s, federally subsidized family planning clinics were not permitted to discuss abortion. In the past, the government has made it illegal to send information through the mail that the First Amendment otherwise protects. A federal agency that provides funds for public radio stations rejected the application of a university because it broadcasts one hour a week of religious programming. In Section 3.2.2, we will see that Congress used its funding power to require censorship of the Internet in public libraries and schools. No matter what side of these issues you are on, no matter how the policy changes with different presidents or Congresses, the point is that, in many circumstances, when the government pays, it can choose to restrict speech that the Constitution would otherwise protect.

---

* The specific laws, court decisions, and guidelines are complex in some cases. The discussion here is general and simplified.

3.2 Controlling Speech

*I disapprove of what you say, but I will defend to the death your right
to say it.*

—Voltaire's biographer, S. G. Tallentyre (Evelyn Beatrice Hall),
describing Voltaire's view of freedom of speech[7]

3.2.1 Offensive Speech: What Is It? What Is Illegal?

What is offensive speech? What should the law prohibit or restrict on the Web? The answers depend on who you are. It could be political or religious speech, pornography, racial or sexual slurs, Nazi materials, libelous statements, abortion information, antiabortion information, advertising of alcoholic beverages, advertising in general, depictions of violence, discussion of suicide, or information about how to build bombs. There are vehement advocates for banning each of these—and more. The state of Georgia tried to ban pictures of marijuana from the Internet. A doctor argued for regulating medical discussion on the Net so that people would not get bad advice. The Chinese government restricts reporting of emergencies (such as major accidents or disasters) and how the government handles them. The French government approved a law banning anyone except professional journalists from recording or distributing video of acts of violence.

Most efforts to censor the Internet in the United States, including several laws passed by Congress, focus on pornographic and other sexually explicit material, so we use pornography as the first example. Many of the same principles apply to efforts to censor other kinds of material. People discuss sexual activity, of conventional and unconventional sorts, including pedophilia, in graphic detail in cyberspace. The distinctions between categories such as erotica, art, and pornography are not always clear, and different people have very different personal standards. There is much on the Net that is extremely offensive to adults. Some people want to prohibit it altogether. Some seek ways to keep it away from children.

The Internet began as a forum for research and scientific discussion, so the rapid proliferation of pornography shocked some people. It is not, however, a surprising development. The same kind of material was already available in adult magazines, bookstores, and movie theaters. As a writer for *Wired* contends, sexual material quickly invades all new technologies and art forms.[8] He points out that, from cave paintings to frescos in Pompeii to stone carvings at Angkor Wat, erotica have flourished. The printing press produced Bibles and porn. Photography produced *Playboy*. Many of the first videocassettes were pornographic. Hundreds of thousands of subscription websites provide adult entertainment.[9] Whether all this is good or bad—whether it is a natural part of human nature or a sign of degeneracy and evil, whether we should tolerate it or stamp it out—are moral and social issues beyond the scope of this book. People debate pornography endlessly.

In addressing the issue of pornography and of other kinds of speech that offend people, we try to focus specifically on new problems and issues related to computer systems and cyberspace.

What was already illegal?

In 1973, the Supreme Court, in *Miller v. California*, established a three-part guideline for determining whether material is obscene under the law. The First Amendment does not protect obscene material. The criteria are that (1) it depicts sexual (or excretory) acts whose depiction is specifically prohibited by state law, (2) it depicts these acts in a patently offensive manner, appealing to prurient interest as judged by a reasonable person using community standards, and (3) it has no serious literary, artistic, social, political, or scientific value. The second point—the application of community standards—was a compromise intended to avoid the problem of setting a national standard of obscenity in so large and diverse a country. Thus, small conservative or religious towns could restrict pornography to a greater extent than cosmopolitan urban areas.

It has long been illegal to create, possess, or distribute child pornography. We discuss child pornography further in Section 3.2.3, where we consider unexpected applications of the laws.

Straining old legal standards

On the Internet, communities have no physical locations. Instead, they are defined by the people who choose to associate in cyberspace because of common interests. The definition of "community" proved critical in an early Internet case. A couple in California operated a computer bulletin board system (BBS) called Amateur Action that made sexually explicit images available to members. Legal observers generally agreed that the Amateur Action BBS operators would not be found guilty of a crime in California. A postal inspector in Memphis, Tennessee, working with a U.S. attorney there, became a member of the BBS (the only member in Tennessee[10]) and downloaded sexually explicit images in Memphis. The couple, who lived and worked in California, were prosecuted in Tennessee and found guilty of distributing obscenity under the local community standards. Both received jail sentences. A spokesman for the American Civil Liberties Union (ACLU) commented that

Different national standards: Section 5.4.1

prosecutions like this one meant that "nothing can be put on the Internet that is more racy than would be tolerated in the most conservative community in the U.S."[11] For this reason, some courts have recognized that "community standards" is no longer an appropriate tool for determining what is acceptable material. (For different national standards, see Section 5.4.1.)

The Net also changed the meaning of "distribution." Did the BBS operators send obscene files to Tennessee? BBSs were accessed through the telephone system. Anyone, from anywhere, could call in if they chose. The postal inspector in Tennessee initiated the telephone call to the BBS and initiated the transfer of the files. He selected and downloaded them. Critics of the prosecution of the BBS operators argued that it is as if the postal inspector went to California, bought pornographic pictures, and brought them home to Memphis—then had the seller prosecuted under Memphis community standards.[12]

3.2.2 CENSORSHIP LAWS AND ALTERNATIVES

Our sole intent is to make the Internet safer for our youth.

—Department of Justice spokesman[13]

Even where the protection of children is the object, the constitutional limits on government action apply.

—Justice Antonin Scalia[14]

Major Internet censorship laws

In the 1990s, as more nontechnical people began using the Internet, a variety of religious organizations, antipornography groups, and others began a campaign to pass federal legislation to censor the Internet. Increasing publicity about porn on the Net and increasing political pressure led Congress to pass the Communications Decency Act (CDA) of 1996.[15] In the CDA and the censorship laws that followed, Congress attempted to avoid an obvious conflict with the First Amendment by focusing on children. The CDA made it a crime to make available to anyone under 18 any communication that is obscene or indecent.

It can be difficult to design a law that keeps inappropriate material from children while allowing access for adults. The Supreme Court ruled on this problem in *Butler v. Michigan*, a significant 1957 case striking down a Michigan law that made it illegal to sell material that might be damaging to children. Justice Frankfurter wrote that the state must not "reduce the adult population of Michigan to reading only what is fit for children."[16] The CDA restricted indecent material accessible by children, but a child can access almost anything on the Net. Thus, opponents said, it would have violated Justice Frankfurter's dictum, not just in Michigan but throughout the country.

Opponents of the CDA gave examples of information that is legal in print but might be cause for prosecution if available online: the Bible, some of Shakespeare's plays, and serious discussions of sexual behavior and health problems like AIDS. Supporters of the CDA argued that this was overreaction. No one would be prosecuted, they said, for such material. The lack of clear standards, however, can lead to uneven and unfair prosecutions. The uncertainty about potential prosecution could have a chilling effect on those who provide information for adults that might not be suitable for children.

The Supreme Court ruled unanimously, in *American Civil Liberties Union et al. v. Janet Reno*, that the censorship provisions of the CDA were unconstitutional. The courts made strong statements about the importance of protecting freedom of expression in general and on the Internet. The decisions against the CDA established that "the Internet deserves the highest protection from government intrusion."

- Distinguish speech from action. Advocating illegal acts is (usually) legal.
- Laws must not chill expression of legal speech.
- Do not reduce adults to reading only what is fit for children.
- Solve speech problems by least restrictive means.

Figure 3.1   Freedom of speech guidelines.

Figure 3.1 summarizes principles courts use to help determine if a censorship law is constitutional. When the government is pursuing a legitimate goal that might infringe on free speech (in this case, the protection of children), it must use the least restrictive means of accomplishing the goal. The courts found that the then newly developing filtering software was less restrictive and more desirable than censorship. The judges also commented, "The government can continue to protect children from pornography on the Internet through vigorous enforcement of existing laws criminalizing obscenity and child pornography."[17]

Congress tried again, with the Child Online Protection Act (COPA), in 1998. This law was more limited than the CDA. COPA made it a federal crime for commercial websites to make available to minors material "harmful to minors" as judged by community standards. Once again, First Amendment supporters argued that the law was too broad and would threaten art, news, and health sites. Courts evaluating COPA noted that because the Web is accessible everywhere, the community-standards provision would restrict the entire country to the standards of the most conservative community. The courts said COPA restricts access to a substantial amount of online speech that is lawful for adults, and COPA's requirements that adults provide identification to view material not appropriate for minors would have an unconstitutional chilling effect on free speech. After more than 10 years of lawsuits and appeals, the Supreme Court declined to hear the last government appeal, and COPA died in 2009.

Congress passed the Children's Internet Protection Act (CIPA) in 2000 to require libraries and schools to use filter software on Internet terminals. When public libraries first installed Internet terminals, there were problems. People used the terminals to look at "X-rated" pictures, within view of children or other library users who found them offensive. Some people tied up terminals for hours viewing such material while others waited to use the terminals. Children accessed adult sexual material. Children and adults accessed extremist political sites and racist material. Librarians around the country tried to satisfy library users, parents, community organizations, civil libertarians, and their own Library Bill of Rights (which opposes restricting access to library materials because of age). Some installed polarizing filters on terminals or built walls around terminals so that the screens were visible only from directly in front (both to protect the privacy of the user and to shield other users and employees from material they find objectionable). Most set time limits on use of terminals. Some librarians asked patrons to stop viewing pornography, just as they would ask someone to stop making noise. Some installed filtering software on all terminals, some on only terminals in the children's section. Some required parental supervision for children using the Internet, and some required written parental permission.

CIPA sought to override these methods. The authors of CIPA attempted to avoid the courts' objections to the CDA and COPA by using the federal government's funding power. CIPA requires that schools and libraries that participate in certain federal programs (receiving federal money for technology) install filtering software on all Internet terminals to block access to sites with child pornography, obscene material, and material "harmful to minors." Of course, many schools and libraries rely on those funds. Civil liberties organizations and the American Library Association sued to block CIPA.[18] The Supreme Court ruled that CIPA does not violate the First Amendment. CIPA does not require the use of filters. It does not impose jail or fines on people who provide content on the Internet. It sets a condition for receipt of certain federal funds. Courts often accept such conditions. The court made it clear that if an adult asks a librarian to disable the filter on a library Internet terminal the adult is using, the librarian must do so. Of course, some adults are unaware of the filter software, unaware that they can legally request it be turned off, or unwilling to call attention to themselves by making the request.

Outside of public schools and libraries, the trend of judicial decisions is to give the Internet First Amendment protection similar to that of print media, that is, the highest degree of protection.

Video games

Violent video games have been the focus of criticism since they began appearing. Some are very gory; some depict murder and torture; some focus on violence against women and members of specific ethnic and religious groups. Are they bad for children? Are they more dangerous than other forms of violence and violent sexism and racism that a minor sees in books or other media? Should we ban them?

Some argue that the interactivity of video games has a more powerful impact on children than passively watching television or reading a violent story. Others point out that children have played at killing each other (cops and robbers, cowboys and Indians) for generations. Does falling down "dead" on the grass compare to the repeated, explosive gore of a video game? At what age is a child mature enough to decide to play a violent video game: 12? 18? Who should decide what games a child plays: parents or legislators? Parents are not always with their children. They regularly worry that peer pressure overrides parental rules and guidance.

A California law banned sale or rental of violent video games to minors. In 2011, the Supreme Court ruled that the law violated the First Amendment. The Court pointed out that violence and gore are common in classic fairy tales (for example, the grim Grimm Brothers), cartoons (Elmer Fudd always shooting at Bugs Bunny), superhero comics, and literature teenagers are required to read in high school. Many video games are extremely disgusting, but the Court said that "disgust is not a valid basis for restricting expression."[19] The Court considered research on the impact of video games on children's feelings of aggression and found that the impacts were small and differed little from the impacts of other media.

Alternatives to censorship

What alternatives to censorship are available to protect children from inappropriate material on the Net (and to shield adults from material that is offensive to them)? Are

Talking about bombs—or farming

Several terrorists who set off bombs in the United States and other countries researched bomb-making techniques on the Internet. Students who carried bombs into schools learned how to make them on the Internet. As far back as 1995, within a few weeks of the bombing of the Oklahoma City federal building, the Senate's terrorism and technology subcommittee held hearings on "The Availability of Bomb Making Information on the Internet." There are many similarities between the controversy about bomb-making information on the Net and the controversy about pornography. As with pornography, bomb-making information was already widely available in traditional media, protected by the First Amendment. It also has legitimate uses. Information about how to make bombs can be found in the print version of the *Encyclopedia Britannica* and in books in libraries and bookstores. The U.S. Department of Agriculture distributed a booklet called the "Blasters' Handbook"—farmers use explosives to remove tree stumps.[20]

Arguing to censor information about bombs on the Internet, Senator Dianne Feinstein said, "There is a difference between free speech and teaching someone to kill."[21] Arguing against censorship, a former U.S. attorney said that "information-plus," (i.e., information used in the commission of a criminal act) is what the law should regulate. Senator Patrick Leahy emphasized that it is "harmful and dangerous *conduct*, not speech, that justifies adverse legal consequences." This was already, in essence, established legal principle outside of cyberspace. There are, of course, existing laws against using bombs to kill people or destroy property, as well as laws against making bombs or conspiring to make them for such purposes.

Congress passed a law mandating 20 years in prison for anyone who distributes bomb-making information knowing or intending that it will be used to commit a crime. Although there have been several incidents since then in which people built and used bombs made with information from the Internet, no one has been tried under this law.[22] It is difficult to determine (and prove) what a person posting the information knows and intends about its uses.

there solutions that do not threaten to diminish free discussion of serious subjects or deny sexually explicit material to adults who want it? As we see for many problems, there are a variety of solutions based on the market, technology, responsibility, and education, as well as on enforcement of existing laws.

The development of software filters is an example of a quick market response to a problem. Many families with children use filtering software (some of which is free). Software filters work in a variety of ways. They can block websites with specific words, phrases, or images. They can block sites according to various rating systems. They can contain long lists of specific sites to block. Parents can choose categories to filter (e.g., sex or violence), add their own list of banned sites, and review a log their child's activity. But filters cannot do a perfect job. In fact, at first, many did a very poor job. They screened out both too much (sites about Middlesex and Essex) and too little (missing some obviously objectionable material). Filters blocked sites containing political discussion and educational material (for example, the home page of a university's biology department and the websites of a candidate for Congress containing statements about abortion and gun control). Filters improved with time, but it is not possible to completely eliminate errors and subjective views about what is too sexual or too violent or too critical of a religion, what medical information is appropriate for children of what age, what is acceptable to say about homosexuality, and so on. None of the solutions we describe in this book for problems generated by new technologies are perfect. They have strengths and weaknesses and are useful in some circumstances and not others. Parents can weigh pros and cons and make their choices. The weaknesses, however—particularly the blocking of legal material—do present a free speech issue when legislators mandate filters or when public institutions use filters.

Wireless carriers set strict "decency" standards for companies providing content for their networks. Their rules are detailed and stricter than what the government can prohibit.[23] Commercial services, online communities, and social networking sites develop policies to protect members. Methods include expelling subscribers who post or email material banned by law or the site's policies, removing offensive material, and aiding law enforcement with investigations of child pornography or attempts to meet and molest children. Social network sites developed technology to trace members who post child pornography. In response to market demand, companies offer online services, websites, and cellphone services targeted to families and children. Some allow subscribers to lock children out of certain areas. Parents can set up accounts without email for their children or set up a specified list of addresses from which their children's accounts can receive email. The video game industry developed a rating system that provides an indication for parents about the amount of sex, profanity, and violence in a game.[24] Some online game sites restrict their offerings to nonviolent games and advertise that policy. Many online services distribute information with tips on how to control what children view. The websites of the

FBI and organizations such as the National Center for Missing and Exploited Children[25] provide information about risks to children and guidelines for reducing them.

Parents have a responsibility to supervise their children and to teach them how to deal with inappropriate material and threats. But technology certainly has changed the risks to children and made the parents' job more difficult. If a young child tried to buy a ticket for an X-rated movie at a movie theater or to buy an adult magazine in a store, a cashier would see the child and refuse (at least, most of the time). In a supermarket or a playground, a parent or other observer might see a "stranger" talking to a child. A potential child molester online is not visible. The home used to be a safe haven from pornography and violent or hateful materials. Parents could relax when a child was playing in his or her bedroom. With Internet connections and cellphones, that is no longer true.

3.2.3 CHILD PORNOGRAPHY AND SEXTING

Child pornography includes pictures or videos of actual minors (children under 18) engaged in sexually explicit conduct.* Laws against creating, possessing, or distributing child pornography predate the Internet. They cover a broad range of images, many of which would not meet the definition of illegally obscene material if the person depicted were an adult.

Production of child pornography is illegal primarily because its production is considered abuse of the actual children, not because of the impact of the content on a viewer. The adults who produce child pornography often coerce or manipulate children into posing or performing. (The mere possession of child pronography does not directly abuse children, but the Supreme Court accepted the ban on possession on the argument that the buyers or users of the images encourage their production.) It is not automatically illegal to make or distribute sexually explicit movies or photos in which an adult actor plays a minor. In other words, the legal basis for child pornography laws is to prevent using, abusing, and exploiting children, not portraying them. Law enforcement agents regularly make arrests for distribution of child pornography by email, chat rooms, social media, and cellphone. They use surveillance, search warrants, sting operations, and undercover investigations to build their cases and make the arrests.

Congress extended the law against child pornography to include "virtual" children, that is, computer-generated images that appear to be minors, as well as other images where real adults appear to be minors. The Supreme Court ruled that this violated the First Amendment. Justice Anthony Kennedy commented that this extension "proscribes the visual depiction of an idea—that of teenagers engaging in sexual activity—that is a fact of modern society and has been a theme in art and literature throughout the ages."[26]

---

* This is a simplification. The laws include more detail and definitions.

However, the Court accepted a later law that provides harsh penalties for certain categories of computer-generated images and cartoon-type images that appear to be a minor.

Sexting means sending sexually suggestive or explicit text or photos, usually by cellphone or social media. The phenomenon we discuss here involves children, particularly teenagers under 18, sending nude or seminude photos of themselves or their boyfriends or girlfriends to each other or to classmates.* This practice is horrifying to parents, who recognize the dangers it poses to their children. One common result of sexting is severe embarrassment and taunting when the pictures become widely distributed. In an extreme case, after an ex-boyfriend redistributed pictures of an 18-year-old girl, she killed herself. Many young people (like many adults) do not think about how quickly something intended for one person or a small group spreads to a large audience, nor how difficult it is to remove something from cyberspace once it is out there. They do not think about the impact for their future personal and career relationships.

Child pornography laws were intended to apply to adults who commit a repugnant abuse of children. But cellphones and sexting led to application of the laws in unanticipated ways. Prosecutors have brought child pornography charges against children for sexting. Possession of child pornography is illegal, so children who have pictures of friends under 18 on their phones that prosecutors think meet the definition of child pornography are potentially in violation. Is sending nude or sexually suggestive photos of oneself a form of expression? Is it foolish and potentially damaging behavior by an immature person that parents and school officials should deal with? Should it be a criminal felony with severe penalties that can include being put in a sex-offender database for many years?

Some prosecutors may see the threat of prosecution as the only tool they have to stop young people from doing something they will strongly regret in the future. Some may be imposing their moral standards on other people's children. In one case, a 14-year-old girl was prosecuted after refusing a deal that required she attend a counseling class and write an essay about her actions. A court ruled that using a threat of prosecution in this way was to compel speech (the essay) and, thus, violated the First Amendment. Tools that might be useful in schools trying to discourage sexting (such as counseling and essays) are not acceptable when forced by the government.

Legislatures in a few states have revised their state's laws in a variety of ways to reduce the penalties for sexting. Details vary. For example, some have made it a misdemeanor, rather than a felony, if a young person sends an illegal photo to another young person of similar age. Some have reduced or eliminated penalties if photos are distributed (among minors) with the consent of the person in the picture. Revising child pornography laws to deal appropriately with sexting is essential, but that alone is not sufficient. Sexting, and especially distributing explicit photos of schoolmates with the intent to embarrass them,

---

* Sexting is certainly not limited to teenagers. At least two members of Congress have resigned over sexting scandals.

are problems that should be addressed through education about the consequences of such actions, parental involvement, school policies, reasonable punishments, and so forth.

3.2.4 Spam

What's the problem?

The term *spam*, in the context of electronic communications, was adopted in the 1990s to mean unsolicited bulk email.* It now applies to text messages, tweets, and phone calls as well. Details of a precise definition, depending on how one defines "bulk" and "unsolicited," can be critical to discussions about how to deal with spam, especially when we consider laws to restrict it.

Spam has infuriated users of the Internet since the 1990s. Most, but not all, spam is commercial advertising. Spam developed because email is extremely cheap compared to printed direct-mail advertising. Some businesses and organizations compile or buy huge lists of email addresses and send their unsolicited messages. Some build lists by using automated software that surfs the Web and collects anything that looks like an email address.

Spam angers people because of both the content and the way it is sent. Content can be ordinary commercial advertising, political advertising, solicitations for funds from nonprofit organizations, pornography and advertisements for it, fraudulent "get rich quick" scams, and scams selling fake or nonexistent products. Topics come in waves, with ads for Viagra, ads for low mortgage rates, promotions for various stocks, and Nigerian refugees who need help getting $30,000,000 out of Africa. Some spammers disguise their

 Spamming for identity theft: Section 5.3

return address so that bounced mail from closed or invalid accounts does not bother them. ISPs filter out email from known spammers, so many disguise the source and use other schemes to avoid filters. Criminal spammers hijack large numbers of computers by spreading viruses that allow the spammer to send huge amounts of spam from the infected machines, called "zombies."

How much spam travels through the Internet? The first case that created an antispam furor involved advertising messages sent by a law firm to 6000 bulletin boards or newsgroups in 1994. At that time, any advertising or postings not directly related to the topic of the group raised the ire of Net users. More recently, one man was accused of running a zombie network that sent billions of emails per day. Another spammer was arrested for clogging Facebook with 27 million spam messages.[27]

Why not just ban spam? We will see some reasons in the next few pages.

---

* Spam is the name of a spiced meat product sold in cans by Hormel Foods. The use of the word in the context of email comes from a Monty Python skit in which some characters repeatedly shouted, "Spam, spam, spam," drowning out other conversation.

Cases and free speech issues

In 1996, about half of the email received at AOL was spam, and a lot of it came from an email advertising service called Cyber Promotions. AOL installed filters to block mail from Cyber Promotions. Cyber Promotions obtained an injunction against AOL's use of filters, claiming AOL violated its First Amendment rights. Thus began the battle over the legal status of spam.

Cyber Promotions' case was weak, and the court soon removed the injunction. Why did AOL have the right to block incoming spam? The spam used AOL's computers, imposing a cost on AOL. AOL's property rights allow it to decide what it accepts on its system. AOL is a membership organization; it can implement policies to provide the kind of environment it believes its members want. Finally, AOL is a private company, not a government institution. On the other side, some civil liberties organizations were uneasy about allowing AOL to filter email because AOL decided what email to block from its members. They argued that because AOL is large, it is a lot like the Post Office, and it should not be allowed to block any mail.

Over the next few years, AOL filed several lawsuits and sought injunctions to stop spammers from sending unsolicited bulk mailings to its members. Notice the subtle shift: Cyber Promotions sought an injunction to stop AOL from filtering out its email. AOL sought injunctions to stop spammers from sending email. Filters do not violate a spammer's freedom of speech, but does an order not to send the mail violate freedom of speech? We listed several arguments why a service provider should be free to filter incoming mail. Do any of the arguments support injunctions against the spammers? One does: the argument that the spam uses the recipient company's property (computer system) against its wishes and imposes a cost on the recipient. AOL and other services won multimillion-dollar settlements from Cyber Promotions and other spammers. But how far does, or should, the owner's control extend? A former Intel employee, Ken Hamidi, maintained a website critical of Intel. He sent six emailings to more than 30,000 Intel employees over a period of less than two years. He disguised his return address, making it difficult for Intel to block his email. Intel sought a court order prohibiting him from sending more email to its employees (at work). Note that in this case the spam was not commercial. Intel argued that freedom of speech gave Hamidi the right to operate his own website, but it did not give him the right to intrude in Intel's property and use its equipment to deliver his messages. Intel argued that the email was a form of trespass. The California Supreme Court ruled in favor of Hamidi. The Court said that Hamidi's bulk emailing was not trespass, because it did not damage Intel's computers or cause economic harm to the company. The dissenting judges argued that Intel's property rights over its computers should allow the company to exclude unwanted email.[28]

Amnesty International has long used its network of thousands of volunteers to flood government officials in various countries with mail when a political prisoner is being tortured or is in imminent danger of execution. Suppose an organization sends the same

An issue for designers and users of filters

We saw that filters are not perfect. They block more or less than the material one wants blocked, and often they block both more and less. If the filter is intended to block sexually explicit material from young children, it might be acceptable to err on the side of blocking some inoffensive material to be sure of preventing the undesirable material from getting through. On the other hand, if the filter is for spam, most people would not mind a few spam messages getting through but would be quite unhappy if some of their nonspam email was thrown away.

email to every member of Congress (or to a list of businesses) each time someone visits the site and clicks to send it. Will we have different points of view about whether this is free speech or spam, depending on how sympathetic we are to the specific organization's message?

Reducing the spam problem

Freedom of speech does not require the intended listener, or message recipient, to listen. Businesses and programmers created a variety of filtering products to screen out spam at the recipient's site, by blocking email from specified addresses, by blocking messages with particular words, and by more sophisticated methods. Many people now see very little spam because their mail service provider filters it out.

Many businesses subscribe to services that provide lists of spammers to block. Aggressive antispam services list not only spammers but also ISPs, universities, businesses, and online services that do not take sufficient action to stop members of their community from sending spam. Such action encourages managers to do something—for example, limit the number of outbound messages from one account. How much discretion should an antispam service have in deciding whom to include on its list of spammers? Harris Interactive, which conducts public opinion surveys by email ("Harris polls"), sued the Mail Abuse Prevention System (MAPS) for including Harris on its blacklist. Harris claimed that the people receiving its email signed up to receive it. MAPS claimed Harris did not meet its standards for assuring the recipients' consent. Harris claimed a competing polling company recommended it for the spammer list.[29] Harris claimed inclusion on the list cut it off from about half of its survey participants and harmed its business. This case illustrates the potential for "gaming" the system by competitors and the differences of opinion that can arise about who is a spammer.

It is interesting to review how attitudes about spam filtering have changed. We saw that when AOL began agressively filtering to block spam, some Internet groups compared the filtering to censorship. Even though AOL was not a government entity, it was large and millions of people received their mail at AOL. People worried that the precedent of a large corporation filtering email for any reason could lead to corporations filtering email because of content they did not like. Now, many advocacy groups and customers of communications services see spam filtering as valuable and essential.

Spam is cheap. Thus, another idea for reducing it is to increase its cost to the sender. Proposals include certified email schemes and schemes in which email senders pay a tiny charge to the recipient for each email message they send. For certified email, the certifier checks out senders who sign up for the service and, for a small charge per message, certifies that their mail is not spam. The certifier makes agreements with ISPs and email service providers that they deliver certified mail to their members, images and links included, without putting the mail through filters. The messages appear in the recipient's mailbox with an indication that they are "certified."

Many groups object to the very idea of charging any fee to send email. For example, Richard Cox of Spamhaus, an international antispam organization, commented that "an e-mail charge will destroy the spirit of the Internet."[30] Critics say charges might reduce use of email by poor people and nonprofit organizations. Critics of certified mail schemes, such as Spamhaus and the Electronic Frontier Foundation, believe they give ISPs incentive not to improve filters, particularly if the service provider gets part of the certification fee. ISPs also would have an incentive to overfilter—that is, to filter out legitimate email so that more senders will need to pay for certification.

Antispam laws

The impact of antispam laws and decisions about their constitutionality can be quite significant. A man convicted for spamming in Virginia was sentenced to nine years in jail. Virginia's law prohibited anonymous, unsolicited, bulk email. The conviction was reversed when the state's Supreme Court ruled that the law violated the First Amendment. The federal CAN-SPAM Act[31] applies to email sent to computers and mobile devices. It targets commercial spam and covers labeling of advertising messages (for easier filtering), opt-out provisions, and methods of generating emailing lists. Commercial messages must include valid mail header information (that is, faking the "From" line to disguise the sender is prohibited) and a valid return address. Deceptive subject lines are prohibited. Criminal penalties apply for some of the more deceptive practices and for sending spam from someone else's computer without authorization (a process that can be accomplished by viruses that take over another computer).[32] In the first application of the law, four people were charged with sending sales pitches for fraudulent weight-loss products and disguising their identities.

Many antispam organizations opposed the CAN-SPAM Act because they preferred to see spam banned altogether (as it is in some countries), rather than legitimized by the regulation. Many businesses supported CAN-SPAM. The law has been helpful in reducing problem spam from legitimate businesses. We can filter it out and we can get off the mailing list. People who send spam that includes fraudulent "get rich quick" schemes or ads for child pornography clearly do not care about what is legal. They are not likely to obey laws to identify themselves. Such laws make it easier to fine or jail them by convicting them of violating antispam regulations in cases where there is insufficient evidence for convictions based on the content of the messages.* Is this a benefit or a threat to free speech and due process?

Spammers continually find new ways around spam blockers. The difficulty of distinguishing spam from real mail with absolute certainty suggests that the cycle of new spam techniques and better blocking techniques will continue. Because antispam laws must avoid conflicts with freedom of speech, and because the most abusive spammers ignore laws, laws can reduce spam but are not likely to eliminate the problem.

3.2.5 CHALLENGING OLD REGULATORY STRUCTURES AND SPECIAL INTERESTS

Most people would not consider ads for wine and real estate on the Web to be offensive material. However, special interest groups tried to remove them. Such groups lobby (often successfully) for laws to restrict uses of new technologies that they see as threats to their income and influence. Most of the cases we discuss here have free speech implications. Several involve regulatory laws that restrict advertising and sales on the Web. Such regulations have noble purposes, such as protecting the public from fraud. They also have the effect of entrenching the already powerful, keeping prices high, and making it more difficult for new and small businesses or independent voices to flourish.

Several companies sell self-help software to assist people in writing wills, premarital agreements, and many other legal documents. The software includes legal forms and instructions for filling them out. It is a typical example of empowering ordinary people and reducing our dependence on expensive experts. A Texas judge banned Quicken legal software from Texas with the argument that the software amounted to practicing law without a Texas license. The Texas legislature later changed its law to exempt software publishers.

When people started publishing online newsletters about certain types of investments, they discovered that they were violating 25-year-old regulations requiring government licenses. License requirements included fees, fingerprinting, a background check, and presenting a list of subscribers on demand to the Commodity Futures Trading Commission (CFTC), the federal agency that administers the regulations. Publishers who did not register with the CFTC could be fined up to $500,000 and jailed up to five years. The regulations were designed for traders who handle other people's money, but the CFTC applied them to people selling investment newsletters or software to analyze commodity futures markets. A federal judge ruled that the CFTC regulations were a prior restraint on speech and violated the First Amendment both for Internet publishers and for traditional newsletter publishers. By raising an issue of free speech on the Web, this case led

---

* Prohibition-era gangster Al Capone went to jail for income-tax evasion because prosecutors could not convict him of other crimes.

to termination of a long-standing unconstitutional restraint of free speech in traditional media as well.[33]

The Web provides the potential for reducing prices for many products by eliminating the "middleman." Small producers, who cannot afford expensive distributors or wholesalers, can sell directly to consumers nationwide. But not if the business was a small winery. Thirty states in the U.S. had laws restricting the shipping of out-of-state wines directly to consumers. The laws protected large wholesaling businesses that typically get 18%–25% of the price and buy mostly from large wineries or those that sell expensive wines. The laws also protected state revenue; state governments cannot collect sales taxes on many out-of-state sales. State governments argued that the laws prevented sales to minors. This was a weak argument in states that permit direct shipments from in-state wineries. New York also banned *advertising* out-of-state wines directly to consumers in the state. A winery that advertised its wines on the Web ran a risk because the website is accessible to consumers in New York. Winery operators challenged the New York wine law, arguing that it unconstitutionally restricted freedom of speech, interfered with interstate commerce, and discriminated against out-of-state businesses.[34] The Supreme Court ruled that bans on out-of-state shipments directly to consumers were unconstitutional.

The governments of California and New Hampshire attempted to require that operators of websites like ForSaleByOwner.com get state real estate licenses in those states because they list homes for sale within the states. The license requirements are irrelevant and expensive for such sites, and state laws allow newspapers to publish real estate ads, both in the papers themselves and on their websites, without a real estate license. Federal courts ruled that these requirements for real estate licenses violate the First Amendment rights of website operators. The rulings protect the same First Amendment rights for websites as for older media and also reduce the powers of a special interest (in this case, real estate brokers) to restrict competition.

In France, the tax rate on ebooks is 19.6%. The tax on printed books is 5.5%. A law in France prohibits stores from giving big discounts on printed books. Small book sellers asked the French government for similar regulation for ebooks. While I was writing this, the French government planned to reduce the ebook tax but delayed the reduction. Perhaps the popularity of ebooks and discounts will lead to reversal of the old law restricting discounts of printed books.

3.3 Posting, Selling, and Leaking Sensitive Material

> *Free speech is enhanced by civility.*
> —Tim O'Reilly[35]

Most of our discussion so far focused on censorship laws, laws prohibiting distribution of or access to certain kinds of material. Legal material that could be sensitive in some way raises social and ethical issues. Examples include legal "adult" entertainment material, Nazi materials, personal information about other people, and maps and other information that might be of use to terrorists. Intentional publishing of leaked (perhaps stolen) sensitive material for political or social purposes raises social and ethical issues (as well as legal issues). In this section, we consider some of these.

Policies of large companies

Policy reversals by several large websites illustrate some of the dilemmas about posting legal material that is offensive to many people. When Yahoo expanded its online store for adult material (erotica, sex videos, and so forth—all legal), many users complained. Critics objected that because Yahoo is a large, mainstream company, its action gave acceptability to pornography. Yahoo reversed policy and removed ads for adult material. This brought complaints from other people that the company "caved in" to pressure from its mainstream advertisers and users. Some people believe that it is wrong for a large, influential business, like Google, Craigslist, Amazon, or Yahoo, for example, to ban any legal material from its services because the effect is similar to government censorship.

Various online companies have policies against posting hate material, bomb-making information, and other unpleasant or risky material. Apple rejects smartphone apps it finds objectionable; it will not sell them in its app store. Many auctions sites prohibit sales of some kinds of legal products. Large retailers restrict sales to minors of video games with violence, nudity, and sex. Does the legal right of adults to purchase or read something (a negative right, to be free from arrest) impose an ethical or social obligation on a business to provide it? The main justification for an affirmative answer is, as we mentioned above, equating the large social impact of a large company with censorship. On the other hand, in a free society where the government does not decide what we can read or view, it is more important for sellers and individuals to take seriously their role and responsibility in deciding what material they will make available. Also, a private company has property rights in its business that include making decisions about what to sell. If most of the public considers some material inappropriate for mainstream websites and stores, then response to customer pressure will probably keep it from such venues. It will still be available from specialty sites and dealers.

What about search engine providers? Do they have a social or ethical obligation to provide complete search results to all queries, or do they have a social or ethical obligation to omit very offensive sites from search results? The people who set policy in such companies face difficult questions. How should a search engine respond to a search for "nude pictures of college students"? How should it respond to a search for graphic pictures of torture by a government or by terrorists? Search engines provide an extraordinarily valuable and fundamental service. We do not want them to discriminate against unpopular opinions or most forms of controversial material. We want to find news and, sometimes, unpleasant facts. Yet recognition of antisocial or risky uses of some material might lead to ethical decisions to decline to present it prominently, or at all.

A website with risks

Consider websites an individual or small organization might set up. To make the discussion concrete, we consider a site about suicide for terminally ill patients in constant, severe pain. The points we raise here apply to other kinds of sensitive information as well. What should the site organizers consider?* First, even if the site is not advertised, search engines will find it. Depressed teenagers and depressed adults will find it. What we put on a public website is public, available to everyone worldwide. The organizers should think about potential risks and research them. Then what? One option is to decide not to set up the site at all. Suppose the site organizers decide to proceed because they believe their plan has significant value for the intended audience. What can they do to reduce risks? Perhaps require a password to access the site. How would someone obtain a password? Would a simple waiting period reduce the risk for temporarily depressed people? Would the password requirement discourage access by intended users because of privacy concerns? Do you have an ethical responsibility to avoid helping 15-year-olds commit suicide? Can you assume they would find the information to do so somewhere else and that the responsibility to decide is theirs? Do you have an ethical responsibility to help a terminally ill person in pain to commit suicide? Or will your site offer a service some people want but with risks to others that you need to minimize?

People who post risky material have an ethical responsibility to seriously consider questions such as these. The answers are sometimes not obvious or easy. Freedom of speech is not the deciding factor.

Whether thinking about setting up a website with sensitive information or thinking about passing along a funny but embarrassing video of a friend, we sum up a few guidelines: Consider potential risks. Consider unintended readers or users. Consider ways to prevent access by unintended users. Remember that it can be difficult to withdraw material once released.

Leaks

The Web is a convenient and powerful tool for whistleblowers. People can anonymously post documents and make them available to the world. Small organizations and large news companies set up websites specifically to receive and publish leaked documents. Corruption and abuse of power in businesses and governments are common topics. Some leaks serve valuable social purposes. On the other hand, because it is easy to leak a large cache of someone else's documents, people sometimes do so carelessly. Sensitive material, leaked irresponsibly, can harm innocent people.

Throughout, we should remember that leaking begins with a strong ethical case against it. Leaked documents are often obtained by hacking into someone else's computer or by an insider who violates a confidentiality agreement. The documents belong to

---

* Some people consider suicide itself, and any encouragement of it, to be immoral. For the sake of this discussion, we assume the people setting up the site do not.

someone; they are being stolen or used without the owner's permission. A leak can cause serious damage to a person or organization without their doing anything wrong. Freedom of speech and press do not legitimate stealing files and publishing them, nor do they excuse acting irresponsibly. This does not mean that leaking is always wrong. It means that the reasons for leaking the material must be strong enough to overcome the ethical arguments against it, and the publisher of the leaked material must handle it responsibly.

To analyze the ethics of specific leaks, we consider the type of material released, the value to society, and the risks to society and innocent individuals. We also look at additional issues related to release of very large numbers of documents and some responsibilities of anyone setting up a site to accept and publish leaked material.

Documents that include significant evidence of serious wrongdoing are reasonable candidates for leaks. Wrongdoing might be corruption; political repression; mass murder by armies in international (or internal) wars; serious violations of laws or professional ethics; safety lapses in large systems that affect the public; dishonest practices by a business, scientists, or police; and coverups of such activities—to cite just a very few categories. Another class of documents describe internal discussions and decision making in businesses, organizations, or governments, and candid reports on products and events. There is justification for leaking these if they provide evidence of wrongdoing or risk, but not merely to embarrass people or damage a competitor or organization one disapproves of.

In this discussion, we use two controversial examples that are too broad and complex to fully analyze here. They help to illustrate the questions to consider when evaluating leaks, and—I hope—they generate more discussion. One is the large set of U.S. military and diplomatic documents that WikiLeaks made public.* The other, sometimes called "Climategate," is a collection of emails and other documents from the Climate Research Unit at the University of East Anglia in England, one of the major centers of research on global warming.

The Climategate emails leaked in 2009 and 2011 showed that researchers at the University of East Anglia pursued a variety of methods to deny access to their temperature data by scientists who question some aspects of global warming. Denying access to the data is a violation of scientific practice. The emails also described efforts to stop scientific journals from publishing papers by scientists who are considered skeptics about global warming and to attack the reputations of some of those scientists. Investigations by the British government and other groups concluded that the emails did not show scientific misconduct, but the research center had broken Britain's Freedom of Information Act. The reports criticized various procedures the research group used but not its scientific conclusions. Some emails discussed criticisms and uncertainties related to details of the argument that human activity causes global warming. Researchers discuss such uncertain-

---

* Earlier, a lot of the material WikiLeaks made public fit reasonable criteria for justifiable, or admirable, leaks. Examples include documents exposing corruption in various governments and exposing murders by police in Kenya.

ties in papers and conferences, but news reports often exclude them. Is it important for the public to know what is in the emails? What criteria argue for or against these leaks?[36]

WikiLeaks released U.S. military documents related to the wars in Iraq and Afghanistan, including videos of shooting incidents. When a long, costly war is controversial, does the public have a right to see the internal reports and vivid video that can inform the debate? Wikileaks released a large set of confidential U.S. diplomatic cables that included, among much else, discussions of the personalities of foreign leaders. Does the value of informing the public outweigh the value of confidential, frank internal discussion when developing diplomatic policies?

When evaluating the ethics of leaking documents on political or highly politicized issues, it can be difficult to make judgments that are independent of our views on the issues themselves. Some people believe that our judgments of the leaks should *not* be independent of the issues: If we oppose U.S. foreign policy, the WikiLeaks leaks are good. If we are skeptical about global warming, the climate research leaks are good. Of course, if we hold the opposite views, we might evaluate the leaks oppositely. This does not help us to develop good criteria for evaluating the ethics of leaking and for guiding us if we come to have access to sensitive data. We can make a much stronger case for ethical criteria by which to evaluate leaks if we are willing to apply the same criteria to leaking similar material on both sides of a political issue.

Potentially dangerous leaks

WikiLeaks released a secret U.S. government cable listing critical sites, such as telecommunications hubs, dams, pipelines, supplies of critical minerals, manufacturing complexes, and so on, where damage or disruption would cause significant harm. Some might defend publication of the list by arguing that it encourages better protection of the sites or that terrorists already know about the sites, but the risks seem to overwhelm any public value of this leak. Other documents detailed discussions between U.S. government officials and an oppostion leader in a country with a very repressive government. Some cables named whistleblowers, confidential informants, human rights activists, intelligence officers, and Chinese people (in business, academia, and the Chinese government) who provided information about social and political conditions in China. The release of these documents put those people at risk. Other documents named people who escaped from repressive countries, potentially endangering their families.* Some leaks do not endanger lives, but they infringe privacy or threaten people's jobs, reputations, freedom, and other values. Those who provide the material and those who publish it have an ethical responsibility to avoid or minimize harming innocent people.[37]

---

* There were indications that names were removed in some cases. The leaker of the Climategate emails used automated software to remove personal contact information and other personal information in the emails (though some remained, according to some reports).

Releasing a huge mass of documents

The U.S. government documents that WikiLeaks made public included approximately 250,000 diplomatic cables* and thousands of other documents. The Climategate leaks included thousands of documents. Did the leakers review and evaluate all the documents they released to be sure they met reasonable criteria to justify the leaks? Should they have? In the spirit of the Web, leakers can now let the public search through the documents for those of special interest. This can be valuable, but it can be wrong. Recall that an important justification for leaking documents that belong to someone else is that the leaker knows they contain information that the public should see. If the vast majority of the information does not meet the criteria for ethical leaking, then it may be hard to justify publishing the entire set of documents. The documents might be interesting to the public, but in most cases that is not sufficient justification. On the other hand, selective disclosure can distort information by presenting it without context. The best choice might not be easy.

Privacy and confidentiality are important to individuals and to the legitimate functioning of businesses and governments. Privacy and confidentiality are not absolute rights, but they are significant values. Leakers have as much ethical reponsibility to respect privacy (even for people they dislike or disagree with) as do governments and businesses. Thus, justification for overriding privacy and publishing confidential documents should be strong and reasonably specific.

Leaking of government documents is a special case. In some ways it is more justifiable to leak or publish government documents; in other ways less justifiable. The public has a reasonable claim to a right to know what is being done in its name and with its money. On the other hand, criminal investigations and national security often require secrecy. Many states and free countries have laws requiring disclosure of certain public records and laws such as the Freedom of Information Act that allow public access to government records in many situations. The legal processes can be tedious and ineffective sometimes, but the processes should be tried, if they apply, before resorting to hacking to get files or obtaining them from an insider. Sometimes, leaks may be the only way to expose corruption and coverups.

Responsibilities of operators of websites for leaks

Suppose a person or organization decides to establish a site to publish leaked documents that serve an important public purpose. In addition to giving serious consideration to the various points we have raised, the site operators have responsibilities to avoid abuse of the site. The site must have sufficient security to protect the whistleblowers—the people who supply the documents. The operators should have a well-thought-out policy about how to handle requests or demands from law enforcement agencies (of various countries) for

---

* After Wikileaks released selected cables, the entire set was made public on the Web, either accidentally or intentionally. Either way, failure to protect the documents was a failure of responsibility.

the identity of a person supplying documents. The intent of some leaks is to sabotage a competitor or a political opponent. Verification of the authenticity and validity of leaked documents can be difficult, but it is a responsibility of the site operators. Serious harm to innocent individuals, businesses, economies, and communities can result from publishing inaccurate or forged documents and sometimes from authentic but maliciously leaked documents.

As a German newspaper observed, "When delicate information is at stake, great prudence is demanded so that the information doesn't fall into the wrong hands and so that people are not hurt."[38] Freedom of speech and of the press leave us with the ethical responsibility for what we say and publish.

3.4 Anonymity

The Colonial press was characterized by irregular appearance, pseudonymous invective, and a boisterous lack of respect for any form of government.

—"Science, Technology, and the First Amendment," U.S. Office of Technology Assessment

Common Sense

From the description quoted above, the Colonial press—the press the authors of the First Amendment to the U.S. Constitution found it so important to protect—had a lot in common with the Internet, including controversy about anonymity.

Jonathan Swift published his political satire *Gulliver's Travels* anonymously. Thomas Paine's name did not appear on the first printings of *Common Sense*, the book that roused support for the American Revolution. The Federalist Papers, published in newspapers in 1787 and 1788, argued for adoption of the new U.S. Constitution. The authors, Alexander Hamilton, James Madison, and John Jay, had already served the newly free confederation of states in important roles. Jay later became chief justice of the Supreme Court, Hamilton the first secretary of the Treasury, and Madison president. But when they wrote the Federalist Papers, they used a pseudonym, Publius. Opponents of the Constitution, those who believed it gave too much power to the federal government, used pseudonyms as well. In the 19th century, when it was not considered proper for women to write books, writers such as Mary Ann Evans and Amantine Lucile Aurore Dupin published under male pseudonyms, or pen names (George Eliot and George Sand). Prominent professional and academic people use pseudonyms to publish murder mysteries, science fiction, or other nonscholarly work, and some writers—for example, the iconoclastic H. L. Mencken—used pseudonyms for the fun of it.

Positive uses of anonymity

> *Anonymous pamphleteering is not a pernicious, fraudulent practice,*
> *but an honorable tradition of advocacy and of dissent. Anonymity is*
> *a shield from the tyranny of the majority.*
>
> —U.S. Supreme Court

In the United States, the First Amendment protects political speech, but there are still many ways in which the government can retaliate against its critics. There are also many personal reasons why someone might not want to be known to hold certain views. Anonymity provides protection against retaliation and embarrassment. On the Internet, people talk about personal topics such as health, gambling habits, problems with teenage children, religion, and so on. Many people use pseudonyms ("handles," aliases, or screen names) to keep their real identity private. Victims of rape and of other kinds of violence and abuse and users of illegal drugs who are trying to quit are among those who benefit from a forum where they can talk candidly without giving away their identity. (Traditional in-person support and counseling groups use only first names, to protect privacy.) Whistleblowers, reporting on unethical or illegal activities where they work, may choose to release information anonymously. In wartime and in countries with oppressive governments, anonymity can be a life-or-death issue.

Businesses provide a variety of sophisticated tools and services that enable us to send email and surf the Web anonymously. Reporters, human rights activists, and ordinary people use anonymous email to protect themselves. The founder of a company that provided anonymous Web surfing services said the company developed tools to help people in Iran, China, and Saudi Arabia get around their governments' restrictions on Internet access.[40] Many people use anonymous Web browsers to thwart the efforts of businesses to collect information about their Web activity and build dossiers for marketing purposes.

We might think the main benefit of anonymizing services is protection for individuals —protecting privacy, protecting against identity theft and consumer profiling, and protecting against oppressive governments. However, businesses, law enforcement agencies, and government intelligence services are also major customers. A business might want to keep its research and planning about new products secret from competitors. If competitors can get logs of websites that a company's employees visit, they might be able to figure out what the company is planning. Anonymous Web surfing aids law enforcement investigations. Suppose law enforcement agents suspect a site contains child pornography, terrorist information, copyright-infringing material, or anything else relevant to an investigation. If they visit the site from their department computers, they might be blocked or see a bland page with nothing illegal.* Also, when law enforcement agents go "under-

---

* Websites can determine the IP addresses (that is, the sequence of numbers that identifies a particular domain or computer on the Web) of a visitor and can block access from specified addresses or put up alternate pages for those visitors.

Anonymous remailer services

Johan Helsingius set up the first well-known anonymous email service in Finland in 1993. (Users were not entirely anonymous; the system retained identifying information.) Helsingius originally intended his service for users in the Scandinavian countries. However, the service was extremely popular and grew to an estimated 500,000 users worldwide. Helsingius became a hero to dissidents in totalitarian countries and to free speech and privacy supporters everywhere. He closed his service in 1996 after the Church of Scientology and the government of Singapore took action to obtain the names of people using it. By then, many other similar services had become available.

To send anonymous email using a "re-mailer" service, one sends the message to the remailer, where the return address is stripped off and the message is re-sent to the intended recipient. Messages can be routed through many intermediate destinations to more thoroughly obscure their origins. If someone wants to remain anonymous but receive replies, he or she can use a service where a coded ID number is attached to the message when the remailer sends it. The ID assigned by the remailer is a pseudonym for the sender, which the remailer stores. Replies go to the remailer site, which forwards them to the original person.

Some anonymity services use encryption schemes to prevent even the company that operates them from identifying the user.

cover" and pretend to be a member or potential victim of an online criminal group, they do not want their IP address to expose them. A senior CIA official explained the CIA's use of anonymity services online: "We want to operate anywhere on the Internet in a way that no one knows the CIA is looking at them."[41]

Negative uses of anonymity

We are not exempt from ordinary ethics and laws merely because we use the Internet or sign comments with an alias rather than a real name.

Anonymity in cyberspace protects criminal and antisocial activities. People use it for fraud, harassment, and extortion, to distribute child pornography, to libel or threaten others with impunity, to steal confidential business documents or other proprietary information, and to infringe copyrights. Anonymous postings can spread false rumors that seriously damage a business, manipulate stock, or incite violence. Anonymity makes it difficult to track wrongdoers. Like encryption, anonymity technology poses challenges to law enforcement.

Anonymity can mask illegal surveillance by government agencies—or legal but repressive surveillance in unfree countries. The CIA helped fund an anonymizer start-up company. The company's anonymity service had flaws that made it possible to determine a user's identity. The company had announced that the CIA had thoroughly reviewed the product, leading to speculation that the CIA knew about the flaws and was happy to have a company offering an anonymizing service that the CIA could circumvent.[42]

Is anonymity protected?

For those not using true anonymity services, secrecy of our identity in cyberspace depends both on the privacy policies of service providers and the sites we visit—and on the laws and court decisions about granting subpoenas for disclosure. How well protected are our real identities? How strongly should they be protected?

A business or organization can get a subpoena ordering an ISP to disclose a person's real identity. In many cases, businesses seek names of people who post criticism, protected by the First Amendment, but who might be employees whom the business would fire. Free speech advocates argue that judges should examine the individual case and determine if the evidence is strong enough that the organization requesting the identity is likely to win a lawsuit—and only then issue a subpoena for the person's real name. Some recommend that ISPs be required to notify a member when the ISP receives a subpoena for the member's identity, so the person has an opportunity to fight a subpoena in court. These suggestions can help protect criticism while holding people responsible for illegal speech.

Because of its potential to shield criminal activity or because they consider it incompatible with politeness and netiquette (online etiquette), some services and online communities choose to discourage or prohibit anonymity. On the other hand, websites that host debate on controversial issues or discussion of socially sensitive topics often consider anonymity to be a reasonable way to protect privacy and encourage open, honest discussion. If those responsible for individual services and websites make policy decisions about anonymity, the policies can be flexible and diverse, adapted to specific services and clienteles.

Many legal issues about anonymity are similar to those in the law enforcement controversies we discussed in Chapter 2. Law enforcement agencies have been able to trace many criminal suspects through the Web (including members of the hacking group called Anonymous). Should it be the responsibility of law enforcement to develop tools to find criminals who hide behind anonymity, or should the task be made easier by requiring that we identify ourselves? Does the potential for harm by criminals who use anonymity to hide from law enforcement outweigh the loss of privacy and restraint on freedom of speech for honest people who use anonymity responsibly? Is anonymity an important protection against possible abuse of government power? Should people have the right to use available tools, including anonymizers, to protect their privacy? We can send hardcopy mail without a return address. Should there be more restrictions on anonymity on the Net than in other contexts?

> *An instance of the inexplicable conservatism and arrogance of the*
> *Turkish customs authorities was recently evidenced by the prohibition*
> *of the importation of typewriters into the country. The reason advanced*
> *by the authorities for this step is that typewriting affords no clew to*
> *the author, and that therefore in the event of seditious or opprobrious*

*pamphlets or writings executed by the typewriter being circulated
it would be impossible to obtain any clew by which the operator of
the machine could be traced . . . . The same decree also applies to
mimeograph and other similar duplicating machines and mediums.*

—*Scientific American*, July 6, 1901[43]

3.5   The Global Net: Censorship and Political Freedom

*The coffee houses emerged as the primary source of news and rumor.
In 1675, Charles II, suspicious as many rulers are of places where the
public trades information, shut the coffee houses down.*

—Peter L. Bernstein[44]

3.5.1   Tools for Communication, Tools for Oppression

Authoritarian governments have taken steps to cut, or seriously reduce, the flow of information and opinion throughout history.* The vibrant communication made possible by the Internet threatens governments in countries that lack political and cultural freedom. For a long time, the "conventional wisdom" among users and observers of the Internet was that it is a protection against censorship and a tool for increased political freedom. Email and fax machines played a significant role during the collapse of the Soviet Union and the democracy demonstrations in China's Tiananmen Square. Websites with content that is illegal in one country can be set up in some other country. People in countries that censor news can access information over the Web from elsewhere. Facebook and cellphones were key tools in organizing the 2011 Arab Spring. Dissidents in Iran, Vietnam, various Middle Eastern countries, and elsewhere use Skype to communicate because of its strong encryption. There are many more examples.

Unfortunately, but not surprisingly, oppressive governments learned and adopted countermeasures to block the flow of information. They use sophisticated interception and surveillance technologies to spy on their citizens more thoroughly than before. In the rest of this section, we describe censorship and interception tools that oppressive regimes (and some democracies) use.

In countries such as China and Saudi Arabia, where the national government owns the Internet backbone (the communications lines and computers through which people access information), the governments install their own computers between their people and the

---

* In Poland, for example, before the communist government fell in 1989, it was illegal to make a photocopy without permission from government censors. Other governments have banned satellite dishes and residential telephones.

outside world. They use sophisticated firewalls and filters to block what they do not want their people to see. The government of Saudi Arabia blocks pornography and gambling, as many countries might, but it also blocks sites on the Bahai faith, the Holocaust, and religious conversion of Muslims to other faiths. It blocks sites with information about anonymizers, tools to thwart filters, and encryption.

Turkey banned YouTube for about two years. Pakistan banned Internet telephony. Burma (Myanmar) banned use of the Internet or creation of Web pages without official permission. It banned posting of material about politics, as well as posting of any material deemed by the government to be harmful to its policies. (Under an earlier law, possession of an unauthorized modem or satellite dish was punishable by a jail term of up to 15 years.) Many countries in the Middle East limit Internet access. Vietnam uses filtering software to find and block anticommunist messages coming from other countries.*

Some countries ban Skype. Others subvert it. Before the revolution in Egypt in 2011, the Egyptian government, for example, used spyware to intercept Skype communications. They did not break Skype's encryption scheme. Instead, it appears they planted spyware on people's computers that intercepted a communication before it was encrypted on the sender's computer or after it was decrypted on the recipient's computer. During the revolution, the government temporarily shut down the Internet and cellphone service entirely.

In the 1990s, when fewer people used the Web, the Chinese government required users of the Internet to register with the police. In China and other long-unfree countries, governments are struggling with the difficulties of modernizing their economy and technology while maintaining tight control over information. Now, with hundreds of millions of Web users, the government strictly controls and censors what people read and what they post. Chinese regulations prohibit "producing, retrieving, duplicating and spreading information that may hinder public order." Banned or censored sites and topics have included Facebook, Google, the *New York Times*, discussion of democracy, religious sites, human rights organizations, news and commentary about Taiwan and Tibet, information about censorship (and how to evade it), economic news, and reports of major accidents or natural disasters and outbreaks of diseases. The government blocked both the Chinese-language and English-language Wikipedia sites for about a year. Thousands of censors monitor websites. When Chinese citizens began texting to communicate about banned topics, the government set up a system to filter the messages.[45] After ethnic protests turned violent in one region, China cut communications, then blocked Internet access in the region for 10 months.

The government of Iran, at various times, blocked the sites of amazon.com, Wikipedia, the *New York Times*, and YouTube. It also blocked a site advocating the end of the

---

* Where the technology has not caught up, governments restrict old communications media. A rival of Zimbabwe's president Robert Mugabe in Zimbabwe's 2001 presidential election was charged with possession of an unlicensed two-way radio.

practice of stoning women. Reporters Without Borders said that Iran blocked access to more than five million websites in recent years. Generally, the government says it blocks sites to keep out decadent Western culture. Iran also jams satellite TV broadcasts. The government uses sophisticated online surveillance tools and trained cyber police to spy on dissidents. Their system examines individual packets of email, phone conversations, images, social-network communications, and so forth.

In some countries, government agents, using social media, pretend to be dissidents and distribute information about planned protests; the police arrest anyone who comes. Some governments (e.g., Tunisia and Libya before the revolutions in 2011) intercepted communications and used spyware on sites such as Facebook and Yahoo to collect passwords, find the names of dissident bloggers, and take down pages critical of the government. Some governments (e.g., China, Iran, Russia, Vietnam) ban or discourage email services and social networking sites based in the West and set up their own—which, of course, they control.[46] As we will see in Section 3.5.2, restrictive governments are increasingly using their leverage over companies that want to do business in their countries to enforce censorship requirements and other content standards.

Will the Internet and related communications technologies be tools for increasing political freedom, or will they give more power to governments to spy on, control, and restrict their people?

> *The office of communications is ordered to find ways to ensure that the use of the Internet becomes impossible. The Ministry for the Promotion of Virtue and Prevention of Vice is obliged to monitor the order and punish violators.*
>
> —Excerpt from the Taliban edict banning all Internet use in Afghanistan, 2001[47]

3.5.2   AIDING FOREIGN CENSORS AND REPRESSIVE REGIMES

> *Freedom of expression isn't a minor principle that can be pushed aside when dealing with a dictatorship.*
>
> —Reporters Without Borders[48]

Providing services, obeying local laws

Search engine companies, social media companies, and news and entertainment companies based in free countries offer services in countries with strict censorship and repressive governments. To operate within a country, companies must follow the laws of the country. What are the trade-offs between providing services to the people and complying with the government's censorship requirements? To what extent does, or should, the prospect of a huge business opportunity in a new country affect a company's decision? How do companies deal with the censorship requirements? What are their ethical responsibilities?

The Chinese sites of Yahoo and MSN comply with local law and omit news stories that offend the government. Microsoft said it censored terms like "freedom" and "democracy" on its Chinese portal. Microsoft also shut down a Chinese journalist's blog on its MSN Spaces site that criticized the Chinese government.[49] Yahoo provided information to the Chinese government that helped identify at least two people who were then jailed for pro-democracy writing. Yahoo said it was required to comply with Chinese law and the company had not been told the reason for the government request for the information.

To operate in China, the Chinese government requires Skype to work in a joint venture with a Chinese communications company (TOM), use a modified version of the Skype software, and filter out sensitive topics from text chat. According to a study by a Canadian university, the modified software allowed widespread surveillance, and TOM stored information from millions of messages.

Google has long promoted the ideal of access to information. Google held out longer than some companies, refusing to censor its search engine, although it had taken some steps toward restricting access to information in China. In 2006, Google disappointed many free speech and human rights advocates by introducing a Chinese version in China, google.cn, that would comply with Chinese law. Its search results did not show sites with banned content. Google concluded that the company could not provide a high level of service in China without a local presence. Thus, the agreement to operate in China and block material the government considers sensitive was a decision that some access is better than no access. Google co-founder Sergey Brin, who was born in the Soviet Union and experienced totalitarian government, was uneasy with the 2006 censoring decision. Google stopped operating the censored search engine in 2010. The company withdrew most operations from China but offered its search service through Hong Kong, which, though part of China, has different laws. The main impetus for the change was a highly sophisticated hack attack originating in China on Google and about 30 other companies. A primary goal of the attack appeared to be access to Gmail accounts of Chinese human rights activists, angering Brin and others at Google. Google's initial refusal to censor, its reversal in 2006, and its reversal again in 2010 illustrate the difficulty of deciding how to deal with repressive governments. Later, Google increased operations in China not subject to censorship, such as product searching and the Android operating system.

When U.S. or other non-Chinese companies set up branches in China and comply with restrictive laws, should we view them as providing more access to information in China than would otherwise exist, albeit not as much as is technically possible? Should we view them as appropriately respecting the culture and laws of the host country? Should we view them as partners in the Chinese government's ethically unacceptable restrictions on debate and access to information by its citizens?

Mark Zuckerberg, CEO of Facebook, suggested that the advantages of social networking in China outweigh the restrictions. We can view this argument, similar to the arguments from other companies for complying with demands of authoritarian governments, as a utilitarian argument. If a company turns over the names of people who violate censorship laws, the government arrests a small number of dissidents, but a very large number of people benefit from the increased services and communications. If one considers longer-term effects, however, one must consider that the work of a small number of dissidents can have a huge impact on the freedom of the society as a whole. One can make other utilitarian arguments (strong and weak). The arrest of a dissident might spur a protest ultimately bringing more freedom—or a brutal crackdown. A rights-based ethical system might accept providing a search or social media service that is somewhat limited. The people have the right (ethical, even if not legal) to seek and share information, but the service provider is not ethically obligated to provide it 100%. However, a rights-base view tells us it is wrong to help jail a person for expressing his views on politics or for criticizing the government. Should companies draw a line, perhaps agreeing to restrict access to information but refusing to disclose information that a government can use to jail someone for publishing his or her views? A government might need to identify a person whom it suspects of stalking, fraud, posting child pornography, or other crimes. A service provider might want to provide information in such criminal cases. If the government does not disclose the reason for a request, or is dishonest about the reason, how can a service provider make an ethical decision?

> *We're allowing too much, maybe, free speech in countries that haven't experienced it before.*
>
> —Adam Conner, a Facebook lobbyist[50]

> *Don't be evil.*
>
> —Google's informal corporate motto

Selling surveillance tools

It is perhaps not surprising that repressive governments intercept communications and filter Internet content. It is disturbing that companies in Western democracies (including England, Germany, France, and the United States) sell them the tools to do so. Companies sell governments sophisticated tools to filter Internet content, to hack cellphones and computers, to block text messages, to collect and analyze massive amounts of Internet data, to plant spyware and other malware (malicious software), to monitor social networks, and to track cellphone users. The companies say the tools are for criminal investigations (as well as detecting and filtering undesirable content) and do not violate the laws of the country using them. Of course, countries with repressive governments have criminals and terrorists too. Do we trust these governments to use the tools only against the bad guys, in ways consistent with human rights? Is it ethical for companies in free countries to sell the tools to repressive governments?

We don't really get into asking, "Is this in the public interest?"

—An organizer of a trade show for companies selling hacking and interception gear to governments[51]

3.5.3 SHUTTING DOWN COMMUNICATIONS IN FREE COUNTRIES

Governments in relatively unfree countries that tightly control communications shut down access to the Internet or shut down cellphone service now and then. These events evoke criticism in the free world, where few expected it could happen. Then the British government and some U.S. cities considered it, and the transit system in San Francisco blocked cellphone service for a few hours, raising new issues for communications in free countries. Giving governments authority to shut down communications poses obvious threats to freedom of speech, ordinary activities, and political liberty. Is it reasonable in limited situations when public safety is at risk? Does shutting communication services in free countries give excuses to dictators? Can we make a clear distinction between short-term responses to violent mobs in free countries and censorship and repression of political discussion in unfree countries? As background for thinking about these questions, we consider the incidents in Britain and the United States.

Mobs of hooligans (that old-fashioned word seems to fit) rampaged through neighborhoods in London and other British cities setting fires, looting businesses, and beating up people who tried to protect themselves or their property. They planned and coordinated their attacks using cellphones, Twitter, BlackBerry Messenger, and similar tools. During the violence, people in the government (and others) argued that Research In Motion should shut down BlackBerry Messenger. (It did not.) After the riots, the British government considered seeking legislation authorizing it to shut down communications systems such as social media and messaging systems in such situations. It decided, at least for the time being, not to seek such power. Several U.S. cities that experienced similiar coordinated violence considered laws to authorize government agencies to block communications, but none passed such laws.

Shortly after the violence in England, the Bay Area Rapid Transit system (BART) in the San Francisco Bay Area shut off wireless service in some of its subway stations after learning of a plan to "use mobile devices to coordinate . . . disruptive activities and communicate about the location and number of BART Police."[52] BART owns the communications equipment; it said its contracts with cell service companies allow it to shut off the service when it thinks necessary. The managers of a private business, expecting violence on or near their property, have the right to shut off their wireless service; refuse entry to anyone carrying, say, a baseball bat; or close up if they think it a wise measure to protect the public and the business. If BART were a private company, there would be arguments on both sides of the question of whether its action was wise, but it would not raise the First Amendment issues of a government-ordered shutdown. (Some of the arguments, and the distinction between government and private action, are similar to those concerning the right of a computer service to filter out spam; see Section 3.2.4.)

BART is a government agency, but it shut down its own wireless service in its own space. Did it threaten freedom of speech, or was it a legitimate safety decision?

What can be done, short of shutting down communications, to reduce the use of such systems for planning mass violence? The membership policies of various social media companies ban threats of violence. Facebook, for example, monitors posts to enforce its ban. The companies can close the accounts of those who violate the agreements, but it is unlikely that such companies would be able to act quickly enough to stop a violent event. In past riots, police collected information from social media and phones of people they arrested, and in doing so they learned of plans for more violent attacks and were prepared to prevent them. While helpful, this also seems like weak protection. But what are the consequences of giving governments the authority to shut down communications? Police can abuse this power, preventing legitimate protests and demonstrations, as repressive governments do. A large-scale shut down would inconvenience (and possibly harm) innocent people. In the United States, the Supreme Court would probably declare unconstitutional a law that authorized a government agency to order a private communications service to shut down. What else can be done?

> *It may be BART's equipment, but that doesn't mean that they have*
> *the freedom to do whatever they want to with it.*
>
> —Michael Risher, ACLU attorney[53]

3.6 Net Neutrality Regulations or the Market?

Direct censorship is not the only factor that can limit the amount and variety of information available to us on the Internet. The regulatory structure affects the availability of services and the degree of innovation. Large companies often lobby for laws and regulations to restrict competition: The U.S. television networks delayed cable for more than a decade. For decades, broadcasting companies lobbied to keep low-power radio stations (called "micro radio") virtually illegal. "Net neutrality" refers to a variety of proposals for restrictions on how telephone and cable companies interact with their broadband customers (primarily for Internet services) and how they set charges for services. There are two different but related issues, sometimes blurred in the arguments: (1) whether the companies that provide the communications networks should be permitted to exclude or give different treatment to content based on the content itself, on the category of content, or on the company or organization that provides it, and (2) whether the companies that provide the communications networks should be permitted to offer content providers and individual subscribers different levels of speed and priority at different price levels. The latter is sometimes called "tiered" service—that is, different levels of service with different charges. Very large companies are on both sides of the debate, as are organizations and prominent people who want to preserve the openness and vitality of the Net.

Advocates of "net neutrality" want the government to mandate that telecommunications companies treat all legal content that travels through their broadband lines and wireless networks the same way. Equal treatment includes charging all customers the same rate for sending information over the Internet and not giving priority to any particular content or customer. Net neutrality would restore part of the concept of common carrier (as described in Section 3.1), based partly on the view that telephone companies (now telephone and cable) have a monopoly on transmission of information and that companies that control transmission should not be permitted to control access to content as well. Many Internet content providers, including individual bloggers and large companies such as eBay, Microsoft, Amazon, Netflix, and Google, argue for net-neutrality rules. Without the rules, some argue, they will have to pay higher rates and communications companies will give special treatment to their own content providers. Some groups argue that allowing communications companies to set varying rates would be devastating for the Internet as it would squeeze out independent voices.

Charging different rates for products and services is not unusual and makes economic sense in many areas. Research journals charge libraries a higher subscription rate than they charge individuals, because more people read each library copy. Many businesses give large-quantity discounts. Some institutions and businesses—hospitals, for example—pay a higher rate for services such as electricity under contracts that guarantee higher priority for repairs or emergency service when necessary. We all have a choice of paying standard delivery charges for products we buy online or paying more for faster delivery. People pay to drive in express lanes on freeways; the price might vary with the time of day and level of traffic. Thus, the notion that every customer should pay the same amount does not have intrinsic merit. Does it have merit for the Internet? Would it make sense for communications carriers to, say, contract with video suppliers to provide faster delivery of videos for a fee?

Supporters of neutral pricing fear that lack of pricing regulation will erode the diversity of the Internet. Only big companies and organizations will be able to afford the prices necessary to ensure that their content moves fast enough to be relevant. Content that individuals and smaller organizations provide will get lost. Some argue that flexible pricing will give telecommunications companies too much power over content on the Internet. Supporters of net neutrality see tiered service as a threat to innovation, democratic participation, and free speech online. Vinton Cerf, Vice President and Chief Internet Evangelist at Google* and a highly respected Internet pioneer, sees the neutrality of the carriers, the lack of gatekeepers and centralized control, as key factors responsible for the success of the Net and innovations like blogging and Internet telephony. He argues that there is not enough competition in the network operator industry to protect against abuses.[54]

---

* Really, that's his title.

Opponents of net neutrality argue that neutrality regulations will slow the advance of high-speed Internet connection and improvements in infrastructure. Before the FCC relaxed older regulations (in 2003–2005), telecommunications companies had little incentive to invest in broadband capacity. In the few years afterward, they invested hundreds of billions of dollars. Speeds increased, prices fell, and the added capacity was essential for new phenomena such as streaming movies. Continued investment in broadband is necessary for growth in areas such as online backup services, all the data we receive on cellphones, applications of remote sensors, innovations in education services, and so on. Opponents of additional regulations say there should be no major new regulation without evidence of harm in the current system. David Farber, another highly respected Internet pioneer, opposes neutrality legislation: "We don't want to inadvertently stall innovation by imposing rules or laws the implications of which are far from clear."[55] Some who support free markets oppose mandated uniform pricing on principle, as an unethical interference in the free choices of sellers and buyers.

The huge surge in traffic due to smartphones and tablets heightened issues of net neutrality. By 2010, video made up more than 75% of mobile data traffic. Does it make sense to treat such traffic differently? Should it have high priority (like voice calls) because delays are annoying to the customer? Should it have lower priority because it uses so much bandwidth? Should service providers make these decisions, or should Congress and the FCC make them? When people watch a video on a smartphone, they often do not watch the whole thing. A company developed techniques to send a video to the user in segments as he or she watches (without increasing delays), rather than sending the entire video as fast as possible. The company said this approach could cut data transfer in half. Can regulators write net neutrality rules that allow or encourage such technological solutions for reducing traffic, or will rigid rules stifle or discourage them?

The legal status of net neutrality is still unclear. When Comcast slowed some traffic from certain specific sites in 2007, the FCC said the company violated FCC guidelines and ordered it to stop. A federal court ruled that the FCC did not have legal authority to do so. Congress has not given the FCC authority to make rules for the Internet. The FCC issued rules, anyway, in 2011; court challenges are underway.

EXERCISES

Review Exercises

3.1   Briefly explain the differences between common carriers, broadcasters, and publishers with respect to freedom of speech and control of content.

3.2   Describe two methods parents can use to restrict access by their children to inappropriate material on the Web.

3.3   What was one of the main reasons why courts ruled the censorship provisions of the Communications Decency Act in violation of the First Amendment?

3.4   What is one way of reducing spam?

3.5   What documents did WikiLeaks make public?

3.6   Give an example of an anonymous publication more than 100 years ago.

3.7   Mention two methods some governments use to control access to information.

General Exercises

3.8   A government actively censors blogs which criticize it. What are some possible reasons for the policy? Does it violate the First Amendment? Is it reasonable?

3.9   The criteria for determining if material is obscene differ among countries and cultures. What effect has the Internet had on such sensibilities? Do you think they can be preserved? If so, explain how. If not, explain why.

3.10   What policy for Internet access and use of filtering software, if any, do you think is appropriate for (a) members of a library (b) employees of a software development company? Do you believe that the Internet should be censored for the general public as well?

3.11   Many social networking services, notably Facebook, are only open to users above a certain age. Give reasons for and against such a requirement. Is it reasonable?

3.12   Gambling websites are illegal in most countries. Discuss some arguments for and against this law.

3.13   Library staff members in two cities filed complaints with the federal Equal Employment Opportunity Commission (EEOC) arguing that they were subjected to a "hostile work environment." The libraries where they worked did not provide filters on Internet terminals. Staffers were forced to view offensive material on the screens of library users and pornographic printouts left on library printers. Discuss the conflict between a hostile work environment and freedom of speech in this situation. Without considering the current laws, how would you resolve the conflict here?

3.14   A depressed young woman commits suicide following instructions she obtained from a website. Should the website author be held responsible for the act? Can the Internet in general be blamed for it?

3.15   You are writing software that blocks advertisements on websites. Given that many websites are funded by such advertisements, discuss the ethics of such a blocking software. What do you think is a reasonable definition of an advertisement in this context?

3.16   Federal regulations and laws in some states (some long-standing, some passed specifically for the Internet) prohibit or restrict many kinds of online sales. For example, laws restrict sale of contact lenses, caskets, and prescription medicines on the Web. Laws prohibit auto manufacturers from selling cars directly to consumers on the Internet.* The Progressive Policy Institute estimated that such state laws cost consumers at least $15 billion a year.[56]

For which of these laws can you think of good reasons? Which seem more like the anticompetitive laws described in Section 3.2.5?

---

* The specific items whose sale or purchase online is prohibited or restricted may have changed.

3.17 Several companies, such as Apple, actively filter applications available from their app stores. Discuss the ethics of doing so. If you believe that filtering is ethical under some circumstances, formulate a reasonable policy for filtering.

3.18 A website that publishes leaked documents posts the contents of the Yahoo email account of a candidate for president during the election campaign.

(a) Describe some types of things that might be among the leaked documents that would be valuable to opponents of the candidate.

(b) Describe some things that might be among the leaked documents that could hurt a campaign but do not indicate any wrongdoing.

(c) Devise standards for the ethics of posting the contents of the account that you would be comfortable with no matter whether you support or oppose the candidate.

3.19 You are aware of a study that concludes that California's emergency systems, including hospitals, emergency supplies, police, and so forth, are not sufficient for responding to the magnitude of earthquake likely to occur in the next 30 years. The study has not been released to the public, and you are thinking of leaking it to a website that publishes leaked documents. List benefits of leaking the study and risks of doing so. List any other questions you consider relevant to making the decision. Indicate how different answers to some of the questions might affect your decision.

3.20 Amateur astronomers around the world have been locating and tracking satellites—both commercial and spy satellites—and posting their orbits on the Web.[57] Some intelligence officials argue that if enemies and terrorists know when U.S. spy satellites are overhead, they can hide their activities. What issues does this problem raise? Should astronomers refrain from posting satellite orbits? Why, or why not?

3.21 Someone posted a video on a popular video site showing a group of men with clubs enter a building and beat unarmed people. The site's policy prohibits posting videos with graphic violence. When a viewer complained, the site removed the video. Other viewers appealed the removal, saying the video documented abuse of prisoners in a Russian prison camp. Suppose you are a manager at the site. Develop a plan for dealing with such videos. Will you repost the video? Explain the issues you considered.

3.22 An antiabortion website posted lists of doctors who perform abortions and judges and politicians who support abortion rights. It included addresses and other personal information about some of the people. When doctors on the list were injured or murdered, the site reported the results. A suit to shut the site for inciting violence failed. A controversial appeals court decision found it to be a legal exercise of freedom of speech. The essential issue is the fine line between threats and protected speech, a difficult issue that predates the Internet. Does the fact that this is a website rather than a printed and mailed newsletter make a difference? What, if any, issues in this case relate to the impact of the Internet?

3.23 The European Union has laws that restrict the percentage of audio-visual media programming (originally primarily television, but now including Internet content) produced outside the EU. Canada has similar restrictions on radio and television content. People in the Canadian film industry have proposed quotas on foreign movies. The reasons given include protecting a country's culture and protecting their content companies from foreign competition.

(a) Do you think such restrictions are reasonable? Do you think they will remain effective with the expansion of online media in recent years? Give reasons.

(b) The United States does not have such quotas on foreign programming or movies. Why do you think this is the case?

3.24 It is illegal for tax-exempt charitable groups to do political lobbying. The websites of many such organizations have links to sites of organizations that do lobbying. For example, a tax-exempt think tank has links to Handgun Control, Inc. and the National Rifle Association, so visitors can find relevant research materials on both sides of gun-control issues. The Internal Revenue Service (IRS) announced an investigation into whether such links violate the rules for tax-exempt status. What do you think they should conclude? How would various possible decisions by the IRS affect the Web?

3.25 A company sells spyware that can intercept and record phone communications and email on a variety of email services. The company sells the software to government agencies in the United States (or your country, if you are outside the United States) that want it to pursue criminals and terrorists. Using ethical criteria from Chapter 1 and legal or constitutional criteria (from Chapter 2 as well as this one, or based on your country's constitution if you are outside the United States), evaluate the decision to sell the software.

3.26 Using ethical criteria from Chapter 1, evaluate the decision to sell the software described in the previous exercise to a repressive government.

3.27 In Section 3.6, we discussed arguments about proposals for charges for faster delivery of content over the Internet. What do you think are likely impacts of such charges? Give reasons. Use analogies from other fields.

3.28 Assume you are a professional working in your chosen field. Describe two new problems, related to the material in this chapter, that may occur in the next ten years. (If you cannot think of anything related to your professional field, choose another field that might interest you.)

3.29 Think back a few years and describe a problem, related to issues in this chapter, that has been resolved by electronic technology or devices.

Assignments

These exercises require some research or activity.

3.30 Find out whether your country restricts access to any websites from its computer systems. What is its policy for determining which sites to restrict? What do you think of the policy?

3.31 At the time I wrote this, Facebook, banned in China since 2009, planned to establish a presence there. It would have to comply with China's censorship requirements and requirements to provide user information to the government. Is Facebook now in China? If so, how has it dealt with the censorship and reporting requirements?

Class Discussion Exercises

These exercises are for class discussion, perhaps with short presentations prepared in advance by small groups of students.

3.32 Under laws in Germany that protect the privacy of criminals who have served their sentence, a murderer took legal action to force Wikipedia to remove its article about his case. Discuss the conflict between privacy and freedom of speech raised by this case.

3.33 To what extent is violent material on the Web and in computer games responsible for shootings in schools? What should be done about it, without violating the First Amendment?

3.34 A computer system manager at a public university noticed that the number of Web accesses to the system jumped dramatically. Most of the increased accesses were to one student's home page. The system manager discovered that his home page contained several sexually oriented pictures. The pictures were similar to those published in many magazines available legally. The system manager told the student to remove the pictures. A female student who accessed the pictures before they were removed filed a grievance against the university for sexual harassment. The student who set up the home page filed a grievance against the university for violation of his First Amendment rights.

Divide the class into four groups: representatives for the female student, the male student, and the university (one group for each grievance). A spokesperson for each group presents arguments. After open discussion of the arguments, take a vote of the class on each grievance.

3.35 The CAN-SPAM law applies to commercial email; political messages are exempt. Present arguments that laws to restrict or regulate spam should treat both categories of bulk email the same way. Present arguments to justify different treatment of these two categories.

3.36 Discuss the questions in Section 3.3 about ethical responsibilities for setting up a website with information about suicide for terminally ill people in pain. Discuss analogous questions for setting up a website with information about how to make explosives for a legitimate purpose (perhaps demolition or clearing farm land). If answers differ for the two situations, identify the attributes or principles that lead to different answers.

3.37 After an incident of nasty verbal attacks and death threats to a blogger from people who disagreed with something she wrote, Tim O'Reilly and Jimmy Wales proposed a Bloggers Code of Conduct. Find a copy of the code that developed from this proposal (or another code of conduct for bloggers). Evaluate it. Discuss its compatibility with freedom of speech. Should bloggers follow the code?

3.38 Is the control that large companies such as Google have over Internet search results a threat to freedom of speech?

3.39 Should Skype continue to operate in China under the joint venture with TOM, as described in Section 3.5.2? Why or why not?

3.40 (a) In a riot such as the one in England in 2011, where rioters planned and coordinated their activites using (among other things) BlackBerry Messenger, should Research In Motion (RIM) shut down Messenger temporarily? Assume the government does not have the legal authority to order the shut down, but law enforcement agencies and government officials have asked RIM to shut the service to prevent more violence.

(b) A cybersecurity bill in the U.S. Senate (which did not pass) had a provision that some critics believed could have given the government authority to shut down the Internet in an emergency. Should the government have such authority?

3.41 The net neutrality rules issued by the FCC in 2011 treated wired and wireless communication networks differently (allowing more flexibility to operators of wireless networks). Give some reasons for treating them differently. Give some reasons why they should be treated the same. What do you think makes the most sense?

BOOKS AND ARTICLES

- Floyd Abrams, *Speaking Freely: Trials of the First Amendment*, Viking Penguin, 2005.

- Robert Corn-Revere, "Caught in the Seamless Web: Does the Internet's Global Reach Justify Less Freedom of Speech?" Cato Institute, July 24, 2002.

- Electronic Privacy Information Center, *Filters and Freedom 2.0: Free Speech Perspectives on Internet Content Controls*, www.epic.org, 2001.

- Mike Godwin, *Cyber Rights: Defending Free Speech in the Digital Age*, Times Books, Random House, 1998.

- Marjorie Heins, *Not in Front of the Children: "Indecency," Censorship, and the Innocence of Youth*, Hill & Wang, 2001.

- Nat Hentoff, *Free Speech for Me—But Not for Thee: How the American Left and Right Relentlessly Censor Each Other*, Harper Collins, 1992.

- Peter Huber, *Law and Disorder in Cyberspace*, Oxford Univ. Press, 1997. Criticizes FCC regulation of telecommunications, showing examples where regulations have delayed introduction of new technologies.

- Anthony Lewis, *Freedom for the Thought That We Hate: A Biography of the First Amendment*, Basic Books, 2008.

- Lyrissa Barnett Lidsky, "Silencing John Doe: Defamation and Disclosure in Cyberspace," *Duke Law Journal*, 49:4, February 2000, pp. 855–946. (Available at www.law.duke.edu.)

- Rebecca MacKinnon, *Consent of the Networked: The Worldwide Struggle for Internet Freedom*, Basic, 2012.

- Evgeny Morozov, *The Net Delusion: The Dark Side of Internet Freedom*, PublicAffairs, 2011.

- "Science, Technology, and the First Amendment, Special Report," Office of Technology Assessment, U.S. Dept. of Commerce, Washington, DC, Jan. 1988 (Report NO. OTA-CIT-369).

- Scott Shane, *Dismantling Utopia: How Information Ended the Soviet Union*, I. R. Dee, 1994.

- Ithiel de Sola Pool, *Technologies of Freedom*, Harvard University Press, 1983. This book describes the history, rights, restrictions, and responsibilities of the various communications technologies in depth.

- Eugene Volokh, "Freedom of Speech in Cyberspace from the Listener's Perspective: Private Speech Restrictions, Libel, State Action, Harassment, and Sex," *Univ. of Chicago Legal Forum*, 1996, pp. 377–436.

- Tim Wu, *The Master Switch: The Rise and Fall of Information Empires*, Knopf, 2010.

NOTES

1. From a speech by Mike Godwin at Carnegie Mellon University, November 1994, quoted with permission. (The speech is excerpted, including part of the quotation used here, in Mike Godwin, "alt.sex.academic.freedom," *Wired*, February 1995, p. 72.)

2. "Internet 2010 in Numbers," Pingdom, royal.pingdom.com/2011/01/12/internet-2010-in-numbers, viewed Nov. 22, 2011.

3. Eric M. Freedman, "Pondering Pixelized Pixies," *Communications of the ACM*, August 2001, 44:8, pp. 27–29.

4. "High Court Rules Cable Industry Rights Greater Than Broadcast's," *Investors Business Daily*, June 28, 1994.

5. Title V, Section 230.

6. Advertising wine on the Internet was protected in a 2006 case in Minnesota. Earlier cases concerned advertising of

tobacco, legal gambling, vitamin supplements, alcohol content of beer, prices of prescription drugs, and Nike's claim that it did not use sweatshop labor. Lee McGrath, "Sweet Nectar of Victory," *Liberty & Law*, Institute for Justice, June 2006, vol. 15, no. 3, pp. 1, 10. Robert S. Greenberger, "More Courts Are Granting Advertisements First Amendment Protection," *Wall Street Journal*, July 3, 2001, pp. B1, B3.

7. In *The Life of Voltaire*, Smith, Elder & Company, 1904. See also Fred S. Shapiro, ed., *The Yale Book of Quotations*, Yale University Press, 2007. The quotation is often incorrectly attributed to Voltaire himself.

8. Gerard van der Leun, "This Is a Naked Lady," *Wired*, Premiere Issue, 1993, pp. 74, 109.

9. Dick Thornburgh and Herbert S. Lin, eds., *Youth, Pornography and the Internet*, National Academy Press, 2002, books.nap.edu/catalog/10261.html.

10. Mike Godwin, "Sex, Cyberspace, and the First Amendment," *Cato Policy Report*, Jan./Feb. 1995, 17(1), p. 10.

11. Robert Peck, quoted in Daniel Pearl, "Government Tackles a Surge of Smut on the Internet," *Wall Street Journal*, Feb. 8, 1995, p. B1.

12. For a commentary on the many issues in this case, see Mike Godwin, "Virtual Community Standards," *Reason*, November 1994, pp. 48–50.

13. Brian Roehrkasse, quoted in Bloomberg News, "U.S. Need for Data Questioned," *Los Angeles Times*, Jan. 26, 2006, articles.latimes.com/2006/jan/26/business/fi-leahy26, viewed Nov. 22, 2011.

14. In *Brown v. Entertainment Merchants Association*, the Supreme Court decision invalidating California's ban on sale or rental of violent video games to minors, 2011.

15. Passed as Title V of the Telecommunications Act of 1996.

16. *Butler v. Michigan*, 352 U.S. 380(1957).

17. Adjudication on Motions for Preliminary Injunction, *American Civil Liberties Union et al. v. Janet Reno* (No. 96-963) and *American Library Association et al. v. United States Dept. of Justice* (No. 96-1458).

18. *ALA v. United States*.

19. *Brown v. Entertainment Merchants Association*.

20. Brock Meeks, "Internet as Terrorist," *Cyberwire Dispatch*, May 11, 1995, cyberwerks.com/cyberwire/cwd/cwd .95.05.11.htm. Brock Meeks, "Target: Internet," *Communications of the ACM*, August 1995, 38(8), pp. 23–25.

21. The quotations in this paragraph are from Meeks, "Internet as Terrorist."

22. David Armstrong, "Bomb Recipes Flourish Online Despite New Law," *Wall Street Journal*, Jan. 18, 2001,

pp. B1, B8. One man accepted a plea bargain for a year in jail.

23. Amol Sharma, "Wireless Carriers Set Strict Decency Standards for Content," *Wall Street Journal*, Apr. 27, 2006, pp. B1, B4.

24. Entertainment Software Ratings Board, www.esrb.org.

25. www.missingkids.com.

26. In the decision striking down the Child Pornography Prevention Act (*Ashcroft v. Free Speech Coalition*). More arguments against the law are in Freedman, "Pondering Pixelized Pixies." Arguments on the other side appear in Foster Robberson, "'Virtual' Child Porn on Net No Less Evil Than Real Thing," *Arizona Republic*, Apr. 28, 2000, p. B11.

27. John Letzing, "'Spam King' Surrenders," *Wall Street Journal*, Aug. 4, 2011, online.wsj.com/article/BT-CO-20110804-726251.html, viewed Nov. 23, 2011.

28. *Intel Corporation v. Hamidi*, news.findlaw.com/wp/docs/ intel/intelhamidi63003opn.pdf, viewed Oct. 22, 2011.

29. Jayson Matthews, "Harris Interactive Continues Spam Battle with MAPS," siliconvalley.internet.com/news/ article/0,2198,3531_434061,00.html, August 9, 2000, viewed Apr. 9, 2001.

30. Quoted in Tom Espiner, "Antispam Group Rejects E-Mail Payment Plan," CNET News, news.com.com, Feb. 7, 2006, viewed Nov. 27, 2011.

31. The full name is the Controlling the Assault of Non-Solicited Pornography and Marketing Act.

32. Federal Trade Commission, "CAN-SPAM Act: A Compliance Guide for Business," September 2009, business.ftc.gov/documents/bus61-can-spam-act-compliance-guide-business, viewed Oct. 22, 2011.

33. John Simons, "CFTC Regulations on Publishing Are Struck Down," *Wall Street Journal*, June 22, 1999, p. A8. Scott Bullock, "CFTC Surrenders on Licensing Speech," *Liberty & Law*, Institute for Justice, April 2000, 9:2, p. 2.

34. *Swedenburg v. Kelly*.

35. Quoted in Brad Stone, "Web Gurus Aim to Bring Civility to a Bad-Tempered Blogosphere," *New York Times*, Apr. 9, 2007, www.technewsworld.com/story/56774 .html, viewed June 21, 2007.

36. A person or organization using the name foia.org leaked the climate research emails. (FOIA is the acronym for "Freedom of Information Act.") I read some (not all) documents at foia2011.org/index.php?id=402. I read numerous articles with quotes from the emails and responses from the CRU researchers. "University of East Anglia Emails: The Most Contentious Quotes," *The Telegraph*, Nov. 23, 2009, www.telegraph.co.uk/earth/environment/

globalwarming/6636563/University-of-East-Anglia-emails-the-most-contentious-quotes.html, viewed Nov. 27, 2011. Antonio Regalado, "Climatic Research Unit Broke British Information Law," *Science*, Jan. 28, 2010, news.sciencemag.org/scienceinsider/2010/01/climate-researc.html, viewed Dec. 23, 2011. Larry Bell, "Climategate II: More Smoking Guns from the Global Warming Establishment," *Forbes*, Nov. 29, 2011, www.forbes.com/sites/larrybell/2011/11/29/climategate-ii-more-smoking-guns-from-the-global-warming-establishment, viewed Dec. 23, 2011. "Cherry-Picked Phrases Explained," University of East Anglia, Nov. 23, 2011, www.uea.ac.uk/mac/comm/media/press/CRUstatements/rebuttalsandcorrections/phrases explained, viewed Dec. 23, 2011.

37. Tim Lister, "WikiLeaks Lists Sites Key to U.S. Security," CNN U.S., Dec. 6, 2010, articles.cnn.com/2010-12-06/us/wikileaks_1_wikileaks-founder-julian-assange-diplomats-homeland-security?_s=PM:US, viewed Aug. 20, 2011. Tim Lister and Emily Smith, "Flood of WikiLeaks Cables Includes Identities of Dozens of Informants," CNN U.S., Aug. 31, 2011, articles.cnn.com/2011-08-31/us/wikileaks.sources_1_diplomatic-cables-wikileaks-websites?_s=PM:US, viewed Oct. 22, 2011.

38. *Die Welt*, quoted in Floyd Abrams, "Don't Cry for Julian Assange," *Wall Street Journal*, Dec. 8, 2011, online.wsj.com/article/SB10001424052970204323904577038293325281030.html, viewed Dec. 26, 2011.

39. *McIntyre v. Ohio Elections Commission*, 514 U.S. 334, 115 S.Ct. 1511 (1995).

40. Jeffrey M. O'Brien, "Free Agent," *Wired*, May 2001, p. 74.

41. Neil King, "Small Start-Up Helps CIA Mask Its Moves on Web," *Wall Street Journal*, Feb. 12, 2001, pp. B1, B6.

42. Declan McCullagh, "SafeWeb's Holes Contradict Claims," *Wired News*, Feb. 12, 2002, www.wired.com/news/politics/0,1283,50371,00.html.

43. Quoted in Robert Corn-Revere, "Caught in the Seamless Web: Does the Internet's Global Reach Justify Less Freedom of Speech?" chapter in Adam Thierer and Clyde Wayne Crews Jr., eds. *Who Rules The Net? Internet Governance and Jurisdiction*, Cato Institute, 2003.

44. Peter L. Bernstein, *Against the Gods: The Remarkable Story of Risk*, John Wiley & Sons, 1996, p. 89.

45. Louisa Lim, "China to Censor Text Messages," BBC News, July 2, 2004, news.bbc.co.uk/2/hi/asia-pacific/3859403.stm.

46. For more on how governments use the Net to thwart freedom movements, see Evgeny Morozov, *The Net Delusion: The Dark Side of Internet Freedom*, PublicAffairs, 2011.

47. Barry Bearak, "Taliban Will Allow Access to Jailed Christian Aid Workers," *New York Times*, Aug. 26, 2001, www.nytimes.com/2001/08/26/world/taliban-will-allow-access-to-jailed-christian-aid-workers.html?pagewanted=all&src=pm, viewed Nov. 26, 2011.

48. In "Google Launches Censored Version of its Search-Engine," Jan. 25, 2006, www.rsf.org.

49. Elinor Mills, "Google to Censor China Web Searches," CNET News.com, Jan. 24, 2006. news.com.com/Google+to+censor+China+Web+searches/2100-1028_3-6030784.htm.

50. Quoted in L. Gordon Crovitz, "Facebook's Dubious New Friends," *Wall Street Journal*, May 2, 2011, online.wsj.com/article/SB10001424052748703567404576293233665299792.html, viewed Nov. 27, 2011.

51. Quoted in Jennifer Valentino-DeVries, Julia Angwin, and Steve Stecklow, "Document Trove Exposes Surveillance Methods," *Wall Street Journal*, Nov. 19, 2011, online.wsj.com/article/SB10001424052970203611404577044192607407780.html, viewed Nov. 26, 2011.

52. "Statement on Temporary Wireless Service Interruption in Select BART Stations on Aug. 11," BART, Aug. 12, 2011, www.bart.gov/news/articles/2011/news20110812.aspx, viewed Oct. 22, 2011. See also Geoffrey A. Fowler, "Phone Cutoff Stirs Worry About Limit on Speech," *Wall Street Journal*, Aug. 16, 2011, online.wsj.com/article/SB10001424053111904253204576510762318054834.html, viewed Oct. 18, 2011.

53. Quoted in Fowler, "Phone Cutoff Stirs Worry."

54. Alan Davidson, "Vint Cerf Speaks Out on Net Neutrality," Google Blog, googleblog.blogspot.com/2005/11/vint-cerf-speaks-out-on-net-neutrality.htm, Nov. 8, 2005.

55. March 2006, quoted on the website of Hands Off the Internet, handsoff.org, viewed July 31, 2006.

56. Robert D. Atkinson, "Leveling the E-Commerce Playing Field: Ensuring Tax and Regulatory Fairness for Online and Offline Businesses," Progressive Policy Institute, www.ppionline.org, June 30, 2003.

57. Massimo Calabresi, "Quick, Hide the Tanks!" *Time*, May 15, 2000, p. 60.

4

INTELLECTUAL PROPERTY

*The Congress shall have Power To . . . promote the Progress of
Science and useful Arts, by securing for limited Times to Authors
and Inventors the exclusive Right to their respective Writings
and Discoveries . . .*

—U.S. Constitution, Article I, Section 8

4.1 Principles, Laws, and Cases

4.1.1 What Is Intellectual Property?

Have you made a video set to a popular song and put it on the Web? Have you recorded
a televised movie to watch later in the week? Have you downloaded music from the Web
without paying for it? Have you watched a streaming video of a live sports event? Do you
know which of these actions are legal and which are illegal, and why? Is it legal for a search
engine to copy videos and books in order to display excerpts? How should intellectual
property owners respond to new technologies that make it easy to copy and distribute
their property without permission? How do copyright owners abuse copyright? If you
are developing software for an online retail site, can you implement one-click shopping
without permission of a patent holder? Will enforcement of strict notions of copyright and
patent smother the creativity enabled by modern technology? We begin our exploration of
these and other issues about intellectual property by explaining the concept of intellectual
property and reviewing principles of intellectual property laws.

Copyright is a legal concept that defines rights to certain kinds of intellectual property.
Copyright protects creative works such as books, articles, plays, songs (both music and
lyrics), works of art, movies, software, and videos. Facts, ideas, concepts, processes,
and methods of operation are not copyrightable. Patent, another legal concept that
defines rights to intellectual property, protects inventions, including some software-based
inventions.

In addition to copyright and patents, various laws protect other forms of intellectual
property. They include trademarks and trade secrets. This chapter concentrates more on
copyright than other forms of intellectual property because digital technology and the
Internet affect copyright so strongly. Patent issues for software and Web technologies are
quite important and controversial. We discuss them in Section 4.5.

The key to understanding intellectual property protection is to understand that the
thing protected is the intangible creative work—not its particular physical form. When
we buy a novel in book form, we are buying a physical collection of paper and ink. When
we buy a novel as an ebook, we are buying certain rights to an electronic-book file. We
are not buying the intellectual property—that is, the plot, the organization of ideas, the
presentation, the characters, and the events that form the abstraction that is the intangible
"book," or the "work." The owner of a physical book may give away, lend, or resell the

one physical book he or she bought but may not make copies (with some exceptions). The legal right to make copies belongs to the owner of the intangible "book"—that is, the owner of the copyright. The principle is similar for software, music, movies, and so on. The buyer of a software package is buying only a copy of it or a license to use the software. When we buy a movie on disc or via streaming video, we are buying the right to watch it, but not the right to play it in a public venue or charge a fee.

Why does intellectual property have legal protection? The value of a book or a song or a computer program is much more than the cost of printing it, putting it on disk, or uploading it to the Web. The value of a painting is higher than the cost of the canvas and paint used to create it. The value of intellectual and artistic works comes from the creativity, ideas, research, skills, labor, and other nonmaterial efforts and attributes their creators provide. Our property rights to the physical property we create or buy include the rights to use it, to prevent others from using it, and to set the (asking) price for selling it. We would be reluctant to make the effort to buy or produce physical things if anyone else could just take them away. If anyone could copy a novel, a computer program, or a movie for the small price of the copying, the creator of the work would receive very little income from the creative effort and would lose some of the incentive for producing it. Protection of intellectual property has both individual and social benefits: it protects the right of artists, authors, and inventors to compensation for what they create, and, by so doing, it encourages production of valuable, intangible, easily copied, creative work.

The author of a particular piece of intellectual property, or his or her employer (e.g., a newspaper or a software company), may hold the copyright or may transfer it to a publisher, a music recording company, a movie studio, or some other entity. Copyrights last for a limited time—for example, the lifetime of the author plus 70 years. After that, the work is in the *public domain*; anyone may freely copy and use it. Congress has extended the time period for copyright control more than a dozen times. The extensions are controversial, as they hold more material out of the public domain for a long time. For example, the movie industry lobbied for and obtained an extension of its copyright protection period from 75 years to 95 years when the first Mickey Mouse cartoon was about to enter public domain.

U.S. copyright law (Title 17 of the U.S. Code[1]) gives the copyright holder the following exclusive rights, with some very important exceptions that we will describe:

- To make copies of the work
- To produce derivative works, such as translations into other languages or movies based on books
- To distribute copies
- To perform the work in public (e.g., music, plays)
- To display the work in public (e.g., artwork, movies, computer games, video on a website)

Restaurants, bars, shopping centers, and karaoke venues pay fees for the copyrighted music they play.* Moviemakers pay for the right to base a movie on a book, even if they make significant changes to the story.

Making a copy of a copyrighted work or a patented invention does not deprive the owner or anyone else of the work's use. Intellectual property differs from physical property in this way. Thus, taking intellectual property by copying is different from theft of physical property, and copyright law does not prohibit *all* unauthorized copying, distribution, and so on. A very important exception is the "fair use" doctrine, which we discuss in Section 4.1.4. Uses of copyrighted material that the copyright owner has not authorized and that one of the exceptions in the law does not permit are infringements of the copyright and are subject to civil and/or criminal penalties.

Most of the discussions in this chapter are within a context that accepts the legitimacy of intellectual property protection but revolve around its extent, how new technology challenges it, and how it can or should evolve. Some people reject the whole notion of intellectual property as property, and hence, copyrights and patents. They see these mechanisms as providing government-granted monopolies, violating freedom of speech, and limiting productive efforts. This issue is independent of computer technology, so we do not cover it in depth in this book. However, the discussion of free software, in Section 4.4, overlaps arguments about the legitimacy of copyright in general.

4.1.2   Challenges of New Technologies

> *Copyright law will disintegrate.*
>
> —Nicholas Negroponte[2]

> *New technologies have been disrupting existing equilibria for centuries,*
> *yet balanced solutions have been found before.*
>
> —Pamela Samuelson[3]

Previous technologies raised challenges to intellectual property protection. For example, photocopiers made copying of printed material easy. However, such earlier technologies were not nearly as serious a challenge as digital technology. A complete photocopy of a book is bulky, sometimes of lower print quality, awkward to read, and more expensive than a paperback. Computers and communications technologies made high-quality copying and high-quantity distribution extremely easy and cheap. Technological factors include the following:

---

* Not all do, of course, but it is the accepted, and legal, practice.

- Storage of all sorts of information (text, sound, graphics, video) in standard digitized formats; the ease of copying digitized material and the fact that each copy is a "perfect" copy
- High-volume, relatively inexpensive digital storage media, including hard disks for servers and small portable media such as DVDs, memory sticks, and flash drives
- Compression formats that make music and movie files small enough to download, copy, and store
- Search engines, which make it easy to find material, and the Web itself
- Peer-to-peer technology, which permits easy transfer of files over the Internet by large numbers of strangers without a centralized system or service; and later, file-hosting services that enable storage and sharing of large files (e.g., movies)
- Broadband (high speed) Internet connections that make transfer of huge files quick and enable streaming video
- Miniaturization of cameras and other equipment that enable audience members to record and transmit movies and sports events; and, before that, scanners, which simplify converting printed text, photos, and artwork to digitized electronic form
- Software tools for manipulating video and sound, enabling and encouraging non-professionals to create new works using the works of others

In the past, it was generally businesses (newspapers, publishers, entertainment companies) and professionals (photographers, writers) who owned copyrights, and it was generally businesses (legal and illegal) that could afford the necessary copying and production equipment to infringe copyrights. Individuals rarely had to deal with copyright law. Digital technology and the Internet empowered us all to be publishers, and thus to become copyright owners (for our blogs and photos, for example), and they empowered us all to copy, and thus to infringe copyrights.

The first category of intellectual property to face significant threats from digital media was computer software itself. Copying software used to be common practice. As one writer said, it was "once considered a standard and acceptable practice (if it were considered at all)."[4] People gave copies to friends on floppy disks, and businesses copied business software. People traded *warez* (unauthorized copies of software) on computer bulletin boards. Software publishers began using the term "software piracy" for high-volume, unauthorized copying of software. Pirated software included (and still includes) word processing programs, spreadsheet programs, operating systems, utilities, games, and just about any consumer software sold. Some, such as new versions of popular games, often appear on unauthorized sites or for sale in other countries before their official release. The software industry estimates the value of pirated software in billions of dollars.

In the early 1990s, one could find on the Internet and download unauthorized copies of popular humor columns (copied from newspapers), lyrics of popular songs, and some images (e.g., Walt Disney Company characters, Playboy pinups, and myriad Star Trek items). Music files were too large to transfer conveniently. Tools for listening to music on computers were unavailable or awkward to use; devices for recording or copying digital music were expensive. Technology improved and prices fell. (CD recorders sold for about $1000 when first introduced, and for $99 within about three years.)

The audio data compression format MP3, introduced in the mid-1990s, reduced the size of audio files by a factor of about 10–12. People could download an MP3 song from the Internet in a few minutes. Hundreds of MP3 sites appeared, making thousands of songs available. MP3 has no mechanism for preventing unlimited or unauthorized copying. Many songwriters, singers, and bands willingly made their music available, but most trading of MP3 files on the Net was unauthorized.

In the 2000s, more new technology (e.g., sophisticated file-sharing schemes, inexpensive video cameras, video editing tools, and video-sharing sites) enabled members of the public to provide entertainment for each other—and to post and share professional videos owned by others. Copying music and movies became easy, fast, cheap, and ubiquitous. The scope of the term "piracy" expanded to include high-volume, unauthorized copying of any form of intellectual property. It can mean individuals posting unauthorized files to legitimate file-sharing sites; underground groups trading unauthorized copies; or highly profitable, multimillion-dollar businesses (mostly outside the United States) that encourage members to upload and share files, knowing that most of the files are unauthorized copies.

The content industries claim that about one-quarter of Internet traffic worldwide consists of copyright-infringing material.[5] The entertainment industry, like the software industry, estimates that people copy, trade, and sell billions of dollars of its intellectual property without authorization each year. The dollar amounts from industry sources might be inflated,* but the amount of unauthorized copying and distribution of music, video, and other forms of intellectual property is huge. Entertainment companies and other content providers are losing significant income and potential income that they could earn from their intellectual property. As we seek solutions to this problem, though, we should recognize that "the problem" looks different from different perspectives. What does it mean to solve the problems of technology's impact on intellectual property rights? What are the problems for which we seek solutions?

To consumers, who get movies and music online, the problem is to get them cheaply and conveniently. To writers, singers, artists, actors—and to the people who work in production, marketing, and management—the problem is to ensure that they are paid for the time and effort they put in to create the intangible intellectual-property products we

---

* Some figures seem to assume that everyone who downloads a movie or song for free illegally would buy it at full price if it were not available for free.

enjoy. To the entertainment industry, to publishers and software companies, the problem is to protect their investment and expected, or hoped-for, revenues. To the millions who post amateur works using the works of others, the problem is to continue to create without unreasonably burdensome requirements and threats of lawsuits. To scholars and various advocates, the problem is how to protect intellectual property, but also to protect fair use, reasonable public access, and the opportunity to use new technologies to the fullest to provide new services and creative work. We explore problems and solutions from several perspectives in this chapter.

The two quotations at the beginning of this section date from 1995, when the significant threat to copyright from digital media became clear. Users and observers of digital media and of the Internet debated whether copyright would survive the enormously increased ease of copying and the habits and expectations that developed about sharing information and entertainment online. Some argued that copyright would survive, mostly because of firm enforcement of copyright law. Others said the ease of copying would win out; most content would be free or almost free. These positions seem more compatible today than they did at first. Enforcement has been fierce, but much legal content is free or cheap due to improved technology and the many services that provide free content sponsored by advertising.

4.1.3 A BIT OF HISTORY

A brief history of copyright law will provide background and help illustrate how new technologies require changes or clarifications in law.[6]

The first U.S. copyright law, passed in 1790, covered books, maps, and charts. It protected them for 14 years. Congress later extended the law to cover photography, sound recordings, and movies. The definition of an unauthorized copy in the Copyright Act of 1909 specified that it had to be in a form that could be seen and read visually. Even with the technologies of the early 20th century, this requirement was a problem. A court applied it in a case about copying a song onto a perforated piano-music roll. (Automatic pianos played such rolls.) A person could not read the music visually from the piano roll, so the copy was not judged a violation of the song's copyright, even though it violated the spirit and purpose of copyright.[7] In the 1970s, a company sued for protection of its chess-playing program, implemented on a read-only-memory (ROM) chip in its handheld computer chess game. Another company sold a game with the identical program; they likely copied the ROM. But because the ROM could not be read visually, a court held that the copy did not infringe the program's copyright.[8] Again, this did not well serve the purpose of copyright. The decision did not protect the creative work of the programmers. They received no compensation from a competitor's sales of their work.

In 1976 and 1980, Congress revised copyright law to cover software. "Literary works" protected by copyright include computer databases that exhibit creativity or originality[9] and computer programs that exhibit "authorship," that is, contain original expression of ideas. Recognizing that technology was changing rapidly, the revised law specifies that copyright applies to appropriate literary works "regardless of the nature of the material objects . . . in which they are embodied." A copy could be in violation of a copyright if the original can be "perceived, reproduced, or otherwise communicated by or from the copy, directly or indirectly."

One significant goal in the development of copyright law, illustrated by the examples above, has been devising good definitions to extend the scope of protection to new technologies. As copying technologies improved, another problem arose: a lot of people will break a law if it is easy to do so and the penalties are weak. In the 1960s, growth in illegal sales of unauthorized copies of recorded music (e.g., on tape) accompanied the growth of the music industry. In 1982, high-volume copying of records and movies became a felony. In 1992, making a small number of copies of copyrighted work "willfully and for purposes of commercial advantage or private gain" became a felony. In response to the growing phenomenon of sharing files for free on the Internet, the No Electronic Theft Act of 1997 made it a criminal offense to willfully infringe copyright (for works with total value of more than $1000 within a six-month period) even if there is no commercial advantage or private gain. The penalties can be severe. After huge growth in sales of unauthorized copies of movies, Congress made it a felony offense to record a movie in a movie theater—one of the ways copies get to those who reproduce and sell them illegally. Critics of these laws argue that the small offenses covered do not merit the severe penalties.

Why did copyright laws get more restrictive and punishing? Generally, creators and publishers of copyrighted works, including print publishers, movie companies, music publishers, sound recording companies (record labels), and the software industry support stronger copyright protection. Congress often delegates the drafting of laws in complex areas to the industries involved. For most of the 20th century, the intellectual property industries drafted laws heavily weighted toward protecting their assets. On the other side, librarians and academic and scientific organizations generally opposed strict rules reducing the public's access to information. Most people were unaware of or indifferent to copyright issues. But digital media, and especially the growth of the Web, focused attention on issues about how much control copyright owners should have. In the 1990s, cybercitizens and organizations such as the Electronic Frontier Foundation joined librarians and others to fight what they view as overly restrictive copyright law. The content industries continue to be powerful lobbyists for their point of view. Web service companies and organizations (such as Google, Facebook, and Wikipedia) add some balance to the lobbying and public debate.

4.1.4 THE FAIR USE DOCTRINE

Copyright law and court decisions attempt to define the rights of authors and publishers consistent with two goals: promoting production of useful work and encouraging the use and flow of information. The fair use doctrine allows uses of copyrighted material that contribute to the creation of new work (such as quoting part of a work in a review) and uses that are not likely to deprive authors or publishers of income for their work. Fair uses do not require the permission of the copyright holder. The notion of fair use (for literary and artistic works) grew from judicial decisions. In 1976, U.S. copyright law explicitly included it. It applies to software also. The 1976 copyright law predated the widespread use of personal computers. The software issues addressed pertained mainly to large business systems, and the law did not address issues related to the Web at all. Thus, it did not take into account many situations where questions of fair use now arise.

The law identifies possible fair uses, such as "criticism, comment, news reporting, teaching (including multiple copies for classroom use), scholarship, or research."[10] It lists four factors to consider in determining whether a particular use is a "fair use":

1. The purpose and nature of the use, including whether it is for commercial purposes or nonprofit educational purposes. (Commercial use is less likely to be fair use.)

2. The nature of the copyrighted work. (Use of creative work, such as a novel, is less likely than use of factual work to be fair use.)

3. The amount and significance of the portion used.

4. The effect of the use on the potential market for or value of the copyrighted work. (Uses that reduce sales of the original work are less likely to be considered fair.)

No single factor alone determines whether a particular use is a fair use, but the last one generally gets more weight than the others.

Court decisions about copyright must be consistent with the First Amendment. For example, courts interpret the fair use principle broadly to protect creation of parodies of other works. In many situations, it is not obvious whether a use is a fair use. Courts interpret and apply the guidelines in specific cases. Law scholars say that results of fair use cases are often notoriously difficult to predict. The uncertainty itself can chill free speech. Fear of an expensive legal case can reduce creation of valuable new work that makes fair use of other works.

4.1.5 ETHICAL ARGUMENTS ABOUT COPYING

There is intrinsic "fuzziness" about the ethics of copying. Many people who get their music, movies, or software from unauthorized sources realize they get "something for nothing." They benefit from the creativity and effort of others without paying for it. To most people, that seems wrong. On the other hand, much copying does not seem wrong. We explore some of the reasons and distinctions.

Copying or distributing a song or computer program does not decrease the use and enjoyment any other person gets from his or her copy. This fundamental distinction between intellectual property and physical property is a key reason why copying is ethical in far more circumstances than taking physical property. However, most people who create intellectual property in entertainment, software, and so on, are doing so to earn income, not for the benefit of using their product themselves. If movie theaters and websites could show, or stream, copies of movies without paying for them, far fewer people and companies would invest money, time, energy, and creative effort in making movies. If search engines could scan any book and offer free downloads without an agreement with the publisher, publishers would probably not sell enough copies to cover costs; they would stop publishing. The value of intellectual property is not just the direct use and enjoyment one gets from a copy. Its value is also as a product offered to consumers to earn money. That is an aspect of the property that one can steal from the copyright holder. When people widely copy intellectual property without permission, they diminish the value of the work as an asset to the owner. That is why a lot of copying is wrong.

Supporters of unauthorized file-sharing services and people who advocate loose restrictions on copying intellectual property argue that permitting copying for, say, trying out a song or computer program before buying it benefits the copyright owner because it encourages sales. Such uses seem ethical, and indeed, since a lot of the "wrong" in unauthorized copying stems from depriving owners of income from their product, the fourth of the fair use guidelines considers the impact on the market for the product. However, we should be careful not to go too far in usurping a copyright holder's decisions. Many businesses give free samples and low-priced introductory offers to encourage sales, but that is a business decision. The investors and employees of the business take the risk for such choices. A business normally makes its own decisions about how it markets its product, not consumers who want free samples, nor even the courts.

People who copy for personal use or distribute works of others without charge usually do not profit financially. Personal use is, reasonably, more likely to be fair use (both ethically and legally) than is commercial use, but is personal use always fair? Is financial gain always relevant? In some contexts, a profit motive, or financial gain, is a factor in concluding that an activity is wrong. In other contexts, it is irrelevant. Vandals do not profit financially from their action, but vandalism is unethical (and a crime) because it destroys—or reduces the value of—someone's property. A profit motive is not a significant factor in determining where to protect freedom of speech. Freedom of speech is an important social, ethical, and legal principle for book, magazine, newspaper, and website publishers, most of whom are in business to make a profit. Many kinds of abusive or threatening speech are unrelated to financial gain but are unethical.

Here are some arguments people make in support of personal copying or posting content on the Web without authorization (in situations that are not clearly fair use) and some counterpoints to consider. The responses below do not mean that unauthorized copying or use of someone else's work is always wrong—in many cases it is not. These are brief suggestions for analyzing the arguments.

- *I cannot afford to buy the software or movie or pay the royalty for use of a song in my video.* There are many things we cannot afford. Not being able to afford something does not justify taking it.

- *The company is a large, wealthy corporation.* The size and success of the company do not justify taking from it. Programmers, writers, and performing artists lose income too when copying is common.

- *I wouldn't buy it at the retail price (or pay the required fee) anyway. The company is not really losing a sale or losing revenue.* The person is taking something of value without paying for it, even if the value to that person is less than the price the copyright owner would charge. There are times when we get things of value without paying. Our neighborhood looks better when our neighbors paint their houses. People do us favors. It can be easy to ignore a crucial distinction: Who makes the decision?

- *Making a copy for a friend is just an act of generosity.* Philosopher Helen Nissenbaum argued that someone who copies software for a friend has a countervailing claim against the programmer's right to prohibit making the copy: the "freedom to pursue the virtue of generosity."[11] Surely we have a liberty (i.e., a negative right) to be generous, and we can exercise it by making or buying a gift for a friend. It is less clear that we have a claim right (a positive right) to be generous. Is copying the software an act of generosity on our part or an act that compels involuntary generosity from the copyright owner?

- *This violation is insignificant compared to the billions of dollars lost to piracy by dishonest people making big profits.* Yes, large-scale commercial piracy is worse. That does not imply that individual copying is ethical. And, if the practice is widespread, the losses become significant.

- *Everyone does it. You would be foolish not to.* The number of people doing something does not determine whether it is right. A large number of people in one peer group could share similar incentives and experience (or lack thereof) that affect their point of view.

- *I want to use a song or video clip in my video, but I have no idea how to get permission.* This is a better argument than many others. Technology has outrun the business mechanisms for easily making agreements. The "transaction costs," as economists call them, are so high that a strict requirement for obtaining permission slows development and distribution of new intellectual property.

- *I'm posting this video (or segment of a TV program) as a public service.* If the public service is entertainment (a gift to the public), the observations above about copying as a form of generosity are relevant here. If the public service is to express an idea or make some statement about an important issue, the posting might be analogous to creating a review or a parody. In some cases, these might be reasonable fair uses with social value. Simply posting a complete program, or a substantial portion of one, is probably not a fair use.

Laws are not always good guides for ethical decisions, but the fair use guidelines do a respectable job of identifying criteria to help distinguish fair and unfair copying. Because of the complexity of the issues, there will always be uncertainty in the application of the guidelines, both ethically and legally. The guidelines might need expansion and clarification to cover new media, but they give us a good framework that corresponds to sensible ethical criteria.

4.1.6 SIGNIFICANT LEGAL CASES

The fair use doctrine is important for different contexts. First, it helps us figure out under what circumstances we as consumers can legally copy music, movies, software, and so on. Second, developers of new software, recording devices, game players, and other products often must copy some or all of another company's software as part of the process of developing the new product. The new product might compete with the other company's product. Is such copying a fair use? We look at cases that cover these contexts. Some of the cases also involve the degree of legal responsibility a company has for copyright violations by users of its products or services. This point is important for many Web-based services, some that implicitly or explicitly encourage unauthorized uses of the works of others.

Sony vs. Universal City Studios (1984)

The Sony case was the first case about private, noncommercial copying of copyrighted work that the Supreme Court decided.[12] It concerns videotape recording machines, but it is cited in Web-based entertainment cases and in cases about new kinds of digital recording devices.

Two movie studios sued Sony for contributing to copyright infringement because some customers used its Betamax video cassette recording machines to record movies shown on television. Thus, this case raised the important issue of whether copyright owners can sue makers of copying equipment because some buyers use the equipment to infringe copyrights. First, we focus on the other issue the Supreme Court decided in the Sony case: whether recording a movie for personal use was a copyright infringement or a fair use. People copied the entire movie. Movies are creative, not factual, works. Thus, factors (2) and (3) of the fair use guidelines argue against the taping. The purpose of recording the movie was to view it at a later time. Normally the consumer reused the tape after viewing the movie, making it an "ephemeral copy." The copy was for a private, noncommercial purpose, and the movie studios could not demonstrate that they suffered any harm. The Court interpreted factor (2), the nature of the copyrighted work, to include not simply whether it was creative or factual, but also the fact that the studios receive a large fee for broadcasting movies on television, and the fee depends on having a large audience of people who view the movies for free. So factors (1), (2), and (4) argue for fair use. The Court ruled that recording a movie for viewing at a later time was a fair use.

The fact that people copied the entire work did not necessitate a ruling against fair use, although many examples of fair use apply only to small excerpts. The fact that the copying was a private, noncommercial use was significant. The Court said that private, noncommercial uses should be presumed fair unless there is realistic likelihood of economic harm to the copyright holder.

On the issue of the legitimacy of the Betamax machine, the Court said makers of a device with substantial legal uses should not be penalized because some people use it to infringe copyright. This is a very important principle.

Reverse engineering: game machines

In the Sony case, the Supreme Court's decision said that noncommercial copying of an entire movie can be fair use. In several cases involving game machines, the courts ruled that copying an entire computer program for a *commercial* use was fair, largely because the purpose was to create a new product, not to sell copies of another company's product. The first case is *Sega Enterprises, Ltd. v. Accolade, Inc.* Accolade made videogames to run on Sega machines. To make their games run properly, Accolade needed to figure out how part of Sega's game-machine software worked. Accolade copied Sega's program and decompiled it (i.e., translated it from machine code to a form in which they could read and understand it). This is *reverse engineering*. Sega sued; Accolade won. Accolade was making new games. The court viewed Accolade's activities as fitting the purpose of fair use—that is, to encourage production of new creative work. The fact that Accolade was a commercial entity was not critical. Although Accolade's games might reduce the market for Sega's games, that was fair competition. Accolade was not selling copies of Sega's games.[13] In *Atari Games v. Nintendo*, the court also ruled that making copies of a program for reverse engineering (to learn how it works so that a company can make a compatible product) was not copyright infringement. It is a fair "research" use.

The court applied similar arguments in deciding in favor of Connectix Corporation in a suit by Sony Computer Entertainment, Inc. Connectix copied Sony's PlayStation BIOS (the basic input–output system) and reverse engineered it to develop software that emulates the PlayStation console. Game players could then buy the Connectix program and play PlayStation games on their computers without buying the PlayStation console. Connectix's program did not contain any of Sony's code, and it was a new product, different from the PlayStation console. The copying of the BIOS was fair use.[14]

These decisions show how courts interpret fair use for situations not imagined when the guidelines were written. Reverse engineering is an essential process for creating new products that must interact with other companies' hardware and software.

Sharing music: the Napster case

When Big Steel and the auto industry were under pressure during the
'70s from low-cost imports, their first instinct was not to change their
outmoded manufacturing plants but to beseech the courts to bar the
outlanders. The record industry has taken a similar tack.

—Karl Taro Greenfeld[15]

Napster opened on the Web in 1999 as a service allowing users to copy songs in MP3 files from the hard disks of other users. It was wildly popular and had more than 50 million users little more than a year later. Almost 100 million MP3 files were available on the service. Webnoize found that almost 75% of college students it surveyed used Napster. It was well known that Napster users copied and distributed most of the songs they traded without authorization. Eighteen record companies sued for copyright infringement and asked for thousands of dollars in damages for each song traded on Napster. The record companies won.[16]

The Napster case is important for many reasons. The fact that so many people participated in an activity that courts decided was illegal is an indication of how new technology challenges existing law and attitudes about what is acceptable. Many people thought the success of Napster meant the end of copyright. Instead the court decision showed that the legal system can still have a powerful impact. The arguments in the case apply to many other sites and services on the Internet.

The issues in the lawsuit against Napster were the following:

- Was the copying and distribution of music by Napster users legal under the fair use guidelines?
- If not, was Napster responsible for the actions of its users?

Napster argued that the sharing of songs by its users was a legal fair use. Let's review the fair use guidelines and how they apply.

Copying songs via Napster does not fit any of the general categories of purposes covered by fair use (e.g., education, research, news), but neither does copying movies on tapes. The *Sony v. Universal City Studios* case showed that the Supreme Court is willing to include entertainment as a possible fair use purpose.

Napster argued that sharing songs via its service was fair use because people were making copies for personal, not commercial, use. Copyright experts said "personal" meant very limited use—say, within a household—not trading with thousands of strangers.

Songs (lyrics and music) are creative material. Users copied complete songs. Thus, fair use guidelines (2) and (3) argue against fair use, but, as the Sony case indicated, they do not necessarily outweigh other factors.

The final, and perhaps most important, point is the impact on the market for the songs—that is, the impact on the income of the artists and music companies that hold the copyrights. Napster argued that it did not hurt record industry sales; users sampled music on Napster and bought the CDs they liked. The music industry claimed Napster severely hurt sales. Survey and sales data did not unequivocally support either side. Sales data showed sales rising significantly during most years in the 1990s, and dropping or rising only slightly in 2000. For example, music sales in the United States (the largest market) dropped 1.5% in 2000. Sales of singles were down 46%.[17] We do not know if Napster was the only reason for the declines, but it is reasonable to conclude that the huge volume of copying on Napster had a negative impact on sales and that the impact would grow.

Many legal observers thought the large-scale copying by Napster users was illegal copyright infringement, not fair use, and that is how the court ruled.

But was Napster responsible for copyright infringement by its users? Napster did not keep copies of songs on its computers. It provided lists of available songs and lists of users logged on at any time. Users transferred songs from each other's hard disks using peer-to-peer software downloaded from Napster. Napster argued that it was similar to a search engine and that a new law, the Digital Millennium Copyright Act (which we discuss at length in Sections 4.2.2 and 4.2.3), protected it from responsibility for copyright violations by its users. The record companies argued that the law requires companies to make an effort to prevent copyright violations and that Napster did not take sufficient steps to eliminate unauthorized songs or users who committed violations.

Napster cited the Sony Betamax case, in which the court said the maker of devices with substantial legitimate uses is not liable for users of the device who infringe copyrights, even if the maker knows some will. Napster had substantial legitimate uses in promoting new bands and artists who were willing to let users copy their songs. The recording industry argued that Napster was not a device or new technology, and it was not asking to ban a technology or shut Napster down. The record companies objected to how Napster *used* widely available technology to aid copyright infringement. It wanted Napster to stop listing songs without permission of the copyright owners.

Sony's relationship with a customer ended when the customer bought the Betamax machine. Napster interacted with its members in providing access to songs they copied. The court said Napster was liable because it had the right and ability to supervise its system, including the copyright-infringing activities, and had a financial interest in those activities. Napster was a business. Although it did not charge for copying songs, it expected the free copying to attract users so that it would make money in other ways.

The court ruled in 2001 that Napster "knowingly encourages and assists in the infringement of copyrights."[18] Napster faced civil suits that could have required payments of billions of dollars in damages. After some ineffective attempts to remove unauthorized songs from its song lists, Napster shut down. Another company bought the "Napster" name and set up a legal streaming music subscription service.

What consumers want from the entertainment industry

Why was Napster so popular? When I asked my college students (while the illegal version of Napster was thriving in 2000), many shouted out "It's free!" That's the obvious reason, but it was not the only one. My students quickly generated a list of other desirable features of Napster. They could get individual songs without having to buy a whole CD to get the ones they wanted. They could sample songs to see if they really wanted them. Through Napster, they had access to a huge "inventory," not limited to one particular store or music label. They could get songs that were not commercially available. They liked the convenience of getting their music online. They could download and play a song from anywhere; they did not need to have a physical CD with them. The Napster site provided information about singers and musicians. Users could chat online with other users while they downloaded songs in the background. Thus, Napster used a variety of then-new technologies to provide flexibility, convenience, and services, in addition to free music.

The record companies did not embrace the new technologies. They expected their customers to continue to buy CDs from stores or order on the Web and wait a few days for shipping. They were used to the old paradigm of getting paid by each customer for each copy and were reluctant to allow or accept distribution of songs in file formats that people could easily copy.

When people began to post video clips from television shows and movies about five years later, content owners reacted like the record companies. They tried to stop the phenomenon rather than seek new business models to make it work.

More file sharing: MGM v. Grokster

About the time of the Napster decision, numerous companies and Web sites (Gnutella, Morpheus, Kazaa, and others) sprang up to provide a new kind of peer-to-peer file-sharing service. These systems enabled copying of files among users on the Internet without a central service, like Napster, to sue when users infringe copyrights. Within months of Gnutella's appearance, more than a million files were available. Many were unauthorized MP3 music files and unauthorized software. In *MGM v. Grokster*, the music and movie industry sued Grokster and StreamCast Networks (the owner of Morpheus). Although the companies did not provide a central service or list of music files available on the disks of users (as did Napster), they provided the software for sharing files. Technologists and supporters of file sharing argued that peer-to-peer file-transfer programs had potential for many productive, legal uses. (They were correct.) However, the Supreme Court ruled unanimously that intellectual property owners could sue the companies for encouraging copyright infringement. (At about the same time, an Australian court made a similar ruling against Kazaa.)

The Napster and Grokster decisions made it clear that businesses that encourage copyright infringement and provide tools to do so as a fundamental part of their business

Plagiarism and copyright

Plagiarism is the use of someone else's work (usually written work), representing it as one's own. Among students, it typically means copying paragraphs (with perhaps small changes) from websites, books, or magazines and incorporating them, without attribution, into a paper the student submits for a class assignment. It also includes buying a term paper and submitting it as one's own work. Novelists, nonfiction writers, and journalists sometimes plagiarize sections or complete works from other authors. Plagiarism was a problem before there were computers, but word processors and the Web have made it easier by making so much information available and making copying as easy as cut and paste.

Most often, the author of the plagiarized material does not know of or authorize its use, so plagiarism often includes copyright infringement. If the material is in the public domain or if someone agrees to write a paper for another, it is not copyright infringement, but it still might be plagiarism.

Plagiarism is dishonest. It misappropriates someone else's work without permission (usually) and without credit. In academia, it is a lie to the instructor, a false claim to have done an assignment oneself. In journalism or publishing, it is a lie to the employer or publisher and to the public. Plagiarism violates school rules and is considered a serious breach of professional ethics.

Thousands of high schools and colleges submit student term papers and essays to a service, turnitin.com, that checks them for plagiarism. Turnitin compares the student work to its database of millions of student papers and to material on the Web and in journal archives. The service builds its database of student papers by adding those submitted for checking. Several students sued the company for infringing their copyrights by adding their papers to the database. A federal appeals court ruled that turnitin.com's storage of student term papers is a fair use. Turnitin copied the entire paper and is a commercial entity. However, the facts that it provides a service very different from writing a term paper and that its service does not reduce the market for a student's paper weighed more strongly.[19]

Social conventions can influence the determination of what is plagiarism. For example, the public and book publishers generally know that ghostwriters write books for politicians and celebrities even when only the politician's or celebrity's name appears as the author. Few call this practice plagiarism.

---

model cannot operate legally in the United States. Many file-sharing companies settled suits with the entertainment industry, paying millions of dollars. Many shut down. Critics of the decisions worried that they threatened development of new peer-to-peer technology and applications.

"Look and feel"

Does copyright apply to user interfaces? The term "look and feel" of a program refers to features such as pull-down menus, windows, icons, and finger movements and the specific ways one uses them to select or initiate actions. Two programs that have similar user interfaces are sometimes called "workalike" programs. The internal structure and programming could be entirely different. One program might be faster or have other advantages. Should the look and feel of a program be copyrightable? Does a workalike program infringe the copyright of the earlier program it resembles?

In the 1980s and 1990s, some companies won copyright infringement suits against others whose software had similar look and feel. An appeals court, reversing one such case, ruled that menu commands are "a method of operation," explicitly excluded from copyright protection. They are, the court said, like the controls of a car.[20] The trend of court decisions has been against copyright protection for "look and feel." Courts ruled that features such as overlapping windows, pull-down menus, and common operations like cut and paste are outside the scope of copyright.

The main argument in favor of protecting a user interface is that it is a major creative effort. Thus, the usual arguments for copyright and patent apply (e.g., rewarding and encouraging innovation). On the other hand, standard user interfaces increase productivity of users and programmers. We do not have to learn new interfaces for each program or device. Programmers do not have to "reinvent the wheel"—that is, design a new interface just to be different. They can concentrate on developing the truly new aspects of their programs. The value of similar interfaces for browsers, smartphones, and so on, is now well recognized and taken for granted.*

4.2 Responses to Copyright Infringement

4.2.1 DEFENSIVE AND AGGRESSIVE RESPONSES FROM THE CONTENT INDUSTRIES

The entertainment industry employs numerous approaches in its efforts to prevent unauthorized use of its products. Its methods include technology to detect and thwart copying, education about copyright law and reasons to protect intellectual property, lawsuits (both reasonable and abusive), lobbying for expansions of copyright law (both reasonable and not), lobbying to restrict or prohibit technologies that aid copyright infringement, and new business models to provide digital content to the public in convenient forms.

Ideas from the software industry

A variety of techniques for protecting software developed early, with varying success. For example, software companies encoded an expiration date in free sample versions of software; the software destroyed itself after that date. Some expensive business software included a hardware *dongle*, a device that the purchaser has to plug into a port on the computer so that the software will run, thus ensuring that the software runs on only

---

* Several companies have patents on the screen technologies that enable touch commands.

International piracy

Some countries traditionally have not recognized or protected intellectual property, including copyrights, patents, and trademarks. Counterfeiting of brand name products, from blue jeans to expensive watches and medicines, is common in some parts of the world. Ignoring foreign copyrights on books and other printed material has long been common practice in many countries as well. Thus, software, music, and movie piracy in these countries are variants of an old phenomenon. Websites that sell or share games, software, and entertainment files without authorization thrive in many countries.

The Business Software Alliance (BSA), a software industry organization, estimates that piracy accounts for 42% of personal computer software in use worldwide. The regions with the highest rates are Central and Eastern Europe and Latin America.[21] (Obviously, it is difficult to get accurate figures for illegal activities. BSA makes estimates by considering the number of computers sold, the expected average number of software packages on each computer, and the number of software packages sold.)

Many countries with high piracy rates do not have a significant software industry. Thus, they do not have domestic programmers and software companies to lobby for protection of software. The lack of a domestic software industry may be an effect, as well as a contributing cause, of weak legal protection for software. It is difficult for such an industry to develop when it cannot recover its investment in software development. The fact that the major software companies are from other countries, and rich ones, may make both the people and the governments less inclined to take action to reduce unauthorized sales. In the United States, with its many legitimate sellers of entertainment and software, customers are likely to know when they are buying illegal products or sharing unauthorized files. In countries where it is common to purchase food unpackaged in outdoor markets, customers might not think there is anything unusual (or wrong) about the way unauthorized vendors sell software

and music. It could be easier for a consumer to find a street vendor selling, say, a U.S. movie on DVD, than to find an authorized dealer. Another reason for piracy in some countries is that the economies are weak and the people are poor. (Some U.S. movie companies sell DVDs in China at relatively low prices to attract customers away from the illegal market.) Thus, culture, politics, economic development, low incomes, and lax enforcement of intellectual property laws are all contributing factors.

The BSA calculated that the software piracy rate in China was 98% in 1994. The U.S. government has repeatedly pressured China's government to improve intellectual property protection, and China has repeatedly announced programs to do so, but with relatively little impact. As China's economy has grown, its government has made more effective efforts to reduce illegal production, sale, and use of intellectual property. Recognition that poor intellectual property protection hindered its own content industries contributed to increased copyright protection in China. For example, under pressure from a Chinese company that represents U.S. music companies and owns rights to thousands of Chinese songs, China's major search engine removed thousands of links to sites that offered pirated songs. Court decisions against infringement of foreign copyrights and jail sentences for offenders increased. In China, personal computer manufacturers used to sell their machines bare, without an operating system. This practice encouraged people to buy cheap, unauthorized copies. In 2006, the Chinese government required that all PCs be sold with an authorized operating system preinstalled. Also, according to the BSA, the Chinese government significantly reduced the use of unauthorized software by its own government agencies. The BSA reports that the software piracy rate in China dropped to 78% in 2010. (A Chinese study, based on surveys, reported a 45% rate for 2010.)[22] For comparison, the BSA gives a rate of 20% for the United States.

Decoys

Some music companies adopted a clever tactic to discourage unauthorized file sharing: They put a large number of damaged music files, called "decoys," on file-sharing sites. The decoys might, for example, fail to download properly or be full of scratchy noises. The idea was that people would become frustrated and stop using the file-sharing sites if a large percentage of the songs they tried to download would not play properly. Movie companies adopted the tactic too, scattering many fake copies of new movies on the Internet.

one machine at a time. Diskettes containing consumer software had "copy protection" to ensure that you could not copy it (or that a copy would not run). Some software requires activation or registration with a special serial number. Some of these systems were "cracked"—that is, programmers found ways to thwart the protection mechanisms. Many companies dropped these techniques, largely because consumers dislike the inconvenience that accompanies them. Some of these early access controls later developed into the more sophisticated digital rights management schemes for entertainment and ebooks that we discuss later in this section.

Software industry organizations, dubbed "software police," were active in business offices before they began policing cyberspace. In most cases, violations of copyright law were so clear that the business or organization agreed to big fines rather than go to trial. Software copying by businesses decreased, due in part to better understanding of the ethical issues involved and in part to fear of fines and exposure in a business climate that gradually came to view large-scale copyright violation as not acceptable.

Law enforcement agencies raided swap meets, warehouses, and other sites and prosecuted sellers of pirated software (and, later, music CDs and movie DVDs). Courts handed out severe penalties for organized, large-scale efforts. For example, the owner of iBackup received a prison sentence of more than seven years and was ordered to pay restitution of more than $5 million after pleading guilty to illegally copying and selling software worth more than $20 million. Similarly, a man who repeatedly recorded new movies on his camera in movie theaters and made pirate copies to sell received a sentence of seven years in jail.

Banning, suing, and taxing

Via both lawsuits and lobbying, the intellectual property industries have delayed, restricted, or prevented services, devices, technologies, and software that make copying easy and that people are likely to use widely in ways that infringe copyrights, although they also have many legal uses. The technology for consumer CD-recording devices for music was available in 1988, but lawsuits filed by record companies delayed its introduction. A group of companies, including a television network and the Walt Disney Company, sued the makers of digital video recording machines that store TV programs and can skip commercials. The movie and record industries delayed introduction of DVD players by threatening to sue companies that make them if consumers could copy movies on the devices. The Recording Industry Association of America (RIAA) sued in 1998 and obtained a restraining order to stop Diamond Multimedia Systems from shipping its Rio machine, a portable device to play MP3 music files. Diamond eventually won, partly because the court interpreted the Rio as a player, not a recorder, that allowed people to play their music at different locations—just as the Sony decision (Section 4.1.6) said people could watch TV shows at different times.[23] Some observers believe that Apple's iPod would not have been possible if the RIAA's lawsuit against the Rio had succeeded.

As new companies introduced a variety of new products and services to deliver entertainment in flexible and convenient ways, the costs of fighting industry lawsuits effectively shut some of them down—with no trial to decide whether their products were legal.

The entertainment industry pushed hard for laws and industry agreements to require that makers of personal computers and digital recorders and players build copy-protection mechanisms into their products. It pressured device makers to design their systems so that files in unprotected formats do not play well—or at all. Such requirements could reduce illegal copying, of course. However, they interfere with use and sharing of homemade works. They complicate sharing of material in the public domain. They restrict legal copying for personal use and other fair uses. Laws requiring or prohibiting specific features violate the freedom of manufacturers to develop and sell products they consider appropriate.

Software and entertainment companies targeted Internet service providers, threatening legal action against those whose subscribers operate file-sharing services or trade unauthorized files via peer-to-peer software, pressuring them to cancel accounts of alleged offenders. The entertainment industry sued or took other legal action against thousands of people for downloading or sharing unauthorized music files. Letters to college students threatened fines of thousands of dollars. Eventually, recognizing that the lawsuits angered customers and were not particularly effective in stopping copying and sharing, the industry cut back on the policy of mass lawsuits. Instead, the industry made agreements under which ISPs warn customers who transfer music or movies illegally and may close the accounts of customers who ignore the warnings.

As an alternative to banning devices that increase the likelihood of copyright infringement, several governments, including most in the European Union, tax digital media and equipment to pay copyright holders for losses expected from unauthorized copying. They introduced special taxes on photocopiers and magnetic tape in the 1960s and later added taxes on personal computers, printers, scanners, blank DVDs, recorders, iPods, and cellphones. Advocates of these taxes argue that makers of copying equipment are responsible for losses their equipment causes for intellectual-property owners and that the tax schemes are a reasonable compromise in a situation where it is difficult to catch each infringer.

Analogies and perspective

Should we ban or restrict software, a technology, a device, or research because it has the potential for illegal use, or should we ban only the illegal *uses*? This question addresses a principle covering much more than copyright infringement. In Chapter 2, we described the FBI's and NSA's pressure for banning telephone technology that is difficult to tap and encryption schemes that were difficult for them to crack. Law enforcement agencies advocate banning anonymous Web browsing and email, because they can hide criminal activity. The issue of banning or restricting tools that have criminal uses arises in numerous areas unrelated to computer technology. Some U.S. cities prohibit sale of spray paint to minors, because they might paint graffiti on walls. Of course, they might paint a table. Some cities ban chewing gum, because some people discard the gum on the street, making a mess. Many countries prohibit ordinary people from owning guns to protect their homes or businesses, because some people misuse guns. Laws ban drug paraphernalia, because people might use it with illegal drugs. Some of these laws make prevention of specific crimes easier. For example, it

might be hard to find the person who painted graffiti, but it is easy to reduce the sale of spray paint by threatening shop owners with fines.

In a free society, which should win: the freedom of people to develop and use tools for legal purposes, or the prevention of potential crimes? Those who reject the policy of banning a tool that has both legitimate and illegal uses argue its absurdity by taking it to its extreme: Should we ban matches because arsonists use them? Others argue that we should look at each application individually, considering the risks of harm. Proponents and lobbyists for bans on tools usually rank the damage they could cause (in general or to the interests of their clients) more highly than the loss of freedom and convenience to those who would use the tool honestly and productively. We can rarely predict all the creative and innovative (legal) uses of a new technology. Bans, delays, and expensive restrictions often cost all of society the unforeseen benefits. The technologies listed in Section 4.1.2 as causes of problems for intellectual-property protection are the foundation of incredible benefits that we enjoy.

Critics argue that the taxes make equipment more expensive, penalize equipment makers unfairly, charge honest users unfairly, and politicize the difficult job of fairly distributing the money collected.

Digital rights management

Digital rights management technologies (DRM) are a collection of techniques that control access to and uses of intellectual property in digital formats. DRM includes hardware and software schemes using encryption and other tools. DRM implementations embedded in text files, music, movies, ebooks, and so on, can prevent saving, printing, making more than a specified number of copies, distributing a file, extracting excerpts, or fast-forwarding over commercials.

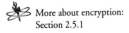 More about encryption: Section 2.5.1

There are many criticisms of digital rights management. DRM prevents fair uses as well as infringing uses. It can prevent extraction of small excerpts for review or for a fair use in a new work, for example. You cannot play or view protected works on old or incompatible machines and operating systems (e.g., Linux). We have long had the right to lend, resell, rent out, or give away a physical book, record, or CD that we owned. (These activities do not require making a copy.) If we could not lend or give a book to a friend, the friend might buy a copy, providing income to the copyright owner. But in 1908, the Supreme Court established the principle that the copyright owner has the right only to the "first sale" of a copy.[24] Publishers, especially of textbooks, which resell often, lobbied for legislation requiring a royalty to the publisher on each resale; they were unsuccessful. DRM enables the content seller to prevent lending, selling, renting, or giving away a purchased copy.

DRM differs in a fundamental way from the banning, suing, and taxing we described earlier. Companies that use DRM on their products are not interfering with other people or businesses. They are offering their own products in a particular way. It is a way that has disadvantages to the public, but surely a publisher should be free to offer its products in whatever form it chooses. If the car model we want to buy comes only in black, white, or green, we cannot demand that the company provide one in orange. But we can buy one and paint it orange. Can we do the equivalent with intellectual property wrapped in DRM? In the next section, we will see that a law says we often cannot.

4.2.2   THE DIGITAL MILLENNIUM COPYRIGHT ACT: ANTICIRCUMVENTION

Congress passed the Digital Millennium Copyright Act (DMCA) in 1998. This very important law has two significant parts. The "anticircumvention" provisions prohibit circumventing technological access controls and copy-prevention systems implemented by copyright owners in intellectual property. The "safe harbor" provisions protect websites from lawsuits for copyright infringement by users of the site. We discuss the anticurcumvention provisions in this section and safe harbor in the next one.

Circumventing access controls

Programmers and researchers regularly find ways to crack or thwart (or "circumvent") DRM, sometimes to infringe copyright on a large scale and sometimes for a variety of legal purposes. The "anticircumvention" provisions of the DMCA prohibit making, distributing, or using tools (devices, software, or services) to circumvent DRM systems used by copyright holders. (There are exceptions. We mention some later.) These provisions are extremely controversial. The law provides for heavy penalties and fines for violators. The ideal purpose of the DMCA is to reduce piracy and other illegal uses of intellectual property. However, it criminalizes actions that do not infringe any copyrights. It outlaws devices and software that have legitimate purposes, which court decisions protected before the DMCA. Content companies use the law in ways that threaten fair use, freedom of speech, research, competition, reverse engineering, and innovation. We give some examples.[25]

The first major legal cases based on the DMCA involved the Content Scrambling System, or CSS, a protection scheme for movies. Three programmers, including 15-year-old Jon Johansen of Norway,* wrote and distributed a program, called DeCSS, that defeated the scrambling.[26] DeCSS could be used to create numerous unauthorized copies. But DeCSS also enables users of the Linux operating system to view (legally purchased) DVDs on their computers. It enables the legal owner of a DVD to view the disk anywhere in the world. (Some movie companies use incompatible codes in Europe and the United States.) Several Hollywood studios sued people who posted DeCSS on their websites. Attorneys in a prominent case argued that people could use DeCSS for fair uses, that banning it violated freedom of speech, and that programmers need to discuss computer code and techniques. None of these arguments mattered much. The judge ruled that DeCSS was illegal under the DMCA and ordered its removal from the Web.[27] Soon after the decision, descriptions of DeCSS appeared on the Web in haiku, bar code, short movies, a song, a computer game, and art.[28] Most of these publications of the code were protests of the judge's decision. They demonstrate how difficult it is to distinguish between expression of an opinion, which the First Amendment strongly protects, and computer code, a form of speech the judge said the government could more easily regulate.† Jon Johansen was tried in Norway under a Norwegian law. The Norwegian court ruled that it was not illegal to break DVD security to view legally purchased DVDs and that the prosecutors had not proved Mr. Johansen used the program to illegally copy movies. In the United States, the movie industry continued to win cases.

A team of researchers responded to a challenge by the Secure Digital Music Initiative (SDMI), an industry consortium, to test its digital watermarking schemes (a form of copyright protection) for music files. The researchers quickly found ways to thwart several of the techniques and planned to present a paper on the flaws in the protection schemes at a conference. The head of the research group, Princeton University computer science professor Edward Felten, said SDMI threatened lawsuits based on the DMCA. He decided not to present the paper.[29] The DMCA has exceptions for actions necessary for encryption research and computer security, but the scope of the exceptions is limited and unclear. This case showed that the DMCA and the industry's threats of lawsuits have a chilling effect on publication of research. Software engineering journals worried about liability for some research papers they might publish. A major book publishing company decided not to publish a planned book on security vulnerabilities in popular game consoles. A computer science professional organization argued that fear of prosecution under the DMCA could

---

* The others chose to remain anonymous.

† Recall that encryption export rules (discussed in Chapter 2), like the DMCA, restricted publication of research and software, but eventually a judge ruled that software is a form of speech.

cause researchers and conferences to leave the United States, eroding its leadership in the field. Felten and other researchers sued for a court ruling that the anticircumvention provisions of the DMCA (when applied to software and research) violate the First Amendment. The case ended after the recording industry and the government issued statements that lawsuits under the DMCA against scientists and researchers studying access control technologies were not appropriate.[30]

Russian programmer arrested for violating the DMCA: Section 5.4.1

We saw in several cases in Section 4.1.6 that courts ruled, before the DMCA, that copying for reverse engineering to produce new products was a fair use. Now, people and companies avoid reverse engineering because the legality under the DMCA remains murky. New, innovative products that might have come to market, but do not because of the DMCA, are invisible.

Smartphones, tablets, game machines, and other devices have mechanisms to prevent installation of software or use of services that the maker of the device does not supply or approve. Cracking such mechanisms is sometimes called *jailbreaking*, unlocking, or *rooting*.* Originally, for example, Apple allowed only AT&T service contracts for iPhones; George Hotz figured out how to circumvent this limitation, as well as limitations on Sony game machines. Jailbreaking certain devices also lets users disable the feature that allows remote deletion of an app from the user's device. These uses do not infringe copyright. However, Apple[31] threatened DMCA lawsuits against a website that hosted discussion of reverse engineering iPods so that they could work with software other than iTunes. Other companies threatened suits for similar dicussions for other devices.

Exemptions

The Library of Congress decides on exemptions to the DMCA's anticircumvention provisions.[32] It now allows circumvention of CSS for fair use purposes. It allows an exemption for research on security vulnerabilities in access controls on CDs, but not as yet for research on such vulnerabilities for, say, video games. It ruled in 2010 that it is legal to alter phones to install third-party software (e.g., apps) or to use an alternate service provider. But the rule does not allow the same actions, for similar purposes, on other devices.[33] There is an exemption for circumventing access controls on ebooks to allow use of text-to-speech software (a useful function for blind people). However, the circumvention is legal only if *all* existing editions of the book have access controls that prevent enabling a read-aloud function or a screen reader.

As these examples illustrate, the exemptions the Library of Congress grants are very narrow. Many allow only a small action that does not infringe copyright and was legal before the DMCA. The exemptions come after years of threats, legal expenses, and delays in innovating new products or using lawfully purchased products. This is a very poor way to structure a law.

---

* I am using the terms informally, not with technical definitions.

4.2.3 The Digital Millennium Copyright Act: Safe Harbor

The "safe harbor" provisions of the DMCA protect websites from lawsuits and criminal charges for copyright infringement when users post infringing material. The site operators must make a good-faith attempt to keep infringing material off their sites. They must remove such material when asked to do so by the copyright owners (often publishers and music and movie companies). They can lose the protection if they profit from the infringing material. Like the safe harbor provisions of the Telecommunications Act of 1996 (Section 3.1.1) for other kinds of illegal content, this was a welcome protection for website owners and the public. It recognized that websites with user content have tremendous social value, but operators could not review everything members post. The safe harbor provisions of the DMCA, along with technological advances in the next several years, encouraged the development of thousands of websites that host user-generated content, including blogs, photos, videos, recipes, reviews, and the myriad other creative works we share on the Web. Holding the sites legally liable for copyright-infringing material a user might post could have severely restricted this phenomenon.

On the other hand, such sites include a huge amount of copyrighted material, from short clips from movies, TV shows, and concerts to entire movies and other shows. Copyright owners request removal of their content (and links to their content) by sending so-called takedown notices. Entertainment companies began sending floods of takedown notices. Infringing material appears and reappears faster than content owners can find it and request its removal.*[34] The entertainment industry and other content companies are unhappy that they have to bear the responsibility and expense of continually searching sites for material that infringes their copyrights and sending the takedown notices. They question the applicability of the safe harbor provision to large commercial websites such as YouTube. The companies argue that the large advertising revenue these sites take in depends in part on the unauthorized content. The safe harbor provision requiring the takedown notices might have been appropriate for legitimate websites of the 1990s whose business plans did not depend on users posting huge amounts of content. Today's sites, they argue, are similar to the peer-to-peer music sites (like Grokster) that made their money on the intellectual property of others without permission. They argue that the sites should have the responsibility of filtering out copyright-infringing material. The burden should not be on the copyright holders. Supporters of the safe harbor provisions fear that weakening safe harbor protection would threaten the many websites that host user-generated material. Viacom sued YouTube and asked for $1 billion in damages.[35] Viacom complained that it found 100,000 of its videos on YouTube. YouTube responded that it complied with the law. It regularly removes video clips when Viacom informs the company that the clips infringe Viacom copyrights. Video-sharing site Veoh won a similar case against a lawsuit by Universal Music both at the trial level and on appeal in 2011.

---

* Google, for example, takes down millions of links to copyright-infringing sites each year.

However, Veoh declared bankruptcy; it cited the huge legal costs. The Viacom case against YouTube, filed in 2007 and still in the courts, could clarify the extent of efforts a site must make to keep out infringing material.* In the meantime, technology has helped reduce the burden. Much of the detection and removal of infringing material is now automated. The content industries, large video sites, and social-networking sites use sophisticated tools to search through user-generated content for copyrighted material posted without authorization.

Although the safe harbor provision was a generally positive and important move, the takedown process has some weaknesses for websites and the public, as well as for the copyright holders. The takedown requirement of the DMCA is clearly open to abuse that threatens free speech and fair competition. Copyright holders are likely to interpret fair use principles narrowly and send takedown notices for material that might be fair use. A study of takedown notices found for about 30% of the notices there is significant question whether the material actually does infringe copyright. The fair use provisions protect much of it—for example, quotations from a book in an unfavorable book review. In one incident, Wendy Seltzer, a law professor, posted a video clip from a football game. YouTube removed it after the National Football League sent a takedown notice, then reposted it when Seltzer claimed it was an educational fair use (demonstrating issues about copyright—the clip included the NFL's copyright notice), then took it down again after the NFL sent another takedown notice. More than half of the notices businesses send to Google demanding removal of links to allegedly infringing Web pages come from competitors of the targeted sites.[36] How can search engine companies and websites evaluate all the takedown notices they receive? How should they respond when they receive a notice that they believe is intended to silence critics or undermine competitors? It is often not obvious how a court will interpret the fair use guidelines. Website operators are likely to protect themselves by complying with requests from large content companies with large legal staffs.

The entertainment industry and other content companies lobby to curtail the safe harbor provisions of the DMCA.[37] They argue that they need more legal tools to shut down pirate sites outside the United States. As in other situations where it is difficult to find or stop the people who are doing what the government wants to stop, the content companies would put more burden of enforcement (and penalties) on legitimate companies. For example, they advocate requiring ISPs to block access to designated infringing sites and requiring payment companies (e.g., Paypal and credit card companies) to stop processing payments to such sites. There is strong debate about how new stringent requirements would affect YouTube, search engines, Flickr, Twitter, and so on, as well as many small sites that do not have the staffs and expertise to comply.   Critics of such requirements warn that the standards the industy uses to identify infringing sites are too

---

* The DMCA is a U.S. law. Lawsuits in Europe have had varying results. YouTube won a case in Spain but lost one in Germany.

vague and broad, that ISP blocking can open security vulnerabilities, and that blocking access and funding, once begun, tends to expand to other purposes and threatens freedom of speech. Piracy continues to be a major headache and cost for the creators and owners of intellectual property. The challenge continues to be finding effective ways to reduce it without burdening legitimate activities and businesses or thwarting innovation and development of new services.

> *Washington regulating the Internet is akin to a gorilla playing a Stradivarius.*
>
> —L. Gordon Crovitz, Information Age columnist for the *Wall Street Journal*[38]

4.2.4 EVOLVING BUSINESS MODELS

> *The more we attempt to provide government protection to the old ways of doing business, the less motivation we provide to the entertainment industry to adapt and benefit from new technology.*
>
> —Les Vadasz, former vice president of Intel[39]

The success of Apple's iTunes, which has sold more than ten billion songs and tens of millions of videos, shows that companies can sell digital entertainment successfully, from the point of view of the customers and the rights holders. After the Supreme Court decision in *MGM v. Grokster* (Section 4.1.6), people who wanted to operate legitimate businesses providing music realized that they had to make agreements with, and payments to, music companies. The entertainment industry initially viewed new distribution technologies, such as peer-to-peer file-sharing, podcasting, and streaming content, as threats—as the movie industry did with video cassette recorders in the 1980s, before it got the idea that it could earn billions by renting and selling movies on cassettes. It seemed to take a long time, but many entertainment companies came to realize that people who share music files are people who like music; they are potential customers. The industry began to explore new business and marketing models. Music subscription services now thrive, with millions of songs available and hundreds of thousands of subscribers. They operate under agreements with the music companies. Similarly, many companies offer (authorized) movie download services.

For years, the music industry fought against distribution of music in (unprotected) MP3 format. Steve Jobs and some people in the entertainment industry argued that DRM was ineffective against piracy. Between 2007 and 2009, a major shift occurred in music sales. EMI Group, Universal Music Group, and Sony (some of the largest music companies in the world) began selling music without DRM. Apple eliminated DRM from its iTunes store for music. The debate about DRM continues within the movie and book industries. Some see DRM as essential to protect against piracy. They fear the industries will suffer severe economic losses if they do not include access controls on digital content. Others point out that pirated movies circulate unprotected. Controls and restrictions on legally sold content encourage irritated consumers to seek out illegal, unprotected copies even though they are willing to pay.

Some entertainment companies and Web content-sharing sites negotiate contracts for the site to pay a share of its ad revenue to the entertainment companies. YouTube and Warner Music Group, for example, worked out such an arrangement for Warner music videos. Sharing sites can use filtering software that examines files as people upload them, looking for digital "fingerprints" of the entertainment company's properties. Depending on agreements between the companies, the site can block a post entirely or pay the entertainment company for its appearance on the site. This is a creative way to allow users to post entertainment company material or include such material in their (usually noncommercial) creations without the overhead and legal liability for getting permissions. It makes sense that the Web companies that benefit from the advertising and have the assets and expertise to develop and use the sophisticated filtering tools make the payments, instead of individual users.

Safe harbor in the cloud?

Cloud services store a customer's files on online servers so that they are synched among the customer's devices and available from anywhere. Some cloud services enable sharing for small organizations or businesses. Cloud storage raises copyright issues. Is copying legally purchased files to and from the cloud a fair use? Will the companies operating the cloud services have any responsibility for unauthorized content their customers store and share on their servers? Unlike on public sites such as YouTube, an individual's content stored in the cloud is not visible to other people or to movie and music companies. The copying is personal from the perspective of the user, but the cloud service operator stores and provides the content to the individual conveniently as part of its business. Since copyright holders do not see what is stored, they do not have the option of sending takedown notices. If cloud services adopt a system of filtering or checking for content that infringes copyright, how will they manage it to protect fair use and the privacy of the user?

What does not work

Some attempts at new business models do not work. Zediva, a small startup in 2011, bought DVDs. It rented them to customers, but it did not send the physical DVD. Instead, it streamed the movie to the renter. Zediva argued that if it could rent the physical DVD without authorization from the studios, as do services such as Netflix under the first sale doctrine (Section 4.2.1), then it should be legal to rent it digitally over the Internet, streaming a movie from one DVD to only one renter at a time. The movie studios argued that streaming a movie is a public performance, which requires authorization. A court agreed and Zediva shut down.[40] Does this interpretation of the law make sense? Should Zediva's variant on streaming be legal?

Some business models appear intended to get around copyright law while helping people distribute illegally copied video. How far can they go? The Pirate Bay case (in Sweden, 2009) addressed the issue of whether the site violated Swedish copyright law by helping users find and download unauthorized copyrighted material (music, movies, computer games) even though the site itself did not host the material. Four organizers of the Pirate Bay were convicted of contributory copyright infringement. The Motion Picture Association of America has sued several other sites that do not host infringing videos but provide links to sites that do. It has won some of the suits. Do these sites differ in any fundamental way from the original Napster and Grokster? Should merely listing or linking to sites with unauthorized files be illegal?

Cyberlockers are services that provide storage of large files on the Web. Members transfer hundreds of thousands of files daily on popular sites. As on Napster more than a decade ago, singers and musicians store files on cyberlockers for free downloads to promote their work. The term cyberlocker, however, often refers to services that either intentionally encourage sharing files (e.g., movies) without authorization or structure their business in ways that make copyright infringement on a huge scale easy. The entertainment industry cites Megaupload, a cyberlocker that did more than $100 million in business (e.g., from membership fees), as an example of this form of piracy. Megaupload operated from Hong Kong and New Zealand, with servers in several countries, including the Netherlands. It had 180 million registered users. It claimed that its terms of use prohibited copyright infringement and that it took down infringing material when notified to do so. Determining whether a particular business illegally contributes to copyright infringement depends on consideration of the factors that are required for safe harbor protection and how seriously the business complies. The U.S. government shut Megaupload in 2012 (by legally seizing its domain names), and police in New Zealand arrested its founder and several employees. Other cyberlocker businesses modified some of their practices to protect themselves from legal action.[41]

4.3 Search Engines and Online Libraries

Copying is essential to many of the operations and services of search engines. In response to search queries, search engines display copies of text excerpts from websites and copies from images or video. In order to respond to user queries quickly, they copy and cache* Web pages and sometimes display these copies to users. Search engine companies copy entire books so that they can search them and display segments in response to user queries. Besides their own copying, search engines provide links to sites that might contain copyright infringing material. Individuals and companies have sued Google for almost every search service it provides (Web text, news, books, images, and video). Should

---

* Caching, generally in computer science, means storing data in specialized memory, frequently updated, to optimize transfer of the data to other parts of a system that use it.

Tools for authorized sharing

Many authors and artists, including those who sell their work on the Web, are willing to share—to a degree. How can they easily—without a publishing company's staff of lawyers and without the overhead of explicit authorization—indicate what they are willing to let others do with their work? From the user perspective, how does someone who wants to copy, say, a photo from someone else's website determine if he or she must get permission or pay a fee? Many people are willing to respect the preferences of an author or artist, but it is often not easy to determine what those preferences are.

Creative Commons,[42] a nonprofit organization, developed a spectrum of licensing agreements inspired by the GNU General Public License for software (Section 4.4). The licenses, which the author or artist announces to viewers by a choice of clickable icons, explicitly permit a selection of actions normally requiring authorization from the copyright owner. They provide a large degree of flexibility. For example, one can allow or disallow copying for commercial uses, require a specified credit line with any use, allow copies or display of the entire work only if there are no changes, allow use of pieces of the work in new works, or put the entire work in the public domain. Like so much on the Web, the use of the licenses and associated software is free. The photo site Flickr is one of the largest users of Creative Commons licensing. Anyone who stores photos on Flickr can indicate what uses he or she permits.

Easy-to-use schemes like this eliminate confusion and expensive overhead. They facilitate and encourage sharing while protecting the wishes of intellectual property owners.

search engines need authorization for the copying essential to search services? Should they be paying fees to copyright owners? As always, uncertainties about the legal status of industry practices can delay innovation. Google boldly introduces new services amid complaints of copyright infringement, but fear of lawsuits has deterred smaller companies that cannot estimate business costs in advance if they do not know their liability. We consider arguments related to a few of the contested practices.

The search engine practice of displaying copies of excerpts from Web pages seems easily to fit under the fair use guidelines. The excerpts are short. Displaying them helps people find the website with the excerpted document—usually an advantage to the site. In most cases, the site from which the search engine copies the excerpt is public, available to anyone who wants to read its content. Web search services are a hugely valuable innovation and tool for the socially valuable goal of making information easily available. In *Kelly v. Arriba Soft,* an appeals court ruled that copying images from Web pages, converting them to thumbnail images (small, low-resolution copies), and displaying the thumbnails to search engine users did not infringe copyrights. In *Field v. Google*, an author sued Google for copying and caching a story he had posted on his website. Caching involves copying entire Web pages. The court ruled that caching Web pages is a fair use. In dismissing a similar suit that challenged both caching and the practice of displaying excerpts from a website, a court compared Google to an ISP that makes copies of Web pages to display them to users. For ISPs, automatically and temporarily storing data to transmit to users does not infringe copyright.[43]

There are, however, some reasonable arguments on the other side. Most major operators of search engines are businesses. They earn significant revenue from advertising. Thus, the copying accomplishes a commercial purpose. The display of short excerpts can reduce income to copyright holders in some situations. A group of Belgian newspapers claimed they lose revenue from subscription fees when Google displays headlines, photos, and excerpts from their news archives. They won a lawsuit against Google (in a Belgian court) in 2007. In response to similar lawsuits and disputes with other news services, Google negotiated licensing agreements to copy and display headlines, excerpts, and photos.

Trademarked search terms

The practice of selling search terms raises intellectual property issues for trademarks. Businesses pay search engine companies to display the business's ads when a user enters specific search terms. What if a business "buys" the name of another company or the names of some of its products? Users searching for one company will see its competitor's ads. A company that makes software for learning foreign languages sued a competitor and Google over this issue. The case (*Rosetta Stone Ltd. v. Google Inc.*), filed in 2009, is still in the courts.

Books online

Project Gutenberg began converting books in the public domain into digital formats in the 1970s. Volunteers typed the entire text of the books—inexpensive scanners were not yet available. The University of California agreed to let Microsoft scan millions of books in its collection that are in the public domain. Google's project of scanning books in major university libraries differs in that Google scans books covered by copyright. Google provides entire books for download, but only those that are in the public domain. For books still under copyright protection, Google Book Search provides short excerpts from the books. Does Google's project infringe copyrights? How does the impact on the market for books differ from the impact of people browsing books in a library? How does it compare to providing excerpts from newspaper articles, as in the Belgian case we described above?

Publishers and authors filed several lawsuits against Google for copying their books. The court so far has rejected several versions of long, complex settlement agreements that Google and the publishers devised in *The Author's Guild et al v. Google, Inc.*. The agreements cover, among other things, sharing of proceeds from sales of out-of-print works, setting prices, and how much of a book Google could display as fair use, without payment. The main reason for the judge's rejection of the agreement in 2011 is that it would give Google significant rights to use books in the future in new ways, not related to the actions that the original lawsuit covered and without approval of copyright owners.

It would also release Google from liability for some future actions. In effect, it rewards Google "for engaging in wholesale copying of copyrighted works without permission."[44]

A French publisher, La Martiniere, won a suit against Google (in France) for scanning its books and putting extracts online without permission. Google and La Martiniere made an agreement to split revenue from digital sales of books.

Similar legal and ethical issues arise again each time technology makes copying and searching of more complex content (movies, for example) possible, especially for content produced explicitly to earn revenue (again, movies, for example). We see that search engine companies sometimes negotiate contracts with major intellectual property owners for displaying excerpts from and/or providing links to content such as images, news archives, television programs, books, and so on. Such contracts recognize that the search companies benefit from the use of another company's intellectual property, that some uses threaten the revenue of the copyright holders, and hence that, for both legal and ethical reasons, a search engine company might need permission to copy and display intellectual property for certain purposes.

4.4 Free Software

In Chapter 1, we talked about all the free stuff on the Web. Individuals post information and create useful websites. Large groups of volunteers, who do not know each other, collaborate on projects such as Wikipedia. Experts share their knowledge and contribute their work. This creation of valuable information "products" is decentralized. It has little or no "management" in the business sense. It flows from incentives other than profits and market pricing. This phenomenon, which some call "peer production," has a predecessor: the free software movement, begun in the 1970s.[45]

4.4.1 What Is Free Software?

Free software is an idea, an ethic, advocated and supported by a large loose-knit group of computer programmers who allow and encourage people to copy, use, and modify their software. The *free* in free software means freedom, not necessarily lack of cost, though often there is no charge. Free software enthusiasts advocate allowing unrestricted copying of programs and making the source code (the human-readable form of a program) available to everyone. Software distributed or made public in source code is *open source*, and the open source movement is closely related to the free software movement. (Commercial software, often called *proprietary software*, is normally sold in object code, the code run by the computer, but not intelligible to people. The source code is kept secret.)

Richard Stallman is the best-known founder and advocate of the free software movement. Stallman began the GNU project in the 1970s (though the GNU name dates from 1983). It began with a UNIX-like operating system, a sophisticated text editor, and many compilers and utilities. GNU now has hundreds of programs freely available and popular among computer professionals and skilled amateur programmers.* In addition, thousands of software packages are available as free software, including audio and video manipulation packages, games, educational software, and various science and business applications.[46]

Free software has many advantages. With freely distributed software, more people can use and benefit from a program. With source code available, any of thousands of programmers can find and fix bugs quickly. Users and programmers can adapt and improve programs. Programmers can use existing programs to create new and better ones. Stallman compares software to a recipe. We can all decide to add a little garlic or take out some salt without paying a royalty to the person who developed the recipe.

To enforce the openness and sharing of free software within the current legal framework that provides copyright protection, the GNU project developed the concept of *copyleft*.[47] Under copyleft, the developer copyrights the program and releases it under an agreement that allows people to use, modify, and distribute it, or any program developed from it, but only if they apply the same agreement to the new work. In other words, no one may develop a new program from a copylefted program and add restrictions that limit its use and free distribution. The widely used GNU General Public License (GPL) implements copyleft. Courts uphold copyright protection for open source software. A federal court said a person who distributes open source software can sue for an injunction against someone who uses the software for commercial products without following the open source licensing agreement.[48]

For a long time, technically savvy programmers and hobbyists were the principal users of free software. Commercial software companies were hostile to the idea. That view changed gradually, then more dramatically, with the Linux operating system.† Linus Torvalds wrote the Linux kernel in 1991. Torvalds distributed it for free on the Internet, and a global network of free software enthusiasts continue development. At first, Linux was difficult to use, not well suited as a consumer or business product. Businesses referred to it as "cult software." Two early users were the company that did the special effects for the movie *Titanic* and the NASA Goddard Space Flight Center. Gradually, small companies began selling a version of Linux along with manuals and technical support, and, eventually, major computer companies, including IBM, Oracle, Hewlett-Packard, and Silicon Graphics, used, supported, and marketed it. Large businesses such as Royal Dutch/Shell and Home Depot adopted Linux. Several movie studios adopted Linux for their special effects and digital animations. Dell sold PCs with Linux installed. Other examples of popular free software include Firefox, the Web browser provided by Mozilla, and Apache, the most widely used program to run websites. Google's mobile operating system, Android, which is Linux-based, has elements of free and open source software.

---

* "GNU" is an acronym for "GNU's Not UNIX." (Programmers like recursive acronyms.)

† Technically, Linux is the kernel, or core part, of the operating system. It is a variant of the earlier UNIX operating system. Other parts are from the GNU project, but the whole operating system is often referred to as Linux.

Major companies began to appreciate the benefits of open source. Several now make source code for their own products public, allowing free use in noncommercial applications. Sun Microsystems licensed the Java programming language under GPL.* Adopting the view of the free software movement, companies expected that programmers would trust the software more if they could see how it operates. Programmers might be more likely to use it and to improve it. IBM placed full-page ads in major newspapers announcing that it "embraced Linux and the open-source movement as a pillar of e-business."[49] IBM donates hundreds of its patents to the open source community. Free software became a competitor for Microsoft, and so those who are critical of Microsoft's products and influence see it as a considerable social benefit.

Critics (and some supporters) of free software point out some of its weaknesses. Much free software is not easy for ordinary consumers to use. Often, there is no technical support number to call for help. (Programmers and users share information about problems and fixes on very active websites.) Because anyone can modify free software, there are many versions and few standards, creating a difficult and confusing environment for nontechnical consumers and businesses. Many businesses want to deal with a specific vendor from whom they can request enhancements and assistance. They are uncomfortable with the loose structure of the free software movement. Some of these weaknesses faded as businesses learned how to work with a new paradigm. New businesses developed to support and enhance free software (like Red Hat for Linux), and more established businesses embraced the movement.

The spirit behind free software and open source spread to other forms of creative work. For example, the Berkeley Art Museum provides digital artworks online with their source files and allows people to download and modify the art.

4.4.2 Should All Software Be Free?

Some people in the free software movement do not believe that copyright should protect software at all. They argue that all software should be open source, free software. Thus, here we consider not the question "Is free software a good thing?" but "Should free software be the only thing?" When considering this question, we must take care to clarify the context of the question. Are we looking at it from the point of view of a programmer or business deciding how to release software? Are we developing our personal opinion about what would be good for society? Or are we advocating that we change the legal structure to eliminate copyright for software, to eliminate proprietary software? We will focus on the last two: Would it be good if all software were free software? And should we change the legal structure to require it?

Free software is undoubtedly valuable, but does it provide sufficient incentives to produce the huge quantity of consumer software available now? How are free software developers paid? Programmers donate their work because they believe in the sharing ethic.

---

* Oracle acquired Sun in 2010.

They enjoy doing what they do. Stallman believes that many good programmers would work like artists for low pay out of commitment to their craft. Contributions, some from computer manufacturers, support some free software efforts. Stallman has suggested government grants to universities as another way of funding software.

Would such funding methods for free software be sufficient? Most programmers work for a salary, even if they write free software on their own time. Would the extra services for which a business could charge bring in enough revenue to support all software development? Would the free software paradigm support the kinds of consumer software sold in millions of copies? What other funding methods could developers use?

A supporter of free software used the analogy of listener-supported radio and television. It is a good analogy for free software, but not one for eliminating proprietary software, because most communities have one listener-supported station and numerous proprietary ones.

Stallman believes that proprietary software—particularly, the aspect that prohibits people from making copies and changes in programs without the software publisher's approval—is ethically wrong. He argues that copying a program does not deprive the programmer, or anyone else, of use of the program. (We saw some counterarguments to this viewpoint in Section 4.1.5.) He emphasizes the distinction between physical property and intellectual property. He also points out that the primary purpose of copyright, as stated in the U.S. Constitution, is to promote progress in arts and sciences, not to compensate writers.[50]

For those who oppose copyright and proprietary software completely, the concept of copyleft and the GNU Public License provide an excellent device for protecting the freedom of free software within the current legal framework. For those who believe there are important roles for both free and proprietary software, they are an excellent device with which the two paradigms can coexist.

4.5 Patents for Inventions in Software*

Whoever invents or discovers any new and useful process, machine, manufacture, or composition of matter, or any new and useful improvement thereof, may obtain a patent therefor, subject to the conditions and requirements of this title.

—U.S. Patent Law (Title 35 U.S. Code, Section 101)

---

* Patent law is extremely complex. I use some terms informally, not in their precise legal meanings. The aim here is to present an overview of the controversies, not a legal analysis.

*A smartphone might involve as many as 250,000 (largely question-
able) patent claims.*

—David Drummond, Chief Legal Officer of Google[51]

Google, Apple, and Microsoft paid billions of dollars to buy thousands of wireless and
smartphone patents. It is generally recognized that the companies do not buy the patents
because they need them for products they are developing. They buy patents so that they
can sue other companies for patent infringement when the other companies sue them
for patent infringement. Google explicitly said it bid (billions of dollars) on thousands
of Nortel patents to "create a disincentive for others to sue Google" and to protect
continued innovation in Android and other projects.[52] It is common for news articles
to refer to "arsenals of patents" and to explicitly call patents "weapons." The large-scale
defensive (and offensive) accumulation of patents is a symptom of problems with patents
for innovations implemented in software and patents for business methods. (Business
methods, in our context, include innovations such as one-click shopping, recommending
products based on a customer's history, privacy controls, pop-up ads, and marketing to
smartphones.) Fierce controversies rage over such patents. One controversy is over whether
there should be patents for business methods and software-based inventions at all. There is
also controversy about many specific patents and about the criteria for granting software-
related patents. Billions of dollars and future technology development depend on how
these controversies are resolved.

How does—and how should—patent law apply to innovations implemented in
software? We will consider both aspects of this question. First, we review the murky state
of patent law in this area.

4.5.1   PATENT DECISIONS, CONFUSION, AND CONSEQUENCES

Patents protect inventions by giving the inventor a monopoly for a specified period
of time.* Patents differ from copyrights in that they protect the invention, not just a
particular expression or implementation of it. Anyone else who wants to use the patented
invention or process must get the authorization of the patent holder, even if the other
person independently came up with the same idea or invention. One device or machine
might involve many patents. Since 1895, for example, thousands of patents (with some
estimates over 100,000), have been issued covering various aspects of the automobile.
Laws of nature and mathematical formulas cannot be patented. Nor are patents to be
granted for an invention or method that is obvious (so that anyone working in the field
would have used the same method) or if it was in use by others before the filing of the
patent application.

---

* Under current law, the period is 20 years from the time of application.

A patent holder can build and sell the patented device or devices using the patented element. Also, the patent holder may license others to do so for a license fee, or royalty. Businesses routinely pay license fees to use patented inventions in their products.

The U.S. Patent and Trademark Office (which I will simply call the Patent Office) evaluates patent applications and decides whether to grant them. In the early days of computing technology, the Patent Office did not issue patents for software. In 1968, it declared computer programs not patentable. In 1981, the Supreme Court said that while software itself is not patentable because it is abstract, a machine or process that includes software, and in which the sole new aspect is the innovation implemented in the software, could be eligible for a patent. In the following decades, the Patent Office issued thousands of patents, and the Federal Circuit court (which handles patent appeals) approved many, interpreting Supreme Court guidelines loosely. Patents now cover encryption algorithms, data-compression algorithms, one-click shopping and other e-commerce techniques, copy-protection schemes, news feeds, location-based services for smartphones, delivery of email to cellphones, and so on. The Patent Office has a backlog of more than 600,000 patent applications. It grants an estimated 40,000 software patents each year. With hundreds of thousands of companies producing software, there are simply not enough patent attorneys to review the patents and determine if a new software product would violate an existing patent.[53]

Courts have made several attempts to clarify the conditions for innovations based in software to be patentable, often issuing decisions that reject prior criteria. Some decisions depended on whether software produced "a useful, concrete, and tangible result," whether a business method "transforms a particular article into a different state or thing," and whether the term "process" in patent law includes "methods." If these phrases and terms do not seem to clarify the criteria, that is the point. A significant Supreme Court ruling in 2007 (*KSR v. Teleflex*) broadened the definition of "obvious" for rejecting patents. In 2010 (*Bilski v. Kappos*), the court reemphasized that a patent must not give control over an abstract idea or mathematical algorithm. The decision declared a previous standard for software patentability to be only a "useful and important clue," not a determining factor, adding more fuzziness.[54] Justice Kennedy summed up the difficulties in making patent decisions and the court's declining to make a clear, general decision about software patents:

> It is important to emphasize that the Court today is not commenting on the patentability of any particular invention, let alone holding that any of the above-mentioned technologies from the Information Age should or should not receive patent protection. This Age puts the possibility of innovation in the hands of more people and raises new difficulties for the patent law. With ever more people trying to innovate and thus seeking patent protections for their inventions, the patent law faces a great challenge in striking the balance between protecting inventors and not granting monopolies over procedures that others would discover by independent, creative application of general principles. Nothing in this opinion should be read to take a position on where that balance ought to be struck.[55]

We saw that application of the fair use criteria for determining copyright infringement leads to uncertain results. The situation for patents is far more confused and unsettled. Judgments in some patent cases are close to or above $1 billion. Uncertainty and lawsuits are expensive, and they delay innovation.

A few cases

Decisions about granting patents are complex, as are decisions about whether a device or method infringes a patent. Reasonable decisions require knowledge of details of the particular case, expertise in the area, and knowledge of history of related technology. Establishing that an invention is not obvious and is not in use is difficult in fast-developing fields such as Web and smartphone technologies, especially when the Patent Office staff must research and process a large number of patent applications. The Patent Office makes mistakes. Various organizations, including the Electronic Frontier Foundation, argue that many patented techniques are not particularly new or innovative. For example, Amazon.com generated a lot of criticism when it sued Barnesandnoble.com for violating its patent on one-click shopping. Many in the industry objected that the government should not have granted the patent in the first place. (The companies settled the suit without disclosing the terms.)

Paul Allen (co-founder of Microsoft) sued several companies (Google, Facebook, Apple, eBay, Netflix, AOL, and others) for violating four early patents related to now widely used e-commerce and Web-viewing features. A judge dismissed the suit in 2011 while the Patent Office reconsiders the patents.[56]

Apple won a patent case against a maker of Android phones. It covers technology that allows a user to tap a touch screen to perform various tasks, such as calling a phone number that is in an email or text message. We can expect more lawsuits over software-related patents for smartphones.

Many Web users remember Amazon innovating the idea of recommending books to customers based on their previous purchases. But Amazon might not have originated the technique for doing so. IBM sued Amazon for violating several of its patents on e-commerce techniques. IBM had obtained a patent on electronic catalogues in 1994, before online retail was common. The patent covers a wide area, including targeted advertising and recommending specific products to a customer. Eventually, Amazon agreed to pay IBM a licensing fee.[57]

Patent trolls

Some companies accumulate thousands of technology patents, including many of the type of software patents and business method patents we are discussing. The firms buy most or all of their patents from individuals or other companies. They do not make any products. They license the patents to others and collect fees. Intellectual Ventures (co-founded by former Microsoft executive Nathan Myhrvold) is an example. The firm has an estimated 30,000 patents.* It says it has collected close to $2 billion in license fees. Some such companies make all or a significant part of their income by suing other companies for patent infringement (for hardware as well as software patents). Critics call these companies "patent trolls," a pejorative term.

Some see the existence of patent-licensing firms as an indication of a serious flaw in the patent system. However, *if* the patents themselves are legitimate (still an open question for many), this business model is not unreasonable. Marketing and negotiating contracts for patent licenses are services that an inventor might have neither the skills for nor the desire to do. A person or company might be better at inventing and patenting new technologies than at implementing them in a successful business. In a highly specialized economy, the existence of firms that buy and license patents is not in itself a negative thing. There are many analogous services in other contexts. (For example, some farmers sell their crop well in advance of harvest to free themselves from risks of market fluctuation. Firms with expertise in economics and risk analysis are the buyers.) However, as many critics of the current state of software patent law observe, when companies collect patents mainly or only to bring lawsuits for patent infringement, the law does not seem to be serving the goal of encouraging innovation well.

4.5.2 To Patent or Not?

In favor of software patents

The main arguments for allowing patents for software-based inventions and certain business methods are similar to those for patents and copyright in general. They reward inventors for their creative work. By protecting rights to the work, they encourage inventors to disclose their inventions so that others can build upon them. They encourage innovation.

Before the digital age, inventions were physical devices and machines. A huge portion of the astounding number of innovative developments in computing and communication technology consists of techniques implemented in software. These inventions have contributed enormous value to all of us. We take many for granted now, but they were truly innovative. Someone thought them up and developed them. Patents help to reward those people ethically and fairly and to encourage more innovation. Patent protection is necessary to encourage the large investment often required to develop innovative systems and techniques.

Businesses routinely pay royalties and license fees for use of intellectual property. It is a cost of doing business, like paying for electric power, raw materials, and so on. Software-related patents fit into this well-established context.

Copyright covers some software, but it is not sufficient for all of it. Software is a broad and varied field. It can be analogous to writing or to invention. A particular computer

---

* Intellectual Ventures obtained some of its patents on inventions it developed.

game, for example, might be analogous to a literary work, like a novel, and copyright would be appropriate. On the other hand, the first spreadsheet program, VisiCalc, introduced in 1979, was a remarkable innovation that had enormous impact on ways of doing business planning and on the sales of computer software and hardware. Similarly, the first hypertext system, the first peer-to-peer system, and many of the innovations that make smartphones so useful have characteristics more like new inventions. Patent might be more appropriate for such innovations.

Against software patents

Critics of software patents include those who oppose software patents in general as a matter of principle and those who conclude that the system developed so far has done a very poor job. Both see patents for software as stifling innovation, rather than encouraging it.

There are now so many software patents that it is difficult for software developers (individuals writing apps or large companies developing new technology) to know if their software infringes patents. Many software developers come up with the same techniques independently, but patent law does not allow them to use their own invention if someone else has patented it. The costs of lawyers to research patents and the risk of being sued discourage small companies from attempting to develop and market new innovations. Businesses cannot sensibly estimate costs of new products and services when lawsuits are so common and results so uncertain. Even large companies, as we indicated earlier, amass patents as defensive weapons for inevitable lawsuits.

If courts uphold patents for software techniques, common e-commerce and smartphone features, and so on, then prices will go up and we will see more incompatible devices and inconsistent user interfaces. In Section 4.1.6, we reviewed earlier controversies about copyrighting user interfaces (the "look and feel" of software systems). The principle that evolved in those cases—that uniformity of interfaces is valuable and that the look and feel should not be copyrightable—suggests a similar principle for patentability of user interfaces for smartphones.

It is difficult to determine what is truly original and to distinguish a patentable innovation from one that preempts an abstract idea, mathematical formula, or fact of nature. (Indeed, many computer scientists see all algorithms as mathematical formulas.) The very fact that there are so many controversial software and business method patents argues against granting these kinds of patents. The Supreme Court has not been able to arrive at clear, consistent legal criteria. This legal confusion suggests that it might be better not to issue patents in these areas.

Evaluating the arguments

Some of the problems of software patents are problems of patents in general. That does not mean we should abandon them; most things have advantages and disadvantages. (It does suggest areas for possible improvement.) Lawsuits over patents for physical inventions are common. (The holder of the 1895 patent on an automobile sued Henry Ford.)

Intellectual property law is a subset of property rights law. For complex areas, it sometimes takes many years to work out reasonable principles.* Software patent holders sue others who independently develop the same techniques, but all patents allow such suits. That is an unfair aspect of patents. Does it do significantly more damage for software-related inventions than for other inventions?

That there has been an enormous amount of innovation in the past decades is obvious. Looking at the same facts and trends, some see patents on software as essential to this innovation, whereas others see them as threatening it. While the patent system has some big flaws, it is likely one of the important factors that contributed to the centuries of innovation in the United States. Legal scholars and software industry commentators emphasize the need for clear rules so that companies can do their work without the threat of changing criteria and unforeseen lawsuits. So, is the idea of patenting software innovations fundamentally flawed, or is it that reasonable criteria have not yet developed? If the latter, is it better to stop granting such patents in the meantime, while better criteria develop, or is it better to continue to issue software patents?

Several Supreme Court justices stated in the *Bilski* case that, while certain patent criteria were useful for the industrial age, the information age and its new technologies need a new approach. We do not have a good new approach yet.

EXERCISES

Review Exercises

4.1   What are the four factors to consider in deciding whether a use of copyrighted material is a fair use?

4.2   Give an example in which plagiarism is also copyright infringement, and give an example in which it is not.

4.3   Summarize the main reasons why the court in the Sony Betamax case ruled that videotaping a movie from television to watch later was not an infringement of copyright.

4.4   Give an example of a device the music or movie industry has tried to ban.

4.5   Give two examples of uses of intellectual property that DRM controls.

4.6   What are the two main provisions of the Digital Millennium Copyright Act?

4.7   List some benefits of free software (in the sense of Section 4.4).

4.8   What was one type of controversial patent for a software-related innovation?

General Exercises

4.9   Describe two things the publishing industry has done to protect its copyrights. For each, tell whether you think the action is justified. Give reasons.

---

* Riparian law is a good example. If you own property that includes part of a river, do you have the right to build a dam, say, to produce energy or make a recreational lake? Do you have a right to a certain amount of clean water flowing by regularly? The two are incompatible; the latter implies that the owner upstream cannot build a dam.

4.10 Your uncle owns a sandwich shop. He asks you to write an inventory program for him. You are glad to help him and do not charge for the program. The program works pretty well, and you discover later that your uncle has given copies to several friends who also operate small food shops. Do you believe your uncle should have asked your permission to give away your program? Do you believe the other merchants should pay you for the copies?

4.11 A political group organized a forum on its website to encourage people to post and comment on individual newspaper articles relevant to political issues of concern to the group. Other participants added their comments, and debate and discussion of the articles continued. Two newspapers sued, arguing that posting the articles violated their copyrights. Analyze the case. How do the fair use guidelines apply? Who should win?[58]

4.12 During the 2008 presidential campaign, a graphic designer found a photo of Barack Obama on the Internet, modified it to look more like a graphic design, and made the very popular "Hope" campaign poster without credit to the photographer or permission from the Associated Press, which owns the photo. AP argued that the designer infringed AP's copyright and that the design, on sweatshirts, etc., produced hundreds of thousands of dollars in income. The designer claimed his use was a fair use. Using the fair use criteria, evaluate the claims.[59]

4.13 You are a teacher. You would like your students to use a software package, but the school's budget does not include enough money to buy copies for all the students. Your school is in a poor neighborhood, and you know most of the parents cannot afford to buy the software for their children.

   (a) List some ways you could try to obtain the software without making unauthorized copies.

   (b) Suppose the methods you try do not work. Will you copy the software or decide not to use it? Give some arguments for and against your position. Explain why you think the arguments on your side are stronger.[60]

4.14 Which of the following activities do you think should be a fair use? Give reasons using copyright law and/or court cases. (If you think the ethically right decision differs from the result that follows from applying the fair use guidelines, explain how and why.)

   (a) Making a copy of a friend's spreadsheet software to try out for two weeks, then either deleting it or buying your own copy.

   (b) Making a copy of a computer game, and playing it for two weeks, then deleting it.

4.15 Describe a situation involving making a copy of a computer program or an entertainment file of some sort for which you think it is difficult to decide if the copying is ethical or not. Explain the reasons for the uncertainty.

4.16 Mr. J wrote the first serious book on the problem of stuttering about 45 years ago. The book is out of print, and Mr. J has died. Mr. J's son wants to make this classic work available to speech pathologists by scanning it and putting it on his Web page. The publisher held the copyright (still in effect), but another company bought out the original publishing company. The son does not know who has the copyright now.

   (a) Analyze this case according to the fair use guidelines. Consider each of the criteria and tell how it applies. Do you think Mr. J's son should post the book?

   (b) Suppose Mr. J's son does put the book on the Web and that the publishing company holding the copyright asks a judge to issue an order for Mr. J to remove it. You're the judge. How would you rule? Why?

4.17 Do you think it is ethical to make drastic changes that are in conflict with the intended mood and nature of a musical composition after expiration of its copyright?

4.18 Service Consultants, a software support company, provides software maintenance service to customers of a software vendor. Service Consultants copied the vendor's program, not to resell the software but to provide service for clients. The vendor sued, and the service company argued that the copying was a fair use. Give arguments for each side. Which side do you think should win? Why?[61]

4.19 Describe an important benefit of the safe harbor provisions of the DMCA. Describe an important weakness of the safe harbor provisions from the perspective of the entertainment industries. Describe an important weakness from the perspective of the public.

4.20 A search engine company copies millions of books in a university library, including books in the public domain and books still protected by copyright. It displays segments—say, a paragraph—in response to user search requests. Analyze how the fair use guidelines apply to this practice for the books still covered by copyright. Should the copying and display be considered fair use, or should the company need permission from the copyright holders? (If you think the ethically right decision differs from the decision that follows from applying the fair use guidelines, explain how and why.)

4.21 The first Mickey Mouse cartoon appeared more than 80 years ago. Give ethical and/or social arguments both for and against each of the following uses of the cartoon or the Mickey Mouse character without authorization from the company that owned or owns the copyright. Tell which side you think is stronger, and why. Do not consider the copyright time period under current law or arguments about the ethics of obeying or breaking laws.

(a) Post a digitized copy of the original cartoon on a video-sharing site.

(b) Use the Mickey Mouse character as the spokeperson in an advertisement very strongly critical of a candidate running for president.

(c) Edit a digitized copy of the original cartoon to improve visual and sound quality, produce copies with the dialog dubbed in various other languages, and sell thousands of copies in other countries.

4.22 Companies selling music or movies (for example) can include digital rights management tools that cause files to self-destruct after a specified amount of time. Give some advantages and disadvantages of this practice. Do you think it is ethical for entertainment businesses to sell content with such a limitation? Why or why not?

4.23 Do you think taxing media and devices that aid copyright infringement (as described on pages 217–200) is a reasonable solution for collecting fees to pay content providers? Give your reasons.

4.24 (a) Suppose the movie industry asks a court to order a website to remove links to other sites that review movies and provide unauthorized (complete) copies of the movies for downloading. Give arguments for each side. What do you think the decision should be? Why?

(b) Suppose a religious organization asks a court to order a website to remove links to other sites that have copies of the organization's copyrighted religious documents. Give arguments for each side. What do you think the decision should be? Why?

(c) If your decisions are the same for both cases, explain what similarity or principle led you to that conclusion. If your decisions differ for the two cases, explain the distinction between the cases.

4.25 Pick two of the actions mentioned in the first paragraph of this chapter and tell whether or not they are legal and why. If there is not enough information given, explain what your answer would depend on.

4.26 Compare the following statements. Are they equally valid (or invalid)? Why or why not? Is home burglary a good analogy for disabling copy protection? Why or why not?

> One side effect of the DMCA's anticircumvention provision is to reduce incentive for the entertainment and publishing industries to develop truly strong protection schemes. The DMCA allows them to use weak schemes and then threaten legal action against anyone who cracks them.
>
> One side effect of laws against burglary is to reduce incentive for homeowners to use sturdy locks. The law allows people to use weak locks and then take legal action against anyone who breaks in.

4.27 In your opinion, which arguments for free software (as in Section 4.4) apply to software as a service (SaaS)? Which do not? Give reasons.

4.28 A cook can modify a recipe by adding or deleting a few ingredients without getting permission or paying a royalty to the person who developed the recipe.

(a) Give an example of modifications of a professional song or a piece of software that is analogous to a cook using the recipe.

(b) Do you think your example satisfies the fair use guidelines? That is, is it very likely courts would consider it a legal fair use? Explain why.

(c) Copyright protects cookbooks. A court would likely find that selling a cookbook in which many of the recipes are slight modifications of recipes in someone's else's cookbook is copyright infringement. Give an example of modifications of a professional song or a piece of software that is analogous to selling such a cookbook.

4.29 Thomas Jefferson and several modern writers used fire as an analogy for copying intellectual property: we can light many candles from one without diminishing the light or heat obtained from the first candle. Suppose a group of people go camping in the wilderness using primitive methods. One person gets a fire started. Others want to start their fire from hers. Give ethical or practical reasons why they might be expected to trade something, perhaps some wild fruit they found, for the use of the fire?

4.30 What effect do you think has the commercialization of software had on computing? How well has it worked? How has it affected the quantity and quality of software produced? Give reasons.

4.31 Do you agree with the view that innovative software should be protected by patents? Give reasons for your opinion. How does your view relate to the principles of free software?

4.32 Did you know, before you read this chapter, that restaurants pay fees for the music they play, community theaters pay fees for the plays they perform, and large companies routinely pay large fees to other companies for use of patented inventions and technologies? Does this long tradition of paying for intellectual property affect your view of the legitimacy of sharing entertainment on the Web without authorization? Give your reasons.

4.33 Think back a few years and describe a problem related to issues in this chapter that has been resolved by electronic technology or devices.

4.34 Think ahead to the next few years and describe a new problem, related to issues in this chapter, likely to develop from digital technology or devices.

Assignments

These exercises require some research or activity.

4.35 Read a license agreement for a software product. It could be a game, operating system, video editor, tax preparation program, and so on.

(a) What does the license agreement say about the number of copies you can make?

(b) Does it specify penalties for making unauthorized copies?

(c) Was the agreement easy to read before purchase (e.g., on the outside of the package or available on a website)?

(d) Do you consider the license agreement to be clearly stated? Reasonable?

4.36 Read the member agreement or policy statement of a website that hosts user videos. Give the name and Web address of the site you chose, and briefly describe it if it is not a well-known site. What does its statement say about posting files that contain or use works of others without authorization?

4.37 Find information about an entertainment industry copyright infringement lawsuit against websites that track torrents. Describe the issues involved, and the result or current status of the case.

4.38 Find and describe the result or current status of *The Author's Guild et al v. Google, Inc.*, the lawsuit against Google for digitizing books without permission (Section 4.3).

4.39 Read the articles by Esther Dyson and Lance Rose from *Wired* (listed in the references below). Write a short essay telling which author's views about the future of intellectual property in the "digital age" have proved more accurate based on events in the years since they wrote the articles.

Class Discussion Exercises

These exercises are for class discussion, perhaps with short presentations prepared in advance by small groups of students.

4.40 A website hosts written works posted by authors. Some people post copyrighted work by other authors without permission. When an author asks the site to remove such material, the site complies and adds the work to its filter database to prevent reposting without permission. An author sues the site claiming the site infringes her copyright by storing her work. Argue the author's case. Argue the site's defense. Evaluate the arguments and decide the case.

4.41 Some people argue that digital rights management violates the public's right to fair uses.

(a) Should a person or company that creates intellectual property have an ethical and/or legal right to offer it for sale (or license) in a form protected by their choice of digital rights management technology (assuming the restrictions are clear to potential customers)? Give reasons.

(b) Should people have an ethical and/or legal right to develop, sell, buy, and use devices and software to remove digital rights management restrictions for fair uses? Give reasons.

4.42 What is your opinion of the Stop Online Piracy Act (SOPA) in the United States?

4.43 Which factor is or will be more important for protection of digital intellectual property: strict copyright laws (and strict enforcement) or technology-based protections (or neither)? Why?

4.44 With respect to copyright issues for digital media and the Web, in what ways are entertainment companies victims? In what ways are entertainment companies villains?

4.45 Debate whether the source code for software should be publicly available (open source) or not (proprietary).

4.46 Discuss to what extent the finger movements we use to navigate on a smartphone touch screen should be patentable.

 ## BOOKS AND ARTICLES

- John Perry Barlow, "The Economy of Ideas: A Framework for Rethinking Patents and Copyrights in the Digital Age," *Wired*, March 1994, pp. 84–90, 126–129.

- Yochai Benkler, "Coase's Penguin, or Linux and *The Nature of the Firm*," *The Yale Law Journal*, December 2002, pp. 369–446, www.yalelawjournal.org/112/3/369_yochai_benkler.html or www.benkler.org/CoasesPenguin.html. An economic analysis of open source software and other forms of peer production.

- Henry Chesbrough, *Open Business Models*, Harvard Business School Press, 2006. How businesses use intellectual property, with emphasis on patents.

- Esther Dyson, "Intellectual Value," *Wired*, July 1995, pp. 136–141, 182–185.

- David D. Friedman, *Law's Order: What Economics Has to Do with Law and Why It Matters*, Princeton University Press, 2000, Chapter 11, "Clouds and Barbed Wire: The Economics of Intellectual Property." Economic pros and cons for intellectual property rights.

- Ben Klemens, *Math You Can't Use: Patents, Copyright, and Software*, Brookings Institution Press, 2005.

- Timothy B. Lee, *Circumventing Competition: The Perverse Consequences of the Digital Millennium Copyright Act*, Cato Institute Policy Analysis No. 564, Mar. 21, 2006.

- Lawrence Lessig, *Free Culture: The Nature and Future of Creativity*, Penguin, 2005.

- Jessica Littman, *Digital Copyright: Protecting Intellectual Property on the Internet*, Prometheus Books, 2001.

- Glyn Moody, *Rebel Code: Inside Linux and the Open Source Revolution*, Perseus, 2001.

- National Research Council, *The Digital Dilemma: Intellectual Property in the Information Age*, National Academy Press, 2000; books.nap.edu/html/digital_dilemma/notice.html.

- Andrew Oram et al., *Peer-to-Peer: Harnessing the Power of Disruptive Technologies*, O'Reilly, 2001.

- L. R. Patterson, *Copyright in Historical Perspective*, Vanderbilt University Press, 1968.

- Eric S. Raymond, *The Cathedral and the Bazaar*, O'Reilly, 1999.

- Lance Rose, "The Emperor's Clothes Still Fit Just Fine," *Wired*, February 1995, pp. 103–106.

- Adam Thierer and Wayne Crews, eds., *Copy Fights: The Future of Intellectual Property in the Information Age*, Cato Institute, 2002.

- Linus Torvalds and David Diamond, *Just for Fun: The Story of an Accidental Revolutionary*, HarperBusiness, 2001.

ORGANIZATIONS AND WEBSITES

- Chilling Effects Clearinghouse, a joint project of Stanford, Harvard, other universities, and the Electronic Frontier Foundation that helps to clarify and protect rights when misuse of intellectual property law chills freedom of speech: chillingeffects.org

- Creative Commons, an organization that provides a variety of free licensing tools for both protecting and sharing intellectual property on the Web: creativecommons.org

- The Electronic Frontier Foundation's page on intellectual property: www.eff.org/issues/intellectual-property

- The GNU project and free software: www.gnu.org/philosophy

- The Motion Picture Association of America: www.mpaa.org/contentprotection

- The Recording Industry Association of America: www.riaa.com

- The Software & Information Industry Association: www.siia.net

NOTES

1. www.copyright.gov/title17

2. Nicholas Negroponte, "Being Digital," *Wired*, February 1995, p. 182.

3. Pamela Samuelson, "Copyright and Digital Libraries," *Communications of the ACM*, April 1995, 38:3, pp. 15–21, 110.

4. Laura Didio, "Crackdown on Software Bootleggers Hits Home," *LAN Times*, Nov. 1, 1993, 10:22.

5. Phil Kurz, "One-quarter of global Internet traffic involves piracy, new study says," *Broadcast Engineering*, Feb. 9, 2011, broadcastengineering.com/ott/one-quarter-global-internet-traffic-involves-piracy-new-study-20110209, viewed Dec. 10, 2011. The figure for the United States is 17%, according to the study.

6. I used several sources for the history in this section. National Research Council, *Intellectual Property Issues in Software*, National Academy Press, 1991. Neil Boorstyn and Martin C. Fliesler, "Copyrights, Computers, and Confusion," *California State Bar Journal*, April 1981, pp. 148–152. Judge Richard Stearns, *United States of America v. David LaMacchia*, 1994. Robert A. Spanner, "Copyright Infringement Goes Big Time," *Microtimes*, Mar. 8, 1993, p. 36.

7. The piano roll case is *White-Smith Publishing Co. v. Apollo*, reported in Boorstyn and Fliesler, "Copyrights, Computers, and Confusion."

8. *Data Cash Systems v. JS & A Group*, reported in Boorstyn and Fliesler, "Copyrights, Computers, and Confusion."

9. In *Feist Publications, Inc. v. Rural Telephone Service Company, Inc.*, the Supreme Court ruled that Rural Telephone Service's telephone directory did not meet the requirement for copyright protection.

10. U.S. Code Title 17, Section 107.

11. Helen Nissenbaum, "Should I Copy My Neighbor's Software?" in Deborah G. Johnson and Helen Nissenbaum, *Computers, Ethics & Social Values*, Prentice Hall, 1995, pp. 201–213.

12. *Sony Corporation of America v. Universal City Studios, Inc.*, 464 U.S. 417(1984). Pamela Samuelson, "Computer Programs and Copyright's Fair Use Doctrine," *Communications of the ACM*, September 1993, 36:9, pp. 19–25.

13. "9th Circuit Allows Disassembly in Sega vs. Accolade," *Computer Law Strategist*, November 1992, 9:7, pp. 1, 3–5. "Can You Infringe a Copyright While Analyzing a Competitor's Program?" *Legal Bytes*, George, Donaldson & Ford, L.L.P., publisher, Winter 1992–93, 1:1, p. 3. Pamela Samuelson, "Copyright's Fair Use Doctrine and Digital Data," *Communications of the ACM*, January 1994, 37:1, pp. 21–27.

14. *Sony Computer Entertainment, Inc. v. Connectix Corporation*, U.S. 9th Circuit Court of Appeal, No. 99-15852, Feb. 10, 2000.

15. Karl Taro Greenfeld, "The Digital Reckoning," *Time*, May 22, 2000, p. 56.

16. Stuart Luman and Jason Cook, "Knocking Off Napster," *Wired*, January 2001, p. 89. Karl Taro Greenfeld, "Meet the Napster," *Time*, Oct. 2, 2000, pp. 60–68. "Napster University: From File Swapping to the Future of Entertainment," June 1, 2000, described in Mary Hillebrand, "Music Downloaders Willing to Pay," *E-Commerce Times*, June 8, 2000, www.ecommercetimes.com/story/3512.html (accessed September 6, 2007).

17. Charles Goldsmith, "Sharp Slowdown in U.S. Singles Sales Helps to Depress Global Music Business," *Wall Street Journal*, Apr. 20, 2001, p. B8.

18. *A&M Records v. Napster*, No. 0016401, Feb. 12, 2001, DC No. CV-99-05183-MHP.

19. *Vanderhye v. IParadigms LLcC*, decided Apr. 16, 2009, U.S. Court of Appeals, Fourth Circuit, caselaw.findlaw.com/us-4th-circuit/1248473.html, viewed Nov. 29, 2011.

20. David L. Hayes, "A Comprehensive Current Analysis of Software 'Look and Feel' Protection," Fenwick & West LLP, 2000, at www.fenwick.com/pub/ip_pubs.

21. "Eighth Annual BSA Global Software Piracy Study," portal.bsa.org/globalpiracy2010, viewed Dec. 14, 2011.

22. 2010 data from Owen Fletcher and Jason Dean, "Ballmer Bares China Travails," *Wall Street Journal*, May 27, 2011, online.wsj.com/article/SB1000142405270230365480457634719024854826.html, and from Wang Yan, "Software Piracy Rate Declining," *China Daily*, May 11, 2011, www.chinadaily.com.cn/china/2010-05/11/content_9831976.htm, both viewed Dec. 14, 2011. 1994 data from Software Publishers Association, "SPA Report on Global Software Piracy."

23. *RIAA v. Diamond Multimedia*, 1999.

24. *Bobbs-Merrill Co. v. Straus*, 1908. The first-sale principle became part of copyright law in 1976.

25. Some of the examples here and many others appear in Root Jonez, "Unintended Consequences: Twelve Years under the DMCA," Electronic Frontier Foundation, March 3, 2010, www.eff.org/wp/unintended-consequences-under-dmca#footnoteref18_9iu0f8l, viewed Dec. 7, 2011.

26. J.S. Kelly, "Meet the Kid Behind the DVD Hack," CNN.com, Jan. 31, 2000, archives.cnn.com/2000/TECH/computing/01/31/johansen.interview.idg/, viewed May 10, 2007.

27. *Universal City Studios, Inc. v. Reimerdes*, 111 F.Supp.2d 294 (S.D.N.Y. 2000).

28. David S. Touretzky, a computer science professor at Carnegie Mellon University, collected many forms of expressing DeCSS on his website, "Gallery of CSS Descramblers," www.cs.cmu.edu/~dst/DeCSS/Gallery; viewed Apr. 12, 2001.

29. The paper leaked and appeared on the Web. It was eventually published at a computer security conference. Scott A. Craver et al, "Reading Between the Lines: Lessons from the SDMI Challenge," www.usenix.org/events/sec01/craver.pdf.

30. Jonez, "Unintended Consequences: Twelve Years under the DMCA." *Felten et al. v. RIAA, SDMI, et al.*. The statement by the ACM, one of the major organizations for professional and academic computer scientists, is at www.acm.org/usacm/copyright/felten_declaration.html.

31. Apple, Inc.

32. Copyright Office, Library of Congress, "Exemption to Prohibition on Circumvention of Copyright Protection Systems for Access Control Technologies," *Federal Register*, v. 71, no. 227, Nov. 27, 2006, www.copyright.gov/fedreg/2006/71fr68472.html, viewed Mar. 15, 2007. For exemptions proposed in 2010 to be decided in 2012, see www.copyright.gov/1201/2010.

33. The Library of Congress considered extending the exemption to more devices in its next set of rules, expected in October, 2012.

34. Geoffrey A. Fowler, Devlin Barrett, and Sam Schechner, "U.S. Shuts Offshore File-Share 'Locker,'" *Wall Street Journal*, Jan. 20, 2012, online.wsj.com/article/SB10001424052970204616504577171060611948408.html, viewed Feb. 19, 2012.

35. *Viacom International, Inc. v. YouTube, Inc.*

36. Jennifer M. Urban and Laura Quilter, "Summary Report: Efficient Process or 'Chilling Effects'? Takedown Notice under Section 512 of the Digital Millennium Copyright Act," mylaw.usc.edu/documents/512Rep-ExecSum_out.pdf; full report in *Santa Clara Journal of High Tech Law and Technology*, March 2006.

37. For example, they supported the Stop Online Piracy Act in 2012.

38. L. Gordon Crovitz, "Horror Show: Hollywood vs. Silicon Valley," *Wall Street Journal*, Nov. 28, 2011, online.wsj.com/article/SB10001424052970204452104577059894208244720.html, viewed Dec. 10, 2011.

39. Les Vadasz, "A bill that chills," *Wall Street Journal*, July 21, 2002, p. A10.

40. Ryan Singel, "Movie Studios Sue Streaming Movie Site Zediva," *Wired*, Apr. 4, 2011, www.wired.com/epicenter/2011/04/mpaa-sues-zediva, and Barbara Ortutay, "Movie Studios Win Lawsuit against Zediva," Oct. 31, 2011, finance.yahoo.com/news/Movie-studios-win-lawsuit-apf-984811847.html, both viewed Dec. 15, 2011.

41. Joe Mullin, "How 'Cyberlockers' Became the Biggest Problem in Piracy," Jan. 19, 2011, paidContent.org, paidcontent.org/article/419-how-cyberlockers-became-the-biggest-problem-in-piracy, viewed Feb. 21, 2012.

42. creativecommons.org

43. *Parker v. Google*, U.S. District Court for the Eastern District of Pennsylvania, 2006. Elinor Mills, "Google wins a court battle," CNET News.com, news.com.com, Mar. 16, 2006.

44. Judge Denny Chin, *The Author's Guild et al v. Google, Inc.*, Mar. 22, 2011, www.nysd.uscourts.gov/cases/show.php?db=special&id=115, viewed Dec. 12, 2011.

45. See Yochai Benkler, "Coase's Penguin, or Linux and *The Nature of the Firm*," *The Yale Law Journal*, December 2002, pp. 369–446, www.yalelawjournal.org/112/3/

369_yochai_benkler.html for an analysis of the phenomenon of peer production.

46. The Free Software Directory, directory.fsf.org/wiki/Main_Page, viewed Dec. 14, 2011.

47. "What Is Copyleft?" www.gnu.org/philosophy.

48. The case involves model train software distributed by Robert Jacobsen.

49. For example in the *Wall Street Journal*, May 11, 2000, p. A7.

50. This is a brief summary of Stallman's views. See his article "Why Software Should Be Free" and many others at the GNU website, www.gnu.org/philosophy.

51. David Drummond, "When Patents Attack Android," *The Official Google Blog*, Aug. 3, 2011, googleblog.blogspot.com/2011/08/when-patents-attack-android.html, viewed Dec. 16, 2011. For a diagram illustrating this statement, see Steve Lohr, "A Bull Market in Tech Patents," *New York Times*, Aug. 16, 2011, www.nytimes.com/2011/08/17/technology/a-bull-market-in-tech-patents.html, viewed Feb. 25, 2012.

52. Kent Walker, "Patents and innovation," *The Official Google Blog*, Apr. 4, 2011, googleblog.blogspot.com/2011/04/patents-and-innovation.html, viewed Dec. 20, 2011. The Nortel patents were sold in a bankruptcy auction.

53. The estimated number of software patents and the observation about the impossibility of checking them are from Christina Mulligan and Timothy B. Lee, "Scaling the Patent System," *NYU Annual Survey of American Law*, forthcoming (abstract at Social Science Research Network, papers.ssrn.com/sol3/papers.cfm?abstract_id=2016968##).

54. Key cases are *Diamond v. Diehr*, 450 U.S. 175 (1981); *State Street Bank & Trust Co. v. Signature Financial Group*, 1998; *In re Bilski*, Federal Circuit, 2008; *Bilski v. Kappos*, June 28, 2010,

www.supremecourt.gov/opinions/09pdf/08-964.pdf, viewed Dec. 26, 2011. See also Daniel Tysver, "Are Software and Business Methods Still Patentable after the Bilski Decisions?" *Bitlaw*, 2010, www.bitlaw.com/software-patent/bilski-and-software-patents.html, viewed Dec. 21, 2011.

55. *Bilski v. Kappos*.

56. Susan Decker, "Paul Allen's Lawsuit against Apple, Google to Remain on Hold," *Bloomberg*, July 14, 2011, www.bloomberg.com/news/2011-07-14/paul-allen-s-lawsuit-against-apple-google-to-remain-on-hold.html, viewed Dec. 19, 2011.

57. Charles Forelle and Suein Hwang, "IBM Hits Amazon with E-Commerce Patent Suit," *Wall Street Journal*, Oct. 24, 2006, p. A3.

58. This exercise is based on the *Los Angeles Times v. Free Republic* case. The court's decision in favor of the newspapers seems inconsistent with the reasoning in the reverse engineering cases described in Section 4.1.6 and other fair use cases. It was criticized by some scholars.

59. The designer, Shepard Fairey, and AP settled out of court in 2011, with some details of the settlement confidential. Fairey later pleaded guilty to fabricating documents and lying during the litigation process.

60. This exercise was sparked by a brief note in Helen Nissenbaum, "Should I Copy My Neighbor's Software?" in Deborah G. Johnson and Helen Nissenbaum, *Computers, Ethics & Social Values*, Prentice Hall, 1995, p 213.

61. In a few such cases the software support companies were found to have infringed copyright. In 2010, Oracle won a large jury award from SAP for actions of its TomorrowNow unit, which provided support for Oracle software.

5

CRIME

5.1 Introduction

Nineteenth-century bank robbers fled the scenes of their crimes on horseback. In the 20th century, they drove getaway cars. In the 21st, they work from a computer. For generations, teenagers have committed pranks and minor crimes. Hacking into school, corporate, and government computer systems was a natural step. Employees embezzled funds from employers by "doctoring" the books. Now they modify or misuse company software. Computing technology and the Internet provide new environments for fraud, stock manipulation, theft, forgery, industrial espionage, and many old and new scams. Hacking—intentional, unauthorized access to computer systems—includes a wide range of activities from minor pranks to huge thefts and shutdowns of services on which lives and livelihoods depend.

Crimes committed with computing technology are more devastating and harder to detect than similar crimes committed without it. A robber who enters a bank and uses a gun gets $2,500–$5000 on average. The average loss from a computer fraud is more than $100,000.[1] A thief who steals a credit card (or a credit card number) gains access to a much larger amount of money than the thief of the past who stole a wallet containing only cash. A hacker who breaks into a retailer's or bank's computer might steal not one or a dozen but thousands or millions of credit card numbers. Identity theft affects millions of people. It can disrupt a victim's life for years. Computer vandalism by teenagers brings business operations of major companies to a halt. Terrorists could sabotage power and communications systems and other critical infrastructure. Global business networks and the Web extend the criminal's reach and make arrests and prosecutions more difficult. With so much sensitive information and infrastructure online, why is security weak enough to allow repeated significant breaches?

Activities that are legal in some countries are illegal in others. But the Web is global. Businesses and individuals are sued and arrested for violating laws of countries that their online business or writing reaches. How serious is this problem, and how can we deal with it?

In this chapter, we examine many of these problems and a variety of approaches for addressing them. The examples we include are representative of dozens or hundreds more.

5.2 Hacking

5.2.1 What is "Hacking"?

The term "hacker," to many people, means an irresponsible, destructive criminal. Hackers break into computer systems. They intentionally release computer viruses. They steal sensitive personal, business, and government information. They steal money, crash websites, destroy files, and disrupt businesses. But other people who call themselves hackers do none of these things. So our first problem is to figure out what "hacker" means and what hackers do.

To organize the discussion, we describe three phases of hacking:

Phase 1—the early years (1960s and 1970s), when hacking was a positive term
Phase 2—from the 1970s to the 1990s, when hacking took on its more negative meanings
Phase 3—beginning in the mid-1990s, with the growth of the Web and of e-commerce and the participation of a large portion of the general public online

The boundaries are not sharp, and each phase includes the kinds of hacking common in the earlier phases. In Sections 5.2.2, 5.2.3, and 5.2.4, we consider hacking for special purposes (political activism, hacking to expose security flaws, and government hacking for military purposes).

Phase 1: The joy of programming

In the early days of computing, a "hacker" was a creative programmer who wrote very elegant or clever programs. A "good hack" was an especially clever piece of code. Hackers were "computer virtuosos." They created many of the first computer games and operating systems. They tended to be outside the social mainstream. Many were high school and college students—or drop-outs. Although they sometimes found ways into systems where they were not authorized users, the early hackers mostly sought knowledge and intellectual challenges—and, sometimes, the thrill of going where they did not belong. Most had no intention of disrupting services; they frowned on doing damage. The *New Hacker's Dictionary* describes a hacker as a person "who enjoys exploring the details of programmable systems and how to stretch their capabilities; . . . one who programs enthusiastically (even obsessively)."[2] Jude Milhon described hacking as "clever circumvention of imposed limits."[3] The limits can be the technical limits of the system one is using, the limits that someone else's security techniques impose, legal limits, or the limits of one's own skills. Her definition is a good one in that it encompasses many of the uses of the term.

"Hacking" still sometimes has the early meaning of clever programming that reflects a high level of skill and that circumvents limits. Fans of Nintendo's Wii videogame console reprogrammed its remote controller to perform tasks Nintendo never imagined. Soon after Apple released the iPhone, hackers found ways to make it operate in ways Apple had tried to prevent. Hundreds of people gather for day-long "hackathons," to work intensely at developing innovative new software products. Another example, of course, is software to circumvent the limits of protection schemes for digital intellectual property (discussed in Section 4.2.2). Hacking often has a whiff, at least, of challenge to powerful institutions.

Phase 2: From the 1970s to the mid-1990s

The meaning, and especially the connotations, of the word "hacker" changed as more people began using computers and more people began abusing them. The word eventually took on its most common meaning today: breaking into computers for which the hacker does not have authorized access. By the 1980s, hacking also included spreading computer viruses, then mostly in software traded on floppy disks. Hacking behavior included pranks, thefts (of information, software, and sometimes money), and *phone phreaking* (manipulating the telephone system). Hackers obtained passwords by sophisticated techniques and by *social engineering*: fooling people into disclosing them.

Hacking a computer at a big research center, corporation, or government agency was a challenge that brought a sense of accomplishment, a lot of files to explore, and respect from one's peers. This "trophy" hacking was often associated with young hackers. Young hackers were especially fond of breaking into Defense Department computers, and they were very successful at it. Clifford Stoll described a more serious case in his book *The Cuckoo's Egg*: a German hacker broke into dozens of U.S. computers, including military systems, in the 1980s, looking for information to sell to the Soviet Union.

A program known as the Internet Worm demonstrated the vulnerability of the Internet as a whole in 1988. A graduate student at Cornell University wrote the worm and released it onto the Internet.* The worm did not destroy files or steal passwords, and there was disagreement about whether its author intended or expected it to cause the degree of disruption that it did. However, it spread quickly to computers running particular versions of the UNIX operating system, jamming them up and preventing normal processing. The worm affected a few thousand computers (a large portion of the Internet at the time). It took a few days for systems programmers to discover, decode, and rid their systems of the worm. The worm disrupted work and inconvenienced a large number of people. This incident raised concern about the potential to disrupt critical computer services and cause social disruption.[4]

Adult criminals began to recognize the possibilities of hacking. Thus, business espionage and significant thefts and frauds joined the list of hacking activities in the 1980s and 1990s. For example, a Russian man, with accomplices in several countries, used stolen passwords to steal $400,000 from Citicorp. He transferred another $11 million to bank accounts in other countries. This incident illustrates the international nature of computer crimes and some of the difficulties it creates for law enforcement. Extraditing the Russian man from London, where he was arrested, to the United States for trial took more than two years.

Phase 3: The growth of the Web and mobile devices

Beginning roughly in the mid-1990s, the intricate interconnectedness of the Web and the increased use of the Internet for email and other communications, for sensitive information, and for economic transactions made hacking more dangerous and damaging—and more attractive to criminal gangs. The kind of accessible information expanded to include

---

*A worm is a program that copies itself to other computers. The concept was developed to make use of idle resources, but it was adopted by people using it maliciously. A worm might destroy files or just waste resources.

credit reports, consumer profiles, medical records, tax records, confidential business information, and other types of information we described in Chapter 2 when we discussed
threats to privacy. With basic infrastructure systems (for example, water and power, hospitals, transportation, emergency services, in addition to the telephone system) accessible
on the Net, the risk increased. Hacking for political motives increased. As the Web spread
globally, so did hacking. We describe examples ranging from new pranks to serious disruptions.

Pranksters modified the U.S. Department of Justice Web page to read "Department
of Injustice" in protest of the Communications Decency Act. They changed the CIA's
site to read "Central Stupidity Agency" and added links to pornography sites.[5]

A teenager crippled a computer system that handled communications between the
airport tower and incoming planes at a small airport. Hackers in England impersonated air
traffic controllers and gave false instructions to pilots. Hackers took over Federal Aviation
Administration (FAA) computers in Alaska, resulting in a shutdown of part of the system.
The hackers also appeared to have access to thousands of FAA passwords.

More than a decade after the Internet Worm, numerous viruses showed that the
Internet, by then much bigger, was still vulnerable. The Melissa virus of 1999 infected approximately a million computers worldwide. In 2000, the "Love Bug," or "ILOVEYOU"
virus, spread around the world in a few hours. It destroyed image and music files, modified
a computer's operating system and Internet browser, and collected passwords. This virus
infected major corporations like Ford and Siemens and 80% of U.S. federal agencies,
including the State Department and the Pentagon, along with members of the British
Parliament and the U.S. Congress. Many businesses and government agencies had to
shut down their email servers. The virus hit tens of millions of computers worldwide and
did an estimated $10 billion in damage.[6]* Viruses and worms such as Code Red, Zotob,
Sasser, and MyDoom caused hundreds of millions or billions of dollars in damage. Some
viruses set up a "back door" on infected computers that allowed later access to sensitive
information such as credit card numbers.

Within about one week, *denial-of-service attacks* shut down almost a dozen major
websites, some for several hours. Victims included Yahoo, eBay, Amazon, E∗Trade,
Buy.com, CNN, and others. In this kind of attack, hackers overload the target site with
hundreds of thousands of requests for Web pages and other information. Programs planted
on numerous other systems (many at universities), to disguise their origin, generate the
requests. Investigators traced the attack to a 15-year-old Canadian who used the name
mafiaboy; he pleaded guilty to a long list of charges. The U.S. government estimated the
cost of this incident at $1.7 billion. One disturbing aspect of this case is that mafiaboy
apparently did not write the destructive programs himself. He found them on the Net,
where other 15-year-olds can find them too.[7]

---

* Damages from such virus attacks are difficult to value precisely; estimates may be rough.

The purposes and techniques of hacking have shifted as the Web and the amount of stored data of all kinds have grown. Hackers steal millions of credit card numbers from large retailers, restaurant chains, banks, and so on. Some are members of organized crime groups; others sell the numbers to organized crime groups. Some demand extortion payments. Such incidents signaled the beginning of the huge problem of credit card fraud and identity theft that we discuss in Section 5.3.

A new type of virus became popular. The virus gives the person who distributed it the power to remotely control the infected computers. Tens of thousands of infected computers (called *zombies*) send spam, contribute to denial-of-service attacks, participate in various kinds of online advertising fraud, and so on. The actual owners of the zombie computers are usually unaware of what their computers are doing. A 21-year-old California man pleaded guilty and was sentenced to almost five years in prison (the longest hacking sentence at that time, 2006) for a collection of offenses related to such a virus. He, according to prosecutors, took over hundreds of thousands of computers (some at military sites), used the infected computers to commit fraud, and "rented" them to others for sending spam and for criminal schemes. In the same year, an antispam expert reported a sophisticated international scam. It involved 20 billion spam messages sent within a two-week period from more than 100,000 computers in more than 100 countries. The messages directed people to e-commerce websites where the unwary ordered products with their credit cards and received nothing. Credit card charges went to a company in Russia. This scam illustrates the growing complexity of crime on the Web combining hacking, spam, phony websites, and international fraud.[8]

As computer systems replaced human ticket sellers for transportation and other services, hackers found more opportunities for theft. For example, New York City accused several people of stealing $800,000 from the city's subway system by taking advantage of an error in the software in the machines that sell fare cards.

Hackers continue to execute pranks and revenge attacks—some quite expensive. Hackers modified the programming at an online gambling site so that everyone won. The site lost $1.9 million. After police raided a popular pirate music site in Sweden, an apparent retaliation attack by hackers shut down the main websites of the Swedish government and police. After Sony sued George Hotz in 2011 for showing how to run unauthorized applications and games on Sony's PlayStation 3, a hacker group launched a denial-of-service attack on Sony and accessed names, birthdates, and credit card information of millions of users of Sony's gaming systems.[9] Hackers attacked companies that criticized or withdrew services from WikiLeaks.

As social networks grew, they became targets of hackers. In 2011, hackers gained access to Facebook member profile pages and posted pornographic and violent images. The hackers had tricked members into running malware. It is a common tactic for hackers to create fake offers of discounts, freebies, or just something funny or interesting. Clicking on it initiates the malware. In this particular attack the purpose might have been to express criticism of a company whose policies the hackers disapprove. Similar attacks encourage a social media friend to view a video. The video site indicates that the user must install software to view the clip; that software is malware. Social networks offer a huge pool of potential victims who are used to sharing.[10]

Hacking of mobile devices (other than stolen laptops) has not yet been a major problem (while I am writing this), but I expect it to become one. With smartphones acting as electronic wallets and tablets synching to all one's data in clouds, they will be attractive targets.

Is "harmless hacking" harmless?

In many cases, it is the excitement and challenge of breaking in that motivates young hackers. Some claim that such hacking is harmless. Is it?

When a system administrator for a computer system at a university, a website, a business, or the military detects an intruder, he or she cannot immediately distinguish a nonmalicious hacker from a thief, terrorist, or spy. The administrator must stop the intrusion. The administrator's responsibility is to protect the system and its data. Thus, at a minimum, the organization will expend time and effort to track down the intruder and shut off his or her means of access. Companies sometimes shut down their Internet connection, at great inconvenience, while investigating and defending against an intruder. Responding to nonmalicious or prank hacking uses resources that might be needed to respond to serious threats.

Uncertainty about the intruder's intent and activities has additional costs for systems that contain sensitive data. According to the head of the computer crime unit at the Department of Justice, after a hacker accessed a Boeing Corporation computer, apparently just to hop to another system, Boeing spent a large sum to verify that the intruder changed no files. Would we be comfortable flying a new Boeing airplane if they had *not* done this? A group of young Danes broke into National Weather Service computers and computers of numerous other government agencies, businesses, and universities in the United States, Japan, Brazil, Israel, and Denmark. Eventually, police caught them. It appeared they had done little damage. But consider the risks. Their activities caused the Weather Service computers to slow down. There was the potential that serious conditions, such as tornadoes, could have gone undetected and unreported.[11] Similarly, if system administrators detect unauthorized access in a medical records system, a credit database, or payroll data, they must stop the intruders and determine whether they copied or changed any records. Uncertainty causes harm, or expense, even if hackers have no destructive intent.

Another problem, of course, is that a hacker with good intentions could make a mistake and do significant damage accidentally. Almost all hacking is a form of trespass. Hackers with nonmalicious intentions should not be surprised that others will often not view them kindly.

5.2.2 Hacktivism, or Political Hacking

Hacktivism is the use of hacking to promote a political cause. Is there ethical justification for such hacking? Should penalties for hacktivists differ from penalties for other hackers? Just as hacking in general ranges from mild to highly destructive activities, so can political hacking. We consider some examples.

Someone posted a pro-drug message on a police department antidrug website. Earlier we mentioned incidents of defacement of U.S. government websites; many make implicit political statements. Three teenagers hacked into the network of an atomic research center in India and downloaded files to protest India's tests of nuclear weapons. Hacktivists targeted the governments of Indonesia and China for their antidemocratic policies. A hacker group hacked into the Bay Area Rapid Transit (BART) system and released emails, passwords, and personal information about a few thousand BART customers. They did this to protest BART's controversial shutdown of wireless communication in several BART stations to thwart a planned protest demonstration.

A fundamental problem with evaluating political hacking is that it can be hard to identify. People who agree with the political or social position of the hackers will tend to see an act as "activism," while those who disagree will tend to see it as ordinary crime (or worse). Is posting a pro-drug message on a police website a political statement against the futility, dishonesty, expense, and international intrusions of U.S. drug policy, or is it the act of a kid showing off? To some political activists, any act that shuts down or steals from a large corporation is a political act. To the customers and owners, it is vandalism and theft.

Suppose we know that a political cause motivates the hackers. How can we begin to evaluate the ethics of their hacktivism? Suppose a religious group, to protest homosexuality, disables a website for gay people. Suppose an environmentalist group, to protest a new housing development, disables a website of a real estate developer. Many of the people who might argue that one of these acts is justifiable hacktivism would argue that the other is not. Yet it would be extremely difficult to develop a sound ethical basis for distinguishing them.

Some academic writers and political groups argue that hacktivism is ethical, that it is a modern form of civil disobedience.[12] Others argue that the political motive is irrelevant, or at the other extreme, that political hacking is a form of cyberterrorism. Civil disobedience has a respected, nonviolent tradition. Henry David Thoreau, Mahatma Gandhi, and Martin Luther King Jr. refused to cooperate with rules they saw as unjust. Peaceful protestors have marched, rallied, and boycotted to promote their goals. Burning down ski resorts (because one would prefer to see the land undeveloped) or abortion clinics (because one opposes abortion) is quite another category of activity. To evaluate incidents of hacktivism, it is helpful to fit them into a scale from peaceful resistance to destruction of other people's property and actions that risk serious harm to innocent people.

Are hacktivists merely exercising their freedom of speech? Freedom of speech does not include the right to hang a political sign in a neighbor's window or paint one's slogans on someone else's fence, even if that "someone else" is a group of people organized as a business or corporation. We have the freedom to speak, but not the right to compel others to listen. Crashing a website or defacing a Web page is comparable to shouting down a speaker with whom one disagrees. Those who believe that the specific content or cause is more important than the principle of freedom of speech defend such actions. It is common for people involved in political causes to see their side as unquestionably morally right, and anyone on the other side as morally evil, not simply someone with a different point of view. This often leads to the view that the freedom of speech, freedom of choice, and property rights of the other side deserve no respect. Peace, freedom, and civil society require that we respect such basic rights and not impose our views on those we disagree with.

Another factor to consider when evaluating hactivism is the political system under which the hacktivists live. From both an ethical and social perspective, in free countries where almost anyone can tweet or post their words and video on the Web for free, it is hard to justify hacking someone else's site to promote a political cause. Activists use the Internet to organize opposition to oil exploration in Alaska that they fear will harm a caribou herd. Activists use free social media to organize mass demonstrations against international meetings of government leaders. Human rights organizations effectively use the Web, Twitter, and Facebook. Groups supporting all kinds of nonmainstream causes, from animal rights to anarchism to odd religions, promote their views in cyberspace. None of this activism requires hacktivism. On the other hand, countries with oppressive governments control the means of communications and prohibit open political discussion, have secret police who kill dissenters, ban some religions, and jail people who express opposition views. In such countries, where openly communicating one's views is impossible or dangerous, there might be good arguments to justify political hacking to get one's message out to the public and, in some cases, to sabotage government activities. The nations in which hacktivism is likely to have the most ethical justification are those least likely to respect acts of civil disobedience.

5.2.3   Hackers as Security Researchers

Since well before the advent of the Web there has been a subculture of hackers who probe computer systems, most often without permission, to find security flaws as an intellectual exercise and, for some, as a public service. They sometimes call themselves "security researchers" to avoid the now negative connotation of the term hacker. In old cowboy movies, the good guys wore white hats and the bad guys wore black hats. So some people use the terms "white hat hacker" and "black hat hacker" for the cowboys of the computer frontier. White hat hackers, for the most part, use their skills to demonstrate system vulnerabilities and improve security. Those who use methods of questionable legality or who publicize vulnerabilities before informing the system owners are sometimes called "gray hats." Many are computer security professionals. Some spent time in jail or on probation for hacking when in their teens. The security researcher who found that some smartphones sent location and ID data to Google and Apple is one example.

Security researcher hackers face ethical dilemmas. The most obvious is: Is it ethical to break into a system without permission, even with good intentions? We discussed this to some degree in the discussion of whether harmless hacking is truly harmless (in Section 5.2.1). Another dilemma is: How can people responsibly inform potential victims of security vulnerabilities without informing malicious hackers who would exploit them? Some post details about security weaknesses on the Internet. Some work quietly with software companies. Most computer professionals are very critical of the first approach. Responsible security professionals do not announce security flaws to the public as soon as they discover them. They inform the software company or system manager responsible for the software and allow time for them to prepare patches (corrections) or close security holes before making a public announcement. They believe that when a security researcher hacker discovers a security weakness in a system, he or she should do the same.

Although the topics are somewhat different, the discussion of the ethics of publishing sensitive leaked material in Section 3.3 has relevance here. In particular, two critical aspects to consider are how important the information is to the public and how much harm might be done by publishing it.

Many security researcher hackers are very scornful of big software companies both because of the large number of security flaws in their products and because they are slow to plug leaks even when they know of them. The hackers argue that these businesses do not behave responsibly toward the public. Publicizing security problems spurs the companies to take action. This argument has some truth to it. Hackers and security consultants say they repeatedly warn companies of flaws that allow access by hackers, but the companies do not respond until malicious hackers exploit the flaws and cause significant problems. Some businesses and government agencies have so much confidence in their systems that they refuse to believe anyone can break in. A man who copied patient files from a medical center said he did it to publicize the system's vulnerability, not to use the information. He disclosed portions of the files to a journalist after the medical center said that no one had copied patient files.[13] Should we view him as a whistleblower or a criminal? Members of a group called Goatse Security collected the email addresses of more than 100,000 iPad owners from an AT&T website. The site displayed the email address of an iPad owner to anyone who entered the iPad ID number; it did not require a password. A spokesperson for Goatse Security said they notified the media about the security flaw after AT&T fixed it. Did they act responsibly or irresponsibly and criminally?[14] A security researcher discovered a major flaw in the Internet's domain name server system (the system that translates Web addresses, say, www.yourbank.com

to IP addresses*) that could have allowed hackers to redirect and steal any information transmitted on the Net. He kept the problem secret while working with several companies to develop a patch, and then announced the patch and said he would make details of the problem—and how to exploit it—public in 30 days. The 30-day limit, he said, encouraged companies to install the patch and encouraged others who knew of the flaw not to disclose it sooner.

Exposing security flaws is not a legitimate justification for most hacking, but, as a side effect, it does sometimes speed up security improvements. As software companies, financial companies, and online retailers began taking security more seriously, some began treating well-intentioned hackers as allies rather than enemies.

5.2.4 HACKING AS FOREIGN POLICY

> *[K]eystrokes originating in one country can impact the other side of the globe in the blink of an eye. In the 21st century, bits and bytes can be as threatening as bullets and bombs.*

—William J. Lynn III, Deputy Defense Secretary [15]

Hacking by governments—for economic and military espionage and to disable enemies (or future enemies)—has increased dramatically in the past few years. The first cyber attack apparently coordinated with a military attack occurred in 2008 when the Russian military moved into Georgia (the former Soviet republic). Georgian government websites were attacked and some disabled. Internet security experts and the Georgian government thought it very likely that the Russian government was responsible. The source of the attack could not be definitely determined, a frequent problem with cyberattacks. In 2011, the government of Iran attempted to hack into the computers and phones of United Nations nuclear inspectors who were attempting to learn whether Iran's nuclear facilities are for military purposes. Whether Iran's intelligence agency was able to extract sensitive information (what the inspectors found, who assisted the inspectors, and so on) was uncertain.

Many cyber attacks come from China, and once again, it is difficult to prove that the government is behind them. However, the nature and sophistication of the attacks, as well as the type of targets lead security researchers to believe that they are the work of government agencies, not civilian hackers. For example, a Chinese government-owned company sent false messages to the Internet routing system to reroute a large amount of Internet traffic through servers in China. The intended (and eventual) destinations of the rerouted traffic included U.S. military agencies and Congress. Clearly, someone (or a government) that does this could spy on, tamper with, or disrupt communications.

---

* That is, the Internet Protocol address, a string of numbers that identifies a website.

Hackers stole several terabytes of information about the design of one of the Pentagon's new and extremely expensive fighter jets. The computer attack appeared to originate in China. Hackers, apparently in China, had high-level and widespread access to the computer system of a large U.S. telecommunications company for almost 10 years. They stole technical documents, research reports, business plans, and email. Security experts report that Russian and Chinese hackers broke into computer networks that control the U.S. electric power grid. They left behind code that could disrupt the system if activated. Hackers intruded on U.S. satellites to the point where they could control, damage, or destroy them (but did not do so). Hackers, apparently in China, systematically hacked oil and gas companies worldwide.[16]

A 2011 attack on the Gmail accounts of White House staffers, China policy experts, military officials, human rights activists, and others originated in a Chinese city where a major Chinese national security division is located. This attack used email carefully written in government jargon about State Department reports to fool the recipients into thinking the email was authentic. High-level government officials (and other people targeted) disclosed their passwords, allowing the hackers to read their email for months.[17]

If the attacks we described are the work of foreign governments, they pose a huge threat to safety and national security. Even if not, they demonstrate the potential for hackers with ill intent to cause significant damage to communication, financial, military, and power systems.

The Pentagon announced that it would consider and treat some cyber attacks as acts of war, and the United States might respond with military force. Countries targeted with cyber attacks must determine whether a foreign government or terrorist organization

Stuxnet

Stuxnet is an extremely sophisticated worm program that targets a particular type of control system and, beginning in 2008, damaged equipment in a uranium enrichment plant in Iran. The focus on Iran's nuclear program and the sophistication of Stuxnet led to speculation that the Israeli and/or U.S. government created it. In 2012, journalist David Sanger published extensive research indicating that the two governments did indeed produce Stuxnet.

Is such cyber sabotage against Iran justified? (Is it better than a military attack by Israel on Iran's nuclear facilities?) Will China, Russia, or other governments cite Stuxnet as an excuse for their own cyber intrusions into the United States and other countries?

Stuxnet eventually spread from Iran and infected equipment in other countries. Wars regularly include deaths of civilians and incidents where military units accidentally kill fighters on their own side. How common and how serious will analogous side effects of cyber attacks be?[18]

(or teenager) organized the attack. What level of certainty should there be before a counterattack? When is a cyber attack an act of war? What responses are appropriate? Perhaps more importantly, how can we make critical systems safer from attacks?

5.2.5 SECURITY

The fact that I could get into the system amazed me.

—Frank Darden, a member of the Legion of Doom, which hacked the BellSouth telephone system[19]

Hacking and the spread of viruses are as much a comment on the security of computers, telecommunication systems, and the Web as they are on the skills and ethics of the hackers. Hacking is a problem; so is poor security. We talked about responsibility for security of personal data when we discussed privacy in Chapter 2, and we say more when we discuss identity theft in Section 5.3. It is hard to overemphasize the importance of responsible, effective security.

A variety of factors contribute to security weaknesses. They come from the history of the Internet and the Web, from the inherent complexity of computer systems (especially the software and communications systems that run phones, the Web, industrial systems, and the many interconnected devices we use), from the speed at which new applications develop, from economic and business factors, and from human nature. We will describe and illustrate some of these influences.

In its early years, the Internet was primarily a communications medium for researchers. The focus was on open access, ease of use, and ease of sharing information. The Internet was not designed for security against malicious intruders, teenage explorers, or organized criminals. Many early systems did not have passwords. Few early systems connected to telephone networks, so protection against intruders was not a concern. Security depended primarily on trust. The World Wide Web developed as a communications tool for physics researchers. Again, security was not a primary design concern. Security on the early Web was extremely weak. When businesses and government agencies began to set up websites, Internet security expert Dan Farmer ran a program to probe the websites of banks, newspapers, government agencies, and pornography sellers for software loopholes that made it easy for hackers to invade and disable or damage the sites. Of the 1700 sites he examined, he found that about two-thirds had security weaknesses—and only four sites apparently noticed that someone was probing their security. Farmer's warnings had little effect.

Attitudes about security in businesses, organizations, and government agencies were slow to catch up with the risks. Gradually, computer scientists responded to increased security threats with improved security technology, and entrepreneurs and the market responded with the development of many security firms and consultants offering a variety of software products and services. Security techniques and practices improved dramatically. Many government agencies, businesses, and organizations have up-to-date, high-quality security, but there are still serious weaknesses. News reports of major break-ins and security lapses appear almost weekly. Numerous government studies warn of vulnerabilities and the potential for sophisticated attacks on critical infrasturcture.

It might not be surprising that, initially, computer security at universities and businesses was weak. It is unsettling, however, that it has been so easy to hack into military systems, other government agencies, and defense contractors. In 1998, the U.S. deputy defense secretary described a series of attacks on numerous U.S. military computers as "the most organized and systematic attack the Pentagon has seen to date."[20] Two boys, aged 16 and 17, had carried them out. A security expert described one hacking attack on Defense Department computers that did not contain classified information as the modern equivalent of a kid sneaking into a Pentagon cafeteria. Maybe. On the other hand, we should expect Pentagon security to be good enough to keep a kid out of its cafeteria. As we noted in Section 5.2.4, foreign governments are replacing teenagers as the major threat to defense systems. Their resources and expertise far surpass those of teenagers. In 2011, the deputy defense secretary said that in the previous decade, intruders stole plans (from the government and defense industry firms) for aircraft avionics, satellite communications systems, network security protocols, missile tracking systems, satellite navigation devices, surveillance drones, and jet fighters. The *New York Times* described a theft (by a foreign intelligence service) of 24,000 Defense Department documents as "one of its worst digital attacks in history"—a description that reappears in hacking reports repeatedly as hackers steal more and more sensitive information.[21]

Security in other government agencies is weaker than in the Defense Department. For example, the Government Accountability Office (GAO) reported that computer security at NASA was so weak that hackers could easily disrupt such functions as the tracking of spacecraft. The same report described Environmental Protection Agency (EPA) computers as "riddled with security weaknesses." Hackers were able to use the EPA's system to launch hacking attacks on other agencies. The U.S. Transportation Department warned of numerous vulnerabilities in the air traffic control system and the potential for sophisticated attacks on air traffic control by foreign governments. Its report said that almost all ATC facilities had insufficient controls for detecting intrusions. A review in 2011 recommended that users be required to enter an ID and password—a requirement that should have long been in place by then.[22]

Encryption is a particularly valuable security tool. It is often not used sufficiently and appropriately, by both governments and businesses, because it can be inconvenient and expensive. For example, the video feeds on U.S. predator drones (unmanned aricraft used in Iraq) were not encrypted. Insurgents in Iraq used $26 software, available on the Internet, to intercept the feeds. Access to the video feeds gave them valuable information about surveillance and attacks. It also might give them the potential to modify the feeds.

U.S. military officials had known the feeds were unprotected since the 1990s (when they used drones in Bosnia). They reconsidered the issue in 2004, but they assumed adversaries would not know how to exploit this security hole. Adding encryption to the system is expensive, but even if omitting it in the 1990s was a reasonable trade-off, they clearly should have updated the decision.[23] Underestimating the skills of opponents and unwillingness to pay for stronger security are frequent underlying causes of vulnerabilities in both government and business systems.

In several major thefts of consumers' personal data from retailers, the databases included unencrypted credit card numbers and other security numbers read from the magnetic strips on the cards. Hacking attacks on major security firms show that even such firms often leave sensitive data (including credit card numbers) on their systems unencrypted. Retailer TJX used a vulnerable, out-of-date encryption system to protect data transmitted between cash registers and store computers on its wireless network. Investigators believe hackers used high-power antennas to intercept data, decoded employee passwords, and then hacked into the company's central database. Over a period of about 18 months, the hackers stole millions of credit and debit card numbers and critical identification information for hundreds of thousands of people. (Stolen numbers were used fraudulently in at least eight countries.) The investigation revealed other security problems. The problems included transmission of debit card transaction information to banks without encryption and failure to install appropriate software patches and firewalls.[24]

In addition to technical security tools such as encryption, there are numerous market pheonomena that can help improve security. For example, just as some home insurance companies give discounts for deadbolt door locks and fire extinguishers in a home, insurance companies that offer insurance for hacker attacks require that their customers use high-quality computer security technology. Some software and security companies hire hackers to attack and find flaws in systems they are developing. Some pay consulting fees to teams of students and faculty at universities to find security weaknesses in their products so that they can fix the flaws before destructive hackers exploit them.

Another factor leading to weak security for systems that affect the general public is the speed of innovation and people's desire for new things fast. Hackers and security professionals regularly find gaping holes each time a new product, application, or cyberspace phenomenon appears. Competitive pressure spurs companies to develop products with insufficient thought or budget devoted to analyzing potential security risks and protecting against them. The culture of sharing and the phenomenon of users developing applications and games for social networks and smartphones come with vulnerabilities as well as all the wonderful benefits. Consumers buy the new products and services and download the apps with far more interest in convenience and dazzling new features than in risks and security.

Many incidents of stolen sensitive data (including some we described in Section 2.1.2) involve stolen portable devices such as laptops and phones. This is one example where individuals, organizations, government agencies, and businesses embraced an advance in technology (portable devices with huge data storage) with little thought to the risks and when few security measures were available. Laptop security is now a booming business. There are systems that track stolen or lost laptops and allow the owner to erase files remotely. Fingerprint readers can control access to a device. Companies learned to use more physical protections, such as cables to secure laptops to heavy furniture in offices or hotels, and to train employees to be more careful with portable devices.

More and more appliances and machinery—from microwave ovens to cars to factory machinery to heart monitors—are going online. Doctors access and control medical devices over the Net. Automated fleets of cars will communicate with each other to drive safely on highways. These appliances and machines are vulnerable. Already, security researchers have manipulated the security system in a car by sending messages to the system over a cellular communication network, unlocking the car and starting its engine. Others used simple off-the-shelf hardware to send fake traffic and weather information to navigation systems in cars.[25] The focus in developing new applications is on making them work. Often, there is insufficient thought to protecting against malicious interference. We have seen (in Section 5.2.1) that some hackers think misdirecting airplane pilots is fun and that satellites and critical infrastructure such as power grids are vulnerable. The potentially dangerous and destructive consequences of malicious hacking of such systems impose a strong degree of responsibility for security on those who design the systems.

Responsibility for security

There are many parallels between security issues for preventing crime and security issues for protecting privacy. There are also similarities with the safety issues we discuss in Chapter 8. Principles and techniques for developing good systems exist, and responsible software designers must learn and use them. The field of computer security is robust and fascinating. System designers can make security from intrusion a major design goal. When a computer system contains valuable or sensitive data, or if many people depend on its smooth operation, the system administrators have a professional and ethical obligation, and in many cases a legal obligation as well, to take reasonable security precautions to protect the system. They must anticipate risks and prepare for them. System developers and administrators must stay up to date about new risks and new security measures. This is often not an easy task, but it is an essential goal and a professional responsibility. No matter how well designed security software and procedures are, the complexity of computer systems means that there will be unexpected security failures. We cannot expect perfection, but we should expect professionalism.

Most people who use smartphones, tablets, and computers have no technical training. Many do not use firewalls or antivirus software, because they do not understand the risks or because they find the security tools too confusing. It does not occur to consumers to ask when buying a new cellphone if their calls are encrypted or easily interceptable. Sellers of any widely used consumer product have an ethical obligation to build in a level of safety appropriate for the general population. Software companies have an ethical obligation to design and implement their products so that they do not expose users to severe security threats.

The security vulnerabilities with the most profound potential threats to the lives and well-being of millions of people are in major infrastructure systems and defense systems. The companies and government agencies that operate these systems have, therefore, a profound responsibility for improving security.

5.2.6 THE LAW: CATCHING AND PUNISHING HACKERS

The law

When teenagers started hacking for the challenge of getting into off-limits computers, there was disagreement not only about whether the activity was a crime under existing law but also about whether it should be. Gradually, state governments passed laws that specifically addressed computer crimes. Congress passed the main federal computer-crime law, the Computer Fraud and Abuse Act (CFAA), in 1984.[26] As a federal law, the CFAA covers areas over which the federal government has jurisdiction: government computers, financial systems, and computers used in interstate or international commerce or communication. That, of course, includes computers connected to the Internet, cellphone systems, and so on. Under the CFAA, it is illegal to access a computer without authorization or to exceed one's authorization (in most cases). Sections of the law address altering, damaging, or destroying information and interference with authorized use of a computer. These cover denial-of-service attacks and the launching of computer viruses and other malicious programs. The CFAA is the main antihacking law, but prosecutors also use other federal laws to prosecute people for crimes related to computer and telecommunications systems. Illegal actions include access to commit fraud, disclosing passwords or other access codes to unauthorized people, and interrupting or impairing government operation, public communication, transportation, or other public utilities. State and federal antihacking laws provide for strong penalties, including prison sentences and fines.

The USA PATRIOT Act includes amendments to the Computer Fraud and Abuse Act. The PATRIOT Act expanded the definition of loss to include the cost of responding to a hacking attack, assessing damage, and restoring systems. It raised the maximum penalty in the CFAA for a first offense to 10 years. It increased penalties for hacking computers used by the criminal justice system or the military. It allows the government to monitor online activity of suspected hackers without a court order. We have observed that hacking covers a wide range of activity—some deserving serious punishment, some comparable to minor offenses kids of all generations commit, and some intended to demonstrate security weaknesses and encourage fixing them. Definitions of the actions to which the PATRIOT Act's antiterrorism provisions apply are broad and include activity few would consider terrorism.

Catching hackers

The people responsible for almost all the hacking incidents we described have been caught. It took only one week to catch the author of the Melissa virus. The FBI traced the denial-of-service attacks in 2000 to mafiaboy and had his real name within a week. Investigators identified four Israeli teenagers who wrote and launched the Goner worm in about the same time. How do hacker trackers do their job?

Initially, the response of law enforcement agencies was ill-informed and embarrassing. John Perry Barlow, a founder of the Electronic Frontier Foundation, colorfully described how he spent two hours explaining the basics of computing and computer networks to an FBI agent who came to question him in 1990. Law enforcement agencies now employ people who are well informed about technical aspects of hacking and the hacker culture. They and security professionals read hacker newsletters and participate in online discussions of hacking, sometimes undercover. Law enforcement agents, some undercover, attend hacker conferences. Security specialists maintain logs of Chat channels used by hackers. Security professionals set up *honey pots*—websites that look attractive to hackers—so that they can record and study everything a hacker does at the site. Law enforcement agents use wiretaps to collect evidence and build their cases against hacking suspects. Investigators identified a number of hackers because they bragged about their exploits.

The field of collecting evidence from computer files and disks is *computer forensics*. (Some use the term *digital forensics*). Computer forensics specialists can recover deleted files, often even if the user has erased and wiped the disks. In Chapter 2, we saw how easy it is to collect and save information about everything we do in cyberspace and to search and match records to build consumer profiles. The same tools that threaten privacy aid in catching criminals. Investigators trace viruses and hacking attacks by using ISP records and the logs of routers, the machines that route messages through the Internet. For example, David Smith, the man who released the Melissa virus, used someone else's AOL account, but AOL's logs contained enough information to enable authorities to trace the session to Smith's telephone line. After a series of high-profile hacking incidents by members of Anonymous, LulzSec, and related groups, police in several countries arrested dozens of members in 2011 and 2012 (though other members continued hacking exploits).

Most people are unaware that word processors and other programs include a lot of "invisible information" in files—in some cases, unique identifying numbers and the author's name. Security experts use such information to trace viruses. The hidden identifying information in files worries privacy advocates—another reminder of the tension between privacy and crime fighting.

Many of the techniques we just described worked because hackers did not know about them. When such methods receive publicity in big cases, hackers learn what mistakes to avoid. Hackers, as well as people seeking privacy, learn how to remove identifying numbers from documents. Hackers learn how to forge such numbers to throw suspicion elsewhere. Thus, the particular methods described here will be less effective when you read this. Law enforcement and security personnel update their skills and tools as hackers change theirs.

Penalties for young hackers

Many young hackers are the modern analogue of other generations of young people who snooped where they did not belong or carried out clever pranks, sometimes breaking a law. In his book *The Hacker Crackdown*, Bruce Sterling describes the phone phreakers of 1878. That is not a typo. The new American Bell Telephone company initially hired teenage boys as operators, some of whom disconnected calls and crossed lines on the switchboard, connecting people to strangers. The boys were also, like many teenage hackers, rude.[27] The phone company learned its lesson and replaced teenage boys with woman operators.

We want young hackers to mature, to learn the risks of their actions, and to use their skills in better ways. Most of them do grow up and go on to successful, productive careers. We do not want to turn them into resentful, hardened criminals or wreck their chances of getting a good job by putting them in jail. This does not mean that we should not punish young hackers if they trespass or cause damage. Kids do not mature and become responsible without good direction or if we reward their irresponsibility. The point is that we should not overreact and overpunish. Some young hackers will become the great innovators of the next generation. Steve Wozniak created the Apple computer, co-founded the Apple company, and, after Apple's success, donated large amounts of money to medical research and other valuable efforts. But before he was building Apples, Wozniak was building blue boxes, devices that enabled people to make long-distance phone calls without paying for them. Nobel Prize winner Richard Feynman used "hacker" techniques when he was a young physicist working on the highly secret atomic bomb project at Los Alamos National Laboratory in the 1940s. He hacked safes (not computers) containing classified work on the bomb. He found or guessed the combinations and delighted in opening the safes at night and leaving messages for the authorized users informing them that security was not as good as they thought.[28]

Many exploits of young hackers are pranks, trespass, and vandalism. They usually do not include financial gain for the hacker (though, as we observed in Section 4.1.5 in the context of copyright infringement, lack of financial gain is often not significant in determining whether actions are wrong). Difficult penalty issues arise for hackers who are young, hackers who do not intend to do damage, and hackers who, through accident, ignorance, or immature irresponsibility, do vastly more damage than they can pay for. How can we distinguish between young hackers who are malicious and likely to commit more crimes and those who are likely to become honest and productive professionals? What penalties are appropriate? Clearly, offenses related to unauthorized access vary in degree, and penalties should likewise vary, as they do for trespass, vandalism, invasion of privacy, fraud, theft, and sabotage.

In many hacking cases, especially those involving young people, the hacker pleads guilty. The evidence is clear, and the hacker and prosecutor work out a plea bargain. At first, most hackers younger than 18 received relatively light sentences including two or three years probation, community service, and sometimes a fine or order to pay restitution. The 15-year-old who disabled an airport radio system got probation even though his exploits could have endangered people. In 2000, a 16-year-old was sentenced to six months in a juvenile detention facility. He was the first juvenile incarcerated for hacking. He had broken into NASA and Defense Department computers and was a member of a hacker group that vandalized government websites. As more young people caused more disruption, the severity of penalties increased.

One of the purposes of criminal penalties is to discourage people from committing crimes. Some people advocate heavy penalties for minor hacking to "send a signal" to others who might be thinking of trying something similar. There is a temptation to do this with hacking because of the costs to the victims and the potential risks to the public. On the other hand, justice requires that punishments fit the specific crime and not be increased dramatically because of the potential of what someone else might do.

Sometimes the company whose computers a hacker invaded gives him a job after catching him. Give a hacker a job instead of a jail sentence? Some computer professionals and law enforcement officials are very critical of this practice of "rewarding" hackers with security jobs. We do not reduce hacking by encouraging young people to think breaking into a computer system is an acceptable alternative to sending a résumé. But, in some cases, the job, the responsibility and respect that go with it, and the threat of punishment for future offenses are enough to turn the hacker's energy and skills toward productive uses. With any criminal law, there is a trade-off between having fixed penalties (for fairness, to avoid favoritism) and flexibility (to consider the particular circumstances). With young people, flexibility is probably more important. Penalties can focus on using the hacker's computer skills in a productive way and on paying victims for damage done (if possible). Deciding on what is appropriate for a particular person is delicate, one of the difficulties prosecutors and judges face with juvenile crime.

How can we dissuade young teens from breaking into computer systems, launching viruses, and shutting down websites? We need a combination of appropriate penalties, education about ethics and risks, and parental responsibility. Parents of many young hackers have no idea what their children are doing. Just as parents have responsibility for teaching their children to avoid unsafe behavior in cyberspace, they also have some responsibility for preventing their children from engaging in malicious, destructive hacking.

Criminalize virus writing and hacker tools?

You can find hacking scripts and computer code for thousands of computer viruses on the Internet. Intentionally or recklessly making such programs available in a context that encourages their destructive use is irresponsible. Should the software itself be illegal? Some law enforcement personnel and security professionals propose making it a crime to write or post computer viruses and other hacking software. A law against writing or publishing viruses and hacking software could keep them from casual hackers. Criminal penalties might dissuade potential teenage hackers, but probably not serious criminals. Such a law could make security work and research more difficult. Security personnel and researchers must be able to possess security and hacker software to effectively do their job.

A law against distributing virus and hacking code would raise issues similar to some we discussed in Chapters 2 and 4 about restricting or banning strong encryption and technologies to circumvent copyright protections. We saw in Chapter 3 that writing about how to make illegal or destructive devices, such as bombs, is not (in most cases) illegal. On the other hand, as a security professional commented, "With a computer virus, the words are the bomb."[29] A federal court ruled that software is a form of speech (see Section 2.5.1), so a law against hacking software or virus software might conflict with the First Amendment. The First Amendment does not protect some kinds of speech, such as inciting a riot. However, encouraging people to commit destructive or illegal actions is generally protected by the First Amendment in situations where the listener has time to reflect and make a decision about whether to act. A person who reads virus code has the opportunity to decide whether to activate the virus.

How do *you* think the law should treat virus code and hacking scripts?

Expansion of the Computer Fraud and Abuse Act

The CFAA predates social networks, smartphones, and sophisticated invisible information collection about our activities in cyberspace. It was intended for malicious and prank hacking. Later applications of the law illustrate how the impact of a law can change and grow with new technology. Some of the new applications can help protect privacy. Some might criminalize common activities of millions of people. We consider the latter first.

Is violating the terms of use of a website a crime under the CFAA's provision about exceeding one's authorized access for the purpose of committing fraud and obtaining something of value?* This question is both a legal and a social one: Does it make sense for violation of terms of use to be a crime? The first major case involved a woman who pretended to be a 16-year-old boy on MySpace, began an online flirting relationship with a 13-year-old girl in her neighborhood (a former friend of the woman's daughter), then broke off the relationship and sent cruel messages. The girl killed herself. The woman's behavior was nasty and unethical. People wanted to see her punished, but it was not clear that she had broken any law. Prosecutors charged her with illegal hacking under the CFAA. They said she exceeded authorized access because she violated MySpace's terms of use requiring that profile information be truthful. A jury convicted the woman, but the judge reversed the conviction. He said in effect that this application of the law was too broad. Normally, a breach of contract is not a criminal offence, and the CFAA does not state or suggest that it has become one. An ordinary, reasonable person does not expect that violating the terms of use of a website is a criminal offense.[30] The decision of one judge, though, does not settle the legal situation. Prosecutions and lawsuits continue to treat violation of terms of use as a crime under the CFAA. Some businesses state in their websites' terms of use that competitors may not use the site for any purpose. Under the broad interpretation of exceeding authorized access, such a business may sue any

---

* This is a simplification of the legal language.

competitor who visits the site. Could someone be prosecuted for lying about his or her age (or attractiveness) on a dating site if the site says members may not provide false or misleading information? Could a high school student be prosecuted for setting up a Gmail account? Gmail's terms of service require that the user be of legal age to form a binding contract; that generally leaves out minors. Who knew?

There are more sensible approaches to handling violations of terms of use. A social network, dating service, or other membership service can terminate the membership of anyone who violates the terms of use to an extent that the organization considers a serious problem. A business can attempt to block access to its website by people (or companies) it wants to exclude—or just accept the fact that if it makes the site public and chooses not to require membership or passwords, then anyone in the public might visit it. If someone violates terms of use and actually commits fraud, theft, or vandalism, appropriate laws against those acts apply.

Another unintended application of the CFAA might help protect privacy. As we discussed in Chapter 2, hidden software on websites or in smartphone apps tracks our online or phone activity. Such software collects information from our phone or other device. When we install an app or visit a website, we implicitly authorize it to interact with our phone or device, using the data necessary to perform its stated purpose. We can interpret going beyond that purpose (if the app or site does not disclose that it does so) as exceeding authorized access. Some prosecutors use the CFAA to bring charges against people or businesses that do unauthorized data collection. The definition of "authorized" is important when prosecutors use the CFAA in this way. The bounds of authorization are often unstated and can be fuzzy. If the line is drawn well, this will be an innovative way of using the CFAA to protect us against surreptitious information collection. If applied too broadly, it could criminalize practices that many consumers accept or like. These cases are new, so it is as yet unclear what the results will be.

The CFAA and personal use of an employer's computer: Section 6.3.2

5.3 Identity Theft and Credit Card Fraud

Con artists and crooks of many sorts have found ample opportunity to cheat unsuspecting people in cyberspace. Some scams are almost unchanged from their pre-Web forms: pyramid schemes, chain letters, sales of counterfeit luxury goods, sales of food-stamp cards, phony business investment opportunities, and so forth. Each generation of people, whatever level of technology they use, needs a reminder that if an investment or bargain looks too good to be true, it probably is. Other scams are new or have evolved to take advantage of characteristics of the Web. In online dating scams, crooks use profiles and photos lifted from social media sites to develop online relationships and convince the unwary to send money for a family emergency or some other false reason. In a particularly offensive scam, people set up websites after disasters such as terrorist attacks and hurricanes to fraudulently collect credit card donations from people who think they are contributing to the Red Cross or funds for victims.

In this section, we examine identity theft and credit card fraud at some length. We look at the thieves' methods and some countermeasures that have emerged. The point is not the particular details but the patterns: insufficient security, big losses, then gradual improvement. People learn the risks. Businesses and individuals respond with new protection mechanisms, and law enforcement agencies acquire skills to catch and convict the crooks and discourage their activity.

5.3.1   STEALING IDENTITIES

We buy products and services from strangers in stores and on the Web. We do our banking and investing online without seeing or knowing the physical location of the company we deal with. We can travel with only a passport and a credit or debit card. We can qualify for a mortgage or a car loan in minutes. As part of providing this convenience and efficiency, our identity has become a series of numbers (credit and debit card numbers, Social Security number, driver's license number, phone number, account numbers) and computer files (credit history, Web activity profile, work history, driving record). The convenience and efficiency engender risks. Remote transactions are fertile ground for many kinds of crime, especially identity theft and its most common result, credit and debit fraud.

Identity theft describes various crimes in which a criminal (or large, well-organized criminal group) uses the identity of an unknowing innocent person. If the thieves get credit (or debit) card numbers, they buy expensive items or sell the numbers to others who use them. If they do not have card numbers, they use other personal information (Social Security number, for example) to open new accounts in the victim's name. In one scam, thieves used names and Social Security numbers of almost 2000 people and applied for their tax refunds. Identity thieves take out loans, buy groceries, raid the victim's bank account, pass bad checks, or use the victim's identity in various other ways for financial gain. A security company executive says a complete identity sells for less than $20.[31]

The Federal Trade Commission receives hundreds of thousands of complaints of identity theft each year. Losses from identity theft amount to billions of dollars per year in the United States, with several million victims. A single incident can affect thousands of people. For example, two U.S. grocery chains reported that data thieves planted malware in the computer systems of their stores and gained access to more than four million credit and debit card numbers. The malware sent the data to a server outside the United States; almost 2000 cases of fraud resulted. Credit card companies and other businesses bear the direct cost of most credit card fraud, but the losses lead to higher charges to consumers. In addition, individual victims might lose a good credit rating, be prevented from borrowing money or cashing checks, be unable to get a job, or be unable to rent an apartment. Creditors might sue the victim for money the criminal borrowed.

The many tactics used for identity theft and credit and debit card fraud, and the many solutions developed in response, illustrate the continual leapfrogging between increased sophistication of security strategies and increased sophistication of criminal strategies. They also illustrate the value of the mix of technology, innovative business policies, consumer awareness, and law to solve the problems. We describe a variety of tactics for identity theft, then consider many approaches to reducing identity theft and reducing its impact on its victims. A few of the methods we describe are no longer used because the other side defeated them or consumers found them too cumbersome. Technology evolves and clever people on both sides of the law develop new ideas. For the general public and for anyone working with sensitive personal data, it is necessary to remain aware and flexible.

Have you received email or a text message from PayPal, Amazon, or a bank asking you to confirm information about your account? Have you received email from the IRS telling you the agency has a tax refund for you? These are examples of fraudulent spam called *phishing* (in the case of email) and *smishing* (in the case of text messaging)*: sending millions of messages fishing for information to use to impersonate someone and steal money and goods. The message tells the victim to click on a link to what purports to be the website of a well-known bank or online company. The phony site asks for account numbers, passwords, and other identifying information. Identity thieves take advantage of our knowledge that there is a lot of online fraud: Several pretexts that appear frequently in phishing scams warn that there has been a breach in the security of your bank or PayPal account and you need to respond to determine whether someone else is misusing your account. Some messages tell the recipient they just made a very big purchase and if the purchase was not really theirs, they should click a link to cancel the order. In a panic, people do—and enter their identifying information when asked for it.

The first defense against phishing is to be extremely wary of clicking on a link in an unsolicited message, especially if the message is about account information. The standard antifraud advice is: If you are uncertain whether the message is authentic but you want to respond, ignore the link and check your account in the usual way. As more people learned to be wary of clicking on links in messages that appear to be from a legitimate company, thieves modified their phishing scams; the message provides a telephone number to call. Those who call hear a request for their account number and other identifying information. This variation is sometimes called *vishing*, for voice phishing. Of course, a phone number provided by phishers is as fake as the links they provide.

Pharming is another technique to lure people to fake websites where thieves collect personal data. Normally when we indicate a website we want to visit, our browser looks up the IP address of the site on one of many Domain Name Servers (DNS), special computers on the Internet for this purpose. Pharming involves planting false Internet addresses in the tables on a DNS that lead the browser to a counterfeit site set up by identity thieves.

---

* SMS is the abbreviation for Short Message Service, the method used for texting on cellphones.

Corrupting a DNS is more difficult than sending a huge number of phishing emails, so it is much less common.

Figure 2.1 lists incidents of loss or theft of large databases containing personal information. In several of those incidents, identity theft and fraud were the goals. Sophisticated criminal rings hack into corporate and government computer networks, steal computers and disks, or pose as legitimate businesses and buy credit records and personal dossiers to obtain information to use in identity theft.

Identity thieves love the millions of résumés that people post on job-hunting sites. They collect addresses, Social Security numbers, birth dates, work histories, and all the other details that help them convincingly adopt the identity of the job seeker. Some identity thieves pose as employers and post fake job announcements; some respond to job hunters and ask for more information, perhaps for a background check. Of course, job-hunting sites are very popular and useful. Now that identity thieves misuse them, people must adapt and be more cautious. That means omitting sensitive data from a posted résumé, not providing sensitive information until you have an actual interview, or finding other ways to determine that the potential employer is authentic. Job sites, once aware of the threat, began to offer services to keep sensitive information private.

Although we focus on criminal groups who use hacking and other technical means to commit identity theft, family members and acquaintances of the victim are responsible for a significant percentage of identity theft. And many identity theft cases result from lost or stolen wallets and checkbooks. We still must use care in protecting our own passwords, documents, Social Security numbers, and so on, in low-tech environments as well as in cyberspace.

5.3.2   Responses to Identity Theft

Authenticating websites

Email programs, Web browsers, search engines, and add-on software (some free) can alert users to likely fraud. Spammers and hackers fake the apparent return address on email, but some mail programs let users check the actual return address. (I find that email claiming to be from PayPal has come from hotmail.com, yahoo.com, Denmark, Germany, and a variety of other unlikely places.) Some mail programs will alert the user if the actual Web address that a link will take you to is different from the one displayed in the text of a message.

Whether someone reaches a website from a link in an email or by browsing or searching, various tools can help determine if the site is safe. Sometimes fake websites are easy to spot because of poor grammar and generally low quality. Software can determine the geographic location of a site reasonably well. If it claims to be a U.S. bank but is located in Romania, it is wise to leave.

Some browsers (and add-on software used with browsers and search engines) will flag websites they consider safe or show alerts for sites known to collect and misuse personal

Tactics and countertactics in credit card and debit card fraud

Credit card fraud began with simple crimes, say, an individual on a shopping spree with a lost or stolen card. At first, the main method was to steal and use (or sell) the actual credit card. Both well-organized theft rings and individual purse snatchers stole credit cards. (They still do.) Several dozen people were convicted in one case where airline employees stole new cards from the mail transported on the airline's airplanes. Charges on the stolen cards ran to an estimated $7.5 million.[32]

Procedural changes helped protect against theft of new cards from the mail. To verify that the legitimate owner received the card, credit card issuers require the customer to call in and provide identifying information to activate a card. This procedure is only as good as the security of the identifying information. At first, credit card companies commonly used the person's Social Security number and mother's maiden name. Several Social Security Administration employees provided the Social Security numbers and mothers' maiden names of thousands of people to a credit card fraud ring so that they could activate stolen cards, according to federal prosecutors.[33] Now credit card companies use caller ID to verify that the authorization call comes from the customer's telephone. Similarly, if you send a change-of-address notification to your credit card company, the company will probably send a confirmation to both your old and new addresses. Why? Thieves who plan to use a stolen credit card number for a long time do not want the owner of the card to see fraudulent charges on the bill and close the account. Thus, they send a change-of-address notice (using a fake address for the new one). A confirmation letter sent to the old address alerts the real card owner.

E-commerce made it easier both to steal card numbers (not cards) and to use the numbers without the physical cards. When retail sales began on the Web, technically trained thieves used software to intercept credit card numbers in transmission from a personal computer to a website. Encryption and secure servers solved much of that problem; without such security, e-commerce could not have thrived.

A simple change in a business policy helped to thwart thieves who searched the trash near stores or banks for receipts with card numbers. Large stores and banks began printing only the last four digits on the receipts. Later, a law required this practice.

Thieves surreptitiously install recording devices, called *skimmers*, inside the card readers in stores, gas stations, and restaurants. They collect debit card numbers and PINs, make counterfeit cards, and raid people's bank accounts through ATM machines.

Credit card companies run sophisticated artificial intelligence software to detect unusual spending activity. When the system finds something suspicious, a merchant can ask a customer for additional identification or the credit card company can call a cardholder to verify purchases. The vast amount of data that businesses store about our purchases and other activities—the data that can threaten privacy—enables the credit card company software to make fairly accurate conclusions about whether a charge on our credit card is likely to be fraudulent.

Services like PayPal provide a trusted third party to increase confidence (and convenience) in online commerce and reduce credit fraud. A customer can buy from strangers online without giving them a credit card number. PayPal handles the payment for a small fee. PayPal and other companies that provide online payment services initially lost millions of dollars to fraud. Gradually, PayPal developed clever solutions and sophisticated security expertise.

information. While helpful for cautious users, such tools generate potential problems. Recall in Section 3.2.4 we observed that we might want a filter for pornography to be more restrictive even if it meant preventing a child from accessing some nonporn sites, while a spam filter should be less restrictive so that legitimate messages are not lost. How strict should a Web tool be about marking a site as safe? When a major browser marks as safe only large companies that it has certified, legitimate small businesses on the Web suffer. Mistakes in marking a legitimate site as a known or suspected phishing site could ruin a small business and could result in a lawsuit for the company that provides the rating. It is important from both an ethical and a business perspective to be cautious when designing and implementing such rating systems.

Banks and financial businesses developed techniques to assure customers that they are at an authentic site before the customer enters a password or other sensitive identifying information. For example, when a customer first sets up an account, some banks ask the customer to supply a digital image (say, of a pet dog) or choose one from many at the bank site. Later, whenever the person begins the log-on process by entering his or her name (or other identifier that is not critical for security), the system displays the image. Thus, the site authenticates itself to the customer before the customer authenticates himself or herself by entering a password.

Authenticating customers and preventing use of stolen numbers

In 2006, a Russian man, using a company located in one country and registered in another, bought stock and then broke into many people's online brokerage accounts and bought the same stock through those accounts. The large number of purchases pushed the price up, and the man sold his at a profit.[34] Note that criminal access to a brokerage account can be costly for the rightful owner even if the thief cannot get funds or stock from the account. This and numerous incidents of theft from online bank and investment accounts led to development of better procedures to authenticate customers. How can such businesses distinguish the real account owner from an identity thief armed with a stolen account number and other commonly used identifying information? Some sites store an identification number for the customer's home computer or laptop, then verify the machine used when the customer logs on. Some ask the customer to provide extra information when the account is first opened, then ask for some of that information at login. Some ask the customer to select from a group of several images when the account is opened, then require the customer to identify the image at login. (Note the latter is similar to the website authentication method described earlier, but used in this way it helps to authenticate the user.)

Some security firms offer more sophisticated authentication software using artificial intelligence techniques. The software calculates a risk score based on variation from the time of day a customer usually logs in, the type of browser regularly used, the customer's typical behavior and transactions, and so on. (How would privacy advocates and the public react to the disclosure that an online bank or brokerage firm stores such information about each customer's visits to the site?)

Geographic location tools, like those that tell users the physical location of a website, can tell an online retailer where a customer is. If the customer is not in the country where his or her credit card was issued, or if the customer is in a country with a high fraud rate, the retailer or credit card company can require extra identification.

Authenticating customers remotely is inherently difficult: many people, businesses, and websites must receive information that is necessary and sufficient to identify someone or authorize a transaction. Eventually, someone will lose, leak, or steal that information. To reduce the spread and vulnerability of Social Security numbers, many institutions began asking customers (for example, on the telephone) for only the last four digits. Then, of course, the last four digits became the critical numbers thieves needed to impersonate someone for access to an existing account. Combining several methods of identification, such as caller ID *and* the last four digits of the Social Security number, adds safety.

Credit card issuers and merchants always make trade-offs between security and customer convenience. For purchases in stores, most customers do not want to take the time to provide identification when they use a credit card, or to wait while merchants check it. Requests for ID might offend customers. Most merchants do not check signatures or photos on credit cards. More and more often, we swipe our card through a machine ourselves; a clerk does not look at it at all. For customer convenience and to speed transactions, some stores do not require a signature for small purchases. Others have self-service checkout. Merchants and credit card companies are willing to absorb some fraud losses as part of doing business. Such trade-offs are not new. Retail stores keep small, very expensive items in locked cabinets, but most goods are easily accessible to customers for convenience and efficiency. Openness encourages sales. Retail stores have always accepted some amount of losses from shoplifting rather than offend and inconvenience customers by keeping everything locked up or by searching customers when they leave the store. When a company perceives the losses as being too high, it improves security. When are merchants and credit card companies irresponsibly ignoring simple and important security measures, and when are they making reasonable trade-offs for convenience, efficiency, and avoiding offense to customers?

Reducing the damage of identity theft

Businesses and government agencies that lose personal data now often arrange for free credit-monitoring services for the people affected. Many nonprofit organizations and start-up businesses help people deal with the effects of identity theft. Laws requiring that companies and state government agencies notify people of breaches of their personal information give potential victims the opportunity to take a variety of protective measures. The most common measure is a *fraud alert*. A fraud alert is a flag on your credit record that tells the credit bureau to call you for confirmation when anyone tries to open a new credit account (e.g., for a car loan or credt card) in your name. We can monitor our credit card accounts to detect fraudulent charges quickly. We can even get insurance for identity theft. Consumer advocates argue for laws requiring that companies that lose sensitive personal data pay for damages, including costs for credit monitoring and other protections for consumers whose data they lost.

Identity thieves are ever vigilant for more opportunities. Some pretend to be legitimate companies providing identity-verification services and services to assist identity theft victims. The consumer must provide such companies with exactly the kinds of information the identity thief wants. Consumers must always be cautious.

Reducing the incidence of fraud by identity theft—and its monetary and personal costs—requires continually evolving methods for authenticating the parties on both sides of a transaction. It requires appropriate and evolving responses from merchants, financial institutions, credit card companies, the public, the programmers and entrepreneurs who develop technical protections and services, and the government agencies whose documents we use for identification.

5.3.3   BIOMETRICS

To protect privacy and to reduce credit fraud, identity theft, some kinds of hacking, and some terrorism threats, it is important to identify a person accurately. Thieves make counterfeit credit and debit cards; they guess or steal passwords. Terrorists make counterfeit driver's licenses; they can fake airport employee tags. Is there a foolproof way to identify someone?

Biometrics are biological characteristics that are unique to an individual. They include fingerprints, voice prints, face structure, hand geometry, eye (iris or retina) patterns, and DNA. Uses of DNA in the law enforcement and justice systems are well known. DNA matching has freed numerous innocent people mistakenly convicted of such serious crimes as rape and murder. Along with fingerprints, DNA has been extremely effective for identifying or eliminating suspects in crimes.

Biometric technology for identification applications is a multibillion-dollar industry with many beneficial applications. Some provide convenience that appeals to consumers. One device lets you open the door of your house by touching a scanner with your finger. No keys to lose, forget, or drop while carrying packages. Two main applications are security and fraud prevention. Some states use a face scanner and digital image matching to make sure a person does not apply for extra driver's licenses or welfare benefits under different names. Some computers require a fingerprint match to log on physically or over the Net, reducing access by hackers or laptop thieves. Some cellphones (especially in Japan) use fingerprints, face recognition, or other biometrics to authenticate the owner and protect against theft of information and funds in "electronic wallets" in the phones. To reduce the risks of terrorism, several airports use fingerprint identification systems to ensure that only employees enter restricted areas.

It appears that the use of biometrics will increase dramatically. Do biometrics provide a foolproof identification technology?

Just as people have always found ways around other security mechanisms, from picking locks to phishing, they find ways to thwart biometric identification. Researchers in the United States and Japan fooled fingerprint readers with cadaver fingers and fingers they made from gelatin and Play-Doh. Criminals can wear contact lenses that fool eye scanners.[35] A photo of a smartphone owner can unlock a phone protected by a (weak) face-recognition lock.

When a thief steals a credit card number, we can get a new account with a new number, but if a hacker gets a copy of the file with our digitized thumbprint or retina scan, we cannot get a new one. Identity theft might become easier to prevent, but much worse for a victim when it occurs. Given the weak security of the Web, it is likely that hackers will be able to steal files of biometrics from government agencies and businesses as easily as they steal files with Social Security and credit card numbers. Then they can access other people's biometrically protected accounts by rigging their machines to transmit a copy of the file rather than scanning their own finger or eye.

In Chapter 2, we discussed problems generated by widespread use of Social Security numbers. Biometrics could find many more applications than Social Security numbers. Will biometrics make us more secure? Or will they make it easier to build dossiers on people? Like the face-matching applications described in Section 2.2.4, will they increase surveillance and tracking of our activities?

We have pointed out a few times that we cannot expect perfection. The fact that criminals can thwart biometrics or that biometrics can pose privacy risks does not condemn these technologies. As always, we must have an accurate view of their strengths, weaknesses, and risks, and compare them with alternatives to determine, carefully, for what applications we should use them. By anticipating both privacy risks and methods criminals will use to get around new security measures, we can design better systems. For example, anticipating that iris scanners can be tricked by a photo of an eye, some scanners flash a light at the eye and check that the pupil contracts, as a real one would. Similarly, some fingerprint-matching systems distinguish live tissue from fake fingers, and researchers developed methods to distinguish a photo of a face from a real one. Just as responsible businesses must use up-to-date encryption, those that provide biometric protections must update them regularly.

5.4 Whose Laws Rule the Web?

5.4.1 WHEN DIGITAL ACTIONS CROSS BORDERS

The ILOVEYOU virus infected tens of millions of computers worldwide in 2000, destroying files, collecting passwords, and snarling computers at major corporations and government agencies. Yet prosecutors dropped charges against the Philippine man be-

- Content control/censorship (Topics include politics, religion, pornography, criminal investigations and trials, and many others.)
- Intellectual property
- Gambling
- Hacking/viruses
- Libel
- Privacy
- Commerce (advertising, store hours, sales)
- Spam

Figure 5.1   Some areas where national laws differ.

lieved responsible. The Philippines had no law against releasing a virus at that time. (It passed one soon after.) Should police arrest the man if he visits Canada, the United States, Germany, France, or any of the other countries where the virus did damage?

It is tempting to say yes, he should face arrest in any country where the virus caused damage and releasing viruses is illegal. It might also be reasonable that prosecutions for denial-of-service attacks, theft, fraud, and so on, take place in countries where the damage is done, not solely in the country where the perpetrator acted. But we need to look carefully at the impact of applying the same policy to all laws.

Figure 5.1 lists some of the subject areas in which national laws differ. In addition to outlawing actions that are legal elsewhere, some countries have significantly different procedural laws. For example, in the United States, the government may not appeal acquittals, but in some countries (including other Western democracies), the government may.

The government of Thailand arrested an American citizen while he was in Thailand on a visit and later sentenced him to more than two years in jail. The man had translated parts of a critical biography of the king (published by Yale University Press) and posted them on the Internet from the United States five years earlier. The Thai government had banned the book under its strict laws against insulting the royal family.[36] A Dutch man released a controversial film critical of Islam on the Internet. The film was not illegal in the Netherlands. However, Jordan prosecuted the man on charges of blasphemy and other crimes. Making it difficult or dangerous for him to travel internationally was apparently one of the goals of the organization that filed the complaints in Jordan. Consider an American or French citizen of Chinese ancestry who is a journalist and publishes a blog about the democracy movement in China. The blog is legal where written, but much of its content is illegal in China, because, in the view of the Chinese government, discussion of democracy damages the social order. Would we consider it right if China arrests the journalist on a trip there to visit relatives?

There are risks in Western countries as well. The first major incident of people and businesses charged with crimes for content that is legal where it was posted occurred in France. The U.S. government arrests employees and executives of foreign companies whose services violate U.S. laws but not their own. (We describe some cases in more detail later.) Canadian courts ban reporting court proceedings in some cases—for example, political scandals and gruesome murders. When a Canadian court banned reporting in a case of alleged corruption in the Labour Party, a U.S. blogger who lived near the border reported details of the court proceedings. His blog had 400,000 hits, mostly from Canada. The blogger feared going to Canada for vacation.

Multinational corporations and tourists have always had to learn about and comply with the laws of countries they operated in or visited. At home, in the past, they had only to deal with their home country's laws. The Web changed that. Which country's laws should apply when Web content crosses borders? In several cases so far, governments are acting on the assumption of a principle I call the responsibility-to-prevent-access principle.

> Responsibility to prevent access: It is the responsibility of providers of services and information to make sure their material is not accessible in countries where it is illegal. They may be sued or jailed in those countries if they do not prevent access.

In the next few sections, we describe more incidents and discuss arguments for and against this point of view.

Yahoo and French censorship

Display and sale of Nazi memorabilia are illegal in France and Germany, with some exceptions for historical purposes. Two antiracism organizations sued Yahoo in a French court in 1999 because French people could view Nazi memorabilia offered for sale on Yahoo's U.S.-based auction sites. The French government also brought criminal charges against Yahoo and former CEO Tim Koogle for justifying a crime against humanity. (Yahoo's French sites, based in France, complied with the French law.)[37] These cases raised technical, legal, and social issues.

Yahoo argued that it was not technically feasible to block access from France. On the Internet at that time, one's physical location was difficult to determine. Also, French people could access Yahoo's sites from outside France or use anonymizing services that obscured their location. Yahoo said the use of filters to screen out Nazi material would not suffice, because they would be less than 50% effective and could not distinguish references to Nazis in hate material from references in *The Diary of Anne Frank* or Holocaust memorials.[38] At the time, however, companies were recognizing that people who read, say, the *New York Times* online in Toronto or London would likely prefer to see ads from stores in their cities rather than from New York stores. A few companies were already using software, called geolocation software, to figure out where website visitors were located. The goal was for visitors to see information in their own language and advertising relevant to their own culture, country, or location. The software was fairly new at the time of the Yahoo case, but experts said Yahoo could use a variant of it to screen out 90% of French users. The French court ordered Yahoo to make a serious effort, including using such tools, to block access by French people to its sites outside of France that contain material illegal in France.

The legal issue is whether the French law should apply to Yahoo auction sites on Yahoo's computers located outside of France. As we saw in the discussion of the Amateur Action bulletin board system case in the box in Section 3.2.1, the meaning of the term "distribution" gets fuzzy on the Internet. Should a speaker have an obligation not to make available speech that others do not want to hear (or that governments do not want the people of a country to hear), or should listeners have the task of covering their ears? Should France have the task of blocking access to material from outside its borders?

The social issue concerns the impact on freedom of speech worldwide if countries with more restrictive laws can enforce them in freer countries. Section 3.5 reminds us how restrictive and extensive those censorship laws are.

Tim Koogle did not go to France to attend his trial. Yahoo and Koogle were acquitted because the court decided that permitting the auctions was not "justifying" the Nazi crimes. The decision did not resolve the issue of whether one country's government could or should bring criminal charges against content providers based in another country for content legal in their own country.

Applying U.S. copyright law to foreign companies

If a company sells a product or service on the Web in a country where it is legal, should its employees face arrest and jail if they visit a country where it is illegal? ElcomSoft, a Russian company, sold a computer program that circumvents controls embedded in Adobe Systems Inc.'s electronic books to prevent copyright infringement. A buyer of the program could use it for legal purposes, such as making backup copies or reading an ebook on different devices, but could also use the program to illegally make copyright-infringing copies. The program itself was legal in Russia and in most of the world, but not in the United States. Distribution of software to thwart built-in copyright protection violates the Digital Millennium Copyright Act (Section 4.2.2). When the program's author, Dmitry Sklyarov, came to the United States to present a talk on the weaknesses in control software used in ebooks, he was arrested. He faced a possible 25-year prison term. After protests in the United States and several other countries, the U.S. government let Sklyarov return home but pressed a criminal case against ElcomSoft. A federal jury acquitted the company of criminal charges. ElcomSoft claimed it did not know the program was illegal in the United States and it stopped distributing the program when Adobe complained. Thus, the case did not resolve the basic issue of whether a prosecution would be successful against a company for continuing to distribute a product that is legal in its own country.

Arresting executives of online gambling and payment companies

The United States arrested David Carruthers, a British citizen and then CEO of BetOn-Sports PLC, as he changed planes in Dallas on a flight from England to Costa Rica. The U.S. government also arrested several other executives of BetOnSports and the chairman of Sportingbook, another large British online gambling company. Online betting is legal in England. Internet gambling companies are listed and traded on the London stock exchange. The arrests caused gambling company stocks to drop by $1.5 billion.[39] The U.S. government argues that most of the companies' customers were in the United States, where most online gambling is illegal. The companies, according to the United States, should have blocked access by U.S. citizens. These arrests, under a 1961 law, are particularly aggressive because legal experts, gambling experts, and legislators disagree about whether the law applies to the Internet. Carruthers, facing a possible 20-year jail sentence, pleaded guilty for a lower sentence.[40]

Foreign online gambling companies thrive with U.S. customers if their employees stay out of the United States, so Congress passed the Unlawful Internet Gambling Enforcement Act. It prohibits credit card and online-payment companies from processing transactions between bettors and gambling sites. U.S. credit card companies and online payment companies such as PayPal had already stopped processing gambling transactions (after pressure from the government), but payment-service companies exist in other countries where online gambling, and processing payments for it, are legal. Within months of passing the new law, the U.S. government arrested the founders of a British Internet payment company that processed payments for gambling sites.

You just don't travel to the U.S. any more if you're in that business.

—A London business analyst, after the arrests of two British online gambling company executives in the United States[41]

5.4.2 LIBEL, SPEECH, AND COMMERCIAL LAW

Differences among free countries

Under defamation law, we can sue a person, business, or organization for saying something false and damaging to our reputations in print or in other media such as television or the Web. Libel is written defamation; slander is verbal. In the United States, if the content is true, there is no libel. Libel laws differ, even among countries that share British background and legal history. The United States has strong protection for freedom of speech and for expression of opinion. Public figures, such as politicians and entertainers, have less libel protection than other people. The reasoning is that vigorous, open debate—and ultimately freedom—would suffer if people could not express strong opinions about prominent people. English and Australian law and tradition, on the other hand, place more emphasis on protecting reputations. Michael Jackson won a libel suit against a

British newspaper for a statement that his plastic surgeries "hideously disfigured" him. He probably would not have won such a suit in the United States. In England, people often sue newspapers, and it can be risky to publish details about business and political scandals. Scientists and medical researchers worry about whistleblowing and publishing criticism of research.* The burden of proof differs in different countries. In the United States, the person who is suing has the burden of proving the case. Public figures must prove the published information is false *and* that the publisher knew it was false or acted recklessly. Libel law in some other countries requires that the publisher of the statement in question prove it is true or that the publisher reasonably believed it was true.

The result is that news publishers must block access to articles by people in countries where publication of the articles violates laws. The *New York Times* did so for the first time in 2006. It reprogrammed its geolocation tools, normally used for targeting advertisements, to block people in England from reading a news article. The article described the investigation of suspects arrested in an alleged plot to carry liquid explosives onto airplanes and blow them up. Publishing information damaging to defendants before a trial is illegal in England. It is not illegal in the United States.[42] Any solution to the problem of differing national laws among free countries involves some compromise. The *New York Times*, in explaining its decision to block the terror-plot article, said that although England does not have a First Amendment protecting freedom of the press to the extent the United States does, England does have a free press, and it is reasonable to respect its laws.

The *New York Times* action shows that major news publishers have the legal staffs and the technical tools to handle differences in laws. Suppose someone in the United States sends the blocked *New York Times* article by email to someone in England. Suppose a U.S. blogger with readers in England repeats some of the information in the article. What might happen to these individuals, who do not have a legal staff and geolocation tools, who might not know the article is illegal in another country?

Libel law as a threat to free speech

A U.S. publisher published a book in the United States by a U.S. scholar about the funding of terrorism. Some people in England bought copies over the Web. A Saudi banker who, according to the book, helped fund Osama bin Laden, brought a libel suit in England against the author and won. Out of fear of the same kind of lawsuit, another U.S. publisher canceled a book on a similar topic (also written by an American) that had been selling well. The relative ease of winning libel cases in England led to a phenomenon called *libel tourism*. It has the following characteristics: The person suing for libel in England does not live or work in England. The person or business sued is, in many cases, not located in England. The content in question, in some cases, is not in English. The content was posted

---

* In 2006, in a "landmark" ruling, the British Law Lords (similar to the U.S. Supreme Court) gave news organizations protection from libel suits for responsible journalism of value to the public.

on the Web on servers outside of England. But the content was accessible in England. Such lawsuits squelch freedom of speech and access to information for people in countries other than England where the libel suits would probably fail.

U.S. courts generally enforce foreign court judgments against U.S. residents. Abuse of libel law led to passage of the SPEECH Act of 2010, which makes foreign libel judgments unenforceable in the United States if they would violate the First Amendment. But even if U.S. courts do not enforce such foreign court decisions, foreign governments can seize assets of U.S. companies that are in their country or arrest visiting individuals or executives of companies that do not comply with their censorship orders.

Even when the laws of two countries are almost identical, the location of a trial is very important. A trial in a foreign country means high travel and legal expenses, time away from work and family, a foreign attorney and jury, unfamiliar forms and procedures, and a cultural disadvantage. In U.S. libel cases where the parties are in different states, courts may rule that the libel (and hence the trial) take place where the damage happens. This makes sense for international cases too, at least for reasonably free countries like the United States, Australia, and England. But what happens if we generalize to oppressive governments that use strict libel laws for political purposes?

Saudi Arabia bans "anything damaging to the dignity of heads of state."[43] In Russia, it is a crime to slander government officials. Government officials in Singapore have long used libel laws to bankrupt political opponents who criticize them. The Prime Minister of Singapore and his father, the former Premier, demanded that the Hong Kong–based *Far Eastern Economic Review* remove from its website an interview with a political opponent who criticized them. They sued the publisher and editor for libel. A lawsuit or criminal charges in these countries against a foreign newspaper or a visiting journalist or blogger is more threatening to honest, critical news coverage than holding a libel trial for a U.S. publisher in Australia.

Commercial law

The European Union (EU) severely restricts advertising of medical drugs and devices directed to consumers. Such ads are legal and common on television and on the Web in the United States. The EU has other restrictive laws about marketing. Some countries prohibit or restrict direct price comparisons, product give-aways, and advertising unconditional-return policies or that a business gives a contribution to charity for each sale. (The justification for these laws is that such practices and advertisements confuse or trick consumers. Germany repealed some of these laws, in force for 90 years, in part because of the influence of the Internet.)[44] Should commercial websites with drug ads or price comparisons have to screen out shoppers from countries where they are illegal? Enforcing such laws on foreign sites does not differ, in principle, from France requiring Yahoo to prevent access by French people to auctions with Nazi memorabilia or the United States requiring foreign gambling sites to exclude U.S. citizens.

5.4.3 Culture, Law, and Ethics

If publishers must comply with the laws of almost 200 countries, would they protect themselves by avoiding anything controversial? Will the extraordinary benefits of international news blogging shrink under the burden of learning every other country's laws, the need to block potentially illegal articles, and the chilling effect of uncertainty? Some fear this would destroy the openness and global information flow of the Web, that the Web would come to reflect some combination of Muslim restrictions on discussion of religion, U.S. opposition to online gambling, and Chinese censorship of political discussion. Others argue that companies would adapt and acquire software to handle the appropriate screening.

Jack Goldsmith and Tim Wu, in their book *Who Controls the Internet?*, argue that the "global network is becoming a collection of nation-state networks"[45] and that this is a good thing. The Net, Goldsmith and Wu believe, will be more peaceful and productive if each country controls content within its borders according to its own history, culture, and values. Goldsmith and Wu point out that many people and governments (in both totalitarian countries and democracies) consider the freedom of speech enjoyed in the United States to be excessive. U.S. publishers and bloggers should respect differing national standards and laws and prevent their publications from reaching people in countries that prohibit them.

Critics of their point of view might point out that respecting culture is not the same as respecting laws. Culture evolves over time and is rarely absolute or uniform throughout a country. Governments often claim to be protecting national culture and values when they impose controls on their citizens to maintain their own power or to benefit special interests within their country. Laws, as we saw in our discussion of differences between law and ethics in Chapter 1, have many ignoble sources. Who in China wants censorship of political discussion in cyberspace—the people or the Communist Party, which is trying to maintain political control while it loosens economic control? The United States defends its ban on offshore gambling sites with the argument that it has the right to ban morally objectionable activities. Certainly there are many valid criticisms of gambling on social and ethical grounds, but this argument from the government is not convincing. The federal and state governments allow and tax many forms of legal gambling and profit from monopolies on their state lotteries. It seems likely that anticompetitiveness—not morality—motivates the governments, casinos, and racetracks that oppose offshore online poker playing.

Consider Canada's and France's restrictions on showing U.S. television programs. Some defenders of these laws emphasize protecting their culture from being overrun by U.S. culture. Others (e.g., in Canada) are frank about the purpose being to provide jobs for Canadians and to protect the financial health of the small domestic broadcasting industry. Within each country that has similar protectionist laws (including the United States), there are strongly opposing opinions about whether such laws are unjust intrusions on freedom, whether they help some domestic industries while hurting others, or whether they are reasonable ways to help a local economy. Should governments enforce their protectionist laws on people outside their borders?

Where a large majority of people in a country support prohibitions on certain content, say, discussions of certain religions, is it ethically proper to abandon the basic human rights of free expression and freedom of religion for minorities? Is there a positive ethical value in thwarting a country's censorship laws and providing exactly the material that some governments ban?

5.4.4 POTENTIAL SOLUTIONS

International agreements

International treaties can set common standards or means of resolving international cases among the countries that sign them. Countries in the World Trade Organization (WTO) agree not to prevent their citizens from buying certain services from other countries if those services are legal in their own. This is a good step, a generalization of the principle in the United States that the individual states cannot discriminate against sellers (of legal products) from other states. (Recall the wine shipment and real estate sales cases in Section 3.2.5.) But this WTO agreement does not help when a product, service, or information is legal in one country and not another.

An alternative principle

An alternative to the responsibility-to-prevent-access principle—call it the authority-to-prevent-entry principle—says:

> Authority to prevent entry: The government of Country A can act within Country A to try to block the entrance of material that is illegal there, but may not apply its laws to the people who create and publish the material, or provide a service, in Country B if it is legal there.

This principle might be reasonable for services such as gambling, which is a prominent part of the culture in some countries, illegal in others, and regulated and taxed in still others. It has been the de facto practice for political speech for a long time. For example, the Soviet Union jammed radio broadcasts from Western countries during the "Cold War." It did not have an internationally respected right to order the broadcasters to stop broadcasting. Similarly, Iran jams BBC programs in Persian on satellite TV. Within their borders, national governments have many tools to block information and activities they do not want. As we saw in Section 3.5.2, they require ISPs and search engine companies (within their country) to block access to banned sites. The government of Singapore made it a criminal offense for Singaporeans to subscribe to, import, or reproduce the *Far Eastern Economic Review* after it published an interview the government considered libelous. Of course, people who believe in freedom of speech do not approve of such actions. The authority-to-prevent-entry principle is a compromise. It recognizes that governments are sovereign within their territories. It attempts to reduce the impact of their restrictive laws outside their borders. If influential countries like the United States and France, for example, adopted this principle and refrained from arresting visiting foreigners, their example could apply pressure to less free countries to do the same. They do not appear inclined to do so.

Of course, this principle has weaknesses too. Countries that lack up-to-date cybercrime laws attract people who commit international online crimes, such as major frauds. We want some sensible way for the victims in other countries to take action against them. One reason for the difficulty in developing good solutions to the problem of differing laws in different countries is that there are such widely different kinds of laws. As we saw in Chapter 1, some outlaw truly bad activities that victimize other people. Some impose particular views about acceptable personal beliefs, speech, and nonviolent activities. If all laws were of the first type, there might be much agreement about their enforcement. The problems would be about differences in detail (such as differences between U.S. and British libel law). The responsibility-to-prevent-access principle, the principle many governments currently follow, is dangerous primarily because there are so many laws of the second type. But many people and governments strongly support such laws. It would be quite difficult to find agreement about which laws are the "right" laws, laws a country could rightly enforce outside its borders. Compromises in this context, unfortunately, reduce freedom for the people in the country that is most free in any particular area. Thus, we still need creative development of good solutions for the problem of determining what country's laws apply in cross-border Internet cases.

EXERCISES

Review Exercises

5.1 What did the word "hacker" mean in the early days of computing?

5.2 Is it legal to release a computer virus that puts a funny message on people's screens but does not damage files?

5.3 Give an example of hacking by a government.

5.4 What is phishing?

5.5 Describe one method financial websites use to convince a consumer the site is authentic.

5.6 What is one problem with using biometrics for identification?

5.7 For what Web-based service did the U.S. government arrest several business executives from England?

General Exercises

5.8 Your roommate Chris uses your phone at night while you sleep. Your other roommate Robin takes and uses your study material while you sleep. (Neither has your permission; neither does damage.)

List several characteristics of the two events that are similar (characteristics related to the effects of the events, ethics, legality, risks, etc.). List several characteristics of the two events that are different. Which would offend you more? Why?

5.9   Young, technically oriented hackers argued that, if the owners of a computer system want to keep outsiders out, it is their responsibility to provide better security. Ken Thompson, one of the inventors of UNIX, said, "The act of breaking into a computer system has to have the same social stigma as breaking into a neighbor's house. It should not matter that the neighbor's door is unlocked."[46] Which position do you agree with more? Give your reasons.

5.10   Some people argue that a hacker who defaces a Web page of a government entity such as the White House, Congress, or Parliament should receive harsher punishment than a hacker who defaces a Web page of a private company or organization. Give some arguments for and against this view.

5.11   In Section 5.2.2, we described the incident in which a hacker group hacked into the Bay Area Rapid Transit (BART) system to protest BART's shut down of wireless communication in some BART stations. Was this a form of hacktivism? Was it ethical? Give reasons.

5.12   A hacker group stole client credit card numbers from a security firm and used them to make donations to charities. Part of the purpose of the hack was to demonstrate the weakness of security at the firm. Analyze the ethics of this incident.

5.13   The terms of use of the website for a online service provider prohibit the creation of automated free accounts. Should a person who used a software program to this end be prosecuted for exceeding authorized access to the site? Why or why not?

5.14   Consider the analogy between occasional downtime on the Web as a result of viruses, worms, or denial-of-service attacks and vehicle traffic slowdowns on roads during rush hour or bad weather. Describe similarities; then evaluate. Are both side effects of modern civilization that we have to get used to? How can individuals and businesses reduce the negative impacts on themselves?

5.15   Suppose a 16-year-old uses automatic-dialing software to flood the emergency 911 telephone system with calls, knocking out 911 service. What penalty do you think is appropriate?

5.16   Evaluate arguments in favor of and against passage of a law making denial of service by a website a crime. Would you support such a law? Why or why not?

5.17   Gas stations, some grocery stores, and other stores do not require a signature for credit card purchases. Give arguments for and against this practice. Do you think retailers should always require a signature? Why or why not?

5.18   Discuss the phenomena of domain hacks. Name some innocent and some misleading uses of it. In your opinion, should certain domain hacks be made criminal to prevent malicious use?

5.19   In Section 5.3.2, we gave an analogy between merchants accepting some amount of shoplifting, on the one hand, and merchants and credit card companies accepting some amount of credit card fraud, on the other hand. Identify a strength and a weakness of this analogy.

5.20   We saw that hackers and identity thieves use many techniques and continually develop new ones. Think up a new scheme for obtaining passwords or some type of personal information that might be useful in identity theft. Then describe a possible response to protect against your scheme.

5.21   A search engine maintains a database of the IP addresses of its users. Does this violate the privacy principles in Figure 2.1 of collecting only the data needed and not storing data longer than needed? Explain your answer. Find some search engines that store IP addresses and at least one that does not.

5.22 Suppose fingerprint readers are a standard feature of personal computers and an ISP requires a match to log in. Would requiring a password in addition to the fingerprint be redundant and pointless, or is there a good security reason to require both? Explain.

5.23 Identify several issues raised by this scenario:

> Someone in California posts on amazon.com a very critical review of a new book written by a British author. The review says the writer is an incompentent fool without a single good idea; he can't even express the bad ideas clearly and probably did not graduate from grade school; he should be washing dishes instead of wasting paper and the reader's time. The author sues the reviewer and Amazon for libel.

5.24 If U.S. law enforcement agents in the United States caught the leader of a South American drug gang that smuggles drugs into the United States, they would arrest him. Is this comparable to arresting Dmitry Sklyarov or David Carruthers? (See Section 5.4.1.) Explain similarities and differences.

5.25 Using some of the ethical principles in Chapter 1, analyze the ethics of the action of the U.S. blogger who posted details about the Canadian trial (page 278). Do you think he should have done it?

5.26 During World War II, "Radio Free Europe" broadcast news and other information into Nazi-controlled countries. It was illegal to listen to those broadcasts in those countries. During the "Cold War," the Soviet Union jammed Western radio broadcasts into that country. In the discussion of the Yahoo/France case (Section 5.4.1), we asked: Should a speaker have an obligation not to make available speech that others do not want to hear (or that governments do not want the people of a country to hear), or should listeners have the task of covering their ears? Does your answer for the Yahoo case differ from your answer in the Nazi and Soviet examples? If so, how and why? If not, why not?

5.27 Assume you are a professional working in your chosen field. Describe two new problems related to the material in this chapter that may occur in the next ten years. (If you cannot think of anything related to your professional field, choose another field that might interest you.)

5.28 Think ahead to the next few years and describe a new problem, related to issues in this chapter, likely to develop from digital technology or devices.

Assignments

These exercises require some research or activity.

5.29 Find a dozen news and/or magazine articles about hackers from mainstream media from the past few years. How are hackers described, as criminals or heroes? Give examples.

5.30 The section on hacking by governments (Section 5.2.4) describes incidents of hacking for military or strategic purposes. Find information about hacking in academia. Summarize your findings. What responses are appropriate?

5.31 Find a use of biometrics in your city. Describe the application and its benefits and risks.

Class Discussion Exercises

These exercises are for class discussion, perhaps with short presentations prepared in advance by small groups of students.

5.32   Near the end of Section 5.2.3, we described three examples of disclosing vulnerabilities in computer systems. Discuss and evaluate them. Were they handled responsibly? Discuss the following more general question: Do hackers do a public service by finding and publicizing computer security weaknesses?

5.33   Suppose a denial-of-service attack shuts down two dozen major websites, including retailers, stock brokerages, and large corporate entertainment and information sites, for several hours. The attack is traced to one of the following perpetrators. Do you think different penalties are appropriate, depending on which it is? Explain why. If you would impose different penalties, how would they differ?

(a) A foreign terrorist who launched the attack to cause billions of dollars in damage to the U.S. economy.

(b) An organization publicizing its opposition to commercialization of the Web and corporate manipulation of consumers.

(c) A teenager using hacking tools he found on a website.

(d) A hacker group showing off to another hacker group about how many sites it could shut down in one day.

5.34   How should the U.S. government respond to a hacking attack by China in which the hackers shut down critical military communications for several hours?*

5.35   Should violation of the terms of agreement of a website be a crime? Why or why not? If you think it should depend on the type of site and the type of violation, explain the criteria to make the distinction.

5.36   After WikiLeaks released thousands of confidential U.S. government diplomatic and military documents on the Web (see Section 3.3), hackers conducted a denial-of-service attack on the WikiLeaks website. When major credit card companies stopped processing donations to WikiLeaks, other hackers attacked the credit card companies. For each action, give arguments that it was justifiable hacktivism, and give arguments that it was not. Which position do you agree with? Explain your reasons.

5.37   Do we have an ethical responsibility to maintain up-to-date antivirus protection and other security software on our personal computers to prevent our computers from being infected with remotely controlled software that harms others? Should a law require that everyone install such software? Would your opinion remain the same whether or not we have to pay for such protection?

5.38   Suppose a local community center has invited you, a group of college students, to make a 15-minute presentation about protecting against computer Trojans. Plan and give the presentation.

5.39   A judge in a country where pornography is illegal seized the Web addresses of more than 100 pornographic sites. The website owners do not have a physical presence in that country, nor are their websites hosted on servers in that country. Give arguments for and against the judge's decision.

---

* This is hypothetical; such an attack has not occurred.

BOOKS AND ARTICLES

- Robert Corn-Revere, "Caught in the Seamless Web: Does the Internet's Global Reach Justify Less Freedom of Speech?" Cato Institute, July 24, 2002. (Also appears in Adam Thierer and Clyde Wayne Crews Jr., eds. *Who Rules The Net?*, listed below.) Criticizes arguments in Goldsmith and Wu, *Who Controls the Internet?*, below, in articles that Goldsmith had published earlier.

- Dorothy E. Denning, *Information Warfare and Security*, ACM Press/Addison-Wesley, 1999.

- Dorothy E. Denning and Peter J. Denning, eds., *Internet Besieged: Countering Cyberspace Scofflaws*, ACM Press/Addison-Wesley, 1998. A collection of articles on hacking and Internet security.

- Pam Dixon, *Medical Identity Theft: The Information Crime That Can Kill You*, World Privacy Forum, May 3, 2006, www.worldprivacyforum.org/medicalidentitytheft.html.

- Scott Eltringham, "Prosecuting Computer Crimes," U.S. Department of Justice, Feb. 2007, www.usdoj.gov/criminal/cybercrime/ccmanual/index.html.

- Jack Goldsmith and Tim Wu, *Who Controls the Internet? Illusions of a Borderless World*, Oxford University Press, 2006. Argues in favor of each country strictly enforcing its laws against foreigners to control what enters its borders via the Internet. See Corn-Revere, "Caught in the Seamless Web," above.

- Warren G. Kruse II and Jay G. Heiser, *Computer Forensics: Incident Response*, Addison-Wesley, 2001.

- Steven Levy, *Hackers: Heroes of the Computer Revolution*, Doubleday, 1984.

- Mark Manion and Abby Goodrum, "Terrorism or Civil Disobedience: Toward a Hacktivist Ethic," in Richard A. Spinello and Herman T. Tavani, eds., *Readings in CyberEthics*, Jones and Bartlett, 2001, pp. 463–473. Argues for expanding the ethical justification for civil disobedience to include hacktivism.

- Kevin Mitnick, *Ghost in the Wires: My Adventures as the World's Most Wanted Hacker*, Little, Brown & Co., 2011.

- Charles P. Pfleeger and Shari Lawrence Pfleeger, *Security in Computing*, 4th edition, Prentice Hall, 2007.

- Tsutomu Shimomura and John Markoff, *Take-Down: The Pursuit and Capture of America's Most Wanted Computer Outlaw—By the Man Who Did It*, Hyperion, 1996.

- William Stallings, *Cryptography and Network Security: Principles and Practice*, 5th edition, Prentice Hall, 2010.

- Clifford Stoll, *The Cuckoo's Egg: Tracking a Spy Through the Maze of Computer Espionage*, Doubleday, 1989.

- Adam Thierer and Clyde Wayne Crews Jr., eds. *Who Rules the Net? Internet Governance and Jurisdiction*, Cato Institute, 2003.

NOTES

1. I have seen estimates ranging up to $500,000 for the average, some from computer security firms, which have an incentive to exaggerate. It is difficult to get precise figures, in part because victims are reluctant to report losses.

2. Eric S. Raymond, ed., *New Hacker's Dictionary*, MIT Press, 1993.

3. Quoted in J. D. Bierdorfer, "Among Code Warriors, Women, Too, Can Fight," *New York Times*, June 7, 2001, pp. 1, 9.

4. Jon A. Rochlis and Mark W. Eichin, "With Microscope and Tweezers: The Worm from MIT's Perspective," *Communications of the ACM*, 32:6, June 1989, pp. 689–698.

5. W. Wayt Gibbs, "Profile: Dan Farmer," *Scientific American*, April 1997, pp. 32, 34. Jared Sandberg, "Holes In the Net," *Newsweek*, Feb. 21, 2000, pp. 46–49.

6. Lev Grossman, "Attack of the Love Bug," *Time*, May 15, 2000, pp. 48–56.

7. See grc.com/dos/grcdos.htm for a first-hand report by a hacking victim that covers technical, sociological, and social aspects of the attack, including email from the boy who launched it; viewed June 3, 2001.

8. Victoria Murphy Barret, "Spam Hunter," Forbes.com, July 23, 2007, members.forbes.com/forbes/2007/0723/054.html.

9. The Swedish site was the Pirate Bay; Ivar Ekman, "File-Sharing Crackdown and Backlash in Sweden," *International Herald Tribune*, June 5, 2006, p. 1. Jason Scheier, "Sony Hack Probe Uncovers 'Anonymous' Calling Card," *Wired*, May 4, 2011, www.wired.com/gamelife/2011/05/sony-playstation-network-anonymous, viewed Oct. 25, 2011.

10. Hayley Tsukayama, "Facebook Security Breach Raises Concerns," *Washington Post*, Nov. 15, 2011, www.washingtonpost.com/business/economy/facebook-hack-raises-security-concerns/2011/11/15/gIQAqCyYPN_story.html, viewed Jan. 1, 2012.

11. John J. Fialka, "The Latest Flurries at Weather Bureau: Scattered Hacking," *Wall Street Journal*, Oct. 10, 1994, pp. A1, A6.

12. Mark Manion and Abby Goodrum, "Terrorism or Civil Disobedience: Toward a Hacktivist Ethic," in Richard A. Spinello and Herman T. Tavani, eds., *Readings in CyberEthics*, Jones and Bartlett, 2001, pp. 463–473.

13. Marc L. Songini, "Hospital Confirms Copying of Patient Files by Hacker," *Computerworld*, Dec. 15, 2000, archives.cnn.com/2000/TECH/computing/12/15/hospital.hacker.idg/index.html, viewed Sept. 7, 2007.

14. Two members of the group faced hacking charges.

15. In Cheryl Pellerin, "DOD Releases First Strategy for Operating in Cyberspace," U.S. Department of Defense, July 14, 2011, www.defense.gov/news/newsarticle.aspx?id=64686, viewed Dec. 31, 2011.

16. Many news stories covered these and other incidents. See, for example: US-China Economic and Security Review Commission, "2010 Report to Congress," p. 243, www.uscc.gov/annual_report/2010/10_annual_report.php, viewed Oct. 29, 2011. Alex Spillius, "China and Russia Hack into US Power Grid," *The Telegraph*, Apr. 8, 2009, www.telegraph.co.uk/news/worldnews/asia/china/5126584/China-and-Russia-hack-into-US-power-grid.html, viewed Oct. 25, 2011. Richard Clarke, "China's Cyberassault on America," *Wall Street Journal*, June 15, 2011, online.wsj.com/article/SB10001424052702304259304576373391101828876.html, viewed Oct. 25, 2011. Jim Wolf, "China Key Suspect in US Satellite Hacks: Commission," *Reuters*, Oct. 28, 2011, www.reuters.com/article/2011/10/28/china-usa-satellite-idUSN1E79R1LK20111028, viewed Oct. 28, 2011.

17. This incident was widely reported. See, for example, L. Gordon Crovitz, "China Goes Phishing," *Wall Street Journal*, June 6, 2011, online.wsj.com/article/SB10001424052702303657404576363374283504838.html, viewed Oct. 31, 2011.

18. Jonathan Fildes, "Stuxnet Worm 'Targeted High-Value Iranian Assets,'" *BBC News*, Sept. 23, 2010, www.bbc.co.uk/news/technology-11388018, viewed Oct. 25, 2011. David Sanger, "Obama Order Sped Up Wave of Cyberattacks against Iran," *New York Times*, June 1, 2012, www.nytimes.com/2012/06/01/world/middleeast/obama-ordered-wave-of-cyberattacks-against-iran.html, viewed June 24, 2012.

19. John R. Wilke, "In the Arcane Culture of Computer Hackers, Few Doors Stay Closed," *Wall Street Journal*, Aug. 22, 1990, pp. A1, A4.

20. "Withdrawal Ordered for U.S. Pentagon Hackers," *San Jose Mercury News* (Reuters), Nov. 5, 1998.

21. Thom Shanker and Elisabeth Bulmiller, "Hackers Gained Access to Sensitive Military Files," *New York Times*, July 14, 2011, www.nytimes.com/2011/07/15/world/15cyber.html?pagewanted=all, viewed Dec. 31, 2011. Cheryl Pellerin, "DOD Releases First Strategy for Operating in Cyberspace," U.S. Department of Defense, July 14, 2011, www.defense.gov/news/newsarticle.aspx?id=64686, viewed Dec. 31, 2011.

22. "NASA Needs to Remedy Vulnerabilities in Key Networks," Government Accountability Office, Oct. 15, 2009, www.gao.gov/products/GAO-10-4. "Information Security: Fundamental Weaknesses Place EPA Data and Operations at Risk," Government Accountability Office, July 2000, www.gao.gov/archive/2000/ai00215.pdf. Associated Press, "U.S. Review Finds Widespread Lapses in Computer Security," *Wall Street Journal*, Apr. 6, 2001, p. B6. "Extradition Fight Lost in Computer Hackings," *San Diego Union-Tribune*, Apr. 4, 2007, p. A8. Jaikumar Vijayan, "Audit Finds 700 High-Risk Vulnerabilities in Air Traffic Systems," *ComputerWorld*, May 7, 2009, www.computerworld.com/s/article/9132663/, viewed Dec. 31, 2011. The 2011 review of the air traffic control system is at www.oig.dot.gov/sites/dot/files/Vulnerability%20Assessment%20of%20FAA%20Air%20Trafffic%20Control%20System_0.pdf, viewed Dec. 31, 2011.

23. William J. Lynn III, "Defending a New Domain," *Foreign Affairs*, Sept./Oct. 2010, www.foreignaffairs.com/articles/66552/william-j-lynn-iii/defending-a-new-domain, viewed Oct. 29, 2011.

24. Joseph Pereira, "How Credit-Card Data Went Out Wireless Door," *Wall Street Journal*, May 4, 2007, pp. A1, A12. In 2011, hackers collected unencrypted sensitive client data from a firm that analyzes international security for government agencies, banks, oil companies, and other large companies. Source: www.telegraph.co.uk/technology/news/8980453/ Anonymous-Robin-Hood-hacking-attack-hits-major-firms.html.

25. Elinor Mills, "Expert Hacks Car System, Says Problems Reach to SCADA Systems," CNet News, July 26, 2011, news.cnet.com/8301-27080_3-20083906-245/expert-hacks-car-system-says-problems-reach-to-scada-systems, viewed Oct. 28, 2011. Joris Evers, "Don't let your navigation system fool you," CNET News.com, Apr. 20, 2007, news.com.com, viewed Apr. 30, 2007.

26. For a summary of the CFAA and how it applies, see "Computer Fraud and Abuse Act (CFAA)," Internet Law Treatise, ilt.eff.org/index.php/Computer_Fraud_and_Abuse_Act_(CFAA), viewed Oct. 27, 2011. The date of the CFAA is sometimes given as 1986, when Congress passed the first of several amendments.

27. Bruce Sterling, *The Hacker Crackdown: Law and Disorder on the Electronic Frontier*, Bantam Books, 1992, pp. 13–14.

28. Craig Bromberg, "In Defense of Hackers," *New York Times Magazine*, Apr. 21, 1991, pp. 45–49. Gary Wolf, "The World According to Woz," *Wired*, Sept. 1998, pp. 118–121, 178–185. Richard P. Feynman, *Surely You're Joking, Mr. Feynman: Adventures of a Curious Character*, W. W. Norton, 1984, pp. 137–155.

29. Peter Tippett, quoted in Kim Zetter, "Freeze! Drop That Download!" *PC World*, Nov. 16, 2000; www.pcworld.com/resource/printable/article/0,aid,34406,00.asp. The article includes pros and cons of criminalizing virus writing and a discussion of other means of reducing viruses.

30. *United States v. Drew*, 259 F.R.D. 449 (C.D.Cal.), 2009.

31. Kim Zetter, "Identity Thieves Filed for $4 Million in Tax Refunds Using Names of Living and Dead," *Wired*, April 8, 2010, www.wired.com/threatlevel/2010/04/fake-tax-returns, viewed Nov. 8, 2011. Alfred Huger, vice president of Symantec Security Response, quoted in Riva Richmond, "PC Hackers Gain Savvy in Stealing Identities," *Wall Street Journal*, Mar. 21, 2007, p. B4B.

32. Barbara Carton, "An Unsolved Slaying of an Airline Worker Stirs Family to Action," *Wall Street Journal*, June 20, 1995, p. A1, A8.

33. Saul Hansell, "U.S. Workers Stole Data on 11,000, Agency Says," *New York Times*, Apr. 6, 1996, p. 6.

34. Robert Lemos, "Stock Scammer Gets Coal for the Holidays," *The Register*, Dec. 28, 2006, www.theregister.co.uk/2006/12/28/sec_freezes_stock_scammer_accounts, viewed Feb. 16, 2007.

35. William M. Bulkeley, "How Biometric Security Is Far from Foolproof," *Wall Street Journal*, Dec. 12, 2006, p. B3.

36. Gareth Finighan, "U.S. Citizen Jailed for More than Two Years in Thailand," *Daily Mail*, www.dailymail.co.uk/news/article-2071468/Joe-Gordon-US-citizen-jailed-Thailand-posting-online-excerpts-book-banned-king.html, Dec. 8, 2011, viewed Dec. 27, 2011.

37. Lisa Guernsey, "Welcome to the Web. Passport, Please?" *New York Times*, Mar. 15, 2001, pp. D1, D8.

38. Mylene Mangalindan and Kevin Delaney, "Yahoo! Ordered to Bar the French from Nazi Items," *Wall Street Journal*, Nov. 21, 2000, pp. B1, B4.

39. Pete Harrison, "Online Gambling Stocks Dive Again," Reuters UK, Sept. 7, 2006, www.gamesandcasino.com/gambling-news/online-gambling-stocks-dive-again-as-us-doj-holds-gaming-executive-again/147.htm, viewed Jan. 3, 2012.

40. Pete Harrison, "Sportingbet Arrest Sparks Fears of Wider Crackdown," Reuters, Sept. 8, 2006, go.reuters.com. Bloomberg News, "Gambling Executive Sentenced to Prison," *New York Times*, Jan. 8, 2010, www.nytimes.com/2010/01/09/business/09gamble.html, viewed Nov. 11, 2011.

41. Quoted in Harrison, "Sportingbet Arrest Sparks Fears."

42. Tom Zeller, Jr., "Times Withholds Web Article in Britain," *New York Times*, Aug. 29, 2006, www.nytimes.com/2006/08/29/business/media/29times.html, viewed Aug. 30, 2006.

43. Robert Corn-Revere, "Caught in the Seamless Web: Does the Internet's Global Reach Justify Less Freedom of Speech?" Cato Institute, July 24, 2002, p. 7.

44. Neal E. Boudette, "German Shoppers May Get 'Sale Freedom,'" *Wall Street Journal*, Jan. 23, 2002, p. B7D.

45. Jack Goldsmith and Tim Wu, *Who Controls the Internet? Illusions of a Borderless World*, Oxford University Press, 2006, p. 149.

46. In Donn Seeley, "Password Cracking: A Game of Wits," *Communications of the ACM*, June 1989, 32:6, pp. 700–703, reprinted in Peter J. Denning, ed., *Computers under Attack: Intruders, Worms, and Viruses*, Addison-Wesley, 1990, pp. 244–252.

6

WORK

6.1 Changes, Fears, and Questions

Computers free us from the repetitious, boring aspects of jobs so that we can spend more time being creative and doing the tasks that require human intelligence. Computer systems and the Internet provide quick, reliable access to information so that we work smarter and more efficiently. But people still do the work. Nurses care for the elderly, and construction workers build buildings. Architects use computer-aided design systems, but they still design buildings. Accountants use spreadsheets and thus have more time for thinking, planning, and analysis. But will computers design buildings? Will audits be automated?

The introduction of computers into the workplace generated many fears. Many social critics, social scientists, politicians, unions, and activists saw virtually all potential effects of computers on work as highly threatening. They foresaw mass unemployment due to increased efficiency. (Some argued, at first, that money spent on computers was a waste because computers *decreased* efficiency.) They argued that requiring workers to acquire computer skills was too heavy a burden, and that the need for increased technical training and skills would widen the earning gap between those who obtain the new skills and those who do not. They saw telecommuting as bad for workers and society. They expected offshoring (hiring people or companies in other countries to perform services that workers in one's home country used to do) to eliminate a huge number of jobs.

Although the dire predictions were wrong, the many and widespread rapid changes raise significant social questions. How do we deal with the dislocations and retraining needs that result when computing technology and the Internet eliminate jobs? "Telecommuting" has become part of our vocabulary, describing the phenomenon of working at a distance from the traditional company office or factory, connected in cyberspace. What are its advantages and disadvantages? How does it affect the physical distribution of population and businesses? Employees have powerful smartphones, tablets, and other devices that can make their work easier. Should they use their own devices for work? What risks need to be considered?

At the same time that information technology gives some workers more autonomy, it gives employers increased power to monitor the work, communications, movements, and online activity of employees and to observe what their employees do away from work (e.g., in social media). These changes affect productivity, privacy, and morale. Why do employers monitor employees? Should monitoring be limited?

In this chapter, we explore these questions.

6.2 Impacts on Employment

> *But nowhere is there any mention of the truth about the information*
> *highway, which is mass unemployment.*

—David Noble, "The Truth About the Information Highway"[1]

6.2.1 JOB DESTRUCTION AND CREATION

The fear that computing technology and the Internet would cause mass unemployment might seem absurd now. Yet, since the beginning of the Industrial Revolution, technology has generated fears of mass unemployment. In the early 1800s, the Luddites (of whom we say more in Chapter 7) burned weaving looms because they feared the looms would eliminate their jobs. A few decades later, a mob of seamstresses and tailors destroyed sewing machines because of the same fears.[2]

More recently, in the 1950s and 1960s, factory automation came under (verbal) fire from presidential candidate John F. Kennedy and industry and labor groups for threatening to bring the menace of increased unemployment and poverty. The quotation at the beginning of this section is about the information highway (a term commonly used for the Internet in the 1990s), but social scientists argued that it applied as well to all computer technology. Technology critics such as Jeremy Rifkin consider the reduction in the human labor and time required to produce goods and services to be one of the horrific consequences of computers and automation. In 2011, President Obama suggested that the high unemployment rate at the time was related to people using ATMs instead of bank tellers and airport check-in kiosks instead of live agents.[3]

Perhaps such viewpoints appeared to be right in the first few decades of computer use. As the use of ATMs grew, the number of bank tellers dropped by about 37% between 1983 and 1993. The number of telephone switchboard operators dropped from 421,000 in 1970 to 164,000 in 1996. The jobs of building, selling, and repairing typewriters have disappeared. Engineers used slide rules since the 17th century. Electronic calculators made them obsolete; the jobs of manufacturing and selling them evaporated. Railroads computerized their dispatch operations and eliminated hundreds of employees. The loss of jobs continued with the development of the Web and other electronic technologies. Travel agencies closed as consumers made airplane reservations online. The jobs of 35,000 electric meter readers disappeared as utility companies installed devices that send meter readings to company computers. Similar technology monitors vending machines and oil wells, reducing the number of people needed to check on them in person. Shopping on the Internet and self-service checkout systems in stores reduced the need for sales clerks. Hundreds of music stores closed and jobs in the printing industry declined as music, magazines, newspapers, and books went digital. Digital cameras put film processors out of work; Kodak, founded in 1880, laid off thousands of employees and filed for bankruptcy protection in 2012. As use of cellphones increased, the number of employees in the wired telecommunications industry dropped by more than 120,000.[4]

There is no doubt that technology in general and computing technology in particular eliminate jobs. Human labor is a resource. By making tasks more efficient, computers reduce the number of workers required to carry out the tasks. The goals of technology include a reduction in the resources needed to accomplish a result and an increase in productivity and standard of living. If we look back at our examples of lost jobs, we see that many of them accompanied increased productivity. While the number of telephone operators was dropping by more than 60% between 1970 and 1996, the number of long-distance calls increased from 9.8 billion to 94.9 billion.* Manufacturing productivity in the United States more than doubled between 1980 and 2002.[5] Productivity growth fluctuates, but the trend is upward.

A successful technology eliminates some jobs, but creates others. With a sewing machine, a seamstress could make more than two shirts a day. Rather than loss of jobs, the sewing machine meant a reduction in the price of clothes, more demand, and ultimately hundreds of thousands of new jobs.[6]† It is obvious now that computers created new products and services, whole new industries, and millions of jobs. From the electronic calculators that replaced slide rules to the networks and cellphones that replaced telephone operators to the social networking services that created a new phenomenon, the new devices and services all represent new jobs. The World Wide Web contributed to the creation of about 100,000 new Internet-related jobs in 1996. By 1997, more than 109,000 people worked in the cellular communications industry in the United States. By 1998, the Semiconductor Industry Association reported that chip makers employed 242,000 workers, directly, in the United States and 1.3 million workers indirectly. The chip industry, which did not exist before the microprocessor was invented in the 1970s, ranked fourth among U.S. industries by annual revenue. Although e-commerce and automatic checkout in stores reduces demand for sales clerks, that does not mean there are fewer people in these jobs. Employment increased 3% in the retail sector between 2003 and 2006, while employment overall increased 6%, according to the Economic Policy Institute. Contrary to predictions in the early 1990s, the number of bank tellers climbed to new highs in 2008, and the Bureau of Labor Statistics (BLS) forecast continued increases through 2018.[7]

---

* In the 1940s, human operators, plugging wires into boards, did almost all the routing and switching of telephone calls. The volume of telephone calls in the United States has increased so much that, if this work were done manually instead of electronically, it would require more than half the adult population of the country as telephone operators.[8]

† Sewing machines were first marketed to factory owners, just as computers were first used by large companies. Isaac Singer had the insight to sell them directly to women, in a parallel to the eventual shift from corporation-owned mainframes to personal computers for consumers.

Countless new products and services based on computer technology create jobs: iPods, medical devices, 3-D printers, navigation systems, smartphones and apps for them, and so on and on. The Facebook app industry alone accounted for between 180,000 and 235,000 fulltime jobs in the United States in 2011. New technologies and products create jobs in design, marketing, manufacture, sales, customer service, repair, and maintenance. New technical jobs also create jobs for such support staff as receptionists, janitors, and stock clerks. The enormous growth of retail sales on the Web contributed to an increase in jobs in the package shipping industry. U.S. consumers spend billions of dollars for personal computer software each year and billions more on online services (such as online tax preparation). Computer and Internet technology generated all the jobs at Google, Apple, eBay, Hulu, Amazon, Microsoft, Twitter, Zappos—and thousands more companies. Forrester Research estimated that governments and businesses worldwide spent $1.6 trillion on information technology. That money paid for a very large number of jobs.[9]

A harpist described how a series of technologies eliminated the jobs of musicians:[10] Piano rolls, automated player pianos, and recordings replaced the live piano player at silent movies. Juke boxes replaced live bands in bars. Records and then digital music replaced live orchestras and bands at Broadway shows, dance performances, and weddings. There is another way to look at the same changes. A few hundred years ago, listening to professional-quality music was a rare luxury for most people. Only the wealthy could hire professional musicians to perform for them. Technology, including electricity, radio, CDs, DVDs, iPods, smartphones, data-compression algorithms, and the Web brought the cost of an individual "performance" in a private home (or out on a hiking trail) down so low that music is available to almost anyone. The effect on employment? Tens of thousands of musicians make a living, and some make a fortune, in jazz, country, classical, zydeco, new age, rock, and rap music. In the long term, if technology brings the cost of a product or service down far enough to expand the market, more people will work in that field, be it music or package delivery.

Some of the same technologies that eliminate jobs help people get new ones. In the past, job seekers did research on jobs and companies in libraries and by telephone. The Web and social media make more information and services available to a job seeker with much more convenience and for a lower price. We post résumés on job sites. We learn about job openings from tweets. We learn about a company's reputation among its employees on a variety of forums. We can learn about climate, schools, entertainment, and religious facilities in distant towns before spending time and money to travel for an interview. We can interview at distant companies without traveling: some conduct job interviews at online virtual communities. Companies recruit via social media and specially designed online games. Online training programs help people learn new skills.

Airplanes, automobiles, radio, television, computers, much medical technology, and so on, did not exist before the 20th century. The use of telephones and electricity was minimal. Throughout the 20th century, there was an enormous increase in technology and a decrease in jobs in such areas as agriculture and saddle making. If technology's overall impact was to destroy jobs, there should have been fewer people working in 2000 than in 1900. But, with a population that approximately quadrupled between 1900 and 2000, the U.S. unemployment rate was 4% in 2000, lower than throughout most of the century. (One segment of the population is working less: children. In 1870, the average age for starting work was 13; by 1990, it was 19. In the early 20th century, children worked long days on farms and in factories and mines. Technology eliminated many of the jobs they did.)

Many new jobs created by computer technology are ones not imagined or possible before. They range from jobs of great social value (e.g., making life-saving and life-enhancing devices) to entertainment and sports (e.g., computer game designers, professional computer game players, and video game coaches). Fifteen years ago, who would have thought that people would buy (and hence others would produce, market, and sell) ringtones for their phones? Who would have imagined that there would be tens of thousands of job openings for smartphone software experts?

What is the overall effect of computerization on employment rates? Does it create more jobs than it destroys? Measuring the effects of computers alone is difficult, because other factors influence employment trends, but we can look at some overall numbers. In the United States, in the ten years between 1993 and 2002 (a decade of increasing computer and Web use), 309.9 million jobs ended—a huge number to anyone who has not seen these figures before. But 327.7 million jobs were added in the same period, for a net increase of 17.8 million jobs. This "job churn," roughly 30 million jobs opening and closing each year,* is typical of a flexible economy. In stagnant economies, people do not change jobs often.[11]

Consider the times of significant unemployment in the United States in the last century. Technology did not cause the Great Depression in the 1930s. Economists and historians attribute the depression to a variety of factors including "business cycles," the then-new Federal Reserve Bank's inept manipulation of interest rates, and that old standby, "greed." Unemployment was high in the early 1980s and in the early 1990s. But growth in use of computers has been dramatic and continuous, especially since the mid-1970s, when personal computers began to appear. Mortgage policies (of financial institutions and the government) were a major cause of the recession that began in 2007; technology was not the cause.

The Organisation for Economic Co-operation and Development (OECD), an international organization whose members include most of Western Europe, North America, Japan, Australia, and New Zealand, studied employment trends in 25 countries. OECD concluded that unemployment stems from "policies . . . [that] have made economies rigid, and stalled the ability . . . to adapt."[12] The study suggested that "unemployment

---

* Roughly half are seasonal jobs that appear and disappear each year.

should be addressed not by seeking to slow the pace of change, but rather by restoring economies' and societies' capacity to adapt to it." Unemployment in many European countries is often higher than in the United States. But Europe is not more technologically advanced or computerized than the United States. The differences have more to do with differences in flexibility in the economies and other political, social, and economic factors. The OECD report says that "history has shown that when technological progress accelerates, so do growth, living standards, and employment."[13]

We saw that new technology reduces employment in specific areas and in the short term, but it is obvious that computer technology did not and does not cause mass unemployment. Those who continually predict mass unemployment see only the old, preexisting jobs that are lost. They lack the imagination or the knowledge of history and economics to see that people create new jobs. The next big breakthrough in technology, perhaps a major advance in artificial intelligence (AI) or robotics, will generate the same scary projections.

Long-term net social gains from new jobs are not of much interest to a person who is fired. The loss of a job is immediate and personal and can be devastating to the individual and his or her family. When large numbers of people lose their jobs in one small community or within a short time, difficult social problems occur. Thus, there is a need for people (individual workers, employers, and communities) and institutions (e.g., schools) to be flexible and to plan for change. There are roles for education professionals who do long-range planning, for entrepreneurs and nonprofit organizations that provide training programs, for large companies that can retrain their employees, for financial institutions that fund start-up companies, and so on.

> *Why not use spoons?*
>
> —The apocryphal response from a man who saw thousands of workers
> digging at a construction site with shovels. When he asked why they were
> not using modern excavation equipment, he was told that using shovels
> created more jobs.

But are we earning less?

Economists agree that the average hourly pay of manufacturing workers quadrupled (in constant dollars) between 1909 and the mid-1970s. They disagree about what happened after that. Wages appeared to decline as much as 10% after 1970. This is sometimes cited as an indication that the value of human work is declining as computers take over tasks people used to do. However, fringe benefits rose significantly, increasing total compensation by about 17% according to some experts, but other experts disagree. Some economists believe the apparent decline resulted from improper computation of the Consumer Price Index.[14] Two researchers, Michael Cox and Richard Alm, decided to avoid the problems of using income and inflation data and, instead, they looked at a long list of direct measures of consumption and leisure. For example, they reported that in the last quarter of the 20th century, attendance at operas and symphonies doubled (per person), recreation spending more than tripled (per person), and spending on toys quadrupled (per child). From 1970 to 2010, the average number of televisions and automobiles per household increased, and the percentage of new homes with air conditioning rose from 49% to 88%. Cox and Alm also calculated how much time an average worker had to work to earn enough money to buy food and luxuries. The cost, in the average worker's work time, of 100 miles of air travel dropped by 40%, while the cost of a coast-to-coast phone call dropped to one-tenth the work time required in 1970. It might not be surprising that the cost of high-tech services dropped so much. The cost, in worker's time, of many basic foods also dropped. Technology is likely responsible for a large share of the reductions. In addition, comparing income and cost data misses improvements in product quality, safety, convenience, and comfort due to technology.[15]

Since the beginning of the Industrial Revolution, working hours have declined. We no longer routinely work 10–12 hour days, six days a week (unless we choose to). People can count working hours, like income data, in various ways, supporting different conclusions. Some economists report a significant decline in working hours since the 1950s. Others say working hours have not declined significantly. Many people continue to work more hours while income rises because they have higher expectations. They consider the lifestyle now possible to be essential. Another reason, according to labor economist Ronald Ehrenberg, is that aspects of the tax and compensation structure encourage employers to have regular workers work overtime rather than hire additional employees.[16] A third reason is that taxes take a larger percentage of income than they did in the past. People have to work more hours for the same take-home pay. Thus it is not clear at all that we are earning less, and if we are, the causes are more likely social, political, and economic factors rather than the impact of technology.

6.2.2 Changing Skills and Skill Levels

Some who are concerned about the impact of computers on employment acknowledge that, in the past, technology led to new jobs and products. They argue that the impact of computing technology is different and more negative. Computers differ from earlier technologies in several key ways.

Computers eliminate a much wider variety of jobs than any single new technological advance in the past. The impact of new machines or technologies tended to be concentrated in one industry or activity. Earlier automation eliminated primarily manufacturing jobs, but computers automate services, such as those of electric meter readers and secretaries, just as easily. The transition to new jobs is more difficult because of the broad impact. The pace of improvement in speed, capability, and cost for computing and communication technology is much faster than for any previous technology. The pace itself causes more job disruption as people continually face job elimination and the need to retrain.

The new jobs created by computing technology are different from the jobs eliminated. The hundreds of thousands of new computer engineering and systems analyst jobs require a college degree. The jobs of telephone operator and factory worker do not. At the same time, computers eliminate more high-skilled jobs than older technologies. Will jobs diverge into two distinct groups: high-paying jobs for a highly skilled and highly trained intellectual elite, and fewer low-paying jobs for people without computer skills and advanced education?

Although it often seems that our times and problems are new and different from what came before, similar concerns arose for other technologies. The steam engine and electricity brought enormous change in jobs, making many obsolete. When economists Claudia Goldin and Lawrence Katz researched earlier periods of rapid technological development, they found that the education system quickly adapted to train children in the necessary skills. They pointed out that a bookkeeper in 1890 had to be highly skilled, whereas a bookkeeper in 1920 was a high school graduate using an early form of an adding machine. In the 19th century, skilled workers earned increasingly more than manual laborers, but the trend reversed in the early 20th century, because more people went to high school and the new technologies of that era reduced the skill level needed for white-collar jobs. Normally, as demand increases for new skills, people acquire them. For example, in 1900, only 0.5 people out of every 1000 in the United States worked as an engineer. After the huge growth in technology during the 20th century, 7.6 out of every 1000 people were engineers.[17] Something went awry with this natural process in recent years. When unemployment was extraordinarily high in 2009–2011, many thousands of jobs went unfilled in engineering and other high-tech fields because there were insufficient qualified applicants. Colleges and graduate schools produced large numbers of trained people, but, for example, 62% of those earning doctorates in electrical engineering were foreign students, and most had to return to their countries because of immigration restrictions.[18] Why are American students not choosing computer science and engineering?

Complex interactive computer systems guide workers through steps of jobs that required extensive training before. Performance-support software and training software empower lower-skilled workers and make the training process for complex jobs cheaper, faster, and easier. Such systems, for example, guide auditors through an audit of a securities firm, help employees at financial institutions carry out transactions, and train sales people. The National Association of Securities Dealers reported that its auditors were fully competent after one year using such a system, compared to two and a half years without it. They saved more than $400,000 in annual training costs. Companies are more willing to hire people without specific skills when they can train new people quickly and use automated support systems. The benefits occur throughout a wide range of job levels. Several large companies, including Walgreens, hire previously unemployable people with mental and physical disabilities. They perform their jobs with the help of electronic gadgets and computer systems. Some of the systems are specially designed.

Some are the ordinary computer and automation tools that workers use in many work-places.[19]

The BLS expects many jobs to be available that require little, if any, computer skill. Areas in which the BLS expects the most new jobs created through 2018 include nursing, home health aid, retail and office clerks, and food preparation and service.[20]

Do automated systems mean fewer jobs for high-skilled workers? Will human intelligence in employment be "devalued"? Software makes decisions that used to require trained, thinking human beings. Computers could take over many white-collar, professional jobs. Computer programs analyze loan applications and decide which to approve. Some programs are better than people at predicting which applicants are likely to default on their loans. Design jobs have become automated. For example, software to design the electrical layout for new housing developments can do in several minutes a job that would have taken a high-paid employee 100 hours.[21] Even computer programming is automated. Some computer programs write computer programs, reducing the need for trained programmers. Although it still requires highly trained engineers, there is a large degree of automation in the layout of computer chips. Programming tools enable nonspecialists to do certain kinds of programming, design Web pages, and so on.

The printing press put scribes out of work when writing was a skill possessed by only a small, "highly trained" elite. Recall from Chapter 1 that machines that did simple arithmetic in the 17th and 18th centuries shocked and disturbed people. People thought arithmetic required uniquely human intelligence. In the past, human imagination and desires continued to find new fields of work, both physical and mental, to replace those no longer needed. They continue to do so today. In spite of the trend to automate high-skill jobs, the BLS projects that the number of management, financial, software, and other professional jobs will increase significantly through 2018, and that computer software engineer will be one of the fastest-growing occupations.[22]

6.2.3 TELECOMMUTING

Computer and communication technologies dramatically changed the way we work and where we work. These technologies encourage smaller businesses and more independent consultants and contractors—"information entrepreneurs," as they are sometimes called. It is easier for workers to work part time for different employers or clients, thus encouraging more information workers to become self-employed. Individuals and small businesses operate globally via the Web. Craftsmakers sell crafts, programmers sell their programming services, musicians sell music, and so on. Many of these people work from home some or all of the time. The Internet and wireless communications made it possible for people who are employees of large companies, as well, to work away from their desk and away from their company office. The Internet made it possible for companies to locate in small towns and work with dispersed consultants instead of having hundreds or thousands of employees in larger population centers. Millions of people work without "going to work," that is, without going to their employer's (or their own) business offices. I will use the terms "telecommuting" and "telework" for several variations of such work paradigms. The most common meaning is working for an employer at a computer-equipped space in the employee's home. Some definitions include running one's own business from home using computers and telecommunications. In some jobs, such as sales and technical support, the office is mobile. Many people work on a laptop in a coffee shop, outdoors in a park, and on airplanes. In many fields, professional people no longer have to live in the same city or state as their employer. Definitions of telecommuting vary, so estimated numbers do also. One study reported that more than 33 million people in the United States telecommute at least one day per month.[23]

Telecommuting is common now, so it might be surprising that local governments and labor unions attempted to stop it in the 1980s.* The view of various unions at the time seemed to be that most computer at-home work would be data-entry work done by low-paid women in sweatshop conditions. The AFL-CIO advocated a government ban on all computer at-home work.[24] The efforts to stop computer work at home quickly turned futile. The mistaken views about who would do computer work at home and what the working conditions would be are reminders to be cautious about banning or restricting a new phenomenon before its applications and benefits, as well as problems, develop.

Benefits

Telecommuting reduces overhead for employers and, in some cases, increases productivity. Productivity studies in areas where work is easy to measure (e.g., data entry) showed productivity gains of 15%. Replacing or shrinking large downtown offices, where real estate and office rentals are expensive, can generate significant savings. Many employees report that telecommuting has made them more productive, more satisfied with their jobs, and more loyal to their employers. One survey found that a large majority of workers whose jobs could permit teleworking would prefer to do so at least once a week.[25]

Telecommuting, and telecommunications generally, make it easier to work with clients, customers, and employees in other countries: at home, one can more easily work a few hours at night that are compatible with foreign time zones. Telecommuting reduces rush-hour traffic congestion and the associated pollution, gasoline use, and stress. Telecommuting reduces expenses for commuting and for work clothes. It saves time that workers can use for exercise, sleep, or more interaction with friends and family. It provides previously unavailable work options for some elderly or disabled people for whom commuting is physically difficult and expensive. It allows work to continue after blizzards, hurricanes, or other disasters close roads or discourage travel. Roughly 58% of woman-owned businesses are home-based businesses.[26] Telecommuting, and the flexible

---

* For example, in the 1980s, the city of Chicago ordered a couple to stop using a computer at home to write textbooks and educational software because Chicago zoning laws restricted home work that used mechanical or electrical equipment.

hours it permits, can help reduce child-care expenses and give parents more time with their children. Employees and employers benefit when a person can accept a job with a company in a distant state without having to move. They can live in rural areas instead of big cities and suburbs if they prefer (in "electronic cottages," to use futurist Alvin Toffler's words). Two-career couples can work for companies hundreds or thousands of miles apart.

Problems

Many early telecommuters were volunteers, people who wanted to work at home. They were more likely to be independent workers. (Many were computer programmers.) As more businesses began to require employees to move their offices to their homes, problems arose, for both employees and employers.

Some employers see resentment among employees who must work at the office. Some found that the corporate loyalty of telecommuters weakened. Lacking immediate supervision, some people are less productive, while others work too hard and too long. The ease of working with people around the world leads some to work odd hours to match the time zones of clients. Some employees need better direction about what work and how much work their employer expects them to do at home. Being at home with children is an advantage for some telecommuters, but a distraction for others. Reducing the boundary between home and work causes stress for some workers and their families.

Some employees complain that the costs of office space and overhead that have been reduced for the employer have simply been shifted to the employee who must give up space at home for the office. Some employees believe that by working at home they miss mentoring relationships and opportunities for advancement. For many people, the social interactions and camaraderie at work are a significant part of pleasant working conditions, so social isolation and low morale can be problems.

Problems led some companies to cut back telecommuting programs. Like many of the options new technologies (or social trends) provide, telecommuting may be very desirable for some employees and employers and of no use to others. But it is possible to reduce many problems related to telecommuting. Numerous communication technologies (e.g., email, texting, tweeting, video conferencing) help telecommuters to stay in touch with coworkers. Employers address the social-isolation problem by holding regular meetings and encouraging other activities such as employee sports leagues, where employees interact in person. Telecommuters reduce isolation by participating in activities of professional associations and other social networks. Some companies found significant improvements in employee satisfaction with their telecommuting jobs when they encourage such interactions.

Side effects

Aside from the direct advantages and disadvantages, teleworking has several side effects that might change various business and social aspects of how we live and work.

How does telework affect our sense of community? The Industrial Revolution led to a major shift in work patterns: jobs moved to offices and factories. Working at home in the late 20th century seemed new and unusual, but before the Industrial Revolution, most people worked at, or close to, home. Even in the past few centuries, working at home has not been uncommon. Writers traditionally work at home. Farmers work in the fields, but the farm office was in the house. Doctors, especially in small towns, had their medical offices in their homes. Shopkeepers often had an apartment behind or above the store. Perhaps writers are closest to modern information workers who telecommute in that they tend to work in isolation. Is that why we have an image of writers spending the evenings at coffee houses or at intellectual "salons" talking with other intellectuals? In the past, social isolation was not considered a problem for people who worked in or near their homes. They lived, worked, and socialized in communities. They had the grange, the church, and the community center. Urban policy researcher Joel Kotkin observes that telecommuting may encourage a return to involvement in one's local community.[27] Is he correct? Will being there all day, doing errands locally, eating in local restaurants, and so on, generate an interest in the safety, beauty, and vitality of the community that is less likely to develop when one returns home after dark, tired from a day at the office? On the other hand, now that we can communicate with people all over the world on the Internet, will home workers stay inside, communicating with unseen business and social acquaintances, and be just as unlikely to know their neighbors as many commuters are?

6.2.4 A GLOBAL WORKFORCE

Offshoring

Over many decades in the 20th century, as transportation and communications improved, manufacturing jobs moved from wealthier countries to less wealthy countries, especially in Asia. The difference in pay rates was large enough to make up for the extra transportation costs. The Internet and the Web reduced "transportation" costs for many kinds of information work to almost zero. With the ease of working with people and companies in other countries, "offshoring of jobs"* has become a phenomenon and a political issue.

Data processing and computer programming were among the first service jobs to go offshore, many to India. The lure is the large pool of low-skilled workers, in the first case, and well-trained, English-speaking computer programmers, in the second. The example most well known to American consumers is the move of customer-service call centers and software "help desks" to India and other countries. Offshoring takes many other forms too. Companies send "back-office" jobs, such as payroll processing, to other countries. Some

---

* The term "outsourcing" refers to the phenomenon where a company pays other companies to build parts for its products or provide services (such as marketing, research, or customer service) instead of performing those tasks itself. This is very common. Generally, but not always, the companies that do the work are in the same country as the company that hires them. The term "offshoring" refers to hiring companies or employees in other countries.

hire companies in other countries to manage their computers and networks. Actuaries in India process insurance claims for a British insurance company. Doctors in the United States dictate notes on patient visits and send digitized voice files to India, where medical scribes transcribe them and return text files. Rather than contracting with companies in another country, some large companies set up divisions (for example, for research and development) offshore.

As offshoring of skilled work, sometimes called "knowledge work," increased dramatically, more worries arose about threats of job loss, now for high-paying jobs held by the middle class. Companies send off work in legal services, aircraft engineering, biotech and pharmaceutical research, and stock analysis and other financial services. Individuals and small businesses hire people in other countries for services such as tutoring and designing logos and websites. Information technology jobs still make up the largest segment of offshored jobs, and India and China are the main destinations.* In some fields, a significant reason for offshoring is that there are not enough trained professionals in the United States. For example, Steve Jobs told President Obama in 2011 that Apple had 700,000 factory workers in China because 30,000 engineers are needed on site in the factories and Apple cannot find enough qualified engineers in the United States. Jobs also said it is easy to build a factory in China but very difficult in the United States because of regulations and unnecessary costs.[28]

The impact of offshoring

The BLS reports that a very small percentage of mass layoffs (50 or more people for more than a month) come from offshoring jobs. However, offshoring will probably increase. How far can it go? Economist Alan Blinder, a former vice chair of the Federal Reserve, studied the types of knowledge and service jobs that could be performed at distant places—candidates for offshoring in the near future.[29] He estimated that 28–42 million people currently work in such jobs in the United States. Thus, he sees offshoring as potentially very disruptive. However, Blinder emphasizes that offshoring means massive transition, not massive unemployment.

Many social scientists, politicians, and organizations view the globalization of the workforce as a terribly negative phenomenon, one of the negative results of information and communications technology and corporate greed for increased profit. From the prospective of workers in developed countries, they argue, it means millions fewer jobs, accompanied by lower pay and a reduced standard of living.

The lost jobs are obvious. Our discussion in Section 6.2.1 about jobs eliminated and created by computer and communications technology suggests we consider how offshoring creates new jobs. Lower labor costs and increased efficiency reduce prices for consumers. Lower prices encourage more use and make new products and services feasible.

---

* Additional destinations include Canada, Brazil, and Ireland, among others.

Inshoring: Two perspectives

Americans working for foreign companies

Americans used to import cars from Japan. Now Japanese car makers build cars in the United States. Otto Bock Health Care, a German company that makes sophisticated microprocessor-controlled artificial limbs, "offshores" research, development, and manufacturing to several countries including the United States (and China). The German software company SAP employs thousands of people in the United States. Offshoring for a German company means "inshoring" for the United States. People in the United States work for Sony, Ikea, Bayer, Novartis, Unilever, Toyota. Overall, almost 5% of U.S. workers work for foreign companies, and those jobs pay more than the U.S. median. Indeed, as the information technology industry grew in India, large Indian companies began offshoring thousands of jobs to the United States and Europe. In a global, interconnected economy, offshoring is one more way of providing products and services to consumers more effectively.

Indian perspectives[30]

For many years, Indian computer scientists and engineers flocked to the United States for jobs, wealth, and entrepreneurial opportunities, while Indian IT companies performed services and provided call centers for foreign companies. Critics, from the Indian perspective, feared a talent drain. They worried that India was not growing its own high-tech industry. Some companies that had developed their own software products stopped doing so, in order not to compete with the U.S. companies for which they provide services.

Over time, more positive results seemed to develop. India's information-technology companies began to provide sophisticated services well beyond the call centers many Americans encounter. They develop and service software. "Offshored" jobs provide professional training and experience, including experience working in a global business environment. They provide confidence and high salaries that permit the savings so helpful for taking risks and starting one's own company. An Indian entrepreneur observes that Indian culture generally had a negative view of entrepreneurs, but that is changing. Some highly trained Indian computer scientists and engineers who went to the United States for jobs are returning to work or start businesses at home. Providing information technology services for foreign companies, from low-level services to highly sophisticated work, is now a multibillion-dollar industry in India.

Manufacturing of computer hardware went offshore early. That was responsible for part of the drop in the cost of hardware; the resulting lower prices contributed to the enormous growth of the industry. The United States is an exporter of services (banking, engineering, and accounting, for example). The same technologies that facilitate offshoring make it easier and cheaper for U.S. service companies to sell more of their services to other countries. Offshoring creates jobs for both low- and high-skilled workers in less wealthy countries. The combination of increased income and reduced prices for goods and services helps grow the economies of these countries. This is likely to yield more jobs on both sides.

Blinder believes that we should plan for a major shift in the United States toward jobs that require presence. His examples, from taxi driver to doctor, include both low-skill and high-skill jobs. He opposes attempts to stop offshoring, but he also warns that we must prepare by shifting emphasis in education. He expects that the flexibility of the U.S. economy will help it adapt more quickly and successfully to offshoring than developed countries with more rigid economies.[31] As we observed in Section 6.2.1 about technology-induced job loss, long-term gains from new jobs are little comfort to people who lose theirs. Helpful responses to the personal and social disruptions offshoring can cause include those we mentioned in Section 6.2.1, among them: flexibility, planning, and changes in educational programs.

Problems and side effects of offshoring

As customers and companies have found, offshoring has problems.

Consumers have many complaints about customer service call centers in foreign countries: Foreign accents are difficult to understand. Service personnel are not familiar with the product or service the consumer is asking about—they just read from a manual. The workers experience problems too. Because of time differences, customer service workers in India work at night. Some find the relatively high pay worth the disruption to their lives; others quit. Problems of customer satisfaction, training, and less-than-expected savings led some companies to conclude that offshoring did not work well for them. (Some developed other cost-saving arrangements. For example, a hotel chain and flower seller agreed to share call center employees in the United States.)

Employees in companies that send projects offshore find they need new job skills. A software engineer, for example, might need to manage people and projects in other countries. Managers and businesspeople find they must schedule meetings during the work hours of workers in another country.

Some small technology companies have found that increased demand for highly skilled workers in India has already forced salaries up. One U.S. entrepreneur said salaries of engineers he hired in India went from 25% of U.S. salaries to 75% within two years. Hiring them is no longer worthwhile for his company.

The problems of offshoring should not surprise us. A theme running through this book is that new things often have unexpected problems. We discover them and find solutions, adapt to changes, or decide not to use certain options. Basic economics tells us that salaries will rise in offshoring destinations. When the gap between salaries in the home and destination countries is no longer big enough to cover the other expenses of offshoring, the trend will decline.

When products cross borders, bullets don't.

—Unknown

Ethics of hiring foreign workers

There is much controversy about both the economics and ethics of offshoring. In this section, we apply some of the ethical theories from Chapter 1 to analyze the practice from an ethical perspective. This is a good example for trying to distinguish economic advantage from ethical arguments. Several countries have passed legislation to restrict the hiring of foreign workers for some industries. The discussion here might provide insight into the ethics of such legislation. Here is the scenario we examine:

> You are a manager at a software company about to begin a large software project. You will need to hire dozens of programmers. Using the Internet for communication and software delivery, you can hire programmers in another country at a lower salary than programmers in your country. Should you do this?[32]

For the discussion, we assume the software company is in the United States and the manager is choosing between U.S. and Indian programmers.

The people most obviously affected by the decision in this case are the Indian programmers and the U.S. programmers you might hire. To generate some ideas, questions, and observations about these two groups, we will use utilitarianism and Kant's principle about treating people as ends in themselves. How can we compare the impact on utility from the two choices? The number of people hired will be about the same in either case. There does not appear to be any reason, from an ethical point of view, for placing a higher weight on the utility of one group of programmers merely because of their nationality. Shall we weigh the utilities of the programmers according to the number of dollars they will receive? That favors hiring the U.S. programmers. Or should we weigh utility by comparing the pay to the average salary in each country? That favors hiring the Indians. The utility obtained from a job for an individual programmer depends on the availability of other jobs. Are there more opportunities to earn a comparable income in the United States or in India? We see that a calculation of net utility for the programmers depends on how one evaluates the utility of the job for each group of programmers.

What happens when we apply Kant's principle? When we hire people for a job, we are interacting with them in a limited role. We are making a trade, money for work. The programmers are a means to an end: producing a marketable product at a reasonable price. Kant does not say that we must not treat people as a means to an end, but rather that we should not treat them merely as such. Kant does not seem helpful here, especially if we observe that the hiring decision does not treat the potential programmers of the two countries differently in a way that has to do with ends and means.

Are you taking advantage of the Indian programmers, perhaps exploiting them by paying them less than you would have to pay the U.S. programmers? Some people believe it is unfair to both the U.S. and Indian programmers that the Indians get the jobs by charging less money. It is equally logical, however, to argue that paying the higher rate for U.S. programmers is wasteful, or charity, or simply overpayment. What makes either pay level more "right" than the other? Buyers would like to pay less for what they buy, and sellers would like to get a higher price for their goods and services. There is nothing inherently unethical about choosing the cheaper of two products, services, or employees.

We can argue that treating the Indian programmers as ends in themselves includes respecting the choices and trade-offs they make to better their lives according to their own judgment, in particular in offering to work for lower wages than U.S. programmers. But there are special cases in which we might decide otherwise. First, suppose your company is doing something to limit the other options of the Indian programmers. If your company is lobbying for U.S. import restrictions on software that Indian firms produce, for example, thus decreasing the availability of other programming jobs in India, then you are manipulating the programmers into a situation where they have few or no other choices. In that case, you are not respecting their freedom and allowing them to compete fairly. You are, then, not treating them as ends in themselves. We will assume for the rest of the discussion that your company is not doing anything like this.

Another reason we might decide that the Indian programmers are not being treated as ends in themselves, or with respect for their human dignity, is that their working conditions would be worse than the working conditions that U.S. workers expect (or that law in the United States requires). The programmers might not get medical insurance. They might work in rundown, crowded offices lacking air-conditioning. Is hiring them to work in such conditions unethical, or does it give them an opportunity to improve conditions in their country? Whether or not it is ethically required, there are several reasons why you might pay more (or provide better working conditions) than the law or market conditions in India require: a sense of shared humanity that motivates you to want to provide conditions you consider desirable, a sense of generosity (i.e., willingness to contribute to the improvement of the standard of living of people in a country less rich than your own), and benefits for your company. Paying more than expected might get you higher morale, better productivity, and increased company loyalty.[33]

Often, in various countries, a large group of potential workers (foreigners, recent immigrants, ethnic minorities, low-skilled workers, teenagers) is willing to work for lower than the standard pay. Governments have passed laws to require that the same salary be paid to all. The main argument is that such laws will prevent employers from exploiting the less advantaged workers. Historically, one of the effects of these laws is that the traditionally higher-paid group gets most of the jobs. (Often that has been the intent of the law.) In this case, the almost certain result would be hiring the U.S. programmers. The law, or an ethical requirement that the pay of the Indian programmers and the U.S. programmers be the same, would protect the high incomes of programmers in the United States and the profits of companies that pay higher salaries. New workers or businesses that are trying to compete by lowering prices generally oppose such requirements.

Your decision affects other people besides the programmers: your customers, the owners or stockholders of your company, and, indirectly and to a smaller degree, many people in other businesses. Hiring the Indian programmers increases the utility of your company and customers. The customers benefit from the lower price of the product, and the owners of the company benefit from the profits. If the product is successful, your company might pay for advertising, distribution, and so on, providing jobs for others in the United States. On the other hand, if you hire U.S. programmers, they will spend more of their earnings in the United States than the Indian programmers, generating jobs and income for others in the United States. If the product is not profitable because of higher programming costs, the company could go out of business, with a negative impact on all its employees, owners, and suppliers. To which of all these people do you have responsibilities or obligations? As a manager of the company, you have an obligation to help make the product and the company successful, to manage the project to make a profit (not in a manner independent of ethical considerations, as we noted in Chapter 1, but consistent with them). Unless the owners of the company have a policy to improve the standard of living of people in other countries or to "Buy American," your obligation to them includes hiring competent workers at the best price. You have some responsibility for the fate of other company employees who might lose their jobs if you do a poor job of managing the project. You do not have any special obligation to other service providers you could hire, nor to people seeking jobs as programmers in either country.

Although hiring lower-paid workers in other countries is often described as ethically suspect, this discussion suggests that there is no strong ethical argument for that view.

6.3 Employee Communication and Monitoring

6.3.1 Learning About Job Applicants

Employers have long done various forms of screening, including criminal background checks, on prospective employees. The Web and social media provide a vast new collection of information on job applicants.* Some employers read applicants' blogs to learn how well they write. Some hire companies that specialize in performing extensive background checks using publicly available social media. The *New York Times* lists a variety of behaviors that one company includes in the dossiers it provides to employers about prospective employees: racist remarks, references to drugs, sexually explicit material, displays of weapons or bombs, and violent activity. (It includes positive information too— for example, charitable work.) The company does not include race, religion, and other information that laws prohibit companies from asking about, but, of course, now it is not difficult for an employer to find such information in social media.[34]

Many privacy advocates object to social media searches on job applicants. Some argue that employers should restrict the information they collect about applicants to what is

---

* In Section 6.3.2, we look at the issue of employers firing employees because of material in social media.

directly related to job qualifications. Marc Rotenberg, president of the Electronic Privacy Information Center, expressed the view that "employers should not be judging what people in their private lives do away from the workplace."[35] This view has merit and might be the best policy for many employers.[36]

It is important to maintain and protect a barrier between work and personal activities. Most people work (and engage in social activities such as the community softball team) with people whose religion, hobbies, and tastes in humor differ from theirs. There is great value in interacting with diverse people. It is better to avoid employment policies with a side effect of stifling expression of those differences outside of work. However, there does not appear to be a convincing ethical argument that an employer *must* consider only information related to the specific job an employee will do, ignoring all other aspects of how the employee will behave at work. Some things an employer might learn about an applicant could affect safety and security at the workplace, the image the company wishes to maintain, and the likelihood of future lawsuits related to an employee's behavior. An employer has no ethical obligation to hire a specific applicant. The number of people hired is not likely to be affected by a policy of using social media information, so (if we value each applicant equally) the overall utility, in the utilitarian sense, is not affected. Employers use a variety of screening methods to efficiently reduce a large pool of applicants to a small number for further consideration. Some routinely reject people who do not have a college degree, even though some of those people could do the job well. An employer that frequently hires suboptimal employees (either by applying poor screening criteria or by not using—or by misusing—relevant social media information) may see its operations suffer. The employer has the most stake in choosing applicants who are likely to be an asset to the company or organization.

Making a responsible and reasonable employment decision based on social media information can be difficult. A person who posts a dozen photos of himself or herself surrounded by a variety of guns might be an avid hunter or sport shooter who would be an excellent employee. Or he or she might be one of those rare people who come to work one day and shoot fellow employees. Information in social media might be inaccurate. A person other than the applicant might have posted questionable material. Some employers are overcautious and decline to hire an applicant if something negative turns up, without exploring the context or determining the accuracy of the information. Is this unethical or a poor policy or an acceptable (if sometimes unwise) choice to emphasize caution and efficiency?

There are ways to help protect applicants' privacy and reduce the consequences of errors when employers choose to do social media searches. One is to use a "third-party" company to perform the searches. The company that is hiring employees never sees information that is deemed to be inappropriate (by law or by the policies of the hiring company or by the policies of the search company). This can protect the applicant's privacy and protect the employer from complaints that it used inappropriate information in the hiring decision. An employer can (and should) make its policy about searches clear to

Verifying workers[37]

It is illegal for an employer in the United States to hire an illegal immigrant or a legal immigrant without legal authority to work. Some employers hire illegal workers knowingly and some hire them unknowingly. Over the years there have been many proposals and pilot programs in which employers verify each job applicant's legal status by checking an automated system maintained by a federal government agency. The current system, E-Verify, uses data from the Social Security Administration and the Department of Homeland Security (DHS). Approximately 200,000 employers use E-Verify. Some states require it, and the federal government requires it for federal contractors. Some people advocate requiring that all employers get approval from E-Verify for each new person hired.

One threat of such a system is the loss of liberty to work. "It is absolutely unprecedented," said congressman Steve Chabot, "to say that the government must grant affirmative permission every time any employee is hired."[38] Any large and frequently changing database is bound to have errors. The U.S. Government Accountability Office (GAO) reported that E-Verify immediately verifies 97.4% of applicants as authorized to work. The system incorrectly rejects 0.3% whom it later approves after a process to correct the error. The government considers the rest unauthorized to work. The initial rejection rate is higher in areas with large immigrant populations. Among other reasons, inconsistencies in the spelling of names cause rejections. The 0.3% initially rejected but approved after a correction process does not include all the incorrect rejections of legal workers. There are many reasons why legal applicants do not appeal a rejection or are not successful in their appeal. The GAO reported that individuals face formidable challenges in getting errors corrected. In some cases, the employer simply declines to hire the applicant without telling him or her why. On the other hand, the GAO reports that the system approves more than half of the applicants who are truly unauthorized to work in the United States because of identity theft and employer dishonesty. (Of course, this rate is difficult to determine precisely.)

Approximately 60 million people in the United States change jobs or enter the workforce every year. If the system becomes mandatory, an error rate of 0.3% incorrect initial rejections would affect 180,000 people who are legal workers each year.

Summing up other risks, the Electronic Frontier Foundation and other critics said: "A nationwide mandatory E-Verify system would be one of the largest and most widely accessible databases of private information ever created in the U.S. Its size and openness would present an irresistible target for identity thieves. Additionally, because the system would cover everyone eligible to work in the United States, it could quickly expand to a host of other uses . . . "[39]

Does the system do its intended job well enough to balance the risks to privacy and the right to work?

applicants. Search companies can have a policy that they perform social media searches only if the applicant consents. The search company can inform an applicant if it provides the employer with negative information, so the applicant has an opportunity to correct errors or explain the context of the information. Some companies that do social media searches follow these policies.

Some people, about to seek a job, try to clean up their online persona. They remove raunchy material, change their "favorite book" to one that appears intellectual, and so on. Some craft online profiles as carefully as people craft résumés. Of course, this means that some profiles are not reliable descriptions of a person, but that is no longer a surprise. On the other hand, some people naively think their blogs are invisible to prospective employers. They criticize the companies they are interviewing with and wonder why they did not get the job. In either case, it is extremely difficult to remove all the negative information and photos a person (or his or her friends) released to cyberspace.

It is common for people to google someone they have begun to date—or almost anyone they meet. We should not be surprised that employers learn about potential employees via social media. We might hope for a civility, a courtesy, a social convention that we—and employers—do not look at what was not intended for us (or them). Is this foolish? Is it achievable? Is it consistent with the culture of the Web and social media?

6.3.2 RISKS AND RULES FOR WORK AND PERSONAL COMMUNICATIONS

Employers have always monitored the work of their employees. The degree of detail and frequency of the monitoring has varied depending on the kind of work, economic factors, and available technology. Logs or time clocks measured total hours worked. Supervisors listened in on the work of telephone operators and customer service representatives. The electronic monitoring capabilities that employers use now are the modern version of the time clock and telephone extension. These capabilities have made old methods more efficient and new kinds of much more extensive monitoring possible. Most precomputer monitoring was not constant, because the supervisor had many workers to oversee and other work to do. Workers usually knew when the supervisor was present to observe them. Now, monitoring can be constant, more detailed, and unseen by the worker. Newspaper editors, senior lawyers, and customer service supervisors can remotely observe the computer screens of the workers they supervise. In retail environments, software monitors transactions at the cash registers, looking for suspicious patterns (for example, a large number of refunds, voids, or sales of cheap items) that might indicate employee theft.* The vast growth of storage capabilities means that employers can store enormous amounts of surveillance information for a long time.

Email, smartphones, social networking, Twitter, and so on, enhance work-related communications and make a lot of work more efficient and more pleasant, benefiting

---

* Theft by retail-store employees exceeds losses from shoplifting.[40]

both employers and employees. They can also be a distraction, a security leak, and a source of lawsuits. Personal social media content, outside of work, can get a person fired. We focus in this section on workplace rules for use of these tools and at monitoring employee communications and cyberspace activity at work and outside work.

Separating—or merging—work and personal communications

In many work environments, employers prohibit employees from using their work email, computers, and other devices for personal use. Among other reasons, content in some personal messages coming from a business address could embarrass the business or subject it to legal problems. (Where businesses archive all email, it could later embarrass the employee.)

What about employees using personal email accounts, social media, laptops, smartphones, and other devices for work? As cellphones have become smarter and more people have gotten used to a variety of ever-new electronic gadgets and social media applications, many workers (especially professional workers) find the tools their employers provide to be less convenient or less versatile. Telecommuters are likely to use the same computer for both personal and work activities. It might seem surprising that some employers prohibit employees from using personal media and devices for work. We consider some of the reasons.

From the employer's perspective, there are two main problems with use of personal devices for work. One is the overhead of managing and maintaining systems to work with the variety of brands and operating systems on the employees' various devices. The other, more serious, is security of company information and operations. Security on some smartphones is not as strong as on, for example, BlackBerry devices that employers favor. An employee might carry a personal device to more places with more opportunity to lose it or for someone to steal it. When an employee leaves the company for any reason, the employer cannot demand the he or she turn over a personal phone or tablet—even though it likely contains confidential client information and company files.

In government agencies, email is part of the official record and is subject to public disclosure (with some exceptions). Some government officials use their personal email specifically to keep communications "off the record." This practice subverts rules about openness in government. It also can have serious security risks. In Chapter 5, we mentioned that a hacking attack on the Gmail accounts of high-level government officials originated in a Chinese city where a major Chinese national security division is located. The U.S. government assured the public that personal email, not government email, was compromised. It is not unlikely, however, that the hackers expected to find, and did find, sensitive government content.

Some employers accept the trend toward using personal devices for work and develop policies and rules to reduce risks. Simple examples include requiring that employees always use a password to access their device. More sophisticated are techniques to remotely erase a device if it is lost or stolen—or if the employee leaves the company. Information on some devices can be separated into a personal area and a secure work area, where only the latter is remotely erased. If such a separation is not utilized and an employer erases the entire device, the employee might lose a huge amount of valuable personal information. The policy about erasing a device must be made clear to employees.[41]

We explained in Section 5.2.5 that the original intent and design of the Internet and the Web was to share information, not to create a secure environment. The same is true for social media and many popular consumer wireless devices. As we saw in Chapter 5, the openness of the Internet led to many problems of intrusions, privacy loss, thefts of information, and malicious disabling of computer systems and websites. Similar problems afflict personal devices and software that employees use for work. Thus, security remains a significant issue for employers.

Some employers have a policy that employees may not install any software on their (work) computers or laptops other than what the employer provides. Some employers, for example, prohibit games. To someone who travels for work, this might seem silly or overly restrictive. Why not install a game to play while commuting or on a plane? Why not download music to listen to while working? Again, one of the main reasons is security: to protect against viruses or other malware that could disable the system or leak confidential company information or personal data. (In one case, investigators believe that after an Arizona police officer installed peer-to-peer software, hackers used it to collect personal information, photos, and email addresses of several police officers.) Another purpose is to keep copyright-infringing software off the employer's computers to avoid legal trouble. What degree of restrictions make sense? The answer varies with the particular industry and the kind of work done.

Monitoring employer systems

Roughly half of major companies in the United States sometimes monitor the email or voice mail of their employees on company systems. Various surveys find high percentages of employees at businesses and government agencies use the Web at work for nonwork purposes. Visits to "adult" and pornography sites, when the Web was new, gave way to sports, shopping, gambling, and stock-investment sites, then to watching videos, downloading music, and networking with friends. Many major companies use software tools that provide reports on employee Web use. The tools rank sites by frequency of visits or create reports on an individual employee's activity, for instance. About 25% of companies in a 2011 survey block access to social network sites.[42] Monitoring raises privacy issues. Employers claim they have a right and a need to monitor the use of their facilities and what employees are doing at work. Controversies stem from disagreements about the reasons for monitoring and the appropriate boundary between the employers' rights and the employees' privacy.

Purposes of monitoring employee communications include training, measuring or increasing productivity, checking compliance with rules for communications, and detecting behavior that threatens the employer in some way. Figure 6.1 lists a variety of purposes.

- Protect security of proprietary information and data.
- Prevent or investigate possible criminal activities by employees. (This can be work related, such as embezzlement, or not work related, such as selling illegal drugs.)
- Check for violations of company policy against sending offensive or pornographic messages.
- Investigate complaints of harassment.
- Comply with legal requirements in heavily regulated industries.
- Prevent personal use of employer facilities (if prohibited by company policy).
- Locate employees.
- Find needed business information when the employee is not available.

Figure 6.1 Reasons for monitoring employee communications.

Many large companies rank leaking of proprietary information as a serious problem. Some businesses filter all outgoing messages for content that violates laws or company policy, could damage relations with customers, or could expose the company to lawsuits. The box on page 318 describes an application of email filtering in the stock brokerage industry. The health industry is another example where very strict federal rules apply to patient information to protect privacy; health businesses and organizations must ensure that employees do not violate the rules. Other problems are harassment (including sexual harassment, cases with pending divorces, and love triangles), sending jokes to thousands of people, running a business using the company's address, personal communications, and running betting pools on football and basketball games. Employee email led to lawsuits against more than 15% of companies in one survey, and 26% of employers said they had fired employees for misusing company email.[43] Most companies that read employee communications do it infrequently, primarily when there is a complaint or some other reason to suspect a problem. At the other extreme, some employers routinely intercept messages entering and leaving the company site. Some supervisors snoop to find out what employees are saying about them or the company.

Is nonwork Web use at work a serious problem for employers, or is it the modern equivalent of reading a newspaper, listening to the radio, or making a quick personal phone call at one's desk? One large U.S. company found that on a typical day, employees viewed 50,000 YouTube videos and listened to 4000 hours of music. These activities caused a significant slowdown of the company's Internet service.[44] Another obvious concern about nonwork Web activity is that employees are not working the hours they are paid to work. (On the other hand, a company found that one of its top-performing employees spent more than an hour a day managing his own stocks on the Web. The company did not care because his performance was good.) Some psychologists argue

Filtering professional email

Most major stock brokerage companies use email filters to detect illegal, unethical, and offensive email sent by their brokers. Stock brokers are not supposed to exaggerate the prospects of investments, downplay the risks, or pressure clients to buy or sell. Filters search for keywords such as "risk-free," vulgarities, and sexist or racist terms. They use AI techniques for more sophisticated analysis of messages.[45]

Is this an example of increased monitoring that technology makes possible? Not entirely. To protect the public, the New York Stock Exchange previously required that a supervisor read all written communication from brokers to clients. When email replaced mailed letters, the volume increased so much that supervisors could no longer read all the mail. Email filtering replaced human review of all messages with human review of only those selected by the filter.

Brokers use email for a greater variety of messages than they did printed letters—including personal messages, which now may be exposed to filters and archiving requirements. Does routine filtering violate the privacy of the brokers? If it does, do the trade-offs justify it? What rules are brokerage companies likely to establish for use of social media by brokers to communicate with clients?

that allowing some personal online activity improves employee morale and efficiency. Companies remain concerned about security and other risks. Viruses and other malicious software that an employee might download have the potential to disrupt company operations or to access sensitive data about the company or its customers and clients. Also, some companies want to avoid the embarrassment of having their employees reported to be visiting pornographic sites, perhaps racist sites, or even job-hunting sites.

Law and cases for employer systems

Monitoring for purposes listed in Figure 6.1 is generally legal in the United States and other countries.[46] The Electronic Communications Privacy Act (ECPA) prohibits interception of email and reading of stored email without a court order, but the ECPA makes an exception for business systems. It does not prohibit employers from reading employee email on company systems. Some privacy advocates and computer ethicists advocate a revision of the ECPA to prohibit or restrict employers from reading employee email.

ECPA: Section 2.6.1

In one case, a company fired two employees after a supervisor read their email messages criticizing him. A judge ruled that the company could read the email because it owned and operated the system. In another case, a court accepted monitoring of a discussion about a boss because the discussion could affect the business environment. Courts have made similar decisions in other cases. In addition, courts generally allow employers to look at messages an employee sends or receives on personal email accounts if the employee uses the employer's computer system or mobile device to do so. In a few cases, courts ruled against an employer for reading email sent at work but on a personal account between an employee and the employee's attorney. The longstanding principle of attorney-client privilege protects such correspondence. However, in at least one case in which the employee used the company's email system for correspondence with her attorney in violation of a clear policy that prohibits personal use of the company system, the court ruled in favor of the employer who read the messages.[47] A court ruling summed up a typical conclusion: "[T]he company's interest in preventing inappropriate and unprofessional comments, or even illegal activity, over its e-mail system would outweigh [the employee's] claimed privacy interest in those communications."[48]

Employees do not give up all privacy when they enter an employer's premises. The bathrooms belong to the employer too, but camera surveillance in bathrooms is generally not acceptable. Courts have sometimes ruled against employers if there was a convincing case that monitoring was done to snoop on personal and union activities or to track down whistleblowers. Workers have a legal right to communicate with each other about work conditions, and the National Labor Relations Board, which decides cases about worker–employee relations, ruled in some cases that they may do so on company systems. Thus, employers may not prohibit all nonbusiness communications.[49]

Court decisions sometimes depend on a conclusion about whether an employee had a reasonable "expectation of privacy." Several decisions emphasize the importance of a company having a clear policy statement. An employer should inform employees clearly about whether it permits personal use of employer-provided communications and computer systems and whether, and under what circumstances, the employer will access employee messages and files. The employer should make clear how it treats messages in personal accounts sent through the employer's equipment. A clear policy removes some of the guesswork about expectations of privacy.*

 Expectation of privacy: Section 2.2.2

Clear policy statements are important from an ethical perspective as well. Respect for an employee's privacy includes warning the employee about when someone is observing his or her apparently private actions or communications (except in special circumstances such as a criminal investigation). Giving or accepting a job in which an employee will use an employer's equipment carries an ethical obligation on both parties to abide by the policy established for that use. From a practical perspective, a clear policy can reduce disputes and abuses (by employees or employers).

So far, we have been discussing cases in which an employee argues that an employer invaded the employee's privacy. Is an employee who violates an employer's policies about use of the employer's computer systems committing a crime? Prosecutors have brought

---

* Some court decisions indicate that an employer does not have to specify each specific technology that the policy covers. The employee should assume that a policy for the employer's laptops and phones, for example, applies to a tablet or a newly invented device.

criminal charges against employees for doing so. In Section 5.2.6, we described unintended applications of the Computer Fraud and Abuse Act (CFAA). This is another. The CFAA was intended for hacking. Several courts have allowed prosecutions of employees, saying the wording of the law (if not the intent) covers violations of an employer's policies. Others reject this interpretation, saying it would make federal criminals of millions of ordinary people who play a game or do some shopping on a work computer in violation of the employer's rules.

Personal social media

Almost a third of multinational companies said in a survey that they took disciplinary action against employees for misuse of social networks.[50] In many instances, employers learn about questionable content after hearing complaints or after another employee shows it to a supervisor. Basing disciplinary action on personal, nonwork social media is more controversial than monitoring employer communications systems because it extends employer control beyond the workplace.

   Are there good reasons for employers to be concerned about what their employees post in such places? Is it reasonable for employers to fire employees for content of their blogs, tweets, or posts on social networks? Consider some of the wide variety of reasons for such firings. A school district fired a teacher because of a photo of her drinking in a bar. A school district declined to rehire a teacher who communicated with students on a social network and included pictures of naked men with his profile. An actor was fired for tweeting jokes about the horrific tsunami in Japan. A restaurant fired a server for complaining on a social network about an inconsiderate, low-tipping customer; the server had included the name of the restaurant. A police department demoted two officers for a cartoon video on YouTube that poked fun at the operation of a local jail. A nonprofit social services organization fired five employees for a discussion on Facebook criticizing their working conditions and the job performance of another employee.[51] These examples suggest a variety of concerns for the employer, from protection of students to protection of the employer's image and reputation (reasonably in some examples, unreasonably where criticism is deserved). Content in social media is often widely distributed; thus, the impact is far stronger than that of a private conversation.

   A frequent question is whether employer restrictions on nonwork social media violate an employee's freedom of speech. Employers prohibit various kinds of speech—for example, disparaging the employer or its customers in public, trash talking about competitors (a common restriction for sports teams), disclosure of any information about clients (a common restriction in health and financial fields), and any discussion of new products or business plans. These are conditions of the job; they do not violate the First Amendment (unless, in some cases, when the employer is the government). On the other hand, people should be free to discuss and criticize working conditions and to report abuses of power. The social service agency said the five employees it fired violated its policy against bullying and harassment, but a judge said that a law allowing discussion of working conditions protects their discussion. Clearly, some discussions will fall on one side of the permissible line and others will not. A decision about the ethics of the firing in many cases depends on the actual content of the material in question, how widely it was distributed, the type of employer, and perhaps other criteria. What about the restaurant server? In what ways might her action differ from that of the social service employees?

Was the police officer who poked fun at the local jail acting in a way "unbecoming an officer," or was he exercising his freedom of speech? In a less controversial firing (but more ugly incident), an Australian police force fired four officers and disciplined more than a dozen others for circulating racist, homophobic, and pornographic email, joking about the death of an Indian man. In this case, the officers used department computers. Would the firings and discipline have been less justifiable if they had used personal email or social media?

A problem, for both ethics and law, consists of defining a reasonable boundary between, on the one hand, the employer's property rights, protection of company assets and reputation, protection of clients or the public, and the need to monitor for possible legal and liability problems, and, on the other hand, actions that invade privacy and restrict employees' reasonable freedom of expression. The most reasonable policy is not always obvious, not always the same in the view of both parties, not the same for all types of businesses, and not always clear when new situations arise.

Monitoring location and equipment usage

Employers supply smartphones and other location devices that tell a supervisor where an employee is at all times. In the box on page 322, we illustrate some issues of location surveillance with one example—long-haul truckers. Heavy equipment companies install similar monitoring devices in their equipment. One company learned that their workers let engines run to keep the air conditioning on while they ate lunch in the vehicle's cab. The company stopped the practice, which had used up thousands of dollars in extra fuel. Is this an advantage (saving money and energy), or is it unfair to the workers?

Electronic identification badges that serve as door keys raise similar issues. They provide increased security for a business, but they allow monitoring of the movements of employees. Nurses in some hospitals wear badges that track their location; a supervisor at a terminal can see where each nurse is. That means supervisors can see who someone eats lunch with and when they go to the bathroom. On the other hand, they can also locate nurses quickly in emergencies. Would a call on a public-address system do just as well?

City governments give cellphones to employees so that supervisors can determine where employees are at all times (while at work). Building inspectors in Massachusetts refused the phones, calling them an invasion of privacy. Is it reasonable for a nurse or a city employee working out in the field to expect his or her location, while working, to be private? Should employer policies permit employees to turn off locating devices when they are on a break? Again, good sense is valuable in making reasonable choices. Most decisions about such questions are wise or unwise, rather than ethically required or ethically prohibited.

Tracking truckers[52]

In the late 1980s, shippers began installing tracking systems in their long-haul trucks. Now, most trucks have such devices. They can report the location and speed of the vehicle, as well as such other details as when the driver turns on the headlights.

These systems enable more precise planning of pick-ups and deliveries, increases in efficiency, reductions in energy use, and reductions in expenses. Companies can use data on speed and rest periods to ensure that drivers follow safety rules. Trucks loaded with valuable goods and construction vehicles themselves are targets for thieves. Owners recovered more than a hundred stolen trucks in one year because the thieves did not know about the tracking devices. Before cellphones were available, the tracking systems facilitated communication about schedule changes, road conditions, breakdowns requiring a mechanic, and so on.

The main disadvantage is that many drivers saw the system as an intrusion on their privacy, a "Big Brother" device watching their every move. Companies can micromanage the driver's actions and decisions, decreasing individual discretion. When the devices were first introduced, some truckers wrapped foil over the transmitter or parked for naps under highway bridges.

Do the benefits of tracking and monitoring outweigh the privacy intrusion, or is this an example of computer technology inappropriately infringing on privacy and worker autonomy? Does the advent of cellphones reduce the advantages significantly?

EXERCISES

Review Exercises

6.1 List two job categories where the number of jobs declined drastically as a result of computerization.

6.2 List two job categories where the number of jobs increased drastically with increasing use of computers.

6.3 What has been one of the impacts on India of offshoring U.S. jobs to India?

6.4 What are two advantages and two disadvantages of telecommuting?

6.5 Give two examples of material on social networking sites that got someone fired.

6.6 What is one risk of using one's personal phone for work?

6.7 Give two reasons for a company to install software to filter all email sent by employees (from work).

General Exercises

6.8 List four examples from Section 1.2 that reduce or eliminate jobs. Tell specifically what jobs they reduce or eliminate.

6.9 Why is it difficult to determine the number of jobs eliminated and created by computers?

6.10 List ten jobs that existed 20 years ago, but have since been rendered obsolete by technology.

6.11   In many parts of the world, the replacement of skilled labor by computers and robots have sparked massive protests. Give arguments both for and against these protests. Which do you think is stronger? Why?

6.12   Apply one of John Rawls' ideas (in Section 1.4.2) to the analysis of the scenario in Section 6.2.4 about whether to hire U.S. programmers or Indian programmers.

6.13   Give some reasons why it might be difficult for companies to find qualified job applicants for some positions such as electrical engineers, network specialists, software developers, and Java programmers.

6.14   In the context of the appropriateness of employers obtaining information on job applicants from social media, discuss whether or how a racist joke told by an applicant during a job interview differs from a racist joke on the applicant's social media page.

6.15   Describe two new uses that might be made of the E-Verify system described in the box in Section 6.3.1. Indicate their advantages and disadvantages briefly.

6.16   Should there be laws banning some kinds of home-based work and not others (e.g., sewing vs. work by professional people who use computers)? Why, or why not? If you think there should be restrictions on some kinds of home work, what principles should apply in deciding which kinds?

6.17   Professional baseball players are not allowed to "trash talk" their opponents in public—for example, at press conferences and in interviews. A team reprimanded a player for tweeting disparaging remarks about an opponent. Is it reasonable for the team to include Twitter in the prohibition on trash talk? Is prohibiting remarks on Twitter a violation of the player's freedom of speech? Do you have another interpretation or analysis of the situation? Explain your position. [53]

6.18   Consider the case of an employee fired for posting pictures on a social media website showing her at a party while on sick leave. What factors would you consider in deciding if the firing was reasonable?

6.19   A company secretly records all telephonic conversations carried out by employees during working hours. Do you think this is appropriate? Why? If you think it is appropriate in some workplaces and not others, give examples and formulate criteria for deciding which.

6.20   Some organizations proposed federal legislation to prohibit monitoring of customer-service or data-entry employees with more than five years of experience. Give reasons for and against monitoring experienced employees.

6.21   Consider a proposed law to require all long-haul trucks to have electronic monitoring devices to ensure that truckers obey laws requiring rest breaks. Government inspectors would review the collected data instead of reviewing the paper logs required previously. Give arguments for and against such a law. Do you think it is a good idea? How does this question differ from the decision of a shipping company to install such devices in its trucks?

6.22   Consider the reasons given in Figure 6.1 for employers to monitor employee communications. For which do you think it is appropriate to have regular, ongoing monitoring for all employees, and for which do you think an employer should access employee communications only when a problem occurs and only for the particular employees involved? Give reasons.

6.23   You work for a large architectural firm. Develop a policy for online social networking by employees at work.

6.24 Suppose your employer prohibits you from using your own computer and the software of your choice at work, citing requirements of consistency amongst employees that you believe to be ill-informed and baseless. How would you react to this?

6.25 Assume you are a professional working in your chosen field. Describe specific things you can do to reduce the impact of any two problems we discussed in this chapter. (If you cannot think of anything related to your professional field, choose another field that might interest you.)

6.26 Think ahead to the next few years and describe a new problem, related to issues in this chapter, likely to develop from digital technology or devices.

Assignments

These exercises require some research or activity.

6.27 The ECPA does not prohibit universities from reading student email on its computers, just as it does not prohibit businesses from reading employee email on company computers. Find your university's policy about access to student computer accounts and email (on university computers) by professors and university administrators. Describe the policy. Tell what parts you think are good and what should change.

6.28 Find a case where an applicant was accepted or rejected owing primarily to information on the applicant's social media pages. Do you think the result was acceptable? Why?

Class Discussion Exercises

These exercises are for class discussion, perhaps with short presentations prepared in advance by small groups of students.

6.29 Discuss cases from history where people have reacted negatively to advances in technology, or cases of mass outsourcing that have eliminated jobs. What reasons were put forth by the protesters? Do you agree with them?
  If there is little controversy about the answer to the question above (as I suspect will be the case), try to identify reasons why so many people react negatively to advances in technology that eliminate some jobs.

6.30 One ethical argument against offshoring jobs is that employee health and safety requirements are not as strong in some countries as they are in the United States. Evaluate this argument.

6.31 Choose any three of the following employers, and discuss arguments for and against a policy to do a social-media search on job applicants.
  (a) A university hiring graduate students
  (b) The Secret Service
  (c) A small establishment selling sandwiches

6.32 (a) Is it an invasion of privacy for an employer to search the Web for information by and about a job applicant? Explain.
  (b) Does refraining from hiring a person who frequently posts or tweets extreme political views violate that person's freedom of speech? Does it matter whether the employer is private or a government agency? Explain.

(c) Should there be legal restrictions on the kinds of information about a job candidate that a prospective employer can look at on the Web (beside what is already illegal)?

6.33 Consider an automated system that large companies can use to process job applications. For jobs such as truck drivers, cleaning staff, and cafeteria workers, the system selects people to hire without interviews or other involvement of human staffers. Describe advantages and disadvantages of such a system.

6.34 In recent years, only about 22% of students earning college degrees in computer science in the United States were women. This is down from a peak of 37% in 1985.[54] Why do you think relatively few women major in computer science? What characteristics or images of the field might discourage women?

6.35 Walking through a public park on their way back to work after lunch, four employees of a large Internet services company begin clowning around and singing silly and raunchy songs. One of them captures the scene on his cellphone and later posts it on a major video site. In the video, the company logo is clearly visible on the tee-shirts the employees are wearing. The company fires the employee who posted the video and has not yet decided on action against the others. Discuss arguments for and against the firing. What disciplinary action, if any, is appropriate for the other employees?

6.36 Do you believe that teaching hacking techniques is ethical? Would your opinion change if the instruction was purely to educate people on exposing security flaws and so on ("ethical" hacking), but the techniques learnt could nevertheless be used for nefarious purposes?

BOOKS AND ARTICLES

- Clair Brown, John Haltiwanger, and Julia Lane, *Economic Turbulence*, University of Chicago Press, 2006.

- Gregory Clark, *A Farewell to Alms: A Brief Economic History of the World*, Princeton University Press, 2007. This and the Diamond book below present two quite different views on the sources of human progress. Clark emphasizes culture.

- Jared Diamond, *Guns, Germs, and Steel: The Fate of Human Societies*, W. W. Norton & Company, 2005. This and the Clark book above present two quite different views on the sources of human progress. Diamond emphasizes geography.

- Nancy Flynn, *Blog Rules: A Business Guide to Managing Policy, Public Relations, And Legal Issues*, AMACOM, 2006. Workplace blogging policies from the employer perspective.

- Ronald Kutscher, *The Impact of Technology on Employment in the United States: Past and Future*, Farmer Press, 1987.

- Jack Nilles, "Teleworking: Working Closer to Home," *Technology Review*, April 1982, pp. 56–62. An early article that foresaw many of the advantages and disadvantages of telework.

- Jeremy Rifkin, *The End of Work*, Tarcher, 1996 (updated edition 2004).

- Jeffrey M. Stanton and Kathryn R. Stam, *The Visible Employee: Using WorkPlace Monitoring and Surveillance to Protect Information Assets—Without Compromising Employee Privacy or Trust*, Information Today, Inc., 2006.

1. CPU: Working in the Computer Industry, Computer Professionals for Social Responsibility, Feb. 15, 1995, www.cpsr.org/prevsite/program/workplace/cpu.013 .html, viewed Apr. 3, 2007.

2. J. M. Fenster, "Seam Stresses," *Great Inventions That Changed the World*, American Heritage, 1994.

3. Interview with Ann Curry, *Today*, NBC, June 14, 2011, described in Rebecca Kaplan, "Obama Defends Economic Policies, Need for Tax Increases In 'Today' Interview," *National Journal*, June 14, 2011, www.nationaljournal.com/whitehouse/obama-defends-economic-policies-need-for-tax-increases-in-today-interview-20110614, viewed Nov. 8, 2011. The video of the interview is at today.msnbc.msn.com/id/26184891/vp/43391550#43391550.

4. Associated Press, "Electronic Dealings Will Slash Bank Jobs, Study Finds," *Wall Street Journal*, Aug. 14, 1995, p. A5D. W. Michael Cox and Richard Alm, *Myths of Rich and Poor: Why We're Better Off than We Think*, Basic Books, 1999, p. 129. G. Pascal Zachary, "Service Productivity Is Rising Fast—and So Is the Fear of Lost Jobs," *Wall Street Journal*, June 8, 1995, p. A1. Lauren Etter, "Is the Phone Company Violating Your Privacy?" *Wall Street Journal*, May 13–14, 2006, p. A7.

5. Cox and Alm, *Myths of Rich and Poor*, p. 129. Alejandro Bodipo-Memba, "Jobless Rate Skidded to 4.4% in November," *Wall Street Journal*, Dec. 7, 1998, pp. A2, A8.

6. Fenster, "Seam Stresses"

7. "High-Tech Added 200,000 Jobs Last Year," *Wall Street Journal*, May 19, 1998. "Chip-Industry Study Cites Sector's Impact on U.S. Economy," *Wall Street Journal*, Mar. 17, 1998, p. A20. Andrea K. Walker, "Retailer's Mass Firing Reflects Sector's Woes," *Baltimore Sun*, Mar. 29, 2007. Fatemeh Hajiha, "Employment Changes from 2001 to 2005 for Occupations Concentrated in the Finance Industries," U.S. Bureau of Labor Statistics, www.bls.gov/oes/2005/may/changes.pdf, viewed Aug. 6, 2007. "Tellers," *Occupational Outlook Handbook, 2010–11 Edition*, U.S. Bureau of Labor Statistics, www.bls.gov/oco/ocos126.htm, viewed Nov. 18, 2011.

8. George F. Gilder, *Microcosm*, Simon & Schuster, 1989, p. 46.

9. Il-Horn Hann *et al.*, "The Facebook App Economy," Center for Digital Innovation, Technology and Strategy, Robert H. Smith School of Business, University of Maryland, Sept. 19, 2011, www.rhsmith.umd.edu/digits/pdfs_docs/research/2011/AppEconomyImpact091911.pdf, viewed Feb. 11, 2012. Lance Whitney, "IT Spending to Recover This Year, Forrester Says," CNet News, Jan. 12, 2010,

news.cnet.com/8301-1001_3-10433116-92.html, viewed July 28, 2011.

10. Kimberly Rowe, in a letter to the editor, *Wall Street Journal*, Aug. 31, 2006, p. A9.

11. Daniel E. Hecker, "Occupational Employment Projections to 2012," *Monthly Labor Review*, February 2004, pp. 80–105 (see p. 80), www.bls.gov/opub/mlr/2004/02/art5full.pdf, viewed Apr. 13, 2007.

12. This quote and the one that follows are from "The OECD Jobs Study: Facts, Analysis, Strategies (1994)," www.oecd.org/dataoecd/42/51/1941679.pdf, viewed Apr. 8, 2007.

13. "The OECD Jobs Study," p. 21.

14. Theodore Caplow, Louis Hicks, and Ben J. Wattenberg, *The First Measured Century: An Illustrated Guide to Trends in America*, AEI Press, 2001, p. 160. Cox and Alm, *Myths of Rich and Poor*, pp. 18–19.

15. Cox and Alm, *Myths of Rich and Poor*, pp. 60, 59, 10, 43. U.S. Census Bureau: www.census.gov/const/C25Ann/sftotalmedavgsqft.pdf and www.census.gov/const/C25Ann/sftotalac.pdf, viewed Aug. 22, 2011. The cost, in work time, of some products and services increased in the same time period. Increases for tax-preparation fees, Amtrak tickets, and the price of a first class stamp perhaps result from more complex tax laws and monopolies. Increases in the average cost of a new car are partly due to the increase in features of new cars.

16. Paul Wallich, "The Analytical Economist," *Scientific American*, Aug. 1994, p. 89.

17. Phillip J. Longman, "The Janitor Stole My Job," *U.S. News & World Report*, Dec. 1, 1997, pp. 50–52. Caplow *et al.*, *The First Measured Century*, p. 31.

18. "Foreign Students Received 1,048 of last year's 1,694 Electrical Engineering Ph.D.s," Democratic Leadership Counsel, Feb. 2, 2011, www.dlc.org/ndol_ci.cfm?kaid=108&subid=900003&contentid=255236, viewed Nov. 6, 2011.

19. Longman, "The Janitor Stole My Job;" Amy Merrick, "Erasing 'Un' from 'Unemployable,'" *Wall Street Journal*, Aug. 2, 2007, pp. B1, B6.

20. U.S. Department of Labor, Bureau of Labor Statistics, "Employment Projections: Occupations with the Largest Job Growth, 2008–18," www.bls.gov/emp/ep_table_104.htm, viewed July 28, 2011.

21. Zachary, "Service Productivity Is Rising Fast."

22. U.S. Department of Labor, Bureau of Labor Statistics, "Occupational Outlook Handbook 2010–11 Edition," www.bls.gov/oco; "Computer software engineers," www.bls.gov/oco/ocos303.htm.

23. The Dieringer Research Group Inc., "Telework Trendlines 2009," February 2009, www.worldatwork.org/

waw/adimLink?id=31115, viewed Aug. 5, 2011. Other sources give higher numbers.

24. They might have had another motivation. An AFL-CIO official, Dennis Chamot, also commented, "It's very difficult to organize workers dispersed over a wide geographical area." (Quoted in David Rubins, "Telecommuting: Will the Plug Be Pulled?" *Reason*, Oct. 1984, pp. 24–32.)

25. Rockbridge Associates, "2005/2006 National Technology Readiness Survey," Robert H. Smith School of Business, University of Maryland, July 12, 2006, www.smith.umd.edu/ntrs/NTRS-2005-06.pdf, viewed Apr. 13, 2007.

26. "Half of U.S. Respondent Businesses Were Home-Based, Majority Self-Financed, Census Bureau Reports," U.S. Census Bureau, June 14, 2011, www.census.gov/newsroom/releases/archives/business_ownership/cb11-110.html, viewed Nov. 2, 2011.

27. Joel Kotkin, "Commuting via Information Superhighway," *Wall Street Journal*, Jan. 27, 1994, p. A14.

28. Walter Isaacson, *Steve Jobs*, Simon & Schuster, 2011, Chapter 41.

29. Linda Levine, "Unemployment Through Layoffs and Offshore Outsourcing," Congressional Research Service, Dec. 22, 2010, assets.opencrs.com/rpts/RL30799_20101222.pdf, viewed July 29, 2011. Alan S. Blinder, "Offshoring: The Next Industrial Revolution?", *Foreign Affairs*, March/April 2006, www.foreignaffairs.org/20060301faessay85209/alan-s-blinder/offshoring-the-next-industrial-revolution.html, viewed Apr. 5, 2007.

30. The ideas in this discussion come from Corie Lok, "Two Sides of Outsourcing," *Technology Review*, Feb. 2005, p. 33.

31. Blinder, "Offshoring: The Next Industrial Revolution?"

32. My thanks to my student Anthony Biag, whose questions in class on this issue prompted me to include it in this book.

33. Foreign-owned firms usually pay more than domestic employers. For example, a study of Indonesia, "Do foreign-owned firms pay more?" by Ann E. Harrison and Jason Scorse of the University of California, Berkeley (International Labour Office, Geneva, Working Paper #98, www.ilo.org/empent/Publications/WCMS_101046/lang–en/index.htm, viewed Aug. 17, 2006, link updated Oct. 22, 2011) found that foreign-owned manufacturers paid unskilled workers 5–10% more and skilled workers 20–35% more than comparable domestic employers.

34. Jennifer Preston, "Social Media History Becomes a New Job Hurdle," *New York Times*, July 20, 2011, www.nytimes.com/2011/07/21/technology/social-media-history-becomes-a-new-job-hurdle.html?pagewanted=all, viewed Aug. 4, 2011.

35. In Preston, "Social Media."

36. Searching social media is generally legal in the United States and other countries. Italy is an exception. Italy prohibits monitoring social network activity of employees or seeking information from social networks about job candidates, according to "Employee Misuse of Social Networking Found at 43 Percent Of Businesses, According to Proskauer International Labor & Employment Group Survey," The Metropolitan Corporate Counsel, Aug. 1, 2011, www.metrocorpcounsel.com/current.php?artType=view&EntryNo=12529, viewed Nov. 4, 2011.

37. Sources for this box include: Department of Homeland Security, U.S. Citizen and Immigration Services www.uscis.gov/portal/site/uscis (click on Employment Verification), viewed July 31, 2011. Michael Chertoff, "Myth vs. Fact: Worksite Enforcement," July 9, 2008, Leadership Journal Archive, Department of Homeland Security, www.dhs.gov/journal/leadership/labels/E-Verify.html, viewed Aug. 2, 2011. "Deciphering the Numbers on E-Verify's Accuracy," Immigration Policy Center, Feb. 11, 2009, www.immigrationpolicy.org/just-facts/deciphering-numbers-e-verifys-accuracy, viewed Aug. 2, 2011. "Immigration: You Can't Rely on E-Verify," editorial in *Los Angeles Times*, May 27, 2011, articles.latimes.com/2011/may/27/opinion/la-ed-arizona-20110527, viewed July 31, 2011. Government Accountability Office, "Employment Verification," December 2010, www.gao.gov/new.items/d11146.pdf, viewed Aug. 2, 2011.

38. Quoted in Joe Davidson, "House Panel Backs Telephone Process to Verify Authorization of New Hires," *Wall Street Journal*, Sept. 22, 1995, pp. A2, A14.

39. Adi Kamdar, "EFF Denounces Flawed E-Verify Proposal That Would Trample on Worker Privacy," July 1, 2011, www.eff.org/deeplinks/2011/07/eff-denounces-flawed-e-verify-proposal, viewed July 31, 2011.

40. In one scam, an employee scans and charges for cheap items but bags expensive ones for the customer who is an accomplice. Richard C. Hollinger and Lynn Langton, "2005 National Retail Security Survey," University of Florida, 2006, pp. 6–8. Security Research Project, University of Florida, soccrim.clas.ufl.edu/criminology/srp/srp.html. Richard C. Hollinger, National Retail Security Survey 2002, reported in "Retail Theft and Inventory Shrinkage," retailindustry.about.com/od/statistics_loss_prevention/l/aa021126a.htm, viewed Aug. 17, 2006. Calmetta Coleman, "As Thievery by Insiders Overtakes Shoplifting, Retailers Crack Down," *Wall Street Journal*, Sept. 8, 2000, p. A1.

41. Roger Cheng, in his article "So You Want to Use Your iPhone for Work? Uh-oh," (*Wall Street Journal*, Apr. 25, 2011, pp. R1,R4), describes in depth the problems and potential solutions discussed here and more.

42. American Management Association and ePolicy Institute, "2007 Electronic Monitoring & Surveillance Survey," Feb. 28, 2008, press.amanet.org/press-releases/177/2007-electronic-monitoring-surveillance-survey, viewed Nov. 3, 2011. "Employee Misuse of Social Networking Found at 43 Percent Of Businesses."

43. American Management Association and ePolicy Institute, "2006 Workplace E-mail, Instant Messaging & Blog Survey," www.epolicyinstitute.com/survey2006 Summary.pdf, link updated Oct. 22, 2011.

44. Emily Glazer, "P&G Curbs Employees' Interent Use," *Wall Street Journal*, Apr. 4, 2012, online.wsj.com/article/SB10001424052702304072004l5773241428470063 40.html, viewed Apr. 8, 2012.

45. Alex Markels, "I Spy: Wall Street Gets Sneaky Software to Keep an Eye on Broker-Client Email," *Wall Street Journal*, Aug. 21, 1997, pp. C1, C23.

46. Italy is an exception, as noted above.

47. *Stengart v. Loving Care Agency, Inc.*, New Jersey Supreme Court, Mar. 30, 2010. *Curto v. Medical World Communications, Inc. Holmes v. Petrovich Development Company, LLC.* See also "Fact Sheet 7: Workplace Privacy and Employee Monitoring," Privacy Rights Clearinghouse, www.privacyrights.org/fs/fs7-work.htm, viewed Nov. 3, 2011.

48. *McLaren v. Microsoft*, Texas Court of Appeal No. 05-97-00824CV, May 28, 1999, cyber.law.harvard.edu/privacy/McLaren_v_Microsoft.htm, viewed Sept. 10, 2007.

49. *Leinweber v. Timekeeper Systems*, 323 NLRB 30 (1997), "E-Mail Law Expands," www.infowar.com/law/99/law_072099a_j.shtml.

50. "Employee Misuse of Social Networking Found at 43 Percent of Businesses."

51. Kabrina Krebel Chang, "Facebook Got Me Fired," Boston University School of Management, May 18, 2011, www.bu.edu/builders-leaders/2011/05/18/facebook-got-me-fired, viewed Nov. 3, 2011. Chang's article mentions several cases and includes valuable discussion of the principles involved. *Spanierman, v. Hughes, Druzolowski, and Hylwa*, www.ctemploymentlawblog.com/uploads/file/hughes.pdf, viewed Nov. 3, 2011. Jacob Sullum, "Renton Police Drop Cyberstalking Investigation of Cartoon Creator, Pursue Harassment Claim Instead," *Reason Hit & Run*, Sept. 7. 2011, reason.com/blog/2011/09/07/renton-police-drop-cyberstalki, viewed Nov. 4, 2011. (The department tried to obtain the identity of an officer who anonymously released a series of satiric "Mr. Fuddlesticks" cartoons about the demotion and about serious police misconduct in the department. The department claimed the cartoons constituted cyberstalking and harassment and that they created a hostile work environment. The department was severely criticized and ridiculed for its behavior in this incident.) The social service organization is Hispanics United of Buffalo. The case and result are summarized in "Administrative Law Judge Finds New York Nonprofit Unlawfully Discharged Employees Following Facebook Posts," National Labor Relations Board, Sept. 7, 2011, www.nlrb.gov/news/administrative-law-judge-finds-new-york-nonprofit-unlawfully-discharged-employees-following-fac, viewed Nov. 7, 2011.

52. Stuart F. Brown, "Trucking Gets Sophisticated," *Fortune*, July 24, 2000, pp. 270B–270R. James R. Hagerty, "'Big Brother' Keeps an Eye on Fleet of Heavy Equipment," *Wall Street Journal*, June 1, 2011, p. B1.

53. Thanks to Julie L. Johnson for suggesting the idea for this exercise.

54. National Science Foundation, "Science and Engineering Indicators 2008, Chapter 2: Higher Education in Science and Engineering," www.nsf.gov/statistics/seind08/c2/c2s4.htm, viewed Aug. 26, 2011.

7

Evaluating and Controlling Technology

In this chapter we consider such questions as these: Does the openness and "democracy" of the Web increase distribution of useful information or inaccurate, foolish, and biased information? How can we evaluate complex computer models of physical and social phenomena? How does access to digital technology differ among different populations? Is computing technology evil? Why do some people think it is? How should we control technology to ensure positive uses and consequences? How soon will robots be more intelligent than people? What will happen after that?

Whole books focus on these topics. The presentations here are necessarily brief. They introduce some of the issues and arguments.

7.1 Evaluating Information

> *A little learning is a dang'rous thing;*
> *Drink deep, or taste not the Pierian spring;*
> *There shallow draughts intoxicate the brain,*
> *And drinking largely sobers us again.*
>
> —Alexander Pope, 1709[1]

7.1.1 The Need for Responsible Judgment

Expert information or the "wisdom of the crowd"?

> *We can get the wrong answer to a question quicker than our fathers*
> *and mothers could find a pencil.*
>
> —Robert McHenry[2]

There is a daunting amount of information on the Web—and much of it is wrong. Quack medical cures abound. Distorted history, errors, outdated information, bad financial advice—it is all there. Marketers and public relations firms spread unlabeled advertisements through blogs, social media, and video sites. Search engines have largely replaced librarians for finding information, but search engines rank Web pages by popularity (at least partly) and give prominent display to content providers who pay them; librarians do not. Wikipedia, the biggest online encyclopedia, is immensely popular, but can we rely on its accuracy and objectivity when anyone can edit any article at any time? On social journalism sites, readers submit and vote on news stories. Is this a good way to get news? The nature of the Internet encourages people to post their immediate thoughts and reactions without taking time for contemplation or for checking facts. How do we know what is worth reading in contexts where there are no editors selecting the well-written and well-researched?

When we see a video of a currently popular performer singing with Elvis Presley, we know we are watching creative entertainment—digital magic at work. But the same technology can deceive. Video-manipulation tools (and increased bandwidth) provide the opportunity for "forging" people. A company developed an animation system that modifies video images of a real person to produce a new video in which the person is speaking whatever words the user of the system provides. Another system analyzes recordings of a person's voice and synthesizes speech with the voice, inflections, and tones of that person. Combined, these systems will likely have many uses, including entertainment and advertising, but clearly people can also use them to mislead in highly unethical ways.[3] How do we know when someone is manipulating us?

Example: Wikipedia

To explore some issues of information quality, we consider Wikipedia. Wikipedia is a collaborative project among large numbers of strangers worldwide. It is huge, free, participatory, noncommercial, ad-free, and written by volunteers. The English edition has almost four million articles, more than 10 times as many as the long-respected Encyclopaedia Britannica, first published in 1768 and online since 1994.[4] Wikipedia is one of the Internet's most-used reference sites. But are its entries true, honest, and reliable?

We expect encyclopedias to be accurate and objective. Traditionally, expert scholars selected by editorial boards write encyclopedias. Volunteers, not carefully selected scholars, write and continually edit and update Wikipedia articles. Anyone who chooses to participate can do so. People worry that the lack of editorial control means no accountability, no standards of quality, no way for the ordinary person to judge the value of the information. They argue that because hundreds of millions of people—anyone at all—can write or edit articles, accuracy and quality are impossible. Truth does not come from populist free-for-alls. Members of the staffs of political candidates have distorted the Wikipedia biographies of their candidates to make their bosses look better. Opponents and enemies regularly vandalize profiles of prominent people. The staff of a federal agency removed criticisms of the agency from its Wikipedia article. Discredited theories about historic events such as the terrorist attacks on September 11, 2001, and the assassination of John F. Kennedy reappear regularly. A lawyer reported that one party in a case edited Wikipedia entries to make information appear more favorable to that party. (Jurors are not supposed to consult online sources about a trial, but some do.) Removing false information, hoaxes, and the like requires constant effort, according to Wikipedia volunteers. The Encyclopaedia Britannica has had errors and oddities, but the nature of Wikipedia makes it prone to more. Anonymity of writers encourages dishonesty. Open, volunteer, instant-publishing systems cannot prevent errors and vandalism as easily as publishers of printed books or closed, proprietary online information sources.

In spite of the errors, sloppiness, bad writing, and intentional distortions, most of Wikipedia is, perhaps surprisingly, of high quality and extraordinary value. Why? What protects quality in large, open, volunteer projects? First, although anyone *can* write and edit Wikipedia articles, most people do not. Thousands write and edit regularly, not millions. Most are educated and have expertise in the subjects they write about. They correct articles promptly. (Wikipedia saves old versions, so it can restore an article someone has vandalized.) After well-publicized incidents of manipulation of articles, Wikipedia's managers developed procedures and policies to reduce the liklihood of such incidents. For example, they lock articles on some controversial topics or people; the public cannot directly edit them.

We, as users, can (and must) learn to deal appropriately with side effects or weaknesses of new paradigms. Even though so much of Wikipedia is excellent and useful, we learn that someone might have wrecked the accuracy and objectivity of any individual article at any hour. We learn that articles on technology, basic science, history, and literature are more likely to be reliable that those on politics, controversial topics and people, and current events. We learn to use Wikipedia for background, but to check facts and alternative points of view. Should we judge Wikipedia (and, by extension, the mass of information on the Web) by the excellent material it provides or by the poor-quality material it includes?

> *Written by fools for the reading of imbeciles.*
>
> —An evaluation of newspapers, not websites, by a character in Joseph Conrad's novel *The Secret Agent* (1907)

The "wisdom of the crowd"

People ask all sorts of questions on Yahoo! Answers (and other sites like it) about dating, make-up, food, college ("Are online college classes as good as classroom classes?"), and wide-ranging technical, social, economic, and political issues ("If we can produce enough food to feed everyone in the world, why don't we?") Of course, a lot of answers are ill-informed. The questioner designates the posted answer he or she deems the best. What qualifies the questioner, presumably a person who does not know the answer, to judge the worthiness of the replies? To what extent does the ease of posting a question reduce the likelihood that a person will seek out well-researched or expert information on the subject? There are obviously questions for which this kind of forum might not provide the best results. (An example might be: Is it safe to drink alcohol while using an acne medicine?) However, the first two sample questions I quoted above are likely to generate a lot of ideas and perspectives. Sometimes that is exactly what the questioner wants. Without the Web, if someone asked questions like those of only a few friends, the answers might be less varied and less useful.

Some health sites on the Web encourage the public to rate doctors, hospitals, and medical treatments. Are such ratings valuable or dangerous? Will they motivate doctors and hospitals to change their practices to achieve higher ratings at the expense of good medical care? Steve Case, co-founder of AOL and founder of a health site that emphasizes ratings by the public, argues that if millions of people participate, the results will be very useful. Others are extremely suspicious of "the wisdom of the crowd." And there is always concern about manipulation. Websites have sprung up to buy and sell votes to get prominent display for articles on social media sites. What are the implications of such practices for sites where the public rates medical care? Will providers of new or questionable medical treatments generate fake favorable reviews and votes? Will responsible operators of sites that display material based on rankings or votes anticipate manipulation and protect against it?

Let's pause briefly to put the problems of incorrect, distorted, and manipulated information in perspective. Quack medical cures and manipulative marketing are hardly new. Product promotions not labeled as advertising date back hundreds of years. Eighteenth-century opera stars paid people to attend performances and cheer for them or boo their rivals. "Hatchet jobs" in the form of news articles, books, ads, and campaign flyers have dishonestly attacked politicians long before the Web existed. There are plenty of poorly written and inaccurate books. Historical movies merge truth and fiction, some for dramatic purposes, some for ideological purposes. They leave us with a distorted idea of what really happened. Two hundred years ago, cities had many more newspapers than they do today. Most were opinionated and partisan. At supermarket counters, we can buy newspapers with stories as outlandish as any online. The *New York Times* is a prime example of a respected newspaper, staffed by trained journalists, with an editorial board in charge. Yet one of its reporters fabricated many stories. Numerous other incidents of plagiarism, fabrication, and insufficient fact-checking have embarrassed newspapers and television networks.

OK, the problems of unreliable information are not new. But they are problems, and the Web magnifies them. So we consider two questions: How good is the wisdom of the crowd? And how can we distinguish good sources of information on the Web?

Researchers find that crowds do, in fact, generate good answers to certain kinds of questions. When a large number of people respond, they produce a lot of answers, but the average, or median, or most common answer is often a good one. This works well when the people are isolated from each other and express independent opinions. Some researchers think a large (independent) group is likely to be more accurate than a committee of experts for a variety of questions such as estimating economic growth or how well a new product or movie will do. (A Canadian mining company, perhaps hoping for such a phenomenon, posted a large set of geological data on the Web and held a contest to choose areas to look for gold.) However, when people see the responses provided by others, some undesirable things happen. People modify their responses so that the set of responses becomes less diverse, and the best answer may no longer stand out. People become more confident from reinforcement even though accuracy has not improved. The wisdom of crowds depends on diversity and independence. In social networks (as well as in-person teams working on projects in businesses, organizations, and government agencies), peer pressure and dominant personalities can reduce the wisdom of the group.[5]

How can we distinguish good sources of information on the Web? Search engines and other services at first ranked sites by the number of people who visit them. Some developed more sophisticated algorithms to consider the quality of information on sites where users provide content. (In response, some sites added editors and fact-checking to improve quality.) A variety of people and services review and rate sites and blogs. Critics of the quality of information on the Web and the lack of editorial control disdain such ratings as merely popularity contests, contending, for example, that the Internet gratifies the "mediocrity of the masses."[6] For blogs, as for Wikipedia or health care sites, they argue that popularity, voting, and consensus do not determine truth. That is correct, but there is no magic formula that tells us what is true and reliable either on the Web or off the Web. That a large number of people visit a website does not guarantee quality, but it provides some information. (Why have newspapers long published "best seller" lists for books?) We can choose to read only blogs written by Nobel Prize winners and college professors, if we wish, or only those recommended by friends and others we trust. We can choose to read only product reviews written by professionals, or we can read reviews posted by the public and get an overview of different points of view.

Over time, the distinction between the online equivalents of responsible journalism and supermarket tabloids becomes clear. Good reputations develop, just as they have for decades offline. Many university libraries provide guides for evaluating websites and the information on them. (I list some at the end of this chapter.) One good step is to determine who sponsors the site. If you cannot determine the sponsor of a site, you can consider its information as reliable as the information on a flyer you might find under your car's windshield wiper when you park in a busy parking lot. Ultimately, we must find sites, reviewers, ratings, editors, experts, and other sources we trust. Good judgment and skepticism are always useful.

> *The only way to preserve the wisdom of the crowd is to protect the independence of the individual.*
>
> —Jonah Lehrer[7]

Vulnerable viewers

Since you are reading this book, you probably are a student, a reasonably well-educated person who is learning how to analyze arguments and make good judgments. You can develop skills to evaluate material you read on the Web. But what about people who have less education or ability? For example, what risks does bad information pose to children who find it on the Web? Some critics of the Web worry most about the impact of inaccurate information on such vulnerable people. The fears of some seem to edge toward a belief that we (or experts, or the government) should somehow prevent such information from appearing. The many strong arguments for freedom of speech in general are arguments against any centralized or legally mandated way of accomplishing this. What can we do to improve the quality of information? Basic social and legal forces help (to a degree): freedom of speech (to provide responses, corrections, alternative viewpoints, and so on), teachers and parents, competition, fraud and libel laws—and people who care, who volunteer to write, review, and correct online information. What else can we do to reduce access to dangerously wrong information by vulnerable people?

Narrowing the information stream

All the problems of junk and nonsense on the Web notwithstanding, the Web now gives us access to more high-quality, up-to-date information than libraries did in the past. Consider current events, politics, and controversial issues. We can read and listen to thousands of news sources on the Web from our own and other countries, getting different cultural and political perspectives on events. We can read the full text of government documents—bills, budgets, investigative reports, congressional testimony and debate— instead of relying on a few sentences quoted from an official news release or a sound bite from a biased spokesperson. We can search archives of millions of news articles from the past 200 years. We can follow websites, blogs, tweets, and social media news of conservatives, liberals, libertarians, tea party activists, environmentalists, evangelical Christians, animal rights activists, and so on, far more easily and cheaply than when we had to seek out and susbscribe to their print newsletters and magazines. But what do people actually do? Some get all their news and interpretation of events from a small number of sites that reflect a specific political point of view. Online tools make it easy: you just set up your bookmarks and feeds and never look anywhere else, except at other sites recommended by the ones you frequent. Some critics see the Web as significantly encouraging political narrowness and political extremes by making it easy for people to avoid seeing alternative opinions.

The phenomenon of using the information that is easy to get applies to other fields be- sides politics, of course. I hear sad complaints from librarians and experienced researchers: Too many students and professionals believe whatever they read in Wikipedia. Researchers "reinvent the wheel" (or apply for grants to do so) because they do not read relevant work in their field published in the past and available only in paper journals. Because there is so much on the Web, it is too easy to ignore what is not there. How serious is the problem of ignoring older, undigitized work? Is it a temporary problem that will go away when virtually all research is available electronically?

A researcher analyzed millions of academic articles published over 50 years and found that as journals moved online, authors tend to cite fewer articles, more recent ones, and articles from a narrower set. The speculation is that researchers using search engines to find articles related to their work select from among the ones that appear high in search results—the ones that are already cited frequently. Those articles might indeed be the most important, but this approach reinforces previous choices and can lead researchers to miss less popular but very relevant work. Researchers have far more (and easier) access to articles and journals online than they had in the stacks of libraries. However, as the author of the study says, searching online "puts researchers in touch with prevailing opinions, but this may accelerate consensus and narrow the range of findings and ideas built upon."[8] The effect of accelerating consensus and narrowing results is similar to what researchers saw with the wisdom of the crowd when crowd members were not

Idiots and dunderheads

A fool and his money are soon parted.
—Old English proverb

New technologies can have the unintended side effect of diminishing older skills. Computing technology has reduced the use of cursive writing, for example. Microsoft made a conscious decision with the effect of diminishing language skills. The thesaurus in Microsoft Word 2000 (and some later versions) lists the verb "trick" as the only meaning for "fool." It omits noun synonyms "clown," "blockhead," "idiot," "ninny," "dunderhead," "ignoramus," and others—all present in earlier versions. Standard references such as dictionaries and Roget's Thesaurus contain some of these and more choices.

Microsoft said it eliminated words "that may have offensive uses."[9]* Was this a dunderheaded decision that dulls the language and reduces literacy? Do producers of widely used reference works have an ethical responsibility to report the substance of their field accurately, or a social responsibility to remove potentially offensive words from the language?

* Microsoft restored some synonyms meaning a foolish person but continues to omit the more colorful and more offensive terms.

independent, though the mechanism is different. Clearly, it is good for researchers to be aware of this phenomenon and to broaden their searches when appropriate. The number of scholarly papers published each year has grown enormously (to, very roughly, a million yearly). Is it the tendency to use search tools in a somewhat lazy way—or the sheer number of papers—that causes some valuable work to be missed?

If we receive too much information that does not interest us, we stop reading it. To counter this problem, Facebook implemented algorithms to filter news feed updates from friends based on how recently a member communicated with them. But of course, sometimes we want to hear from those people we have not heard from in a long time. What better methods could Facebook use? And is this relevant to social issues beyond personal relationships? It is. Eli Pariser, president of (liberal) MoveOn.org, includes conservatives among his Facebook friends because he wants to be aware of views different from his own. Over time, he realized he was no longer receiving updates from them (because he did not communicate with them regularly). Although Facebook members can turn off the filtering of news feeds, most people are not aware of it. Pariser considered the problem of filtered information so disturbing that he wrote a book about it.[10] What lessons can we learn from Facebook's filtering? It is not ideal to use Facebook as our main source of access to political discussion. Facebook's choice of a default setting (filtering turned on) might not be best (but, then again, most people might prefer it). More fundamentally, the problem of determining what information is relevant and desired does not have an easy or obvious solution. We observed (in the box in Section 3.2.4) that in some situations filtering out too much is better than filtering out too little, while in other situations the opposite is true. Any solution that a search engine or social media service adopts will not be perfect. However, when people do not know that they are seeing filtered information, they do not know to turn off the filter or to look elsewhere for more information. There should be a clear indication when filters are active and an explanation of what they do.

How else does the Web narrow information streams? In Chapter 2 we saw that search engines personalize results for users based on their location, past searches, profile information, and other criteria. Given the huge amount of information on the Web, this fine tuning helps us find what we want quickly. It is very valuable. However, it does mean that when we are searching for something outside our usual context, including perhaps information on controversial subjects, we might have to make an effort to look a little harder.

Do the various aspects of the Internet that narrow our information stream significantly diminish access to different points of view on controversial social and political topics? Members of radical political groups (left and right) and cults got information and opinions from narrow sources well before the Web. Does the Web encourage or increase ideological isolation? Does it simply reflect the choices that some people have often made in the past? Does it make it more likely that we will see a variety of points of view? When we criticize aspects of the Web, it is helpful to look to human nature and the past for perspective. It is also helpful to look toward an ideal to suggest improvements.

Abdicating responsibility

> *I have a spelling checker.*
> *It came with my PC.*
> *It plainly marks four my revue,*
> *Miss steaks aye can knot sea.*
> *Eye ran this poem threw it,*
> *I'm sure your pleased too no.*
> *It's letter perfect in it's weigh,*
> *My checker tolled me sew.*
>
> —Jerrold H. Zar, "Candidate for a Pullet Surprise"[11]

The tools and technologies we use encourage certain practices and consequences by making them easier. The spelling-checker verse above humorously illustrates the problem of doing what the tool makes easy and ignoring other important tasks. Software can check the spelling of all the words in a document faster than a person can find the first one by flipping through the pages of a printed dictionary. But a simple spell checker looks up each word only to discover whether it is in its dictionary. It does not check whether the writer uses the word properly.*

---

* Grammar checkers were rudimentary when the poem first circulated on the Internet. They would now catch some of the errors.

The convenience of using a computer system and abdication of responsibility to exercise judgment can encourage a mental laziness with serious consequences. A trucker in Britain got his truck stuck on a small farm road after ignoring a sign saying the road was not suitable for large vehicles. He was unquestioningly following the directions of a navigation system. A newspaper editor in Pakistan received a letter to the editor by email and inserted it into the newspaper without reading beyond the title. The letter was an attack on the prophet Muhammad. Angry Muslims set fires in the newspaper office. Several editors were arrested and charged with blasphemy, sometimes punishable by death.[12] Back when newspaper content was still typeset and copyedited, such an accident would have been unlikely.

Businesses make decisions about loan and insurance applications with the help of software that analyzes risks. School districts make decisions about the progress of students and the careers of administrators on the basis of computer-graded and -calibrated tests. They sometimes make bad decisions because of ignorance of the kinds of errors that limitations of the system can cause. Law enforcement agents arrested people when a check of an FBI database showed an arrest warrant for someone with a similar name. Do officers think that because the computer displayed the warrant, the system has decided that the person they are checking is the wanted person? Or does an officer understand that the system simply displays any close matches and that the responsibility for the arrest decision lies with the officer?

Sometimes reliance on a computer system rather than human judgment becomes "institutionalized" in the sense that an organization's management and the legal system can exert strong pressure on individual professionals or employees to do what the computer says. In bureaucracies, a decision maker might feel that there is less personal risk (and less bother) in just accepting what the software produces rather than doing additional checking or making a decision the software does not support. Computer programs advise doctors on treatments for patients. It is critical to remember that, in complex fields, the computer systems might provide valuable information and ideas but might not be good enough to substitute for an experienced professional's judgment. In some institutions, when something goes wrong, "I did what the program recommended" is a stronger defense (to superiors or against a lawsuit) than "I did what my professional judgment and experience recommended." Such institutions are encouraging abdicatation of personal responsibility, with potentially harmful results.

7.1.2 COMPUTER MODELS

> *Likeness to truth is not the same thing as truth.*
>
> —Peter L. Bernstein[13]

Evaluating models

Computer-generated predictions based on mathematical models of subjects with important social impact frequently appear in the news. Figure 7.1 shows a few examples. A mathematical model is a collection of data and equations describing, or simulating, characteristics and behavior of the thing studied. The models and simulations of interest to us here require so much data and/or computation that they must be run on computers. Researchers and engineers do extensive modeling to simulate both physical systems, such as the design for a new car or the flow of water in a river, and intangible systems, such as parts of the economy. Models allow us to simulate and investigate the possible effects of different designs, scenarios, and policies. They have obvious social and economic benefits: They help train operators of power plants, submarines, and airplanes. They enable us to consider alternatives and make better decisions, reducing waste, cost, and risk. They enable us to project trends and plan better for the future.

Although the models we consider are abstract (i.e., mathematical), the meaning of the word "model" here is similar to its meaning in "model airplane." Models are simplifications. Model airplanes generally do not have an engine, and the wing flaps might not move. In a chemistry class, we could use sticks and balls to build models of molecules to help us understand their properties. The molecule models might not show the components of the individual atoms. Similarly, mathematical models do not include equations for every factor that could influence the outcome. They often include simplified

---

- Population growth
- The cost of a proposed government program
- The effects of second-hand smoke
- When we will run out of a critical natural resource
- The effects of a tax cut on the economy
- The threat of global warming
- When a big earthquake is likely to occur

Figure 7.1   Some problems studied with computer models.

equations because the correct ones are unknown or too complicated. For example, we use a constant known as the acceleration of gravity in a simple equation to determine when an object dropped from a high place will hit the ground. We ignore the effect of wind in the equation, but, on some days, wind could make a difference.

Physical models are usually not the same size as the real thing. Model planes are smaller; the molecule model is larger. In mathematical models, it is time rather than physical size that often differs from reality. Computations done on a computer to model a complex physical process in detail often take more time than the actual process takes. For models of long-range phenomena, such as population growth and climate change, the computation must take less time than the real phenomenon for the results to be useful.

Predictions from expensive computers and complex computer programs impress people, but models vary enormously in quality. Some are worthless. Others are very reliable. Politicians and special interest groups use model predictions to justify multibillion-dollar programs and laws with significant impact on the economy and the standard of living and choices of millions of people. It is important for both computer professionals and the general public to have some idea of what is in such computer programs, where their uncertainties and weaknesses might lie, and how to evaluate their claims. It is the professional and ethical responsibility of those who design and develop models for public issues to describe honestly and accurately the results, assumptions, and limitations of their models.

The following questions help us determine the accuracy and usefulness of a model.

1. How well do the modelers understand the underlying science or theory (be it physics, chemistry, economics, or whatever) of the system they are studying? How well understood are the relevant properties of the materials involved? How accurate and complete are the data?

2. Models necessarily involve assumptions and simplifications of reality. What are the assumptions and simplifications in the model?

3. How closely do the results or predictions of the model correspond with results from physical experiments or real experience?

Among three models developed to predict the change in health care costs that would result if the United States adopted a national health system, the predictions varied by hundreds of billions of dollars. Two of the models predicted large increases and one predicted a drastic decrease.[14] Why was there such a difference? There are both political and technical reasons why models might not be accurate. Political reasons, especially for this example, are probably obvious. In addition to technical reasons that the questions above suggest (incomplete knowledge of the system being modeled, incomplete or inaccurate data, and faulty assumptions or oversimplification), other reasons are that computing power could be inadequate for the number of computations needed to model the full complexity of the system, and the difficulty, if not impossibility, of numerically quantifying variables that represent human values and choices.

- How many times do parents reuse a cloth diaper before discarding it? (Values ranged from 90 to 167.)

- Should the model give credit for energy recovered from incineration of waste? Or does pollution from incineration counterbalance the benefit?

- How many cloth diapers do parents use each time they change a baby? (Many parents use two at once for increased protection.) Numbers in the models ranged from 1.72 to 1.9.

- How should the model count pesticides used in growing cotton?

Figure 7.2 Factors in diaper life cycle modeling.

Are reusable (washable cloth) diapers better for the environment than disposable diapers? When environmentalists proposed bans and taxes on disposable diapers, this controversy consumed almost as much energy as diaper manufacturing. Several modelers developed computer models to study the question. We call this particular kind of model a life cycle analysis. It attempts to consider the resource use and environmental effects of all aspects of the product, including manufacture, use, and disposal. To illustrate how difficult such a study might be, Figure 7.2 lists a few of the questions about which the modelers made assumptions. Depending on the assumptions, the conclusions differed.[15] It is worth noting also that the models focused on one quality—environmental impact. To make a personal decision, we might consider the results of such a model (if we think it reliable), and we might also consider other factors such as cost, aesthetics, convenience, comfort, and health risks.

The U.S. Army Corps of Engineers uses mathematical models to predict how long an artifically constructed or replenished beach will last before waves wash it away. Two geologists have explained weaknesses in these models.[16] Among other simplifying assumptions, the models assume that all waves have the same wavelength, that all waves come from the same direction, and that all grains of sand are the same size. A model uses only 6 of 49 parameters that might affect the amount of sand washed away. Even if these 6 are the most important (or if the model included all 49), the appropriate values for a particular beach are uncertain. Often, say the critics, the beaches do not last as long as the models predict, partly because the models do not accurately provide for relevant but irregular natural phenomena such as big storms.

Example: Modeling car crashes*

Car crash analysis programs use a technique called the finite-element method. They superimpose a grid on the frame of a car, dividing the car into a finite number of small

* An earlier version of this section appeared in my chapter, "Social and Legal Issues," in *An Invitation to Computer Science* by G. Michael Schneider and Judith L. Gersting, West Publishing Co., 1995. (Used with permission.)

pieces, or elements. The grid is entered into the program, along with data describing the specifications of the materials making up each element (e.g., density, strength, and elasticity). Suppose we are studying the effects on the structure of the car from a head-on collision. Engineers initialize data to represent a crash into a wall at a specified speed. The program computes the force, acceleration, and displacement at each grid point and the stress and strain within each element. It repeats these calculations to show what happens as time passes in small increments. These programs require intensive computation to simulate 40–100 milliseconds of real time from the impact.

A real crash test can cost several hundred thousand dollars. It includes building and testing a unique prototype for a new car design. The crash analysis programs allow engineers to consider alternatives—for example, to vary the thickness of steel for selected components, or change materials altogether—and discover the effect without building another prototype for each alternative. But how good are the programs?

How well is the physics of car crashes understood? How accurate and complete are the data? Force and acceleration are basic principles. The physics involved in these programs is straightforward. Engineers know the relevant properties of steel, plastics, aluminum, glass, and other materials in a car fairly well. However, although they understand the behavior of the materials when force is applied gradually, they know less about the behavior of some materials under abrupt acceleration, as in a high-speed impact, and their behavior near or at breaking point. There are good data on the density, elasticity, and other characteristics of materials used in the model.

What simplifications do the programs make? The grid pattern is the most obvious. A car is smooth, not made up of little blocks. Also, time is continuous. It does not pass in discrete steps. The accuracy of a simulation depends in part on how fine the grid is and how small the time intervals are. Current computer speeds allow updating the calculations on fine grids with small time intervals (e.g., one millionth of a second).

How do the computed results compare to actual crash tests on real cars? High-speed cameras record real crash tests. Engineers attach sensors to the car and mark reference points on the frame. They compare the values the sensors record with values the program computes. They physically measure the distortion or displacement of the reference points, then compare these measurements to the computed positions of the points. Starting with the results of the physical crash, the engineers use elementary physics to calculate backward and determine the deceleration and other forces acting on the car. They compare these to the values computed in the simulation. The conclusion? Crash analysis programs do an extremely good job. In part because of the confidence that has developed over time in the validity of the results, engineers use variations of the same crash analysis modeling programs in a large variety of other impact applications, including those in Figure 7.3.

Engineers who work with the crash analysis programs do not believe that they will or should eliminate physical crash testing. The computer program is an implementation of theory. Results could be poor if something happens that the program designers simply did

- Predict damage to a hazardous waste container if dropped.
- Predict damage to an airplane windshield or nacelle (engine covering) if hit by a bird.
- Determine whether beer cans would get dented if an assembly line were speeded up.
- Simulate a medical procedure called balloon angioplasty, where doctors insert a balloon in a blocked artery and inflate it to open the artery. The computer program helps researchers determine how to perform the procedure with less damage to the arterial wall.
- Predict the action of airbags and the proper location for sensors that inflate them.
- Design interior parts of cars to reduce injuries during crashes (e.g., from the impact of a steering wheel on a human chest).
- Design bicycle and motorcycle helmets to reduce head injuries.
- Design cameras to reduce damage if dropped.
- Forecast effects of earthquakes on bridges and buildings.

Figure 7.3   Other uses of crash analysis programs.

not consider. The crash analysis programs are excellent design tools that enable increases in safety with far less development cost. The physical crash test is confirmation.

Example: Modeling climate

The earth has Ice Ages and warm interglacial periods. We are now in an interglacial period that is more than 11,000 years old. Within such periods, climate varies over time and in different parts of the world. For example, the Northern Hemisphere experienced both a medieval warm period about a thousand years ago and a later colder period (roughly 1550–1850), sometimes called the Little Ice Age.

Climate change is a very complex phenomenon. Solar radiation warms the earth. Some of the heat is reflected back, and gases trap some in the atmosphere. The latter phenomenon is known as the greenhouse effect. Without it, the temperature on the earth would be too cold to support life. Water vapor is the main greenhouse gas, but there are several other significant greenhouse gases as well. Among those whose concentration has been increased by human activity (in particular, burning of fossil fuels), carbon dioxide (CO_2) is most important. An upward trend in CO_2 concentration began roughly 16,000 years ago. However, since the beginning of the Industrial Revolution, CO_2 concentration has been increasing at a faster rate.* Between the period 1850–1899 and the period 2001–

---

* CO_2 concentration has increased by almost 40% since 1750.[17] The older data come from measurements of gases trapped in ice cores drilled in Antarctica and Greenland.

2005, average global temperature rose roughly 0.76°C.*[18] The increase has been steeper since roughly 1980. The global temperature increase raised concern about the threat of excess global warming, possibly caused by human-induced increase of CO_2 and other greenhouse gases in the atmosphere. Global warming predictions are based on computer models of climate. We consider those models. Since 1990, the Intergovernmental Panel on Climate Change (IPCC), sponsored by the United Nations and the World Meteorological Organization, has published comprehensive reports on the science of climate change and the quality and projections of climate models roughly every five years. Much of the information in this section comes from those reports.[19]

Climate models, like the car crash analysis models, calculate relevant variables for grid points and elements (grid boxes) for specified simulated time intervals. The grid circles the earth, rises through the atmosphere, and goes down into the ocean. The models contain information about the sun's energy output; the orbit, inclination, and rotation of the earth; geography (a map of land masses); topography (mountains, etc.); clouds; sea and polar ice; soil and air moisture; and a large number of other factors. Equations simulate atmospheric pressure, temperature, wind speed and direction, moisture, precipitation, ocean currents, and so forth. Researchers use climate models to study several aspects of future climate. They try, for example, to determine the effect of doubling CO_2 concentration in the atmosphere. (Current trends suggest the concentration will have doubled, from its approximate level at the beginning of the 20th century, by some time in the 21st century.†) Models also project the likely increase in global temperature, sea level, and other climate characteristics in various scenarios with assumptions about population, industrial and economic activity, energy use, and so on, for the rest of this century. Another task for the models is to distinguish how much warming is caused by human activity and how much is natural. The IPCC has concluded that it is "extremely likely" that human activity has had a substantial warming effect on climate since 1750.[20]

Climate models have improved over the few decades that scientists have been developing and working with them. The models used in the 1980s and 1990s were quite limited. Here is a brief sampling of simplifications, assumptions, and factors modelers did not fully understand: The models did not distinguish day and night.[21] They used a fairly coarse grid (with points roughly 500 kilometers apart). They did not include the El Niño phenomenon. They made assumptions about methane (a greenhouse gas) that scientists later determined were incorrect. They did not include aerosols (small particles in the air) that have a cooling effect. Clouds are extremely important to climate, but many processes involved with the formation, effects, and dissipation of clouds were not particularly well understood. The IPCC summarized in 2001: "As has been the case since the first IPCC Assessment Report in 1990, probably the greatest uncertainty in future projections of

---

* With an error range of ±0.19.

† Other greenhouse gases are included too by converting their amount and effect to the equivalent number of units of CO_2.

climate arises from clouds and their interactions with radiation. . . . Clouds represent a significant source of potential error in climate simulations."[22] The extremely simplified representations of the oceans in these models was another very significant weakness. Computing power was insufficient to do the many calculations to simulate ocean behavior. When run on past data, some of the early climate models predicted temperature increases three to five times as high as what actually occurred over the previous century. The 1990 IPCC report predicted that temperature would increase 0.3°C per decade (with an error range of 0.2°–0.5°C). The actual temperature increase over the next two decades was lower than that.[23] Thus, it should not be surprising that there was much skepticism about the climate models and their projections.

Current models are more detailed and complex. Increased computer power allows the use of finer grids (with points spaced roughly 100–300 kilometers apart) and more experiments with the models. Increased data collection and basic science research have been improving the understanding of the behavior and interactions of climate system components. The models project that doubling the concentration of greenhouse gases in the atmosphere will cause a global temperature increase within the range 2°–4.5°C. The models project warming of 0.2°C per decade for the next few decades and a sea level rise of between 8 and 23 inches by the end of the 21st century.[24]

How well is the science understood? How accurate are the data? Climatologists know an enormous amount about climate. The models incorporate a huge amount of good science and data. But the amount not known is also large.

Much of the variation in model results comes from the still troublesome lack of full understanding of clouds. When the earth warms, water evaporates, and the additional water vapor in the atmosphere absorbs more thermal energy, warming the atmosphere farther. On the other hand, water vapor forms clouds, which reflect incoming solar radiation with a cooling effect. Thus, clouds have positive (destabilizing) and negative (stabilizing) feedback effects. The basic science of the mechanisms is fairly well understood, but not the complexity and magnitude of the feedbacks.[25]

A related area of uncertainty has been the impact of variations in output from the sun. Recent research on the interactions between solar activity, cosmic rays (radiation from space), and cloud formation suggests that solar activity might have an impact on cloud formation, and thus on warming, that the climate models do not include. The research is at an early stage, the theory is controversial, and the magnitude of the impact is unknown. Experiments are continuing.[26]

There is insufficient data on many phenomena for the period before satellites collected data. For example, the IPCC lists among "key uncertainties" insufficient data to draw conclusions about trends in thickness of Antarctic sea ice.

The temperature data sets that models use for temperature over the past century have been a source of some contention. They include many kinds of limitations (for example, few monitoring stations in the oceans and remote land areas) and errors. In 2011, the Berkeley Earth Surface Temperature project completed a multiyear effort analyzing temperature data from 15 different data sets. It reviewed algorithms and statistical methods used to develop the data sets, and it developed new statistical methods to try to overcome problems in the previous methods. It developed and published a new global surface temperature record and provided an uncertainty analysis.[27] Climate science researchers had much praise for the quality of the work in this project and for Berkeley Earth's decision to openly publish its methodology.

What are the assumptions and simplifications in the models? Ideally, equations derived from the underlying science (generally, physics and chemistry) would model all the processes that affect climate. This is not possible, because it would require too much computation time and because all the underlying science is not known. Simplified equations, called parametrizations, represent many processes; they seem to give realistic results but are not derived from scientific theory. The specific parametrizations vary among the models, reflecting the choices of the modelers.

The IPCC acknowledges that the underlying complexity of the problem still hampers the accuracy of projections for future climate change. That is, even the extremely powerful computers of today are not sufficient to achieve an ideal level of resolution (grid size) and to include simulation of more processes that affect climate.[28]

The model projections based on scenarios (rather than a specific increase in greenhouse gas concentration) include numerous assumptions about technological development, political control of emissions, population, economic development, energy use, and so on, throughout a century.

Science and fiction

Why do science fiction movies about global warming show the buildings of cities underwater? The entertainment industry exaggerates and dramatizes, of course. Why does an exhibit in a science museum show water up to the middle of the Statue of Liberty (about 200 feet above sea level)? A climate scientist once said: "[T]o capture the public's imagination," "we have to offer up scary scenarios, make simplified dramatic statements, and make little mention of any doubts we may have. . . . Each of us has to decide what the right balance is between being effective and being honest."[29] Although he said he hoped climate scientists could be both effective and honest, there is clearly an ethical problem when we trade honesty for something else. Is it a good idea? A 20-inch rise in sea level would be a very significant problem, but one we can tackle. Tens or hundreds of feet of sea level rise would be an enormous disaster. Exaggeration might lead people to take constructive action. Or exaggeration might lead to overreaction and counterproductive, expensive actions, draining resources from effective approaches. If we hope to solve real potential problems (such as flooding in low-lying areas), we must first identify them accurately.

How well do predictions of the models correspond with actual experience? The models predict seasonal variations and other actual broad-scale phenomena. The general patterns of predictions by different models are similar. For example, they all predict warming, and they all predict that more of the warming would take place near the poles and in winter. Many models now do a good job predicting air temperature near the surface of the earth (that is, close to observed temperatures) for the recent past. The models do well enough that the IPCC expresses many of its projections as very likely or likely.

For more than a decade at the beginning of the 21st century, global temperature fluctuated but did not rise overall. The models did not indicate that this would happen. Scientists are devising and testing theories to account for it. The amount of water vapor in the stratosphere is a key suspect.[30] Models designed to project long-term trends might not predict short-term variations well. Thus, we do not know yet if the first decade of the century was a short-term variation or whether it will require revisions in the models.

7.2 The "Digital Divide"[31]

The term *digital divide* refers to the fact that some groups of people (the "haves") enjoy access to and regularly use the various forms of modern information technology, while others (the "have-nots") do not. The focus of the discussion about "the digital divide" has shifted over time. In the 1990s, the focus was on access to computers and the Internet for poor people, people in rural areas, and certain demographic groups within the United States (and other developed countries). As more people acquired digital technology and Internet access, focus shifted to a divide among those who have broadband and those who do not. There is also more focus now on the digital divide between developed countries and poor countries.

7.2.1 TRENDS IN COMPUTER ACCESS

Once upon a time, everyone in the world had equal access to personal computers and the Internet. They did not exist, and we all had none. Later, a small, elite minority enjoyed these new, expensive tools. As the technology began to spread and its value became clearer, people became more concerned about the gap in access. Poor children and children of some ethnic minorities had less access to computers both in schools and at home. In the early 1990s, only about 10% of Net users were women. By 1997, the gender gap had vanished,[32] but other gaps remained.* Black and Hispanic households were about half as likely as the general population to own a computer. Access in rural and remote regions lagged behind the cities.

---

* A gender gap remains among those who work in information technology fields. Only about one-quarter are women, and the percentage of women undergraduates interested in the computer science major dropped drastically between 2000 and 2009.

Cost is one factor that affects access by the general population. Ease of use is another. At first, personal computers and the Internet were difficult to use. Software innovations, such as point-and-click graphical user interfaces, Web browsers, and search engines made computer use significantly more comfortable for ordinary people. With lower prices, more useful applications, and ease of use, ownership and access spread quickly. The data I found about the extent of computer ownership and Web access differ in specific numbers, but all showed the same trends: In 1990, 22% of households in the United States owned a computer. In 2001, 84% of homes with children in middle and high school had Internet access. That was a significantly higher percentage of households overall, suggesting that families perceived access to be important for their children and allocated their spending accordingly.[33]

Individuals, businesses, community organizations, foundations, and government programs contributed to the spread of computers and Internet access. Internet cafés sprang up from Alaska to Cairo in the 1990s when Net access from home was relatively uncommon. The federal government and local governments spent billions of dollars on technology for schools. By the end of the 1990s, most public libraries provided Internet access for the public for free. By 2000, 98% of high schools had Internet access. At about the same time, African Americans, people 65 and older, and Hispanics increased their use of the Internet significantly. Groups with low access in earlier years began to catch up. The gaps among Hispanic, black, and white people almost completely disappeared among those with the same education levels.[34] By 2011, there were more than 300 million cellphone subscriptions in the United States. Computing and new communication technology reached more households much more quickly than earlier technologies such as telephone, television, electricity, and automobiles.

Virtually all technological innovation is first available to the rich (or others willing to pay the initially high price). The early purchases finance improvements in design and production techniques that bring the price down. Prices of many consumer products follow this pattern. Telephones and televisions were originally luxuries of the rich. Now, almost everyone in developed countries has them. (By 2006, there were more televisions than people in the United States.) When first introduced in the 1980s, compact disk music players cost $1000. Now we play music and video on our phones. Computer prices plunged more dramatically than prices of most other products, even while the memory, speed, and variety of input/output devices and software increased enormously.* The vast resources of the Internet are available for about what home telephone service used to cost. The phenomenon that new technologies and inventions first are expensive luxuries, then become cheaper and spread throughout the population, has led some observers to conclude that it is more accurate to think of people as "haves" and "have-laters" rather than "haves" and "have-nots."[35]

---

* For example, the cost of disk storage fell from hundreds of dollars per megabyte in the 1980s to about $100 a terabyte (one million times as much space) by 2012.

Access to broadband connection is a newer version of a digital divide. The same demographic groups that were the have-laters with respect to Internet access in the 1990s had less broadband access in the first decade of the 2000s, with similar disadvantages. Without broadband access, it is more difficult to find employment opportunities, access news and information, and make use of some online health information and tools. Children are less likely to graduate from high school. People without broadband are less likely to create Internet content. According to Connected Nation, in 2011 only 46% of low-income households with children and 37% of low-income minority households with children had broadband at home, compared to 66% of households nationally. (About 20% of all U.S. households had broadband in 2003.) The largest barrier to adopting broadband, according to people surveyed, was cost, followed by digital literacy and not believing that the Internet was relevant to their lives. In 2011, the FCC approved a program to extend broadband service to rural areas of the United States. Businesses and nonprofit organizations started a program to address cost and digital literacy. Under this initiative, major cable carriers offer broadband service at a low price to low-income customers. Best Buy, Microsoft, America's Promise Alliance, and United Way, among many others, provide digital literacy training.[36]

A related digital divide exists among content consumers and content producers on the Internet. Internet users create blogs, Web pages, videos, and product reviews. Being a content creator empowers a user to communicate his or her message to a large number of people. The Internet can be a strong agent for change for those who have the skills, education, and tools to create content. Content creators tend to be people who access the Internet frequently from multiple places using multiple gadgets. They also are more educated.[37] The content-production divide shows a gap among users based on socioeconomic status. How should we view the Internet content-production divide? Before the Internet, a very small percent of people wrote books and articles and produced movies and television shows. The vast majority of people were content consumers only. Is the current divide less of a social problem than the pre-Internet divide because so many more people can now create content, or is it more of a problem than before because it isolates a smaller part of the population that cannot?

7.2.2 THE GLOBAL DIVIDE AND THE NEXT BILLION USERS

Approximately two billion people worldwide use the Internet, a fivefold increase over roughly a decade.[38] From one perspective, that is an extraordinary accomplishment in a very short time. From another perspective, it means that about five billion people do not use the Internet. Lack of access to the Internet in much of the world has the same causes as lack of health care, education, and so on: poverty, isolation, poor economies, and politics.

Both nonprofit organizations and huge computer companies have ongoing projects to spread computer access to more people in developing countries. Some companies use the catchphrase "the next billion users" to describe the people their programs address. For the companies, these programs create good will and—if successful in improving the standard of living and economies of the target countries—a large future customer base. Companies have trained hundreds of thousands of teachers to use technology effectively in classrooms in China, India, and other countries.

One Laptop per Child is a nonprofit organization that supplies an inexpensive laptop computer specially designed for elementary school children in developing countries. The laptop works in extreme heat or cold, extremes of humidity, and dusty or rainy environments. The power requirements are very low. The program provided an important lesson: giving out computers and walking away will not close the digital divide. The success of the program in implementing the technology into school curricula depends on the presence of supporting social and technical infrastructures such as electricity, networks, tech support, parental support, teacher attitudes towards technology, and administrative school support. Purely financial resources can be less important than these factors.[39]

Some people active in movements to shrink the "digital divide" emphasize the need to provide access in ways appropriate to the local culture. For example, one website argues that access can hurt the poor "by loosening the bonds of tradition." In many countries, access "is one-way, entertainment-oriented, commercial." Access might accelerate the exodus of untrained, unprepared young people from rural areas into cities.[40] How significant are these concerns? What can be done to alleviate them?

Only a few years ago, most people in the world had never made a telephone call. By the end of 2010, there were five billion cellphone subscriptions.*[41] Almost every time I have read about a program to bring Internet access or cellphones to rural, third-world adults over the past several years, the most immediate uses are similar. Farmers use the Internet to learn about better farming techniques and to get up-to-date pricing information for their crops. Fishermen use their cellphones to find a nearby village where they will get a good price for their catch. As the technology spreads, food production and economic well-being improve. Some see each new digital divide as a serious social problem. What is perhaps most surprising is how quickly most of these divides shrink and how much more quickly they shrink than did previous technological divides between rich and poor, men and women, black and white, or developed and undeveloped countries.

7.3 Neo-Luddite Views of Computers, Technology, and Quality of Life

> *The microchip is . . . made of silicon, or sand—a natural resource*
> *that is in great abundance and has virtually no monetary value. Yet the*

---

* That does not mean that five billion people had cellphones. In wealthier areas, some people have more than one.

combination of a few grains of this sand and the infinite inventiveness of the human mind has led to the creation of a machine that will both create trillions of dollars of added wealth for the inhabitants of the earth in the next century and will do so with incomprehensibly vast savings in physical labor and natural resources.

—Stephen Moore[42]

Quite apart from the environmental and medical evils associated with them being produced and used, there are two moral judgments against computers. One is that computerization enables the large forces of our civilization to operate more swiftly and efficiently in their pernicious goals of making money and producing things . . . And secondly, in the course of using these, these forces are destroying nature with more speed and efficiency than ever before.

—Kirkpatrick Sale[43]

7.3.1 CRITICISMS OF COMPUTING TECHNOLOGIES

The quotations above, both from 1995, illustrate the extreme divergence of views about the anticipated value of computer technology. Evaluations cover the spectrum from "miracle" to "catastrophe." Although most of this book discusses problems that arise with the use of computers, the Internet, and other digital communications technologies, the implicit (and sometimes explicit) view has been that these technologies are a positive development bringing us many benefits. The potential for loss of freedom and privacy via government surveillance and the building of consumer dossiers is a serious danger. Computer crime is expensive, and changes in employment are disruptive. Our discussion of systems failures in the next chapter warns us that some potential applications can have horrifying risks. We might urgently try to prevent implementation of some applications and urgently advocate for increased protection from risks, yet not consider the threats and risks as reasons for condemning the technology as a whole. For the most part, we have looked at new risks and negative side effects as problems that occur in the natural process of change, either problems we need to solve or the price we pay for the benefits, part of a trade-off. Many people with quite different political views share this attitude, although they disagree about the significance of specific computer-related problems and about exactly how to solve them.

On the other hand, there are people who utterly reject the view that computing technology is a positive development with many important benefits. They see the benefits as few and overwhelmingly outweighed by the damage done. Neil Postman says that voting, shopping, banking, and getting information at home online is a "catastrophe." There are fewer opportunities for people to be "co-present," resulting in isolation from neighbors. Richard Sclove and Jeffrey Scheuer argue that electronic communication will erode family and community life to the point that people will mourn the loss of depth and meaning in their lives.[44] A comment made by one reviewer of this book illustrates the difference in perspective. He objected to the "gift of fire" analogy I use to suggest that computers can be very useful and also very dangerous. The reviewer thought "Pandora's box" was more appropriate. Pandora's box held "all the ills of mankind." Kirkpatrick Sale, author of *Rebels Against the Future*, used to demonstrate his opinion of computers by smashing one with a sledgehammer at public appearances.

In England in 1811–1812, people burned factories and mills in efforts to stop the technologies and social changes that were eliminating their jobs. Many were weavers who had worked at home on small machines. They were called Luddites.* For 200 years, the memory of the violent Luddite uprising has endured as the most dramatic symbol of opposition to the Industrial Revolution. The term "Luddite" has long been a derisive description for people who oppose technological progress. More recently, critics of technology have adopted it as an honorable term. Kirkpatrick Sale and many others who share his viewpoint call themselves neo-Luddites, or simply Luddites.

What do the neo-Luddites find so reprehensible about computers? Some of their criticisms are problems that also trouble people whose view of computing technology is generally positive, problems we discussed in earlier chapters. One of the differentiating characteristics of the neo-Luddites is that they focus on these problems, seeing no solutions or trade-offs, and conclude that computers are a terribly bad development for humankind. Among their specific criticisms are the following:

- Computers cause massive unemployment and de-skilling of jobs. "Sweatshop labor is involved in their manufacture."[45]

- Computers "manufacture needs"; that is, we use them just because they are there, not because they satisfy real needs.

- Computers cause social inequity.

- Computers cause social disintegration; they are dehumanizing. They weaken communities and lead to isolation of people from each other.

- Computers separate humans from nature and destroy the environment.

- Computers benefit big business and big government most.

- Use of computers in schools thwarts development of social skills, human values, and intellectual skills in children. They create an "ominous uniformity of knowledge" consistent with corporate values.[46]

---

* The name Luddite comes from General Ned Ludd, the fictitious, symbolic leader of the movement.

- Computers do little or nothing to solve real human problems. For example, Neil Postman, in response to claims of the benefits of access to information, argues that "if families break up, children are mistreated, crime terrorizes a city, education is impotent, it does not happen because of inadequate information."[47]

Some of these criticisms might seem unfair. The conditions in computer factories hardly compare to conditions in the sweatshop factories of the early Industrial Revolution. In Chapter 6, we saw that computers eliminate some jobs, and that the pace of computerization causes disruptions, but the case that computers, and technology in general, cause massive unemployment is not convincing. Blaming computers for social inequity in the world ignores thousands of years of history. Postman is right that inadequate information is not the source of most social problems. A computer in the classroom does not replace good parents in the home. But should this be a criticism of computers and information systems? Access to information and communication can assist in solving problems and is not likely to hurt. The main problem for ordinary people, Postman says, is how to find meaning in life. We need answers to questions like "Why are we here?" and "How are we supposed to behave?"[48] Is it a valid criticism of computing technology that it does not solve fundamental social and philosophical problems that have engaged us for thousands of years?

To the neo-Luddites, the view that computers are fundamentally malevolent is part of a wider view that almost all of technology is malevolent. To the modern-day Luddites, computer technology is just the latest, but in many ways the worst, stage in the decline of what was good in human society. Computers are worse than earlier technologies because of their enormous speed and flexibility. Computers increase the negative trends that technology causes. Thus, if one points out that a particular problem blamed on computers already existed because of an earlier technology, Luddites consider the distinction to be a minor one.

The depth of the antipathy to technology in the Luddite view is perhaps made clearer by attitudes toward common devices most of us use daily. For example, Sale has said, "I find talking on the phone a physical pain, as well as a mental anguish." Sven Birkerts, another critic of computers, says that if he lived in 1900, he would probably have opposed the telephone.* Speaking of the invention of the printing press, Sale laments that "literacy . . . destroys orality." He regards not only computers but civilization as a catastrophe. Some of us see modern medicine as a life-saving and life-enhancing boon to humanity; some Luddites point out that it gave us the population explosion and extended senility.[49]

---

* Critics of telephones complained that they replaced true human interaction with disembodied, remote voices. They actually expanded and deepened social relationships for isolated people—for example, women in general (farm wives, in particular) and the elderly.[50]

Having read and listened to the arguments of technology enthusiasts and technology critics, I find it striking that different people look at the same history, the same society, the same products and services, the same jobs—and come to diametrically opposed conclusions about what they see. There is a fundamental difference between the world views of supporters and opponents of technology. It is more than the difference between seeing a glass as half full or half empty. The difference seems to be one of contrasting views about what should be in the glass. Supporters of technology see an upward trend in quality of life, beginning with people living at the mercy of nature with an empty glass that technology has been gradually filling. Neo-Luddites view the glass as originally full when people lived in small communities with little impact on nature; they see technology as draining the glass.

The neo-Luddite view is associated with a particular view of the appropriate way of life for human beings. For example, Sale's first point, in the quotation at the beginning of this section, makes the moral judgment that making money and producing things is pernicious. His introductory remark and his second point barely hint at the unusually high valuation he places on not disturbing nature (unusually high even in the contemporary context, where there is much awareness of the importance of protecting the environment). We explore these views further.

7.3.2   Views of Economics, Nature, and Human Needs

Luddites generally have a negative view of capitalism, business, markets, consumer products, factories, and modern forms of work. They see the profit-seeking goals of businesses as in fundamental conflict with the well-being of workers and the natural environment. They see work in factories, large offices, and business in general as dehumanizing, dreary, and bad for the health of the workers. Hence, for example, the Luddite criticisms of the clock. Neil Postman describes the invention of the clock as "the technology of greatest use to men who wished to devote themselves to the accumulation of money."[51]

Choice of words, making subtle differences in a statement, sometimes illustrate the difference in perspective between Luddites and non-Luddites. What is the purpose of technology? To the Luddites, it is to eliminate jobs to reduce the costs of production. To proponents of technology, it is to reduce the effort needed to produce goods and services. The two statements say nearly the same thing, but the first suggests massive unemployment, profits for capitalists, and a poorer life for most workers. The second suggests improvements in wealth and the standard of living.

The Luddite view combines a negative attitude toward business with a high estimation of the power of corporations to manipulate and control workers and consumers. For example, Richard Sclove describes telecommuting as being "imposed by business." (Interestingly, one of the common criticisms of the Industrial Revolution was that working in factories instead of at home weakened families and local community.)

Luddites make particularly strong criticisms of automobiles, of cities, and of most technologies involved in communications and transportation. Thus, it is worth noting that most of us get both personal and social benefits from them. Cities are centers of culture, wealth production, education, and job opportunities.[52] Modern transportation and communication reduce the price of products and increase their variety and availability. For example, we can eat fresh fruits and vegetables all year. We can look up menus and movie schedules on our smartphone to find what we want. We can shop worldwide on the Web. We can commute a long distance to take a better job without having to sell our house and move. If we move to a new city for college or a job, modern conveniences such as airplanes, telephones, and the Internet make the separations less unpleasant. We can visit more often in person. We can share greetings and activities with friends and family members via social media. Luddites and other critics of technology do not value these advantages highly. In some cases, in their point of view, the advantages are merely ameliorating other problems technology causes. For example, Postman quotes Sigmund Freud's comment, "If there had been no railway to conquer distances, my child would never have left his native town and I should need no telephone to hear his voice."[53]

Does the technology create the need for itself?

A common criticism of capitalism is that it survives by convincing us to buy products we do not need. Luddites argue, similarly, that technology causes production of things we do not need. This contrasts with the market-oriented view that sees consumer choices as determining which products, services, and businesses succeed or fail (in the absence of government favoritism, subsidies, and restrictions). We examine the issue of created needs.

Sale argued that small, portable computers do not "meet any known or expressed need," but companies produced them simply because miniaturization of computing components made it possible. People have bought many millions of laptops, tablet computers, and cellphones. The number of uses is phenomenal. So, does a mobile computer meet a need? It depends on what we mean by "need." Do we need to do homework in the backyard or listen to music on an iPod? Does an architect or contractor need a laptop at a construction site? Those who emphasize the value of individual action and choices argue that needs are relative to goals, and goals are held by individuals. Thus, should we ask whether "we," as a society, need portable computers? Or should this be an individual decision with different responses? Many people demonstrate, by their purchases, that they want portable computers. Anyone who does not feel a desire or need for one does not have to buy one. The Luddites, who believe that advertising, work pressure, or other external forces manipulate buyers, reject this individual-oriented approach.

Environmental and anti-technology groups use computers and the Web. The editor of *Wild Earth*, who considers himself a neo-Luddite, said he "inclines toward the view

Wal-Mart and e-commerce versus downtown and community[54]

Does electronic commerce force changes on communities that no one wants? Richard Sclove and Jeffrey Scheuer think so.[55] They use the analogy of a Wal-Mart store draining business from downtown shops, resulting in the decline of the downtown community, a "result that no consumers wanted or intended." They generalize from the Wal-Mart scenario to cyberspace. As we conduct more economic transactions electronically, we lose more local stores, local professional and social services, and convivial public spaces like the downtowns of small towns. Consumers are "compelled" to use electronic services, "like it or not." Other strong critics of technology share the underlying point of view of Sclove and Scheuer, so it is worth examining their argument.

The Wal-Mart analogy is a good one. The scenario is useful for illustrating and clarifying some issues about the impact of e-commerce on communities. Suppose, say Sclove and Scheuer, that a new Wal-Mart store has opened just outside of town and about half the town residents begin to do about a third of their shopping there, while the others continue to do all their shopping downtown. Everyone shops downtown, and everyone wants the downtown stores to remain. But downtown stores have lost about 16.5% of their sales, and many will not survive. Sclove and Scheuer describe this as an "involuntary transformation" that no consumer wanted or intended. It occurs, they say, because of a "perverse market dynamic." The changes, however, are not involuntary or perverse. The core of the problem with Sclove's and Scheuer's interpretation is their failure to make two important distinctions: the distinction between wanting something and the willingness to pay for it, and the distinction between something being coerced or involuntary, on the one hand, and being unwanted, unintended, or unexpected on the other.

Consider a simpler situation for a moment. Suppose we poll the adult residents of a small town with a population of, say, 3000 and ask if they would like to have a fine French restaurant in town. Almost everyone says yes. Will a French restaurant open in the town? Probably not. Almost everyone wants it, yet there is not enough potential business for it to survive. There is a market dynamic at work, but it is not perverse. The fact that consumers want a particular service, store, or product is irrelevant if not enough people are willing to pay the prices that make the business viable. In Sclove's

and Scheuer's Wal-Mart scenario, the downtown stores could stay in business if the people were willing to pay higher prices to make up for the 16.5% of revenue lost to Wal-Mart. But we know that if the stores raise prices, they will almost certainly lose even more customers. The town residents are not willing to pay what it costs to keep the downtown stores in business. You might object: The townspeople did not have to pay the higher prices before. Why now? Because now the people who shop at Wal-Mart—or online—*have another choice*. Whatever price advantage or convenience lured them, they were not getting that benefit before. Again, a market dynamic is at work, but not a perverse one: competition.

The second issue about the Wal-Mart/e-commerce scenario is whether the change is an "involuntary" transformation. Sclove and Scheuer say that, as local businesses decline, people will be compelled to use electronic services, like it or not. Is this accurate? No more so than Wal-Mart shoppers or cyberspace enthusiasts were compelled to shop downtown (or from other offline stores), like it or not, before they had the new option. The new status quo is no more involuntary than the previous one. Although no one wants to see the downtown decline, the actions that could lead to that result are all voluntary. When a new store opens (online or offline), no one is forced to shop there. The impact on the downtown stores might not have been obvious to all the townspeople at the beginning (although now it is common enough that they might anticipate it), but an unexpected or unintended result is not the same as a coerced result. In a free society, individuals make millions of decisions based on their knowledge and preferences. This decentralized, individualized decision making produces a constantly changing pattern of stores, services, and investments (not to mention social and cultural patterns). No one can predict exactly what the result will be, and no one intends a particular picture of the economy or society, but (apart from government subsidies, prohibitions, and regulations) the actions of the consumers and merchants are voluntary. No one person can expect to have exactly the mix of shopping options (or other community characteristics) that he or she wants. If the result flows from the myriad decisions that consumers and producers make, it is not coerced. It is the process, not the result, that tells us whether an outside force is coercing people.

Do we need cellphones?

Hundreds of thousands of people have heart attacks in the United States each year. Treatment received in the first few minutes can be critical to their survival. A fire department in California helped develop a smartphone app that alerts people trained in CPR if they are near the location where a person is having a heart attack, perhaps in the same office building, shopping center, or neighborhood. The app provides the location of the victim and the locations of any nearby emergency defibrillator devices, so a trained person can get to the scene quickly and has the tools to save a life.

that technology is inherently evil," but he "disseminates this view via E-mail, computer, and laser printer."[56] An interviewer reported that in 2007, after a long career attacking computers, Kirkpatrick Sale was using a laptop. The question is: Are Sale and the editor of *Wild Earth* using computer equipment because of an artificial need or because it is useful and helpful to them? Sale sees the use of computers as an uncomfortable compromise. The use of computers, he says, insidiously embeds into the user the values and thought processes of the society that makes the technology.[57]

The argument that capitalists or technologies manipulate people to buy things they do not really want, like the argument that use of computers has an insidiously corrupting effect on computer users, displays a low view of the judgment and autonomy of ordinary people. It is one thing to differ with another person's values and choices. It is another to conclude that, because of the difference, the other person is weak and incapable of making his or her own decisions. The Luddite view of the appropriate way of life puts little value on modern comforts and conveniences or on the availability of a large variety of goods and services. Perhaps most people value these things more highly than the Luddites do. To get a clearer understanding of the Luddite view of a proper life style, we consider some of their comments on the relationship of humans and nature.

Nature and human life styles

Luddites argue that technology has made no improvement in life, or at best improvements of little importance. Sale's list of benefits includes speed, ease, and mass access—all of which he disdains. Sale says that although individuals might feel their lives are better because of computers, the perceived benefits are "industrial virtues that may not be virtues in another morality." He defines moral judgment as "the capacity to decide that a thing is right when it enhances the integrity, stability, and beauty of nature and is wrong when it does otherwise."[58] Jerry Mander, founder of the Center for Deep Ecology and author of books critical of technology and globalization, points out that thousands of generations of humans got along without computers, suggesting that we could do just fine without them too. While some people evaluate trade-offs between negative side effects of pesticides and the benefits of reducing diseases or protecting food crops, Mander's objections to technology lead him to the conclusion that there can be no "good" pesticide. While many people work on technological, legal, and educational approaches to reducing the gasoline usage of automobiles, Mander says there can be no "good" automobile.[59]

What are the underlying premises behind these comments by Sale and Mander? We consider Sale's comment on moral judgment first. Many debates about the environment set up a humans-versus-nature dichotomy.[60] This is not the true conflict. Nature, biodiversity, forests, a hospitable climate, clean air and water, open space away from cities— these are all important and valuable to humans. So is shelter from the rain, cold, and heat. So are life-saving medicines and medical techniques. Conflicts about the environment are not conflicts between humans and nature. They are conflicts between people with different views about how to meet human needs. In contrast to Sale's statement, moral judgment, to many people, and for many centuries, has meant the capacity to choose that which enhances human life, reduces misery, and increases freedom and happiness. Sale's comment chooses nature, not humanity, as the primary standard of moral value.

Whether an automobile (or computing device) is "good," by a human-centered standard, depends on whether it meets our needs, how well it does so, at what cost (to the environment and society, as well as to our bank account), and how well it compares to alternatives. Critics of modern technologies point out their weaknesses but often ignore the weaknesses of alternatives—for example, the millions of acres once needed to grow feed for horses and the hundreds of tons of horse manure dropped on the streets of cities each day, a century ago.[61] Mander's comment about automobiles again raises the issues of our standard of value and our need for a product or service. Candles, gas lamps, and kerosene lamps filled homes with fumes and soot. Do we need electricity? Do we need hot water on tap, movies, and symphony orchestras? Or do we need nothing more than food and shelter? Do we need an average life expectancy of more than 25 years? Do we want to merely exist—do we *need* even that?—or do we want long, happy, comfortable lives filled with time for love, interesting activities, and an opportunity to use our marvelously inventive brains?

> *The Web is alive, and filled with life, nearly as complex and, well,*
> *natural as a primordial swamp.*
>
> —John Perry Barlow[62]

Accomplishments of technology

It is easy to miss the extreme changes in quality of life that have taken place over the past few centuries. We mention here a scattering of examples.

Technology and the Industrial Revolution have had a dramatic impact on life expectancy. A study in 1662 estimated that only 25% of people in London lived to age

Environmental impacts of computing technology

I had thought of including a section in this book on environmental impacts of computers, mobile devices, and the Internet. As I looked for data, I concluded that attempts to quantify environmental benefits and costs would be subject to the same weaknesses and criticisms of models that we discussed in Section 7.1.2. It is extremely difficult to measure impacts and to determine how to compare to impacts of technologies and activities that computing technology replaces. However, we can make some observations.

Production of computers is energy intensive and uses hazardous materials. Because of these materials, disposal is an issue, as it is for flourescent light bulbs. Running and cooling the millions of servers on the Internet in the United States accounts for about 2% of U.S. electric power usage,[63] more than the U.S. auto industry and less than the chemical industry. There are estimates that production of computers uses roughly twice as much energy as operating them.

On the other hand, digitally controlled machinery uses less power than older electromechanical controls. Digital sensors and controls for regulating lighting, heating, air conditioning, and farm irrigation (among many other examples) save resources by determining just what is needed and thus reduce waste. Microprocessors control hybrid cars, reducing gasoline use. Telecommuting, e-commerce, and online libraries and information sites significantly reduce the need for driving and flying and thus, the need for fuel. One fiber-optic cable, with about 150 pounds of silica, carries more messages than a ton of copper wire.[64]

Digital storage of documents, data, photos, and so on, reduce the need for paper (and the amount of trash produced.) Specific examples suggest the reductions: A large insurance company reduced its use of paper by 100 million pages in a nine-month period by storing its manuals digitally instead of printing them. A computerized system for recording insurance claims replaced more than 30 million index cards. We use email and texting instead of sending letters and cards on paper. Electronic payments eliminate paper bills and checks. We read books, newspapers, magazines, and so on, on tablets, e-readers, and smartphones, reducing paper use. The decline in business for the U.S. Postal Service and printed newspapers, while population and economic activity grow, are indications of these reductions. But do we actually use less paper than we did before? I could not find clear data for total paper use. However, between 2001 and 2011, annual consumption of newsprint for daily newspapers in the United States dropped by an estimated 61%, and the number of pieces of first class mail dropped by about 24%.[65]

We take, post, and share far more photos (billions per month) than we did when we made prints and slides. This is one example of a phenomenon that occurs in many fields: as a product or service becomes more efficient and cheaper, we use more of it. It seems that people have certain levels of cost that they are willing to accept. We do more and use more when the cost goes down. Perhaps we have increased our use of resources as we have increased our use of computing technology. Certainly, we shift resources from areas where there are savings to other uses, including improved medical technology, more music and video, easier access to education, and other products and services that bring us benefits.

26. Records from 18th-century French villages showed that the median age of death was lower than the median age of marriage. Until recent generations, parents had to endure the deaths of most of their children. Starvation was common. In the United States, life expectancy at birth increased from 47.3 years in 1900 to 77.9 in 2007. Worldwide average life expectancy increased from approximately 30 in 1900 to approximately 64 in 2006. Science and technology (along with other factors such as education) reduced or almost eliminated typhoid, smallpox, dysentery, plagues, and malaria in most of the world. Deaths at work, during travel, and by accidents declined dramatically.[66]

In the early 2000s, Americans spent less than 10% of family income on food, compared to approximately 47% in 1901. Agronomist Norman Borlaug, who won a Nobel Peace Prize for his work in improving agricultural productivity, reported that when new forms of wheat and crop management were introduced in India, yields rose from 12.3 million tons in 1965 to 73.5 million tons in 1999. In about the same timeframe, U.S. production of its 17 most important crops increased from 252 million tons to 596 million tons, but used 25 million fewer acres. Nicholas Eberstadt, an expert on population, reported that food supplies and gross domestic product have been growing faster than population for decades in most areas of the world, in both developing and developed countries.[67]

The benefits of telecommunications and information technology are enormous in developing countries. A report of a United Nations Conference on Trade and Development, for example, observes that developing economies can make productivity gains worth billions of dollars by encouraging the growth of electronic commerce. The report said that "it is because the internet revolution is relevant not just to the high-tech, information-intensive sectors but also to the whole organisation of economic life that . . . developing countries stand a better chance of sharing in its benefits earlier than in previous technological revolutions."[68]

Technology is certainly not the only factor in improving quality of life. Progress against disease, discomfort, and early death depends on the stability, freedom, and flexibility of political and economic systems as well. Measuring quality of life is subjective, and some find other measures more important than the few we cited above. But, for many people, these data suggest that technology has contributed much to human well-being.

7.4 Making Decisions About Technology

No one voted for this technology or any of the various machines and processes that make it up.

—Kirkpatrick Sale[69]

7.4.1 QUESTIONS

We saw, in Section 7.3, that the determination of what are true needs depends on our choice of values. Throughout this book, we saw controversies about specific products, services, and applications of computer technology (for example, personalized advertising, anonymous Web surfing, and face recognition systems). How should we make decisions about the basic question of whether to use a whole technology, or major segments of it, at all? Who would make such decisions?

Most people in science, engineering, and business accept, almost without question, the view that people can choose to use a technology for good or ill. Some critics of technology disagree. They argue that technologies are not "neutral." Neil Postman says, "Once a technology is admitted [to our culture], it plays out its hand; it does what it is designed to do."[70] This view sees the technologies themselves as being in control.

In the view of some critics of computing technology, big corporations and governments make decisions about uses of the technology without sufficient input or control by ordinary people. Kirkpatrick Sale's lament at the beginning of this section expresses this view: there was never a vote on whether we should have computers and the Internet. Some people argue that we should not use a new technology at all until we have studied it, figured out its consequences, and made a determination that the consequences are acceptable. The idea is that if the technology does not meet certain criteria, we would not permit its development and use.

This view leads to a few basic questions. Can a society choose to have certain specific desirable modern inventions while prohibiting others or prohibiting whole technologies? How well can we predict the consequences of a new technology or application? Who would make the decisions? We consider the first question here and the others in the next few sections.

How finely can we make decisions about acceptable and unacceptable technologies? In response to a criticism that the tribal life he extolled would have no pianos, no violins, no telescope, no Mozart, Sale replied, "[I]f your clan thought that the violin was a useful and nonharmful tool, you could choose to invent that."[71] Perhaps critics of computing technology who recognize its value to disabled people would permit development of applications for them. The question is whether it is possible for a clan or society to choose to invent a violin or a book reader for blind people without the technological and economic base on which development of these products depends. That base includes the freedom to innovate, a large enough economy to get materials from distant sources, and a large number of potential applications that make the research, development, and production of the basic ingredients of these products economically feasible. It is unlikely that anyone would even think of developing a book reader for the blind if some of the components did not already exist in prior products (for example, perhaps, a photocopy machine).

Telemedicine: A bad application of technology?

In Chapter 1, we described long-distance medicine, or telemedicine, as a benefit of computer technology. Computer and communications networks make possible remote examination of patients and medical test results, and they make possible remotely controlled medical procedures. You should be able to think of potential privacy and safety problems with such systems. You might think of other objections as well. Should we ban telemedicine?

Several states passed laws prohibiting the practice of telemedicine by doctors who are not licensed in that state. The main argument they give for the laws is safety, or concern about out-of-state "quacks." The laws will "keep out the charlatans and snake-oil salesmen," according to one supporter.[72] Also, telemedicine could increase the influence of large, well-financed medical centers—to the detriment of local physicians in private practice. Large hospitals might become the "Wal-Marts of medicine," says one writer. Telemedicine might make medical care even more impersonal than it is already.

Is concern for patients the real reason for the laws? The arguments about charlatans and quacks seem weak, considering that the laws target doctors who are licensed, but in another state. Many doctors who support the bans see telemedicine as a significant competitive threat. As the director of one state medical board put it, "They're worried about protecting their turf."[73] The laws restrict competition and protect established special interests—a risk of any mechanism designed to prohibit a new technology or product.

7.4.2 THE DIFFICULTY OF PREDICTION

A brief look at the development of communications and computer technology suggests the difficulty of evaluating the consequences and future applications of a new technology. Early computers were developed to calculate ballistics trajectories for the military. The PC was originally a tool for doing computation and writing documents. No one but a few visionaries imagined most of their current uses. Each new technology finds new and unexpected uses. When physicists began developing the World Wide Web, who would have predicted online auctions, social networking, or sharing home video? Would anyone have predicted even a small fraction of the ways we use smartphones? Postman's statement that a technology does "what it is designed to do" ignores human responsibility and choice, innovation, discoveries of new uses, unexpected consequences, and social action to encourage or discourage specific applications. Computer scientist Peter Denning takes a different view: "Although a technology does not drive human beings to adopt new practices, it shapes the space of possibilities in which they can act: people are drawn to technologies that expand the space of their actions and relationships."[74] Denning says people adopt technologies that give them more choices. Note that he does not say more choices of consumer products, but more actions and relationships. Don Norman also suggests that society influences the role of a technology when he says, "The failure to predict the computer revolution was the failure to understand how society would modify the original notion of a computational device into a useful tool for everyday activities."[75]

- *The telephone is so important, every city will need one!*
  —Anonymous

- *My personal desire would be to prohibit entirely the use of alternating currents. They are unnecessary as they are dangerous.*
  —Thomas Edison, 1899

- *I think there is a world market for maybe five computers.*
  —Thomas J. Watson, chairman of IBM, 1943

- *Computers in the future may . . . only weigh 1.5 tons.*
  —*Popular Mechanics*, 1949

- *There is no reason for any individual to have a computer in their home.*
  —Ken Olson, president of Digital Equipment Corp., 1977

- *The U.S. will have 220,000 computers by the year 2000.*
  —Official forecast by RCA Corporation, 1966. The actual number was close to 100 million.

Figure 7.4   Predictions.[76]

How well can a government committee, a think tank, or a computer industry executive predict the consequences of a new technology? The history of technology is full of wildly wrong predictions—some overly optimistic, some overly pessimistic. Consider the quotations in Figure 7.4. Some scientists were skeptical of air travel, space travel, and even railroads. (They believed that passengers would not be able to breathe on high-speed trains.) The quotations in Figure 7.4 reflect a lack of imagination about the myriad uses people would find for each new technology, about what the public would like, and about what they would pay for. They demonstrate humorously that many experts can be utterly wrong. We examine the prediction problem more seriously and in more depth by considering arguments made by computer scientist Joseph Weizenbaum in 1975 against the development of a particular computer technology: speech recognition systems.[77] We now have more than 35 years of hindsight. However, many inexpensive applications of speech recognition had already appeared by the early 1990s. Here are Weizenbaum's objections, accompanied by comments from our perspective today.

- *"The problem is so enormous that only the largest possible computers will ever be able to manage it."* Speech recognition software runs on smartphones.
- *". . . a speech-recognition machine is bound to be enormously expensive, . . . only governments and possibly a very few very large corporations will therefore be able to afford it."* Millions of people own smartphones and other devices that include speech recognition.

- *"What can it possibly be used for?"* Much more than I will mention here. (Speech recognition technology is a multibillion-dollar industry.) We can search the Web from a cellphone by speaking what we want instead of typing. We can call a business, speak the name of the person we want to reach, and automatically connect to that person's extension. Other customer-service applications include checking airline flight schedules, getting stock quotes and weather information, conducting banking transactions, and buying movie tickets on the phone by speaking naturally instead of pushing buttons.

  Recall some of the applications described in Sections 1.2.3 and 1.2.4: training systems (e.g., for air traffic controllers and for foreign languages) and tools that help disabled people use computers and control appliances in their homes. People who suffer from repetitive strain injury use speech recognition input instead of a keyboard. IBM advertised speech-input software for poets, so they can concentrate on poetry instead of typing. People with dyslexia use speech recognition software so they can write by dictation.

  Speech translation systems recognize speech and translate it into other languages. Full translation is still a difficult problem, but tourists, business people, social service workers, hotel reservations clerks, and many others use specialized versions.

  Voice-activated, hands-free operation of cellphones, car stereos, and other appliances in automobiles eliminates some of the safety hazard of using these devices while driving.

- *The military planned to control weapons by voice command, "a long step toward a fully automated battlefield."* Some argue that we should have the best possible weapons to defend ourselves. Others argue that, if wars are easier to fight, governments fight more of them. If countries fight wars with remotely controlled automated weapons and no humans on the battlefield, is that an improvement over wars in which people are slaughtered? What if only one side has the high-tech weapons? Would that cause more wars of aggression? Is there any technology that the military cannot or does not use? Should we decline to develop strong fabrics because the military can use them for uniforms? Clearly, military use of high-tech tools raises serious ethical and policy questions. Are these questions sufficient reason to abandon or condemn a technology?

- *Governments can use speech recognition to increase the efficiency and effectiveness of wiretapping.* Abuses of wiretapping concerned Weizenbaum (e.g., tapping done by oppressive governments). He does not explicitly mention wiretapping of criminal suspects. One can argue that governments can use the same tool beneficially in legal wiretapping of suspected criminals and terrorists, but it is true that speech recognition, like many other technological tools, can be a danger in the hands of governments. Protection from such abuses depends in part on the recognition of the importance of strictly controlling government power and in part on the appropriate laws and enforcement mechanisms to do so.

Discussion of Weizenbaum's objections is important for several reasons. (1) Although Weizenbaum was an expert in artificial intelligence, of which speech recognition is a subfield, he was mistaken in his expectations about the costs and benefits. (2) His objections about military and government use highlight the dilemma: Should we decline to develop technologies that people can misuse, or should we develop the tools because of their beneficial uses, and use other means, including our votes and our voices, to influence government and military policy? (3) Weizenbaum's argument against development of a technology because of its expected cost is similar to arguments expressed by others about current and future computer applications and other technologies. For example, a common objection to some new medical technologies is that they are so expensive that only the rich will be able to afford them. This shortsighted view can result in the denial of benefits to the whole population. For many new inventions, prices are high at first but quickly come down. A computer chip developed to float on the retina of the eye and send visual signals to the brain has the potential to restore sight to some blind people. The initial cost was $500,000. Should we ban it because it would be available only to the very rich? The developer of the chip expected the cost to come down to $50 with mass production.

Weizenbaum was not trying to evaluate computer technology as a whole but was focusing on one specific application area. If we are to permit the government, or experts, or the people via a majority vote to prohibit development of certain technologies, it is essential at least that we be able to estimate the consequences—both risks and benefits—of the technology fairly accurately. We cannot do this. The experts cannot do it.

But what if a technology might threaten the survival of the human race? We consider such an example in the next section.

7.4.3   INTELLIGENT MACHINES AND SUPERINTELLIGENT HUMANS— OR THE END OF THE HUMAN RACE?

Prominent technologists such as Hans Moravec, Ray Kurzweil, and Vernor Vinge describe a not-very-distant future in which intelligence-enhancing devices, artificial intelligence, and intelligent robots change our society and our selves in profound ways.* The more optimistic scenarios include human use of intelligent machines and services of many kinds. People might acquire advanced mental powers through brain implants and computer–brain interfaces. When someone has a stroke, doctors might remove the damaged part of a brain and replace it with a chip that performs the lost functions, perhaps with a large amount of extra memory or a chip to access the Web directly. Why wait for a stroke? Once the technology is available, healthy people will likely buy and install such implants.

---

* I include some references at the end of the chapter.

MIT robotics researcher Rodney Brooks, for example, suggests that by 2020 we might have wireless Internet interfaces that doctors can implant in our heads. He says people might be just as comfortable with them as they are now getting laser eye surgery at a mall.[78] Will such implants make someone less human than a heart transplant or pacemaker does? What social problems will intelligence enhancement cause in the next few decades? What philosophical and ethical problems arise when we combine human and machine intelligence in such intimate ways?

Going farther into the future, will we "download" our brains to long-lasting robot bodies? If we do, will we still be human?

The technological singularity

The term *technological singularity* refers to the point at which artificial intelligence or some combined human–machine intelligence advances so far that we cannot comprehend what lies on the other side. It is plausible, says computer scientist Vinge, that "we can, in the fairly near future, create or become creatures who surpass humans in every intellectual and creative dimension. Events beyond such a singular event are as unimaginable to us as opera is to a flatworm."[79]

Some technologists welcome the idea of the human race transforming into an unrecognizable race of superintelligent, genetically engineered creatures within this century. Others find it horrifying—and others unlikely. Some see potential threats to the survival of the human race. They see the possibility of the machines themselves achieving human-level intelligence, then rapidly improving themselves to a superhuman level. Once robots can improve their design and build better robots, will they "outcompete" humans? Will they replace the human race, just as various species of animals displace others? And will it happen soon, say within the next 20 years or so?

Two estimates support these scenarios. One is an estimate of the computing power of the human brain. The other is based on Moore's Law, the observation that the computing power of new microprocessors doubles roughly every 18 to 24 months. If the progress of hardware power continues at this rate, then by roughly 2030 computer hardware will be about as powerful as a human brain, sufficiently powerful to support the computation requirements of intelligent robots.

Both those who think an extreme advance in machine intelligence or human–machine intelligence is likely in the near future and those who criticize these ideas provide several reasons why it might not happen. Here are some of them. First, hardware progress might slow down. Second, we might not be able to develop the necessary software in the next few decades, or at all. Developments in AI, particularly in the area of general intelligence, have been much slower than researchers expected when the field began. Third, the estimates of the "hardware" computing power of the human brain (the sophistication of the computing power of neurons) might be drastically too low. Finally, some philosophers argue that robots programmed with AI software cannot duplicate the full capability of the human mind.

Responding to the threats of intelligent machines

Whether the singularity occurs within a few decades, or later, or not at all, many in the relevant fields foresee general-purpose intelligent machines within your lifetime. By its definition, we cannot prepare for the aftermath of the singularity, but we can prepare for more gradual developments. Many of the issues we explored in previous chapters are relevant to enhanced intelligence. Will software bugs or other malfunctions kill thousands of people? Will hackers hack brains? Will a large division open up between the superintelligent and the merely humanly intelligent? We saw that protections for safety and privacy in computer systems are often weak because they were not designed in from the start. It is valuable to think about potential problems of superintelligent systems and intelligence enhancement for humans well before they confront us so that we can design the best protections.

Bill Joy is cofounder of Sun Microsystems and a key developer of Berkeley Unix and the Java programming language. In his article "Why the Future Doesn't Need Us,"[80] Joy describes his worries about robotics, genetic engineering, and nanotechnology. He observes that these technologies will be more dangerous than technologies of the 20th century (such as nuclear weapons) because they will be self-replicating and will not require rare and expensive raw materials and huge factories or laboratories. Joy foresees profound threats, including possibly the extinction of the human race.

What protections do people who fear for the future of the human race recommend? Joy describes and criticizes some before suggesting his own. Space enthusiasts suggest creating colonies in space. Joy observes that it will not happen soon enough. If it does, it might save the human race but not the vast majority of humans on earth. If colonists take the current technologies with them, the threat goes too. A second solution is to develop protections that can stop the dangerous technologies from getting out of control. Futurist Virginia Postrel suggests "a portfolio of resilient responses."[81] Joy argues that we could not develop "shields" in time, and if we could, they would necessarily be at least as dangerous as the technologies they are supposed to protect us against. Joy recommends "relinquishment," by which he means we must "limit development of the technologies that are too dangerous, by limiting our pursuit of certain kinds of knowledge." He cites, as earlier examples, treaties to limit development of certain kinds of weapons and the United States's unilateral decision to abandon development of biological weapons. However, relinquishment has the same kinds of weaknesses Joy attributes to the approaches he rejects: they are "either undesirable or unachievable or both." Enforcing relinquishment would be extraordinarily difficult, if not impossible. As Joy recognizes, intelligent robots and the other technologies that concern him have huge numbers of potentially beneficial applications, many of which will save lives and improve quality of life. At what point should governments stop pursuit of knowledge and development? Ethical professionals will refuse to participate in development of some AI applications, but they too face the difficult problem of where to draw the line. Suppose we develop the technology to a point where we get useful applications with legal and technological safety controls. How will we prevent visionary or insane scientists, hackers, teenagers, aggressive governments, or terrorists from circumventing the controls and going beyond the prohibited level? Joy sees a relinquishment verification program on an unprecedented scale, in cyberspace and in physical facilities, with privacy, civil liberties, business automony, and free markets seriously curtailed. Thus, relinquishment means not only that we might lose development of innovative, beneficial products and services. We would lose many basic liberties as well.

Although we can find flaws with all proposals to protect against the dangers of powerful technologies, that does not mean we should ignore the risks. We need to choose appropriate elements from the various proposals and develop the best protections we can.

Prediction is difficult, especially about the future.[82]

7.4.4 A Few Observations

We have presented arguments against the view that we should evaluate and perhaps ban new technologies at the start. Does this mean that no one should make decisions about whether it is good to develop a particular application of a new technology? No. The arguments and examples suggest two things: (1) that we limit the scope of decisions about development of new technology, perhaps to particular products, and (2) that we decentralize the decision-making process and make it noncoercive, to reduce the impact of mistakes, avoid manipulation by entrenched companies who fear competition, and prevent violations of liberty. We cannot often predict the decisions and the results of decisions made by individual engineers, researchers, programmers, entrepreneurs, venture capitalists, customers, and teenagers who tinker in their garages, but they have a valuable robustness. The fundamental problem is not *what* decision to make about a particular technology. Rather, it is to select a decision-making *process* that is most likely to produce what people want, to work well despite the difficulty of predicting consequences, to respect the diversity of personal opinions about what constitutes a desirable life style, and to be relatively free of political manipulation.

When we consider the most extreme potential developments, such as superintelligent robots, what level of certainty of dire consequences should we require before restricting the freedom to develop technologies and products that might have marvelous benefits?

EXERCISES

Review Exercises

7.1   What is one significant criticism of Wikipedia?

7.2   What questions do we use to evaluate computer models?

7.3   What is one common use of Internet access in rural areas of developing countries?

7.4   Give one of the neo-Luddite criticisms of electronic commerce.

7.5   Give an example of a mistaken prediction made about computers.

General Exercises

7.6   Consider a music talent contest where the winner depends on the votes of viewers. Is it an ethical obligation of the site operators to ensure that votes are not bought and sold, or is it merely a good business policy? Or is it both?

7.7   Describe the easy availability of pornography on the Internet, with respect to its effect on children. What are some methods which might be used to safeguard children from pornography?

7.8   Describe an example of hacking for each of the following categories. Elaborate on the third one; give some arguments for each side.

(a) There is no ethical problem; it is clearly ethical.

(b) No complex argument is needed; it is clearly unethical.

(c) Deciding whether it is ethical or not is not simple. There are reasonable arguments on both sides, or the context might be important.

7.9   Some religion-based cellphone services charge less for calls to others in the same network of religion-based phones. Is this a positive way of reinforcing a community or an encouragement for insularity? Give reasons for your answer.

7.10 Rewrite the spelling-checker verse (in Section 7.1.1), correcting all the mistakes without using a computer or other electronic device. (There are more than a dozen mistakes.)

7.11 Give examples of situations where computers increase and decrease productivity.

7.12 Approximately 6000 languages are spoken in the world. This number is declining rapidly as a result of increased communication and transportation, globalization of business and trade, and so on—all side effects of increased technology in general and of the Internet in particular. What are the advantages and disadvantages of losing languages? Overall, is it a significant problem?

7.13 Write three questions whose answers you would need for a life-cycle analysis model comparing the environmental impact of plastic carry-bags with paper carry-bags. (Use the questions for diapers in Figure 7.2 as a guide.) Consider manufacture, transportation, use, and disposal.

7.14 Suppose a computer program uses the following data to determine in how many years an important natural resource (say, copper) will run out.

- The number of tons in the known reserves of the resource.
- The average amount of the resource used per person (worldwide) per year.
- The total population of the world.
- An estimate of the rate of population increase for the next few decades.

(a) List all the reasons you can think of why this program is not a good predictor of when we will run out of the resource.

(b) In 1972, a group called the Club of Rome published a study using computer models that implied that the world would run out of several important natural resources in the 1980s. Today, even with the enormously increased demand from China and other developing countries, we have not run out. Why do you think many people accepted the predictions in the study?

7.15 In your opinion, should schools ban their students from using certain technologies in the classroom? Would your opinion change if the ban extended outside the classroom as well? Explain with examples of technologies which are candidates for such a ban.

7.16 How widely adopted is broadband Internet in your country? What factors prevent perfect adoption? How is it likely to change in the near future? Is this "digital divide" a significant problem?

7.17 What fraction of citizens of your country have access to the Internet? Is there a "digital divide" between people who are Internet-savvy and those who are not? Do other sociological reasons contribute to this divide, if any?

7.18 Analyze the effect of social networking on social practices. Do you think its influence has been largely positive or negative? What measures do you suggest to overcome the negative aspects, if any?

7.19 A large number of college students enroll in online degree programs. Discuss some advantages and disadvantages (to the students and to society in general) of students getting degrees online instead of at traditional colleges where they are co-present with faculty and other students.

7.20 Name some conventional businesses or industries that are under threat from e-commerce. Does this constitute unfair competition? What can be done to ensure that these businesses do not go bankrupt? Do we have an ethical obligation to ensure this?

7.21 Internet chess is a worldwide phenomena, and several grandmasters play regularly on online chess servers. What effect do you think Internet play has on a game? Is this a desirable trend? State both advantages and disadvantages.

7.22 Analyze the following argument that we are forced to have a cellphone. Is it convincing?

Some people do not want to own or use a cellphone. Technology advocates say if you don't want one, you don't have to buy one. But this is not true. We have to have one. Before cellphones became popular, there were coin-operated telephones all over, on street corners, in and near stores, in restaurants, at gas stations, and so on. If we needed to make a call while away from home or work, we could use a pay phone. Now most pay phones are gone, so we have to have a cellphone whether we want to or not.

7.23 Which of the Luddite criticisms of computers listed in Section 7.3.1 do you consider the most valid and significant? Why?

7.24 Recall the discussion in the box "Wal-Mart and e-commerce versus downtown and community" (Section 7.3.2), and consider these questions: Do people have a right to shop in small neighborhood stores rather than online? Do people in a small town have a right to eat in a French restaurant? Distinguish between negative and positive rights (Section 1.4.2).

7.25 Sclove and Scheuer saw e-commerce as a major threat to local "brick and mortar" businesses. Give a few specific examples of ways in which online businesses and services contribute to the success of local businesses. What kinds of local businesses are least likely to be hurt by online competition?

7.26 Some governments adapted software originally developed to help parents and Internet service providers block access to material inappropriate for children to block access to political and religious discussions. With regard to this, discuss the phenomena of Internet censorship. What are its positive and negative aspects? Does your country censor the Internet? If so, what rationale is given by the government?

7.27 Some neo-Luddites acknowledge that computing technology is beneficial to many people, but they see the main beneficiaries as government and big business. They say the key question is: Who benefits most? Consider the following questions and discuss the issue of who benefits most.

When a drug company develops a new cancer drug and its executives make millions of dollars as the stock goes up, while people who had that cancer live 20 extra years, who benefits most? Who benefits most from social media: governments, businesses, or ordinary users?

7.28 Philosophers have argued over the notions of weak versus strong artificial intelligence. Which possibility do you find more convincing? Give your reasons. What ethical concerns are attached to this debate?

7.29 Some biometric techniques analyze a person's face to grant or deny access. Describe some potentially useful and some potentially threatening or risky applications.

7.30 Assume you are a professional working in your chosen field. Describe specific things you can do to reduce the impact of any two problems we discussed in this chapter. (If you cannot think of anything related to your professional field, choose another field that might interest you.)

7.31 Think ahead to the next few years and describe a new problem, related to issues in this chapter, likely to develop from digital technology or devices.

Assignments

These exercises require some research or activity.

7.32 Find an article in Wikipedia on a subject that you already know a lot about. Read and review the article. Is it accurate, well done, complete?

7.33 The Internet sometimes provides unreliable and conflicting medical advice. Identify at least two examples of this. Describe the sites and explain the basis of your characterization of them. How can this harmful trend be regulated or inhibited?

7.34 Investigate the Folding@home project. What do you think of the potential of such collaborative distributed computing? What ethical issues are attached to it?

7.35 Research the phenomena of Internet memes. Why do you think they exist? Do you think the Internet has a "culture" of its own?

7.36 Research Moore's law. How far has it remained valid? Do you think it will hold true in the future? What implications would this have on our future? Give your reasons.

7.37 Self-driving cars are an active area of research. Suppose someone described these devices ten years ago as a potential invention and asked: Will they fill any real needs? How do you think most people would have answered? What is your answer now?

Class Discussion Exercises

These exercises are for class discussion, perhaps with short presentations prepared in advance by small groups of students.

7.38 To counter the problem of unreliable information on the Web, do you think all information should be screened or verified by experts? How far do you think this is possible? In this context, discuss Citizendium as opposed to Wikipedia.

7.39 Some critics of tools that enable us to specify the kinds of information we receive on the Web argue that the tools encourage fragmentation of society along political lines. Some argue that when most people got their news from three TV networks, there was a more cohesive, shared background of information. How serious is the problem of people seeing only one political point of view on the Web?

7.40 Discuss the technique of search engine optimization (SEO). Do you consider it to be an ethical practice? If your answer would depend on the situation, in what situations would you consider it to be ethical (and in what situations not)?

7.41 What do you think of the phenomenon of cloud computing, in which your data is stored on someone else's server? Would you consider this to be a violation of your privacy—a loss of control over your data—or would the advantages outweigh the risks? Discuss arguments both for and against the issue.

7.42 What are some skills, traditions, and/or social conventions that have been created due to computer, phone, and Internet technology? Have they replaced any conventions that existed before? In your opinion, has the change been positive or negative? Give an example of each.

7.43 Which of the following models do you think would produce very accurate results? Which do you think would be less reliable? Give your reasons.

   (a) A model developed by a team of mathematicians in 1895, using projections of population growth, economic growth, and traffic increase, to project the tonnage of horse droppings on the city streets in 1995

   (b) A model to predict the effect of an income tax change on government revenue

   (c) A model to predict the position of the moon in relation to the earth 30 years from now

   (d) A model to predict how much optical fiber a major city will need 30 years from now

   (e) A model to predict how much carbon dioxide the burning of fossil fuel for energy will emit worldwide 30 years from now

   (f) A model to predict the speed of a new racing-boat hull design under specified wind conditions

   (g) A model to project temperature increase and sea level rise over the next several centuries from a quadrupling of CO_2 concentration in the atmosphere (which the model assumes would happen in 140 years)[83]

7.44 What effect has the "digital divide" had on society? How do digital divides differ from social divisions that occurred with the introduction of earlier, nondigital information and communication technologies?

7.45 In the Prometheus myth, Zeus, the king of the gods, was furious at Prometheus for teaching science and technological skills to mankind because they made people more powerful. Zeus was jealous of his power and determined to withhold fire from mankind so that people would have to eat their food raw. Zeus and the Luddites represent different viewpoints on who benefits most from technology.

　(a) Give arguments in support of Zeus' view that technology helps the less powerful, reducing the advantage of the more powerful.

　(b) Give arguments in support of the Luddite view that technology helps the more powerful (e.g., governments and large corporations) most.

7.46 Read Bill Joy's article and the reply by Virginia Postrel (see the references at the end of the chapter). Whose arguments are more convincing? Why?

BOOKS AND ARTICLES

- John Attarian, "Spiritual and Cultural Perils of Technological Progress," *The Social Critic*, Winter 1998, pp. 10–18.

- Ronald Bailey, ed., *Earth Report 2000: Revisiting the True State of the Planet*, McGraw Hill, 2000. Includes much data on improvements in the environment, resource usage, food and energy production, and so on.

- Sven Birkerts, *The Gutenberg Elegies: The Fate of Reading in an Electronic Age*, Faber and Faber, 1994. Birkerts is a critic of computers; he writes on a typewriter.

- John Brockman, ed., *Is the Internet Changing the Way You Think?*, Harper Perennial, 2011.

- Rodney A. Brooks, *Flesh and Machines: How Robots Will Change Us*, Pantheon Books, 2002 (also, Vintage, 2003).

- Theodore Caplow, Louis Hicks, and Ben J. Wattenberg, *The First Measured Century: An Illustrated Guide to Trends in America*, AEI Press, 2001.

- Benjamin M. Compaine, ed., *The Digital Divide: Facing a Crisis or Creating a Myth*, MIT Press, 2001.

- W. Michael Cox and Richard Alm, *Myths of Rich and Poor: Why We're Better Off Than We Think*, Basic Books, 1999.

- Peter J. Denning, ed., *Talking Back to the Machine: Computers and Human Aspiration*, Copernicus, 1999.

- Michael Dertouzos, *The Unfinished Revolution: Human-Centered Computers and What They Can Do for Us*, Harper-Collins, 2001.

- Peter H. Diamandis and Steven Kotler, *Abundance: The Future Is Better than You Think*, Simon and Schuster, 2012.

- Hubert L. Dreyfus, *On the Internet*, Routledge, 2001. Criticisms of hyperlinks and the organization of information on the Internet.

- Hubert Dreyfus, *What Computers Still Can't Do: A Critique of Artificial Reason*, MIT Press, 1992. How well did Dreyfus's arguments hold up? Can computers now do some of the things he said they could not do?

- Samuel C. Florman, *Blaming Technology: The Irrational Search for Scapegoats*, St. Martin's Press, 1981.

- Merritt Ierley, *Wondrous Contrivances: Technology at the Threshold*, Clarkson Potter, 2002. Looks at expectations for and attitudes about many earlier technological devices.

- Jean-Noel Jeanneney, *Google and the Myth of Universal Knowledge: A View from Europe*, Univeristy of Chicago Press, 2006. The author is president of the France's Bibliotèque Nationale (National Library).

- Bill Joy, "Why the Future Doesn't Need Us," *Wired*, April 2000, www.wired.com/wired/archive/8.04/joy.html. A response by Virginia Postrel is listed below.

- Ray Kurzweil, *The Singularity Is Near: When Humans Transcend Biology*, Viking, 2005.

- Todd Lappin, "Déjà Vu All Over Again," *Wired*, May 1995, pp. 175–177, 218–222. A comparison of predictions of the social impact of radio 75 years ago and the predictions for the Internet.

- Jerry Mander and Edward Goldsmith, eds., *The Case against the Global Economy and for a Turn Toward the Local*, Sierra Club Books, 1996. Extremely critical of computer technology, automation, and technology in general. Argues that globalization should be halted and reversed.

- Joel Mokyr, *The Lever of Riches: Technological Creativity and Economic Progress*, Oxford University Press, 1990.

- Stephen Moore and Julian Simon, *It's Getting Better All the Time: The 100 Greatest Trends of the 20th Century*, Cato Institute, 2000.

- Hans Moravec, *Robot: Mere Machine to Transcendent Mind*, Oxford University Press, 2000.

- Donald A. Norman, *Things That Make Us Smart: Defending Human Attributes in the Age of the Machine*, Addison-Wesley, 1993.

- Eli Pariser, *The Filter Bubble: What the Internet Is Hiding from You*, Penguin Press, 2011.

- Roger Penrose, *The Emperor's New Mind: Concerning Computers, Minds, and the Laws of Physics*, Oxford University Press, 2002. Penrose argues that artificial intelligence cannot duplicate the full range of human intelligence.

- Neil Postman, *Technopoly: The Surrender of Culture to Technology*, Alfred A. Knopf, 1992.

- Virginia Postrel, *The Future and Its Enemies*, The Free Press, 1998.

- Virginia Postrel, "Joy, to the World," *Reason*, June 2000, www.reason.com/news/show/27725.html. A response to Bill Joy's article listed above.

- Kirkpatrick Sale, *Rebels Against the Future: The Luddites and Their War Against the Industrial Revolution: Lessons for the Computer Age*, Addison-Wesley, 1995.

- C. P. Snow, "The Two Cultures and the Scientific Revolution." In this speech, Snow argues that people in the humanities and people in the sciences have fundamentally different views of science and technology. The speech appears, with an update, in C. P. Snow, *The Two Cultures: And a Second Look*, Cambridge University Press, 1964.

- Mark Stevenson, *An Optimist's Tour of the Future*, Avery, 2011.

- Clifford Stoll, *High Tech Heretic: Reflections of a Computer Contrarian*, Anchor Books, 2000.

- James Surowieki, *The Wisdom of Crowds*, Anchor, 2005.

- Vernor, Vinge, "The Coming Technological Singularity: How to Survive in the Post-Human Era," presented at the VISION-21 Symposium (sponsored by NASA Lewis Research Center and the Ohio Aerospace Institute), March 30-31, 1993, www-rohan.sdsu.edu/faculty/vinge/misc/singularity.html.

- William Wresch, *Disconnected: Haves and Have-Nots in the Information Age*, Rutgers University Press, 1996.

ORGANIZATIONS AND WEBSITES

- American Library Association, "Using Primary Sources on the Web": www.ala.org/rusa/sections/history/resources/pubs/usingprimarysources

- Johns Hopkins University library, "Evaluating Information Found on the Internet":

  www.library.jhu.edu/researchhelp/general/evaluating/

- University of California, Berkeley, library, "Evaluating Web Pages: Techniques to Apply & Questions to Ask": www.lib.berkeley.edu/TeachingLib/Guides/Internet/Evaluate.html

NOTES

1. From Pope's poem "An Essay on Criticism." In Greek mythology, the Pierian spring in Macedonia inspired the Muses and others who drank from it. Pope's poem turned it into a metaphor for knowledge.

2. Quoted in Stacy Schiff, "Know It All: Can Wikipedia Conquer Expertise?" *New Yorker*, July 31, 2006, www.newyorker.com/archive/2006/07/31/060731fa_fact, viewed Jan. 2, 2012. McHenry was an editor at the Encyclopedia Britannica.

3. Robert Fox, "News Track: Everybody Must Get Cloned," *Communications of the ACM*, August 2000, 43:8, p. 9. Lisa Guernsey, "Software Is Called Capable of Copying Any Human Voice," *New York Times*, July 31, 2001, pp. A1, C2.

4. "Wikipedia: Size Comparisons," Wikipedia, en.wikipedia.org/wiki/Wikipedia:Size_comparisons, viewed Jan. 2, 2012.

5. Jan Lorenz, Heiko Rauhut, Frank Schweitzer, and Dirk Helbing, "How Social Influence Can Undermine the Wisdom of Crowd Effect," *Proceedings of the National Academy of Sciences*, May 10, 2011, www.pnas.org/content/early/2011/05/10/1008636108.full.pdf, viewed Jan. 6, 2012. James Surowieki, *The Wisdom of Crowds*, Anchor, 2005. A course on decision making taught by Michael Roberto and an article by Jonah Lehrer led me to these ideas and references.

6. Joseph Rago, "The Blog Mob," *Wall Street Journal*, Dec. 20, 2006, p. A18.

7. Jonah Lehrer, "When We're Cowed by the Crowd," *Wall Street Journal*, May 28, 2011, online.wsj.com/article/SB10001424052702304066504576341280447107102.html, viewed Jan. 6, 2012.

8. James A. Evans, "Electronic Publication and the Narrowing of Science and Scholarship," *Science*, July 18, 2008 (Vol. 321, no. 5887, pp. 395–399), www.sciencemag.org/content/321/5887/395.abstract, viewed Jan. 6, 2012. I learned of this article from an article by Jonah Lehrer.

9. From Microsoft's explanation of its policy, quoted in Mark Goldblatt, "Bowdlerized by Microsoft," *New York Times*, Oct. 23, 2001, p. A23, www.nytimes.com/2001/10/23/opinion/bowdlerized-by-microsoft.html, viewed Jan. 6, 2012.

10. Eli Pariser, *The Filter Bubble: What the Internet Is Hiding from You*, Penguin Press, 2011.

11. Parts of this poem have circulated on computer networks and appeared in newspapers. The full version (36 lines), slightly different from the one I used, appeared in the *Journal of Irreproducible Results*, Jan./Feb. 1994, 39(1), p. 13. Zar attributes the title to Pamela Brown and the opening lines to Mark Eckman.

12. Barry Bearak, "Pakistani Tale of a Drug Addict's Blasphemy," *New York Times*, Feb. 19, 2001, pp. A1, A4.

13. *Against the Gods: The Remarkable Story of Risk*, John Wiley & Sons, 1996, p. 16.

14. Amanda Bennett, "Strange 'Science': Predicting Health-Care Costs," *Wall Street Journal*, Feb. 7, 1994, p. B1.

15. Cynthia Crossen, "How 'Tactical Research' Muddied Diaper Debate," *Wall Street Journal*, May 17, 1994, pp. B1, B9.

16. Orrin H. Pilkey and Linda Pilkey-Jarvis, "Why Mathematical Models Just Don't Add Up," *The Chronicle of Higher Education*, May 25, 2007, chronicle.com/weekly/v53/i38/38b01201.htm, viewed July 21, 2007.

17. "Recent Greenhouse Gas Concentrations," Carbon Dioxide Information Analysis Center, Oak Ridge National Laboratory, U.S. Dept. of Energy, December 2011, cdiac.ornl.gov/pns/current_ghg.html, viewed Feb. 6, 2012.

18. Summary for Policy Makers, p. 5, in S. Solomon *et al.*, eds., *Climate Change 2007: The Physical Scientific Basis*, Cambridge University Press, 2007, www.ipcc.ch/pdf/assessment-report/ar4/wg1/ar4-wg1-spm.pdf, viewed Feb. 9, 2012.

19. The IPCC reports (published by Cambridge University Press): S. Solomon *et al.*, eds., *Climate Change 2007: The Physical Scientific Basis*, 2007 (Technical Summary at ipcc-wg1.ucar.edu/wg1/wg1-report.html, viewed July 17, 2007). J. T. Houghton *et al.*, eds., *Climate Change 2001: The Scientific Basis*, 2001. J. T. Houghton *et al.*, eds., *Climate Change 1995: The Science of Climate Change*, 1996. J. T. Houghton, B. A. Callander, and S. K. Varney, eds., *Climate Change 1992: The Supplementary Report to the IPCC Scientific Assessment*, 1992. J. T. Houghton, G. J. Jenkins, and J. J. Ephraums, eds., *Climate Change: The IPCC Scientific Assessment*, 1990. Various IPCC reports are available at www.ipcc.ch/publications_and_data/publications_and_data_reports.shtml. I also used a large variety of other books and articles for background.

20. Solomon, Technical Summary, *Climate Change 2007*, p. 81.

21. One reason why this distinction is important is that temperature records for large areas of the northern hemisphere showed a larger rise in the nighttime winter lows than in the daytime summer highs (a potentially benign or beneficial form of warming).

22. D. L. Albritton *et al.*, "Technical Summary," in J. T. Houghton *et al.*, eds., *Climate Change 2001*, pp. 21–83; see p. 49.

23. National Oceanic and Atmospheric Administration, National Climatic Data Center, "State of the Climate Global Analysis Annual 2011," Dec. 2011, www.ncdc.noaa.gov/sotc/global/2011/13, viewed Feb. 10, 2012.

24. Solomon, Technical Summary, *Climate Change 2007*, Table TS.6, p. 70.

25. Solomon, Technical Summary, *Climate Change 2007*, p. 70. "Greenhouse Gases Frequently Asked Questions," National Oceanic and Atmospheric Administration National Climatic Data Center, www.ncdc.noaa.gov/oa/climate/gases.html, viewed Jan. 14, 2012.

26. Geoff Brumfiel, "Cloud Formation May Be Linked to Cosmic Rays," *Nature*, Aug. 24, 2011, www.nature.com/news/2011/110824/full/news.2011.504.html#B1, viewed Jan. 16, 2012. Pallab Ghosh, "Cloud Simulator Tests Climate Models," BBC News, Aug. 24, 2011, www.bbc.co.uk/news/science-environment-14637647, viewed Jan. 17, 2012.

27. Berkeley Earth Surface Temperature project: berkeleyearth.org.

28. Solomon, Technical Summary, *Climate Change 2007*, TS.6: "Robust Findings and Key Uncertainties," pp. 81–91.

29. Stephen Schneider, quoted in Jonathan Schell, "Our Fragile Earth," *Discover*, Oct. 1989, pp. 44–50.

30. National Oceanic and Atmospheric Administration, "State of the Climate Global Analysis Annual 2011." Susan Solomon *et al.*, "Contributions of Stratospheric Water Vapor to Decadal Changes in the Rate of Global Warming," *Science*, March 5, 2010, pp. 1219–1223, mls.jpl.nasa.gov/library/Solomon,%20S_3734D5B7d01.pdf, viewed Jan. 16, 2012. Richard A. Muller *et al.*, "Decadal Variations in the Global Atmospheric Land Temperatures," Berkeley Earth Surface Temperature project, berkeleyearth.org/pdf/berkeley-earth-decadal-variations.pdf, viewed Jan. 16, 2012.

31. I thank Ellen Kraft for her work on the revision and updating of this section.

32. See, for example, Jon Katz, "The Digital Citizen," *Wired*, December 1997, pp. 68–82, 274–275.

33. Most of the data in this paragraph come from polls and studies by Pew Research Center, Forrester Research, Luntz Research Companies, Ipsos-Reid Corporation, Nielsen//NetRatings, the U.S. Commerce Department, and others, reported in various news media.

34. Susannah Fox and Gretchen Livingston, "Latinos Online," Pew Research Center, Mar. 14, 2007, pewresearch.org/pubs/429/latinos-online, viewed Mar. 21, 2007.

35. To the best of my knowledge, Marvin Minsky first used the term "have-lates," as a substitute for "have-nots;" I prefer to use "have-laters" rather than "have-lates."

36. "Chairman Julius Genachowski Remarks on Broadband Adoption," Federal Communications Commission, Nov., 9, 2011, www.fcc.gov/document/chairman-genachowski-remarks-broadband-adoption, viewed Nov. 14, 2011 (by Ellen Kraft). Peter Svensson, "Cable Cos. to Offer $9.95 Broadband for Poor Homes," Associated Press, Nov. 9, 2011, abclocal.go.com/wpvi/story?section=news/technology&id=8424807, viewed Jan. 18, 2012.

37. Jen Schradie, "The Digital Production Gap: The Digital Divide and Web 2.0 Collide," *Poetics*, Vol. 39, No. 2, April 2011, pp. 145–168.

38. "Increased Competition Has Helped Bring ICT Access to Billions," United Nations International Telecommunication Union, Jan. 2011, www.itu.int/net/pressoffice/stats/2011/01/index.aspx, viewed Jan. 18, 2012.

39. One Laptop per Child: one.laptop.org, viewed Feb. 8, 2012. Ruy Cervantes *et al.*, "Infrastructures for Low Cost Laptop Use in Mexican Schools," *Proceedings of the 2011 Annual Conference on Human Factors in Computing Systems*, www.ics.uci.edu/~nsambasi/CHI2011_

Infrastructures.pdf, viewed Nov. 14, 2011 (by Ellen Kraft).

40. The quotes are from "Nine Digital Divide Truths," Digital Divide.org, www.digitaldivide.org/dd/truths.htm, viewed Mar. 27, 2007.

41. "Increased Competition Has Helped Bring ICT Access to Billions," United Nations International Telecommunication Union, Jan. 2011, www.itu.int/net/pressoffice/stats/2011/01/index.aspx, viewed Jan. 18, 2012.

42. Stephen Moore, "The Coming Age of Abundance," in Ronald Bailey, ed., *The True State of the Planet*, Free Press, 1995, p. 113.

43. "Interview with the Luddite" (Kevin Kelly, interviewer), *Wired*, June 1995, pp. 166–168, 211–216 (see pp. 213–214).

44. Alexandra Eyle, "No Time Like the Co-Present" (interview with Neil Postman), *NetGuide*, July 1995, pp. 121–122. Richard Sclove and Jeffrey Scheuer, "On the Road Again?: If Information Highways Are Anything Like Interstate Highways—Watch Out!" in Rob Kling, ed., *Computerization and Controversy: Value Conflict and Social Choices*, 2nd ed., Academic Press, 1996, pp. 606–612.

45. Kirkpatrick Sale, *Rebels Against the Future: The Luddites and Their War Against the Industrial Revolution: Lessons for the Computer Age*, Addison-Wesley, 1995, p. 257.

46. Jerry Mander, *In the Absence of the Sacred: The Failure of Technology and the Survival of the Indian Nations*, Sierra Club Books, 1991, p. 61.

47. Neil Postman, *Technopoly: The Surrender of Culture to Technology*, Alfred A. Knopf, 1992, p. 119.

48. Eyle, "No Time Like the Co-Present."

49. Harvey Blume, "Digital Refusnik" (interview with Sven Birkerts), *Wired*, May 1995, pp. 178–179. "Interview With the Luddite."

50. From a study by sociologist Claude Fisher, reported in Charles Paul Freund, "The Geography of Somewhere," *Reason*, May 2001, p. 12.

51. Postman, *Technopoly*, p. 15.

52. See Jane Jacob's classic *The Economy of Cities*, Random House, 1969.

53. Postman, *Technopoly*, p. 6. The Freud quote is from *Civilization and Its Discontent* (e.g., the edition edited and translated by James Strachey, W. W. Norton, 1961, p. 35).

54. This is a much condensed version of my article "Impacts on Community," *Computers & Society* 27(4), December 1997, pp. 15–17.

55. Sclove and Scheuer, "On the Road Again?"

56. John Davis, quoted in Sale, *Rebels Against the Future*, p. 256.

57. Peter Applebome, "A Vision of a Nation No Longer in the U.S.," *New York Times*, Oct. 18, 2007, www.nytimes.com/2007/10/18/nyregion/18towns

.html, viewed Jan. 7, 2012. Sale, *Rebels Against the Future*, p. 257.

58. The quotes are from "Interview With the Luddite," p. 214 and p. 213. Sale expresses this point of view also in *Rebels Against the Future*, p. 213.

59. Sale, *Rebels Against the Future*, p. 256.

60. This dichotomy has always struck me as strange, because it almost suggests that humans are alien creatures who arrived on earth from somewhere else. We evolved here. We are part of nature. A human's house is as natural as a bird's nest, though, unlike birds, we have the capacity to build both ugly and beautiful things.

61. Martin V. Melosi, *Garbage in the Cities: Refuse, Reform, and the Environment: 1880–1980*, Texas A&M University Press, 1981, p. 24–25.

62. In "George Gilder and His Critics," *Forbes ASAP*, Oct. 9, 1995, pp. 165–181.

63. According to engineer Steve Rosenstock, Edison Electric Institute, reported in Steve Hargreaves, "The Internet: One Big Power Suck," *CNN Money*, May 9, 2011, money.cnn.com/2011/05/03/technology/internet_electricity/index.htm, viewed Feb. 9, 2012.

64. Optical fiber: Ronald Bailey, ed., *Earth Report 2000: Revisiting the True State of the Planet*, McGraw Hill, 2000, p. 51.

65. William M. Bulkeley, "Information Age," *Wall Street Journal*, Aug. 5, 1993, p. B1. "Newstrack" ("Claims to Fame"), *Communications of the ACM*, February 1993, p. 14. Vertical Research Partners (verticalresearchpartners.com), reported in Jennifer Levitz, "Tissue Rolls to Mill's Rescue," *Wall Street Journal*, Feb. 16, 2012, p. A3. U.S. Postal Service.

66. Ian Hacking, *The Emergence of Probability*, Cambridge University Press, 1975, p. 108. C. P. Snow, "The Two Cultures and the Scientific Revolution," in *The Two Cultures: And a Second Look*, Cambridge University Press, 1964, pp. 82–83. The population data are from *Health, United States, 2010*, Table 22, p. 134, National Center for Health Statistics, Center for Disease Control, www.cdc.gov/nchs/data/hus/hus10.pdf, viewed Jan. 8, 2012, and from the United Nations, reported in Nicholas Eberstadt, "Population, Food, and Income: Global Trends in the Twentieth Century," pp. 21, 23 (in Bailey, *The True State of the Planet*) and in Theodore Caplow, Louis Hicks, and Ben J. Wattenberg, *The First Measured Century: An Illustrated Guide to Trends in America*, AEI Press, 2001, pp. 4–5. Nonvehicular accidental deaths declined from 72 per 100,000 people in 1900 to 19 per 100,000 people in 1997 (Caplow *et al.*, *The First Measured Century*, p. 149).

67. Moore, "The Coming Age of Abundance," p. 119. Eberstadt, "Population, Food, and Income," p. 34. Family income spent on food: Stephen Moore and Julian L. Simon, *It's Getting Better All the Time: The 100*

Greatest Trends of the 20th Century, Cato Institute, 2000, p. 53, and U.S. Department of Agriculture Economic Research Service, "Food CPI, Prices and Expenditures: Food Expenditure Tables," Table 7, www.ers.usda.gov/Briefing/CPIFoodAndExpenditures/Data/, viewed Mar. 21, 2007. Ronald Bailey, "Billions Served" (interview with Norman Borlaug), *Reason*, April 2000, pp. 30–37. Julian L. Simon, "The State of Humanity: Steadily Improving," *Cato Policy Report*, Sept./Oct. 1995, 17:5, pp. 1, 10–11, 14–15.

68. United Nations, "E-Commerce and Development Report 2001," quoted in Frances Williams, "International Economy & the Americas: UNCTAD Spells Out Benefit of Internet Commerce," *Financial Times*, Nov. 21, 2001.

69. Sale, *Rebels Against the Future*, p. 210.

70. Postman, *Technopoly*, p. 7.

71. "Interview with the Luddite."

72. Bill Richards, "Doctors Can Diagnose Illnesses Long Distance, to the Dismay of Some," *Wall Street Journal*, Jan. 17, 1996, pp. A1, A10.

73. Richards, "Doctors Can Diagnose Illnesses Long Distance."

74. Peter J. Denning, "The Internet After 30 Years," in Dorothy E. Denning and Peter J. Denning, eds., *The Internet Besieged*, Addison Wesley, 1998, p. 20.

75. Donald A. Norman, *Things That Make Us Smart: Defending Human Attribute in the Age of the Machine*, Addison-Wesley, 1993, p. 190.

76. Telephone: Norman, *Things That Make Us Smart*, p. 191. Edison and Watson: Chris Morgan and David Langford, *Facts and Fallacies: A Book of Definitive Mistakes and Misguided Predictions*, St. Martin's Press, 1981 (Watson: p. 44). *Popular Mechanics*, March 1949, p. 258. Olson: Christopher Cerf and Victor Navasky, *The Definitive Compendium of Authoritative Misinformation*, Pantheon Books, 1984, p. 208, 209. Olson made the comment at a convention of the World Future Society. RCA: Thomas Petzinger Jr., "Meanwhile, from the Journal's Archives," *Wall Street Journal*, Jan. 1, 2000, p. R5.

77. Joseph Weizenbaum, *Computer Power and Human Reason: From Judgment to Calculation*, W. H. Freeman and Company, 1976, pp. 270–272.

78. Rodney Brooks, "Toward a Brain–Internet Link," *Technology Review*, November 2003, www.technologyreview.com/Infotech/13349/, viewed July 18, 2007.

79. "Superhuman Imagination," interview with Vernor Vinge by Mike Godwin, *Reason*, May 2007, pp. 32–37.

80. *Wired*, April 2000, www.wired.com/wired/archive/8.04/joy.html, viewed Sept. 7, 2007.

81. Virginia Postrel, "Joy, to the World," *Reason*, June 2000, www.reason.com/news/show/27725.html, viewed Sept. 7, 2007.

82. This statement has been attributed to both Neils Bohr and Albert Einstein; I could not find a reliable source for either.

83. Scientists at the National Oceanic and Atmospheric Administration use such a model ("Climate Impact of Quadrupling CO2," Geophysical Fluid Dynamics Laboratory, National Oceanic and Atmospheric Administration, www.gfdl.noaa.gov/climate-impact-of-quadrupling-co2, viewed Jan. 14, 2012).

8

ERRORS, FAILURES, AND RISKS

8.1 Failures and Errors in Computer Systems

8.1.1 An Overview

"Navigation System Directs Car Into River"

"Data Entry Typo Mutes Millions of U.S. Pagers"

"Flaws Found in Software That Tracks Nuclear Materials"

"Software Glitch Makes Scooter Wheels Suddenly Reverse Direction"

"IRS Computer Sends Bill for $68 Billion in Penalties"

"Robot Kills Worker"

"California Junks $100 Million Child Support System"

"Man Arrested Five Times Due to Faulty FBI Computer Data"

These headlines describe real incidents. Most computer applications, from consumer software to systems that control communications networks, are so complex that it is virtually impossible to produce programs with no errors. In the next few sections, we describe a variety of mistakes, problems, and failures—and some factors responsible for them. Some errors are minor. For example, a word processor might incorrectly hyphenate a word that does not fit at the end of a line. Some incidents are funny. Some are tragic. Some cost billions of dollars. Studying these failures and risks contributes to understanding their causes and helps prevent future failures.

Are computer systems too unreliable and too unsafe to use? Or, like many news stories, do the headlines and horror stories emphasize the bad news—the dramatic but unusual events? We hear reports of car crashes, but we do not hear that drivers completed 200,000 car trips safely in our city today. Although most car trips are safe, there is a good purpose for reporting crashes: It teaches us what the risks are (e.g., driving in heavy fog) and it reminds us to be responsible and careful drivers. Just as many factors cause car crashes (faulty design, sloppy manufacturing or servicing, bad road conditions, a careless or poorly trained driver, confusing road signs, and so on), computer glitches and system failures also have myriad causes, including faulty design, sloppy implementation, careless or insufficiently trained users, and poor user interfaces. Often, there is more than one factor. Because of the complexity of computer systems, it is essential to follow good procedures and professional practices for their development and use. Sometimes, no one does anything clearly wrong, but an accident occurs anyway. Occasionally, the irresponsibility of software developers and managers is comparable to driving while very drunk.

If the inherent complexity of computer systems means they will not be perfect, how can we distinguish between errors we should accept as trade-offs for the benefits of the system and errors that are due to inexcusable carelessness, incompetence, or dishonesty?

How good is good enough? When should we, or the government, or a business decide that a computer system or application is too risky to use? Why do multimillion-dollar systems fail so miserably that the firms and agencies that pay for them abandon them before completion? We cannot answer these questions completely, but this chapter provides some background and discussion that can help us in forming conclusions. It should help us understand the problems from the perspective of several of the roles we play:

- *A computer user.* Whether we use our own tablet computer or a sophisticated, specialized system at work, we should understand the limitations of computer systems and the need for proper training and responsible use.

- *A computer professional.* If you are planning a career as computer professional (system designer, programmer, or quality assurance manager, for example), studying computer system failures should help you become a better professional. Understanding the source and consequences of failures is also valuable if you will be responsible for buying, developing, or managing a complex system for a hospital, airport, or business. The discussions of the examples in this chapter include many implicit and explicit lessons about how you can avoid similar problems.

- *An educated member of society.* There are many personal decisions and social, legal, and political decisions that depend on our understanding of the risks of computer system failures. We could be on a jury. We could be an active member of an organization lobbying for legislation. We could be deciding whether or not to have surgery performed by a robot. Also, we can apply some of the problem-solving approaches and principles in this chapter to professional areas other than computer systems.

We can categorize computer errors and failures in several ways—for example, by the cause, by the seriousness of the effects, or by the application area. In any scheme to organize the discussion, there will be overlap in some categories and mixing of diverse examples in others. I use three categories: problems for individuals, usually in their roles as consumers; system failures that affect large numbers of people and/or cost large amounts of money; and problems in safety-critical applications that may injure or kill people. We will look at one safety-critical case in depth (in Section 8.2): the Therac-25. This computer-controlled radiation treatment machine had a large number of flaws that resulted in the deaths of several patients. In Sections 8.3 and 8.4, we try to make some sense of the jumble of examples. Section 8.3 looks at underlying causes in more depth and describes professional practices and other approaches to preventing failures and handling them properly when they occur. Section 8.4 puts the risks in perspective in various ways.

The incidents described here are a sampling of the many that occur. Robert Charette, an expert on software risk management, emphasizes that computer system errors and failures occur in all countries, in systems developed for businesses, governments, and nonprofit organizations (large and small) "without regard to status or reputation."[1] In most cases, by mentioning specific companies or products, I do not mean to single those out as unusual offenders. One can find many similar stories in news reports, software engineering journals, and in The Risks-Forum Digest organized by Peter Neumann.[2] Neumann collects thousands of reports describing a wide range of computer-related problems.

8.1.2 PROBLEMS FOR INDIVIDUALS

Billing errors

The first few errors we look at are relatively simple ones whose negative consequences were undone with relative ease.

- A woman received a $6.3 million bill for electricity. The correct amount was $63. The cause was an input error made by someone using a new computer system.
- The IRS is a constant source of major bloopers. When it modified its programs to avoid billing victims of a Midwest flood, the computer generated erroneous bills for almost 5000 people. One Illinois couple received a bill for a few thousand dollars in taxes—and $68 billion in penalties. In one year the IRS sent 3000 people bills for slightly more than $300 million. One woman received a tax bill for $40,000,001,541.13.
- The auto insurance rate of a 101-year-old man suddenly tripled. Rates depend on age, but the program handled ages only up to 100. It mistakenly classified the man as a teenager.
- Hundreds of Chicago cat owners received bills from the city for failure to register dachshunds, which they did not own. The city used two databases to try to find unlicensed pets. One database used DHC as the code for domestic house cat, and the other used the same code for dachshund.

Programmers and users could have avoided some of these errors. For example, programmers can include tests to determine whether a billing amount is outside some reasonable range or changed significantly from previous bills. In other words, because programs can contain errors, good systems have provisions for checking their results. If you have some programming experience, you know how easy it would be to include such tests and generate a list of cases for a person to review. These errors are perhaps more humorous than serious. Big mistakes are obvious. They usually get fixed quickly. They are worth studying, because the same kinds of design and programming errors can have more serious consequences in different applications. In the Therac-25 case (Section 8.2), we will see that including tests for inconsistent or inappropriate input could have saved lives.

How close to perfection should we expect billing systems to be? A water-utility company sent a customer an incorrect bill for $22,000. A spokesman for the company pointed out that one incorrect bill out of 275,000 monthly bills is pretty good. It is better than a 99.999% accuracy rate. Is that reasonable? At some point, the expense of improving a system is not worth the gain, especially for applications where the impact of the error is small and errors can be detected (once they occur) and corrected at much lower cost than it would take to try to prevent them.

Inaccurate and misinterpreted data in databases

Credit bureau records incorrectly listed thousands of New England residents as not having paid their local property taxes. An input error appeared to be the cause of the problem. People were denied loans before someone identified the scope of the problem and the credit bureau corrected it. Like $40 billion tax bills, a systematic error affecting thousands of people is likely to get noticed. The relevant company or agency is likely to fix it quickly. More serious, perhaps, are all the errors in individual people's records. In one case, a county agency used the wrong middle name in a report to a credit bureau about a father who did not make his child-support payments. Another man in the same county had the exact name reported. He could not get credit to buy a car or a house. A man applied for jobs at several retail stores. They all turned him down. Eventually he learned that the stores used a database to screen applicants, and it listed him as a shoplifter. A real shoplifter had given the police the innocent man's identification from a lost wallet.

It is difficult to get accurate and meaningful error rates for major databases with information about millions of people. Also, we need to distinguish between a spelling error in someone's address and an incorrect report that someone bounced several checks. The results of numerous surveys and studies vary considerably, but they indicate that a high percentage of credit records have serious errors.

Errors affecting job applicants: Section 6.3.1

Federal law requires states to maintain databases of people convicted of sex crimes against children and to release information about them to the public. A family was harassed, threatened, and physically attacked after their state posted an online list of addresses where sex offenders live. The state did not know the offender had moved away before the family moved in. A man murdered two men in Washington state after getting their addresses from the state's sex offender database, and another man killed two men listed in Maine's online registry. One of them was in the database because, as a teenager, he had sex with his girlfriend who was a few weeks below the age of consent. While technically not an error in the database, this case illustrates the need for careful thought about what a database includes and how it is presented to the public, especially if it involves a highly charged subject.

A high school excluded a 14-year-old boy from football and some classes without explanation. He eventually learned that school officials thought he had been using drugs while in junior high school. The two schools used different disciplinary codes in their computerized records. The boy had been guilty of chewing gum and being late. This case is very similar to the case of the dachshund/cat confusion described earlier—except that the consequences were more significant. Both cases illustrate the problems of relying on computer systems without taking the responsibility of learning enough about them to use them properly.

When errors occur in databases used by law enforcement agencies, the consequences can include arrests at gunpoint, strip searches, and time in jail with violent criminals. For example, two adults went to jail and a child to a juvenile home for 24 hours while police determined that they really had rented the rental car they were driving. The car rental company had listed the car as stolen. An adoption agency ran a routine check on an applicant and found a conviction for grand larceny. In fact, the applicant had taken part in a college prank—stealing a restaurant sign—years before. He had apologized and paid for the damage, and the charges had been dropped. The error could have caused the agency to deny the adoption. Police arrested a Michigan man for several crimes, including murders, committed in Los Angeles. Another man had assumed his identity. It is understandable that the FBI's National Crime Information Center (NCIC) database showed the innocent man as wanted—someone using his name was committing crimes. However, the innocent man was arrested five times; the database was not corrected. The military imprisoned a man for five months because NCIC mistakenly reported that he was AWOL.* A college professor returning from London spent two days in jail after a routine check with NCIC at Customs showed that he was a wanted fugitive. NCIC was wrong— for the third time—about this particular man. Police stopped and frisked an innocent driver because his license plate number incorrectly appeared as the license number of a man who had killed a state trooper. The computer record did not include a description of the car. (NCIC now includes digitized photographs and fingerprints to help reduce the number of incidents in which police detain an innocent person.)[3]

After the terrorist attacks in 2001, the FBI gave a "watch list" to police departments and businesses such as car rental agencies, banks, casinos, and trucking and chemical firms. Recipients emailed the list to others, and eventually thousands of police departments and thousands of companies had copies. Many incorporated the list into their databases and systems that screened customers or job applicants. Although the list included people who were not suspects but whom the FBI wanted to question, some companies labeled the list "Suspected terrorists." Many entries did not include date-of-birth, address, or other identifying information, making mistaken identifications likely. Some companies received the list by fax and typed misspelled names from blurred copies into their databases. The FBI stopped updating the list but did not tell the recipients; thus, many entries became obsolete.[4] Even if someone corrects an error in the original database, problems may not be over for the affected person. Copies of incorrect or mislabeled data remain in other systems.

Several factors contribute to the frequency and severity of the problems people suffer because of errors in databases and misinterpretation of their contents:

---

* AWOL means "absent without official leave."

- A large population (Many people have identical or similar names, and most of our interactions are with strangers.)
- Automated processing without human common sense or the power to recognize special cases
- Overconfidence in the accuracy of data stored on computers
- Errors (some due to carelessness) in data entry
- Failure to update information and correct errors
- Lack of accountability for errors

The first factor is unlikely to change. It is the context in which we live. The second is partly a side effect of the speed and processing ability of computer technology, but we can reduce its negative impacts with better system specifications and training of users. The remaining factors in the list above are all within our control as individuals, professionals, and policy makers. We discuss them throughout this chapter.

> *It is repugnant to the principles of a free society that a person should ever be taken into police custody because of a computer error precipitated by government carelessness. As automation increasingly invades modern life, the potential for Orwellian mischief grows.*
>
> —Arizona Supreme Court[5]

8.1.3   System Failures

Modern communications, power, medical, financial, retail, and transportation systems depend heavily on computer systems. They do not always function as planned. We give examples of failures, with some indications of the causes. For computer science students and others who might contract for or manage custom software, one aim is to see the serious impacts of the failures—and to see what you want to work hard to avoid. The lessons of adequate planning and testing, of having backup plans in case of failures, and of honesty in dealing with errors apply to large projects in other professions as well.

Millions of BlackBerry users did not get their email for nine hours after the company installed a faulty software update. Customers of AT&T lost telephone service for voice and data for hours because of a software error in a four-million-line program. A three-line change in a two-million-line telecommunications switching program caused a failure of telephone networks in several major cities. Although the program underwent 13 weeks of testing, it was not retested after the change—which contained a typo. American Express Company's credit card verification system failed during the Christmas shopping season. Merchants had to call in for verification, overwhelming the call center. Log-ins overloaded Skype's peer-to-peer network system when a huge number of people rebooted

BlackBerry thumb and RSI

Millions of children play games on small electronic devices, and millions of adults answer email on portable electronic gadgets with mini keypads. In many professions, people type on a keyboard for hours each day. Most of the risks we describe in this chapter result from errors in software, poor system design, or inaccurate and misinterpreted information. Here, we look at physical phenomena known as BlackBerry thumb, gamer's thumb, Nintendonitis, repetitive strain injury (RSI), and by a variety of other terms. Repetitive strain injury, the more formal term, covers a variety of injuries or pain in thumbs, fingers, wrists, and arms (and sometimes neck and shoulders). You may have seen computer programmers, prolific bloggers, or secretaries wearing wrist braces, called splints—a common sign of RSI. These injuries can make ordinary activities painful or impossible and can prevent people from working.

RSI is not a new disease. There are references to similar problems in the 18th and 19th centuries afflicting clerks and scribes (we used to call this "writer's cramp"), women who milked cows, and others whose work required repetitive hand motions. RSI problems occur among gymnasts, sign language interpreters for the deaf, "pushup enthusiasts," auto workers, seamstresses, musicians, carpenters, meat processors, and workers in bakery factories. (An article in the *Journal of the American Medical Association* listed 29 occupations with common RSI problems.)[6] Computer game players and smartphone and keyboard users are among the newest significant group of RSI sufferers.

Thousands of people suffering from RSI sued keyboard makers and employers in the 1990s. They charged that the companies were at fault and should pay for medical costs and damages to the victims. Many of the suits resulted in dismissals or decisions for the defendants. The uncertainty of causation (defects in the devices or improper use) made it difficult to win such suits. Some judges and others compare the complaints to ordinary aches and pains from overexercising or overusing a normally safe tool or device. What would we think of an RSI lawsuit against the maker of a tennis racket or a violin?

Attention to proper ergonomic design of keyboards and workstations reduced RSI problems for keyboard users. We can now buy split, twisted, and otherwise nontraditionally shaped keyboards—each one implementing some manufacturer's idea of what will be more comfortable and reduce strain. But modifying equipment alone does not solve the problem. RSI experts stress the importance of training in proper technique (including the importance of rest breaks, posture, and exercises). One can install free software that interrupts the user at regular intervals for rest breaks and software-guided exercises. Speech input devices might also reduce RSI caused by keyboard use. (But we might discover an increase in strain of the vocal cords.) Partly because of growing recognition of the RSI problem, and partly as protection against lawsuits, computer companies now provide information about proper use and arrangement of keyboards. Some game device makers package their product with reminders for users to take rest breaks.

Adult users of any tool or toy should learn proper techniques for its use. Young children need parental supervision or rules for electronic devices, as they might, for example, about wearing a helmet when riding a bicycle. Employers have a responsibility to provide training in proper and safe use of tools. Being aware of the potential for RSI might or might not encourage game players and tweeters to take breaks and rest their hands and fingers. Mothers and doctors tell us repeatedly that we should sit up straight, exercise often, and eat our vegetables. Many people do not follow this advice—but, once we have the information, we can choose what to do with it.

Balance is very important for hand comfort. You'll be surprised at how quick your wrist will ache if the knife is not balanced properly.
—George McNeill, Executive Chef, Royal York Hotel, Toronto (on an advertisement for fine cutlery)

their computers after installing routine Windows updates. A majority of Skype's Internet phone users could not log in for two days.

When a Galaxy IV satellite computer failed, many systems we take for granted stopped working. Pager service stopped for an estimated 85% of users in the United States, including hospitals and police departments. Airlines that got their weather information from the satellite had to delay flights. The gas stations of a major chain could not verify credit cards. Some services were quickly switched to other satellites or backup systems. It took days to restore others.[7]

Every few years, the computer system of one of the world's large stock exchanges or brokerages fails. An error in a software upgrade shut down trading on the Tokyo Stock Exchange. A glitch in an upgrade in the computer system at Charles Schwab Corporation crashed the system for more than two hours and caused intermittent problems for several days. Customers could not access their accounts or trade online. A computer malfunction froze the London Stock Exchange for almost eight hours—on the last day of the tax year, affecting many people's tax bills.[8]

A failure of Amtrak's reservation and ticketing system during Thanksgiving weekend caused delays because agents had no printed schedules or fare lists. Virgin America airline switched to a new reservation system a month before Thanksgiving. Its website and check-in kiosks did not work properly for weeks.[9]

The $125 million Mars Climate Orbiter disappeared when it should have gone into orbit around Mars. One team working on the navigation software used English-measure units while another team used metric units. The investigation of the loss emphasized that while the error itself was the immediate cause, the fundamental problem was the lack of procedures that would have detected the error.[10]

An inventory management system caused severe losses for businesses that used it. The system had been developed and written for one computer and operating system, then modified and sold to run on another. The modified system sometimes did not accept purchase orders, causing an expensive backlog in orders. Printing invoices took minutes instead of seconds. The system gave incorrect information about inventory and prices. Several users claimed that although the company that sold the system received complaints of serious problems from many customers, the company told customers the problems they were having were unique. Eventually, the company agreed it "did not service customers well" and the program should have undergone more extensive testing. The sources of the problems included technical difficulties (converting software to a different system), poor management decisions (inadequate testing of the modified system on the new platform), and, according to the customers, dishonesty in promoting the system and responding to the problems.[11]

Voting systems

The U.S. presidential election of 2000 demonstrated some of the problems of old-fashioned election machines and paper or punch-card ballots. Vote counters found these

Destroying careers and summer vacations[12]

CTB/McGraw-Hill develops and scores standardized tests for schools. Millions of students take its tests each year. An error in CTB's software caused it to report test results incorrectly—substantially lower than the correct scores—in several states. In New York City, school principals and superintendents lost their jobs because their schools appeared to be doing a poor job of teaching students to read. Educators endured personal and professional disgrace. One man said he applied for 30 other superintendent jobs in the state but did not get one. Parents were upset. Nearly 9000 students had to attend summer school because of the incorrect scores. Eventually, CTB corrected the error. New York City's reading scores had actually risen five percentage points.

Why was the problem not detected sooner, soon enough to avoid firings and summer school? School testing officials in several states were skeptical of the scores showing sudden, unexpected drops. They questioned CTB, but CTB told them nothing was wrong. They said CTB did not tell them that other states experienced similar problems and also complained. When CTB discovered the software error, the company did not inform the schools for many weeks, even though the president of CTB met with school officials about the problem during those weeks.

What lessons can we learn from this case? Software errors happen, of course. People usually notice significant mistakes, and they did here. But the company did not take seriously enough the questions about the accuracy of the results and was reluctant to admit the possibility—and later the certainty—of errors. It is this behavior that must change. The damage from an error can be small if the error is found and corrected quickly.

CTB recommended that school districts not use scores on its standardized tests as the sole factor in deciding which students should attend summer school. But New York City did so. In a case with a similar lesson, Florida state officials relied on computer-generated lists of possible felons to prevent some people from voting, even though the database company supplying the lists said the state should do additional verification.[13] Relying solely on one factor or on data from one database is temptingly easy. It is a temptation that people responsible for critical decisions in many situations should resist.

ballots sometimes difficult to read or ambiguous. Recounting was a slow tedious process. Many people saw electronic systems as the solution. In 2002, Congress passed the Help America Vote Act and authorized $3.8 billion to improve voting systems. By the 2006 elections, only a very small percentage of Americans voted with paper ballots. The rush to electronic voting machines demonstrated that they too could have numerous faults. Here are some of the problems that occurred: Some electronic voting systems just crashed—voters were unable to vote. Machines in North Carolina failed to count more than 400 votes because of a technical problem. One county lost more than 4000 votes because the machine's memory was full. A programming error generated 100,000 extra votes in one Texas county. A programming error caused some candidates to receive votes actually cast for other candidates.

Security against vote fraud and sabotage is a significant issue in elections. Programmers or hackers can intentionally rig software to give inaccurate results. Depending on the structure of the system, independent recounting may be difficult. Security researchers strongly criticized electronic voting machines. They said the machines had insecure encryption techniques (or none at all), insufficient security for installation of upgrades to software, and poor physical protection of the memory card on which the system stores votes. One research group demonstrated a system's vulnerability to a virus that essentially took over the machine and manipulated the vote results. They found that voting system developers lacked sufficient security training. Programmers omitted basic procedures such as input validation and boundary checks. Researchers opened the access panel on a voting machine with a standard key that is easily available and used in office furniture, electronic equipment, and hotel minibars. There were certification standards for voting systems, but some flawed systems were certified; the standards were inadequate.[14] In some counties, election officials gave voting machines to high school students and other volunteers to store at home and deliver to polling places on election day.

Many of the failures that occurred result from causes we will see over and over: lack of sufficient planning and thought about security issues, insufficient testing, and insufficient training. (In this application, the task of training users is complex. Thousands of ordinary people volunteer as poll workers and manage and operate the machines on election day.) An underlying cause is haste. In projects like these, the desire of states to obtain federal grants encourages haste. The grants have short limits on how soon the states must spend the money,

Long before we voted on computers, Chicago and parts of Texas were infamous for vote fraud. In some cities, election officials found boxes full of uncounted paper ballots after an election was over. Reasonable accuracy and authenticity of vote counts are essential in a healthy democracy. Electronic systems have the potential for reducing some kinds of fraud and accidental loss of ballots, but they introduce a host of other problems that must be addressed. The first step is to recognize that developing them requires a high degree of professionalism and a high degree of security. In the near future, we will probably vote online. Sadly, it is likely that, at least at first, online voting systems will be highly vulnerable to fraud.

> *Those who cast the votes decide nothing. Those who count the votes decide everything.*
>
> —Attributed to Joseph Stalin (Premier of the Soviet Union)[15]

Stalled airports: Denver, Hong Kong, and Malaysia

Ten months after the $3.2 billion Denver International Airport airport was supposed to have opened, I flew over the huge airport. It covers 53 square miles, roughly twice the size of Manhattan. It was an eerie sight—nothing moved. There were no airplanes or people at the airport and no cars on the miles of wide highway leading to it. The opening was rescheduled at least four times. The delay cost more than $30 million per month in bond interest and operating costs. The computer-controlled baggage-handling system, which cost $193 million, caused most of the delay.[16]

The plan for the baggage system was quite ambitious. Outbound luggage checked at ticket counters or curbside counters was to travel to any part of the airport in less than 10 minutes via an automated system of carts traveling at up to 19 miles per hour on 22 miles of underground tracks. Similarly, inbound luggage would go to terminals or transfer directly to connecting flights anywhere in the airport. Carts, bar-coded for their destinations, carried the bags. Laser scanners throughout the system tracked the 4000 carts and sent information about their locations to computers. The computers used a database of flights, gates, and routing information to control motors and switches to route the carts to their destinations.

The system did not work as planned. During tests over several months, carts crashed into each other at track intersections. The system misrouted, dumped, and flung luggage. Carts needed to move luggage went by mistake to waiting pens. Both the specific problems and the general underlying causes are instructive. Some of the specific problems:

- *Real-world problems.* Some scanners got dirty or knocked out of alignment and could not detect carts going by. Faulty latches on the carts caused luggage to fall onto the tracks between stops.

- *Problems in other systems.* The airport's electrical system could not handle the power surges associated with the baggage system. The first full-scale test blew so many circuits that the test had to be halted.

- *Software errors.* A software error caused the routing of carts to waiting pens when they were actually needed.

No one expects software and hardware of this complexity to work perfectly when first tested. In real-time systems,* especially, there are numerous interactions and conditions that designers might not anticipate. Mangling a suitcase is not embarrassing if it occurs during an early test and if the problem is fixed. It is embarrassing if it occurs after the system is in operation or if it takes a year to fix. What led to the extraordinary delay in the Denver baggage system? There seem to have been two main causes:

- *The time allowed for development and testing of the system was insufficient.* The only other baggage system of comparable size was at Frankfurt Airport in Germany. The company that built that system spent six years on development and two years testing and debugging. BAE Automated Systems, the company that built the Denver system, was asked to do it in two years. Some reports indicate that

---

* Real-time systems are systems that must detect and respond to or control activities of objects or people in the real world within time constraints.

because of the electrical problems at the airport, there were only six weeks for testing.

- *Denver made significant changes in specifications after the project began.* Originally, the automated system was to serve United Airlines, but Denver officials decided to expand it to include the entire airport, making the system 14 times as large as the automated baggage system BAE had installed for United at San Francisco International Airport.

As a *PC Week* reporter said, "The bottom-line lesson is that system designers must build in plenty of test and debugging time when scaling up proven technology into a much more complicated environment."[17] Some observers criticized BAE for taking on the job when the company should have known that there was not enough time to complete it. Others blamed the city government for poor management, politically motivated decisions, and proceeding with a grandiose but unrealistic plan.

Opening day at the new airports in Hong Kong and Kuala Lumpur were disasters. The ambitious and complex computer systems at these airports were to manage *everything*: moving 20,000 pieces of luggage per hour and coordinating and scheduling crews, gate assignments for flights, and so on. Both systems failed spectacularly. At Hong Kong's Chek Lap Kok airport, cleaning crews and fuel trucks, baggage, passengers, and cargo went to the wrong gates, sometimes far from where their airplanes were. Airplanes scheduled to take off were empty. At Kuala Lumpur, airport employees had to write boarding passes by hand and carry luggage. Flights, of course, were delayed; food cargo rotted in the tropical heat.

At both airports, the failures were blamed on people typing in incorrect information. In Hong Kong, it was perhaps a wrong gate or arrival time that was dutifully sent throughout the system. In Kuala Lumpur, mistakes by check-in agents unfamiliar with the system paralyzed it. "There's nothing wrong with the system," said a spokeman at the airport in Malaysia. A spokesman at Hong Kong made a similar statement. They are deeply mistaken. One incorrect gate number would not have caused the problems experienced at Hong Kong. Any system that has a large number of users and a lot of user input must be designed and tested to handle input mistakes. The "system" includes more than software and hardware. It includes the people who operate it. As in the case of the Denver airport, there were questions about whether political considerations, rather than the needs of the project, determined the scheduled time for the opening of the airports.[18]

Abandoned systems

The flaws in some systems are so extreme that the systems end up in the trash after wasting millions, or even billions, of dollars. A large British food retailer spent more than $500 million on an automated supply management system; it did not work. The Ford Motor Company abandoned a $400 million purchasing system. The California and Washington state motor vehicle departments each spent more than $40 million on computer systems

- Lack of clear, well-thought-out goals and specifications
- Poor management and poor communication among customers, designers, programmers, and so on
- Institutional or political pressures that encourage unrealistically low bids, unrealistically low budget requests, and underestimates of time requirements
- Use of very new technology, with unknown reliability and problems, perhaps for which software developers have insufficient experience and expertise
- Refusal to recognize or admit that a project is in trouble

Figure 8.1 Why abandonned systems failed.

before abandoning them because they never worked properly. A consortium of hotels and a rental car business spent $125 million on a comprehensive travel-industry reservation system, then canceled the project because it did not work. The state of California spent more than $100 million to develop one of the largest and most expensive state computer systems in the country: a system for tracking parents who owe child support payments. After five years, the state abandoned the system. After spending $4 billion, the IRS abandoned a tax-system modernization plan; a Government Accountability Office report blamed mismanagement. The FBI spent $170 million to develop a database called the Virtual Case File system to manage evidence in investigations, then scrapped it because of many problems. A Department of Justice report blamed poorly defined and changing design requirements, lack of technical expertise, and poor management. (The FBI's next major attempt at a paperless case-management system was scheduled for completion in 2009 but delayed at least until 2012.)[19] There are many more such examples.

Software expert Robert Charette estimates that from 5% to 15% of information technology projects are abandoned before or soon after delivery as "hopelessly inadequate." Figure 8.1 includes some reasons he cites.[20] Such large losses demand attention from computer professionals, information technology managers, business executives, and public officials who set budgets and schedules for large projects.

Legacy systems

After US Airways and America West merged, they combined their reservations systems. The self-service check-in kiosks failed. Long lines at ticket counters delayed thousands of passengers and flights. Merging different computer systems is extremely tricky, and problems are common. But this incident illustrates another factor. According to a vice president of US Airways, most airline systems date from the 1960s and 1970s. Designed for the mainframe computers of that era, they, in some cases, replaced reservations on 3 × 5 paper cards. These old systems "are very reliable, but very inflexible," the airline executive said.[21] These are examples of "legacy systems"—out-of-date systems (hardware, software, or peripheral equipment) still in use, often with special interfaces, conversion software, and other adaptations to make them interact with more modern systems.

The problems of legacy systems are numerous. Old hardware fails and replacement parts are hard to find. Old software often runs on newer hardware, but it is still old software. Programmers no longer learn the old programming languages. Old programs often had little or no documentation, and the programmers who wrote the software or operated the systems have left the company, retired, or died. If there were good design documents and manuals, they probably no longer exist or cannot be found. Limited computer memory led to obscure and terse programming practices. A variable a programmer might now call "flight_number" would then have been simply "f."

The major users of computers in the early days included banks, airlines, government agencies, and providers of infrastructure services such as power companies. The systems grew gradually. A complete redesign and development of a fully new, modern system would, of course, be expensive. It would require a major retraining project. The conversion to the new system, possibly requiring some downtime, could also be very disruptive. Thus, legacy systems persist.

We will continue to invent new programming languages, paradigms, and protocols—and we will later add on to the systems we develop as they age. Among the lessons legacy systems provide for computer professionals is the recognition that someone might be using your software 30 or 40 years from now. It is important to document, document, document your work. It is important to design for flexibility, expansion, and upgrades.

8.1.4   What Goes Wrong?

Computer systems fail for two general reasons: the job they are doing is inherently difficult, and sometimes the job is done poorly. Several factors combine to make the task difficult. Computer systems interact with the real world (including both machinery and unpredictable humans), include complex communications networks, have numerous features and interconnected subsystems, and are extremely large. Automobiles, passenger airplanes, and jet fighters contain millions of lines of computer code.[22] A smartphone has several millions of lines of code. Computer software is "nonlinear" in the sense that, whereas a small error in a mechanical system might cause a small degradation in performance, a single typo in a computer program can cause a dramatic difference in behavior.

The job can be done poorly at any of many stages, from system design and implementation to system management and use. (This characteristic is not unique to computer systems, of course. We can say the same about building a bridge, a house, a car, or any complex system.) Figure 8.1 (in Section 8.1.3) summarized high-level, management-related causes of system failures. Figure 8.2 lists more factors in computer errors and system failures. The examples we described illustrate most of them. We comment on a few.

- Design and development:
  Inadequate attention to potential safety risks
  Interaction with physical devices that do not work as expected
  Incompatibility of software and hardware, or of application software and the operating system
  Not planning and designing for unexpected inputs or circumstances
  Confusing user interfaces
  Insufficient testing
  Reuse of software from another system without adequate checking
  Overconfidence in software
  Carelessness
- Management and use:
  Data-entry errors
  Inadequate training of users
  Errors in interpreting results or output
  Failure to keep information in databases up to date
  Overconfidence in software by users
  Insufficient planning for failures; no backup systems or procedures
- Misrepresentation, hiding problems; inadequate response to reported problems
- Insufficient market or legal incentives to do a better job

Figure 8.2   Some factors in computer system errors and failures.

Overconfidence

Overconfidence, or an unrealistic or inadequate understanding of the risks in a complex system, is a core issue. When system developers and users appreciate the risks, they have more motivation to use the techniques that are available to build more reliable and safer systems and to be responsible users. How many people do not back up their files or contact lists until after their computers crash or they lose their phones?

Some safety-critical systems that failed had supposedly "fail-safe" computer controls. In some cases the logic of the program was fine, but the failure resulted from not considering how the system interacts with real users or real-world problems (such as loose wires, fallen leaves on train tracks, a cup of coffee spilled in an airplane cockpit, and so on).

Unrealistic estimates of reliability or safety can come from genuine lack of understanding, from carelessness, or from intentional misrepresentation. People without a high regard for honesty, or who work in an organization that lacks a culture of honesty and focus on safety, sometimes give in to business or political pressure to exaggerate safety, to hide flaws, to avoid unfavorable publicity, or to avoid the expense of corrections or lawsuits.

Reuse of software: the Ariane 5 rocket and "No Fly" lists

Less than 40 seconds after the first launch of France's Ariane 5 rocket, the rocket veered off course and was destroyed as a safety precaution. The rocket and the satellites it was carrying cost approximately $500 million. A software error caused the failure.[23] The Ariane 5 used some software designed for the earlier, successful Ariane 4. The software included a module that ran for about a minute after initiation of a launch on the Ariane 4. It did not have to run after takeoff of the Ariane 5, but a decision was made to avoid introducing new errors by making changes in a module that operated well in Ariane 4. This module did calculations related to velocity. The Ariane 5 travels faster than the Ariane 4 after takeoff. The calculations produced numbers bigger than the program could handle (an "overflow" in technical jargon), causing the system to halt.

A woman named Jan Adams, and many other people with first initial J and last name Adams, were flagged as possible terrorists when they tried to board an airplane. The name "Joseph Adams" is on a "No Fly" list of suspected terrorists (and other people considered safety threats) that the Transportaton Security Agency had given to the airlines. To compare passenger names with those on the "No Fly" list, some airlines used old software and strategies designed to help ticket agents quickly locate a passenger's reservation record (e.g., if the passenger calls in with a question or to make a change). The software searches quickly and "casts a wide net." That is, it finds any possible match, which a sales agent can then verify. In the intended applications for the software, there is no inconvenience to anyone if the program presents the agent with a few potential matches of similar names. In the context of tagging people as possible terrorists, a person mistakenly "matched" will likely undergo questioning and extra luggage and body searches by security agents.

Do these examples tell us that we should not reuse software? One of the goals of programming paradigms such as object-oriented code is to make software elements that can be widely used, thus saving time and effort. Reuse of working software should also increase safety and reliability. After all, it has undergone field testing in a real, operational environment; we know it works. At least, we think it works. The critical point is that it works in a different environment. It is essential to reexamine the specifications and design of the software, consider implications and risks for the new environment, and retest the software for the new use.

8.2 Case Study: The Therac-25

8.2.1 THERAC-25 RADIATION OVERDOSES

The benefits of computing technology to health care are numerous and very impressive. They include improved diagnosis, monitoring of health conditions, development of new drugs, information systems that speed treatment and reduce errors, devices that save lives, and devices that increase the safety of surgeries. Yet one of the classic case studies of a deadly software failure is a medical device: a radiation treatment machine.

The Therac-25 was a software-controlled radiation-therapy machine used to treat people with cancer. Between 1985 and 1987, Therac-25 machines at four medical centers gave massive overdoses of radiation to six patients. In some cases, the operator repeated an overdose because the machine's display indicated that it had given no dose. Medical personnel later estimated that some patients received more than 100 times the intended dose. These incidents caused severe and painful injuries and the deaths of three patients. Why is it important to study a case as old as this? To avoid repeating the errors. Medical physicists operating a different radiation-treatment machine in Panama in 2000 tried to circumvent a limitation in the software in an attempt to provide more shielding for patients. Their actions caused dosage miscalculations. Twenty-eight patients received overdoses of radiation, and several died.[24] It seems that dramatic lessons need repetition with each new generation.

What went wrong with the Therac-25?

Studies of the Therac-25 incidents showed that many factors contributed to the injuries and deaths. The factors include lapses in good safety design, insufficient testing, bugs in the software that controlled the machines, and an inadequate system of reporting and investigating the accidents. (Articles by computer scientists Nancy Leveson and Clark Turner and by Jonathan Jacky are the main sources for this discussion.[25])

To understand the discussion of the problems, it will help to know a little about the machine. The Therac-25 is a dual-mode machine. That is, it can generate an electron beam or an x-ray photon beam. The type of beam needed depends on the tumor being treated. The machine's linear accelerator produces a high-energy electron beam (25 million electron volts) that is dangerous. Patients must not be exposed to the raw beam. A computer monitors and controls movement of a turntable that holds three sets of devices. Depending on the intended treatment, the machine rotates a different set of devices in front of the beam to spread it and make it safe. It is essential that the proper protective device be in place when the electron beam is on. A third position of the turntable uses a light beam instead of the electron beam to help the operator position the beam precisely in the correct place on the patient's body.

8.2.2 Software and Design Problems

Design flaws

The Therac-25 followed earlier machines called the Therac-6 and Therac-20. It differed from them in that it was fully computer controlled. The older machines had hardware safety interlock mechanisms, independent of the computer, that prevented the beam from firing in unsafe conditions. The design of the Therac-25 eliminated many of these hardware safety features. The Therac-25 reused some software from the Therac-20 and Therac-6. The developers apparently assumed the software functioned correctly. This assumption was wrong. When new operators used the Therac-20, there were frequent shutdowns and blown fuses, but no overdoses. The Therac-20 software had bugs, but the hardware safety mechanisms were doing their job. Either the manufacturers did not know of the problems with the Therac-20, or they completely missed the serious implications.

The Therac-25 malfunctioned frequently. One facility said there were sometimes 40 dose-rate malfunctions in a day, generally underdoses. Thus, operators became used to error messages appearing often, with no indication that there might be safety hazards.

There were a number of weaknesses in the design of the operator interface. The error messages that appeared on the display were simply error numbers or obscure messages ("Malfunction 54" or "H-tilt"). This was not unusual for early computer programs when computers had much less memory and mass storage than they have now. One had to look up each error number in a manual for more explanation. The operator's manual for the Therac-25, however, did not include an explanation of the error messages. The maintenance manual did not explain them either. The machine distinguished between errors by the amount of effort needed to continue operation. For certain error conditions, the machine paused, and the operator could proceed (turn on the electron beam) by pressing one key. For other kinds of errors, the machine suspended operation and had to be completely reset. One would presume that the machine would allow one-key resumption only after minor, non-safety-related errors. Yet one-key resumption occurred in some of the accidents in which patients received multiple overdoses.

Atomic Energy of Canada, Ltd. (AECL), a Canadian government corporation, manufactured the Therac-25. Investigators studying the accidents found that AECL produced very little documentation concerning the software specifications or the testing plan during development of the program. Although AECL claimed that they tested the machine extensively, it appeared that the test plan was inadequate.

Bugs

Investigators were able to trace some of the overdoses to two specific software errors. Because many readers of this book are computer science students, I will describe the bugs. These descriptions illustrate the importance of using good programming techniques. Because some readers have little or no programming knowledge, I will simplify the descriptions.

After the operator entered treatment parameters at a control console, a software procedure called Set-Up Test performed a variety of checks to be sure the machine was in the correct position, and so on. If anything was not ready, this procedure scheduled itself to rerun the checks. (The system might simply have to wait for the turntable to move into place.) The Set-Up Test procedure can run several hundred times while setting up for one treatment. A flag variable indicated whether a specific device on the machine was in the correct position. A zero value meant the device was ready; a nonzero value meant it must be checked. To ensure that the device was checked, each time the Set-Up Test procedure ran, it incremented the variable to make it nonzero. The problem was that the flag variable was stored in one byte. After the 256th call to the routine, the flag overflowed and showed a value of zero. (If you are not familiar with programming, think of this as an automobile's odometer rolling over to zero after reaching the highest number it can show.) If everything else happened to be ready at that point, the program did not check the device position, and the treatment could proceed. Investigators believe that in some of the accidents, this bug allowed the electron beam to be on when the turntable was positioned for use of the light beam, and there was no protective device in place to attenuate the beam.

Part of the tragedy in this case is that the error was such a simple one, with a simple correction. No good student programmer should have made this error. The solution is to set the flag variable to a fixed value, say 1, rather than incrementing it, to indicate that the device needs checking.

Other bugs caused the machine to ignore changes or corrections made by the operator at the console. When the operator typed in all the necessary information for a treatment, the program began moving various devices into place. This process could take several seconds. The software checked for editing of the input by the operator during this time and restarted the set-up if it detected editing. However, because of bugs in this section of the program, some parts of the program learned of the edited information while others did not. This led to machine settings that were incorrect and inconsistent with safe treatment. According to the later investigation by the Food and Drug Administration (FDA), there appeared to be no consistency checks in the program. The error was most likely to occur with an experienced operator who was quick at editing input.

In a real-time, multitasking system that controls physical machinery while an operator enters—and might modify—input, there are many complex factors that can contribute to subtle, intermittent, and hard-to-detect bugs. Programmers working on such systems must learn to be aware of the potential problems and to use good programming practices to avoid them.

8.2.3 Why So Many Incidents?

There were six known Therac-25 overdoses. You may wonder why hospitals and clinics continued to use the machine after the first one.

The Therac-25 had been in service for up to two years at some clinics. Medical facilities did not immediately pull it from service after the first few accidents because they did not know immediately that it caused the injuries. Medical staff members considered various other explanations. The staff at the site of the first incident said that one reason they were not certain of the source of the patient's injuries was that they had never seen such a massive radiation overdose before. They questioned the manufacturer about the possibility of overdoses, but the company responded (after the first, third, and fourth accidents) that the machine could not have caused the patient injuries. According to the Leveson and

Turner investigative report, they also told the facilities that there had been no similar cases of injuries.

After the second accident, AECL investigated and found several problems related to the turntable (not including any of the ones we described). They made some changes in the system and recommended operational changes. They declared that they had improved the safety of the machine by five orders of magnitude, although they told the FDA that they were not certain of the exact cause of the accident. That is, they did not know whether they had found the problem that caused the accident or just other problems. In making decisions about continued use of the machines, the hospitals and clinics had to consider the costs of removing the expensive machine from service (in lost income and loss of treatment for patients who needed it), the uncertainty about whether the machine was the cause of the injuries, and, later, when that was clear, the manufacturer's assurances that they had solved the problem.

A Canadian government agency and some hospitals using the Therac-25 made recommendations for many more changes to enhance safety; they were not implemented. After the fifth accident, the FDA declared the machine defective and ordered AECL to inform users of the problems. The FDA and AECL spent about a year (during which the sixth accident occurred) negotiating about changes in the machine. The final plan included more than two dozen changes. They eventually installed the critical hardware safety interlocks, and most of the machines remained in use after that with no new incidents of overdoses.[26]

Overconfidence

In the first overdose incident, when the patient told the machine operator that the machine had "burned" her, the operator told her that was impossible. This was one of many indications that the makers and some users of the Therac-25 were overconfident about the safety of the system. The most obvious and critical indication of overconfidence in the software was the decision to eliminate the hardware safety mechanisms. A safety analysis of the machine done by AECL years before the accidents suggests that they did not expect significant problems from software errors. In one case where a clinic added its own hardware safety features to the machine, AECL told them it was not necessary. (None of the accidents occurred at that facility.)

The hospitals using the machine assumed that it worked safely, an understandable assumption. Some of their actions, though, suggest overconfidence, or at least practices that they should have avoided. For example, operators ignored error messages because the machine produced so many of them. A camera in the treatment room and an intercom system enabled the operator to monitor the treatment and communicate with the patient. (The operator uses a console outside the shielded treatment room.) On the day of an accident at one facility, neither the video monitor nor the intercom was functioning. The operator did not see or hear the patient try to get up after an overdose. He received a second overdose before he reached the door and pounded on it. This facility had successfully treated more than 500 patients with the machine before this incident.

8.2.4 Observations and Perspective

From design decisions all the way to responding to the overdose accidents, the manufacturer of the Therac-25 did a poor job. The number and pattern of problems in this case, and the way they were handled, suggest serious irresponsibility. This case illustrates many of the things that a responsible, ethical software developer should not do. It illustrates the importance of following good procedures in software development. It is a stark reminder of the consequences of carelessness, cutting corners, unprofessional work, and attempts to avoid responsibility. It reminds us that a complex system can work correctly hundreds of times with a bug that shows up only in unusual circumstances—hence the importance of always following good safety procedures in operation of potentially dangerous equipment. This case also illustrates the importance of individual initiative and responsibility. Recall that some facilities installed hardware safety devices on their Therac-25 machines. They recognized the risks and took action to reduce them. The hospital physicist at one of the facilities where the Therac-25 overdosed patients spent many hours working with the machine to try to reproduce the conditions under which the overdoses occurred. With little support or information from the manufacturer, he was able to figure out the cause of some of the malfunctions.

To emphasize that safety requires more than bug-free code, we consider failures and accidents involving other radiation treatment systems. Three patients received overdoses in one day at a London hospital in 1966 when safety controls failed. Twenty-four patients received overdoses from a malfunctioning machine at a Spanish hospital in 1991; three patients died. Neither of these machines had computer controls.[27] Two news reporters reviewed more than 4000 cases of radiation overdoses reported to the U.S. government. Here are a few of the overdose incidents they describe. A technician started a treatment, then left the patient for 10–15 minutes to attend an office party. A technician failed to carefully check the prescribed treatment time. A technician failed to measure the radioactive drugs administered; she just used what looked like the right amount. In at least two cases, technicians confused microcuries and millicuries.* The underlying problems were carelessness, lack of appreciation for the risk involved, poor training, and lack of sufficient penalty to encourage better practices. (In most cases, the medical facilities paid small fines or none at all.)[28]

Most of the incidents we just described occurred in systems without computers. For some, a good computer system might have prevented the problem. Many could have occurred whether or not the treatment system was controlled by a computer. These

---

* A curie is a measure of radioactivity. A millicurie is one thousand times as much as a microcurie.

examples remind us that individual and management responsibility, good training, and accountability are important no matter what technology we use.

8.3 Increasing Reliability and Safety

Success actually requires avoiding many separate possible causes of failure.

—Jared Diamond[29]

8.3.1 Professional Techniques

The New York Stock Exchange installed a $2 billion system with hundreds of computers, 200 miles of fiber-optic cable, 8000 telephone circuits, and 300 data routers. The exchange managers prepared for spikes in trading by testing the system on triple and quadruple the normal trading volume. On one day, the exchange processed 76% more trades than the previous record. The system handled the sales without errors or delays.[30] We have been describing failures throughout this chapter. Many large, complex computer systems work extremely well. We rely on them daily. How can we design, build, and operate systems that are likely to function well?

To produce good systems, we must use good software engineering techniques at all stages of development, including specifications, design, implementation, documentation, and testing. There is a wide range between poor work and good work, as there is in virtually any field. Professionals, both programmers and managers, have the responsibility to study and use the professional techniques and tools that are available and to follow the procedures and guidelines established in the various relevant codes of ethics and professional practices. (The Software Engineering Code of Ethics and Professional Practice and the ACM Code of Ethics and Professional Conduct, in Appendix A, are two important sets of general guidelines for the latter.)

Management and communications

Management experts use the term *high reliability organization* (HRO) for an organization (business or government) that operates in difficult environments, often with complex technology, where failures can have extreme consequences (for example, air traffic control, nuclear power plants).[31] Researchers have identified characteristics of HROs that perform extremely well. These characteristics can improve software and computer systems in both critical and less critical applications. One characteristic is "preoccupation with failure." That means always assuming something unexpected can go wrong—not just planning, designing, and programming for all problems the team can foresee, but always being aware that they might miss something. Preoccupation with failure includes being alert to cues that might indicate an error. It includes fully analyzing near failures (rather than assuming the system "worked" because it averted an actual failure) and looking for systemic reasons for an error or failure rather than focusing narrowly on the detail that was wrong. (For example, *why* did some programmers for the Mars Climate Orbitor assume measurements were in English units while others assumed metric?)

Another feature of successful organizations is loose structure. It should be easy for a designer or programmer to speak to people in other departments or higher up in the company without going through rigid channels that discourage communication. An atmosphere of open, honest communication within the organization and between a company and client are essential for learning of problems early and reducing the effort required to handle them.

There is much more to the field of organizational features that encourage success. It is well worthwhile for project managers, founders of start-up companies, and anyone in management to devote time to studying it.

Safety-critical applications

A subfield of computer science focuses on design and development of safety-critical software. Safety specialists emphasize that developers must "design in" safety from the start. There are techniques of hazard analysis that help system designers identify risks and protect against them. Software engineers who work on safety-critical applications should have special training. Software expert Nancy Leveson emphasizes that with good technical practices and good management, you can develop large systems right: "One lesson is that most accidents are not the result of unknown scientific principles but rather of a failure to apply well-known, standard engineering practices."[32]

To illustrate two important principles in safety-critical applications, I will use as examples accidents that destroyed two space shuttles, each killing the seven people onboard. Computer systems and software were not the cause, but these tragedies make the points well. Burning gases leaked from a rocket shortly after launch of the *Challenger* and destroyed it. The night before the scheduled launch, the engineers argued for a delay. They knew the cold weather posed a severe threat to the shuttle. We cannot prove absolutely that a system is safe, nor can we usually prove absolutely that it will fail and kill someone. An engineer reported that, in the case of the *Challenger*, "It was up to us to prove beyond a shadow of a doubt that it was not safe to [launch]."[33] For the ethical decision maker, the policy should be to suspend or delay use of the system in the absence of a convincing case for safety, rather than to proceed in the absence of a convincing case for disaster. In the second accident, a large piece of insulating foam dislodged and struck the wing of the *Columbia* space shuttle as it launched. NASA knew this happened, but pieces of foam had dislodged and struck the shuttle on other flights without causing a major problem. Thus NASA managers declined to pursue available options to observe and repair the damage. *Columbia* broke up when reentering the earth's atmosphere at the end of its mission. This tragedy illustrates the danger of complacency. An organization focused on safety must explore ambiguous risks. Tragedies are less likely if the organization has established policies and procedures to evaluate such risks.[34]

Specifications

Companies that do well expend extensive effort to learn the needs of the client and to understand how the client will use the system. Good software developers help clients better understand their own goals and requirements, which the clients might not be good at articulating. The long planning stage allows for discovering and modifying unrealistic goals. One company that developed a successful financial system that processes one trillion dollars in transactions per day spent several years developing specifications for the system, then only six months programming, followed by carefully designed, extensive testing.

User interfaces and human factors

If you are editing a document and you try to quit without saving your changes, what happens? Most programs will remind you that you have not saved your changes and give you a chance to do so. The designers of the programs know that people forget or sometimes click or type the wrong command. This is a simple and common example of considering human factors in designing software—one that has avoided personal calamities for millions of people.

Well-designed user interfaces can help avoid many problems. System designers and programmers need to learn from psychologists and human-factors experts who know principles and practices for doing a good job.* User interfaces should provide clear instructions and error messages. They should be consistent. They should include appropriate checking of input to reduce major system failures caused by typos or other errors a person will likely make.

The crash of American Airlines Flight 965 near Cali, Colombia, illustrates the importance of consistency (and other aspects of good user interfaces). While approaching the airport, the pilot intended to lock the autopilot onto the beacon, called Rozo, that would lead the plane to the airport. The pilot typed "R," and the computer system displayed six beacons beginning with "R." Normally, the closest beacon is at the top of the list. The pilot selected it without checking carefully. The beacon at the top of the list was "Romeo" and was more than 100 miles away, near Bogota. The plane turned more than 90 degrees and headed for Romeo. In the dark, it crashed into a mountain, killing 159 people.[35]

In the lawsuits that followed, juries attributed blame mostly to pilot error. The pilot chose the wrong beacon without checking and continued to descend at night after the plane made a large, unexpected turn. One jury assigned some of the responsibility to the companies that provided the computer system. While it is clear that the pilot could have

---

* See, for example, the books by Shneiderman, Tufte, Nielsen, and Norman in the list of references at the end of the chapter.

and should have avoided the crash, it is also clear that the inconsistency in the display—not putting the nearest beacon at the top of the list—created the dangerous situation.

Crashing into mountains was a major cause of air travel fatalities. The Cali crash triggered the adoption of a ground proximity warning system (GPWS) to reduce such crashes. Older radar-based systems sometimes gave warning only 10 seconds before a potential impact. The GPWS contains a digital map of the world's topography. It can give a pilot up to a minute of warning if a plane is too close to a mountain and automatically displays a map of nearby mountains. Dangerous peaks are shown in red. The GWPS is likely responsible for preventing crashes in several incidents in which pilots incorrectly set an altimeter, attempted to land with poor visibility, mistook building lights for airport lights, and so on. No commercial U.S. airliner has crashed into a mountain since the GPWS was implemented.[36]

As an illustration of more principles that can help build better and safer systems, we consider several aspects of automated flight systems. An expert in this area emphasizes the following points:[37]

- *The user needs feedback to understand what the system is doing at any time.* This is critical when a pilot must suddenly take over if the automation fails or if he or she must turn it off for any reason. One example is having the throttle move as a manually operated throttle would, even though movement is not necessary when the automated system is operating.

- *The system should behave as an experienced user expects.* Pilots tend to reduce their rate of climb as they get close to their desired altitude. On the McDonnell Douglas MD-80, the automated system maintains a climb rate that is up to eight times as fast as pilots typically choose. Pilots, concerned that the plane might overshoot its target altitude, made adjustments, not realizing that their intervention turned off the automated function that caused the plane to level out when it reached the desired altitude. Thus, because the automation behaved in an unexpected way, the airplane climbed too high—exactly what the pilot was trying to prevent. (The incidence of the problem declined with more training.)

- *A workload that is too low can be dangerous.* Clearly, an overworked operator is more likely to make mistakes. One of the goals of automation is to reduce the human workload. However, a workload that is too low can lead to boredom, inattention, or lack of awareness of the current status. That is a danger if the pilot must take over in a hurry.

Redundancy and self-checking

Redundancy and self-checking are two techniques important in systems on which lives and fortunes depend. Redundancy takes several forms. On aircraft, several computers can control an accuator on, say, a wing flap. If one computer fails, another can do the job. Software modules can check their own results—either against a standard or by computing the same thing in two different ways and then comparing to see if the two results match. A more complex form of redundancy, used, for example, in flight control systems in aircraft, aims to protect against consistently faulty assumptions or methods of one programming team. Three independent teams write modules for the same purpose, in three different programming languages. The modules run on three separate computers. A fourth unit examines the outputs of the three modules and chooses the result obtained by at least two out of three. Safety experts say that even when programmers work separately, they tend to make the same kinds of errors, especially if there is an error, ambiguity, or omission in the program specifications.[38] Thus, this type of "voting" redundancy, while valuable in many safety-critical applications, might not overcome problems in other areas of the software development process.

Testing

It is difficult to overemphasize the importance of adequate, well-designed testing of software. Testing is not arbitrary. There are principles and techniques for doing a good job. Many significant computer system failures in previously working systems occurred soon after installation of an update or upgrade. Even small changes need thorough testing. Unfortunately, many cost-conscious managers, programmers, and software developers see testing as a dispensable luxury, a step you can skimp on to meet a deadline or to save money. This is a common but foolish, risky, and often irresponsible attitude.

A practice called independent verification and validation (IV&V) can be very useful in finding errors in software systems. IV&V means that an independent company (that is, not the one that developed the program and not the customer) tests and validates the software. Testing and verification by an independent organization is not practical for all projects, but many software developers have their own testing teams that are independent of the programmers who develop a system. The IV&V team acts as "adversaries" and tries to find flaws. IV&V is helpful for two reasons. The people who designed and/or developed a system think the system works. They think they thought about potential problems and solved them. With the best of intentions, they tend to test for the problems they have already considered. Also, consciously or subconsciously, the people who created the system may be reluctant to find flaws in it. Their testing may be half-hearted. Independent testers bring different perspectives, and for them, success in finding flaws is not emotionally or professionally tied to responsibility for those flaws.

You might have used a *beta version* of a product or heard of *beta testing*. Beta testing is a near-final stage of testing. A selected set of customers (or members of the public) use a complete, presumably well-tested system in their "real-world" environment. Thus, this is testing by regular users, not software experts. Beta testing can detect software limitations and bugs that the designers, programmers, and testers missed. It can also uncover confusing aspects of user interfaces, the need for more rugged hardware, problems that occur when interfacing with other systems or when running a new program on older computers, and many other sorts of problems.

We are what we repeatedly do. Excellence, therefore, is not an act, but a habit.

—Will Durant, summarizing Aristotle's view in his *Nicomachean Ethics*[39]

8.3.2 Trust the Human or the Computer System?

How much control should computers have in a crisis? This question arises in many application areas. We address it in the context of aircraft systems.

Like antilock braking systems in automobiles that control braking to avoid skidding (and do a better job than human drivers), computer systems in airplanes control sudden sharp climbs to avoid stalling. Some airplanes automatically descend if they detect cabin depressurization and the pilot does not take action quickly.

The Traffic Collision Avoidance System (TCAS) detects a potential in-air collision of two airplanes and directs the pilots to avoid each other. The first version of the system had so many false alarms that it was unusable. In some incidents, the system directed pilots to fly toward each other rather than away, potentially causing a collision instead of avoiding one. TCAS was improved, however. It is a great advance in safety, according to the head of the Airline Pilots Association's safety committee.[40] The TCAS systems functioned correctly when a Russian airplane carrying many children and a German cargo plane got too close to each other. The systems detected a potential collision and told the Russian pilot to climb and the German pilot to descend. Unfortunately, the Russian pilot followed an air traffic controller's instruction to descend, and the planes collided. In this example, the computer's instructions were better than the human's. A few months after this tragedy, the pilot of a Lufthansa 747 ignored instructions from an air traffic controller and followed instructions from the computer system instead, avoiding a midair collision. U.S. and European pilots are now trained to follow TCAS instructions even if they conflict with instructions from an air traffic controller.

Pilots are trained to immediately turn off autopilot systems when TCAS signals a potential collision. They manually maneuver the plane to avoid the collision. That might change. Pilots of the Airbus 380, the world's largest passenger airplane, are trained to allow its autopilot system to control the plane when a midair collision threatens. The aircraft maker says that pilots sometimes overreact to collision warnings and make extreme maneuvers that can injure passengers or cause a collision with other air traffic in the area. The policy is controversial among pilots.[41]

Computers in some airplanes prevent certain actions even if the pilot tries them (for example, banking at a very steep angle). Some people object, arguing that the pilot should have ultimate control in case unusual action is needed in an emergency. Based on accident statistics, some airlines believe otherwise: that preventing pilots from doing something "stupid" can save more lives than letting them do something bold and heroic, but outside the program limitations, in the very rare cases where it might be necessary.

8.3.3 Law, Regulation, and Markets

Criminal and civil penalties

Legal remedies for faulty systems include suits against the company that developed or sold the system and criminal charges when fraud or criminal negligence occurs. Families of Therac-25 victims sued; they settled out of court. A bank won a large judgment against a software company for a faulty financial system that caused problems a user described as "catastrophic." Several people have won large judgments against credit bureaus for incorrect data in credit reports that caused havoc in their lives.

Many contracts for business computer systems limit the amount the customer can recover to the actual amount spent on the computer system. Customers know when they sign the contract that there is generally no coverage for losses incurred because the system did not meet their needs for any reason. Courts uphold such contract limitations. If people and businesses cannot count on the legal system upholding the terms of a contract, contracts would be almost useless. Millions of business interactions that take place daily would become more risky and therefore more expensive. Because fraud and misrepresentation are not, of course, part of a contract, some companies that suffer large losses allege fraud and misrepresentation by the seller in an attempt to recover some of the losses, regardless of whether the allegations have firm grounding.

Well-designed liability laws and criminal laws—not so extreme that they discourage innovation, but clear and strong enough to provide incentives to produce good systems— are important legal tools for increasing reliability and safety of computer systems and accuracy of data in databases, as they are for protecting privacy and for protecting customers in other industries. After-the-fact penalties do not undo the injuries that occurred, but the prospect of paying for mistakes and sloppiness is incentive to be responsible and careful. Payments compensate the victim and provide some justice. An individual, business, or government that does not have to pay for its mistakes and irresponsible actions will make more of them. (In many contexts, the government does not permit lawsuits against it.)

Unfortunately, there are many flaws in liability law in the United States. People often win multimillion-dollar suits when there is no scientific evidence or sensible reason to hold the manufacturer or seller of a product responsible for accidents or other negative impacts. Abuse of the liability lawsuit system almost shut down the small-airplane manufacturing industry in the United States for years. The complexity of large computer systems make designing liability standards difficult, but this is a necessary task.

Regulation and safety-critical applications

Is there legislation or regulation that can prevent life-threatening computer failures? A law saying that a radiation machine should not overdose a patient would be silly. We know that it should not do that. We could ban the use of computer control for applications where an error could be fatal, but such a ban is ill advised. In many applications, the benefits of using computers are well worth the risks.

A widely accepted option is regulation, possibly including specific testing requirements and requirement for approval by a government agency before a new product can be sold. The FDA has regulated drugs and medical devices for decades. Companies must do extensive testing, provide huge quantities of documentation, and get government approval before they sell new drugs and some medical devices. Arguments in favor of such regulation, both for drugs and for safety-critical computer systems, include the following: Most potential customers and people who would be at risk (e.g., patients) do not have the expertise to judge the safety or reliability of a system. It is better to prevent use of a bad product than to rely on after-the-calamity remedies. It is too difficult and expensive for ordinary people to sue large companies successfully.

If the FDA had thoroughly examined the Therac-25 before it was put into operation, it might have found the flaws before any patients were injured. However, we should note some weaknesses and trade-offs in the regulatory approach.[42] The approval process is extremely expensive and time consuming. The multiyear delays in introducing a good product cost many lives. Political concerns affect the approval process. Competitors influence decisions. Also, there is an incentive for bureaucrats and regulators to be overcautious. Damage caused by an approved product results in bad publicity and possible firing for the regulator who approved it. Deaths or losses caused by the delay or failure to approve a good new product are usually not obvious and get little publicity.

Leveson and Turner, in their Therac-25 article, summarize some of these dilemmas:

> The issues involved in regulation of risky technology are complex. Overly strict standards can inhibit progress, require techniques behind the state of the art, and transfer responsibility from the manufacturer to the government. The fixing of responsibility requires a delicate balance. Someone must represent the public's needs, which may be subsumed by a company's desire for profits. On the other hand, standards can have the undesirable effect of limiting the safety efforts and investment of companies that feel their legal and moral responsibilities are fulfilled if they follow the standards. Some of the most effective standards and efforts for safety come from users. Manufacturers have more incentive to satisfy customers than to satisfy government agencies.[43]

Professional licensing

Another controversial approach to improving software quality is mandatory licensing of software development professionals. Laws require licenses for hundreds of trades and professions. Licensing requirements typically include specific training, the passing of competency exams, ethical requirements, and continuing education. The desired effect is to protect the public from poor quality and unethical behavior. The history of mandatory licensing in many fields shows that the actual goals and the effects were and are not always very noble. In some trades (plumbing, for example), the licensing requirements were devised to keep black people out. Requirements for specific degrees and training programs, as opposed to learning on one's own or on the job, tend to keep poorer people from qualifying for licenses. Economic analyses have shown that the effect of licensing is to reduce the number of practitioners in the field and keep prices and income for licensees higher than they would otherwise be—in many cases, without any improvement in quality.[44] Some see a requirement for a government-approved license as a fundamental violation of the freedom to work (that is, of the negative right, or liberty, to work, in the terms of Section 1.4.2).

Clashes between licensing laws and the Web: Section 3.2.5

There are voluntary approaches to measuring or certifying qualifications of software personnel—for example, a diploma from a respected school and certification programs by professional organizations—particularly for advanced training in specialized areas.

Taking responsibility

In some cases of computer errors, businesses pay customers for problems or damages (without a lawsuit). For example, Intuit offered to pay interest and penalties that resulted from errors in flawed income-tax programs. When United Airlines mistakenly posted ticket prices on its website as low as about $25 for flights between the United States and Europe, it honored tickets purchased before it corrected the error. United, at first, charged the buyers the correct fare and probably had the legal right to do so, but the airline concluded that having angry customers would cost more than the tickets. We noted that business pressures can lead to cutting corners and releasing defective products. Business pressure can also be a cause for insistence on quality and maintaining good customer relations. Good business managers recognize the importance of customer satisfaction and the reputation of the business. Also, some businesses have an ethical policy of behaving responsibly and paying for mistakes, just as a person would pay for accidentally breaking a neighbor's window with a misdirected softball.

Other market mechanisms besides consumer backlash encourage a quality job and provide ways to deal with the risk of failures. Insurance companies have an incentive to evaluate the systems they insure and require that certain standards are met. Some businesses pay a higher rate for "uninterrupted" satellite communications service. That is, the service company would switch their communications quickly to other satellites in case of a failure. Businesses that can withstand a few hours of interruption need not pay for that extra protection. Organizations whose communications are critical to public safety, such as police departments and hospitals, should take responsibility to ensure they have appropriate backup service, possibly paying extra for the higher level of service.

How can customers protect themselves from faulty software? How can a business avoid buying a seriously flawed program? For high-volume consumer and small-business software, one can consult the many websites that review new programs, or consult one's social network. Specialized systems with a small market are more difficult to evaluate before purchase. We can check the seller's reputation with the Better Business Bureau. We can consult previous customers and ask how well the seller did the job. Online user groups for specific software products are excellent sources of information for prospective and current customers. In the case of the Therac-25, the users eventually spread information among themselves. If the Web had existed at the time of the accidents, it is likely that the problems would have been identified sooner and that some of the accidents would not have happened.

8.4 Dependence, Risk, and Progress

8.4.1 Are We Too Dependent on Computers?

Many people who write about the social impacts of computers lament our dependence on computing technology. Because of their usefulness and flexibility, computers, cellphones, and similar devices are now virtually everywhere. Is this good? Or bad? Or neutral? The word "dependence" often has a negative connotation. "Dependence on computers" suggests a criticism of our use of the technology and its gadgets. Is that appropriate?

In Holland, no one discovered the body of a reclusive, elderly man who died in his apartment until six months after his death. Eventually someone noticed that he had a large accumulation of mail. This incident was described as a "particularly disturbing example of computer dependency." Many of the man's bills, including rent and utilities, were paid automatically. His pension check went automatically to his bank account. Thus, "all the relevant authorities assumed that he was still alive."[45] But who expects the local gas company or other "relevant authorities" to discover a death? The problem here, clearly, was the lack of concerned family, friends, and neighbors. I happened to be present in a similar situation. An elderly, reclusive woman died in her home. Within two days, not six months, the mailman noticed that she had not taken in her mail. He informed a neighbor, and together they checked the house. It did not matter whether her utility bills were paid automatically.

On the other hand, many people and businesses are not prepared to do without the computer systems and electronic devices they use every day. Many drivers would be lost if their navigation system failed. A BlackBerry email blackout disrupted the work of bankers, technology workers, talent agents, and others who depend on constant communication— some who receive more than 500 emails per day. A physician commented that modern hospitals and clinics cannot function efficiently without medical information systems. Modern crime fighting depends on computers. Some military jets cannot fly without the assistance of computers. In several incidents, computer failures or other accidents knocked out communications services. Drivers could not buy gasoline with their credit cards. "Customers were really angry," said a gas station manager. More than 1000 California state lottery terminals were down; people could not buy tickets or collect winnings. A supermarket manager reported, "Customers are yelling and screaming because they can't get their money, and they can't use the ATM to pay for groceries."[46]

Is our "dependence" on electronic technology different from our dependence on electricity, which we use for lighting, entertainment, manufacturing, medical treatments—just about everything? Is our "dependence" on computers different from a farmer's dependence on a plow? Modern surgery's dependence on anesthesia?

Computers, smartphones, and plows are tools. We use tools because we are better off with them than without them. They reduce the need for hard physical labor and tedious routine mental labor. They help us be more productive, or safer, or more comfortable. When we have a good tool, we can forget (or no longer even learn) the older method of performing a task. If the tool breaks down, we are stuck. We cannot perform the task until someone fixes it. That can mean that no telephone calls get through for several hours. It might mean the loss of a large amount of money, and it can mean danger or death for some people. But the negative effects of a breakdown do not condemn the tool. To the contrary, for many applications (not all), the inconveniences or dangers of a breakdown are a reminder of the convenience, productivity, or safety the tool provides when it is working. The breakdown can remind us, for example, of the billions of communications, carrying voice, text, photos, and data, that are possible or more convenient or cheaper because of the technology.

Some misconceptions about dependence on computers come from a poor understanding of the role of risk, confusion of "dependence" with "use," and blaming computers for failures where they were only innocent bystanders. On the other hand, abdication of responsibility that comes from overconfidence or ignorance is a serious problem. There are valid technical criticisms of dependence when a system design allows a failure in one component to cause a major breakdown. There are valid criticisms of dependence when businesses, government agencies, and organizations do not make plans for dealing with systems failures. The wise individual is grateful for ATMs and credit cards, but keeps a little extra cash at home in case they do not work. The driver with a navigation system might choose to keep a map in the car.

8.4.2   Risk and Progress

> *Electricity lets us heat our homes, cook our food, and enjoy security and entertainment. It also can kill you if you're not careful.*
>
> —"Energy Notes" (Flyer sent with San Diego Gas & Electric utility bills)

We trust older technologies when we turn on a light or ride a bicycle. As the tools and technologies we use become more complex and more interconnected, the amount of damage that results from an individual disruption or failure increases, and we sometimes pay the costs in dramatic and tragic events. If a person out for a walk bumps into another person, neither is likely to be hurt. If both are driving cars at 60 miles per hour, they could be killed. If two jets collide, or one loses an engine, several hundred people could be killed. However, the death rate per mile traveled is lower for air travel than for cars.

Most new technologies were not very safe when first developed. If the death rate from commercial airline accidents in the United States were the same now as it was 50 years ago, 8,000 people would die in plane crashes each year. In some early polio vaccines, the virus was not totally inactivated. The vaccines caused polio in some children. We discover and solve problems. Scientists and engineers study disasters and learn how to prevent them and how to recover from them. A disastrous fire led to the development of fire hydrants—a way to get water to the fire from the water pipes under the street. Automobile engineers used to design the front of an automobile to be extremely rigid, to protect passengers in a crash. But people died and suffered serious injuries because the car frame transmitted the force of a crash to the people. The engineers learned it was better to build cars with "crumple zones" to absorb the force of impact.[47] Software engineering textbooks use the Cali crash, described in Section 8.3.1, as an example so that future software specialists will not repeat the mistakes in the plane's computer system. We learn. Overall, computer systems and other technologies have made air travel safer. In the first decade of this century, there was roughly one fatal accident per four million commercial flights, down 60% from 10 years earlier.[48]

The death rate from motor vehicle accidents in the United States declined almost 80% from 1965 to 2010 (from 5.30 per 100 million vehicle miles traveled to 1.13 per 100 million vehicle miles traveled).[49] Why? One significant factor is increased education about responsible use (i.e., the campaign against drunk driving). Devices that protect people when the system fails (seat belts and airbags) are another. Other systems help avoid accidents: Rear-view cameras help drivers avoid hitting a child when backing up. "Night vision" systems detect obstacles and project onto the windshield an image or diagram of objects in the car's path. Electronic stability systems have sensors that detect a likely roll-over, before the driver is aware of the problem, and electronically slow the engine. As use of technology, automation, and computer systems has increased in virtually all work places, the risk of dying in an on-the-job accident dropped from 39 among 100,000 workers (in 1934) to 5 in 100,000 in 2008.[50]

There are some important differences between computers and other technologies. Computers make decisions; electricity does not. The power and flexibility of computers encourages us to build more complex systems—where failures have more serious consequences. The pace of change in computer technology is much faster than that in other technologies. Software is not built from standard, trusted parts as is the case in many engineering fields. These differences affect the kind and scope of the risks we face. They need our attention as computer professionals, workers and planners in other fields, and as members of the public.

Observations

Throughout this chapter, we have made several points:

1. Many of the issues related to reliability and safety for computers systems have arisen before with other technologies.

2. There is a "learning curve" for new technologies. By studying failures, we can reduce their occurrence.

3. Much is known about how to design, develop, and use complex systems well and safely. Ethical professionals learn and follow these methods.

4. Perfection is not an option. The complexity of computer systems makes errors, oversights, and failures likely.

5. Comparing the risks of using computer technologies with the risks of using other methods, and weighing the risks against the benefits, give us important perspective.

This does not mean that we should excuse or ignore computer errors and failures because failures occur in other technologies. It does not mean we should tolerate carelessness or negligence because perfection is not possible. It does not mean we should excuse accidents as part of the learning process, and it does not mean we should excuse accidents because, on balance, the contribution of computer technology is positive.

The potential for serious disruption of normal activities and danger to people's lives and health because of flaws in computer systems should always remind the computer professional of the importance of doing his or her job responsibly. Computer system developers and other professionals responsible for planning and choosing systems must assess risks carefully and honestly, include safety protections, and make appropriate plans for shutdown of a system when it fails, for backup systems where appropriate, and for recovery.

Knowing that one will be liable for the damages one causes is strong incentive to find improvements and increase safety. When evaluating a specific instance of a failure, we can look for those responsible and try to ensure that they bear the costs of the damage they caused. It is when evaluating a particular application area or when evaluating the technology as a whole that we should look at the balance between risks and benefits.

EXERCISES

Review Exercises

8.1   List two cases described in this chapter in which insufficient testing was a factor in a program error or system failure.

8.2   List two cases described in this chapter in which the provider did an inadequate job of informing customers about flaws in the system.

8.3   What was one cause of the delay in completing the Denver airport?

8.4   What is one case in which reuse of software caused a serious problem?

8.5   What is one characteristic of successful high reliability organizations?

8.6   Describe one principle of human-interface design that is particularly important in safety-critical applications.

General Exercises

8.7   (a) Suppose you write a computer program to add two integers. Assume that each integer and their sum will fit in the standard memory unit the computer uses for integers. How likely do you think it is that the sum will be correct? (If you run the program a million times on different pairs of integers, how many times do you think it would give the correct answer?)

   (b) Suppose a utility company has a million customers and it runs a program to determine whether any customers have overdue bills. How likely do you think it is that the results of the program will be completely correct?

   (c) Probably your answers to parts (a) and (b) were different. Give some reasons why the likely number of errors would be different in these two examples.

8.8   Consider the case described in Section 8.1.2 in which a school assumed a boy was a drug abuser because two schools used different disciplinary codes in their computerized records. Describe some policies or practices that can help prevent such problems.

8.9   In response to the lack of scientific knowledge about whether or how computer keyboards cause RSI, a plaintiff's lawyer who handled more than 1000 RSI lawsuits commented that "the law can't wait on science."[51] Give some arguments to support this statement (as it applies to RSI lawsuits). Give some arguments against it. Do you agree with the statement? Why?

8.10   List several possible reasons why a car rental company might mistakenly list one of its rented cars as stolen. (See page 384.) Which of these could better software or better policies prevent? Which are the kinds of mistakes that would be difficult or impossible to prevent?

8.11   Suggest design features in databases that can encourage updating or can help reduce problems resulting from out-of-date information.

8.12   Consider the standardized-test score reporting error described in the box in Section 8.1.3. Suppose the test company had reported scores to the schools as significantly higher, rather than lower, than the correct scores. Do you think the schools would have questioned the scores? Do you think anyone would have discovered the error? If so, how? Give a few examples of situations where you think people would not report computer errors. For each example, give your reason (e.g., optimism, ignorance, gullibility, dishonesty, others).

8.13   The U.S. Immigration and Naturalization Service (INS) sent visa approval notifications for two of the September 11 hijackers six months after they crashed airplanes into the World Trade Center. No one had updated the INS database to cancel the visas (which the INS had approved before September 11). This incident generated a lot of publicity embarrassing for the INS. What policy or process could have avoided this error? Is it reasonable to expect that the INS should have prevented it?

8.14   Many college students attend several colleges before they eventually graduate. It would be a convenience for students if they could order a complete transcript (say, for job applications) from the federal student database discussed in Section 2.4.1.* Describe ways in which getting transcripts from the database might be riskier than getting them from the individual colleges.

8.15 Suppose you are on a consulting team to design a voting system for your state in which people can vote by logging on to a website (from a computer, smartphone, or other Internet-connected device). What are some important design considerations? Discuss some pros and cons of such a system. Overall, do you think it is a good idea?

8.16 Find several provisions of the Software Engineering Code of Ethics and Professional Practice (Appendix A.1) that were violated in the Therac-25 case.

8.17 In the discussion of high reliability organizations, we said that one important practice is being alert to cues that might indicate an error. What cues were missed or ignored in the Therac-25 case by the manufacturer, and what cues were missed or ignored by some users?

8.18 Identify one ethical failure that occurred in all three of these cases: the inventory management system (Section 8.1.3), the standardized-test score reporting error (Section 8.1.3), and the Therac-25.

8.19 Several models of a medical infusion pump in use worldwide had a defect, called "key-bounce." When a user typed the dosage on the keypad, a key pressed once could bounce and cause the digit to record twice. Thus, a dose of 2 units might become 22 units. The pump could give a patient an overdose of drugs. More than five years after the company was warned of problems with the pumps, the FDA issued a recall notice.[52] Identify several things that various people did, and probably did, that were wrong.

8.20 Suppose you are responsible for the design and development of a computer system to control an amusement park ride. Sensors in the seats will determine which seats are occupied, so the software can consider weight and balance. The system will control the speed and duration of the ride. The amusement park wants a system where, once the ride starts, a person is not needed to operate it.

      List some important things that you can or should do to ensure the safety of the system. Consider all aspects of development, technical issues, operating instructions, and so on.

8.21 What features are included in modern database systems to prevent data loss? In this context, research the ACID properties of such systems.

8.22 Who are the "good guys"? Pick two people or organizations mentioned in this chapter whose work helped make systems safer or reduced the negative consequences of errors. Tell why you picked them.

8.23 We mentioned that some cellphones contain a few million lines of computer code. How many lines of code would your computer operating system contain? Estimate how many pages this code would take up if printed. (State your assumptions.)

8.24 Research automated diagnosis via expert systems. What sources for error exist in these systems? Historically, how far have these systems been successful in effecting correct and efficient treatment?

---

* The actual database proposal does not include providing services such as transcripts for individual students.

8.25 A person who had spent the entire month vacationing received an electricity bill of $0. Understandably, he ignored it. A month later, his electricity supply was discontinued for nonpayment of the bill! To what degree is each of the following people responsible: the electricity company, the person who wrote the billing program, the software company that sells the billing software, the lead developer of the project? What, if anything, did each do wrong, and what could reduce the chance of such a problem in the future? Are there any other people who bear some of the responsibility? (You cannot give a full and definite answer without more detailed information. Where necessary, indicate what additional information you need and how it would affect your answer.)

8.26 The FDA maintains a registry of more than 120,000 drugs. An investigation by the Department of Health and Human Services found that the information on about 34,000 drugs was incorrect or out of date. Nine thousand drugs were missing from the directory.[53] Describe several possible risks of the database being so out of date. Give as many possible reasons as you can think of why the database was out of date.

8.27 There is a story that a major retail company "lost" a warehouse from its inventory system for three years. The warehouse received no goods and shipped none. A separate system handled payroll, so the employees continued to get paychecks. To what extent is this a computer failure? What other important factors are part of the problem?

8.28 How would you be affected if you could not use the Internet for a week?

8.29 Choose a noncomputer activity that you are familiar with and that has some risks (e.g., skateboarding, scuba diving, or working in a restaurant). Describe some of the risks and some safety practices. Describe analogies with risks related to computer systems.

8.30 What aspects of successful high reliability organizations (Section 8.3.1) were lacking in the Therac case? What factors in the space shuttle disasters (Section 8.3.1) appear also in the Therac-25 case?

8.31 Software developers are sometimes advised to "design for failure." Give some examples of what this might mean.

8.32 This exercise is for computer science students or others who write software. Describe how you could put exception handling or automatic backups into a program you wrote. If you have done so, describe the project and the methods.

8.33 Assume you are a professional working in your chosen field. Describe specific things you can do to reduce the impact of any two problems we discussed in this chapter. (If you cannot think of anything related to your professional field, choose another field that might interest you.)

8.34 Think ahead to the next few years and describe a new problem, related to issues in this chapter, likely to develop from digital technology or devices.

Assignments

These exercises require some research or activity.

8.35 Read a few items in the current issue of the Risks Digest (www.csl.sri.com/users/risko/risks.txt). Write a summary of two items.

8.36 Recently, there has been a study claiming that office devices such as photocopiers and scanners pose health problems. Find the study. What were its conclusions?

8.37 Find a journalistic or scientific article published within the past year that discusses significant downtime of a major Web service. Write a summary of the article, and a commentary on the article's analysis of the problem. Include a full citation for the article.

Class Discussion Exercises

These exercises are for class discussion, perhaps with short presentations prepared in advance by small groups of students.

8.38 Assume that the family of one of the victims of the Therac-25 has filed three lawsuits. They are suing a hospital that used the machine, the company that made the machine (AECL), and the programmer who wrote the Therac-25 software. Divide students into six groups: attorneys for the family against each of the three respondents, and attorneys for each of the three respondents. Each group is to present a five-minute summation of arguments for its case. Then, let the class discuss all aspects of the case and vote on the degree of responsibility of each of the respondents.

8.39 Consider the following scenario. A state's highway patrol keeps records of stolen cars in its computer system. There is no routine process for updating records when stolen cars are recovered. The system still listed a car as stolen a few years after it had been recovered and the owner sold it. A highway patrol officer shot and killed the new owner of the car during a traffic stop. The officer thought the car was stolen and that the driver was acting suspiciously. An investigation concluded that the officer "acted in good faith." To what extent should the error in the database affect the family's wrongful-death lawsuit against the highway patrol. Suggest a feature the database should have that might prevent such incidents.

8.40 A factory contains an area where robots do all the work. There is a fence around the area. Human workers are not supposed to enter while the robots are working. When anyone opens the gate in the fence, it automatically cuts off power to the robots. A worker jumped over the fence to repair a robot that was malfunctioning. Another robot, bringing parts to the malfunctioning robot, accidentally pinned the worker against a machine, killing him.

Suppose your class is a consulting team hired (by a neutral party) to investigate this case and write a report. Consider several factors relevant in safety-critical systems. What was done right? What was done wrong? Is there important information not included in this summary of the case that you would ask about? If so, what? What degree of blame do you assign to the software company that designed the robot system, the company that operates the factory, and the worker? Why? What changes, if any, should the factory operators make to reduce the likelihood of more deaths?

BOOKS AND ARTICLES

- W. Robert Collins, Keith W. Miller, Bethany J. Spielman, and Phillip Wherry, "How Good Is Good Enough?" *Communications of the ACM*, January 1994, 37(1), pp. 81–91. A discussion of ethical issues about quality for software developers.

- Paul Stephen Dempsey, Andrew R. Goetz, and Joseph S. Szyliowicz, *Denver International Airport: Lessons Learned*, McGraw-Hill, 1997.

- Richard Epstein, *The Case of the Killer Robot*, John Wiley and Sons, 1996.

- Richard P. Feynman, *What Do You Care What Other People Think?*, W. W. Norton & Co., 1988. Includes Feynman's report on the investigation of the explosion of the *Challenger* space shuttle, with many insights about how to, and how not to, investigate a system failure.

- Jonathan Jacky, "Safety-Critical Computing: Hazards, Practices, Standards, and Regulation," in Charles Dunlop and Rob Kling, eds., *Computerization and Controversy*, Academic Press, 1991.

- Nancy G. Leveson, *Safeware: System Safety and the Computer Age*, Addison Wesley, 1995.

- Nancy G. Leveson and Clark S. Turner, "An Investigation of the Therac-25 Accidents," *IEEE Computer*, July 1993, 26(7), pp. 18–41.

- Jakob Nielsen, *Designing Web Usability: The Practice of Simplicity*, New Riders Publishing, 2000.

- Donald Norman, *The Invisible Computer: Why Good Products Can Fail, the Personal Computer Is So Complex, and Information Appliances Are the Solution*, MIT Press, 1998.

- Donald Norman, *The Psychology of Everyday Things*, Basic Books, 1988. A study of good and bad user interfaces on many everyday devices and appliances.

- Ivars Peterson, *Fatal Defect: Chasing Killer Computer Bugs*, Times Books (Random House), 1995.

- Henry Petrovski, *To Engineer Is Human: The Role of Failure in Successful Design*, St. Martin's Press, 1985. This book is more about engineering in general, not computer systems design, but the principles and lessons carry over.

- Shari L. Pfleeger and Joanne Atlee, *Software Engineering: Theory and Practice*, 4th ed., Pearson Prentice Hall, 2010.

- Ben Shneiderman, Catherine Plaisant, Maxine Cohen, and Steven Jacobs, *Designing the User Interface: Strategies for Effective Human-Computer Interaction*, 4th ed., Addison Wesley Longman, 2009.

- Edward Tufte, *Envisioning Information*, Graphics Press, 1990.

- Edward Tufte, *Visual Explanations*, Graphics Press, 1997.

- Aaron Wildavsky, *Searching for Safety*, Transaction Books, 1988. On the role of risk in making us safer.

NOTES

1. Robert N. Charette, "Why Software Fails," *IEEE Spectrum*, September 2005, www.spectrum.ieee.org/sep05/1685, viewed Dec. 8, 2006.

2. *The Risks Digest: Forum on Risks to the Public in Computers and Related Systems*, archived at catless.ncl.ac.uk/risks.

3. Dan Joyce, email correspondence, May 17, 1996 (the adoption case). Study by the Office of Technology Assessment, reported in Jeffrey Rothfeder, *Privacy for Sale*, Simon & Schuster, 1992. "Jailing the Wrong Man," *Time*, Feb. 25, 1985, p. 25. David Burnham, "Tales of a Computer State," *The Nation*, April 1983, p. 527. Evelyn Richards, "Proposed FBI Crime Computer System Raises Questions on Accuracy, Privacy," *Washington Post*, Feb. 13, 1989, p. A6. "Wrong Suspect Settles His Case of $55,000," *New York Times*, Mar. 6, 1998, p. 30. Peter G. Neumann, "Risks to the Public in Computer and Related Systems," *Software Engineering Notes*, April 1988, 13:2, p. 11. Herb Caen, *San Francisco Chronicle*, July 25, 1991.

4. Ann Davis, "Post-Sept. 11 Watch List Acquires Life of Its Own," *Wall Street Journal*, Nov. 19, 2002, p. A1.

5. *Arizona v. Evans*, reported in "Supreme Court Rules on Use of Inaccurate Computer Records," *EPIC Alert*, Mar. 9, 1995, v. 2.04.

6. Edward Felsenthal, "An Epidemic or a Fad? The Debate Heats Up over Repetitive Stress," *Wall Street Journal*, July 14, 1994, p. A1. R. L. Linscheid and J. H. Dobyns, "Athletic Injuries of the Wrist," *Clinical Orthopedics*, September 1985, pp. 141–151. J. D. Stedt, "Interpreter's Wrist: Repetitive Stress Injury and Carpal Tunnel Syndrome in Sign Language Interpreters," *American Annals of the Deaf*, 1992, 137(1), 40–43. David M. Rempel, Robert J. Harrison, Scott Barnhart, "Work-Related Cumulative Trauma Disorders of the Upper Extremity," *Journal of the American Medical Association*, 267(6), Feb. 12, 1992, pp. 838–842.

7. Frederic M. Biddle, John Lippman, and Stephanie N. Mehta, "One Satellite Fails, and the World Goes Awry," *Wall Street Journal*, May 21, 1998, p. B1.

8. Reuters, "Glitch Closes Tokyo Stock Exchange," *The New Zealand Herald*, Nov. 2, 2005, nzherald.co.nz, viewed Dec. 12, 2006. Julia Flynn, Sara Calian, and

Michael R. Sesit, "Computer Snag Halts London Market 8 Hours," *Wall Street Journal*, Apr. 6, 2000, p. A14.

9. Jack Nicas, "Jet Lagged: Web Glitches Still Plague Virgin America," *Wall Street Journal*, Nov. 23, 2011, online.wsj.com/article/SB1000142405297020371070 4577053110330006178.html, viewed Nov. 23, 2011.

10. mars.jpl.nasa.gov/msp98/orbiter, viewed Dec. 19, 2006.

11. Thomas Hoffman, "NCR Users Cry Foul over I Series Glitch," *Computerworld*, Feb. 15, 1993, p. 72. Milo Geyelin, "Faulty Software Means Business for Litigators," *Wall Street Journal*, Jan. 21, 1994, p. B1. Milo Geyelin, "How an NCR System for Inventory Control Turned into a Virtual Saboteur," *Wall Street Journal*, Aug. 8, 1994, p. A1, A5. Mary Brandel and Thomas Hoffman, "User Lawsuits Drag On for NCR," *Computerworld*, Aug. 15, 1994, p. 1.

12. Jacques Steinberg and Diana B. Henriques, "When a Test Fails the Schools, Careers and Reputations Suffer," *New York Times*, May 21, 2001, pp. A1, A10–A11.

13. Andrea Robinson, "Firm: State Told Felon Voter List May Cause Errors," *Miami Herald*, Feb. 17, 2001.

14. Davide Balzarotti, Greg Banks, Marco Cova, Viktoria Felmetsger, Richard Kemmerer, William Robertson, Fredrik Valeur, and Giovanni Vigna, "Are Your Votes Really Counted? Testing the Security of Real-World Electronic Voting Systems," *Proceedings of the International Symposium on Software Testing and Analysis*, July 2008, www.cs.ucsb.edu/~seclab/projects/voting/issta08_ voting.pdf, viewed Nov. 18, 2011. Ed Felton, "Hotel Minibar Keys Open Diebold Voting Machines," Sept. 18, 2006, www.freedom-to-tinker.com/?p=1064, viewed Dec. 6, 2006.

15. Balzarotti et al., "Are Your Votes Really Counted?"

16. The DIA delay was widely reported in the news media. A few of the sources I used for the discussion here are Kirk Johnson, "Denver Airport Saw the Future. It Didn't Work." *New York Times*, Aug. 27, 2005, www.nytimes.com, viewed Dec. 12, 2006; W. Wayt Gibbs, "Software's Chronic Crisis," *Scientific American*, September 1994, 271(3), pp. 86–95; Robert L. Scheier, "Software Snafu Grounds Denver's High-Tech Airport," *PC Week*, 11(19), May 16, 1994, p. 1; Price Colman, "Software Glitch Could Be the Hitch. Misplaced Comma Might Dull Baggage System's Cutting Edge," *Rocky Mountain News*, Apr. 30, 1994, p. 9A; Steve Higgins, "Denver Airport: Another Tale of Government High-Tech Run Amok," *Investor's Business Daily*, May 23, 1994, p. A4; Julie Schmit, "Tiny Company Is Blamed for Denver Delays," *USA Today*, May 5, 1994, pp. 1B, 2B.

17. Scheier, "Software Snafu Grounds Denver's High-Tech Airport."

18. Wayne Arnold, "How Asia's High-Tech Airports Stumbled," *Wall Street Journal*, July 13, 1998, p. B2.

19. Robert N. Charette, "Why Software Fails," *IEEE Spectrum*, September 2005, www.spectrum.ieee.org/sep05/ 1685, viewed Dec. 12, 2006. Virginia Ellis, "Snarled Child Support Computer Project Dies," *Los Angeles Times*, Nov. 21, 1997, p. A1, A28. Peter G. Neumann, "System Development Woes," *Communications of the ACM*, December 1997, p. 160. Harry Goldstein, "Who Killed the Virtual Case File?" *IEEE Spectrum*, September 2005, www.spectrum.ieee.org/sep05/1455, viewed Dec. 12, 2006.

20. Charette, "Why Software Fails."

21. H. Travis Christ, quoted in Linda Rosencrance, "US Airways Partly Blames Legacy Systems for March Glitch," *Computerworld*, Mar. 29, 2007. Linda Rosencrance, "Glitch at U.S. Airways Causes Delays," *Computerworld*, Mar. 5, 2007, www.computerworld.com, viewed Apr. 24, 2007.

22. Robert N. Charette, "This Car Runs on Code," *IEEE Spectrum*, February 2009, spectrum.ieee.org/greentech/advanced-cars/this-car-runs-on-code, viewed Apr. 19, 2011.

23. The report of the inquiry into the explosion is at sunnyday.mit.edu/accidents/Ariane5accidentreport .html, viewed Sept. 12, 2007.

24. "FDA Statement on Radiation Overexposures in Panama," www.fda.gov/cdrh/ocd/panamaradexp.html, viewed Jan. 4, 2007. Deborah Gage and John McCormick, "We Did Nothing Wrong," *Baseline*, Mar. 4, 2004, www.baselinemag.com/article2/0,1397,1543564 ,00.asp, viewed Jan. 2, 2007.

25. Nancy G. Leveson and Clark S. Turner, "An Investigation of the Therac-25 Accidents," *IEEE Computer*, July 1993, 26(7), pp. 18–41. Jonathan Jacky, "Safety-Critical Computing: Hazards, Practices, Standards, and Regulation," in Charles Dunlop and Rob Kling, eds., *Computerization and Controversy*, Academic Press, 1991, pp. 612–631. Most of the factual information about the Therac-25 incidents in this chapter is from Leveson and Turner.

26. Conversation with Nancy Leveson, Jan. 19, 1995.

27. Jacky, "Safety-Critical Computing," p. 615. Peter G. Neumann, "Risks to the Public in Computers and Related Systems," *Software Engineering Notes*, April 1991, 16(2), p. 4.

28. Ted Wendling, "Lethal Doses: Radiation That Kills," *Cleveland Plain Dealer*, Dec. 16, 1992, p. 12A. (I thank my student Irene Radomyshelsky for bringing this article to my attention.)

29. Jared Diamond, *Guns, Germs, and Steel: The Fates of Human Societies*, W. W. Norton, 1997, p. 157.

30. Raju Narisetti, Thomas E. Weber, and Rebecca Quick, "How Computers Calmly Handled Stock Frenzy," *Wall Street Journal*, Oct. 30, 1997, p. B1, B7.

31. One of several articles that discuss characteristics of HROs is Karl E. Weick, Kathleen M. Sutcliffe, and David Obstfeld, "Organizing for High Reliability: Processes of Collective Mindfulness," Chapter 44 in

Crisis Management: Volume III, edited by Arjen Boin, Sage Library in Business and Management, 2008, politicsir.cass.anu.edu.au/staff/hart/pubs/46%20t%20Hart.pdf, viewed Nov. 13, 2011.

32. From an email advertisement for Nancy G. Leveson, *Safeware: System Safety and Computers*, Addison Wesley, 1995.

33. Roger Boisjoly, quoted in Diane Vaughan, *The Challenger Launch Decision: Risky Technology, Culture, and Deviance at NASA*, University of Chicago Press, 1996, p. 41.

34. For a discussion of systemic, organizational issues behind the *Columbia* failure, see Michael A. Roberto, Richard M.J. Bohmer, and Amy C. Edmondson, "Facing Ambiguous Threats," *Harvard Business Review*, November 2006, hbr.org/2006/11/facing-ambiguous-threats/ar/1, viewed Nov. 14, 2011.

35. A particularly good article discussing human factors and the causes of the crash is Stephen Manes, "A Fatal Outcome from Misplaced Trust in 'Data,'" *New York Times*, Sept. 17, 1996, p. B11.

36. Alan Levin, "Airways Are the Safest Ever," *USA Today*, June 29, 2006, p. 1A, 6A. William M. Carley, "New Cockpit Systems Broaden the Margin of Safety for Pilots," *Wall Street Journal*, Mar. 1, 2000, p. A1.

37. Barry H. Kantowitz, "Pilot Workload and Flightdeck Automation," in M. Mouloua and R. Parasuraman, eds., *Human Performance in Automated Systems: Current Research and Trends*, Lawrence Erlbaum, 1994, pp. 212–223.

38. M. Sghairi, A. de Bonneval, Y. Crouzet, J.-J. Aubert, and P. Brot, "Challenges in Building Fault-Tolerant Flight Control System for a Civil Aircraft," *IAENG International Journal of Computer Science*, Nov. 20, 2008, www.iaeng.org/IJCS/issues_v35/issue_4/IJCS_35_4_07.pdf, viewed Nov. 14, 2011. (My thanks to Patricia A. Joseph for finding this reference.) "Airbus Safety Claim 'Cannot Be Proved,'" *New Scientist*, Sept. 7, 1991, 131:1785, p. 30.

39. Will Durant, *The Story of Philosophy: The Lives and Opinions of the World's Greatest Philosophers*, Simon & Schuster, 1926.

40. William M. Carley, "New Cockpit Systems Broaden the Margin of Safety for Pilots," *Wall Street Journal*, Mar. 1, 2000, pp. A1, A10. Kantowitz, "Pilot Workload and Flightdeck Automation," p. 214.

41. Andy Pasztor, "Airbus to Use Computers for Avoiding Collisions," *Wall Street Journal Europe*, May 29, 2006, p. 5.

42. These problems and trade-offs occur often with regulation of new drugs and medical devices, regulation of pollution, and various kinds of safety regulation. They are discussed primarily in journals on the economics of regulation.

43. Leveson and Turner, "An Investigation of the Therac-25 Accidents," p. 40.

44. See, for example, Walter Williams, *The State Against Blacks*, McGraw-Hill, 1982, Chapters 5–7. One year during a construction lull, a state failed everyone who took the building contractor's license exam. It is illegal in 48 states for most software engineers to call themselves software engineers because of licensing laws for engineers. One company had to spend thousands of dollars changing job titles, business cards, and marketing literature to remove the word "engineer." (Julia King, "Engineers to IS: Drop That Title!" *Computerworld*, May 30, 1994, 28(22), pp. 1, 119.)

45. Tom Forester and Perry Morrison, *Computer Ethics: Cautionary Tales and Ethical Dilemmas in Computing*, 2nd ed., MIT Press, 1994, p. 4.

46. Heather Bryant, an Albertson's manager, quoted in Penni Crabtree, "Glitch Fouls Up Nation's Business," *San Diego Union-Tribune*, Apr. 14, 1998, p. C1. Miles Corwin and John L. Mitchell, "Fire Disrupts L.A. Phones, Services," *Los Angeles Times*, Mar. 16, 1994, p. A1.

47. An excellent "Nova" series, "Escape! Because Accidents Happen," aired Feb. 16 and 17, 1999, shows examples from 2000 years of history of inventing ways to reduce the injuries and deaths from fires, and from boat, car, and airplane accidents.

48. FAA Commissioner Marion Blakey, "Keeping Pace with Change," speech at the National Business Aviation Association, Orlando, FL, Oct. 17, 2006, www.faa.gov/news/speeches/news_story.cfm?newsId=7439, viewed Dec. 19, 2006.

49. 2010 data from National Highway Traffic Safety Administration, Fatality Analysis Reporting System Encyclopedia, 2010, www-fars.nhtsa.dot.gov/Main/index.aspx.

50. U.S. Census Bureau, *Statistical Abstract of the United States: 2011*, www.census.gov/compendia/statab/2011/tables/11s0656.pdf. Datum from 1934: "A Fistful of Risks," *Discover*, May 1996, p. 82.

51. Steven Philips, quoted in Felsenthal, "An Epidemic or a Fad?"

52. "Class 1 Recall: Cardinal Health Alaris SE Infusion Pumps," Food and Drug Administration, Aug. 10, 2006, www.fda.gov/cdrh/recalls/recall-081006.html. Jennifer Corbett Dooren, "Cardinal Health's Infusion Pump is Seized Because of Design Defect," *Wall Street Journal*, Aug. 29, 2006, p. D3.

53. "FDA Proposes Rules for Drug Registry," *Wall Street Journal*, Aug. 24, 2006, p. D6.

9

PROFESSIONAL ETHICS
AND RESPONSIBILITIES

9.1 What Is "Professional Ethics"?

The scope of the term "computer ethics" varies considerably. It can include such social and political issues as the impact of computers on employment, the environmental impact of computers, whether or not to sell computers to totalitarian governments, use of computer systems by the military, and the impact of new applications on privacy. It can include personal dilemmas about what to post on the Internet and what to download. In this chapter, we focus more narrowly on a category of professional ethics, similar to medical, legal, and accounting ethics, for example. We consider ethical issues a person might encounter as a computer professional, on the job. Professional ethics includes relationships with and responsibilities toward customers, clients, coworkers, employees, employers, people who use one's products and services, and others whom one's products affect. We examine ethical dilemmas and guidelines related to actions and decisions of individuals who create and use computer systems. We look at situations where you must make critical decisions, situations where significant consequences for you and others could result.

Extreme examples of lapses in ethics in many professional fields regularly appear in the news. In numerous incidents, journalists at prominent news organizations plagiarized or invented stories. A famed and respected researcher published falsified stem cell research and claimed accomplishments he had not achieved. A writer invented dramatic events in what he promoted as a factual memoir of his experiences. These examples involve blatant dishonesty, which is almost always wrong.

Honesty is one of the most fundamental ethical values. We all make hundreds of decisions all day long. The consequences of some decisions are minor. Others are huge and affect people we never meet. We base decisions, partly, on the information we have. (It takes 10 minutes to drive to work. This software has serious security vulnerabilities. What you post on a social network site is available only to your designated friends.) The information is not all accurate, but we must base our choices and actions on what we know. A lie deliberately sabotages this essential activity of being human: absorbing and processing information and making choices to pursue our goals. Lies are often attempts to manipulate people. As Kant might say, a lie treats people as merely means to ends, not ends in themselves. Lies can have many negative consequences. In some circumstances, lying casts doubt on the work or word of other people unjustly. It hurts those people, and it adds unnecessary uncertainty to decisions by others who would have acted on their word. Falsifying research or other forms of work is an indirect form of theft of research funds and other payments. It wastes resources that others could have used productively. It contributes to incorrect choices and decisions by people who depend on the results of the work. The costs and indirect effects of lies can cascade and do much harm.

Many ethical problems are more subtle than the choice of being honest or dishonest. In health care, for example, doctors and researchers must decide how to set priorities for organ transplant recipients. Responsible computer professionals confront issues such as

How much risk (to privacy, security, safety) is acceptable in a system? and What uses of another company's intellectual property are acceptable?

Suppose a private company asks your software company to develop a database of information obtained from government records, perhaps to generate lists of convicted shoplifters or child molesters, perhaps marketing lists of new home buyers, affluent boat owners, or divorced parents with young children. The people who will be on the lists did not have a choice about whether the information would be open to the public. They did not give permission for its use. How will you decide whether to accept the contract? You could accept on the grounds that the records are already public and available to anyone. You could refuse in opposition to secondary uses of information that people did not provide voluntarily. You could try to determine whether the benefits of the lists outweigh the privacy invasions or inconveniences they might cause for some people. You could refuse to make marketing lists but agree to make lists of people convicted of certain crimes, following Posner's principle that negative information, such as convictions, should be in the public domain (see Section 2.5.2). The critical first step, however, is recognizing that you face an ethical issue.

The decision to distribute a smartphone app for paying bills from a phone has an ethical component: Do you know enough about security? The decision to distribute software to convert files from formats with built-in copy protection to formats that people can copy easily has an ethical component. So, too, does the decision about how much money and effort to allocate to training employees in the use of a new computer system. We have seen that many of the related social and legal issues are controversial. Thus, some ethical issues are also.

There are special aspects to making ethical decisions in a professional context, but the decisions are based on general ethical principles and theories. Section 1.4 describes these general principles. It would be good to reread or review it now. In Section 9.2, we consider ethical guidelines for computer professionals. In Section 9.3, we consider sample scenarios.

9.2   Ethical Guidelines for Computer Professionals

9.2.1   Special Aspects of Professional Ethics

Professional ethics have several characteristics different from general ethics. The role of the professional is special in several ways. First, the professional is an expert in a field, be it computer science or medicine, that most customers know little about. Most of the people affected by the devices, systems, and services of professionals do not understand how they work and cannot easily judge their quality and safety. This creates responsibilities for the professional. Customers rely on the knowledge, expertise, and honesty of the professional. A professional advertises his or her expertise and thus has an obligation to provide it.

Second, the products of many professionals (e.g., highway bridges, investment advice, surgery protocols, and computer systems) profoundly affect large numbers of people. A computer professional's work can affect the life, health, finances, freedom, and future of a client or members of the public. A professional can cause great harm through dishonesty, carelessness, or incompetence. Often, the victims have little ability to protect themselves; they are not the direct customers of the professional and have no direct control or decision-making role in choosing the product or making decisions about its quality and safety. Thus, computer professionals have special responsibilities, not only to their customers, but also to the general public, to the users of their products, regardless of whether they have a direct relationship with the users. These responsibilities include thinking about potential risks to privacy and security of data, safety, reliability, and ease of use. They include taking action to diminish risks that are too high.

In Chapter 8, we saw some of the minor and major consequences of flaws in computer systems. In some of those cases, people acted in clearly unethical or irresponsible ways. In many cases, however, there was no ill intent. Software can be enormously complex, and the process of developing it involves communications between many people with diverse roles and skills. Because of the complexity, risks, and impact of computer systems, a professional has an ethical responsibility not simply to avoid intentional evil, but to exercise a high degree of care and follow good professional practices to reduce the likelihood of problems. That includes a responsibility to maintain an expected level of competence and be up to date on current knowledge, technology, and standards of the profession. Professional responsibility includes knowing or learning enough about the application field to do a good job. Responsibility for a noncomputer professional who manages or uses a sophisticated computer system includes knowing or learning enough about the system to understand potential problems.

In Section 1.4.1, we observed that although people often associate courage with heroic acts, we have many opportunities to display courage in day-to-day life by making good decisions that might be unpopular. Courage in a professional setting could mean admitting to a customer that your program is faulty, declining a job for which you are not qualified, or speaking out when you see someone else doing something wrong.

9.2.2 Professional Codes of Ethics

Many professional organizations have codes of professional conduct. They provide a general statement of ethical values and remind people in the profession that ethical behavior is an essential part of their job. The codes provide reminders about specific professional responsibilities. They provide valuable guidance for new or young members of the profession who want to behave ethically but do not know what is expected of them, people whose limited experience has not prepared them to be alert to difficult ethical situations and to handle them appropriately.

There are several organizations for the range of professions included in the general term "computer professional." The main ones are the ACM and the IEEE Computer Society (IEEE CS).[1] They developed the Software Engineering Code of Ethics and Professional Practice (adopted jointly by the ACM and IEEE CS) and the ACM Code of Ethics and Professional Conduct (both in Appendix A). We refer to sections of the Codes in the following discussion and in Section 9.3 using the shortened names SE Code and ACM Code. The Codes emphasize the basic ethical values of honesty and fairness.[*] They cover many aspects of professional behavior, including the responsibility to respect confidentiality,[†] maintain professional competence,[‡] be aware of relevant laws,[§] and honor contracts and agreements.[**] In addition, the Codes put special emphasis on areas that are particularly (but not uniquely) vulnerable from computer systems. They stress the responsibility to respect and protect privacy,[††] to avoid harm to others,[‡‡] and to respect property rights (with intellectual property and computer systems themselves as the most relevant examples).[§§] The SE Code covers many specific points about software development. It is available in several languages, and various organizations have adopted it as their internal professional standard.

Managers have special responsibility because they oversee projects and set the ethical standards for employees. Principle 5 of the SE Code includes many specific guidelines for managers.

9.2.3   Guidelines and Professional Responsibilities

We highlight a few principles for producing good systems. Most concern software developers, programmers, and consultants. A few are for professionals in other areas who make decisions about acquiring computer systems for large organizations. Many more specific guidelines appear in the SE Code and in the ACM Code, and we introduce and explain more in the scenarios in Section 9.3.

Understand what success means. After the utter foul-up on opening day at Kuala Lumpur's airport, blamed on clerks typing incorrect commands, an airport official said, "There's nothing wrong with the system." His statement is false, and the attitude behind the statement contributes to the development of systems that will fail. The official defined the role of the airport system narrowly: to do certain data manipulation correctly,

---

[*] SE Code: 1.06, 2.01, 6.07, 7.05, 7.04; ACM Code: 1.3, 1.4.

[†] SE Code: 2.05; ACM Code: 1.8.

[‡] SE Code: 8.01–8.05; ACM Code: 2.2.

[§] SE Code: 8.05; ACM Code: 2.3.

[**] ACM Code: 2.6.

[††] SE Code: 1.03, 3.12; ACM Code: 1.7.

[‡‡] SE Code: 1.03; ACM Code: 1.2.

[§§] SE Code: 2.02, 2.03; ACM Code: 1.5, 1.6, 2.8.

assuming all input is correct. Its true role was to get passengers, crews, planes, luggage, and cargo to the correct gates on schedule. It did not succeed. Developers and institutional users of computer systems must view the system's role and their responsibility in a wide enough context.

Include users (such as medical staff, technicians, pilots, office workers) in the design and testing stages to provide safe and useful systems. The importance of this guideline is illustrated by the discussion of computer controls for airplanes (Section 8.3.1) where confusing user interfaces and system behavior increased the risk of accidents. There are numerous "horror stories" in which technical people developed systems without sufficient knowledge of what was important to users. For example, a system for a newborn nursery at a hospital rounded each baby's weight to the nearest pound. For premature babies, the difference of a few ounces is crucial information.[2] The responsibility of developers to talk to users is not limited to systems that affect safety and health. Systems designed to manage stories for a news website, to manage inventory in a toy store, or to organize documents and video on a website could cause frustration, waste a client's money, and end up on the trash heap if designed without sufficient consideration of the needs of actual users.

The box nearby illustrates more ways to think about your users.

Do a thorough, careful job when planning and scheduling a project and when writing bids or contracts. This includes, among many other things, allocating sufficient time and budget for testing and other important steps in the development process. Inadequate planning is likely to lead to pressure to cut corners later. (See SE Code 3.02, 3.09, and 3.10.)

Design for real users. In so many cases, computers crashed because someone typed input incorrectly. In one case, an entire paging system shut down because a technician did not press the "Enter" key (or did not hit it hard enough). Real people make typos, get confused, or are new at their job. It is the responsibility of the system designers and programmers to provide clear user interfaces and include appropriate checking of input. It is impossible for software to detect all incorrect input, but there are techniques for catching many kinds of errors and for reducing the damage that errors cause.

Don't assume existing software is safe or correct. If you use software from another application, verify its suitability for the current project. If the software was designed for an application where the degree of harm from a failure was small, the quality and testing standards might not have been as high as necessary in the new application. The software might have confusing user interfaces that were tolerable (though not admirable) in the original application but that could have serious negative consequences in the new application. We saw in Chapter 8 that a complete safety evaluation is important even for software from an earlier version of the same application if a failure would have serious consequences. (Recall the Therac-25 and Ariane 5.)

Be open and honest about capabilities, safety, and limitations of software. In several cases described in Chapter 8, there is a strong argument that the treatment of customers was dishonest. Honesty of salespeople is hardly a new issue. The line between emphasizing your best qualities and being dishonest is not always clear, but it should be clear that hiding known, serious flaws and lying to customers are on the wrong side of the line.

Reinforcing exclusion

A speaker recognition system is a system (consisting of hardware and software) that identifies the person speaking. (This is different from speech recognition, discussed in Section 7.4.2, which identifies the words spoken.) One application of speaker recognition is teleconferencing for business meetings. The system identifies who is speaking and displays that person on everyone's screens. Some speaker recognition systems recognize male voices more easily than female voices. Sometimes when the system fails to recognize female speakers and focus attention on them, they are effectively cut out of the discussion.[3] Did the designers of the system intentionally discriminate against women? Probably not. Are women's voices inherently more difficult to recognize? Probably not. What happened? There are many more male programmers than female programmers. There are many more men than women in high-level business meetings. Men were the primary developers and testers of the systems. The algorithms were optimized for the lower range of male voices.

In his book, *The Road Ahead*, Bill Gates tells us that a team of Microsoft programmers developed and tested a handwriting recognition system. When they thought it was working fine, they brought it to him to try. It failed. All the team members were right-handed. Gates is left-handed.[4]

In some applications, it might make sense to focus on a niche audience or ignore a special audience, but that choice should be conscious (and reasonable). These examples show how easy it is to develop systems that unintentionally exclude people—and how important it is to think beyond one's own group when designing and testing a system. Besides women and left-handed people, other groups to consider are nontechnical users, different ethnic groups, disabled people, older people (who might, for example, need a large-font option), and children.

In these examples, doing "good" or "right" in a social sense—taking care not to reinforce exclusion of specific groups of people—coincides with producing a good product and expanding its potential market.

Honesty includes taking responsibility for damaging or injuring others. If you break a neighbor's window playing ball or smash into someone's car, you have an obligation to pay for the damage. If a business finds that its product caused injury, it should not hide that fact or attempt to put the blame on others.

Honesty about system limitations is especially important for *expert systems* (also called decision systems)—that is, systems that use models and heuristics incorporating expert knowledge to guide decision making (for example, medical diagnoses or investment planning). Developers must explain the limitations and uncertainties to users (doctors, financial advisors, and so forth, and to the public when appropriate). Users must not shirk responsibility for understanding them and using the systems properly.

Require a convincing case for safety. One of the most difficult ethical problems that arises in safety-critical applications is deciding how much risk is acceptable. We repeat a guideline from Section 8.3.1: For the ethical decision maker, the policy should be to suspend or delay use of the system in the absence of a convincing case for safety, rather than to proceed in the absence of a convincing case for disaster.

Pay attention to defaults. Everything, it seems, is customizable: the level of encryption on a cellphone or wireless network, whether consumers who buy something at a website will go on an email list for ads, the difficulty level of a computer game, the type of news stories your favorite news site displays for you, what a spam filter will filter out, what you share and with whom in your social network. So the default settings might not seem important. They are. Many people do not know about the options they can control. They do not understand issues of security. They often do not take the time to change settings. System designers should give serious thought to default settings. Sometimes protection (of privacy or from hackers, for example) is the ethical priority. Sometimes ease of use and compatibility with user expectations is a priority. Sometimes priorities conflict.

Develop communications skills. A computer security consultant told me that often when he talks to a client about security risks and the products available to protect against them, he sees the client's eyes glaze over. It is a tricky ethical and professional dilemma for him to decide just how much to say so that the client will actually hear and absorb it.

There are many situations in which a computer professional has to explain technical issues to customers and coworkers. Learning how to organize information, distinguishing what is important to communicate and what is not, engaging the listener actively in the conversation to maintain interest, and so on, will help make one's presentations more effective and help to ensure that the client or coworker is truly informed.

9.3 Scenarios

9.3.1 Introduction and Methodology

The cases we present here, some based on real incidents, are just a few samples of the kinds that occur. They vary in seriousness and difficulty, and they include situations that illustrate professional responsibilities to potential users of computer systems in the general public, customers or clients, the employer, coworkers, and others. More scenarios appear in the exercises at the end of the chapter.

In most of this book, I have tried to give arguments on both sides of controversial issues without taking a position. Ethical issues are often even more difficult than some of the others we have covered, and there could well be disagreement among computer ethics specialists on some points in the cases considered here. In any real case, there are many other relevant facts and details that affect the conclusion. In spite of the difficulty of drawing ethical conclusions, especially for brief scenarios, I give conclusions for some of these cases. You might face cases like these where you have to make a decision. I do not want to leave the impression that, because a decision is difficult or because some people benefit or lose either way, there is no ethical basis for making the decision. (It seems ethically irresponsible to do so.)

On the other hand, in Section 1.4 we emphasized that there is not always one right answer to an ethical question. Often many responses or actions are ethically acceptable. We also emphasized that there is no algorithm that cranks out the correct answers. We often must use our knowledge of how people behave, what problems have occurred in the past, and so on, to decide what choices are reasonable. Throughout this book we have approached many issues as problem-solving situations. Identity thieves get information in a certain way. How can we make it harder for them while maintaining varied and convenient services for consumers? The Internet exposes children to pornography. How can we reduce that exposure while protecting freedom of speech and access to information for adults? We will see the same approach in some of these ethical scenarios. Rather than concluding that a particular service or product or action is right or wrong, we, as responsible, ethical professionals, look for ways to reduce negative consequences.

How shall we analyze specific scenarios? We now have a number of tools. We can try to apply our favorite ethical theory, or some combination of the theories. We can ask questions that reflect basic ethical values: Is it honest? Is it responsible? Does it violate an agreement we made? We can consult a code of professional ethics. Ethical theories and guidelines might conflict, or we might find no clause in the Codes specifically applicable. The Preamble of the SE Code recognizes this problem and emphasizes the need for good judgment and concern for the safety, health, and welfare of the public.

Although we will not follow the outline below step by step for all the scenarios, our discussions will usually include many of these elements:

1. *Brainstorming phase*
   - List all the people and organizations affected. (They are the *stakeholders*.)
   - List risks, issues, problems, consequences.
   - List benefits. Identify who gets each benefit.
   - In cases where there is not a simple yes or no decision, but rather one has to choose some action, list possible actions.

2. *Analysis phase*
   - Identify responsibilities of the decision maker. (Consider responsibilities of both general ethics and professional ethics.)
   - Identify rights of stakeholders. (It might be helpful to clarify whether they are negative or positive rights, in the sense of Section 1.4.2.)
   - Consider the impact of the action options on the stakeholders. Analyze consequences, risks, benefits, harms, and costs for each action considered.
   - Find sections of the SE Code or the ACM Code that apply. Consider the guidelines in Section 9.2.3. Consider Kant's, Mill's, and Rawls' approaches.

Then, categorize each potential action or response as ethically obligatory, ethically prohibited, or ethically acceptable.
- If there are several ethically acceptable options, select an option by considering the ethical merits of each, courtesy to others, practicality, self-interest, personal preferences, and so on. (In some cases, plan a sequence of actions, depending on the response to each.)

The brainstorming phase can generate a long discussion with humorous and obviously wrong options. In the analysis phase, we might reject some options or decide that the claims of some stakeholders are irrelevant or minor. The brainstorming effort in generating the options and identifying those stakeholders was not wasted. It could bring out ethical and practical considerations and other useful ideas that one would not immediately think of. And it is as helpful to know why some factors do not carry heavy ethical weight as it is to know which ones do.

9.3.2 PROTECTING PERSONAL DATA

Your customer is a community clinic. The clinic works with families that have problems of family violence. It has three sites in the same city, including a shelter for battered women and children. The director wants a computerized record and appointment system, networked for the three sites. She wants a few laptop computers on which staffers can carry records when they visit clients at home and stay in touch with clients by email. She asked about an app for staffers' smartphones by which they could access records at social service agencies. At the shelter, staffers use only first names for clients, but the records contain last names and forwarding addresses of women who have recently left. The clinic's budget is small.

The clinic director is likely to be aware of the sensitivity of the information in the records and to know that inappropriate release of information can result in embarrassment for families using the clinic and physical harm to women who use the shelter. But she might not be aware of the risks of the technologies in the system she wants. You, as the computer professional, have specialized knowledge in this area. It is as much your obligation to warn the director of the risks as it is that of a physician to warn a patient of side-effects of a drug he or she prescribes. (See, for example, ACM Code 1.7 and SE Code 2.07 and 3.12.)

The most vulnerable stakeholders here are the clients of the clinic and their family members, and they do not take part in your negotiations with the director. You, the director, the clinic employees, and the donors or agencies that fund the clinic are also stakeholders.

Suppose you warn the director about unauthorized access to sensitive information by hackers and the potential for interception of records during transmission. You suggest measures to protect client privacy, including, for example, identification codes for clients (not Social Security numbers) that the clinic will use when real names are not necessary. You recommend encryption for transmission of records. You recommend security software to reduce the threat of hackers who might steal data. You tell the director that carrying client records on laptops or phones has serious risks, citing examples of loss and theft of devices containing large amounts of sensitive personal data. You advise that the system encrypt records on laptops, and you suggest that the director buy laptops with extra security features (such as thumbprint readers, so that only authorized employees can access the data, or remote tracking or erasing features). You warn that staffers might be bribed to sell or release information from the system. (Suppose a client is a candidate for the city council or a party in a child-custody case.) You suggest procedures to reduce such leaks. They include a user ID and password for each staff member, coded to allow access only to information that the particular worker needs, a log function that keeps track of who accessed and modified the records, and monitoring and controls on employee email and Web activity. Note that your ability to provide these suggestions is dependent on your professional competence, currency in the field, and general awareness of relevant current events.

The features you recommend will make the system more expensive. If you convince the director of the importance of your recommendations, and she agrees to pay the cost, your professional/ethical behavior has helped improve the security of the system and protect clients.

Suppose the director says the clinic cannot afford all the security features. She wants you to develop the system without most of them. You have several options. You can develop a cheap, but vulnerable, system. You can refuse and perhaps lose the job (although your refusal might convince the director of the importance of the security measures and change her mind). You can add security features and not charge for them. You can work out a compromise that includes the protections you consider essential. All but the first option are pretty clearly ethically acceptable. What about the first? Should you agree to provide the system without the security you believe it should have? Is it now up to the director alone to make an informed choice, weighing the risks and costs? In a case where only the customer would take the risk, some would say yes, it is your job to inform, no more. Others would say that the customer lacks the professional expertise to evaluate the risks. In this scenario, however, the director is not the only person at risk, nor is the risk to her the most significant risk of an insecure system. You have an ethical responsibility to consider the potential harm to clients from exposure of sensitive information and not to build a system without adequate privacy protection.

The most difficult decision may be deciding what is adequate. Encryption of personal records on portable devices might be essential. Monitoring employee Web access is probably not. There is not always a sharp, clear line between sufficient and insufficient protection. You will have to rely on your professional knowledge, on being up to date about current risks and security measures, on good judgment, and perhaps on consulting others who develop systems for similar applications (SE Code 7.08).

Note that although we have focused on the need for privacy protection here, you can overdo such protection. You also have a professional ethical responsibility not to scare a customer into paying for security measures that are expensive but protect against very unlikely risks.

9.3.3   Designing an Email System With Targeted Ads

Your company is developing a free email service that will include targeted advertising based on the content of the email messages—similar to Google's Gmail. You are part of the team designing the system. What are your ethical responsibilities?

Obviously you must protect the privacy of email. The company plans a sophisticated text analysis system to scan email messages and select appropriate ads. No humans will read the messages. Marketing for the free email will make clear that users will see targeted ads. The privacy policy will explain that the content of the email will determine which ads appear. So, the marketing director contends, you have satisfied the first principle of privacy protection, informed consent. What else must you consider to meet your ethical responsibility in offering this service to the public?

The fact that software, not a person, scans the email messages and assigns the ads reduces privacy threats. But what will this system store? Will it store data about which ads it displayed to specific users? Will it store data about which key words or phrases in emails determine the selection of particular ads? Will it store data about who clicked on specific ads? Because the system selects ads based on the content of email, the set of ads displayed to a particular user could provide a lot of information about the person, just as one's search queries do. Some of it will be incorrect or misleading information because of quirks in the ad-targeting methods.

Should we insist that no such data be stored? Not necessarily. Some of it might have important uses. Some records are necessary for billing advertisers, some for analysis to improve ad-targeting strategies, and perhaps some for responding to complaints from email users or advertisers. The system design team needs to determine what records are necessary, which need to be associated with individual users, how long the company will store them, how it will protect them (from hackers, accidental leaks, and so on), and under what conditions it will disclose them.

Now, back up and reconsider informed consent. Telling customers that they will see ads based on the content of their email is not sufficient if the system stores data that can link a list of ads with a particular user. You must explain this to potential users in a privacy policy or user agreement. But we know that most people do not read privacy policies and user agreements, especially long ones. A click might mean legal consent, but ethical responsibility goes further. Independent of what is in the agreement, the designers must think about potential risks of the system and design in protections.

There are ways to reduce potential damage from unintended disclosure of the ads selected for a particular person. For example, if the system does not target based on sensitive topics, such as mortgage foreclosures, health, and religion, then the records the system stores will not have information about those subjects. Thus, for added protection, the designers should consider restrictions on the set of topics the system uses for targeting.

Should the system let users turn off ads completely? The service is free; the advertising will pay for it. Anyone who objects to ads can find another free email service. There is no strong argument that an opt-out option is ethically obligatory. Offering it is admirable, however, and it could be a good business decision, creating good will and attracting people who might then use other company services.

9.3.4 WEBCAMS IN SCHOOL LAPTOPS[5]

> As part of your responsibilities, you oversee the installation of software packages for large orders. A recent order of laptops for a local school district requires webcam software to be loaded. You know that this software allows for remote activation of the webcam.

Remotely operated cameras and microphones can be in televisions, game systems, cellphones, and other appliances. Thus, issues similar to this scenario can arise in many other situations.

Is it your duty to know how your customers will use a product that you supply? Should you inform them, caution them, even require them to take measures to protect the people who will use the product?

Perhaps one of the most challenging questions for anyone doing business is *to whom am I responsible?* The most obvious answer is the paying customer—in this case, the school district. But as the ACM Code points out, our responsibilities go beyond customers, to employers, users and the public (see ACM Code 2.5 and 3.4). In this situation, the stakeholders include not only the school district administration but also the students, parents, teachers, and our own company. Each party has an interest in the security and proper usage of the webcam software, whether they know it or not.

First, find out more about the order. Are these computers going to students or employees? It is possible that employees of the school district have agreed to some sort of privacy policy or have given informed consent. If students are the recipients, then they and their parents need to know about the remote activation capability.

Consider that the school district might not even be familiar with the workings of the software package they ordered. Suppose the school district is unaware that the cameras can be activated remotely. Suppose a dishonest school employee activates several webcams and eavesdrops on students in their homes. The violation is uncovered and accusations fly. Parents want to know why the school would install such software and why it did not provide proper security measures. School administrators, caught completely off guard, want to know why you did not inform them about the risks and offer them additional security. Valuable trust between families and their schools and between you and your customer evaporates—trust that is hard to restore.

Your company is ethically responsible for informing your customers of the risks of a product it sells, whether the company or a third party designed and built it. Approach this responsibility not as a burden—an obligation that might jeopardize the sale—but as a service to your customer. When you inform a customer about a security or privacy risk, suggest solutions or alternatives such as the ability to disable certain functions or an alternative product that might lower or eliminate the risk. Let your customer know that you are there to help them navigate the risks and that your goal is to deliver a product that will meet the requirements of the stakeholders.

As with many scenarios, there might not be a happy ending. It is possible that the school district will turn down your proposal for better security or cannot afford an alternative, more secure product. In these cases, you and your company will have to further weigh the risks to the other parties. Sometimes, your only ethical course of action is to pass on the contract. Awareness and preparation in advance can help avoid such negative situations. Become familiar with all of the products your company offers. If the sale of some of these products can present ethical dilemmas (security, safety, privacy, etc.), then formulate contractual requirements beforehand and present them to any potential customer up front. In the case of the webcam software, you might have a policy in place that allows for installation only on systems meeting some minimum security requirements. Moving these concerns to the front of the negotiating process helps to avoid ethical dilemmas later. In addition, it positions your company as one that is familiar with the risks and benefits of the systems it sells and as a company that subscribes to a high ethical standard.

9.3.5 Publishing Security Vulnerabilities

Three MIT students planned to present a paper at a security conference describing security vulnerabilites in Boston's transit fare system. At the request of the transit authority, a judge ordered the students to cancel the presentation and not to distribute their research. The students are debating whether they should circulate their paper on the Web.* Imagine that you are one of the students.

What are some reasons why you might want to circulate the paper? You might think the judge's order violates your freedom of speech; posting the paper would be a protest. You might want to circulate the paper for the same reasons you planned to present it at a conference: to make other security experts aware of the problems, perhaps to generate work on a security patch, perhaps to spur the transit authority to fix the problems.

Publishing the vulnerabilities has several risks. The transit system could lose a substantial amount of money it people exploit the information. You and your co-authors could

---

* The first part of the scenario is from an actual incident. I don't know if the students considered violating the order; I made up that part.

face legal action for violating the order. The university could face negative consequences because the work was part of a school project.

In the actual case, the transit authority requested a five-month ban to provide time for them to fix the problems. The judge dissolved the order after a week. We have an established legal system where both parties to a disagreement have an opportunity to present their arguments. The system has plenty of flaws, but it is better than most. Maintaining a peaceful, civil society requires that we sometimes accept a decision of an impartial adjudicator. Ignoring a legal decision might be ethical in some circumstances, but not merely if one does not like it.

9.3.6 SPECIFICATIONS

You are a relatively junior programmer working on modules that collect data from loan application forms and convert them to formats required by the parts of the program that evaluate the applications. You find that some demographic data are missing from some forms, particularly race and age. What should your program do? What should you do?

Consult the specifications for the program. Any project should have specification documents approved by the client or managers of the company developing the project (or both). Your company has an ethical and business obligation to ensure that the specifications are complete and to produce a program that meets them. Ethical reasons for this include, but go beyond, doing what the company has agreed to do and has been paid to do.

Suppose you do not find anything in the specs that covers your problem. The next step is to bring the problem to the attention of your manager. Suppose the manager tells you, "Just make the program assume 'white' for race if it's missing. Banks shouldn't discriminate based on race anyway." Do you accept your manager's decision? You should not. You do not have the authority to make a decision not covered by the specifications without consulting the client or higher-level managers in your company who are responsible for the program design. Your manager probably does not have that authority either. The manager's quick and simplistic response suggests that he or she is not acting with informed responsibility. In addition, your company must document whatever decision it makes. That is, the specifications need a revision so that they will be complete (SE Code 3.11).

Why is it important, from an ethical point of view, to consult someone else? Decisions about how a program handles unusual situations might have serious consequences. You (and your manager) might not know enough about the uses of the program to make a good decision. In this example, it is possible that the modules of the program that evaluate the loan application do not use the data on race at all. It is possible that the lender or the government wants data on race to ensure compliance with nondiscrimination policies and laws.

What other consequences could the manager's decision have? Suppose the company later uses some of your modules in another project, say, one that evaluates patients for inclusion in research studies on new drugs. Some diseases and drugs affect people in different ethnic groups differently. Inaccurate data could threaten the health or life of people in the studies and distort the conclusions in ways that harm other people who later use the drugs. But, you say, we emphasized in Chapter 8 and Section 9.2.3 that people who reuse existing software, especially in a safety critical project, should review the software and its specifications to ensure that it meets the standards of the new project. That is their responsibility, you say. But if your way of handling missing data is not in the specifications, how will they know about it? Perhaps someone will notice that the specs are incomplete. Perhaps they will test the modules thoroughly before reusing them and discover what the code does. However, we have seen enough examples of human error to derive a lesson for a responsible professional: Do not count on everyone else to do their jobs perfectly. Do your best to make sure your part is not one of the factors that contribute to a failure.

9.3.7 SCHEDULE PRESSURES

A safety-critical application

> Your team is working on a computer-controlled device for treating cancerous tumors. The computer controls direction, intensity, and timing of a beam that destroys the tumor. Various delays have put the project behind schedule, and the deadline is approaching. There will not be time to complete all the planned testing. The system has been functioning properly in the routine treatment scenarios tested so far. You are the project manager, and you are considering whether to deliver the system on time, while continuing testing and making patches if the team finds bugs.

As we observed in Chapter 8, there are often pressures to reduce software testing. Testing is one of the last steps in development, so when deadlines approach, testing schedules often shrink.

The central issue here is safety. Your company is building a machine designed to save lives, but if it malfunctions, it can kill or injure patients. Perhaps the situation seems obvious: delivering the system on time benefits the company but could endanger the patients—a case of profits versus safety. But we will defer a conclusion until after we analyze the case further.

Who does your decision affect? First, the patients who will receive treatment with the machine. A malfunction could cause injury or death. On the other hand, if you delay release of the machine, some patients it might have cured could undergo surgery instead. We will assume treatment with the new machine is preferable because it is less invasive, requires less hospitalization and recovery time, and overall is less expensive. For some patients, surgery might be impossible, and they could die from their cancer without the new device. A second set of stakeholders is the hospitals and clinics who will purchase the machine. Delay could cause financial losses if they have planned on having the machine at the scheduled time. However, it is reasonable for them to expect that the design and testing are professional and complete. You are deceiving the customers if you do not tell them that you have not completed testing. Third, your decision affects you and your company (including its employees and stockholders). The negative consequences of delaying delivery could include damage to your reputation for managing a project (with possible impact on salary and advancement), loss of reputation, a possible fall in stock price for the company, and loss of other contracts, resulting in reduction of jobs for the company's programmers and other employees. As a project manager, you have an obligation to help the company do well. On the other hand, if the system injures a patient, the same negative consequences are likely to occur, in addition to the human feelings of guilt and remorse as well as significant monetary losses from lawsuits.

This brief examination shows that delivering the system without complete testing could have both negative and positive impacts on patients and on the other stakeholders. The issue is not simply profits versus safety. We assume you are honestly trying to weigh the risks of delivering the system against the costs of delay. However, we must consider a few aspects of human nature that can influence the decision. One is to put more weight on short-term and/or highly likely effects. Many of the costs of delay are fairly certain and immediate, and the risk of malfunction is uncertain and in the future. Also, people tend to use the inherent uncertainties of a situation and the genuine arguments for one side to rationalize making the wrong decision. That is, they use uncertainty to justify taking the easy way out. It might take experience (with both professional and ethical issues), knowledge of cases like the Therac-25, and courage to resist the temptation to put short-term effects ahead of longer-term risks.

Now that we have seen that there are arguments on both sides, we must decide how to weigh them and how to avoid rationalization. First, the machine works well in the routine tests performed so far. The Therac-25 case illustrates that a complex system can function correctly hundreds of times but fail with fatal consequences in unusual circumstances. Your customer might not know this. You, as a computer professional, have more understanding about the complexity of computer programs and the potential for errors, especially in programs that interact with real-world events such as operator input and control of machinery. We assume that careful thought went into devising the original test plan for the machine. You should delay delivery and complete the tests. (See SE Code 1.03 and 3.10 and ACM Code 1.2.)

Some patients will benefit from on-time delivery. Should their interests bear equal weight with those of the patients whom a malfunction might harm? Not necessarily. The machine represents an improvement in medical treatment, but there is no ethical obligation that it be available to the public on a certain date. You are not responsible for the disease of people who rely on existing treatments. Your obligation to the people who will use the machine is to be sure that it is as safe as good professional practice can make it, and that includes proper testing. You do not have an ethical obligation to cure people of cancer. You do have an ethical obligation to use your professional judgment in a way that does not expose people, without their knowledge, to additional harm.[*]

What about your responsibility to your company? Even if we weigh the short-term effects of the delay more highly than the risks of losses that would result from a malfunction, the ethical arguments are on the side of fully testing the machine. Yes, you have a responsibility to help your company be successful, but that is not an absolute obligation. (Recall the discussion of goals and constraints in Section 1.4.3.) Perhaps the distinction would be more obvious if the issue were stealing (from a competitor or a customer perhaps). Your responsibility to the financial success of the company is secondary to ethical constraints. In the present case, avoiding unreasonable risk of harm to patients is the ethical constraint (SE Code 1.02).

Getting a product to market

Most products are not safety-critical ones where flaws might threaten people's lives. Consider this scenario:

> You are a programmer working for a very small start-up company. The company has a modest product line and is now developing a truly innovative new product. Everyone is working 60-hour weeks and the target release date is nine months away. The bulk of the programming and testing is done. You are about to begin the beta testing. (See Section 8.3.1 for an explanation of beta testing.) The owner of the company (who is not a programmer) has learned about an annual industry show that would be ideal for introducing the new product. The show is in two months. The owner talks with the project manager. They decide to skip the beta testing and start making plans for an early release.[6]

Should you protest? Students discussing this scenario generally recognize that the decision is a bad one and that the company should do the beta testing. They ask, however, if the programmer is even in a position to protest. Are you supposed to do what the project manager, your direct supervisor, says? Should you say nothing, speak up, or quit?

Consider this possible outcome: You ask for a meeting with the owner. You explain that the product is not ready, that beta testing is a very important stage of development, and that the company should not skip it. The owner accepts what you say and drops the idea of an early release. The new product, released when originally planned, is a success. You eventually become the head of quality control for the growing company.

This is not a fairy tale. It is an actual case, and the outcome I just described is what actually happened. This case makes a very important point: sometimes people will

---

[*] There are many situations where patients knowingly try risky drugs or treatments. Here, we are assuming that doctors and hospitals do not present the device as risky or experimental, but as a new, presumably safe treatment device.

listen to you, provided, of course, you are respectful, thoughtful, and well prepared. In another actual case a manager within a company, but not the software division, asked a programmer to do something the programmer knew was not a good idea. Although she feared that she might lose her job for refusing a manager's request, she said no and gave a brief explanation. The manager accepted the explanation, and that was the end of the incident. People often ask for things they do not necessarily expect to get. It is important to keep in mind that others might respect your opinion. You might be the only one who recognizes the problem or understands a particular situation. Your responsibilities to your company include applying your knowledge and skill to help avoid a bad decision. In the start-up scenario, speaking up might have had a significant impact on the success of the product and the company. Many people are reasonable and will consider a good explanation or argument. Many, but not all. The CEO of a small electronics company proposed producing a new version of a product within three months. The director of engineering (an excellent, experienced software engineer) wrote up a detailed schedule of all the necessary steps and told the CEO that the project would take more than a year. Note that the software engineer did not simply tell the CEO that the three-month plan was unreasonable. He documented his claim. (SE Code 2.06 and 3.09 apply.) The CEO replaced him with someone who had a "can do" attitude. Although it might seem that the result for the engineer in this case was the opposite of the two previous cases, this is also a case where doing what is professionally responsible corresponds with doing what is good for oneself. The software engineer did not want the stress of working under an extremely unreasonable schedule nor the responsibility for the inevitable failure. Leaving the company was not a bad thing.

9.3.8 SOFTWARE LICENSE VIOLATION

> Your company has a license for a computer program for 25 machines, but you discover that it has been copied onto 80 computers.

The first step here is to inform your supervisor that the copies violate the license agreement. Suppose the supervisor is not willing to take any action? What next? What if you bring the problem to the attention of higher-level people in the company and no one cares? There are several possible actions: Give up; you did your best to correct the problem. Call the software vendor and report the offense. Quit your job.

Is giving up at this point ethically acceptable? My students thought it depended in part on whether you are the person who signed the license agreements. If so, you have made an agreement about the use of the software, and you, as the representative of your company, are obligated to honor it. Because you did not make the copies, you have not broken the agreement directly, but you have responsibility for the software. As practical matters, your name on the license could expose you to legal risk, or unethical managers in your company could make you a scapegoat. Thus, you might prefer to report the violation or quit your job and have your name removed from the license to protect yourself. If you are not the person who signed the license, then you observed a wrong and brought it to the attention of appropriate people in the company. Is that enough? What do Sections 2.02, 6.13, and 7.01 of the SE Code and 1.5 and 2.6 of the ACM Code suggest?

9.3.9 GOING PUBLIC

Suppose you are a member of a team working on a computer-controlled crash-avoidance system for automobiles. You think the system has a flaw that could endanger people. The project manager does not seem concerned and expects to announce completion of the project soon. Do you have an ethical obligation to do something?

Given the potential consequences, yes (see SE Code 1.04; ACM Code 1.2, 2.5). We consider a variety of options. First, at a minimum, discuss your concerns with the project manager. Voicing your concerns is admirable and obligatory. It is also good for your company. Internal "whistleblowing" can help protect the company, as well as the public, from all the negative consequences of releasing a dangerous product. If the manager decides to proceed as planned with no examination of the problem, your next option is to go to someone higher up in the company.

If no one with authority in the company is willing to investigate your concerns, you have a more difficult dilemma. You now have the option of going outside the company to the customer, to the news media, or to a government agency. There is personal risk of course: you might lose your job. There is also the ethical issue of the damage you might do to your company and, ultimately, to the people who would benefit from the system. You might be mistaken. Or you might be correct, but your method of whistleblowing might produce negative publicity that kills a potentially valuable and fixable project. As the ACM Code (1.2) says, "[M]isguided reporting of violations can, itself, be harmful." At this point, it is a good idea to consider whether you are confident that you have the expertise to assess the risk. It could help to discuss the problem with other professionals. If you conclude that the management decision was an acceptable one (and that you are not letting your concern for keeping your job sway your conclusion), this might be the point at which to drop the issue. If you are convinced that the flaw is real, or if you are aware of a careless, irresponsible attitude among the company managers, then you must go further (SE Code 6.13). You are not an uninvolved bystander, for whom the question of ethical obligation might be more fuzzy. The project pays your salary. You are part of the team; you are a participant. Note, also, that this is the kind of situation suggested in the SE Code 2.05, where you may violate a confidentiality agreement.

There have been several dramatic cases where professionals faced this difficult situation. Computer engineers who worked on the San Francisco Bay Area Rapid Transit system (BART) worried about the safety of the software designed to control the trains. Although they tried for many months, they were not successful in their attempts to convince their managers to make changes. Eventually, a newspaper published some of their critical memos and reports. The engineers were fired. During the next few years, several crashes occurred, and there were public investigations and numerous recommendations made for improving safety of the system.[7]

One of the BART engineers made these comments about the process:

> If there is something that ought to be corrected inside an organization, the most effective way to do it is to do it within the organization and exhaust all possibilities there . . . you might have to go to the extreme of publishing these things, but you should never start that way.[8]

It is important, for practical and ethical reasons, to keep a complete and accurate record of your attempts to bring attention to the problem and the responses from the people you approach. The record protects you and others who behave responsibly and could help avoid baseless accusations later.

9.3.10 Release of Personal Information

We will look at two related scenarios. Here is the first:

> You work for the IRS, the Social Security Administration, a movie-rental company, or a social networking service. Someone asks you to get a copy of records about a particular person. He will pay you $500.

Who are the stakeholders? You: you have an opportunity to make some extra money. The person seeking the records: presumably he has something to gain. The person whose records the briber wants: providing the information invades his or her privacy. All people about whom the company or agency has personal information: if you sell information about one person, chances are you will sell more if asked in the future. Your employer (if a private company): If the sale becomes known, the victim might sue the company. If such sales of information become common, the company will acquire a reputation for carelessness and will potentially lose business and lawsuits.

There are many alternative actions open to you: Sell the records. Refuse and say nothing about the incident. Refuse and report the incident to your supervisor. Refuse and report to the police. Contact the person whose information the briber wants and tell him or her of the incident. Agree to sell the information, but actually work with the police to collect evidence to convict the person trying to buy it.

Are any of these alternatives ethically prohibited or obligatory? The first option, selling the records, is clearly wrong. It almost certainly violates rules and policies you have agreed to abide by in accepting your job. As an employee, you must abide by the guarantees of confidentiality the company or agency has promised its customers or the public. Depending on the use made of the information you sell, you could be helping to cause serious harm to the victim. Disclosing the information is also likely illegal. Your action might expose your employer to fines. If someone discovers the leak, the employer and the police might suspect another employee, who could face arrest and punishment. (See ACM Code: 1.2, 1.3, 1.7, 2.6; SE Code: 2.03, 2.05, 2.09, 4.04, 6.05, 6.06.)

What about the second alternative: refusing to provide the records, but not reporting the incident? Depending on company policies (and laws related to certain government agencies; see SE Code 6.06 and ACM Code 2.3), you might be obligated to report any attempt to gain access to the records. There are other good reasons for reporting the incident. Reporting could lead to the capture of someone making a business of surreptitiously and illegally buying sensitive personal information. It could protect you and other innocent employees if someone later discovers the sale of the records and does not know who sold them. (Some ethicists, e.g., deontologists, argue that taking an action because it benefits you is not ethically meritorious. However, one can argue that taking an action that protects an innocent person is meritorious, even if the person is yourself.)

ACM Code 1.2 and 1.7 suggest an obligation to report, but it is not explicit. There might be disagreement about whether you have an ethical responsibility to do more than refuse to sell the information. It is difficult to decide how much you must do to prevent a wrong thing from happening if you are not participating in the wrong act. A recluse who ignores evils and pains around him might not be doing anything unethical, but he is not what we would consider a good neighbor. Acting to prevent a wrong is part of being a good neighbor, good employee, or good citizen; it is ethically admirable—even in situations where it is not ethically obligatory.

Now consider a variation of this scenario.

You know another employee sells records with people's personal information.

Your options include doing nothing, talking to the other employee and trying to get him or her to stop selling files (by ethical arguments or threats of exposure), reporting to your supervisor, or reporting to an appropriate law enforcement agency. The question here is whether you have an obligation to do anything. This scenario differs from the previous one in two ways. First, you have no direct involvement; no one has approached you. This difference might seem to argue for no obligation. Second, in the previous scenario, if you refused to sell the file, the buyer might give up, and the victim's information would remain protected. In the current scenario, you know that a sale of confidential, sensitive information occurred. This makes the argument in favor of an obligation to take action stronger (see SE Code 6.13 and 7.01). You should report what you know.

9.3.11 Conflict of Interest

You have a small consulting business. The CyberStuff company plans to buy software to run a cloud data-storage business. CyberStuff wants to hire you to evaluate bids from vendors. Your spouse works for NetWorkx and did most of the work in writing the bid that NetWorkx plans to submit. You read the bid while your spouse was working on it, and you think it is excellent. Do you tell CyberStuff about your spouse's connection with NetWorkx?

Conflict-of-interest situations occur in many professions. Sometimes the ethical course of action is clear. Sometimes, depending on how small your connection with the people or organizations your action affects, it can be more difficult to determine.

I have seen two immediate reactions to scenarios similar to this one (in discussions among professionals and among students). One is that it is a simple case of profits versus honesty, and ethics requires that you inform the company about your connection to the software vendor. The other is that if you honestly believe you can be objective and fairly consider all bids, you have no ethical obligation to say anything. Which is right? Is this a simple choice between saying nothing and getting the consulting job or disclosing your connection and losing the job?

The affected parties are the CyberStuff company, yourself, your spouse, your spouse's company, other companies whose bids you will be reviewing, and future customers of CyberStuff's cloud storage service. A key factor in considering consequences is that we do not know whether CyberStuff will later discover your connection to one of the bidders. If you say nothing about the conflict of interest, you benefit, because you get the consulting job. If you recommend NetWorkx (because you believe its bid is the best), it benefits from a sale. However, if CyberStuff discovers the conflict of interest later, your reputation for honesty—important to a consultant—will suffer. The reputation of your spouse's company could also suffer. Note that even if you conclude that you are truly unbiased and do not have an ethical obligation to tell CyberStuff about your connection to your spouse's company, your decision might put NetWorkx's reputation for honesty at risk. The appearance of bias can be as damaging (to you and to NetWorkx) as actual bias.

Suppose you take the job and you find that one of the other bids is much better than the bid from NetWorkx. Are you prepared to handle that situation ethically?

What are the consequences of disclosing the conflict of interest to the client now? You will probably lose this particular job, but CyberStuff might value your honesty more highly, and you might get you more business in the future. Thus, there could be benefits, even to you, from disclosing the conflict of interest.

Suppose it is unlikely that anyone will discover your connection to NetWorkx. What are your responsibilities to your potential client as a professional consultant? When someone hires you as a consultant, they expect you to offer unbiased, honest, impartial professional advice. There is an implicit assumption that you do not have a personal interest in the outcome or a personal reason to favor one of the bids you will review. The conclusion in this case hangs on this point. In spite of your belief in your impartiality, you could be unintentionally biased. It is not up to you to make the decision about whether you can be fair. The client should make that decision. Your ethical obligation in this case is to inform CyberStuff of the conflict of interest. (See SE Code Principle 4, 4.03, and 4.05, and ACM Code 2.5.)

9.3.12   KICKBACKS AND DISCLOSURE

You are an administrator at a major university. Your department selects a few brands of security software to recommend to students for their desktop computers, laptops, tablets, and other devices. One of the companies whose software you will evaluate takes you out to dinner, gives you free software (in addition to the security software), offers to pay your expenses to attend a professional conference on computer security, and offers to give the university a percentage of the price for every student who buys its security package.

You are sensitive to the issue of bribery, but the cost of the dinner and software the company gave you is relatively small. The university cannot pay to send you to conferences. Attending one will improve your knowledge and skills and make you better at your job, a benefit to both you and the university. The percentage from the sales benefits the university and thus all the students. This sounds like a good deal for all.

A similar situation arose in the student loan business. Universities recommend loan companies to students seeking student loans. A flurry of news reports disclosed that several universities and their financial aid administrators gave special privileges and preferred recommendations to particular lending companies in exchange for payments to the universities and consulting fees, travel expenses, and other gifts for the administrators. Some financial aid officers defended the practices. Professional organizations scurried to write new ethical guidelines. Some lenders paid heavy fines. The reputations of the universities suffered. The government heavily regulates the lending industry, so we return to the security software scenario to discuss ethical issues, not primarily legal ones.

First of all, does your employer have a policy about accepting gifts from vendors? Even if gifts appear small to you and you are confident that they do not influence your judgment, you are obligated to follow your employer's policy. Violating the policy violates an agreement you have made. Violating the policy could expose the employer to negative publicity (and possibly legal sanctions). (See SE Code 6.05 and 6.06. SE Code 1.06, 4.03, and 4.04 are also relevant to this case.)

Who does not benefit from the arrangement with the software company? Any company that charges less for software of comparable quality. Any company that charges the same or perhaps a little more for a better product. All the students who rely on the recommendation. The university's obligation in making the recommendation is primarily to the students. Will the benefits the administrator and the university receive sway their choice of company to the point where they do not choose the products best for the students?

People want to know when a recommendation represents an honest opinion and when someone is paying for it. We expect universities and certain other organizations to be impartial in their recommendations. When the university selects software to recommend, the presumption is that it is, in the university's opinion, the best for the students. If there are other reasons for the selection, the university should disclose them. Disclosure is a key point. Many organizations encourage their members to get a credit card that provides a kickback to the organization. This is not unethical primarily because the kickback is made clear. It is even a selling point: Use this card and help fund our good cause. However, even if the university makes clear in its recommendation that it benefits financially from sales of the software it recommends, there are good arguments against such an arrangement, arguments similar to those against what the loan administrators did. The cozy relationship between administrators and certain companies can lead to decisions not in the best interests of the students.

9.3.13 A Test Plan

A team of programmers is developing a communications system for firefighters to use when fighting a fire. Firefighters will be able to communicate with each other, with supervisors near the scene, and with other emergency personnel. The programmers will test the system in a field near the company office.

What is the ethical issue? The test plan is insufficient, and this is an application where lives could be at risk. Testing should involve real firefighters inside buildings or in varied terrain, perhaps in an actual fire (perhaps a controlled burn). The programmers who work on the system know how it behaves. They are experienced users with a specific set of expectations. They are not the right people to test the system. Testing must address issues such as: Will the devices withstand heat, water, and soot? Can someone manipulate the controls wearing heavy gloves? Are the controls clear and easy to use in poor light conditions? Will a building's structure interfere with the signal?

In an actual case, the New York City Fire Commissioner halted use of a $33 million digital communications system after a fireman called for help on his radio and no one heard. Firefighters reported other problems during simulation tests. The commissioner commented, "We tested the quality, durability, and reliability of the product, but we didn't spend enough time testing them in the field or familiarizing the firefighters with their use."[9]

9.3.14 Artificial Intelligence and Sentencing Criminals

You are part of a team developing a sophisticated program using artificial intelligence techniques to make sentencing decisions for convicted criminals.

Maybe, in the future, we will have computer systems capable of doing this well without human intervention. It is helpful for judges to review sentencing in cases with similar characteristics, but judges use judgment in deciding sentences (within bounds established in law). Prosecutors and defense lawyers present arguments that a judge considers but software could not. A judge can consider unusual circumstances in the case, the character of the convicted person, and other factors that a program might not handle. Judges sometimes innovate creative new aspects of sentencing. A program that analyzes and chooses from prior cases could not. On the other hand, some judges have a reputation for giving extremely tough sentences, while others are very lenient. Some people argue that software might be more fair than a judge influenced by personal impressions and biases. At this point, however, most of the legal community, and probably the public, would prefer to have human judges make sentencing decisions. Years of experience provide insights that are, at this time, difficult to encode into software. For now, we modify the scenario by adding two words to the original scenario:

> You are part of a team developing a sophisticated program using artificial intelligence techniques to *help judges* make sentencing decisions for convicted criminals.

The system will analyze the characteristics of the crime and the criminal to find other cases that are similar. Based on its analysis of cases, should it then make a recommendation for the sentence in the current case, or should it simply display similar cases, more or less as a search engine would, so that the judge can review them? Or should it provide both a recommended sentence and the relevant cases?

This is clearly an application where it is essential to have experts and potential users involved in the design. The expertise and experience of judges and lawyers are essential for choosing criteria and strategies for selecting the similar cases on which the program bases its recommendation or on which a judge bases a decision. The system's recommendations, if it makes them, must comply with sentencing requirements specified in laws.

The involvement of lawyers can improve more subtle decisions. Consider the question of the ordering of the cases the system displays. Should it order them by date or by the length of the sentence? If the latter, should the shortest or longest sentences come first? This last question suggests that the project's consultants should include both prosecutors and defense lawyers. But probably none of these orderings is best. Perhaps you should order the cases according to an evaluation of their similarity or relevance to the current case. That is a fuzzier criterion than date or length of sentence. Again, it is important to include a variety of experts, with different perspectives, in the design process.

Is the ordering of the selected cases so important? When you are researching some topic, how many pages of search engine results do you look at? Many people rarely go beyond the first page. We expect a judge making a sentencing decision to be more thorough. Experience, however, reminds us that people sometimes are tired or rushed. Sometimes they have too much confidence in results from computer systems. Even when people are deliberate and careful in interpreting output from a computer system, the manner in which the viewers see the data can influence their perceptions. (We saw examples in Chapters 7 and 8. Academic researchers, using search engines, tend to cite papers from a smaller portion of all papers because they do not look beyond the first several pages of search results. School districts ignored warnings that they should not rely solely on results of computer-graded tests when making decisions about assigning students to summer school.) Thus, careful planning, including much consultation with relevant experts, is an ethical requirement in a system that will have significant impact on people's lives.

A company or government agency that develops or installs this system must consider how it will maintain and update the system. Clearly there will be new cases to add. How will the system handle changes in sentencing laws? Should it discard cases decided under the old law? Include them but flag them clearly as predating the change? How much weight should the system give such cases in its selection criteria?

We have not yet answered the question about whether the system should recommend a sentence. A specific recommendation from the system that differs from the judge's initial plan might lead a judge to give a case more thought. Or it might influence a judge more than it should. If the system presents a recommendation, legislators or administrators might begin to think that a clerk or law student, not a judge, can operate the system and handle sentencing. This is not likely in the short term—judges and lawyers would object. It is, however, a possible consequence of apparently sophisticated AI systems making apparently wise decisions in any professional area. A potential drop in employment for judges (or other professionals) is not the main issue. The quality of the decisions is. Thus, an answer to the question will depend in part on the quality of AI technology (and the specific system) at the time of development and on the sensitivity of the application. (See Exercise 6.33 for another application area.)

> Suppose judges in your state use a sentencing decision system that displays similar cases for the judge to review. You are a programmer working for your state government. Your state has just made it a criminal offense to use a cellphone while taking a college exam. Your boss, a justice department administrator, tells you to modify the program to add this new category of crime and assign the same relevancy weights to cases as the program currently does for using a cellphone while driving a car (already illegal in your state).

The first question, one for your boss, is whether the contract under which the system operates allows the state to make changes. For many consumer products, guarantees and service agreements become void if the consumer takes the product apart and makes changes. The same can be true for software. Let's assume the boss knows that the state's contract allows the state to modify the system.

Suppose you know that your boss made the decision quickly and independently. You should say no, with appropriate politeness and reasons. SE Code 3.15 states a very important, often ignored principle: "Treat all forms of software maintenance with the same professionalism as new development." That includes developing specifications—in this example, in consultation with lawyers and judges who understand the law and its subtleties. We raised a sampling of the complex and sensitive issues that go into the design of a system such as this. Modifications and upgrades should undergo as thorough planning and testing.

9.3.15 A Gracious Host

> You are the computer system administrator for a mid-size company. You can monitor the company network from home, and you frequently work from home with some company files on your home computer. Your niece, a college student, is visiting for a week. Her phone battery is dead, and she asks if she can use your computer to check her email. Sure, you say.

You are being a gracious host. What is the ethical problem?

Maybe there is none. Maybe you have an excellent firewall and excellent antivirus software. Maybe you remember that you are logged in to your company system and you log out before letting your niece use the computer. Maybe your files are password protected and you create a separate account on your computer for your niece. But maybe you did not even think about security when your niece asked to use the computer.

Your niece is a responsible person. She would not intentionally snoop or do harm to you or your company. But after checking email, she might check in on her Facebook friends, then look for someone selling cheap concert tickets, then . . . who knows? Maybe her own computer crashed twice in the past six months because of viruses.

Your company network contains employee records, customer records, and plenty of information about company projects, finances, and plans. Depending on what the company does, the system might contain other very sensitive information. Downtime, due to a virus or similar problem, would be very costly for the company. In an actual incident, someone in the family of a mortgage company employee signed up for a peer-to-peer file sharing service and did not properly set the options indicating which files to share. Mortgage application information for a few thousand customers leaked and spread on the Web.

The point of this scenario is that you must always be alert to potential risks. Mixing family and work applications poses risks.

EXERCISES

Review Exercises

9.1   What are two ways professional ethics differ from ethics in general?

9.2   Why did a program developed by Microsoft programmers to read handwriting fail?

9.3   What is one important policy decision a company should consider when designing a system to target ads based on email content?

9.4   Suppose you are a programmer, and you think there is a serious flaw in software your company is developing. Who should you talk to about it first?

General Exercises

9.5   Describe a case at work or in school where someone asked or pressured you to do something you thought unethical.

9.6   Most online services require users to create an account protected by a password. Do you think that this protection should be optional? What are some risks of not requiring a password? From an ethical point of view, which of the options (or others you might think of) are ethically acceptable? Which is best?

9.7   Suppose the service in the previous exercise chooses to provide an option for quick retrieval of user data without a password. What should the default setting for this option be when someone initiates service (on or off)? Why?

9.8   Your company sells a device (smartphone, tablet, or other small portable device) for which owners can download third-party apps from your app store. The company's published policy says that the company will delete an app from users' devices if and only if the company discovers that the app contains malicious software such as a virus that compromises the security of the devices or of sensitive user data on the devices. The company discovers that an app has an undocumented but easily initiated component that displays extremely offensive video showing men insulting and violently attacking Chinese people. The company immediately removes the app from its app store and alerts customers to delete the app from their devices. Should the company remotely delete the app from the devices of all who downloaded it? Give arguments on both sides. Which side do you think is stronger? Why?

9.9   The scenarios in Sections 9.3.2 and 9.3.4 are about different situations, but they share many principles. Identify several principles that these scenarios have in common.

9.10   You have been hired by an online search company to create a system that will suggest results customized according to user's search trends. However, in order to do this, the user's search history must be stored on company servers. What risks to privacy does this entail? What features should you include? How should the company inform users about the system?

9.11   Analyze the following scenario using the methodology of Section 9.3.1. Is the action ethical?

> You work for a software company developing a system to process loan applications for mortgage companies. You will do maintenance on the system after delivery. You are considering building in a back door so that you can easily get in to the system after it is installed at various customer facilities. (This is not in the specifications for maintenance; it is your secret.)

9.12   A factory manager has hired your company to develop and install a surveillance system in a software development company. The system includes software that will monitor phone and email conversations of employees. Supervisors and security personnel can view and hear these in real time in a control room. The factory manager says the purposes are to watch for safety problems and for misuse of resources by workers. What issues, specifications, and policies will you discuss with the manager? Would you set any conditions on taking the job? Explain.

9.13   You work for a company that develops security products. You helped write software for a car door lock that operates by matching the driver's thumbprint. The manager for that project is no longer at the company. A local power station wants your company to develop a thumbprint-operated lock for secure areas of the power station. Your boss says to use the software from the car locks. What is your response?

9.14   Write a scenario to illustrate SE Code 2.05 and ACM Code 1.8.

9.15   You are a manager at a health maintenance organization. You find that one of your employees has been reading people's medical records without authorization. What actions could you take? What will you choose? Why?

9.16   In many cities, wills processed by courts are public records. A business that sells information from local public records is considering adding a new "product," lists of people who recently inherited a large amount of money. Using the methodology of Section 9.3.1, analyze the ethics of doing so.

9.17   You are designing a database to keep track of patients while they are in a hospital. The record for each patient will include special diet requirements. Describe some approaches to deciding how to design the list of diet options from which a user will select when entering patient data. Evaluate different approaches.

9.18   You are an expert in speaker recognition systems. (See the box in Section 9.2.3.) A company asks you to help develop a system to sift through huge quantities of sound files from intercepted phone conversations to find the conversations of specific people. The company plans to sell the system to law enforcement agencies in the United States and other countries where it expects the system to be used in compliance with the country's laws. What questions, if any, will you ask to help make your decision, and how will they affect the decision? If you would accept or reject the job without further information, give your decision and your reasons.

9.19   Review the description of the airplane crash near Cali, Colombia, in Section 8.3.1. Find specific guidelines in Section 9.2.3 and the ethics codes in Appendix A that, if followed carefully, might have avoided problems in the flight management software that contributed to the crash.

9.20   A company that is developing software for a new generation of space shuttles offers you a job. You do not have any training in the specific techniques used in the programs you will be working on. You can tell from the job interview that the interviewer thinks your college program included this material. Should you take the job? Should you tell the interviewer that you have no training or experience in this area? Analyze this scenario, using the methods in Section 9.3.1. Find relevant sections from the ethics codes in Appendix A.

9.21   A small company offers you a programming job. You are to work on new versions of its software product to disable copy protection and other access controls on electronic books. (For this exercise, assume you are in a country that does not outlaw tools to circumvent copy protection as the Digital Millennium Copyright Act does in the United States.) The company's program enables buyers of ebooks to read their ebooks on a variety of hardware devices (fair uses). Customers could also use the program to make many unauthorized copies of copyrighted books. The company's Web page implicitly encourages this practice, particularly for college students who want to avoid the cost of e-textbooks. Analyze the ethics of accepting the job. Find relevant sections from the ethics codes in Appendix A.

9.22   Find at least two examples described in this book where there was a violation of Clause 3.09 of the SE Code.

9.23   Clause 1.03 of the SE Code says, "Approve software only if [it does not] diminish privacy or harm the environment." Search engines can diminish privacy. Do they violate this clause? Should the clause say something about trade-offs, or should we interpret it as an absolute rule? The concluding sentence of Clause 1.03 says, "The ultimate effect of the work should be to the public good." Does this suggest trade-offs? Give another example in which the dilemma in this exercise would be relevant.

9.24 Clause 8.07 in the SE Code says we should "not give unfair treatment to anyone because of any irrelevant prejudices." The guidelines for Section 1.4 of the ACM Code say, "Discrimination on the basis of . . . national origin . . . is an explicit violation of ACM policy and will not be tolerated." Analyze the ethical issues in the following scenario. Do you think the decision in the scenario is ethically acceptable? How do the relevant sections from the two Codes apply? Which Code has a better statement about discrimination? Why?

> Suppose you came to the United States from Iraq 15 years ago. You now have a small software company. You will need to hire six programmers this year. Because of the devastation by the war in your homeland, you have decided to seek out and hire only programmers who are refugees from Iraq.

9.25 Consider the following statements.

1. In addition to a safe social environment, human well-being includes a safe natural environment. Therefore, computing professionals who design and develop systems must be alert to, and make others aware of, any potential damage to the local or global environment.[10]

2. We cannot assume that a computer-based economy automatically will provide enough jobs for everyone in the future. Computer professionals should be aware of this pressure on employment when designing and implementing systems that will reduce job opportunities for those most in need of them.[11]

Compare the two statements from the perspective of how relevant and appropriate they are for an ethical code for computer professionals. Do you think both should be in such a code? Neither? Just one? (Which one?) Give your reasons.

9.26 You are a Web designer. One of your most important clients asks you to design an online store selling sex toys. Such websites are legal in your client's country, but not in yours. You have to decide what to do with the contract. Give some options, and give arguments for and against them. What will you do? Why?

9.27 A Dutch hacker who copied patient files from a University of Washington medical center (and was not caught) said in an online interview that he did it to publicize the system's vulnerability, not to use the information. He disclosed portions of the files (to an individual, not the public) after the medical center said that no patient files had been copied. Analyze the ethics of his actions using the methodology of Section 9.3.1. Was this honorable whistleblowing? Irresponsible hacking?

9.28 The lead developer of your team instructs you to inject malicious code into software that will cause it to fail repeatedly, forcing the user to request support, which they will have to pay for. He threatens to have you fired if you do not comply. Discuss the ethical issues of following or not following his instructions.

9.29 The first case in Section 9.3.7 concerns safety-critical systems. Suppose the software product in the second scenario is an accounting system, or a game, or a photo-sharing system. Which principles or ideas in the analysis of the first scenario apply to the second one? Which do not? Explain your answers.

9.30 You are a high-level manager at an automobile company. You must decide whether to approve a proposed project to add a feature to car models that appeal to young drivers. The feature allows receiving and sending social media updates by voice. What are the issues? Make a decision and explain it, or explain what additional information you would consider before making your decision.

9.31 Suppose there are two large competing telecommunications firms in your city. The companies are hostile to each other. There have been unproven claims of industrial espionage by each company. Your spouse works for one of the companies. You are now interviewing for a job with the other. Do you have an ethical obligation to tell the interviewer about your spouse's job? How is this case similar to and different from the conflict-of-interest case in Section 9.3.11?

9.32 In the conflict-of-interest case in Section 9.3.11, we mentioned that future customers of Cyber-Stuff's cloud storage service are stakeholders, but we did not discuss them further. How does your decision affect them? What are your ethical obligations to them?

9.33 You are developing an app to work with browsers on mobile devices that will tag game sites as safe or unsafe based on criteria about what data the sites collect from the user's device. What ethical responsibilities do you have to the game sites you will rate and to potential users of your app?

9.34 Several professional associations of engineers opposed allowing increased immigration of skilled high-tech workers. Was this ethical? Give arguments for both sides. Then give your view and defend it.

Assignments

These exercises require some research or activity.

9.35 Watch a science fiction movie set in the near future. Describe a computer or telecommunications system in the movie that does not currently exist. Suppose, in the years before the movie takes place, you are on the team that develops it. Identify issues of professional ethics the team should consider.

9.36 Read the privacy agreement of any major online service provider—what data they store, for what purposes they use this data, and so on. Evaluate the decisions they made. Suggest improvements if you can think of any.

Class Discussion Exercises

These exercises are for class discussion, perhaps with short presentations prepared in advance by small groups of students.

9.37 You are the programmer in the clinic scenario (Section 9.3.2). The director has asked you to rank your suggestions for security and privacy protection measures so that she can choose the most important ones while still trying to stay within her budget. Group the suggestions into at least three categories: essential, recommended, and least important. Include explanations you might give her and assumptions you make (or questions you would ask her) to help determine the importance of some features.

9.38 You are an experienced programmer working on part of a project to enable people to control household appliances from their cellphone. (For example, they can turn on the air conditioning while on the way home.) You have figured out that you can do a part of your section of the program in a way that is more efficient than the method described in the specifications. You are confident that your method is correct, and you know that the change will have no impact on other parts of the program. You understand the importance of following specifications, but you also know that any proposed revision generates a long, bureaucratic process that will take weeks and require approvals from many people in both your company and the client company. Is this a case where the trade-offs make it reasonable to use the better method without a revision of the specifications? Explain your response.

9.39   The faculty at a large university requested that the campus store sell an electronic device, Auto-Grader, for students to use when taking machine-scorable tests. Students enter test answers into the device. When done, they send the answers to the instructor's laptop or tablet in the classroom. Once the instructor's computer receives the answers, it immediately grades the test and sends each student's score back to the student's device.

Suppose you are a university dean who must decide whether to allow use of this system. Analyze the decision as both an ethical and practical problem. Discuss potential benefits and problems or risks of using the system. Discuss all the issues (of the kind relevant to the topics of this book) that are relevant to making the decision. Mention any warnings or policies you might include if you approve use of the system.

9.40   As we saw in Section 7.4.3, some people fear that development of intelligent robots could have devastating consequences for the human race. Do you believe that a code of ethics should be programmed into robots to prevent this? Formulate such a code. Research examples of such codes already formulated by futurists and science fiction authors.

BOOKS AND ARTICLES

- Robert M. Anderson, Robert Perrucci, Dan E. Schendel, and Leon E. Trachtman, *Divided Loyalties: Whistle-Blowing at BART*, Purdue University, 1980.

- Ronald E. Anderson, Deborah G. Johnson, Donald Gotterbarn, and Judith Perrolle, "Using the New ACM Code of Ethics in Decision Making," *Communications of the ACM*, February 1993, 36(2), pp. 98–107.

- Michael D. Bayles, *Professional Ethics*, Wadsworth, 1981.

- Vint Cerf, "Ethics and the Internet," *Communications of the ACM*, June 1989, 32(6), p. 710. An early attempt to establish a standard of ethics for the Internet.

- W. Robert Collins, Keith W. Miller, Bethany J. Spielman, and Phillip Wherry, "How Good

Is Good Enough?" *Communications of the ACM*, January 1994, pp. 81–91.

- M. David Ermann and Michele S. Shauf, eds., *Computers, Ethics, and Society*, 3rd. ed., Oxford University Press, 2002.

- Deborah G. Johnson, *Computer Ethics*, 4th ed., Prentice Hall, 2009.

- Michael J. Quinn, *Ethics for the Information Age*, 4th ed., Addison Wesley, 2010.

- James Rachels, *The Elements of Moral Philosophy*, McGraw Hill, 1993.

- Richard Spinello, *CyberEthics: Morality and Law in Cyberspace*, 4th ed., Jones and Bartlett, 2010.

- Herman T. Tavani, *Ethics and Technology: Controversies, Questions, and Strategies for Ethical Computing*, Wiley, 2010.

ORGANIZATIONS AND WEBSITES

- ACM: www.acm.org

- IEEE Computer Society: www.computer.org

NOTES

1. The somewhat outdated full names are the Association for Computing Machinery and the Institute of Electrical and Electronics Engineers.

2. Bob Davis and David Wessel, *Prosperity: The Coming 20-Year Boom and What It Means to You*, Random House, 1998, p. 97.

3. Charles Piller, "The Gender Gap Goes High-Tech," *Los Angeles Times*, Aug. 25, 1998, p. A1.

4. Bill Gates, *The Road Ahead*, Viking, 1995, p. 78.

5. Julie Johnson contributed this scenario and its analysis.

6. I thank Cyndi Chie for giving me this scenario and telling me of the outcome in the actual case.

7. Robert M. Anderson *et al.*, *Divided Loyalties: Whistle-Blowing at BART*, Purdue University, 1980.

8. Holger Hjorstvang, quoted in Anderson *et al.*, *Divided Loyalties*, p. 140.

9. Robert Fox, "News Track," *Communications of the ACM*, 44, no. 6 (June 2001), pp. 9–10. Kevin Flynn, "A Focus on Communication Failures," *New York Times*, Jan. 30, 2003, p. A13.

10. Guidelines of the ACM Code of Ethics and Professional Conduct, Section 1.1.

11. Tom Forester and Perry Morrison, *Computer Ethics: Cautionary Tales and Ethical Dilemmas in Computing*, 2nd ed., MIT Press, 1994, p. 202.

Epilogue

Although most of this book focuses on problems and controversial issues, we celebrate the enormous benefits that computer technology and the Internet have brought us.

Critics of computer technology predicted many very negative consequences that did not occur (for example, mass unemployment). Critics, especially those without a technical background, were less likely to anticipate some of the problems that do occur: hacking, identity theft, spam. Very few people anticipated whole new phenomena such as portable access to the resources of the Internet, social media, and content sharing by millions of members of the public, with their marvelous benefits and new problems.

The human mind, and hence technology, does not stand still. Change always disrupts the status quo. Technology is always shifting the balance of power—between governments and citizens, between hackers and security experts, between people who want to protect their privacy and businesses that want to collect and use personal information. Entrenched powers such as governments or dominant companies in an industry will fight to maintain their position. We can look to governments for solutions to some problems that technology causes, but we should remember that governments are institutions, like businesses and other organizations, with their own interests and incentives.

Because technology brings change, it often brings new problems. With time, we solve or reduce many of the problems, using more or better technology, the market, innovative services and business arrangements, laws, education, and so on. We cannot eliminate all negative effects. We accept some and adapt to a new environment. We make trade-offs.

In some areas, such as privacy of personal data and activities, computer technology has brought profound changes that could fundamentally alter our interactions with the people around us and with our governments. It is essential to think about personal choices and their consequences. It is essential for businesses and computer professionals to think about appropriate guidelines for use of the technology. It is essential to think ahead—to anticipate potential problems and risks and to design products and policies to reduce them. On the other hand, we must be careful not to regulate too soon in ways that would stifle innovation and prevent new benefits.

The issue of banning a tool or technology has come up in several contexts. These included encryption, anonymity on the Web, machines that copy music and movies, software to circumvent copyright protection, intelligent robots, and so on. The difficulty of predicting future beneficial uses of technologies is a strong argument against such bans.

We learn from experience. System failures, even disasters, lead to better systems. However, the observation that perfection is not possible does not absolve us of responsibility for sloppy or unethical work.

There are many opportunities for computer professionals to develop wonderful new products and to use their skills and creativity to build solutions to some of the problems we have discussed. I hope that this book has sparked a lot of ideas. I hope also that the discussion of risks and failures encourages you to exercise the highest degree of professional and personal responsibility.

Appendix A

THE SOFTWARE ENGINEERING CODE
AND THE ACM CODE

A.1 Software Engineering Code of Ethics and Professional Practice*

Software Engineering Code of Ethics and Professional Practice (Version 5.2) as recommended by the ACM/IEEE-CS Joint Task Force on Software Engineering Ethics and Professional Practices and jointly approved by the ACM and the IEEE-CS as the standard for teaching and practicing software engineering.

Software Engineering Code of Ethics and Professional Practice (Short Version)

PREAMBLE

The short version of the code summarizes aspirations at a high level of the abstraction; the clauses that are included in the full version give examples and details of how these aspirations change the way we act as software engineering professionals. Without the aspirations, the details can become legalistic and tedious; without the details, the aspirations can become high sounding but empty; together, the aspirations and the details form a cohesive code.

Software engineers shall commit themselves to making the analysis, specification, design, development, testing and maintenance of software a beneficial and respected profession. In accordance with their commitment to the health, safety and welfare of the public, software engineers shall adhere to the following Eight Principles:

1. PUBLIC – Software engineers shall act consistently with the public interest.

2. CLIENT AND EMPLOYER – Software engineers shall act in a manner that is in the best interests of their client and employer consistent with the public interest.

---

3. PRODUCT – Software engineers shall ensure that their products and related modifications meet the highest professional standards possible.

4. JUDGMENT – Software engineers shall maintain integrity and independence in their professional judgment.

5. MANAGEMENT – Software engineering managers and leaders shall subscribe to and promote an ethical approach to the management of software development and maintenance.

6. PROFESSION – Software engineers shall advance the integrity and reputation of the profession consistent with the public interest.

7. COLLEAGUES – Software engineers shall be fair to and supportive of their colleagues.

8. SELF – Software engineers shall participate in lifelong learning regarding the practice of their profession and shall promote an ethical approach to the practice of the profession.

Software Engineering Code of Ethics and Professional Practice (Full Version)

Preamble

Computers have a central and growing role in commerce, industry, government, medicine, education, entertainment, and society at large. Software engineers are those who contribute by direct participation or by teaching, to the analysis, specification, design, development, certification, maintenance, and testing of software systems. Because of their roles in developing software systems, software engineers have significant opportunities to do good or cause harm, to enable others to do good or cause harm, or to influence others to do good or cause harm. To ensure, as much as possible, that their efforts will be used for good, software engineers must commit themselves to making software engineering a beneficial and respected profession. In accordance with that commitment, software engineers shall adhere to the following Code of Ethics and Professional Practice.

The Code contains eight Principles related to the behavior of and decisions made by professional software engineers, including practitioners, educators, managers, supervisors, and policy makers, as well as trainees and students of the profession. The Principles identify the ethically responsible relationships in which individuals, groups, and organizations participate and the primary obligations within these relationships. The Clauses of each Principle are illustrations of some of the obligations included in these relationships. These obligations are founded in the software engineer's humanity, in special care owed to people affected by the work of software engineers, and the unique elements of the practice of software engineering. The Code prescribes these as obligations of anyone claiming to be or aspiring to be a software engineer.

It is not intended that the individual parts of the Code be used in isolation to justify errors of omission or commission. The list of Principles and Clauses is not exhaustive. The Clauses should not be read as separating the acceptable from the unacceptable in professional conduct in all practical situations. The Code is not a simple ethical algorithm that generates ethical decisions. In some situations standards may be in tension with each other or with standards from other sources. These situations require the software engineer to use ethical judgment to act in a manner which is most consistent with the spirit of the Code of Ethics and Professional Practice, given the circumstances.

Ethical tensions can best be addressed by thoughtful consideration of fundamental principles, rather than blind reliance on detailed regulations. These Principles should influence software engineers to consider broadly who is affected by their work; to examine if they and their colleagues are treating other human beings with due respect; to consider how the public, if reasonably well informed, would view their decisions; to analyze how the least empowered will be affected by their decisions; and to consider whether their acts would be judged worthy of the ideal professional working as a software engineer. In all these judgments concern for the health, safety and welfare of the public is primary; that is, the "Public Interest" is central to this Code.

The dynamic and demanding context of software engineering requires a code that is adaptable and relevant to new situations as they occur. However, even in this generality, the Code provides support for software engineers and managers of software engineers who need to take positive action in a specific case by documenting the ethical stance of the profession. The Code provides an ethical foundation to which individuals within teams and the team as a whole can appeal. The Code helps to define those actions that are ethically improper to request of a software engineer or teams of software engineers.

The Code is not simply for adjudicating the nature of questionable acts; it also has an important educational function. As this Code expresses the consensus of the profession on ethical issues, it is a means to educate both the public and aspiring professionals about the ethical obligations of all software engineers.

PRINCIPLES

Principle 1: Public

Software engineers shall act consistently with the public interest. In particular, software engineers shall, as appropriate:

1.01. Accept full responsibility for their own work.

1.02. Moderate the interests of the software engineer, the employer, the client, and the users with the public good.

1.03. Approve software only if they have a well-founded belief that it is safe, meets specifications, passes appropriate tests, and does not diminish quality of life, diminish privacy, or harm the environment. The ultimate effect of the work should be to the public good.

1.04. Disclose to appropriate persons or authorities any actual or potential danger to the user, the public, or the environment, that they reasonably believe to be associated with software or related documents.

1.05. Cooperate in efforts to address matters of grave public concern caused by software, its installation, maintenance, support, or documentation.

1.06. Be fair and avoid deception in all statements, particularly public ones, concerning software or related documents, methods and tools.

1.07. Consider issues of physical disabilities, allocation of resources, economic disadvantage, and other factors that can diminish access to the benefits of software.

1.08. Be encouraged to volunteer professional skills to good causes and contribute to public education concerning the discipline.

Principle 2: Client and Employer

Software engineers shall act in a manner that is in the best interests of their client and employer, consistent with the public interest. In particular, software engineers shall, as appropriate:

2.01. Provide service in their areas of competence, being honest and forthright about any limitations of their experience and education.

2.02. Not knowingly use software that is obtained or retained either illegally or unethically.

2.03. Use the property of a client or employer only in ways properly authorized, and with the client's or employer's knowledge and consent.

2.04. Ensure that any document upon which they rely has been approved, when required, by someone authorized to approve it.

2.05. Keep private any confidential information gained in their professional work, where such confidentiality is consistent with the public interest and consistent with the law.

2.06. Identify, document, collect evidence, and report to the client or the employer promptly if, in their opinion, a project is likely to fail, to prove too expensive, to violate intellectual property law, or otherwise to be problematic.

2.07. Identify, document, and report significant issues of social concern, of which they are aware, in software or related documents, to the employer or the client.

2.08. Accept no outside work detrimental to the work they perform for their primary employer.

2.09. Promote no interest adverse to their employer or client, unless a higher ethical concern is being compromised; in that case, inform the employer or another appropriate authority of the ethical concern.

Principle 3: Product

Software engineers shall ensure that their products and related modifications meet the highest professional standards possible. In particular, software engineers shall, as appropriate:

3.01. Strive for high quality, acceptable cost, and a reasonable schedule, ensuring significant tradeoffs are clear to and accepted by the employer and the client, and are available for consideration by the user and the public.

3.02. Ensure proper and achievable goals and objectives for any project on which they work or propose.

3.03. Identify, define, and address ethical, economic, cultural, legal and environmental issues related to work projects.

3.04. Ensure that they are qualified for any project on which they work or propose to work by an appropriate combination of education, training, and experience.

3.05. Ensure an appropriate method is used for any project on which they work or propose to work.

3.06. Work to follow professional standards, when available, that are most appropriate for the task at hand, departing from these only when ethically or technically justified.

3.07. Strive to fully understand the specifications for software on which they work.

3.08. Ensure that specifications for software on which they work have been well documented, satisfy the users' requirements, and have the appropriate approvals.

3.09. Ensure realistic quantitative estimates of cost, scheduling, personnel, quality, and outcomes on any project on which they work or propose to work and provide an uncertainty assessment of these estimates.

3.10. Ensure adequate testing, debugging, and review of software and related documents on which they work.

3.11. Ensure adequate documentation, including significant problems discovered and solutions adopted, for any project on which they work.

3.12. Work to develop software and related documents that respect the privacy of those who will be affected by that software.

3.13. Be careful to use only accurate data derived by ethical and lawful means, and use it only in ways properly authorized.

3.14. Maintain the integrity of data, being sensitive to outdated or flawed occurrences.

3.15 Treat all forms of software maintenance with the same professionalism as new development.

Principle 4: Judgment

Software engineers shall maintain integrity and independence in their professional judgment. In particular, software engineers shall, as appropriate:

4.01. Temper all technical judgments by the need to support and maintain human values.

4.02 Only endorse documents either prepared under their supervision or within their areas of competence and with which they are in agreement.

4.03. Maintain professional objectivity with respect to any software or related documents they are asked to evaluate.

4.04. Not engage in deceptive financial practices such as bribery, double billing, or other improper financial practices.

4.05. Disclose to all concerned parties those conflicts of interest that cannot reasonably be avoided or escaped.

4.06. Refuse to participate, as members or advisors, in a private, governmental or professional body concerned with software related issues, in which they, their employers or their clients have undisclosed potential conflicts of interest.

Principle 5: Management

Software engineering managers and leaders shall subscribe to and promote an ethical approach to the management of software development and maintenance. In particular, those managing or leading software engineers shall, as appropriate:

5.01 Ensure good management for any project on which they work, including effective procedures for promotion of quality and reduction of risk.

5.02. Ensure that software engineers are informed of standards before being held to them.

5.03. Ensure that software engineers know the employer's policies and procedures for protecting passwords, files, and information that is confidential to the employer or confidential to others.

5.04. Assign work only after taking into account appropriate contributions of education and experience tempered with a desire to further that education and experience.

5.05. Ensure realistic quantitative estimates of cost, scheduling, personnel, quality, and outcomes on any project on which they work or propose to work, and provide an uncertainty assessment of these estimates.

5.06. Attract potential software engineers only by full and accurate description of the conditions of employment.

5.07. Offer fair and just remuneration.

5.08. Not unjustly prevent someone from taking a position for which that person is suitably qualified.

5.09. Ensure that there is a fair agreement concerning ownership of any software, processes, research, writing, or other intellectual property to which a software engineer has contributed.

5.10. Provide for due process in hearing charges of violation of an employer's policy or of this Code.

5.11. Not ask a software engineer to do anything inconsistent with this Code.

5.12. Not punish anyone for expressing ethical concerns about a project.

Principle 6: Profession

Software engineers shall advance the integrity and reputation of the profession consistent with the public interest. In particular, software engineers shall, as appropriate:

6.01. Help develop an organizational environment favorable to acting ethically.

6.02. Promote public knowledge of software engineering.

6.03. Extend software engineering knowledge by appropriate participation in professional organizations, meetings, and publications.

6.04. Support, as members of a profession, other software engineers striving to follow this Code.

6.05. Not promote their own interest at the expense of the profession, client, or employer.

6.06. Obey all laws governing their work, unless, in exceptional circumstances, such compliance is inconsistent with the public interest.

6.07. Be accurate in stating the characteristics of software on which they work, avoiding not only false claims but also claims that might reasonably be supposed to be speculative, vacuous, deceptive, misleading, or doubtful.

6.08. Take responsibility for detecting, correcting, and reporting errors in software and associated documents on which they work.

6.09. Ensure that clients, employers, and supervisors know of the software engineer's commitment to this Code of ethics, and the subsequent ramifications of such commitment.

6.10. Avoid associations with businesses and organizations which are in conflict with this code.

6.11. Recognize that violations of this Code are inconsistent with being a professional software engineer.

6.12. Express concerns to the people involved when significant violations of this Code are detected unless this is impossible, counter-productive, or dangerous.

6.13. Report significant violations of this Code to appropriate authorities when it is clear that consultation with people involved in these significant violations is impossible, counter-productive, or dangerous.

Principle 7: Colleagues

Software engineers shall be fair to and supportive of their colleagues. In particular, software engineers shall, as appropriate:

7.01. Encourage colleagues to adhere to this Code.

7.02. Assist colleagues in professional development.

7.03. Credit fully the work of others and refrain from taking undue credit.

7.04. Review the work of others in an objective, candid, and properly-documented way.

7.05. Give a fair hearing to the opinions, concerns, or complaints of a colleague.

7.06. Assist colleagues in being fully aware of current standard work practices including policies and procedures for protecting passwords, files, and other confidential information, and security measures in general.

7.07. Not unfairly intervene in the career of any colleague; however, concern for the employer, the client or public interest may compel software engineers, in good faith, to question the competence of a colleague.

7.08. In situations outside of their own areas of competence, call upon the opinions of other professionals who have competence in that area.

Principle 8: Self

Software engineers shall participate in lifelong learning regarding the practice of their profession and shall promote an ethical approach to the practice of the profession. In particular, software engineers shall continually endeavor to:

8.01. Further their knowledge of developments in the analysis, specification, design, development, maintenance, and testing of software and related documents, together with the management of the development process.

8.02. Improve their ability to create safe, reliable, and useful quality software at reasonable cost and within a reasonable time.

8.03. Improve their ability to produce accurate, informative, and well-written documentation.

8.04. Improve their understanding of the software and related documents on which they work and of the environment in which they will be used.

8.05. Improve their knowledge of relevant standards and the law governing the software and related documents on which they work.

8.06 Improve their knowledge of this Code, its interpretation, and its application to their work.

8.07 Not give unfair treatment to anyone because of any irrelevant prejudices.

8.08. Not influence others to undertake any action that involves a breach of this Code.

8.09. Recognize that personal violations of this Code are inconsistent with being a professional software engineer.

This Code was developed by the ACM/IEEE-CS joint task force on Software Engineering Ethics and Professional Practices (SEEPP):

Executive Committee: Donald Gotterbarn (Chair), Keith Miller and Simon Rogerson;

Members: Steve Barber, Peter Barnes, Ilene Burnstein, Michael Davis, Amr El-Kadi, N. Ben Fairweather, Milton Fulghum, N. Jayaram, Tom Jewett, Mark Kanko, Ernie Kallman, Duncan Langford, Joyce Currie Little, Ed Mechler, Manuel J. Norman, Douglas Phillips, Peter Ron Prinzivalli, Patrick Sullivan, John Weckert, Vivian Weil, S. Weisband and Laurie Honour Werth.

A.2 ACM Code of Ethics and Professional Conduct*

Adopted by ACM Council 10/16/92.

PREAMBLE

Commitment to ethical professional conduct is expected of every member (voting members, associate members, and student members) of the Association for Computing Machinery (ACM).

This Code, consisting of 24 imperatives formulated as statements of personal responsibility, identifies the elements of such a commitment. It contains many, but not all, issues professionals are likely to face. Section 1 outlines fundamental ethical considerations, while Section 2 addresses additional, more specific considerations of professional conduct. Statements in Section 3 pertain more specifically to individuals who have a leadership role, whether in the workplace or in a volunteer capacity such as with organizations like ACM. Principles involving compliance with this Code are given in Section 4.

The Code shall be supplemented by a set of Guidelines, which provide explanation to assist members in dealing with the various issues contained in the Code. It is expected that the Guidelines will be changed more frequently than the Code.

The Code and its supplemented Guidelines are intended to serve as a basis for ethical decision making in the conduct of professional work. Secondarily, they may serve as a basis for judging the merit of a formal complaint pertaining to violation of professional ethical standards.

It should be noted that although computing is not mentioned in the imperatives of Section 1, the Code is concerned with how these fundamental imperatives apply to one's conduct as a computing professional. These imperatives are expressed in a general form to emphasize that ethical principles which apply to computer ethics are derived from more general ethical principles.

It is understood that some words and phrases in a code of ethics are subject to varying interpretations, and that any ethical principle may conflict with other ethical principles in specific situations. Questions related to ethical conflicts can best be answered by thoughtful consideration of fundamental principles, rather than reliance on detailed regulations.

CONTENTS AND GUIDELINES

1. General Moral Imperatives.
2. More Specific Professional Responsibilities.

---

* ACM CODE OF ETHICS AND PROFESSIONAL CONDUCT. Copyright © 1997 by the Association for Computing Machinery, Inc. and the Institute for Electrical and Electronics Engineers, Inc.

3. Organizational Leadership Imperatives.

4. Compliance with the Code.

5. Acknowledgments.

1. General Moral Imperatives.

As an ACM member I will . . .

1.1 Contribute to society and human well-being.

This principle concerning the quality of life of all people affirms an obligation to protect fundamental human rights and to respect the diversity of all cultures. An essential aim of computing professionals is to minimize negative consequences of computing systems, including threats to health and safety. When designing or implementing systems, computing professionals must attempt to ensure that the products of their efforts will be used in socially responsible ways, will meet social needs, and will avoid harmful effects to health and welfare.

In addition to a safe social environment, human well-being includes a safe natural environment. Therefore, computing professionals who design and develop systems must be alert to, and make others aware of, any potential damage to the local or global environment.

1.2 Avoid harm to others.

"Harm" means injury or negative consequences, such as undesirable loss of information, loss of property, property damage, or unwanted environmental impacts. This principle prohibits use of computing technology in ways that result in harm to any of the following: users, the general public, employees, employers. Harmful actions include intentional destruction or modification of files and programs leading to serious loss of resources or unnecessary expenditure of human resources such as the time and effort required to purge systems of "computer viruses."

Well-intended actions, including those that accomplish assigned duties, may lead to harm unexpectedly. In such an event the responsible person or persons are obligated to undo or mitigate the negative consequences as much as possible. One way to avoid unintentional harm is to carefully consider potential impacts on all those affected by decisions made during design and implementation.

To minimize the possibility of indirectly harming others, computing professionals must minimize malfunctions by following generally accepted standards for system design and testing. Furthermore, it is often necessary to assess the social consequences of systems to project the likelihood of any serious harm to others. If system features are misrepresented to users, coworkers, or supervisors, the individual computing professional is responsible for any resulting injury.

In the work environment the computing professional has the additional obligation to report any signs of system dangers that might result in serious personal or social damage.

If one's superiors do not act to curtail or mitigate such dangers, it may be necessary to "blow the whistle" to help correct the problem or reduce the risk. However, capricious or misguided reporting of violations can, itself, be harmful. Before reporting violations, all relevant aspects of the incident must be thoroughly assessed. In particular, the assessment of risk and responsibility must be credible. It is suggested that advice be sought from other computing professionals. See principle 2.5 regarding thorough evaluations.

1.3 Be honest and trustworthy.

Honesty is an essential component of trust. Without trust an organization cannot function effectively. The honest computing professional will not make deliberately false or deceptive claims about a system or system design, but will instead provide full disclosure of all pertinent system limitations and problems.

A computer professional has a duty to be honest about his or her own qualifications, and about any circumstances that might lead to conflicts of interest.

Membership in volunteer organizations such as ACM may at times place individuals in situations where their statements or actions could be interpreted as carrying the "weight" of a larger group of professionals. An ACM member will exercise care to not misrepresent ACM or positions and policies of ACM or any ACM units.

1.4 Be fair and take action not to discriminate.

The values of equality, tolerance, respect for others, and the principles of equal justice govern this imperative. Discrimination on the basis of race, sex, religion, age, disability, national origin, or other such factors is an explicit violation of ACM policy and will not be tolerated.

Inequities between different groups of people may result from the use or misuse of information and technology. In a fair society, all individuals would have equal opportunity to participate in, or benefit from, the use of computer resources regardless of race, sex, religion, age, disability, national origin or other such similar factors. However, these ideals do not justify unauthorized use of computer resources nor do they provide an adequate basis for violation of any other ethical imperatives of this code.

1.5 Honor property rights including copyrights and patent.

Violation of copyrights, patents, trade secrets and the terms of license agreements is prohibited by law in most circumstances. Even when software is not so protected, such violations are contrary to professional behavior. Copies of software should be made only with proper authorization. Unauthorized duplication of materials must not be condoned.

1.6 Give proper credit for intellectual property.

Computing professionals are obligated to protect the integrity of intellectual property. Specifically, one must not take credit for other's ideas or work, even in cases where the work has not been explicitly protected by copyright, patent, etc.

1.7 Respect the privacy of others.

Computing and communication technology enables the collection and exchange of personal information on a scale unprecedented in the history of civilization. Thus there is increased potential for violating the privacy of individuals and groups. It is the responsibility of professionals to maintain the privacy and integrity of data describing individuals. This includes taking precautions to ensure the accuracy of data, as well as protecting it from unauthorized access or accidental disclosure to inappropriate individuals. Furthermore, procedures must be established to allow individuals to review their records and correct inaccuracies.

This imperative implies that only the necessary amount of personal information be collected in a system, that retention and disposal periods for that information be clearly defined and enforced, and that personal information gathered for a specific purpose not be used for other purposes without consent of the individual(s). These principles apply to electronic communications, including electronic mail, and prohibit procedures that capture or monitor electronic user data, including messages, without the permission of users or bona fide authorization related to system operation and maintenance. User data observed during the normal duties of system operation and maintenance must be treated with strictest confidentiality, except in cases where it is evidence for the violation of law, organizational regulations, or this Code. In these cases, the nature or contents of that information must be disclosed only to proper authorities.

1.8 Honor confidentiality.

The principle of honesty extends to issues of confidentiality of information whenever one has made an explicit promise to honor confidentiality or, implicitly, when private information not directly related to the performance of one's duties becomes available. The ethical concern is to respect all obligations of confidentiality to employers, clients, and users unless discharged from such obligations by requirements of the law or other principles of this Code.

2. More Specific Professional Responsibilities.

As an ACM computing professional I will . . .

2.1 Strive to achieve the highest quality, effectiveness and dignity in both the process and products of professional work.

Excellence is perhaps the most important obligation of a professional. The computing professional must strive to achieve quality and to be cognizant of the serious negative consequences that may result from poor quality in a system.

2.2 Acquire and maintain professional competence.

Excellence depends on individuals who take responsibility for acquiring and maintaining professional competence. A professional must participate in setting standards for appropriate levels of competence, and strive to achieve those standards. Upgrading technical knowledge and competence can be achieved in several ways: doing independent study; attending seminars, conferences, or courses; and being involved in professional organizations.

2.3 Know and respect existing laws pertaining to professional work.

ACM members must obey existing local, state, province, national, and international laws unless there is a compelling ethical basis not to do so. Policies and procedures of the organizations in which one participates must also be obeyed. But compliance must be balanced with the recognition that sometimes existing laws and rules may be immoral or inappropriate and, therefore, must be challenged. Violation of a law or regulation may be ethical when that law or rule has inadequate moral basis or when it conflicts with another law judged to be more important. If one decides to violate a law or rule because it is viewed as unethical, or for any other reason, one must fully accept responsibility for one's actions and for the consequences.

2.4 Accept and provide appropriate professional review.

Quality professional work, especially in the computing profession, depends on professional reviewing and critiquing. Whenever appropriate, individual members should seek and utilize peer review as well as provide critical review of the work of others.

2.5 Give comprehensive and thorough evaluations of computer systems and their impacts, including analysis of possible risks.

Computer professionals must strive to be perceptive, thorough, and objective when evaluating, recommending, and presenting system descriptions and alternatives. Computer professionals are in a position of special trust, and therefore have a special responsibility to provide objective, credible evaluations to employers, clients, users, and the public. When providing evaluations the professional must also identify any relevant conflicts of interest, as stated in imperative 1.3.

As noted in the discussion of principle 1.2 on avoiding harm, any signs of danger from systems must be reported to those who have opportunity and/or responsibility to resolve them. See the guidelines for imperative 1.2 for more details concerning harm, including the reporting of professional violations.

2.6 Honor contracts, agreements, and assigned responsibilities.

Honoring one's commitments is a matter of integrity and honesty. For the computer professional this includes ensuring that system elements perform as intended. Also, when one contracts for work with another party, one has an obligation to keep that party properly informed about progress toward completing that work.

A computing professional has a responsibility to request a change in any assignment that he or she feels cannot be completed as defined. Only after serious consideration and with full disclosure of risks and concerns to the employer or client, should one accept the assignment. The major underlying principle here is the obligation to accept personal accountability for professional work. On some occasions other ethical principles may take greater priority.

A judgment that a specific assignment should not be performed may not be accepted. Having clearly identified one's concerns and reasons for that judgment, but failing to procure a change in that assignment, one may yet be obligated, by contract or by law, to proceed as directed. The computing professional's ethical judgment should be the final guide in deciding whether or not to proceed. Regardless of the decision, one must accept the responsibility for the consequences.

However, performing assignments "against one's own judgment" does not relieve the professional of responsibility for any negative consequences.

2.7 Improve public understanding of computing and its consequences.

Computing professionals have a responsibility to share technical knowledge with the public by encouraging understanding of computing, including the impacts of computer systems and their limitations. This imperative implies an obligation to counter any false views related to computing.

2.8 Access computing and communication resources only when authorized to do so.

Theft or destruction of tangible and electronic property is prohibited by imperative 1.2 - "Avoid harm to others." Trespassing and unauthorized use of a computer or communication system is addressed by this imperative. Trespassing includes accessing communication networks and computer systems, or accounts and/or files associated with those systems, without explicit authorization to do so. Individuals and organizations have the right to restrict access to their systems so long as they do not violate the discrimination principle (see 1.4). No one should enter or use another's computer system, software, or data files without permission. One must always have appropriate approval before using system resources, including communication ports, file space, other system peripherals, and computer time.

3. Organizational Leadership Imperatives.

As an ACM member and an organizational leader, I will . . .

BACKGROUND NOTE: This section draws extensively from the draft IFIP Code of Ethics, especially its sections on organizational ethics and international concerns. The ethical obligations of organizations tend to be neglected in most codes of professional conduct, perhaps because these codes are written from the perspective of the individual member. This dilemma is addressed by stating these imperatives from the perspective of the organizational leader. In this context "leader" is viewed as any organizational member who has leadership or educational responsibilities. These imperatives generally may apply to organizations as well as their leaders. In this context "organizations" are corporations, government agencies, and other "employers," as well as volunteer professional organizations.

3.1 Articulate social responsibilities of members of an organizational unit and encourage full acceptance of those responsibilities.

Because organizations of all kinds have impacts on the public, they must accept responsibilities to society. Organizational procedures and attitudes oriented toward quality and the welfare of society will reduce harm to members of the public, thereby serving public interest and fulfilling social responsibility. Therefore, organizational leaders must encourage full participation in meeting social responsibilities as well as quality performance.

3.2 Manage personnel and resources to design and build information systems that enhance the quality of working life.

Organizational leaders are responsible for ensuring that computer systems enhance, not degrade, the quality of working life. When implementing a computer system, organizations must consider the personal and professional development, physical safety, and human dignity of all workers. Appropriate human-computer ergonomic standards should be considered in system design and in the workplace.

3.3 Acknowledge and support proper and authorized uses of an organization's computing and communication resources.

Because computer systems can become tools to harm as well as to benefit an organization, the leadership has the responsibility to clearly define appropriate and inappropriate uses of organizational computing resources. While the number and scope of such rules should be minimal, they should be fully enforced when established.

3.4 Ensure that users and those who will be affected by a system have their needs clearly articulated during the assessment and design of requirements; later the system must be validated to meet requirements.

Current system users, potential users and other persons whose lives may be affected by a system must have their needs assessed and incorporated in the statement of requirements. System validation should ensure compliance with those requirements.

3.5 Articulate and support policies that protect the dignity of users and others affected by a computing system.

Designing or implementing systems that deliberately or inadvertently demean individuals or groups is ethically unacceptable. Computer professionals who are in decision making positions should verify that systems are designed and implemented to protect personal privacy and enhance personal dignity.

3.6 Create opportunities for members of the organization to learn the principles and limitations of computer systems.

This complements the imperative on public understanding (2.7). Educational opportunities are essential to facilitate optimal participation of all organizational members. Opportunities must be available to all members to help them improve their knowledge and skills in computing, including courses that familiarize them with the consequences and limitations of particular types of systems. In particular, professionals must be made aware of the dangers of building systems around oversimplified models, the improbability of anticipating and designing for every possible operating condition, and other issues related to the complexity of this profession.

4. Compliance with the Code.

As an ACM member I will . . .

4.1 Uphold and promote the principles of this Code.

The future of the computing profession depends on both technical and ethical excellence. Not only is it important for ACM computing professionals to adhere to the principles expressed in this Code, each member should encourage and support adherence by other members.

4.2 Treat violations of this Code as inconsistent with membership in the ACM.

Adherence of professionals to a code of ethics is largely a voluntary matter. However, if a member does not follow this code by engaging in gross misconduct, membership in ACM may be terminated.

This Code and the supplemental Guidelines were developed by the Task Force for the Revision of the ACM Code of Ethics and Professional Conduct: Ronald E. Anderson, Chair, Gerald Engel, Donald Gotterbarn, Grace C. Hertlein, Alex Hoffman, Bruce Jawer, Deborah G. Johnson, Doris K. Lidtke, Joyce Currie Little, Dianne Martin, Donn B. Parker, Judith A. Perrolle, and Richard S. Rosenberg. The Task Force was organized by ACM/SIGCAS and funding was provided by the ACM SIG Discretionary Fund. This Code and the supplemental Guidelines were adopted by the ACM Council on October 16, 1992.

Index

An italic page number indicates a definition or fundamental explanation.